Dictionary of
Aviation

second edition

Also published by Bloomsbury Reference:

Dictionary of
Aviation

second edition

David Crocker

BLOOMSBURY

A BLOOMSBURY REFERENCE BOOK

www.bloomsbury.com/reference

Originally published by Peter Collin Publishing
as *Dictionary of Aeronautical English*

First published 1999
Second edition published 2005

Bloomsbury Publishing Plc
38 Soho Square, London W1D 3HB

British Library Cataloguing-in-Publication Data
A catalogue record for this book is available from the British Library

ISBN 0 7475 7219 4

Text Production and Proofreading
Katy McAdam, Sandra Anderson, Heather Bateman, Emma Harris

All papers used by Bloomsbury Publishing are natural, recyclable
products made from wood grown in well-managed forests. The
manufacturing processes conform to the environmental regulations
of the country of origin.

Text processed and computer typeset by Bloomsbury
Printed and bound in Italy by Legoprint

Preface

English is the universal language of communication used in civil aviation. This dictionary provides the basic vocabulary of terms used by pilots, cabin staff, maintenance crews, ground staff and travellers worldwide. The terms are those used in everyday work on aircraft, and cover parts of the aircraft, manipulating the aircraft on the ground and in the air, instructions to passengers, conversations with air traffic control, weather, emergencies, etc.

Unlike conventional aeronautical dictionaries, the *Dictionary of Aviation* defines vocabulary often found in conjunction with the purely technical terms as well as the technical terms themselves. Simple explanations are presented in simple language, making the dictionary ideal for those working towards a private or commercial pilot's licence, as well as trainee maintenance engineers and more experienced professionals. We also give examples to show how the words are used in context.

We have selected quotations from various specialised magazines to show the words and phrases as they are used in real-life situations. The supplements at the back give further information in the form of tables.

We are particularly grateful to the staff at Qatar Aeronautical College for their help in the production of the first edition of this dictionary. Thanks are also due to Stephen Copeland and Gavin Rowden for specialist advice and helpful suggestions during the preparation of this new edition.

The information contained in this dictionary is not to be regarded as a substitute for formal training in a given discipline.

Pronunciation Guide

The following symbols have been used to show the pronunciation of the main words in the dictionary.

Stress is indicated by a main stress mark (') and a secondary stress mark (,). Note that these are only guides, as the stress of the word changes according to its position in the sentence.

Vowels		Consonants	
æ	back	b	buck
ɑː	harm	d	dead
ɒ	stop	ð	other
aɪ	type	dʒ	jump
aʊ	how	f	fare
aɪə	hire	g	gold
aʊə	hour	h	head
ɔː	course	j	yellow
ɔɪ	annoy	k	cab
e	head	l	leave
eə	fair	m	mix
eɪ	make	n	nil
əʊ	go	ŋ	sing
ɜː	word	p	print
iː	keep	r	rest
i	happy	s	save
ə	about	ʃ	shop
ɪ	fit	t	take
ɪə	near	tʃ	change
u	annual	θ	theft
uː	pool	v	value
ʊ	book	w	work
ʊə	tour	x	loch
ʌ	shut	ʒ	measure
		z	zone

A

AAIB *abbreviation* Air Accident Investigation Branch

AARA *abbreviation* air to air refuelling area

abbreviate /ə'bri:vieɪt/ *verb* to shorten a word or a text ○ *Air Traffic Control is usually abbreviated to ATC.* □ **abbreviated weather report** a shortened weather report

abbreviation /ə,bri:vi'eɪʃ(ə)n/ *noun* the short form of a word or text ○ *Aeronautical charts use abbreviations and symbols.* ○ *Km is the abbreviation for kilometre.*

COMMENT: Abbreviations can cause confusion. They may range from those which have a very specific meaning as defined by an authoritative body, to others which may come about because of personal usage in note-making, etc. ICAO approved abbreviations may differ from those used in JARs. AC can mean 'alternating current' or 'altocumulus'. CPL is generally taken to mean Commercial Pilot's Licence but the ICAO definition is Current Flight Plan. Advances in technology have significantly increased the number of abbreviations with which pilots and engineers must be familiar. Abbreviations in this dictionary include those with generally accepted definitions and others with specific ICAO definitions.

ability /ə'bɪlɪti/ *noun* the power, knowledge or skill needed to do something ○ *Strength is the ability of a material to support a load.* □ **he has great ability** he has good skills or is very clever

able /'eɪb(ə)l/ *adjective* skilful and competent □ **to be able to** to have the power, knowledge, skill or strength to do something ○ *Is she able to carry this heavy suitcase?*

able-bodied /,eɪb(ə)l 'bɒdɪd/ *adjective* referring to a person who has no physical disabilities ○ *Physically disadvantaged as well as able-bodied people can gain a PPL.*

abnormal /æb'nɔ:m(ə)l/ *adjective* not normal

abnormality /,æbnɔ:'mælɪti/ *noun* something that is not normal, expected or correct, and is therefore possibly worrying ○ *Any abnormality in engine performance should be checked.*

abnormal load /æb,nɔ:m(ə)l 'ləʊd/ *noun* a load which is heavier than normal

abort /ə'bɔ:t/ *verb* **1.** to stop something taking place ○ *They had to abort the landing because of a violent storm* **2.** to end something before it has finished

absolute /'æbsəlu:t/ *adjective* complete, total □ **absolute necessity** something that you cannot manage without under any circumstances □ **absolute silence** a condition in which no sound of any kind can be heard

absolute ceiling /,æbsəlu:t 'si:lɪŋ/ *noun* the maximum height above sea level at which an aircraft can maintain horizontal flight

absolute humidity /,æbsəlu:t hju:'mɪdəti/ *noun* the vapour concentration or mass of water in a given quantity of air

absolute pressure /ˌæbsəluːt ˈpreʃə/ *noun* a unit of force per unit of area without comparison to other pressure ○ *Aircraft show absolute pressure in inches of mercury on the inlet manifold pressure gauge.*

absolute value /ˌæbsəluːt ˈvæljuː/ *noun* the size or value of a number regardless of its sign ○ *The absolute value of –64.32 is 64.32.*

absolute zero /ˌæbsəluːt ˈzɪərəʊ/ *noun* the lowest temperature possible, 0 °K, or –273.15 °C

absorb /əbˈzɔːb/ *verb* to take in ○ *Warm air absorbs moisture more easily than cold air.* ○ *Our bodies absorb oxygen.* □ **to absorb information** to understand and remember something ○ *Only a few passengers absorb the pre-departure safety information.*

absorption /əbˈzɔːpʃən/ *noun* the act of taking something in ○ *There is absorption of energy by the tyre when the aircraft lands.*

AC *abbreviation* **1.** alternating current **2.** altocumulus (*ICAO*)

ACARS *abbreviation* airborne communication, addressing and reporting system

ACAS /ˈeɪkæs/ *abbreviation* airborne collision avoidance system

ACC *abbreviation* area control centre

accelerate /əkˈseləreɪt/ *verb* to increase speed ○ *After start-up, the engine accelerates up to idling speed.* ○ *The aircraft accelerated down the runway and took off.* Opposite **decelerate**

acceleration /əkˌseləˈreɪʃ(ə)n/ *noun* **1.** the act of increasing the speed of something or of going faster. Opposite **deceleration** (NOTE: Acceleration can be felt as an aircraft begins its take-off run.) **2.** a force that pulls outwards and is caused by a change in direction rather than a change in speed ○ *Acceleration forces can be felt during aerobatic manoeuvres.*

acceleration due to earth's gravity *noun* the pulling force exerted on a body by the Earth. It has an international standard value of 9.80665 metres per second per second. Abbreviation **g**

accelerometer /əkˌseləˈrɒmɪtə/ *noun* an instrument that measures an aircraft's acceleration

accept /əkˈsept/ *verb* **1.** to be able to take or receive ○ *Some units accept electrical inputs from the autopilot.* **2.** to take or receive something when it is given to you ○ *She accepted the award on behalf of the whole crew.* □ **to accept a gift**, **to accept a prize** to take a prize which is handed to you **3.** to be willing to receive or admit something □ **to accept the blame** to be willing to admit that you were the person who caused something bad to happen ○ *The airline accepted the blame for the loss of their baggage.* □ **to accept responsibility** to be willing to be answerable for something ○ *The copilot accepted responsibility for the incident.*

acceptable /əkˈseptəb(ə)l/ *adjective* allowed or approved of, although it may not be perfect □ **acceptable level of safety** a good enough standard of safety □ **acceptable limits** the limits generally regarded as correct □ **there must be a continuous flow of clean oil at an acceptable temperature** the temperature of the oil must be within given maximum and minimum figures

acceptance /əkˈseptəns/ *noun* **1.** willingness to believe something or agree to something ○ *There is a growing acceptance that safety is the main priority.* **2.** willingness to do or use something □ **acceptance of new technology** willingness to use new technology

accepted /əkˈseptɪd/ *adjective* believed or recognised ○ *It is accepted that incorrect use of English played a part in the accident.* ○ *It is generally accepted that flying is one of the safest forms of transport.*

access /ˈækses/ *noun* a way to find or get at something □ **to gain access to** to manage to enter a place □ **access to information** the means to get at, retrieve and use information ■ *verb* to find and use □ **to access data**, **to access information** to find, retrieve and use data *or* information

accessibility /ək,sesı'bılıti/ *noun* the ease with which something can be reached or found ○ *Accessibility of components and equipment during servicing enables work to be done more quickly.*

accessible /ək'sesıb(ə)l/ *adjective* easy to get at ○ *It is a good idea to have a set of emergency charts in an accessible place in the cockpit.* ○ *Instruments which need resetting in flight must be accessible to the crew.*

accessory /ək'sesəri/ *noun* a system or piece of equipment of secondary importance ○ *a camera with several accessories* ■ *adjective* of secondary importance ○ *There are many accessory systems which need engine power to operate them – pumps, generators, magnetos, etc.* (NOTE: The noun **accessory** is not connected with the noun **access** or the verb **to access**.)

access panel /'ækses ,pæn(ə)l/ *noun* a part of the aircraft skin which can be easily removed so internal components can be inspected

accident /'æksıd(ə)nt/ *noun* **1.** something which happens which seems to have no cause □ **it was an accident** nobody planned that it should happen or deliberately caused it to happen □ **by accident** by chance □ **we met by accident** we met by chance **2.** an unfortunate or harmful event, something causing damage ○ *An accident must be reported.* ○ *The flight attendant was injured in the accident.*

'Mr Skidmore lost both arms in an accident while serving in the army as a young man, and is believed to be the first pilot in the UK – and possibly the world – to go solo with two artificial arms' [*Pilot*]

accidental /,æksı'dent(ə)l/ *adjective* **1.** happening by accident, not deliberate or planned ○ *There is a safety device to prevent accidental retraction of the undercarriage.* **2.** relating to an accident, or happening as a result of an accident ○ *We were told of his accidental death.*

accompanied /ə'kʌmp(ə)nid/ *adjective* found together with □ **accompanied luggage** luggage which belongs

to one of the passengers and is carried on the same aircraft. ◊ **unaccompanied**

accompany /ə'kʌmp(ə)ni/ *verb* to go together with something else ○ *Engine failure is sometimes accompanied by fire.* □ **Mr Smith was accompanied by his wife and children on the flight to New York** Mr Smith's wife and children were with him on the flight

accomplish /ə'kʌmplıʃ/ *verb* (*in formal technical texts*) to do something ○ *Feathering is accomplished by moving the pilot's control lever.* ○ *Retraction of the undercarriage is accomplished by electrical power.* □ **to accomplish a task** to successfully finish doing something demanding ○ *She was the first woman to accomplish the feat in a single-engined aircraft.*

accomplishment /ə'kʌmplıʃmənt/ *noun* **1.** an achievement ○ *Charles Lindbergh's flight across the Atlantic in May 1927 was a great accomplishment.* **2.** (*in physics*) work done ○ *Power is measured by units of accomplishment correlated with time.*

accordance /ə'kɔːd(ə)ns/ *noun* □ **in accordance with** in agreement with or following something such as rules, instructions or laws ○ *Fuels must be used in accordance with instructions.* □ **in accordance with Buys Ballot's Law** as described by Buys Ballot's Law

'…use full heat whenever carburettor heat is applied, partial hot air should only be used if an intake temperature gauge is fitted and only then in accordance with the Flight Manual or Pilot's Operating Handbook' [*Civil Aviation Authority, General Aviation Safety Sense Leaflet*]

accordingly /ə'kɔːdıŋli/ *adverb* as needed ○ *Check for increasing manifold pressure and reduce power accordingly.*

according to /ə'kɔːdıŋ tuː/ *preposition* **1.** as determined by or in relation to ○ *The force exerted by the pilot on the control column will vary according to a number of factors.* **2.** as written or said by somebody else ○ *According to the copilot, engine vibration was detected in engine number one.* **3.** in agreement with something, e.g. instructions, etc. □ **according to instructions** exactly as said in the instructions □ **according to requirements** as required

account /ə'kaʊnt/ *noun* □ **to take something into account** to remember something and consider it carefully ○ *When planning a flight, wind speed and direction must be taken into account.* ○ *In the event of an in-flight emergency, the aircraft should be landed at the nearest suitably equipped airport, taking into account fuel available.* □ **on no account** under no circumstances, never ○ *On no account should anybody fly an aircraft without carrying out pre-flight checks.*

account for /ə'kaʊnt fə/ *verb* **1.** to make up or constitute ○ *Kevlar and carbon fibre account for a large percentage of the materials used in modern aircraft.* **2.** to provide the main reason for something ○ *High humidity accounted for the longer take-off run.*

accrete /ə'kriːt/ *verb* to increase in amount by slow external addition, to accumulate □ **ice accretes on the rotor** ice builds up on the rotor

accretion /ə'kriːʃ(ə)n/ *noun* increase or accumulation by slow external addition ○ *Ice accretion can cause loss of lift and significantly increase the weight of the aircraft.*

accumulate /ə'kjuːmjʊleɪt/ *verb* to collect and increase ○ *Due to katabatic effects, cold air flows downwards and accumulates over low ground.*

accumulation /ə,kjuːmjʊ'leɪʃ(ə)n/ *noun* the collection and increase of something ○ *Fire in a toilet could present difficulties due to the confined space and possible smoke accumulation.*

accumulator /ə'kjuːmjʊleɪtə/ *noun* **1.** a device for storing energy in hydraulic systems ○ *An accumulator is fitted to store hydraulic fluid.* **2.** an electric circuit in a calculator or computer, in which the results of arithmetical and logical operations are formed

accuracy /'ækjʊrəsi/ *noun* **1.** the state of being correct □ **to check for accuracy** to make certain that the result is correct **2.** the ability to find, hit or show things correctly ○ *The accuracy of*

modern navigational equipment is much greater than older systems.

accurate /'ækjʊrət/ *adjective* **1.** correct ○ *Skill in accurate flying can only be achieved by practice.* □ **accurate results** results which are exactly correct **2.** precise ○ *This watch is very accurate.*

ACFT *abbreviation* aircraft

achieve /ə'tʃiːv/ *verb* **1.** to manage to do something demanding ○ *In order to achieve a safe landing in a crosswind, the correct techniques must be used.* **2.** to obtain ○ *In wind shear conditions, a fly-by-wire system allows the pilot to achieve maximum lift by pulling hard back on the stick without risk of a stall.*

achievement /ə'tʃiːvmənt/ *noun* something difficult that somebody succeeds in doing and feels proud about ○ *For most trainee pilots, making their first solo flight is a great achievement.*

acid /'æsɪd/ *noun* a chemical substance which reacts with a base to form a salt ○ *sulphuric acid (H_2SO_4)* (NOTE: An acid turns a litmus indicator red and has a sour taste.)

acidity /ə'sɪdɪti/ *noun* having an acid content □ **the acidity of a substance** the amount of acid in a substance

acid-proof /'æsɪd pruːf/ *adjective* able to resist the harmful effects of an acid

acid test /,æsɪd 'test/ *noun* a difficult or exacting test of worth or quality ○ *A pilot's ability to react appropriately in an emergency situation is the acid test of his or her professionalism.*

ACMS *noun* a computer which records information from various aircraft systems during flight. Full form **aircraft condition monitoring system**

ACN *abbreviation* aircraft classification number

acoustic /ə'kuːstɪk/ *adjective* referring to sound

acoustic ear muffs /ə,kuːstɪk 'ɪə ,mʌfs/ *plural noun* coverings to protect the ears from loud noise. Also called **ear protectors**, **ear defenders**

acquire /ə'kwaɪə/ *verb* to buy or otherwise obtain ○ *to acquire a new air-*

craft ○ *Speed control is used to acquire and maintain a selected airspeed.*

acquisition /ˌækwɪ'zɪʃ(ə)n/ *noun* the act of buying or otherwise obtaining ○ *Each computer checks data acquisition.* ○ *The image of the airline improved after the acquisition of the new aircraft.*

acronym /'ækrənɪm/ *noun* a word which is made up of the initial letters of a name, and is pronounced as a word ○ *NASA is the acronym for National Aeronautics and Space Administration.* ○ *VASI is the acronym for visual approach slope indicator.*

act /ækt/ *verb* **1.** to behave in a particular way ○ *The crew must act with authority.* **2.** to take the role of ○ *Mountain ranges act as a barrier.* ○ *The governor spill valve also acts as a safety relief valve.* **3.** □ **to act on** to produce an effect ○ *Bending and twisting forces act on a propeller.* ○ *Gravity acts vertically downwards.*

acting /'æktɪŋ/ *adjective* temporarily taking on the responsibilities of somebody ○ *Captain Smith will be acting Chief Flying Instructor while Captain White is absent from work.*

action /'ækʃən/ *noun* **1.** something done or to be done □ **to take action** to so something ○ *If there is a risk of collision, the crew should take the appropriate action.* **2.** an effect

activate /'æktɪveɪt/ *verb* to make a system or a piece of equipment or a procedure start to work or to operate ○ *The system is activated by the pilot or copilot.* ○ *The sounding of the alarm will activate emergency procedures.*

activation /ˌæktɪ'veɪʃ(ə)n/ *noun* the act of making something start to work or to operate ○ *Activation may be mechanical or electrical.*

active /'æktɪv/ *adjective* **1.** live, in action or use □ **the system is active** the system is on and working **2.** not passive □ **in a secondary radar system, the target is active** in a secondary radar system the target transmits a signal while in a primary radar system it does not **3.** □ **active Cb clouds** developing cumulonimbus clouds

active runway /ˌæktɪv 'rʌnweɪ/ *noun* a runway that is being used

'…never cross an active runway without permission from the tower: there may be more than one active runway' [*Civil Aviation Authority, General Aviation Safety Sense Leaflet*]

activity /æk'tɪvɪti/ *noun* a movement or action of some kind ○ *Sunspot activity can affect the amount of solar radiation.*

actual /'æktʃuəl/ *adjective* real ○ *The actual path of the aircraft over the ground is called its track, which may not be the same as the desired course.*

actually /'æktʃuəli/ *adverb* in fact, in reality ○ *The design is such that, although the aircraft loses altitude rapidly, it does not actually stall.*

actuate /'æktʃu,eɪt/ *verb* **1.** to move a device or a part ○ *The fore and aft movement of the control column actuates the elevators.* **2.** to switch on a system or a piece of equipment, or put it into operation ○ *A lever actuates the fire deluge system.* **3.** to put a procedure into action ○ *Receipt of the distress signal will actuate the support facilities at the airport.*

actuation /æktʃʊ'eɪʃ(ə)n/ *noun* **1.** the act of making a device or a part move □ **electrical actuation** the use of an electric motor to make something move □ **mechanical actuation** the use of a mechanical part such as a rod, arm or lever to make something move **2.** a movement made by a device or part

actuator /'æktʃueɪtə/ *noun* a device which changes electrical or hydraulic energy into mechanical motion ○ *The actuator control is sensitive to engine rpm.* ○ *Actuators are classified as either linear or rotary.*

AD *abbreviation* airworthiness directive

A/D *abbreviation* aerodrome

ADA *abbreviation* advisory airspace

adapt /ə'dæpt/ *verb* **1.** to change or modify for special use ○ *The turboprop engine is often used in transport aircraft and can be adapted for use in single-engine aircraft.* **2.** to change to suit new conditions ○ *Crew flying long-haul routes have to adapt to time changes.*

adaptation /ˌædæpˈteɪʃ(ə)n/ *noun* **1.** the act of changing or modifying something for special use ○ *Doppler VOR is an adaptation of VOR to reduce errors caused by location.* **2.** adjustment to new conditions ○ *Adaptation to time changes when travelling west to east takes time.*

adapter /əˈdæptə/ *noun* **1.** a piece of equipment or device which allows a change or modification □ **a 'T' piece adapter** a device for connecting two inputs to one output or vice versa **2.** a device that allows two incompatible devices to be connected

ADC /ˌeɪ diː ˈsiː/ *abbreviation* air data computer

add /æd/ *verb* **1.** to put figures together to form a sum, to make a total ○ *Add the two numbers together to find the sum.* **2.** to put together to make a larger group or a group with different properties ○ *There are only nine chairs, add another one.* ○ *A substance is added to the fuel to clean fuel injectors.*

addition /əˈdɪʃ(ə)n/ *noun* **1.** a mathematical operation consisting in putting numbers together ○ *Addition is normally taught before subtraction, multiplication and division.* ○ *The addition sign is +.* **2.** the act of adding something ○ *With the addition of methanol, the turbine inlet temperature is restored.* **3.** □ **in addition** also □ **in addition to** as well as

additional /əˈdɪʃ(ə)nəl/ *adjective* added or extra

additive /ˈædɪtɪv/ *noun* a chemical substance, often liquid, added to another substance to give it extra qualities ○ *Additives are used in engine oils to prolong the life of the engine.* ○ *Anti-icing additives are used in radiator coolants.*

adequate /ˈædɪkwət/ *adjective* enough, sufficient ○ *The compressor must provide an adequate airflow through the engine.* □ **adequate fuel** enough fuel

ADF *abbreviation* automatic direction finder

adhere /ədˈhɪə/ *verb* to stick as if glued ○ *Clear ice adheres strongly to airframes.*

adhesive /ədˈhiːsɪv/ *noun* glue ■ *adjective* having the sticking quality of glue ○ *adhesive tape* ○ *Adhesive bonding of aluminium parts is widely employed.*

ADI /ˌeɪdiːˈaɪ/ *abbreviation* attitude direction indicator *or* attitude director indicator

adiabatic /ˌædɪəˈbætɪk/ *adjective* **1.** referring to processes through which heat cannot be lost or gained **2.** referring to a change in temperature in a mass of air, which occurs when the air is compressed or expanded by an increase or decrease in atmospheric pressure and does not involve the air losing heat to, or gaining heat from, its surroundings

adiabatic compression /ˌædɪəbætɪk kəmˈpreʃ(ə)n/ *noun* compression caused by atmospheric factors, which makes descending air warm up

adiabatic cooling /ˌædɪəbætɪk ˈkuːlɪŋ/ *noun* a process in which ascending air is cooled by a decrease in atmospheric pressure without heat transfer

adiabatic expansion /ˌædɪəbætɪk ɪkˈspænʃ(ə)n/ *noun* expansion caused by atmospheric factors, which makes ascending air cool down ○ *Cooling by adiabatic expansion may result in cloud formation.*

adiabatic heating /ædɪəˌbætɪk ˈhiːtɪŋ/ *noun* a process in which descending air is heated by an increase in atmospheric pressure without heat transfer

adjacent /əˈdʒeɪs(ə)nt/ *adjective* next to or near ○ *Fire extinguishers should be positioned adjacent to the aircraft during all ground-running operations.*

adjust /əˈdʒʌst/ *verb* to change and improve the position or setting of a piece of equipment ○ *The pilot adjusts the throttle or propeller controls.* □ **to adjust the seat** to move the seat into a position suitable for yourself □ **to**

adjust the volume to increase or decrease the volume to improve the sound quality

adjustable /ə'dʒʌstəb(ə)l/ *adjective* designed to be adjusted ○ *An adjustable stop on the throttle control ensures a positive idling speed.*

adjustment /ə'dʒʌstmənt/ *noun* **1.** a change to improve the setting, position or operation of something ○ *A slight adjustment to the seat will make it much more comfortable to sit in.* **2.** the act of changing something to improve its setting or position ○ *Maximum system pressure is often controlled by adjustment of the main engine-driven pump.*

admit /əd'mɪt/ *verb* to allow to enter ○ *Cold air can be admitted to the cabin through adjustable louvres or shutters.*

adopt /ə'dɒpt/ *verb* to choose to use something as standard equipment or to make it standard procedure ○ *A policy of no smoking on all flights has been adopted by many airlines.* □ **widely adopted** now in standard use with many companies, institutions and organisations

adoption /ə'dɒpʃən/ *noun* the act of using something as standard equipment or making it standard procedure ○ *In spite of the adoption of the axial flow type compressor, some engines retain the centrifugal type.*

ADR *abbreviation* accident data recorder

ADS *abbreviation* automatic dependent surveillance

ADT *abbreviation* approved departure time

advance /əd'vɑːns/ *noun* **1.** a change that improves something □ **enormous advances in aircraft design** great progress or developments in aircraft design **2.** □ **in advance of** ahead of ○ *The Gulf region is three hours in advance of GMT.* ■ *verb* **1.** to move forwards, or move something forwards □ **the throttle lever is advanced** the throttle lever is moved forwards **2.** to make something happen at an earlier time □ **to advance the ignition** to adjust the timing of the ignition so that the spark occurs earlier

advanced /əd'vɑːnst/ *adjective* modern and sophisticated ○ *The A340 is an advanced type of aircraft.*

'…a Seattle-based modification company specializing in advanced winglet designs is developing a lightweight winglet for the Boeing 747 200F' [*Flight International 1–7 May 1996*]

advantage /əd'vɑːntɪdʒ/ *noun* a good or beneficial factor ○ *The multi-wheel combination has the advantage of smaller and lighter undercarriage structures.* □ **to take advantage of** to get benefit from a situation □ **to take advantage of favourable winds** to use tailwinds to increase ground speed and thus save time and money. Opposite **disadvantage**

advantageous /ˌædvən'teɪdʒəs/ *adjective* better □ **the most advantageous** the best ○ *The minimum time path is the most advantageous for economy.*

advect /əd'vekt/ *verb* to move in a horizontal direction due to convection ○ *Dispersal of hill fog takes place when surface heating lifts the cloud base or drier air is advected.*

advection /əd'vekʃ(ə)n/ *noun* the movement of air in a horizontal direction

advection fog /əd'vekʃ(ə)n fɒg/ *noun* fog which forms when warmer moist air moves over a colder surface

advent /'ædvent/ *noun* an arrival, especially of something very important ○ *With the advent of satellite navigation systems, pilots of light aircraft have a more accurate means of knowing their position.*

adverse /'ædvɜːs/ *adjective* **1.** bad or poor ○ *Only in extremely adverse conditions should the crew evacuate the aircraft.* □ **adverse handling characteristics** aspects of an aircraft's handling which are poor **2.** acting or going against you

adverse yaw /'ædvɜːs jɔː/ *noun* yaw caused by aileron drag, in the opposite direction to the direction of the intended turn

advice /əd'vaɪs/ *noun* useful or helpful information ○ *The instructor's advice was of great help to the student* *pilot.* (NOTE: **Advice** has no plural form.)

advisability /əd,vaɪzə'bɪlɪti/ *noun* □ the advisability of something whether something is a good idea or not ○ *Flying manuals often contain guidance on the advisability of flying with a cold.*

advisable /əd'vaɪzəb(ə)l/ *adjective* recommended, suggested ○ *It is advisable to check the condition of the tyres after each landing.*

advise /əd'vaɪz/ *verb* **1.** to inform, to notify ○ *The flight deck advised the cabin crew that descent would start in 20 minutes.* **2.** to recommend, to suggest ○ *Because of the bad weather, the instructor advised the trainee pilot not to fly.* □ **to advise against** to recommend or to suggest that something should not be done

advisory /əd'vaɪz(ə)ri/ *adjective* giving advice and information

advisory airspace /əd,vaɪz(ə)ri 'eəspeɪs/ *noun* airspace containing advisory routes in which air traffic control provide an advisory service but not full control. Abbreviation **ADA**

advisory route /əd'vaɪz(ə)ri ruːt/ *noun* a published route for which there is an advisory service. Abbreviation **ADR**

advisory service /əd'vaɪz(ə)ri ,sɜːvɪs/ *noun* a service in which Air Traffic Control provides advice and information to assist a pilot in the safe conduct of a flight

AEEC *abbreviation* airlines electronic engineering committee

aerate /'eəreɪt/ *verb* to put a gas, especially carbon dioxide or air, into a liquid so that bubbles are formed ○ *Aerated fuel causes problems.* Opposite **de-aerate**

aeration /eə'reɪʃ(ə)n/ *noun* the act of putting a gas, especially carbon dioxide or air, into a liquid ○ *The purpose of the booster pump is to prevent fuel aeration.* Opposite **de-aeration**

aerator /eə'reɪtə/ *noun* a device to put a gas – especially carbon dioxide or air – into a liquid. Opposite **de-aerator**

aerial /'eəriəl/ *adjective* **1.** happening in the air **2.** done by an aircraft in flight ■ *noun* a device to send or receive radio or TV signals ○ *Ice-covering reduces the effectiveness of aerials.* (NOTE: The US English word with this meaning is **antenna**.)

aerial display /'eəriəl dɪs,pleɪ/ *noun* a display of flying skills and aircraft performance

aerial photography /,eəriəl fə'tɒgrəfi/ *noun* photography done from an aircraft in the air

aero- /eərəʊ/ *prefix* **1.** referring to the air ○ *aerodynamic* **2.** referring to aircraft ○ *aero-engine* ○ *aero-tow*

aerobatic /,eərə'bætɪk/ *adjective* referring to aerobatics ○ *Loops and rolls are aerobatic manoeuvres.*

aerobatic aircraft /,eərəbætɪk 'eəkrɑːft/ *noun* an aircraft which is designed to perform aerobatics

COMMENT: One of the most famous competition aerobatic aircraft is the Pitts Special which first flew in 1944.

aerobatic display /,eərəbætɪk dɪs'pleɪ/ *noun* a demonstration, often public, of piloting skill and aircraft performance

aerobatics /,eərəʊ'bætɪks/ *noun* the art of performing spectacular controlled movements in a flying aircraft for the purposes of entertainment or competition ○ *The Russian pilot gave a great display of aerobatics.*

aerobatic team /,eərə'bætɪk ,tiːm/ *noun* a team of pilots and aircraft who perform aerobatics

aerodrome /'eərədrəʊm/ *noun* any area of land or water designed for the taking off and landing of aircraft ○ *Airports and military air bases or stations are types of aerodrome.* ○ *All aerodromes are marked on charts.* Abbreviation **A/D** □ **disused aerodrome** an aerodrome which is no longer in use for the purpose of taking off and landing aeroplanes

aerodrome boundaries /'eərədrəʊm ,baʊnd(ə)riz/ *plural noun* the physical or geographical limits of an aerodrome

aerodrome circuit /ˈeərədrəʊm ˌsɜːkɪt/ *noun* the pattern and direction of aircraft movement in the air around the aerodrome

aerodrome QFE /ˌeərədrəʊm ˌkjuː ef ˈiː/ *noun* the barometric pressure setting at which the altimeter reads zero when the aircraft is on the runway

aerodrome QNH /ˌeərədrəʊm ˌkjuː en ˈeɪtʃ/ *noun* the barometric pressure setting at which the altimeter reads aerodrome elevation when the aircraft is on the runway

aerodrome surveillance monitoring indicator /ˌeərədrəʊm ˌsɜːveɪləns ˈmɒnɪtərɪŋ ˌɪndɪkeɪtə/ *noun* same as **airport surface detection equipment**

aerodrome traffic zone /ˌeərədrəʊm ˈtræfɪk ˌzəʊn/ *noun* an area of protected airspace around an aerodrome, which pilots need permission to enter or to move in. Abbreviation **ATZ**

aerodynamic /ˌeərəʊdaɪˈnæmɪk/ *adjective* **1.** referring to the way in which objects are affected when they move through the atmosphere **2.** referring to a smooth rounded shape which moves easily through the air □ **aerodynamic design** a streamlined shape that enables something to move easily through the air

aerodynamic braking /ˌeərəʊ daɪnæmɪk ˈbreɪkɪŋ/ *noun* the braking effect of drag

aerodynamic forces /ˌeərəʊ daɪnæmɪk ˈfɔːsɪz/ *noun* the forces of the air which act on an aircraft in flight

aerodynamic resistance /ˌeərəʊ daɪnæmɪk rɪˈzɪstəns/ *noun* same as **drag**

aerodynamics /ˌeərəʊdaɪˈnæmɪks/ *noun* the science that deals with the interaction of moving objects with the atmosphere ○ *Aerodynamics is one of the major areas of study for a trainee pilot.*

aerodyne /ˈeərəʊdaɪn/ *noun* an aircraft that is heavier than air and whose lift in flight results from forces caused by its motion through the air, e.g. a plane or helicopter

aero-engine /ˈeərəʊ ˌendʒɪn/ *noun* an engine used in aircraft ○ *Most piston aero-engines are cooled by air.*

aerofoil /ˈeərəʊfɔɪl/ *noun* a surface which is shaped to produce more lift than drag when moved through the air ○ *Wings, ailerons, elevators, fins and propellers are all examples of aerofoils.* (NOTE: The US English word is **airfoil**.)

aeronautical /ˌeərəˈnɔːtɪk(ə)l/ *adjective* referring to aeronautics

aeronautical chart /ˌeərə ˈnɔːtɪk(ə)l ˌtʃɑːt/ *noun* a map used in air navigation which may include topographic features, hazards and obstructions, navigational aids and routes, designated airspace and airports

aeronautical engineer /ˌeərənɔːtɪk(ə)l ˌendʒɪˈnɪə/ *noun* an engineer who specialises in the design of aircraft

aeronautical engineering /ˌeərəʊnɔːtɪk(ə)l ˌendʒɪˈnɪərɪŋ/ *noun* the science or study of the design of aircraft

aeronautical fixed service /ˌeərənɔːtɪk(ə)l ˌfɪkst ˈsɜːvɪs/ *noun* a radio communications service between fixed points that is designed to enable aircraft to travel safely. Abbreviation **AFS**

aeronautical fixed telecommunication network /ˌeərənɔːtɪk(ə)l ˌfɪkst ˌtelikəmjuːnɪˈkeɪʃ(ə)n ˌnetwɜːk/ *noun* a ground-based network of teleprinters that transmits flight plans and similar data between control centres. Abbreviation **AFTN**

aeronautical information circular /ˌeərənɔːtɪk(ə)l ˌɪnfəˈmeɪʃ(ə)n ˌsɜːkjʊlə/ *noun* a notice issued by an aviation authority in which information is given about administrative, technical, safety or operational matters

Aeronautical Information Publication *noun* a document issued by a state in which information is given about aviation in that country. Abbreviation **AIP**

aeronautics /ˌeərəˈnɔːtɪks/ *noun* **1.** the science of aircraft design, construction and operation **2.** the theory and practice of aircraft navigation

aeroneurosis /ˌeərəʊnjʊˈrəʊsɪs/ *noun* anxiety and fatigue in airline pilots as a result of long periods of flying

aeroplane /ˈeərəpleɪn/ *noun* a power-driven, heavier-than-air craft with fixed wings (NOTE: Many people use the words **aeroplane** and **aircraft** as if they had exactly the same meaning. However, aeroplanes, hot-air balloons, helicopters, airships and gliders are all **aircraft**. The US English is **airplane**.)

aeroplane performance /ˌeərəpleɪn pəˈfɔːməns/ *noun* a description in figures of what a plane can do, including, e.g., its speed, rate of climb, and the length of its take-off run

aerostat /ˈeərəʊstæt/ *noun* a hot-air or gas-filled aircraft, e.g. an airship or balloon

aero-tow /ˈeərəˈtəʊ/ *noun* a technique of using a powered aircraft to pull a glider into the air ○ *An aero-tow to 2,000 feet costs $25.*

AFCS *abbreviation* automatic flight control system

AFDS *abbreviation* autopilot flight director system

affect /əˈfekt/ *verb* to have an influence on something, or cause a change in something ○ *Humidity and air density are factors which affect the output of the engine.* Compare **effect**

AFI *abbreviation* assistant flying instructor

AFIC *abbreviation* assistant flying instructor course

AFIS *abbreviation* aerodrome flight information service

AFS *abbreviation* aeronautical fixed service

aft /ɑːft/ *adjective* towards the rear part of the aircraft ○ *The rear part of the fuselage is called the aft section.* □ **aft cabin** the passenger compartment at the back of the aircraft ■ *adverb* rearwards or backwards □ **to move the control column aft** to move the control column backwards. Opposite **fore**, **forward**

after /ˈɑːftə/ *adjective* positioned closer to the rear of an aircraft ■ *adverb* closer to the rear of an aircraft

afterburner /ˈɑːftəbɜːnə/ *noun* a system that injects fuel into the hot exhaust gases of a jet engine in order to increase thrust

AFTN *abbreviation* aeronautical fixed telecommunication network

agent /ˈeɪdʒənt/ *noun* **1.** a chemical substance which causes a change ○ *If de-icing fluid is used as an anti-icing agent it should be sprayed onto the aircraft before the onset of icing.* □ **extinguishing agent** a substance used to put out fires **2.** a person who represents a company or arranges something for a company ○ *the agent for British Airways* ○ *a travel agent*

aggregate /ˈæɡrɪɡət/ *noun* the total obtained by adding ○ *The aggregate of the capacity of all the fuel tanks is 50 gallons.* ■ *verb* to add or come together to form a mass or total ○ *Ice crystals aggregate to form snowflakes.*

AGL *abbreviation* above ground level

agree /əˈɡriː/ *verb* **1.** to have the same idea or opinion about something ○ *The crew agreed with the findings of the investigation.* **2.** to come to an understanding ○ *After hours of discussion, the cabin staff agreed to call off the planned strike.*

agreed /əˈɡriːd/ *adjective* generally accepted ○ *The millibar is an agreed unit of pressure.*

agreement /əˈɡriːmənt/ *noun* **1.** the state of having the same idea or opinion as somebody □ **we are in agreement** we agree **2.** a document in which the things that two or more people or organisations have agreed to do are written down ○ *Regional Air Navigation Agreements*

ahead /əˈhed/ *adverb* in front □ **look ahead** look some distance in front of you □ **straight ahead** directly in front

ahead of /əˈhed əv/ *preposition* **1.** in front of ○ *Air ahead of a cold front is warmer than air behind a cold front.* **2.** in advance of or at an earlier time than ○ *The flight from Paris arrived 10 minutes ahead of schedule.*

AHRS *noun* a sensor which provides information on the pitch, bank and heading of an aircraft. Full form **attitude heading reference system**

AI *abbreviation* attitude indicator

AIAA *abbreviation* area of intense air activity

AIC *abbreviation* aeronautical information circular

aid /eɪd/ *noun* something which helps somebody do something ■ *verb* to help ○ *Computers can aid students in their studies.*

AIDS /eɪdz/ *abbreviation* **1.** airborne integrated data system **2.** aircraft integrated data system

aileron /ˈeɪlərɒn/ *noun* a horizontal control surface hinged to the mainplane, which enables an aeroplane to bank or roll ○ *By rotating the yoke the ailerons are moved and the aircraft rolls into a turn.* (NOTE: The word comes from the French 'aile', meaning 'wing'.)

aim /eɪm/ *noun* a goal or objective ○ *A 100% safe operation is the aim of all airline companies.* ■ *verb* to intend or to try to do something □ **we aim to succeed** we intend to succeed

AIP *abbreviation* Aeronautical Information Publication

air /eə/ *noun* the mixture of gases which forms the Earth's atmosphere ○ *Air enters the cabin through an inlet.*

AIRAC *abbreviation* aeronautical information regulation and control

Air Accident Investigation Branch /ˌeər ˌæksɪd(ə)nt ɪnˌvestɪˈgeɪʃ(ə)n ˌbrɑːntʃ/ *noun* the department of the CAA of the United Kingdom responsible for establishing the cause of accidents. Abbreviation **AAIB**

airborne /ˈeəbɔːn/ *adjective* lifted and kept in the air by aerodynamic forces ○ *Shortly after the aircraft becomes airborne, the undercarriage is retracted.*

airborne installation /ˌeəbɔːn ˌɪnstəˈleɪʃ(ə)n/ *noun* a radio device in an aircraft which operates in conjunction with a ground installation ○ *The airborne installation comprises an antenna, receiver and indicator(s).*

airborne weather radar /ˌeəbɔːn ˈweθə ˌreɪdɑː/ *noun* a radar installation in an aircraft to give the flight crew information about the weather along their route. Abbreviation **AWR**

air-breathing engine /ˌeə ˌbriːθɪŋ ˈendʒɪn/ an engine that burns a mixture of liquid fuel and air (NOTE: There are four types of air-breathing engine: turbo jet, turbo prop, turbofan and ramjet.)

air bridge /ˈeə brɪdʒ/ *noun* a link provided by aircraft that carry people and supplies between two places, especially in situations where travel by land is not possible

Airbus /ˈeəbʌs/ a trademark for a large passenger jet aircraft manufactured by aerospace companies from different European countries working together

air conditioner /ˌeə kənˈdɪʃ(ə)nə/ *noun* a device which filters and cools the air in a room or in an aircraft ○ *In order to obtain maximum engine power, the air conditioner should be switched off for take-off.*

air conditioning /eə kənˈdɪʃ(ə)nɪŋ/ *noun* a system for controlling the temperature of the air in a building or in an aircraft

air-cooled /ˈeə ˌkuːld/ *adjective* cooled by means of a flow of air □ **air-cooled engines** piston aero-engines cooled by air, not water

air corridor /ˈeə ˌkɒrɪdɔː/ *noun* a route that aircraft must take through an area in which flying is restricted

aircraft /ˈeəkrɑːft/ *noun* a machine that is able to travel through the air ○ *Aeroplanes, gliders, balloons, airships, helicopters, etc., are all aircraft.* Abbreviation **ACFT** (NOTE: **Aircraft** has no plural form.)

aircraft classification number /ˌeəkrɑːft ˌklæsɪfɪˈkeɪʃ(ə)n ˌnʌmbə/ *noun* a number expressing the relative effect of an aircraft on a pavement for a specified sub-grade strength. Abbreviation **CAN**

aircraft condition monitoring system /ˌeəkrɑːft kənˌdɪʃ(ə)n ˈmɒnɪt(ə)rɪŋ ˌsɪstəm/ *noun* full form of **ACMS**

aircraft configuration /ˌeəkrɑːft kənˌfɪgəˈreɪʃ(ə)n/ *noun* a particular combination of moveable parts such as flaps and landing gear that affects the aerodynamics of the aircraft

aircraft proximity hazard /ˌeəkrɑːft prɒkˈsɪmɪti ˌhæzəd/ *noun* same as **airprox**

aircraft stability /ˌeəkrɑːft stəˈbɪləti/ *noun* the tendency of an aircraft to return to its original attitude after being deflected

aircrew /ˈeəkruː/ *noun* the pilot, navigator and other crew members of an aircraft

air cushion vehicle /ˌeə ˌkuʃ(ə)n ˈviːɪk(ə)l/ *noun* same as **hovercraft**

air data computer /ˌeə ˌdeɪtə kəm ˈpjuːtə/ *noun* an electronic device which provides information such as air temperature, airspeed and static pressure. Abbreviation **ADC**

air density /ˈeə ˌdensəti/ *noun* the density of the atmosphere

airfield /ˈeəfiːld/ *noun* an area of land given over to runways, taxiways and aprons ○ *When the pressure setting on the altimeter is set to 1013.25 millibars, the pressure altitude of the airfield is known as QNE.*

air filter /ˈeə ˌfɪltə/ *noun* a device to filter solid particles out of the air in engine and ventilation systems

airflow /ˈeəfləʊ/ *noun* **1.** the movement of air over the aircraft as it travels through the atmosphere **2.** a current of air flowing through or past an object or body ○ *The compressor must provide an adequate airflow through the engine.*

airfoil /ˈeərfɔɪl/ *noun* US same as **aerofoil**

airframe /ˈeəfreɪm/ *noun* the body of the aircraft without the engines, instruments and internal fittings ○ *The airframe has to be built to very specific requirements.*

airframe icing /ˈeəfreɪm ˌaɪsɪŋ/ *noun* ice that forms on the aircraft structure as opposed to on components such as carburettors

air gap /ˈeə gæp/ *noun* a space between two things □ **air gap type**

spark plug a spark plug with a space between the electrodes, across which the spark jumps

air intake /ˈeə ˌɪnteɪk/ *noun* the front part of a jet engine where air enters

air lane /ˈeə leɪn/ *noun* a regular route that aeroplanes fly along

airline /ˈeəlaɪn/ *noun* a company which manages air transport services for passengers or goods ○ *Which airline is she working for, Air France or Air Canada?* ○ *Most airlines do not allow passengers to smoke during flight.*

airliner /ˈeəlaɪnə/ *noun* an aeroplane designed to carry large numbers of passengers ○ *Concorde is the world's fastest airliner.*

airline representative /ˌeəlaɪn ˌreprɪˈzentətɪv/ *noun* a person who acts on behalf of an airline, or a person who works for an airline ○ *Passengers should assemble in the departure lounge where an airline representative will meet them.*

airline security area /ˌeəlaɪn sɪ ˈkjʊərɪti ˌeəriə/ *noun* an area in which measures are taken by an airline to ensure the safety of people and property

Airline Transport Pilot's Licence /ˌeəlaɪn ˌtrænspɔːt ˈpaɪləts ˌlaɪs(ə)ns/ *noun* the licence that a person must have to be the pilot-in-command or co-pilot of a public transport aircraft. Abbreviation **ATPL**

airman /ˈeəmən/ *noun* a person who is a member of a country's Air Force

airmanship /ˈeəmənʃɪp/ *noun* all-round skill in piloting an aircraft which includes academic knowledge, common sense, quick reactions, awareness, experience, consideration for other people and property ○ *Keeping a careful lookout for other aircraft in the circuit is good airmanship.*

'I was always told by my airmanship instructor, in an emergency, to find the largest piece of asphalt with the biggest fire trucks' [*INTER PILOT*]

air mass /ˈeə mæs/ *noun* a very large mass of air in the atmosphere in which the temperature is almost constant and which is divided from another mass by a front ○ *Air masses are divided into two* *types according to source region, and these are known as polar and tropical air masses.*

airpark /'eəpɑːk/ *noun* a small airport, usually found near a business or industrial centre

airplane /'eəpleɪn/ *US* same as **aeroplane**

air pocket /'eəpɒkɪt/ *noun* a small area where the air is less dense or where there is a downward air current, and which makes an aircraft lose height suddenly

air pollution /eə pə'luːʃ(ə)n/ *noun* pollution of the air by gas, smoke, ash, etc. ○ *Solid particles in the air include dust, sand, volcanic ash and atmospheric pollution.* Also called **atmospheric pollution**

airport /'eəpɔːt/ *noun* a civil aerodrome designed for the take-off and landing of passenger-carrying aircraft for the general public and/or cargo aircraft ○ *London Heathrow is one of the busiest airports in the world.* Abbreviation **A/P**

airport authority /,eəpɔːt ɔː'θɒrɪti/ *noun* the organisation responsible for the running of an airport

airport security officer /,eəpɔːt sɪ'kjʊərɪti ,ɒfɪsə/ *noun* a person employed by an airport authority to check passengers and baggage for illegal substances or devices, e.g. drugs, guns

airport surface detection equipment /,eəpɔːt ,sɜːfɪs dɪ'tekʃ(ə)n ɪ,kwɪpmənt/ *noun* short-range radar equipment that scans the surface area of an airport and tracks the movement of aircraft and other vehicles on the ground

airprox /'eəprɒks/ *noun* a situation in which aircraft are too close to one another in an area of airspace and there is the possibility of danger to them. Also called **aircraft proximity hazard**

air-sea rescue /,eə siː 'reskjuː/ *noun* a rescue at sea in which aircraft, especially helicopters, are used

airship /'eəʃɪp/ *noun* a powered, gas-filled balloon which can be steered ○ *An*

airship is classified as a lighter-than-air craft.

airshow /'eəʃəʊ/ *noun* a public display of aircraft in flight and on the ground, held at an airfield

airside /'eəsaɪd/ *noun* the part of an airport where the aircraft take off and land, load, or unload

air sock /'eə sɒk/ *noun* same as **windsock**

airspace /'eəspeɪs/ *noun* the part of the atmosphere that is above a particular geographical area and is subject to the laws of a particular country or controlling authority ○ *The Korean 747 flew into Soviet airspace and was shot down.*

airspeed /'eəspiːd/ *noun* the speed of the aircraft relative to the air around it ○ *Maintain a constant airspeed on final approach.*

airspeed indicator /'eəspiːd ,ɪndɪkeɪtə/ *noun* a primary cockpit or flight deck instrument which shows the pilot the speed of the aircraft in relation to the air around it ○ *Airspeed is shown in knots on the airspeed indicator.* Abbreviation **ASI**

COMMENT: The position of the pitot tube and the attitude of an aircraft can affect the accuracy of the airspeed indicator. Aircraft operating handbooks usually have a table to help pilots calculate calibrated airspeed (CAS).

air station /'eə ,steɪʃ(ə)n/ *noun* a small airfield with facilities for the maintenance of aircraft

airstream /'eəstriːm/ *noun* the flow of air caused by the movement of the aircraft through the air ○ *Pressure is built up inside the pitot tube by the airstream.*

COMMENT: Unlike airflow, airstream does not refer to the movement of air around the airframe and its aerodynamic effect.

airstrip /'eəstrɪp/ *noun* a place for aircraft to take off and land that has no facilities and is often temporary

air taxi /'eə ,tæksi/ *noun* a small commercial aircraft used for short flights between places not on a regular airline route

air terminal /'eə ˌtɜːmɪn(ə)l/ *noun* **1.** an airport building with a range of facilities where passengers check in before boarding their plane and where they arrive when their plane lands **2.** a building in a city for receiving passengers who are being transported to or from an airport by train or bus

air terrorism /'eə ˌterərɪz(ə)m/ *noun* violent actions that aim to frighten or kill passengers, disrupt air services, or damage or destroy aircraft in an attempt to achieve a political objective

air-tight /'eə taɪt/ *adjective* closed or sealed so that air cannot get in or out

air-to-air /'eətə'eə/ *adjective* between one airborne aircraft and another ○ *air-to-air communications* □ **air-to-air communications** communications between one airborne aircraft and another

air to air refuelling area /ˌeə tə ˌeə riː'fjuːəlɪŋ ˌeəriə/ *noun* an area of airspace in which tanker aircraft are permitted to refuel other aircraft in flight. Abbreviation **AARA**

air-to-ground visibility /ˌeə tə ˌɡraʊnd ˌvɪzɪ'bɪlɪti/ *noun* a description of how easily seen an object on the ground is from the air ○ *Glare caused by reflection of sunlight from the top of a layer of fog or haze can seriously reduce the air-to-ground visibility.*

air-to-surface /ˌeə tə 'sɜːfɪs/ *adjective* directed from a flying aircraft to a point on the ground

air traffic /'eə ˌtræfɪk/ *noun* aircraft operating in the air or on the airport surface ○ *Students practising circuit flying need to keep a very careful lookout especially at times when there is a lot of air traffic.*

air traffic control /ˌeə ˌtræfɪk kən'trəʊl/ *noun* a service that oversees and guides the movements of aircraft and provides for the safe and efficient flow of air traffic ○ *Controllers in the tower provide an air traffic control service for aircraft in the air around the airfield.* Abbreviation **ATC**

COMMENT: Air Traffic Control's main function is to maintain separation between aircraft operating within Instrument Flight Rules (IFR), but it also provides a service to aircraft using Visual Flight Rules (VFR). Ground control is for aircraft taxiing to and from runways. The tower controls aircraft around an airport, clearing them for take-off or landing. Departure and approach controls monitor and control aircraft around the airport, and en route centres control traffic between airports.

air traffic controller /ˌeə ˌtræfɪk kən'trəʊlə/ *noun* a person who works in air traffic control and whose main task is to ensure correct separation of aircraft in all phases of flight ○ *The air traffic controller approved the emergency landing.* Abbreviation **ATC.** ◊ **controller**

air traffic movements /ˌeə 'træfɪk ˌmuːvmənts/ *plural noun* the number of aircraft taking off and landing ○ *an increase in air traffic movements*

airway /'eəweɪ/ *noun* an area of the sky, usually rectangular in cross-section, along which civil aircraft fly from place to place ○ *Airways provide a high degree of safety by ensuring adequate separation between aircraft.* ○ *Aircraft inside an airway are controlled by ATC.* (NOTE: Airways are usually 10 nm wide with a centreline joining navigational beacons.)

Airways /'eəweɪz/ *noun* a commercial company operating flights (NOTE: Usually used in the names of companies, e.g. British Airways, South African Airways)

airworthiness /'eəˌwɜːðinəs/ *noun* the state of an aircraft with regard to whether it can fly safely, as determined by a national certifying authority

airworthiness directive *noun* a regulation issued by an aviation authority when a problem has been identified with a particular aircraft part. Abbreviation **AD**

airworthy /'eəwɜːði/ *adjective* meeting the standards of a national certifying authority ○ *It is the pilot's responsibility to ensure that the aircraft is airworthy.*

AIS *abbreviation* aeronautical information services

aisle /aɪl/ *noun* a long passageway between the seats in the passenger cabin of an airliner □ **aisle seat** a seat which is by an aisle, as opposed to a window seat

alarm /ə'lɑːm/ *noun* **1.** fear or worry ○ *If the ammeter shows a high level of charge after start-up, it is quite normal and no cause for alarm.* **2.** a warning sound or light ○ *In the event of fire or overheat, the control unit will produce an alarm.* ■ *verb* to frighten or worry ○ *Severe turbulence may alarm passengers.*

alert /ə'lɜːt/ *adjective* fully awake, watchful and ready to deal with any situation ○ *The crew must be alert at all times to the possibility of hijacking, bombs and stowaways.* ■ *noun* a signal, warning everyone to be alert □ **to be on the alert** to be watchful and ready for anything that may happen ■ *verb* to warn ○ *It is the cabin staff's responsibility to alert the flight crew if they see smoke coming from an engine.*

alight /ə'laɪt/ *adjective* on fire ○ *Although the passenger thought he had extinguished his cigarette, it was still alight when he threw it into the waste disposal bin.* ■ *verb* (*formal*) **1.** (*of people*) to leave or get off an aeroplane ○ *At some airports, passengers alight onto the apron when they leave the aircraft.* **2.** (*of aircraft*) to land ○ *An aeroplane may not fly over a city below such a height as would allow it to alight in the event of an engine failure.*

align /ə'laɪn/ *verb* **1.** to position along an axis or line ○ *The nose wheel must be aligned in a fore and aft direction during retraction.* **2.** to set in a correct position in relation to something else ○ *Aligned white marks on the wheel and tyre indicate that there is no creep.*

alignment /ə'laɪnmənt/ *noun* **1.** position in relation to an axis or a line □ **to check the alignment of something** to make sure it is in the correct position relative to an axis or line □ **to maintain alignment with the runway** to keep the aircraft on the imaginary extended centre line of the runway **2.** correct position in relation to something else □

out of alignment not aligned as it should be

alkaline /'ælkəlaɪn/ *noun* a substance with a pH value of more than 7

alleviate /ə'liːvieɪt/ *verb* to reduce or lessen the harmful effect of something ○ *Anti-icing additives are available to alleviate the problem of icing.*

alleviation /ə,liːvi'eɪʃ(ə)n/ *noun* a reduction or lessening of the harmful effect of something ○ *Deep, regular breathing may provide some alleviation from stress.*

allocate /'æləkeɪt/ *verb* to provide something particular for a given purpose ○ *Special seats are allocated to mothers with small children.*

allocation /,ælə'keɪʃ(ə)n/ *noun* the provision of something particular for a given purpose ○ *At the check-in desk, airline staff are responsible for the allocation of seats to passengers.* □ **frequency allocation** the frequency or range of radio frequencies set aside for a particular use ○ *The frequency allocation for VOR is 108–117.975 MHz.*

allow /ə'laʊ/ *verb* to enable, to permit or to authorise ○ *An engine should be run at low rpm after flight to allow engine components to cool.* ○ *Additional fuel is carried to allow for holding en route.* ○ *Passengers are not allowed to smoke on some aeroplanes.*

allowable /ə'laʊəb(ə)l/ *adjective* permitted or authorised ○ *maximum allowable weight* ○ *maximum allowable tyre pressure*

allowance /ə'laʊəns/ *noun* **1.** consideration for possibilities or changing circumstances □ **to make allowances for** to take into account ○ *When estimating flight duration, make allowances for taxiing time.* **2.** something such as money given at regular intervals or for a specific purpose ○ *a travel allowance to cover hotel and restaurant bills.* **3.** the amount of something that somebody is allowed to have

'…with many four and six seat aircraft, it is not possible to fill all the seats, use the maximum baggage allowance, fill all the fuel tanks and remain within the approved centre of gravity limits' [*Civil Aviation*

Authority, General Aviation Safety Sense Leaflet]

alloy /'ælɔɪ/ *noun* a mixture of metals ○ *an alloy of aluminium and lithium*

aloft /ə'lɒft/ *adjective* up in the air

alter /'ɔːltə/ *verb* to change, modify or adjust ○ *If there is a risk of collision, alter course to the right.* ○ *If the rate of descent is too low, alter the throttle setting accordingly.* ○ *The rudder linkage was altered to comply with certification requirements.*

alteration /ˌɔːltə'reɪʃ(ə)n/ *noun* **1.** a change, modification or adjustment ○ *It was discovered that alterations had been made to the log book.* ○ *As a result of the accident, alterations were made to the design of the carburettor heat system.* **2.** the act of making changes, modifications or adjustments □ **heading alteration** the act of making of heading corrections

alternate *adjective* /ɔːl'tɜːnət/ **1.** every other ○ *A, c, e, and g are alternate letters, as are b, d, f, h, etc.* □ **alternate days** every other day ○ *There are outward flights on alternate days, i.e. on Mondays, Wednesdays and Fridays.* **2.** *US* same as **alternative** ■ *noun* /ɔːl'tɜːnət/ an aerodrome of second choice to be used if the aircraft cannot be landed at the aerodrome of first choice because of bad weather, etc. ○ *The point of no return is calculated before departure to cover the chance that both the terminal airfield and its alternate become unavailable during flight.* ■ *verb* /'ɔːltəneɪt/ to happen in turns □ **Captain Smith and Captain Jones alternate as CFI on a daily rota** each captain has one day on duty as CFI followed by a day off, on which the other captain acts as CFI

alternating current /ˌɔːltəneɪtɪŋ 'kʌrənt/ *noun* an electric current which reverses its direction at regular intervals ○ *Resistance to alternating current remains almost constant and is independent of frequency.* Abbreviation **AC**

alternative /ɔːl'tɜːnətɪv/ *adjective* referring to another or a second possibility ○ *A turbine bypass, in the form of an alternative exhaust duct is fitted with*

a valve. □ **an alternative means of doing something** another or different way of doing something ■ *noun* another choice or possibility ○ *In some emergency situations the pilot may have no alternative but to force-land the aircraft as soon as possible.*

alternator /'ɔːltəneɪtə/ *noun* a type of generator designed to produce AC power

altimeter /'æltɪmiːtə/ *noun* a radio instrument for measuring vertical distance or altitude □ **altimeter check** a routine check to ensure that the altimeter pressure setting is correct □ **altimeter display** the display of altitude information, which can be given in analogue or digital form. ◊ **pointer**

altitude /'æltɪtjuːd/ *noun* the vertical distance between an aircraft, or a point or a level, and mean sea-level □ **to lose altitude** to descend from higher to lower altitude □ **cabin altitude** the artificial altitude created in the cabin by pressurisation

alto- /æltəʊ/ *prefix* at a moderate or high altitude

altocumulus /ˌæltəʊ'kjuːmjʊləs/ *noun* small white cumulus clouds which form as a layer at moderate altitude, usually meaning fair weather. Compare **stratocumulus**

altostratus /ˌæltəʊ'strɑːtəs/ *noun* a uniform layer cloud at moderate altitude

aluminium /ˌæljə'mɪniəm/ *noun* a strong, light metal used in the construction of aircraft (NOTE: The US English is **aluminum**.)

COMMENT: In recent years, aluminium has been increasingly replaced by the use of composite materials in the construction of different types of aircraft, from small home-built light aircraft to transport aircraft such as the Airbus A320.

aluminum /ə'luːmɪnəm/ *noun US* same as **aluminium**

AMA *abbreviation* approach monitoring aid

amber /'æmbə/ *adjective* an orange or yellow colour ○ *An amber light flashes on the instrument panel.* (NOTE: Amber is often used to describe the colour of the yellow light in traffic signals.)

ambient /'æmbiənt/ *adjective* referring to the surrounding atmospheric conditions ○ *Fresh ambient air is routed into the cabin.* □ **ambient temperature** the temperature outside the aircraft

ambient pressure /ˌæmbiənt 'preʃə/ *noun* the pressure outside the aircraft

ambiguity /ˌæmbɪ'gjuːɪti/ *noun* something heard or seen which can be understood in more than one way, thus resulting in possible confusion □ **to avoid ambiguity** to avoid misunderstanding or confusion ○ *Correct use of R/T phraseology avoids ambiguity.*

ambiguous /æm'bɪgjuəs/ *adjective* able to be understood in more than one way ○ *It is important that R/T transmissions are not ambiguous.*

AMD *abbreviation* amendment

amend /ə'mend/ *verb* to change, update, improve or correct something □ **he amended the entry in his log book** he corrected or changed the entry in his log book

amendment /ə'mendmənt/ *noun* a change, updating, improvement or correction made, e.g., to a document or procedure ○ *When a terminal aerodrome forecast requires amendment, the amended forecast is indicated by inserting AMD after TAF.*

ammeter /'æmiːtə/ *noun* an instrument for measuring amperes in order to give the strength of an electric current ○ *The centre-zero ammeter tells the pilot the status of the aircraft battery.*

amp /æmp/ *abbreviation* ampere

amperage /'æmpərɪdʒ/ *noun* the strength of an electric current expressed in amperes ○ *Measuring the amperage of a motor can give a rough estimate of the load on the motor.*

ampere /'æmpeə/ *noun* a unit of electric current equal to one volt flowing through an impedance of one ohm ○ *a 13-amp fuse* ○ *Current flow is measured in amperes.* Abbreviation **amp** □ **ampere hours** number of amperes per hour ○ *Battery capacity is rated in ampere hours.*

ample /'æmpəl/ *adjective* plenty of ○ *During the course you will have ample opportunity to demonstrate your skill.* □ **ample time** plenty of time

amplification /ˌæmplɪfɪ'keɪʃ(ə)n/ *noun* the act of increasing the strength of an electrical signal ○ *Amplification of the signal increases the volume.*

amplifier /'æmplɪfaɪə/ *noun* an electronic device for increasing the strength of an electrical signal ○ *If the power supply from the amplifier to the gauge fails, the needle slowly falls to zero.*

amplify /'æmplɪfaɪ/ *verb* to increase the strength of an electrical signal ○ *An electric current is amplified and then transmitted.* (NOTE: **amplifies – amplifying – amplified**)

amplitude /'æmplɪtjuːd/ *noun* the maximum variation of a vibration or oscillation from the position of equilibrium ○ *to calculate fuel required, multiply the duration of the flight by the consumption of the engine at the required power*

AMS *abbreviation* aeronautical mobile service

AMSL *abbreviation* above mean sea level

AMSS *abbreviation* automatic message switching system

anabatic /ænə'bætɪk/ *adjective* referring to a warm flow of air travelling up a hillside or mountainside. Compare **katabatic**

anabatic wind /ˌænəbætɪk 'wɪnd/ *noun* a wind current, caused by solar heating of the land, that rises up a south-facing mountainside ○ *South-facing slopes are most suitable for the anabatic wind.* Compare **katabatic wind**

analog /'ænəlɒg/ *adjective* same as **analogue**

analogous /ə'næləgəs/ *adjective* similar or comparable to ○ *Isobars are analogous to contour lines.*

analogue /'ænəlɒg/ *adjective* **1.** representing a quantity or signal that varies continuously by means of a physical apparatus such as a dial and pointer ○ *The electronic centralised aircraft monitor (ECAM) does not have analogue* *presentation of engine information.* **2.** □ **analogue display (on a clock)** a traditional hands and face display on a clock or dial. Compare **digital display**

analyse /'ænəlaɪz/, **analyze** *verb* to break down into parts and study very closely □ **to analyse fuel** to separate fuel into its different parts to find out what it consists of □ **to analyse a chart** to examine a chart in detail

analysis /ə'næləsɪs/ *noun* breaking down a substance into its parts in order to study them closely ○ *At a crash site, samples of materials are removed for analysis.* (NOTE: The plural form is **analyses** /ə'nælɪsiːz/ .) □ **chart analysis** careful study of charts

anchor /'æŋkə/ *noun* a device connected to and dropped from a boat in order to prevent the boat from moving in the water ■ *verb* to drop an anchor to prevent the boat from moving

anemograph /ə'neməgrɑːf/ *noun* an instrument which maintains a continuous recording of wind direction and speed on a graph ○ *The anemograph gives a continuous recording of wind velocity which is displayed on a chart and reveals gusts, squalls and lulls.*

anemometer /ænɪ'mɒmɪtə/ *noun* an instrument, usually attached to a building, with three or four 'cups' which rotate with the wind thus providing wind-speed information ○ *The strength of the wind can be seen by the speed with which the anemometer rotates.*

aneroid /'ænərɔɪd/ *adjective* not containing or using liquid

aneroid barometer /ˌænərɔɪd bə'rɒmɪtə/ *noun* a barometer which uses an aneroid capsule to sense atmospheric pressure changes

aneroid capsule /ˌænərɔɪd 'kæpsjuːl/ *noun* a thin flexible cylindrical box, usually made of metal, which has most of the air removed from it and which expands and contracts with changes in atmospheric pressure ○ *The aneroid capsule in the barometer is connected to a system of levers which operate a pointer.*

aneroid switch /'ænərɔɪd swɪtʃ/ *noun* a switch operated by an aneroid capsule

angle /'æŋgəl/ *noun* the difference in direction between two lines or surfaces measured in degrees

angle of attack /ˌæŋg(ə)l əv ə'tæk/ *noun* the angle formed between the relative airflow and the chord line of the aerofoil

COMMENT: The angle of attack is related to the flight path of the aircraft, not to the angle the wing makes with the horizontal. If the angle of attack becomes too great, the smooth airflow over the upper surface of the wing will break down. If no corrective action is taken by the pilot, there will be a sudden loss of lift and the aircraft will stall.

angle of incidence /ˌæŋg(ə)l əv 'ɪnsɪd(ə)ns/ *noun* the angle formed between the chord-line of the mainplane and the horizontal when the aircraft is in the rigging position

angle of inclination /ˌæŋg(ə)l əv ˌɪnklɪ'neɪʃ(ə)n/ *noun* the angle formed between a sloping path or surface and a reference point or line which is either horizontal or vertical ○ *Between any two meridians there is an angle of inclination one to the other which varies with latitude.*

angular /'æŋgjʊlə/ *adjective* referring to or forming an angle ○ *The angular difference between the direction of magnetic north and compass north is called variation.*

anneal /ə'niːl/ *verb* to heat and allow to cool slowly in order to strengthen ○ *Sheet and plate magnesium are annealed at the rolling mill.*

annotate /'ænəteɪt/ *verb* to add notes to an existing document, book, chart, etc. ○ *He annotated his report after he was asked to give the exact time of the incident.* ○ *Variation is annotated east or west according to the direction of change.*

annotation /ˌænə'teɪʃ(ə)n/ *noun* the act of adding notes to a document, book, chart, etc., or the notes added

announce /əˈnaʊns/ *verb* to state something publicly or officially ○ *British Airways announce the departure of flight BA152 to New York.*

announcement /əˈnaʊnsmənt/ *noun* a public statement ○ *The captain made a public address (PA) system announcement asking passengers to remain seated.*

annual /ˈænjʊəl/ *adjective* **1.** happening once a year □ **annual inspection** an inspection that happens once a year **2.** over a period of one year ○ *Overload operations should not exceed 5% of annual departures.*

annular /ˈænjʊlə/ *adjective* shaped like a ring

annunciation /ənʌnsiˈeɪʃ(ə)n/ *noun* an announcement or indication on the annunciator panel □ **failure annunciation** signals on the annunciator panel indicating the failure of a system

annunciator /əˈnʌnsieɪtə/ *noun* a device which gives off a sound or light to indicate which of several electrical circuits is active ○ *An annunciator panel may contain a precise warning.*

anode /ˈænəʊd/ *noun* a positive pole or electrode ○ *The positive connector of a battery is usually called the anode and is indicated by the sign +.*

anodise /ˈænədaɪz/, **anodize** *verb* to coat or cover by using electrolysis ○ *Anti-corrosion treatment includes the anodizing of aluminium parts.*

anomalous /əˈnɒmələs/ *adjective* referring to something unusual, unexpected or otherwise departing from what is the normal order or range □ **an anomalous instrument reading** an unusual instrument reading which may require further investigation

anomaly /əˈnɒməli/ *noun* something unusual, unexpected or otherwise not within the normal order or range ○ *Any anomalies in the localiser will be detected during calibration.*

anoxia /æˈnɒksiə/ *noun* a state in which no oxygen reaches the body tissues, resulting in death. ◊ **hypoxia**

COMMENT: Anoxia is a complete lack of oxygen and can, of course, be fatal.

Hypoxia is a lack of sufficient oxygen, the symptoms of which are sometimes difficult to detect.

antenna /ænˈtenə/ *noun US* same as **aerial**

anti- /ˈænti/ *prefix* against, opposing ○ *anti-icing* ○ *anticlockwise* ○ *anti-corrosion*

anticipate /ænˈtɪsɪpeɪt/ *verb* to realise what is likely happen and do what is necessary in readiness □ **during take-offs, pilots should anticipate an engine failure** pilots should think ahead and be ready to act immediately if an engine fails during take-off

anticipation /æn,tɪsɪˈpeɪʃ(ə)n/ *noun* a state in which you realise what is likely to happen and do what is necessary in readiness

anticipation of landmarks /æn,tɪsɪpeɪʃ(ə)n əv ˈlændmɑːks/ *noun* the action of watching out for landmarks, which you know from flight planning should be visible at a particular stage of a flight

anticlockwise /,æntiˈklɒkwaɪz/ *adjective, adverb* referring to a circular movement in the opposite direction to the hands of a clock ○ *Turn the nut anticlockwise to loosen it.* Opposite **clockwise**

anti-collision /,ænti kəˈlɪʒ(ə)n/ *adjective* helping to prevent collisions

anti-collision light /,ænti kə ˈlɪʒ(ə)n laɪt/ *noun* a flashing white light on an aircraft

anti-corrosion /,ænti kəˈrəʊʒ(ə)n/ *adjective* protecting against corrosion, especially rust ○ *an anti-corrosion treatment*

anticyclone /,æntiˈsaɪkləʊn/ *noun* an area of high atmospheric pressure, usually associated with fine dry weather in summer and fog in winter ○ *Winds circulate round an anticyclone clockwise in the northern hemisphere and anticlockwise in the southern hemisphere.*

anti-icing /,ænti ˈaɪsɪŋ/ *adjective* preventing icing ○ *anti-icing additive*

anti-icing fluid /,ænti ˈaɪsɪŋ ,fluːɪd/ *noun* a fluid which prevents icing

anti-skid /ˌænti ˈskɪd/ *adjective* designed to prevent skidding

anvil /ˈænvɪl/ *noun* a metal block which ends in a point, has a rounded bottom and a flat top, and on which horseshoes, etc., are made ○ *A cumulonimbus cloud has a characteristic anvil shape.*

anvil cloud /ˈænvɪl klaʊd/ *noun* a cloud, usually a large dark thundercloud, which has the shape of an anvil

A/P *abbreviation* **1.** airport **2.** autopilot

apart /əˈpɑːt/ *adverb* separated from one another ○ *The jets were only 200 feet apart, vertically.*

aperture /ˈæpətʃə/ *noun* an opening ○ *Any aperture or cut-out in the fuselage structure must be specially strengthened.*

APHAZ *abbreviation* aircraft proximity hazard

APP *abbreviation* **1.** approach **2.** approach control

apparent /əˈpærənt/ *adjective* **1.** obvious, clear ○ *It became apparent that carbon monoxide was entering the cabin.* □ **from the above, it will be apparent that …** from the above, it will be clear that … **2.** seeming or appearing to be ○ *an apparent failure of the system* ○ *The ILS showed an apparent deflection to the right.*

appear /əˈpɪə/ *verb* **1.** to come into view ○ *Another aircraft appeared on the radar screen.* **2.** to seem to be ○ *Although air may appear to be still, it is in fact, moving.*

appearance /əˈpɪərəns/ *noun* **1.** an instance of being seen or coming into view ○ *The appearance of the passenger on the flight deck surprised the crew.* **2.** the way something looks ○ *It may be difficult to recognise a particular stretch of coast in an area simply by its appearance.*

appendix /əˈpendɪks/ *noun* a section containing additional information, often found at the end of a book, etc. ○ *Charts are reproduced as an appendix to the map section.* (NOTE: The plural form is **appendices**.)

applicable /əˈplɪkəb(ə)l/ *adjective* **1.** relevant or appropriate □ **rule 24 is not applicable in this case** rule 24 cannot be used in this case **2.** suitable, necessary, appropriate ○ *Emergency systems are checked when applicable.*

application /ˌæplɪˈkeɪʃ(ə)n/ *noun* **1.** a formal request, often on paper, for employment □ **application form** a form to be filled out by a person looking for a job, and sent back to the organisation offering the job **2.** the act of putting a substance onto something □ **the application of a coat of paint** the covering of something with a coat of paint **3.** the act of using something, e.g. an ability, to carry out a task ○ *When an accident occurs, the application of knowledge and skills is important.*

apply /əˈplaɪ/ *verb* **1.** □ **to apply for a job** to formally ask for employment ○ *He applied for the post of chief engineer but was not successful.* **2.** to put on ○ *to apply a coat of paint* ○ *Apply a plaster to the skin.* **3.** to use something to carry out a task ○ *Apply the same method as in the example.* **4.** to be relevant or relate to ○ *The rules which apply to the measurement of wind velocities on isobaric charts apply equally to contour charts.* (NOTE: **applying – applied**)

appreciable /əˈpriːʃəb(ə)l/ *adjective* **1.** possible to measure ○ *Appreciable weakening may be permitted without risk of failure.* **2.** considerable, large in size or amount □ **there is an appreciable difference between statute miles and nautical miles** there is a big difference between statute miles and nautical miles

appreciate /əˈpriːʃieɪt/ *verb* **1.** to understand or recognise the importance or significance of something ○ *The map reader is in a position to appreciate the relative values of the features seen on the ground.* **2.** to increase in value ○ *The value of the building has appreciated by 100% in 10 years.* Opposite **depreciate 3.** to be thankful or grateful for something ○ *The student appreciated the extra help given by the instructor.*

appreciation /əˌpriːʃiˈeɪʃ(ə)n/ *noun* **1.** understanding ○ *It is essential to have* *an appreciation of the basic gas laws.* **2.** an increase in value ○ *There has been an appreciation of 100% in the value of the building in 10 years.* Opposite **depreciation 3.** thankfulness, gratitude ○ *After gaining her private pilot's licence, the newly-qualified pilot showed her appreciation by sending a letter of thanks to her instructor.*

approach /ə'prəʊtʃ/ *noun* **1.** a path towards something ○ *The approach to the terminal was blocked by an overturned lorry.* **2.** the descent of an aircraft towards the place where it intends to land. Abbreviation **APP 3.** a way of achieving or doing something □ **to take a different approach to a situation** to deal with or to manage a situation in a different way ■ *verb* **1.** to move nearer in place or time to something ○ *The aircraft is approaching a danger area.* □ **nightfall is approaching** it will soon be dark **2.** to have a particular mental attitude towards something ○ *He approaches his studies with great enthusiasm.* **3.** to speak to or get in touch with somebody ○ *You must approach the chief flying instructor regarding your request for a week's holiday.*

approach control /ə'prəʊtʃ kən ˌtrəʊl/ *noun* a control station in an air traffic control centre that guides an aircraft while it is making its approach

approach monitoring aid /ə 'prəʊtʃ ˌmɒnɪtərɪŋ ˌeɪd/ *noun* an instrument or system that helps an air traffic controller to track the position and movements of an aircraft during its approach. Abbreviation **AMA**

approach path /ə'prəʊtʃ pɑːθ/ *noun* the course taken by the aircraft in preparation for landing

approach plate *noun* a document issued by an aviation authority which provides detailed information about how to land at a given airport in very poor visibility

approach to land /ə,prəʊtʃ tə 'lænd/ *noun* the final stage of the flight when the aircraft is manoeuvred into position, relative to the landing area, in preparation for landing ○ *on the approach to land, the aircraft reduces speed and height*

appropriate /ə'prəʊpriət/ *adjective* suitable or needed □ **appropriate action** the action that is needed to deal with the situation

appropriately /ə'prəʊpriətli/ *adverb* in a way that it is suitable or necessary □ **to adjust the mixture appropriately** to adjust the mixture to suit the conditions

approval /ə'pruːv(ə)l/ *noun* permission or agreement □ **with the captain's approval** with the permission of the captain □ **to meet with the approval** to be approved by ○ *The management's plans for restructuring the airline met with the approval of the shareholders.*

approve /ə'pruːv/ *verb* **1.** to allow or agree to something ○ *The air traffic controller approved the emergency landing.* **2.** □ **to approve of** to believe something to be right or good ○ *Nearly everybody approved of the new colour scheme for the furnishings.* □ **he doesn't approve of women being airline pilots** he believes that it is wrong for women to be airline pilots

approx /ə'prɒks/ same as **approximate**, **approximately**

approximate *adjective* /ə 'prɒksɪmət/ not exact, around or about □ **an approximate distance of 60 nm** about 60 nautical miles ■ *verb* /ə 'prɒksɪmeɪt/ to be close to, to be around (NOTE: **Approximate** can be shortened to **approx** or **APRX** (ICAO).)

approximately /ə'prɒksɪmətli/ *adverb* not exactly, around or about ○ *Approximately 2,000 people work in the airport.* (NOTE: **Approximately** can be shortened to **approx** or **APRX** (ICAO).)

approximation /ə,prɒksɪ'meɪʃ(ə)n/ *noun* a calculation which is not exact but near enough, a rough estimate □ **an approximation of aircraft height** a rough estimate of aircraft height

apron /'eɪprən/ *noun* an area of tarmac, concrete, etc., outside a hangar for parking aircraft (NOTE: The US term is **ramp**.)

APRX *abbreviation* (*ICAO*) **1.** approximate **2.** approximately

APU *abbreviation* auxiliary power unit

aquaplaning /'ækwəpleɪnɪŋ/ *noun* sliding in an uncontrolled way over a thin layer of water on the runway ○ *Aquaplaning is caused by a layer of water between the tyre and the runway.*

arbitrary /'ɑːbɪtrəri/ *adjective* decided by chance rather than by careful logical thought, happening without planning or at random ○ *The statute mile is an arbitrary unit of measurement.* (NOTE: The nautical mile is not an arbitrary unit: it is based on calculations which have a wider use. See **arc**.)

arc /ɑːk/ *noun* part of the circumference of a circle ○ *A nautical mile is the length of an arc on the Earth's surface subtended by an angle of one minute at the centre of the Earth.* ■ *verb* to jump across a gap ○ *The spark arcs from one electrode to another.* ○ *The condenser prevents spark plugs from arcing.* ◊ **gap**

Arctic /'ɑːktɪk/ *adjective* referring to the area around the North Pole □ **cold Arctic air** cold air from the Arctic □ **the Arctic Circle** a parallel running round the Earth at latitude 66°32N, to the north of which lies the Arctic region ■ *noun* □ **the Arctic** the area of the Earth's surface around the North Pole, north of the Arctic Circle ○ *The aircraft flew over the Arctic.*

area /'eəriə/ *noun* **1.** a defined part of a surface **2.** a region □ **area forecasts** a weather forecast for a region rather than, e.g., an aerodrome

area control service /,eəriə kən'trəʊl ,sɜːvɪs/ *noun* a unit that provides air traffic control services to flights within the area for which it is responsible

area navigation /,eəriə ,nævɪ'geɪʃ(ə)n/ a method of navigation that permits aircraft to operate on any desired flight path within the area covered by ground-based navigational aids, self-contained navigational aids or a combination of the two. Abbreviation **RNAV**

argument /'ɑːgjʊmənt/ *noun* **1.** a factor ○ *QNH is the pressure at station level reduced to sea level using arguments of station height and an international standard atmosphere.* **2.** a verbal disagreement □ **to have an argument** to disagree openly and verbally with somebody ○ *The investigation revealed that there had been an argument between the commander and the copilot about the advisability of continuing with the final approach to land.* **3.** a reason ○ *One of the arguments in favour of building the new terminal is the increase in opportunities of employment for the local residents.*

arid /'ærɪd/ *adjective* very dry □ **arid terrain** desert □ **an arid, sub-tropical climate** a hot, dry climate

arise /ə'raɪz/ *verb* to come into being, to happen, to show up or to appear ○ *Should any problems arise, report back to me immediately.* (NOTE: **arising – arose – arisen**)

arm /ɑːm/ *noun* **1.** a device similar in function to a human arm, operating as a lever **2.** the horizontal distance from a reference point to the centre of gravity ○ *The principle of the arm is used in weight and balance calculations for an aircraft.* ■ *verb* to make ready for action or use ○ *Door-mounted escape slides are armed before flight.*

armature /'ɑːmətʃə/ *noun* the rotating coils of an electric motor or dynamo ○ *Secondary windings are wound over the primary windings and the whole assembly is known as an armature.*

ARR *abbreviation* arrival

arrange /ə'reɪndʒ/ *verb* **1.** to organise, to plan and prepare ○ *to arrange a meeting* **2.** to put in special position ○ *Charts should be numbered and arranged in order of use.* ○ *A series of dipoles are arranged in a circle.*

arrangement /ə'reɪndʒmənt/ *noun* **1.** a plan ○ *The arrangements for the VIPs are being handled by the public relations department.* **2.** the relative positions of a number of different parts ○ *The diagram shows a simple arrangement of pistons, cylinders and pipes.*

array /ə'reɪ/ *noun* an arrangement of antennas ○ *The localiser antenna array is very wide.*

arrest /ə'rest/ *verb* **1.** to stop or to prevent something from happening □ **to**

arrest the spread of a fire to stop the fire spreading **2.** to hold somebody for breaking the law ○ *He was arrested at the airport.* ■ *noun* the act of holding somebody for breaking the law ○ *His arrest was unexpected.*

arrester /ə'restə/ *noun* a device or substance which prevents or stops something from happening

arrival /ə'raɪv(ə)l/ *noun* the act of reaching somewhere. Abbreviation **ARR** □ **Gulf Air announce the arrival of flight GF147 from Abu Dhabi** flight GF147 from Abu Dhabi has just landed

arrivals /ə'raɪv(ə)lz/ *noun* the part of an airport that deals with passengers who are arriving

arrive /ə'raɪv/ *verb* to reach somewhere □ **the flight from Tokyo arrived at 8.30** the flight from Tokyo landed at 8.30

arrow /'ærəʊ/ *noun* a painted or printed sign which points to something ○ *Non-return valves are marked with an arrow which shows the direction of flow.*

arrow convention /'ærəʊ kən ˌvenʃ(ə)n/ *noun* an agreed method of using arrows when drawing wind triangles

article /'ɑːtɪk(ə)l/ *noun* an object, an item □ **loose articles** things which may move during flight and cause problems

artificial /ˌɑːtɪ'fɪʃ(ə)l/ *adjective* not natural, made by humans ○ *The small needle indicates cabin altitude or the artificial altitude created by the pressurisation system.*

artificial horizon /ˌɑːtɪfɪʃ(ə)l hə 'raɪz(ə)n/ *noun* an instrument that displays the degree of pitch or bank of an aircraft relative to the horizon

ascend /ə'send/ *verb* to rise, to go or move upwards ○ *Hot air ascends.* □ **in ascending order** in order of number or rank with the smallest or less important at the bottom and the largest or more important at the top. Opposite **descend**

ascent /ə'sent/ *noun* a rise, a slow upward movement ○ *the forced ascent of air over high ground* ○ *In a stable atmosphere where the ascent of air is*

forced, precipitation is mostly light and occasionally moderate.

ascertain /ˌæsə'teɪn/ *verb* to find out, to make certain ○ *During pre-flight checks, control surfaces should be moved by hand to ascertain that they have full and free movement.*

ASDE *abbreviation* airport surface detection equipment

ASI *abbreviation* airspeed indicator

ASMI *abbreviation* aerodrome surface movement indicator

aspect /'æspekt/ *noun* **1.** a part of a problem or subject ○ *Vertical motion is an important aspect of meteorology.* □ **safety aspects** matters related to safety **2.** the view from a particular position ○ *The aspect of the runway on final approach helps the pilot to judge height and progress.*

aspect ratio /ˌæspekt 'reɪʃiəʊ/ *noun* the ratio of the length of an aircraft's wing to the average distance between the front and back edge of the wing (NOTE: Aircraft that operate at low speeds, for example gliders, need a high aspect ratio and have long narrow wings. Supersonic aircraft need a low aspect ratio, which is created by swinging the wings back.)

asphyxiation /əsˌfɪksi'eɪʃ(ə)n/ *noun* unconsciousness or death caused by lack of oxygen ○ *Fire may result in the cabin being filled by smoke causing asphyxiation.*

ASR /ˌeɪ es 'ɑː/ *abbreviation* **1.** airport surveillance radar **2.** altimeter setting region

assemble /ə'semb(ə)l/ *verb* **1.** to put a number of parts together ○ *The parts are made in different countries but the plane is assembled in France.* **2.** to gather together ○ *Passengers should assemble in the departure lounge where an airline representative will meet them.*

assembly /ə'sembli/ *noun* **1.** something that is made up of smaller parts **2.** the act of putting parts together to make a whole ○ *Final assembly of the A320 takes place in France.*

assess /ə'ses/ *verb* to check, estimate or find out ○ *Cabin crew must assess if* *their exits are usable.* □ **to assess a situation** to consider all aspects of a situation

assessment /ə'sesmənt/ *noun* a judgement on a situation based on careful thought ○ *The captain's assessment of factors such as aircraft damage, passenger-load, fire, etc., will affect the decision on whether to evacuate the aeroplane or not.*

assign /ə'saɪn/ *verb* to set apart beforehand or allocate for a specific purpose □ **assigned seats** seats selected beforehand for particular people ○ *Crew sit in their assigned seats.* ○ *Individual carriers assign codes to aircraft.*

assist /ə'sɪst/ *verb* to help ○ *If you have any difficulty, cabin staff will assist you.* ○ *When evacuating the aircraft, hand signals by cabin staff assist in directing passengers to the exits.* ◊ **power**

assistance /ə'sɪst(ə)ns/ *noun* help □ **to require assistance** to need help ○ *If a pilot requires assistance, they should contact ATC.* □ **to provide assistance** to give help

associate /ə'səʊsieɪt/ *verb* to come with or be linked to something else ○ *Turbulence is often associated with strong winds.* ○ *The airport authority has to overcome a lot of problems associated with its plans to build a new terminal.*

association /əˌsəʊsi'eɪʃ(ə)n/ *noun* **1.** a group of people who organise themselves into an official body with common objectives and a code of conduct ○ *British Air Line Pilots Association.* **2.** □ **in association with** together with ○ *Rain-ice occurs only rarely over the British Isles and is usually found in association with warm fronts.*

assume /ə'sjuːm/ *verb* **1.** to take as true before there is proof ○ *I assume that she's ill because she's not at work today – but I may be wrong.* **2.** to suppose □ **for our studies we will assume that the earth is a perfect sphere** we know that the Earth is not a perfect sphere but it helps if we accept, for the time being, that it is □ **assuming (that)** accepting or supposing that ○ *Assuming*

that the return flight from the point of no return to A is made on three engines, calculate the distance from D to the point of no return. **3.** to take on, to undertake the duties of somebody ○ *The copilot assumed control of the aircraft after the captain was taken ill during the flight.* **4.** to take a particular bodily position ○ *The correct technique of using the escape slides is to assume a sitting position.*

assumption /ə'sʌmpʃ(ə)n/ *noun* an understanding or belief ○ *The one-in-sixty rule is based on the assumption that one nautical mile subtends an angle of one (at a distance of 60 nautical miles).*

asymmetric /ˌæsɪ'metrɪk/, **asymmetrical** /ˌæsɪ'metrɪk(ə)l/ *adjective* not identical or equal on each side of an imaginary central dividing line. Opposite **symmetric**

asymmetric flight /ˌæsɪmetrɪk 'flaɪt/ *noun* a condition in which one engine, displaced from the aircraft's centre-line is not working

asymmetric power /ˌæsɪmetrɪk 'paʊə/ *noun* power on one side of the aircraft's centre line only

asynchronous /ə'sɪŋkrənəs/ *adjective* **1.** not happening at the same time or rate ○ *An asynchronous orbit is a 24-hour orbit which enables a satellite to remain overhead one part of the Earth's surface.* **2.** not in frequency or phase

asynchronous computer /eɪ ˌsɪŋkrənəs kəm'pjuːtə/ *noun* a computer which does not process information according to the internal clock

ATA /ˌeɪ tiː 'eɪ/ *abbreviation* actual time of arrival

ATC /ˌeɪ tiː 'siː/ *abbreviation* **1.** air traffic control **2.** air traffic controller

ATCC *abbreviation* air traffic control centre

ATCRU *abbreviation* air traffic control radar unit

ATD /ˌeɪ tiː 'diː/ *abbreviation* actual time of departure

ATFM *abbreviation* air traffic flow management

ATIS *abbreviation* Automatic Terminal Information Service

ATM /ˌeɪ tiː ˈem/ *abbreviation* air traffic management

atmosphere /ˈætməsfɪə/ *noun* **1.** a mixture of gases in a mass surrounding the earth ○ *The surrounding atmosphere moves with the earth.* **2.** a unit of measurement of pressure

COMMENT: The main gases found in the atmosphere are nitrogen and oxygen. The atmosphere contains less than 1% carbon dioxide and argon, and also traces of hydrogen, helium, krypton, neon, ozone and xenon.

atmospheric /ˌætməsˈferɪk/ *adjective* referring to the atmosphere ○ *atmospheric density*

atmospheric attenuation /ˌætməsferɪk əˌtenjuˈeɪʃ(ə)n/ *noun* the weakening of a radio signal as it passes through the air

atmospheric pollution /ˌætməsferɪk pəˈluːʃ(ə)n/ *noun* same as **air pollution** ○ *Solid particles in the air include dust, sand, volcanic ash and atmospheric pollution.*

atmospheric pressure /ˌætməsferɪk ˈpreʃə/ *noun* normal air pressure on the surface of the earth

atmospheric refraction /ˌætməsferɪk rɪˈfrækʃən/ *noun* change in direction of waves due to variations in temperature, pressure and humidity, particularly at lower altitudes

atom /ˈætəm/ *noun* the smallest amount of a substance which can take part in a chemical reaction ○ *An atom consists of a nucleus and electrons.*

atomic /əˈtɒmɪk/ *adjective* referring to atoms □ **atomic structure of matter** the structure of materials and substances at their smallest level

atomisation /ætəmaɪˈzeɪʃn/, **atomization** /ˌætəmaɪˈzeɪʃ(ə)n/ *noun* the reduction of liquids to a fine spray ○ *The fuel achieves fine atomisation under pressure.*

atomise /ˈætəmaɪz/, **atomize** *verb* to reduce liquids to a fine spray ○ *The fuel must be atomised or vaporised to combine with the air to permit combustion.*

ATPL *abbreviation* Airline Transport Pilot's Licence

ATS *abbreviation* air traffic services

ATSU *abbreviation* air traffic service unit

attach /əˈtætʃ/ *verb* to join or fix something to something ○ *The ice detector is attached to the fuselage.*

attachment /əˈtætʃmənt/ *noun* **1.** the act of joining or fixing something to something ○ *The attachment of winglets improved the handling characteristics of the aeroplane.* **2.** an accessory which can be attached ○ *The video camera is sold with a number of attachments including a carrying strap and a battery pack.*

attachment point /əˈtætʃmənt pɔɪnt/ *noun* a place on the airframe where something such as an engine is attached by means of bolts ○ *Additional strength is required for the power plant attachment points.*

attain /əˈteɪn/ *verb* to reach, to achieve something, often with difficulty ○ *In order to attain a fuller understanding of gas turbines, it is essential to know something about basic gas laws.*

attempt /əˈtempt/ *noun* a try ○ *Any attempt to increase range by applying more power is of little or no benefit.* ■ *verb* to try ○ *He attempted to land despite the poor visibility but then decided to divert to another airfield where he landed safely.*

attendant /əˈtendənt/ *adjective* accompanying something else ○ *Fuel spillage and attendant fire risk must be minimised.* □ **attendant problems** associated problems ■ *noun* a person employed to help members of the public

attention /əˈtenʃən/ *noun* the ability or power to concentrate on something ○ *The crew's attention is alerted by an automatic display.* □ **attention please** listen carefully to what will be said □ **pay attention** listen to the speaker and concentrate on what is being said

attenuate /əˈtenjueɪt/ *verb* to lose power or strength ○ *A wave becomes attenuated or loses strength as range increases.*

attenuation /əˌtenjuˈeɪʃ(ə)n/ *noun* loss of strength ○ *Atmospheric attenuation is negligible until the upper end of the UHF band when it increases rapidly to limit the highest usable frequency to about 10 GHz.*

attenuative /əˈtenjuətɪv/ *adjective* becoming weaker ○ *Rain has an attenuative effect.*

attitude /ˈætɪtjuːd/ *noun* **1.** the position of the aircraft in the air in relation to the horizon ○ *Angle of attack will vary with changes in engine speed and aircraft attitude.* □ **nose down attitude** the attitude of the aircraft when the nose is at a lower level than the tail **2.** a way of thinking and feeling about or of behaving towards something or somebody □ **he has an excellent attitude towards his training programme** he is positive and motivated in his training programme

attitude heading reference system /ˌætɪtjuːd ˌhedɪŋ ˈref(ə)rəns ˌsɪstəm/ *noun* full form of **AHRS**

attitude indicator /ˈætɪtjuːd ˌɪndɪkeɪtə/ *noun* a flight instrument that gives the pilot information about the position of the aircraft in the air in relation to the horizon ○ *In light aircraft, the attitude indicator is situated on the instrument panel, directly in front of the pilot.* ◊ **pitch, bank**

COMMENT: The attitude indicator is sometimes referred to as the 'artificial horizon'. In instrument flight training, the attitude indicator is the primary reference instrument. It is positioned on the instrument panel directly in front of the pilot.

attract /əˈtrækt/ *verb* **1.** to cause to draw near ○ *If two magnets, with unlike poles are brought together, they will attract each other.* □ **to attract attention** to behave in such a way that people will notice you **2.** to cause people to want to have or do something

attraction /əˈtrækʃən/ *noun* **1.** a force that draws things towards something ○ *The strength of the magnetic force will depend, amongst other things, on the magnitude of attraction at the magnetic source.* **2.** a quality that causes people to want to have or do something ○ *The attraction of flying was the factor which made him decide to train as a pilot.*

attractive /əˈtræktɪv/ *adjective* **1.** referring to something you feel you would like to have ○ *After long talks, the prospective buyer made a financially attractive offer for the aircraft.* **2.** nice to look at

ATZ *abbreviation* aerodrome traffic zone

audible /ˈɔːdɪb(ə)l/ *adjective* possible to hear ○ *The fire detection system should contain an audible warning device.*

audio /ˈɔːdiəʊ/ *noun* an audible sound or sound signal ○ *The diagram shows an amplitude modulation case where the lower frequency of the audio is about 300 Hertz.*

augment /ɔːgˈment/ *verb* to make larger by adding something ○ *The sea breeze may augment the up-slope motion of an anabatic wind.*

aural /ˈɔːrəl/ *adjective* referring to hearing ○ *The aural and visual alerts will continue until the crew take action to cancel them.* (NOTE: **Aural** is sometimes pronounced /ˈaʊrəl/ to show the difference with **oral**.)

authorise /ˈɔːθəraɪz/, **authorize** *verb* to allow officially, to give permission ○ *A signature is required to authorise the repair.*

authorised /ˈɔːθəraɪzd/, **authorized** *adjective* officially allowed, permitted ○ *Aircraft with a maximum authorised weight of 12,500 lb or less.* □ **an authorized person** a person who has been given power to act and perform particular tasks or duties

authoritative /ɔːˈθɒrɪtətɪv/ *adjective* in the manner of somebody with authority, in a commanding way □ **crew must act in an authoritative manner** crew must give firm instructions or orders

authority /ɔːˈθɒrɪti/ *noun* **1.** complete control or power over something ○ *While boarding, the captain has the authority to ask an unruly passenger to leave the aircraft.* **2.** an official or government body with the power to make decisions

auto- /ɔːtəʊ/ *prefix* automatic or automated

autogiro /ˈɔːtəʊˌdʒaɪrəʊ/ *noun* an aircraft that uses a propeller to produce forward motion and has an unpowered horizontal rotor for lift and stability

autoland /ˈɔːtəʊlænd/ *abbreviation* automatic landing

automate /ˈɔːtəmeɪt/ *verb* to make e.g. a device or procedure automatic □ **automated systems** systems which have been made less dependent on direct human control or management

automatic /ˌɔːtəˈmætɪk/ *adjective* **1.** done without needing to think ○ *In the early stages of training, student pilots have to think about the use of the flying controls, but after a while these actions become automatic.* **2.** which works by itself without the need of an operator ○ *The normal activation method is automatic.*

automatic dependent surveillance /ˌɔːtəmætɪk dɪˈpendənt sə ˌveɪləns/ an electronic surveillance system that uses data that aircraft provide automatically via a datalink and is able to identify and track the aircraft

automatic direction finder /ˌɔːtəmeɪtɪd daɪˈrekʃ(ə)n ˌfaɪndə/ *noun* a radio navigation instrument that receives signals from non-directional radio beacons ○ *The needle on the ADF indicator points toward the selected radio signal.* Abbreviation **ADF**

automatic landing /ˌɔːtəmætɪk ˈlandɪŋ/ *noun* automatic flight control system capable of landing an aircraft 'hands-off.' Abbreviation **autoland**

automatic mixture control /ˌɔːtəmætɪk ˈmɪkstʃə kənˌtrəʊl/ *noun* a subsystem in a piston engine which adjusts the flow of fuel to balance changes in air density

automatic pilot /ˌɔːtəmætɪk ˈpaɪlət/ *noun* full form of **autopilot**

Automatic Terminal Information Service /ˌɔːtəmætɪk ˌtɜːmɪn(ə)l ˌɪnfəˈmeɪʃ(ə)n ˌsɜːvɪs/ *noun* a recording of information played continuously on a specified radio frequency which gives pilots the current weather, runway in use, etc. ○ *Students listen to the ATIS to practise their language skills.* Abbreviation **ATIS**

automation /ˌɔːtəˈmeɪʃ(ə)n/ *noun* the automatic operation or automatic control of a piece of equipment, a process, or a system ○ *Automation has speeded up baggage handling.* ○ *Automation of throttle control has removed the need for pilots to monitor airspeed so closely.* ○ *It is possible that the alternate source might provide a reduced level of automation.*

autopilot /ˈɔːtəʊpaɪlət/ *noun* a system which automatically stabilises an aircraft about its three axes, restores the original flight path following an upset and, in some systems, causes the aircraft to follow a preselected airspeed, altitude or heading. Full form **automatic pilot**. Abbreviation **A/P**

auxiliary /ɔːɡˈzɪliəri/ *adjective* secondary, which is used when necessary to help or substitute for something else

auxiliary gearbox /ɔːɡˌzɪliəri ˌɡɪə ˈbɒks/ *noun* a gear box which allows main engine power to be used for secondary systems

auxiliary power unit /ɔːɡˌzɪliəri ˈpaʊə ˌjuːnɪt/ *noun* a small jet engine used to generate electrical power for air-conditioning, etc., when the aircraft is parked on the ground. Abbreviation **APU**

auxiliary rotor /ɔːɡˌzɪliəri ˈrəʊtə/ *noun* the tail rotor of a helicopter

availability /əˌveɪləˈbɪlɪti/ *noun* the fact of being available ○ *The status of an airport is determined by the availability of suitable navigation aids.*

available /əˈveɪləb(ə)l/ *adjective* ready for immediate use ○ *On a multi-engine aircraft, all the fuel must be available for use by any engine.*

average /ˈæv(ə)rɪdʒ/ *adjective* referring to an average ○ *For load sheet purposes, an average weight of the passengers and crew members may be used.* ■ *noun* the total divided by the number of items added ○ *The average of 1, 5, 9, 10 and 15 is 8 (1+5+9+10+15 = 40 ÷ 5 = 8).* ■ *verb* to reach a particular figure as an average ○ *Brake temperatures average around 500°C during normal operations.*

avert /ə'vɜːt/ *verb* to avoid ○ *To avert a collision, he changed direction.*

AVGAS /'ævgæs/ *abbreviation* aviation gasoline

aviation /ˌeɪviˈeɪʃ(ə)n/ *noun* flying an aircraft ○ *Wind speeds in aviation are usually given in knots.*

aviation gasoline /ˌeɪvieɪʃ(ə)n 'gæsəliːn/ *noun* fuel used in piston-engined aircraft. Abbreviation **AVGAS**

aviation law /ˌeɪviˈeɪʃ(ə)n ˌlɔː/ *noun* the laws relating to flying

aviation routine weather report /ˌeɪvieɪʃ(ə)n ˌruːtiːn 'weθə rɪˌpɔːt/ *noun* a weather report issued regularly at intervals of an hour or half an hour describing weather conditions at an airport. Abbreviation **METAR**

aviator /'eɪvieɪtə/ *noun* a person who flies aircraft

avionics /ˌeɪviˈɒnɪks/ *noun* electronic communication, navigation, and flight-control equipment of an aircraft ○ *The trainee engineer is doing an avionics course.* Full form **aviation electronics**

avoid /ə'vɔɪd/ *verb* **1.** to prevent something from happening ○ *She just managed to avoid an accident.* **2.** to keep away from something ○ *Avoid flying close to any person or vessel.* ○ *Cumulonimbus clouds and thunderstorms should be avoided by as great a distance as possible.*

avoidance /ə'vɔɪd(ə)ns/ *noun* an act of avoiding something □ **avoidance of thunderstorms is recommended** it is recommended to keep away from thunderstorms

await /ə'weɪt/ *verb* to wait for ○ *Await instructions from the flight deck.*

aware /ə'weə/ *adjective* knowing and being conscious of something ○ *The*

pilot should be aware of the positions of all other aircraft in the circuit.

awareness /ə'weənəs/ *noun* the state of being aware or conscious of something □ **safety awareness** the state of being familiar with and prepared for any situation in which safety is important

AWR *abbreviation* airborne weather radar

axial /'æksiəl/ *adjective* referring to an axis

axial flow compressor /ˌæksiəl fləʊ kəm'presə/ *noun* a compressor in which the flow of air is along the longitudinal axis of the engine ○ *In spite of the adoption of the axial flow type compressor, some engine retain the centrifugal type.*

axis /'æksɪs/ *noun* **1.** an imaginary line around which a body rotates ○ *The Earth rotates around its own axis.* ○ *An aircraft moves around three axes – vertical, longitudinal and lateral.* ◊ **pitch, roll, yaw 2.** a horizontal or vertical scale on a graph, often referred to as the X axis, the horizontal axis, and the Y axis, the vertical axis ○ *The plot shows the effect of airspeed on lift with airspeed shown on the horizontal axis and lift on the vertical axis.* (NOTE: The plural form is **axes**.)

axle /'æksəl/ *noun* a shaft on which a wheel is mounted ○ *Unequal tyre-pressures, where two wheels are mounted on the same axle, will result in one tyre carrying a greater share of the load than the other.* (NOTE: The wheel either turns round the axle or is fixed to the axle.)

azimuth /'æzɪməθ/ *noun* the horizontal angle or direction of a compass bearing ○ *Where precision approach radar is installed, the controller can inform the pilot if they depart from either the extended centre-line in azimuth or height or both.*

B

back /bæk/ *verb* (*of the wind*) to change direction in an anticlockwise direction. Opposite **veer**

backup /'bækʌp/ *adjective, noun* a second or third system, instrument or computer disk available to be used if the first one fails ○ *The backup system or the backup failed as well.* ○ *Backup generators are driven by the engine.*

backward /'bækwəd/ *adjective* directed towards the back ○ *a backward movement*

backwards /'bækwədz/ *adverb* towards the back ○ *Unlike most aircraft, the C130 can move backwards using its own power.* (NOTE: The US English is **backward**.)

backwash /'bækwɒʃ/ *noun* a backward flow of air produced by an aircraft propeller or jet engine

baffle /'bæf(ə)l/ *noun* a metal plate for preventing the free movement of sound or liquids ○ *Integral fuel tanks can be strengthened by fitting baffle plates.*

baggage /'bægɪdʒ/ *noun* luggage, cases and bags which you take with you when travelling ○ *One passenger had a huge amount of baggage.* ○ *She lost one piece of baggage.* (NOTE: The word **luggage** is also used in British English.) □ **baggage hall** an area where arriving passengers pick up their baggage □ **carry-on baggage** small bags of limited size and weight that passengers are allowed to take with them into the cabin of an aircraft

baggage allowance /ˌbægɪdʒ ə'lauəns/ *noun* the weight of baggage each air passenger is allowed to take

free ○ *There is an accompanied baggage allowance of 18 kilos.*

baggage handling /'bægɪdʒ ˌhændlɪŋ/ *noun* the process by which passengers' baggage is loaded onto an aircraft, or unloaded and moved to the airport terminal

balance /'bæləns/ *noun* **1.** a state in which weight, force or importance are evenly distributed ○ *The propelling nozzle size is extremely important and must be designed to obtain the correct balance of pressure, temperature and thrust.* **2.** the act of staying steady ■ *verb* **1.** to be opposite and equal in weight, force or importance to something else ○ *The pressure exerted by the weight of the atmosphere above the level of the bowl balances a column of mercury in the tube.* **2.** to stay steady, especially when resting on the centre of gravity

'…balance refers to the location of the centre of gravity along the longitudinal axis of the aeroplane' [*Civil Aviation Authority, General Aviation Safety Sense Leaflet*]

ball /bɔːl/ *noun* in an inclinometer, the round object which indicates if a turn is coordinated □ **to step on the ball** to correct a skid or a slip by putting pressure on the rudder on the side to which the ball in an inclinometer has moved during a turn. If the ball has moved to the left, the turn can be corrected by putting pressure on the left rudder, and vice versa.

balloon /bə'luːn/ *noun* a large bag inflatable with hot air or gas to provide lift, but without power ○ *Balloons are sent into the upper atmosphere to col-*

lect information useful to meteorologists.

BALPA /'bælpə/ *abbreviation* British Air Line Pilots Association

band /bænd/ *noun* **1.** a narrow strip ○ *A jet stream is a narrow band of high-altitude strong winds.* **2.** a range of numbers or frequencies between two limits within a radio system

bandwidth /'bændwɪdθ/ *noun* the width of a band of radio frequencies ○ *The sharp setting means the bandwidth is reduced to one kilohertz to minimise noise or interference.*

bank /bæŋk/ *verb* (*of an aircraft*) to rotate or roll around its longitudinal axis to a particular angle ○ *Stresses are increased when the aircraft banks, turns or pulls out of a dive.* ■ *noun* (*of an aircraft*) a rotating or rolling movement around its longitudinal axis to a particular angle ○ *An attitude indicator gives the pilot pitch and bank information.*

bar /bɑː/ *noun* **1.** a long, straight, rigid piece of metal ○ *The part is made from a solid bar of aluminium.* **2.** (*in meteorology*) a unit of atmospheric pressure equal to 1,000 millibars. ◊ **millibar**

barograph /'bærəgrɑːf/ *noun* an instrument for measuring and recording atmospheric pressure ○ *The most common type of barograph is that which utilises an aneroid capsule mechanically connected to a pen.*

barometer /bə'rɒmɪtə/ *noun* an instrument for measuring the atmospheric pressure

barometric /bærə'metrɪk/ *adjective* referring to a barometer □ **barometric pressure** atmospheric pressure as indicated by a barometer

barometric tendency /ˌbærəmetrɪk 'tendənsi/ *noun* the amount of change in pressure with increase in altitude

barrel roll /'bær(ə)l rəʊl/ *noun* a manoeuvre in which an aircraft turns completely over sideways while flying along

barrier /'bæriə/ *noun* **1.** something such as a wall that prevents the movement of something else ○ *Elevation of the ground over which the aircraft flies* can be a dangerous barrier to flight. **2.** something that prevents a person from making progress ○ *His medical problems were a barrier to his successful completion of the course.*

base /beɪs/ *noun* the bottom part or lowest part ■ *verb* to develop or develop something from something else ○ *The operation of the auxiliary power unit is based on the gas turbine engine.* ○ *The principle of vapour cycle cooling is based upon the ability of a refrigerant to absorb heat.*

base leg /'beɪs leg/ *noun* the part of the airfield traffic circuit flown at approximately 90° to the direction of landing, followed by the final approach. ◊ **leg**

basic /'beɪsɪk/ *adjective* referring to the most important but often simplest part of something, from which everything else is derived ○ *This chapter provides a basic understanding from which the study of meteorology can develop.* □ **basic principle** a central or fundamental idea or theory

basic area navigation /ˌbeɪsɪk ˌeəriə ˌnævɪ'geɪʃ(ə)n/ *noun* a standard of performance for navigation that requires an aircraft to remain within 5 nautical miles of the centreline of its course for 95% of the time

basis /'beɪsɪs/ *noun* the central and most important part of something from which everything else is derived ○ *The basis of air navigation is the triangle of velocities.* (NOTE: The plural form is **bases**.)

bat /bæt/ *noun* an object shaped like a table-tennis bat used by a person on the ground to guide an aircraft when it is taxiing or parking

batsman /'bætsmən/ *noun* somebody who uses a pair of bats to guide an aircraft when it is taxiing or parking

battery /'bæt(ə)ri/ *noun* a chemical device that produces electrical current ○ *This piece of equipment is powered by 2 batteries.* ◊ **charger**

bay /beɪ/ *noun* **1.** a space or area in the structure of an aeroplane where equipment can be located ○ *To avoid damage to the wheel bay, the nose wheel must be* *aligned in a fore and aft direction during retraction.* **2.** a part of the coast that curves inwards ○ *the Bay of Bengal*

bayonet fitting /ˌbeɪənɪt ˈfɪtɪŋ/ *noun* a means of attaching something to something, in which an object with two side pins is inserted into a L-shaped slot in another object on some light-bulbs ○ *Magnetic chip detectors are of the bayonet type fitting and can be removed and replaced very quickly.*

beacon /ˈbiːkən/ *noun* a light or radio signal for navigational purposes ○ *If the aircraft turns towards the beacon, signal strength will increase.*

beam /biːm/ *noun* **1.** a long thick metal bar used as a support ○ *A beam is designed with a breaking load of 12 tons but when a three ton load is applied repeatedly, the beam may fail.* **2.** a shaft of light or radiation travelling in one direction, as from a car's headlights ○ *The electron gun produces a stream of fast-moving electrons and focuses them into a narrow beam.*

beam sharpening /ˈbiːm ˌʃɑːpənɪŋ/ *noun* the process of making a radio or light beam narrower ○ *Any system employing beam sharpening is vulnerable to side lobe generation at the transmitter.*

bear /beə/ *verb* **1.** to carry or to hold ○ *The undercarriage has to bear the weight of the aircraft on the ground.* □ **rain-bearing cloud** a cloud carrying moisture which can fall as rain **2.** □ **to bear something in mind** to keep in mind □ **it should be borne in mind** it should be remembered □ **bearing in mind** considering ○ *Bearing in mind that she hadn't flown for three weeks, the student pilot's landings were very good.* **3.** to be able to deal with something without becoming distressed or annoyed ○ *He can't bear the noise.* (NOTE: **bearing – bore – borne**) □ **he can't bear the heat** the heat is too much for him

bearing /ˈbeərɪŋ/ *noun* **1.** the angle, measured in a clockwise direction, of a distant point, relative to a reference direction ○ *To plot a position line from the non-directional radio beacon, it is*

first necessary to convert the relative bearing to a true bearing and then calculate the reciprocal. **2.** a device containing steel balls or needles which allows free rotation of one component around another

Beaufort scale /ˈbəʊfət skeɪl/ *noun* scale from 1–12 used to refer to the strength of wind ○ *Wind speeds can be estimated by using the Beaufort scale of wind force.*

belly flop /ˈbeli flɒp/ *noun* same as **belly landing**

belly landing /ˈbeli ˌlændɪŋ/ *noun* an emergency landing of an aircraft when the wheels have not come down

belt /belt/ *noun* **1.** a long, relatively narrow area □ **high-pressure belt** long narrow area of high pressure □ **precipitation belt** a long narrow area of rain, snow or hail □ **rain belt** long narrow area where rain falls ○ *The cirrus cloud can be 900 miles ahead of the surface front with a rain belt as wide as 200 miles.* **2.** a loop of strong material connecting two pulleys or wheels, one driving the other

belt-driven /ˈbelt ˌdrɪv(ə)n/ *adjective* (*of a wheel*) moved by a belt linked to another wheel which, in turn, is moved by a motor or an engine ○ *Aircraft generators are belt-driven or shaft-driven.*

belt-driven generator /ˌbelt ˌdrɪv(ə)n ˈdʒenəreɪtə/ *noun* a generator whose pulley is turned by a belt attached to an engine-driven pulley

bend /bend/ *noun* a curve ■ *verb* to curve from a straight shape (NOTE: **bending – bent**) □ **to bend downwards** to curve down from a horizontal position □ **to bend upwards** to curve up from a horizontal position ○ *The wings support the weight of the aircraft and they bend upwards in flight.*

bending load /ˈbendɪŋ ləʊd/ *noun* a load that causes a structure to bend

Bernoulli's principle /bɜːˈnuːliːz ˌprɪnsɪp(ə)l/ *noun* ♦ **lift**

beware /bɪˈweə/ *verb* to be careful or to watch out for ○ *Beware of carburettor icing.* ○ *Beware of other aircraft in the circuit.*

beyond /bɪ'jɒnd/ *preposition* further away than ○ *The radio horizon extends beyond the visible horizon.* □ **it is beyond his understanding** he cannot understand it at all, it is too difficult for him to understand

bi- /baɪ/ *prefix* **1.** two **2.** twice

biannual /baɪ'ænjuəl/ *adjective* happening two times a year □ **biannual inspection** an inspection done twice every year

bill /bɪl/ *noun* US same as **note** *noun* 4

bimetallic /ˌbaɪmeˈtælɪk/ *adjective* made of two metals

bimetallic strip /ˌbaɪmetælɪk 'strɪp/ *noun* a strip made of two separate metals with different rates of expansion, joined together side by side so that when the strip is heated, it bends and makes, or breaks, electrical contact ○ *Circuit breakers use a bimetallic strip as the sensing element.*

binary /'baɪnəri/ *adjective* referring to a number system used in computers that only uses the digits 0 and 1 ○ *Logic gates work with binary data.* ○ *Computers only process binary information.*

biplane /'baɪpleɪn/, **bi-plane** *noun* an old aeroplane design with two pairs of wings, one above the other ○ *Most of the aircraft used in the 1914–18 war were biplanes.*

bird strike /'bɜːd straɪk/ *noun* a collision between a bird or birds and an aircraft that is flying

black box /ˌblæk 'bɒks/ *noun* same as **flight data recorder** (NOTE: It is often called the **black box**, although it is not black.)

blade /bleɪd/ *noun* a flattened part of a propeller or rotor □ **blade tip** the end of the blade furthest from the centre of rotation □ **turbine blade** a flat part in a turbine, which has an aerodynamic effect on the air

blade angle /'bleɪd ˌæŋg(ə)l/ *noun* the angle between the blade axis and the axis of rotation ○ *With a variable pitch propeller, the blade angle may be changed in flight.*

blade slip /'bleɪd slɪp/ *noun* a loss of propulsive power from a propeller

caused by the difference between geometric and effective pitch

blade twist /'bleɪd twɪst/ *noun* **1.** a reduction in propeller blade angle from root to tip **2.** the unwanted variation in propeller blade pitch from root to tip caused by aerodynamic loads

blank /blæŋk/ *adjective* **1.** with nothing written, printed or drawn on it ○ *a blank sheet of paper* □ **a blank form** a form without the details filled in **2.** (*of a TV, computer or video screen*) with nothing appearing on it ○ *When he returned to his computer, the screen was blank.*

bleed air /'bliːd eə/ *noun* compressed air from the engine compressor used for cabin pressurisation or to drive other services ○ *Bleed air from the right engine can power items normally powered by the left engine.*

bleed screw /'bliːd skruː/ *noun* a small screw in highest point of a hydraulic system to allow for the removal of air or vapour

blind transmission /ˌblaɪnd trænz 'mɪʃ(ə)n/ *noun* a transmission from one station to another in a situation where two-way communication cannot be established but where it is believed that the called station is able to receive the transmission

block /blɒk/ *noun* a large mass of something ■ *verb* **1.** to prevent something such as a fluid from passing freely through a pipe or channel ○ *At high altitude, any water condensing out of the fuel could freeze and block the filters.* **2.** to prevent a course of action ○ *The government blocked attempts to prevent the building of the new airport.*

blockage /'blɒkɪdʒ/ *noun* **1.** a collection of something blocking a pipe, narrow channel, filter, etc. ○ *Ice crystals may form to cause a blockage of the fuel filter.* **2.** the state of being blocked ○ *The blockage was caused by ice.*

blow /bləʊ/ *noun* **1.** an impact ○ *a blow on the head* **2.** a disappointment ○ *The news of her failure in the examination was a severe blow.* ■ *verb* **1.** (*of the wind or air*) to move ○ *The sea breeze may blow almost parallel to the coast.* **2.** (*of* *a fuse*) to break, as it should, when the circuit is overloaded (NOTE: **blowing – blew – blown**)

blow-back /ˈbləʊ bæk/ *noun* a sudden movement of fluid in the opposite direction to the general flow ○ *A sudden release of pressure may cause a blow-back.*

blower /ˈbləʊə/ *noun* a device for blowing air ○ *Air for combustion is obtained from a blower.*

board /bɔːd/ *noun* **1.** a flat, square or rectangular piece of wood or other material **2.** □ **on board** on an aircraft ○ *The flight plan records the callsign and the number of people on board.* ■ *verb* to get on to an aircraft ○ *In an emergency, many passengers only remember the entrance by which they boarded the aircraft.*

boarding gate /ˈbɔːdɪŋ geɪt/ *noun* the door through which passengers leave the terminal building to get on to an aircraft ○ *Boarding gates 1 – 10 are on the left.*

boarding pass /ˈbɔːdɪŋ pɑːs/ *noun* a temporary pass, issued at the check-in desk, which allows the holder to board the aircraft ○ *Boarding passes must be shown at the gate.* (NOTE: The plural form is **boarding passes**.)

boarding steps /ˈbɔːdɪŋ steps/ *plural noun* stairs used by passengers and crew to get on board an aircraft ○ *Passengers had to wait in the aircraft for 15 minutes before the boarding steps were put in position.*

boarding time /ˈbɔːdɪŋ taɪm/ *noun* the time when passengers are due to board the aircraft ○ *Boarding time is at 13.30 hrs.*

body /ˈbɒdi/ *noun* **1.** the whole of a person or an animal **2.** the main part of a person, but not the arms or legs **3.** the main part of an aeroplane, system, text, etc. ○ *The body of an aircraft is also called the 'airframe'.* ○ *A flow-control valve consists of a body and a floating valve.* **4.** a large mass of liquid or gas □ **body of air** a large quantity of air behaving in a particular way **5.** an object ○ *Acceleration is the rate of change of velocity of a body.*

boil /bɔɪl/ *verb* to heat a liquid until it reaches a temperature at which it changes into gas ○ *Water boils at 100°C.* □ **boiling point** the temperature at which a liquid changes into gas ○ *The boiling point of water is 100°C.*

bolt /bəʊlt/ *noun* **1.** a metal rod with a head, which screws into a nut ○ *The two halves of the wheel are held together by bolts.* **2.** □ **bolt of lightning** one electrical discharge of lightning ■ *verb* to attach with a bolt ○ *Aircraft wheels are constructed in two halves which are bolted together.*

bond /bɒnd/ *noun* the power that holds surfaces together, when they are joined using heat, cold, chemicals or glue ○ *The de-icing boot breaks the bond between the ice and the outer skin.* ■ *verb* to join surfaces together normally using heat, cold, chemicals or glue ○ *The skin is bonded to the internal members by the redux process.*

boom /buːm/ *noun* in some aircraft, a spar that connects the tail to the fuselage

boost /buːst/ *noun* an increase or improvement ○ *The improvement in a country's economy often gives a boost to the airline industry.* ■ *verb* **1.** to make or to help something increase ○ *An oil pump boosts engine oil pressure.* **2.** to increase ○ *The instructor's comments boosted the student pilot's confidence.*

booster /ˈbuːstə/ *noun* a device which increases the force or amount of something

booster pump /ˈbuːstə pʌmp/ *noun* a centrifugal pump often positioned at the lowest point of a liquid fuel tank to ensure positive pressure in the supply lines to the engine ○ *Fuel is fed through a filter and a booster pump.* ○ *The purpose of the booster pump is to prevent fuel aeration.*

boot /buːt/ *noun* one of a set of flat, flexible tubes bonded to the leading edge or wings and other surfaces which, when pressurised with fluid, break up ice ○ *The boots on the leading edge of the wings were damaged by hail.*

bottleneck /'bɒt(ə)lnek/ *noun* a buildup of air traffic causing delays in taking off or landing

bound /baʊnd/ *adjective* □ **bound for** on the way to ○ *an aircraft bound for Paris* □ **the Copenhagen-bound flight** the flight on the way to Copenhagen □ **outward bound** leaving home, especially for another country

boundary /'baʊnd(ə)ri/ *noun* a physical or imaginary limit between two areas ○ *The boundary between two air masses is called the frontal surface.*

boundary layer /ˌbaʊnd(ə)ri 'leɪə/ *noun* the layer of fluid next to the surface over which it is flowing and, because of friction, travelling more slowly than layers further from the surface

bowser /'baʊzə/ *noun* a mobile fuel tank for refuelling aircraft ○ *It is important to prevent the possibility of an electric spark by earthing the aircraft and the bowser.*

Boyle's Law /'bɔɪlz lɔː/ *noun* a scientific principle that states that the volume of a given mass of gas, whose temperature is maintained constant, is inversely proportional to the gas pressure

brace /breɪs/ *verb* **1.** to strengthen a construction using cross-members and/or wires ○ *Early aircraft were of the braced type of construction.* **2.** to take a protective body position in preparation for a crash landing ○ *The cabin-crew will repeat the 'brace' order and brace themselves.* □ **to brace yourself** to quickly prepare yourself mentally and physically for what is shortly to happen

brace position /'breɪs pəˌzɪʃ(ə)n/ *noun* the position that a person is recommended to adopt before impact in a crash, protecting the head with the arms and bringing the legs up underneath the chest

bracket /'brækɪt/ *noun* **1.** a metal support, often triangular or L-shaped □ **component bracket** a metal device to attach and support a component **2.** a range of frequencies within a band of radio frequencies ○ *Terminal VOR is in the frequency bracket 108–112 MHz.* **3.**

□ **round brackets** the printing symbol ( ) used to separate words in a sentence, or within a text □ **square brackets** the printing symbol [ ] used to enclose some types of text

brake /breɪk/ *noun* a device for stopping a vehicle or a machine □ **parking brake** a brake used to prevent the aircraft moving after it has come to a stop ■ *verb* to slow down or to stop by pressing the brakes ○ *He had to brake hard after landing in order to turn off at the correct taxiway.* (NOTE: **braking – braked**)

brake drum /'breɪk drʌm/ *noun* a round hollow part of the brake mechanism, which is attached to the wheel and against which the brake shoes rub, thus preventing the wheel from turning

braking /'breɪkɪŋ/ *noun* the act of putting on the brakes to slow down or to stop ■ *adjective* slowing down ○ *the braking effect of drag* ◇ **action**

breaking load /'breɪkɪŋ ləʊd/ *noun* a load capable of being supported before a structure breaks

breather /'briːðə/ *noun* **1.** a pipe connecting the crankshaft to the atmosphere to prevent build-up of crankcase pressure **2.** a short rest (*informal*) □ **to take a breather** to have a short break, to relax before starting again

breeze /briːz/ *noun* a gentle wind especially near the coast ○ *There's no wind, not even a breeze.* □ **land breeze** a light wind which blows from the land towards the sea ○ *Land and sea breezes occur in coastal areas.* □ **sea breeze** a gentle wind which blows from the sea towards the land ○ *The strength of the sea breeze decreases with height.*

brief /briːf/ *adjective* short □ **brief visit** a visit that lasts only short time □ **brief letter** a letter containing only a few words ■ *noun* general instructions to enable somebody to perform their duties ○ *The inspector's brief is to find out as much as possible about the causes of accidents.* ■ *verb* to give basic information to somebody ○ *Before take-off, cabin crew must brief passengers on the location and use of emergency exits and life jackets.*

briefing /'briːfɪŋ/ noun a short meeting to enable instructions and basic information to be given

British Isles /ˌbrɪtɪʃ 'aɪlz/ plural noun the islands which make up Great Britain and Ireland ○ The climate of the British Isles is affected by the Atlantic Ocean.

British thermal unit /ˌbrɪtɪʃ 'θɜːm(ə)l/ noun the amount of heat needed to raise the temperature of one pound of water by one degree Fahrenheit. Abbreviation **Btu**

brittle /'brɪt(ə)l/ adjective having a tendency to break easily, like thin glass ○ Absorption of oxygen and nitrogen from the air at temperatures above 1,000° F makes titanium brittle.

BRNAV abbreviation basic area navigation

broad /brɔːd/ adjective **1.** very wide ○ a broad river **2.** wide or general ○ Three broad categories of aircraft are considered – rotary wing aircraft, light single-engine aircraft and twin-engine aircraft. Opposite **narrow**

broadcast /'brɔːdkɑːst/ verb to transmit, often to a large number of people, a radio signal or message which requires no answer ○ The cabin crew can use the public address system to broadcast messages to passengers only. (NOTE: **broadcasting – broadcast**) ■ noun a transmission of information relating to air navigation that is not addressed to a specific station or stations

broadly /'brɔːdli/ adverb widely or generally □ **broadly speaking** generally speaking

brush /brʌʃ/ noun **1.** a tool that has lengths of hair or wire fixed into a handle and is mainly used for painting or cleaning **2.** a small, replaceable block of carbon which rubs against the surface of a commutator in a generator or electric motor ○ At high altitude, the air becomes drier and this causes a greatly increased rate of wear on the brushes.

buckle /'bʌk(ə)l/ noun a metal part of a belt used for joining the two ends together ■ verb to bend out of shape because of heat or force ○ Overheating will make the battery plates buckle.

buffet /'bʌfɪt/ noun a shaking movement of the aircraft caused by the breakdown of the airflow over the upper surface of the wing ○ Large aircraft use a stick shaker to supplement the natural stall warning of buffet. ■ verb to push around with great force, as by water or wind ○ The storm buffeted the coast. ○ The aircraft was buffeted by strong crosswinds as it made its final approach to land.

COMMENT: Buffet is a warning to the pilot that the smooth airflow over the wing is breaking down and that he should take corrective action to prevent a stall.

buffeting /'bʌf(ə)tɪŋ/ noun an irregular shaking of a part or the whole of an aircraft during flight, usually caused by strong winds

buffet speed /'bʌfɪt spiːd/ noun the speed at which buffet is first noticed

bug /bʌg/ noun a fault in computer software which causes the program to operate incorrectly

build up /ˌbɪld 'ʌp/ verb to form by accumulation ○ In icing conditions, ice builds up on the leading edges. ◊ **built-up** (NOTE: **building up – built up**)

build-up /'bɪld ʌp/ noun a gradual accumulation ○ a build-up of static electricity

built-up /'bɪlt ˌʌp/ adjective □ **built-up area** an area which is full of houses, shops, offices, and other buildings, and with very little open space

bulb /bʌlb/ noun **1.** a glass ball inside a lamp that gives electric light ○ If a lamp does not work, the bulb may need replacing. **2.** something shaped like a lamp bulb ○ The most common type of hygrometer is the wet and dry bulb thermometer arrangement.

bulkhead /'bʌlkhed/ noun a dividing partition across the structure of the fuselage separating one compartment from another for reasons of safety or strength ○ A fireproof bulkhead is provided to separate the cool area of the engine from the hot area.

bulletin /'bʊlɪtɪn/ *noun* a short report or information on a situation ○ *news bulletin* ○ *weather bulletin* ○ *A terminal aerodrome forecast bulletin may consist of forecasts for one or more aerodromes.*

BUMF ♦ mnemonic

burble /'bɜːb(ə)l/ *noun* a break in the flow of air around an aircraft's wing, which leads to turbulence

burst /bɜːst/ *noun* **1.** a minor explosion caused by increased pressure ○ *The risk of tyre burst through overheating is increased by hard application of the brakes.* **2.** a very short period of activity followed by no activity ○ *The ground installation transmits a code in two short bursts.* □ **burst of energy** a very short period of energy ■ *verb* to explode because of increased pressure or puncture ○ *Metal debris on the runway may cause a tyre to burst.* (NOTE: **bursting – burst**)

busbar /'bʌsbɑː/ *noun* an electrical conductor used to carry a particular power supply to various pieces of equipment ○ *Complex busbars are thick metal strips or rods to which input and output connections are made.*

button /'bʌt(ə)n/ *noun* a little round disc which you push to operate something, e.g. to ring a bell

Buys Ballot's Law /ˌbaɪz 'bæləts ˌlɔː/ *noun* a rule for identifying low pressure areas, based on the Coriolis effect

COMMENT: In the northern hemisphere, if the wind is blowing from behind you, the low pressure area is to the left, while in the southern hemisphere it is to the right.

buzz /bʌz/ *verb* to fly low in an aircraft over people or buildings, or to fly across the path of other aircraft

bypass /'baɪpɑːs/ *noun* **1.** an alternative pipe, channel, etc. ○ *A turbine bypass in the form of an alternative exhaust duct is fitted with a valve.* **2.** same as **shunt**

C

C *symbol* **1.** Celsius **2.** centigrade

CAA *abbreviation* Civil Aviation Authority

cabin /ˈkæbɪn/ *noun* a passenger compartment in an aircraft ○ *Air enters at the front of the cabin and leaves at the rear.*

cabin attendant /ˈkæbɪn əˌtendənt/ *noun* member of the flight crew who looks after passengers, serves food, etc. ○ *If you need something, press the call button and a cabin attendant will respond within a few minutes.* Also called **flight attendant**

cabin compressor and blower system /ˌkæbɪn kəmˌpresə ən ˈbləʊə ˌsɪstəm/ *noun* part of the air conditioning system for the cabin

cabin crew /ˈkæbɪn kruː/ *noun* airline staff who are in direct contact with the passengers and whose in-flight responsibilities include: ensuring correct seating arrangements, serving food and attending to the general well-being of passengers, etc.

cabin environment *noun* the conditions inside the aircraft cabin, including the temperature, the space, the colour scheme, the seating arrangements, etc.

cabin pressure /ˈkæbɪn ˌpreʃə/ *noun* the pressure of air inside the cabin which allows people to breathe normally at high altitudes

cabin pressurisation /ˌkæbɪn ˌpreʃəraɪˈzeɪʃ(ə)n/ *noun* the maintenance of an acceptable atmospheric pressure in an aircraft while flying at high altitude ○ *At 35,000 ft (feet) passengers can breathe freely because of cabin pressurisation.*

cable /ˈkeɪb(ə)l/ *noun* **1.** thick metal wire □ **control cables** thick metal wire linking the pilot's cockpit controls to control surfaces such as the elevators and ailerons **2.** a thick metal wire used for electrical connections ○ *Earth return is by cable to the negative pole of the battery.*

cabotage /ˈkæbətɑːʒ/ *noun* the right of a country to operate internal air traffic with its own airlines and not those of other countries

calculate /ˈkælkjʊleɪt/ *verb* to find out an answer to a problem by working with numbers ○ *The total flight fuel can be calculated by multiplying the time of the flight by kilograms of fuel per hour.*

calculation /ˌkælkjʊˈleɪʃ(ə)n/ *noun* an act of finding out an answer to a problem by working with numbers

calculation of fuel required /ˌkælkjʊleɪʃ(ə)n əv ˌfjuːəl rɪˈkwaɪəd/ *noun* an arithmetic estimation of fuel needed by using time, distance and fuel-consumption factors

calculator /ˈkælkjʊleɪtə/ *noun* an electronic machine for making calculations ○ *Students are not allowed to use calculators in the examination.*

calibrate /ˈkælɪbreɪt/ *verb* to adjust the scale or graduations on a measuring instrument or gauge ○ *The international standard atmosphere is used to calibrate pressure altimeters.*

calibrated airspeed /ˌkælɪbreɪtɪd ˈeəspiːd/ *noun* indicated airspeed corrected for instrumentation and installation errors. Abbreviation **CAS**

calibration /ˌkælɪˈbreɪʃ(ə)n/ *noun* the adjusting of the scale or graduations on a measuring instrument or gauge ○ *The international standard atmosphere is used for the calibration of instruments.*

call button /'kɔːl ˌbʌt(ə)n/ *noun* a button, often on the arm of a passenger seat, which can be pushed when you need help from an attendant

callsign /'kɔːlsaɪn/ *noun* a series of words and/or letters and/or numbers used to identify an aircraft or station ○ *The aircraft's callsign is 'College 23'.* ○ *VOR stations transmit a two or three letter aural Morse callsign.*

calorie /'kæləri/ *noun* the amount of heat required to raise the temperature of 1 gram of water by 1°C, equal to 4.186 joules ○ *After 2 calories have been released the temperature will have risen 2 degrees i.e. to 0°C, and so the freezing process ceases temporarily.* Abbreviation **cal**

calorific /ˌkælə'rɪfɪk/ *adjective* referring to calories □ **calorific value** the heat produced by the complete burning of a given amount of fuel ○ *The calorific value of a fuel is an expression of the heat or energy content released during combustion.*

cam /kæm/ *noun* an oval or egg-shaped wheel which, when rotating, converts circular motion into reciprocating motion ○ *In a piston engine, the shape of each cam is designed to give the correct amount of opening to the valve.*

CAMFAX /'kæmfæks/ *noun* the civil aviation meteorological facsimile network

camplate /'kæmpleɪt/ *noun* a rotating or non-rotating plate with cams on it ○ *The fuel pump consists of a rotor assembly fitted with several plungers, the ends of which bear onto a non-rotating camplate.*

camshaft /'kæmʃɑːft/ *noun* a rotating shaft carrying cams, which opens and closes valves in a piston engine ○ *As the camshaft rotates, the cam will transmit a lifting force.*

canard /'kænɑːd/ *noun* a projection similar to a small wing fitted close to the nose of an aircraft and designed to increase its horizontal stability

candela /kæn'diːlə/ *noun* the SI unit of brightness of a light ○ *The red and green wing tip navigation lights must be at least 5 candela.* (NOTE: It is usually written **cd** with figures.)

candle power /'kænd(ə)l ˌpaʊə/ *noun* a unit to measure the brightness of a light ○ *Estimation of visibility is achieved by noting the distances at which lights of a known candle power can be observed.*

canopy /'kænəpi/ *noun* **1.** a transparent cover, typically on some fighters, light aircraft and gliders, designed to slide backwards and forwards or hinge upwards to allow pilots to enter or leave an aircraft **2.** a covering to protect people in a life raft ○ *The canopy should be erected to provide protection from the weather.*

cantilever /'kæntɪliːvə/ *noun* a beam fixed and supported at one end only ○ *The mainplanes or wings are of cantilever design.*

cap /kæp/ *noun* a top or lid ○ *the exhaust valve cap*

CAP *abbreviation* Civil Aviation Publication

capability /ˌkeɪpə'bɪlɪti/ *noun* the capacity or ability to do something □ **the flare has a day and night capability** the flare is effective in daylight and in the dark

'France has a large capability in the areas of commercial aviation training and simulation' [*Civil Aviation Training*]

capable /'keɪpəb(ə)l/ *adjective* competent, having an ability ○ *Aircraft used in aerobatics must be capable of withstanding the extra loads imposed on the airframe by the manoeuvres.* ○ *In most modern multi-engine jet transport aircraft, each fuel tank is capable of feeding any engine.* □ **a capable person** a person who works well

capacitance /kə'pæsɪtəns/ *noun* the ability of a system of conductors and insulators to store an electrical charge when there is a positive discharge between the conductors ○ *If the supply frequency is low, the voltage has more* *time to build up a larger charge, or capacitance.* (NOTE: Capacitance is measured in farads and can either be a fixed amount or variable amount.)

capacitive /kə'pæsɪtɪv/ *adjective* referring to the ability of a system of conductors and insulators to store an electrical charge ○ *Overspeed is usually a fault in the constant speed drive unit which causes the generator to over-speed and damage the capacitive loads on the aircraft.*

capacitor /kə'pæsɪtə/ *noun* a system of conductors and insulators which store electrical charge (NOTE: A capacitor is used in a circuit to store energy for a short while.)

capacity /kə'pæsɪti/ *noun* **1.** the ability to do something easily ○ *Energy is the capacity for performing work.* **2.** the amount of something which a container can hold ○ *Each cylinder has a capacity of 0.5 litres.* □ **battery capacity** the amount of electrical energy a battery can store and deliver expressed in ampere hours **3.** the ability of an ATC system, in a given area, to provide a normal service, expressed in numbers of aircraft

'…a 500 to 600 seat ultra-high capacity type aircraft is now being studied by Airbus Industrie and Boeing' [*Flight International 1–7 May 1996*]

capillary /kə'pɪləri/ *noun* a very fine or narrow tube

capillary action /kə,pɪləri 'ækʃən/, **capillary flow** /kə'pɪləri fləʊ/ *noun* the action by which a liquid rises up a narrow tube

capsule /'kæpsjuːl/ *noun* a small closed container

captain /'kæptɪn/ *noun* the person in charge of an aircraft ○ *The captain asked all passengers to remain seated until the aircraft had come to a stop.*

captive /'kæptɪv/ *adjective* not free to move

captive balloon /,kæptɪv bə'luːn/ *noun* a balloon which, when in flight, is attached to the ground by a long cable

carbon /'kɑːbən/ *noun* **1.** a non-metallic element, which is a component of living matter and organic chemical

compounds and is found in various forms, e.g. as diamonds or charcoal **2.** a black material with good electrical properties

carbon brush /'kɑːbən brʌʃ/ *noun* a small, replaceable, carbon block found in electric motors, generators and alternators, which provides the passage of electric current

carbon deposits /,kɑːbən dɪ'pɒzɪtz/ *plural noun* residues of burnt oil deposited in the combustion chamber, etc., in the course of the combustion process ○ *Carbon deposits on a spark-plug electrode may cause misfiring.*

carbon dioxide /,kɑːbən daɪ'ɒksaɪd/ *noun* a colourless, odourless, non-toxic gas found in the atmosphere, and also used in fire extinguishers and fizzy drinks ○ *Carbon dioxide can be solidified at low temperature to produce dry ice.* Symbol CO_2

carbon fibre /,kɑːbən 'faɪbə/ *noun* a thin, light and very strong strand of pure carbon which can be combined with other materials to make them stronger

carbon monoxide /,kɑːbən mə'nɒksaɪd/ *noun* a colourless but poisonous gas from incomplete combustion found in the exhausts of spark ignition engines. Symbol CO

carburation /,kɑːbjuː'reɪʃ(ə)n/ *noun* the process of mixing fuel with air in a carburettor ○ *Carburation must ensure that rapid and complete burning will take place within the cylinder.*

carburettor /,kɑːbə'retə/ *noun* a device for mixing air with fuel in the right quantities before combustion ○ *Most carburettors are installed so that they are in a warm position.*

carburettor heat /,kɑːbə'retə hiːt/ *noun* a system for keeping the carburettor and associated components free of ice

carburettor icing /,kɑːbəretə 'aɪsɪŋ/ *noun* a process by which, under particular conditions, ice forms in the venturi tube of the carburettor

cardioid /'kɑːdiɔɪd/ *adjective* shaped like a heart ○ *The cardioid polar dia-*

gram of the magnetic field around a bar-magnet.

carousel /ˌkærə'sel/ *noun* a rotating platform from where arriving passengers can pick up their baggage ○ *Baggage from flight AC123 is on carousel No 4.*

carriage /'kærɪdʒ/ *noun* the act of carrying ○ *Regulations require the carriage of life-rafts when flying over water.*

carrier /'kæriə/ *noun* **1.** a person or organisation that carries people or goods from one place to another ○ *Individual carriers assign codes to aircraft.* **2.** a frame or bag in which objects can be carried

carrier wave /'kæriə weɪv/ *noun* a radio signal that is transmitted continuously at a constant amplitude and frequency ○ *Amplitude modulation has only one pair of usable sidebands each at about one sixth of the signal strength of the carrier.*

carry /'kæri/ *verb* to take somebody or something from one place to another ○ *The aircraft was carrying 120 passengers.* (NOTE: **carrying – carried**)

cartridge /'kɑːtrɪdʒ/ *noun* a removable unit for an air filter ○ *Cabin air filters normally consist of a casing, housing a replaceable filter cartridge.*

CAS *abbreviation* **1.** calibrated airspeed **2.** controlled airspace

case /keɪs/ *noun* **1.** an outer covering, housing or jacket ○ *Cooling air is directed through passages in the engine case to control engine case temperature.* **2.** an example, situation or circumstance ○ *In some special cases, e.g. for landing and take-off, wind directions are measured from magnetic north.*

casing /'keɪsɪŋ/ *noun* a cover that encloses a piece of equipment, etc. ○ *Annular and outer air casing form a tunnel around the spine of the engine.*

CAT /kæt/ *abbreviation* clear air turbulence

catastrophe /kə'tæstrəfi/ *noun* a very bad event or accident, a disaster ○ *the recent air catastrophe off the Nova Scotia coast.* ○ *Although the family were not at home when it happened, the*

crash which destroyed their house was a catastrophe for them.

catastrophic /ˌkætə'strɒfɪk/ *adjective* terrible, disastrous ○ *In a catastrophic accident where many persons may be disabled, those who show signs of life should be rescued first.*

categorise /'kætɪgəraɪz/, **categorize** *verb* to put into groups, classes or categories ○ *Figure 2 categorises the types of wave by frequency band.* ○ *Aircraft can be categorised by weight, number of engines, role, etc.*

category /'kætɪg(ə)ri/ *noun* an official class or group ○ *Load factors vary depending on the category of aircraft.*

cathode /'kæθəʊd/ *noun* a negative electrode or terminal ○ *The cathode is a metal cylinder fitted with an internal heater.*

cathode ray tube /ˌkæθəʊd 'reɪ ˌtjuːb/ *noun* a high-vacuum tube in which cathode rays produce an image on a screen such as a TV screen ○ *Electronic indicating systems show engine indications, systems monitoring and crew alerting functions on one or more cathode ray tubes or liquid crystal displays mounted in the instrument panel.* Abbreviation **CRT**

cause /kɔːz/ *noun* something that makes something else happen, a reason ○ *If the ammeter shows a high state of charge after start up, it is quite normal and no cause for alarm.* ■ *verb* to make something happen ○ *Air in the fuel line can cause an engine to flame-out or stop.*

caution /'kɔːʃ(ə)n/ *noun* **1.** advice or a warning to be careful ○ *If a problem occurs in the spoiler system, a master caution light illuminates.* **2.** care ○ *Proceed with caution.*

cavitation /ˌkævɪ'teɪʃ(ə)n/ *noun* the formation of vapour-filled cavities or holes in liquids and gases, caused by low pressure or high speed ○ *Most reservoirs are pressurised to provide a positive fluid pressure at the pump inlet and thus prevent cavitation and the formation of bubbles.*

cavity /'kævɪti/ *noun* a hole ○ *De-icing fluid flows into the cavity in the* *distributor panels before passing through the porous steel outer skin.*

CB *abbreviation* cumulonimbus

cc /ˌsiː ˈsiː/ *abbreviation* cubic centimetres

cd *symbol* candela

CDI *abbreviation* course deviation indicator

cease /siːs/ *verb* to stop ○ *If fuel, oxygen or heat is removed from the fire triangle, combustion will cease.*

ceiling /ˈsiːlɪŋ/ *noun* **1.** the highest point **2.** the greatest pressure height that can be reached ○ *The aircraft has a ceiling of 50,000 ft.*

celestial /səˈlestiəl/ *adjective* referring to the sky □ **celestial navigation** navigation by using the stars in the sky

cell /sel/ *noun* **1.** a system of positive and negative plates for storage of electricity that form a battery ○ *A battery is a device which converts chemical energy into electrical energy and is made up of a number of cells.* **2.** the central part of a thunder cloud ○ *The life cycle of the thunderstorm cell ends when the downdraughts have spread throughout the cloud.*

Celsius /ˈselsiəs/ *noun* a scale for measuring temperature in which water freezes at 0° and boils at 100°. Symbol **C**. Compare **Fahrenheit**

center /ˈsentə/ *noun, verb US* same as **centre**

centerline /ˈsentəlaɪn/ *noun US* same as **centreline**

centigrade /ˈsentɪɡreɪd/ *noun* a scale for measuring temperature in which water freezes at 0° and boils at 100°. Symbol **C**. Compare **Fahrenheit**

centimetre /ˈsentɪmiːtə/ *noun* a measure of length that is equal to one hundredth of a metre (NOTE: 2.54 cm = 1 inch.)

central /ˈsentrəl/ *adjective* located in the centre or in the middle ○ *The control knob is moved from the central position.*

Central Flow Management Unit (Brussels) /ˌsentr(ə)l fləʊ ˈmænɪdʒmənt ˌjuːnɪt ˌbrʌs(ə)lz/ *noun* a central agency in Brussels that is responsible for air traffic management

throughout the area controlled by the ECAC

centralise /ˈsentrəlaɪz/, **centralize** *verb* to put into the centre or into the middle position ○ *The operating jack centralises the control surface after the turn.*

Central Standard Time /ˌsentrəl ˈstændəd ˈtaɪm/ *noun* the time zone of the east-central part of the USA and Canada, 6 hours behind GMT

centre /ˈsentə/ *noun* **1.** the middle ○ *The plane of the great circle passes through the centre of a sphere.* □ **centre of a circle** mid-point of a circle, point in the middle of a circle **2.** a main building or office ○ *Area Forecasting Centre* ■ *verb* to move to a central position ○ *Centre the control column.* (NOTE: **centred – centring**; the US English is **centered – centering**.)

centre fix /ˈsentə fɪks/ *noun* same as **self-positioning**

centreline /ˈsentəlaɪn/ *noun* a painted or imaginary line running along the centre of the runway (NOTE: It is also written **centre line**; written **centerline** in US English.)

centre of gravity /ˌsentə əv ˈɡrævɪti/ *noun* the point at which a body can be balanced ○ *Distribution of the tanks and the fuel in the tanks is vital in maintaining the aircraft centre of gravity and trim.* Abbreviation **CG**

COMMENT: If the centre of gravity is outside the limits, the aircraft may be difficult or impossible to control.

centrifugal /ˌsentrɪˈfjuːɡ(ə)l, senˈtrɪfjʊɡ(ə)l/ *adjective* moving away from the centre ○ *The blades must be strong enough to carry the centrifugal loads due to rotation at high speed.*

centrifugal force /ˌsentrɪfjuːɡ(ə)l ˈfɔːs/ *noun* outward force caused by turning motion

centrifuge /ˈsentrɪfjuːdʒ/ *noun* a device which uses centrifugal force to separate or remove liquids ■ *verb* to separate liquids by using centrifugal force ○ *The rotating vanes of the breather centrifuge the oil from the mist.*

centripetal /ˌsentrɪˈpiːt(ə)l, sen
ˈtrɪpɪt(ə)l/ *adjective* moving towards
the centre

centripetal force /sen,trɪpɪt(ə)l
ˈfɔːs/ *noun* inward, centre-seeking
force working in opposition to centrifugal force ○ *The magnitude of the centripetal force varies with the square of
the wind speed.* ○ *In a turn, lift provides
the centripetal force.*

certain /ˈsɜːt(ə)n/ *adjective* **1.** particular, some ○ *in certain areas* ○ *at certain times* ○ *under certain circumstances* **2.** sure ○ *There are certain to be
horizontal differences in the mean temperature of a layer.* □ **to make certain**
to make sure ○ *Make certain that the
parking brake is on before doing engine
run-up checks.*

certificate *noun* /sə'tɪfɪkət/ an official document which states that particular facts are true ■ *verb* /sə'tɪfɪkeɪt/ to
award or give a certificate □ **aircraft
which are certificated for flight** aircraft which have the necessary paper-
work to be authorised to fly

certificate of airworthiness /sə
ˌtɪfɪkət əv 'eəwɜːðɪnəs/ *noun* a document issued by an aviation authority
stating that an aircraft meets specific
safety and performance requirements
that allow it to be used in service ○ *An
authorised person may require production of the Certificate of Airworthiness.*
Abbreviation **C of A**

certification /sə,tɪfɪ'keɪʃ(ə)n/ *noun*
the process of giving certificates ○ *The
inferential method of ice detection is
used on flight trials for certification of
aircraft.*

certify /'sɜːtɪfaɪ/ *verb* to authorise or
permit the use of something ○ *The aircraft is certified for aerobatic flight.*

CFI *abbreviation* chief flying instructor

CFMU *abbreviation* Central Flow
Management Unit

CFRP *abbreviation* carbon fibre reinforced plastic

chalk /tʃɔːk/ *noun* a soft white lime-
stone rock that may be used in powder
form or as a shaped stick for writing
with ○ *Oil, which is trapped in the*

*defects, is absorbed by the chalk thus
indicating their positions.*

chamber /'tʃeɪmbə/ *noun* a small
enclosed compartment

chandelle /ʃæn'del/ *noun* a steep
climbing turn in which an aircraft
almost stalls as it uses momentum to
increase its rate of climb

channel /'tʃæn(ə)l/ *noun* a special
frequency band for the transmission of
radio signals ○ *The system operates on
VHF communications between 118 and
135.95 MHz giving 360 channels at 50
kHz spacing.*

character /'kærɪktə/ *noun* **1.** a quality or set of qualities which make something different and separate from something else ○ *The circulation of the
atmosphere is zonal in character.* **2.** an
individual letter, number or symbol
used in printing and writing

characterise /'kærɪktəraɪz/, **char-
acterize** *verb* □ **to be characterised by**
to have qualities or features which make
it different and separate from other
things ○ *The stratosphere is characterised by a temperature structure which is
steady or increases with height.*

characteristic /ˌkærɪktə'rɪstɪk/
adjective typical of a class or group of
things □ **a characteristic feature** a normal feature of the thing in question ■
noun a feature or quality making something different or separate from something else ○ *Air masses have distinct
characteristics which can be used to
separate them on a chart.* □ **handling
characteristics** features of an aircraft
that make it different from other aircraft
when handling it □ **summer characteristics** climatic conditions which are typical of summertime

charge /tʃɑːdʒ/ *noun* **1.** an amount of
electricity ○ *Friction causes a charge of
static electricity.* ○ *The battery was so
old, it would not take a charge.* □ **a high
level of charge** a high amount of electricity **2.** money demanded or paid for
the providing of a service □ **overnight
parking is free of charge** it costs nothing to park overnight ■ *verb* **1.** to pass
electrical current through something
and thereby make it electrically active ○

An installed battery becomes fully charged by the aircraft generator. □ **charged particles** atmospheric particles which have either a positive or negative electrical charge **2.** to take money for a service ○ *We do not charge for overnight parking.*

charger /'tʃɑːdʒə/ *noun* □ **battery charger** device for putting an electrical charge into a battery. ◊ **turbocharger**

chart /tʃɑːt/ *noun* a map for navigational purposes □ **significant weather chart** a weather chart with important weather information marked on it

chase plane /'tʃeɪs pleɪn/ *noun* an aircraft whose role is to escort another aircraft or to photograph it

check /tʃek/ *noun* an examination to make certain that something is as it should be ○ *safety check* ○ *A check was made on the undercarriage and airframe after the pilot reported a heavy landing.* ◊ **run** ■ *verb* to examine something in order to find out if it is correct ○ *It is the pilot's responsibility to check that the aircraft is airworthy.*

'European Union (EU) airports may be empowered to carry out safety checks on foreign airlines' [*Flight International 1–7 May 1996*]

check in /,tʃek 'ɪn/ *verb* to register by giving in your ticket, showing your passport and giving your baggage at an airline desk before a flight ○ *Passengers should check in two hours before departure.*

check-in /'tʃek ɪn/ *noun* an airline desk where passengers register before a flight ○ *The check-in is on the first floor.* □ **check-in time** time at which passengers should check in

check-in counter /'tʃek ɪn ,kaʊntə/, **check-in desk** *noun* counter where passengers check in

checklist /'tʃeklɪst/ *noun* a list of items, often in booklet form, to be checked in a given sequence ○ *Before every flight, the pilot should perform pre-flight checks using a checklist.*

chemical /'kemɪk(ə)l/ *adjective* referring to chemistry ○ *a chemical reaction* ■ *noun* a substance used in or made by a chemical process ○ *a chemical such as anti-ice for propellers*

chemistry /'kemɪstri/ *noun* **1.** the science of chemical substances and their reactions **2.** the nature of something ○ *The basic chemistry of fire can be illustrated by the three sides of a triangle representing fuel, oxygen and heat.*

chief /tʃiːf/ *adjective* most important, main □ **the chief factors** the most important factors

chief flying instructor /,tʃiːf 'flaɪɪŋ ɪn,strʌktə/ *noun* the senior rank of flying instructor. Abbreviation **CFI**

chock /tʃɒk/ *noun* a wooden or metal device placed in front of the wheels of a parked aircraft to prevent it from moving ○ *The accident happened because the chocks had been removed before the engine was started.*

choke /tʃəʊk/ *noun* a valve in a carburettor, which controls the amount of air combining with fuel ■ *verb* **1.** to block a tube, etc., making a liquid unable to move □ **a choked nozzle** a blocked or partly-blocked nozzle **2.** to stop breathing because you have inhaled water or smoke

choke tube /tʃəʊk tjuːb/ *noun* same as **venturi** ○ *Increase in rpm increases the speed of air passing through the choke tube or venturi.*

chopper /'tʃɒpə/ (*informal*) *noun* same as **helicopter** ■ *verb* to transport something or somebody by helicopter, or to travel by helicopter

chord /kɔːd/ *noun* the shortest distance between the leading and trailing edges of an airfoil

chute /ʃuːt/ *noun* same as **parachute** (*informal*)

circle /'sɜːk(ə)l/ *noun* a line forming a round shape, or a round shape formed by objects or people ○ *They stood in a circle on the tarmac.* □ **great circle direction** an imaginary circle on the surface of the Earth which lies in a plane passing through the centre of the Earth

circuit /'sɜːkɪt/ *noun* **1.** a complete route around which an electrical current can flow **2.** the pattern of take-off, climb-out, turn onto crosswind leg, turn onto downwind leg, turn onto base leg, turn onto final approach and landing ○ *When carrying out practice landings at an aerodrome, the pilot should keep a sharp lookout for other aircraft in the circuit.*

circuit board /'sɜːkɪt bɔːd/ *noun* an insulating board which holds components connected into an electrical circuit

circuit-breaker /'sɜːkɪt ˌbreɪkə/ *noun* a small protective device in the circuit which blows or breaks before a dangerous overload of current arises

circuitry /'sɜːkɪtri/ *noun* a system of electrical circuits ○ *In an anti-skid braking system, circuitry is employed which can detect individual wheel deceleration.*

circular /'sɜːkjʊlə/ *adjective* shaped like a circle ○ *Anodes are circular plates with centre holes.* □ **semi-circular** shaped like a half-circle ■ *noun* a document distributed to a large number of people ○ *an aeronautical information circular*

circular slide rule /ˌsɜːkjʊlə 'slaɪd ˌruːl/ *noun* a calculating device on which all manner of conversions and complex calculations can be made to assist in flight planning

circulate /'sɜːkjʊleɪt/ *verb* to move round in such a way as to arrive at the point of departure ○ *Water circulates via the radiator and pump through to the engine block itself.*

circulation /ˌsɜːkjʊ'leɪʃ(ə)n/ *noun* the act of moving round in such a way as to arrive at the point of departure ○ *The general circulation is indicated by the arrows.* □ **cyclonic circulation** the circulation of air which, if viewed from above, is anticlockwise in the northern hemisphere and clockwise in the southern hemisphere

circulatory /ˌsɜːkjʊ'leɪt(ə)ri/ *adjective* moving around a circuit ○ *a self-contained re-circulatory oil system*

circumference /sə'kʌmf(ə)rəns/ *noun* the distance around the edge of a circle ○ *The angle subtended by an arc*

equal to one 360th part of the circumference of a circle is called one degree.

circumstance /'sɜːkʌmstns/ *noun* a condition which affects something in a given situation □ **in some circumstances, under certain circumstances** in some particular situations

cirro- /sɪrəʊ/ *prefix* high altitude, i.e. above 20,000 feet

cirrocumulus /ˌsɪrəʊ'kjuːmjʊləs/ *noun* a layer of broken cloud at about 20,000 feet

cirrostratus /ˌsɪrəʊ'strɑːtəs/ *noun* a layer cloud at about 20,000 feet

cirrus /'sɪrəs/ *noun* a high cloud in a mass of separate clouds which are formed of ice crystals

Civil Aviation Authority /ˌsɪvɪl ˌeɪvi'eɪʃ(ə)n ɔːˌθɒrəti/ *noun* the organisation which licences operators, aircraft and employees for non-military, especially commercial aviation. Abbreviation **CAA**

Civil Aviation Publication /ˌsɪvɪl ˌeɪvi'eɪʃ(ə)n ˌpʌblɪkeɪʃ(ə)n/ *noun* a book, etc., published by the Civil Aviation Authority, each publication having its own reference number ○ *The procedure for obtaining a bearing can be found in CAP 413.* Abbreviation **CAP**

COMMENT: CAA (Civil Aviation Authority) publications are referred to as CAPs and each has a reference number for identification: *the procedure for obtaining a bearing is described in CAP 413.*

clad /klæd/ *verb* to protect by covering ○ *Alloys can be protected from corrosion by cladding the exposed surface with a thin layer of aluminium.*

clamshell door /'klæmʃel dɔː/ *noun* the hinged part of a thrust reverser ○ *Clamshell doors are hydraulically or pneumatically opened, and direct the exhaust gases forwards to produce reverse thrust.*

classification /ˌklæsɪfɪ'keɪʃ(ə)n/ *noun* the act of putting things into groups or classes because they possess particular common features ○ *Classification of aircraft consists of a multi-level diagram with each category divided into sub-categories.* ○ *A full* *classification of layer cloud is given in the table.*

classify /'klæsɪfaɪ/ *verb* to group items so that those with similar characteristics are in the same group ○ *Precipitation is classified as light, moderate or heavy according to its rate of fall.* ○ *The weather associated with visibility reductions by particles suspended in the atmosphere is classified either as fog, mist, haze, or smoke.*

clear /klɪə/ *adjective* **1.** referring to conditions in which it is easy to see, e.g. with no cloud or fog □ **a clear sky** a sky with no cloud □ **a clear winter night** a night with no fog, mist or other conditions which might impair visibility **2.** possible to easily see through **3.** with nothing blocking the way □ **clear runway, the runway is clear** nothing is on the runway □ **keep the exits clear** do not put anything and do not stand in front of the exits **4.** away from **5.** easy to hear □ **clear of cloud** either above or below cloud □ **keep clear (of)** keep away (from) **6.** easy to understand ○ *The explanation is very clear.* **7.** understood **8.** understood □ **is it clear?** do you understand? ■ *verb* **1.** to remove a blockage or some other unwanted effect which prevents a system from working correctly ○ *A heater element is fitted to clear the detector of ice.* **2.** to disappear ○ *In winter frost and fog are slow to clear.* **3.** to make sure that it is all right to do something □ **clear it with the CFI** make sure that the CFI agrees with the request **4.** to officially ask people to quickly leave a given area or place □ **to clear the building** to quickly leave the building

'…the principles of weight and balance should have been learned by all pilots during their initial training, but it is clear that, afterwards, some forget' [*Civil Aviation Authority, General Aviation Safety Sense Leaflet*]

COMMENT: On 27th March 1977 two Boeing 747s collided on the runway at Los Rodeos airport Tenerife in poor visibility, resulting in 575 deaths. A KLM 747 commenced take-off while a Pan Am 747 was still taxiing towards it on the same runway. There was clearly a breakdown in communications, perhaps a misunderstood radio call. The Pan Am aircraft had been asked by the controller, who was unable to see either aircraft due to low cloud, 'Are you clear of the runway?' The KLM aircraft had already commenced the take-off roll without clearance. It is possible that the KLM pilot mistook the call to the other aircraft thinking that he was 'clear to take off'.

clear air turbulence /ˌklɪər eə 'tɜːbjʊləns/ *noun* turbulence encountered in air where no cloud is present (NOTE: CAT is often associated with the jet stream.)

clearance /'klɪərəns/ *noun* **1.** a space made to allow for the movement of hardware relative to other hardware ○ *clearance between rocker arm and valve tip* **2.** official permission ○ *Obtain clearance for IFR flight.* **3.** the disappearance of something unwanted, often rain, fog or snow ○ *Low temperatures caused a delay in the clearance of fog.*

clearance limit /'klɪərəns ˌlɪmɪt/ the point to which an aircraft is allowed to proceed when granted an air traffic control clearance

clear ice /ˌklɪər 'aɪs/ *noun* ice which is glass-like rather than white

clear pass /ˌklɪə 'pɑːs/ *noun* an exam result which is in no doubt

clear to land /ˌklɪə tə 'lænd/ *noun* air traffic control permission to land

climate /'klaɪmət/ *noun* weather conditions particular to a given area ○ *Mediterranean climate* ○ *tropical climate* □ **temperate climate** a type of climate which is neither very hot in summer nor very cold in winter. ◊ **continental**

climatic /klaɪ'mætɪk/ *adjective* referring to climate or weather conditions particular to a given area ○ *The aircraft forward speed and altitude as well as climatic conditions will influence the value of thrust.*

climatic zone /klaɪ'mætɪk zəʊn/ *noun* one of the eight areas of the Earth which have distinct climates

COMMENT: The climatic zones are: the two polar regions (Arctic and Antarctic); the boreal zone in the northern hemisphere, south of the Arctic; two temperate zones, one in the northern hemisphere and one in the southern hemisphere; two subtropical zones, including the deserts; and the equatorial zone which has a damp tropical climate.

climatology /klaɪmə'tɒlədʒi/ *noun* the science of the study of climate ○ *Although pilots do not need to be experts in climatology, they should have a good understanding of the factors which produce changes in the weather.*

climb /klaɪm/ *noun* the act of increasing altitude by use of power ○ *Fine pitch enables full engine speed to be used during take-off and climb.* Opposite **descent** ■ *verb* to increase altitude by use of power ○ *After take-off, the aircraft climbed to 5,000 ft.* Opposite **descend**

climb-out /'klaɪm'aʊt/ *noun* a flight after take-off from 35 feet to 1,500 feet during which undercarriage and flaps are retracted ○ *Turn right after climb-out.*

clockwise /'klɒkwaɪz/ *adjective, adverb* describing a circular movement in the same direction as the hands of a clock ○ *a clockwise direction* ○ *The relative bearing indicated is measured clockwise from the nose of the aircraft.* Opposite **anticlockwise**

clog /klɒg/ *verb* to prevent movement of fluid through a pipe, etc., because of a build-up of solid matter ○ *Most filters allow unfiltered fluid to pass to the system when the filter becomes clogged.*

close /kləʊz/ *verb* to shut ○ *Close the door.*

closure /'kləʊʒə/ *noun* the act of closing or shutting ○ *The voltage regulator is turned on by the closure of the generator control relay.*

cloud /klaʊd/ *noun* a mass of water vapour or ice particles in the sky that can produce rain

COMMENT: The most important types of cloud are the following: **altocumulus**, cloud formed at about 12,000 feet as a layer of rounded mass with a level base; **altostratus**, cloud formed as a continuous layer between 6,000 and 20,000 feet usually allowing the sun or moon to be seen from the surface; **cirrocumulus**, a layer of broken cloud at about 20,000 feet; **cirrostratus**, layer cloud at about 20,000 feet; **cirrus**, cloud made of ice crystals at 25,000 – 40,000 feet appearing as hair-like formations; **cumulonimbus**, cloud formed as a towering mass and often associated with thunderstorms; **cumulus**, cloud formed in rounded masses with a flat base at low altitude, resulting from up currents of air; **nimbostratus**, thick dark layer cloud at low altitude from which rain or snow often falls (nimbus = rain cloud); **stratocirrus**, cloud similar to cirrostratus but more compact; **stratocumulus**, a layer of connected small clouds at low altitude.

cloud base /'klaʊd beɪs/ *noun* the bottom part of a layer of cloud ○ *In general, the lower the cloud base, the less heat is lost by the earth.*

cloud ceiling /'klaʊd ˌsiːlɪŋ/ *noun* the height above the ground or water of the base of the lowest layer of cloud

cloud group /'klaʊd gruːp/ *noun* a collection of different cloud types which have similarities, e.g. stratus clouds

cm *abbreviation* centimetre

co- /kəʊ/ *prefix* together □ **co-axial** having the same axis □ **co-located** having the same location

coalesce /ˌkəʊə'les/ *verb* to join together to form a large mass or number ○ *The moisture in the air coalesces into large water droplets.*

coalescence /ˌkəʊə'les(ə)ns/ *noun* the act of joining together to form a larger mass or number ○ *Coalescence of water vapour in the atmosphere forms larger droplets of water.*

coast /kəʊst/ *noun* an area where the land meets the sea ○ *Valentia is situated on the coast of south west Ireland.*

coastal /'kəʊst(ə)l/ *adjective* referring to the coast □ **coastal area** an area near a coast ○ *Land and sea breezes occur in coastal areas.*

coastal refraction /ˌkəʊst(ə)l rɪ'frækʃən/ *noun* change in direction of waves when a signal crosses a coastline from sea to land

coastline /'kəʊstlaɪn/ *noun* the outline of a coast seen from a distance or on a map ○ *It is normally easy to identify a coastline or island.*

coat /kəʊt/ *noun* a thin covering of a substance such as paint ○ *The coats of paint on a large aircraft significantly increase its weight.* ■ *verb* to cover with a thin layer of a substance such as paint ○ *Metals are coated for protection against corrosion.*

coating /ˈkəʊtɪŋ/ *noun* **1.** a thin layer of a substance ○ *There are two coatings on the inside of CRT screens.* **2.** the act of covering with a thin layer of a substance

cock /kɒk/ *noun* a manually controlled valve or tap to control the flow of a liquid ○ *It is necessary to have a master cock for each engine.*

cockpit /ˈkɒkpɪt/ *noun* the forward area in an aircraft from where the aircraft is controlled by the pilot ○ *In the case of an in-flight oil loss, a warning indicator will light in the cockpit.*

'...in the cockpit of the future there will be two animals, a pilot and a dog. The pilot will be there to feed the dog, and the dog will be there to bite the pilot if he tries to touch anything' [*NYT News Service*]

code /kəʊd/ *noun* **1.** a system of numbers, letters or symbols used to represent language which has to be learned and decoded in order for the receiver to understand the meaning **2.** a series of pulses by which an aircraft transponder replies to a signal from the ground

codeshare /ˈkəʊdʃeə/ *noun* □ **codeshare deal** an agreement between airlines regarding connecting flights ○ *The two airlines have entered into a codeshare deal for flights between Dubai and Bangkok.*

codeshare partner /ˈkəʊdʃeə ˌpɑːtnə/ *noun* an airline which has an agreement with another airline regarding connecting flights

codesharing /ˈkəʊdʃeərɪŋ/ *noun* **1.** a procedure which allows travellers to use connecting flights between one airline and another partner airline for worldwide destinations **2.** an arrangement by which two airlines sell seats on the same flight using their own flight numbers

coefficient /ˌkəʊɪˈfɪʃ(ə)nt/ *noun* a mathematical quantity placed before and multiplying another

C of A *abbreviation* certificate of airworthiness

C of G *abbreviation* centre of gravity

coil /kɔɪl/ *noun* a device consisting of coiled wire for converting low voltage to high voltage ○ *A voltage coil is connected across the generator.*

coiled wire /ˈkɔɪld ˈwaɪə/ *noun* a length of wire twisted round and round ○ *A coiled wire connects the terminal to earth.*

coincide /ˌkəʊɪnˈsaɪd/ *verb* to happen at the same time and/or in the same place ○ *When the aircraft heading is directly into wind or down wind, track and heading coincide.*

coincident /kəʊˈɪnsɪdənt/ *adjective* happening at the same place or at the same time ○ *The Earth's true north and magnetic north poles are not coincident.*

col /kɒl/ *noun* an area of slack pressure gradient between two centres of high or low pressure ○ *The persistence and movement of cols are governed by the movement of the adjacent pressure systems.*

cold front /kəʊld frʌnt/ *noun* an advancing mass of cold air, moving under and lifting warmer air ○ *A cold front brought rainy, windy conditions to the country.*

collapse /kəˈlæps/ *noun* a sudden and complete fall □ **the collapse of a company** the end of the existence of the company ■ *verb* **1.** to fall suddenly and completely ○ *The magnetic field will reach a maximum in one direction, collapse to zero and reach a maximum in the opposite direction.* **2.** to fold or to close suddenly and unintentionally □ **the undercarriage collapsed** (*of an apparatus*) the undercarriage could not support the aircraft and broke or retracted on its own **3.** to faint □ **the passenger collapsed** the passenger fell and became semi- or fully unconscious because of some medical problem

'...as the aeroplane slid off the runway, the left landing gear collapsed' [*Pilot*]

collect /kə'lekt/ *verb* **1.** to gather over a period of time ○ *Any given object will usually collect ice more quickly at high speed.* **2.** to take something or to pick something up from a place

collection /kə'lekʃən/ *noun* **1.** a number of things brought together ○ *a collection of vintage aircraft* **2.** an act of being collected by somebody ○ *The documents are in the office awaiting collection.*

collide /kə'laɪd/ *verb* to bump or to crash into something ○ *The aircraft left the runway and collided with a fire truck.*

collision /kə'lɪʒ(ə)n/ *noun* a crash between two objects, two vehicles, etc. ○ *If there is a risk of collision, alter course to the right.* □ **collision avoidance** the prevention of collisions by taking measures beforehand to ensure that they do not happen

column /'kɒləm/ *noun* **1.** a body of fluid or solid with a tall, narrow shape ○ *Torricelli first demonstrated that the atmosphere has weight by showing that it can support a column of liquid.* **2.** a vertical section of a table in a document ○ *Column four of the table shows the totals of the other three columns.*

combat /'kɒmbæt/ *verb* to fight against ○ *Fire extinguishers are provided to combat fire.*

combat aircraft /ˌkɒmbæt 'eəkrɑːft/ *noun* aircraft designed for warfare

combination /ˌkɒmbɪ'neɪʃ(ə)n/ *noun* two or more things brought together to form one ○ *The combination of wind direction and wind speed is called velocity.*

combine /kəm'baɪn/ *verb* to bring two or more things together to make one ○ *The stabilising channels for ailerons and elevators are combined.* ○ *Thrust and lift combine to overcome drag and gravity.*

combustible /kəm'bʌstəb(ə)l/ *adjective* burning or igniting easily □ **combustible materials** materials which will catch fire easily, e.g. wood, paper, etc.

combustion /kəm'bʌstʃən/ *noun* burning, especially that which takes place in an engine ○ *The heat generated by combustion is considerable.*

combustion chamber /kəm 'bʌstʃ(ə)n ˌtʃeɪmbə/ *noun* the part of the cylinder in a piston engine where the ignition of the fuel/air mixture takes place

combustor /kəm'bʌstə/ *noun* the part of a jet or gas-turbine engine that burns fuel to produce power. It consists of the fuel injection system, the igniter, and the combustion chamber.

command /kə'mɑːnd/ *noun* an order □ **the command to evacuate** the order to leave the aircraft in an emergency □ **in command** having responsibility for and authority over ■ *verb* to order something to be done ○ *The captain commanded the evacuation of the aircraft.*

commander /kə'mɑːndə/ *noun* a pilot in control of, and responsible for, the aircraft and its contents during flight time □ **the commander of an aircraft** the member of the flight crew specified by the operator as being the commander

commence /kə'mens/ *verb* to start to do something □ **commence the evacuation** start getting people out of the aircraft

commercial /kə'mɜːʃ(ə)l/ *adjective* referring to a business activity □ **commercial aviation** flying as a business enterprise

commercial aircraft /kəˌmɜːʃ(ə)l 'eəkrɑːft/ *noun* aircraft used to carry cargo or passengers for payment

Commercial Pilot's Licence /kə ˌmɜːʃ(ə)l 'paɪləts ˌlaɪs(ə)ns/ *noun* the licence that a person requires to be pilot-in-command of public transport aircraft certified for single-pilot operations. Abbreviation **CPL**

common sense /ˌkɒmən 'sens/ *noun* ordinary good sense ○ *You should use your common sense as well as follow the rules if a passenger feels unwell.*

comms /kɒmz/ *abbreviation* communications

communicate /kə'mju:nɪkeɪt/ *verb*
to make contact with somebody in order
to pass information ○ *The cabin attend-*
ants should communicate with the cap-
tain.

communication /kə,mju:nɪ
'keɪʃ(ə)n/ *noun* the act of passing information to somebody usually, but not
always, by using language ○ *Two meth-*
ods of communication are available to
crew members – language and hand
signals.

communication link /kə,mju:nɪ
'keɪʃ(ə)n ,lɪŋk/ *noun* a telephone or
radio connection, as between the
ground crew and flight deck while an
aircraft is preparing for departure

communications /kə,mju:nɪ
'keɪʃ(ə)nz/ *plural noun* a system of
passing information ○ *satellite commu-*
nications ○ *VHF communications are*
allocated the frequency bracket 118–
137 MHz. Abbreviation **comms**

commutator /'kɒmjuteɪtə/ *noun* a
device containing metal bars connected
to the coils of a generator to produce
electrical current ○ *As the power output*
required is DC not AC, a commutator is
fixed at one end of the armature.

compact /kəm'pækt/ *adjective*
small, close together, or not taking
much space ○ *The annular system, as*
used on modern aircraft, provides a
compact system, and, for the same out-
put and mass flow, a shorter system. ■
verb **1.** to make smaller or more dense
by pressing **2.** to compress, by driving
over with heavy machinery ○ *When tax-*
iing on grass, aircraft wheels compact
the earth as the aircraft moves over it.

compaction /kəm'pækʃ(ə)n/ *noun*
the act of pressing things together to
form one, or of compressing something
to make it hard ○ *The speed of impact*
when the aircraft passes through a
snowstorm causes compaction of snow-
flakes into a solid mass on leading
edges and air-intakes.

comparable /'kɒmp(ə)rəb(ə)l/
adjective possible to compare equally
with something else ○ *Titanium is non-*
magnetic and has an electrical resist-

ance comparable to that of stainless
steel.

comparator /kəm'pærətə/ *noun* a
device to compare two things ○ *The*
autopilot comparator monitors the
operation of the elevator and aileron
channels.

compare /kəm'peə/ *verb* to find the
similarities and dissimilarities between
two or more things ○ *When the chart is*
properly orientated, it is easier to com-
pare the distance between landmarks
on the ground with their corresponding
distances on the chart. ○ *An aneroid*
barometer is small compared with a
mercury barometer. (NOTE: **Compare**
with is regarded by some as better
usage than **compare to**.)

comparison /kəm'pærɪs(ə)n/ *noun*
a statement expressing the differences
and similarities between two or more
things ○ *A table showing a comparison*
of fixed points on various temperature
scales is given on page three.

compartment /kəm'pɑ:tmənt/
noun a small space or area in a structure
for a particular purpose ○ *engine com-*
partment □ **crew compartment** the area
reserved for crew

compass /'kʌmpəs/ *noun* an instrument usually with a magnetic needle
which always points to the magnetic
north

compass bearing /'kʌmpəs
,beərɪŋ/ *noun* a direction or position
relative to a fixed point measured in
degrees on a compass

compatibility /kəm,pætɪ'bɪlɪti/
noun the ability of a component to operate successfully with other components
○ *Problems of compatibility caused the*
computerised system to malfunction.

compatible /kəm'pætɪb(ə)l/ *adjec-*
tive referring to a component or system
which can be used with a different component or system without causing any
problems ○ *Computer software*
designed for one particular system may
not be compatible with other systems.

compensate /'kɒmpənseɪt/ *verb* **1.**
to make up for the loss of something ○
The floor covering may be designed to
compensate for temperature, pressuri-

sation and bending loads. ○ *The fall in air temperature increases the air density and so compensates to some extent for the loss of the thrust due to atmospheric pressure.* **2.** to give money to a person or organisation to make up for a physical or financial loss ○ *The money offered by the company did not compensate for the injuries she received in the accident.*

compensation /ˌkɒmpənˈseɪʃ(ə)n/ *noun* money paid to an individual or organisation to replace or make up for physical or financial loss ○ *The company paid out \$2 million in compensation to the families of those who lost their lives in the tragedy.*

compilation /ˌkɒmpɪˈleɪʃ(ə)n/ *noun* the putting together of suitable information ○ *The manual is a compilation of materials used by each of the instructors.*

compile /kəmˈpaɪl/ *verb* to put together a number of pieces of information ○ *Aviation routine weather reports are compiled half-hourly or hourly at fixed times.*

complement /ˈkɒmplɪmənt/ *verb* to fit in with and improve the performance of something ○ *Ultra-sonic detection is used to complement other methods of flaw detection.*

complementary /ˌkɒmplɪˈment(ə)ri/ *adjective* the fact of fitting in with and improving the performance of something ○ *SSR is complementary to the primary radars used by ATC.*

complete /kəmˈpliːt/ *adjective* **1.** containing all the parts it should contain ○ *The centre section can be constructed either as a complete unit or as two separate units.* **2.** absolute and total ■ *verb* **1.** to finish or make whole ○ *The number of revolutions for the crankshaft to complete a full cycle is always two.* □ **complete the work** to continue until the work is finished **2.** to fill in information □ **complete the flight plan** to fill in the required information in the flight plan

completion /kəmˈpliːʃ(ə)n/ *noun* the satisfactory finishing of a task ○ *It is important to carry out an inspection of*

an aircraft after completion of de-icing operations.

complex /ˈkɒmpleks/ *adjective* complicated and therefore possibly difficult to understand ○ *Of all the pre-departure activities, route planning is one of the most complex.* ■ *noun* **1.** a whole made up of many different parts □ **a cumulonimbus cloud complex** a collection of cumulonimbus clouds forming a system **2.** a building made up of many different parts □ **the terminal three complex** the main building and associated buildings which together make up terminal three

complexity /kəmˈpleksɪti/ *noun* the condition of being complex, or a complication ○ *Up-to-date design does not necessarily mean structural complexity.*

complicate /ˈkɒmplɪkeɪt/ *verb* to make more difficult ○ *Map reading is often complicated by seasonal variations.*

complicated /ˈkɒmplɪkeɪtɪd/ *adjective* not easy to understand

complication /ˌkɒmplɪˈkeɪʃ(ə)n/ *noun* a difficulty or problem ○ *The complication with the Mercator's projection is that great circle directions must be converted to rhumb line directions by the application of conversion angle before they can be plotted.*

comply /kəmˈplaɪ/ *verb* to be or do what is required by an instruction or law ○ *Equipment and furnishings of modern jet transports must comply with safety regulations.* ○ *Passengers must comply with the no-smoking signs.* (NOTE: **complying – complied**)

component /kəmˈpəʊnənt/ *noun* **1.** a part of an aircraft, aircraft system or piece of equipment ○ *The undercarriage is made up of a number of different components.* **2.** one part of a force such as wind which consists of a number of different parts **3.** a substance which forms part of a compound

compose /kəmˈpəʊz/ *verb* to make something from a number of parts ○ *The atmosphere is composed of a mixture of gases.*

composite /ˈkɒmpəzɪt/ *adjective* referring to something made up of a number of different parts ○ *composite* *material* ○ *The flight crew route flight plan is a composite document which serves as a navigation log.* ■ *noun* a lightweight but very strong man-made material used in aircraft manufacturing ○ *To make a composite it is necessary to combine the reinforcing glass fibres with special glue or resin.* (NOTE: The word **composite** was originally an adjective, but through frequent usage the term **composite material** has been shortened to **composite**.)

'Canadian Aerospace Group (CAG) is working with Pratt & Whitney Canada on a turboprop-powered version of its Windeagle all-composite light aircraft' [*Flight International 16–22 July 1997*]

COMMENT: Composites are used in the construction of many modern aircraft, from gliders to aircraft such as the Airbus A320, because they are strong and lighter than metals.

composition /ˌkɒmpəˈzɪʃ(ə)n/ *noun* the make-up or structure of something □ **composition of the atmosphere** the combination of gases which make up the atmosphere

compound /ˈkɒmpaʊnd/ *adjective* referring to something made up of two or more parts or substances ■ *noun* a substance made up of two or more components ○ *A chemical compound has qualities that are different from those of the substances from which it is made.* ○ *Advances in sealing compounds have now made fuel tanks less liable to leaks.*

compound wound generator /ˌkɒmpaʊnd ˌwuːnd ˈdʒenəreɪtə/ *noun* a generator which consists of a number of windings

compress /kəmˈpres/ *verb* to put under pressure thereby reducing volume ○ *Pressure is created when a fluid is compressed.*

compressibility /kəmpresəˈbɪlɪti/ *noun* the natural ability of a substance to change volume when under varying pressures ○ *In systems using very high pressure, the compressibility of the liquid becomes important.*

compressible /kəmˈpresəb(ə)l/ *adjective* referring to something that can be compressed ○ *Air is compressible, but water is not.*

compression /kəmˈpreʃ(ə)n/ *noun* an act or instance of putting pressure on something

compression stroke /kəmˈpreʃ(ə)n strəʊk/ *noun* the stage of an internal combustion cycle when the fuel/air mixture comes under pressure from the upward-moving piston

compressive /kəmˈpresɪv/ *adjective* referring to forces caused by pressure on a surface ○ *A strut is designed to withstand compressive loads.*

compressive load /kəmˌpresɪv ˈləʊd/ *noun* a load caused by forces acting in opposite directions towards each other

compressive stress /kəmˌpresɪv ˈstres/ *noun* the resistance of a body to crushing by two forces acting towards each other along the same straight line

compressor /kəmˈpresə/ *noun* a device such as a pump to compress air, in order to increase pressure ○ *A shaft connects the turbine to the compressor.* ◊ **axial**

comprise /kəmˈpraɪz/ *verb* to be made of (NOTE: The correct use of **comprise** is often disputed. Some people regard it as a synonym for the verb **consist of**, while others believe it should be used in an opposite sense: *a tank, pipes, a filter, a pump and a carburettor comprise the fuel system*. It is sometimes used in its passive form: *the fuel system is comprised of a number of different parts*.)

concentrate /ˈkɒnsəntreɪt/ *verb* **1.** to collect in a particular place rather than spread around ○ *Most of the mass of air is concentrated at the lowest levels of the atmosphere.* **2.** to give attention and thought to something in particular ○ *This chapter concentrates on charts.* □ **to concentrate hard** to give all one's thought and attention to something

concentration /ˌkɒnsənˈtreɪʃ(ə)n/ *noun* **1.** the fact of being collected in a particular place rather than spread around ○ *The maximum concentration of ozone is between 20 and 25 km above the Earth's surface.* **2.** the act of giving attention and thought to something ○ *In* *the early stages of training, instrument flying requires great concentration on the part of the student pilot.*

concentric /kən'sentrɪk/ *adjective* having the same centre □ **concentric circles** circles of different diameters but with the same centre point

concept /'kɒnsept/ *noun* an idea or abstract principle ○ *The concept of open skies is not one with which everybody agrees.* □ **a complicated concept** an idea or series of ideas or principles which are difficult to understand

concern /kən'sɜːn/ *noun* **1.** serious interest □ **a matter for concern** something which must be taken very seriously **2.** responsibility ○ *Attention to the welfare of passengers is the concern of the cabin crew.* ○ *Safety is everybody's concern.* □ **this is no concern of ours** this is nothing to do with us ■ *verb* **1.** to cause somebody to feel worried □ **this report concerns me enormously** I am not at all happy about this report **2.** to be about or to be the subject of ○ *If there is serious vibration, the crew should shut down the engine concerned.* □ **this report concerns me** this report is about me **3.** to be of interest and relevance to □ **the regulations concern all employees** the regulations apply to all employees

'…the correct storage and handling of cargo and especially dangerous goods is an area which is of considerable concern to the Federation' [*INTER PILOT*]

concrete /'kɒnkriːt/ *noun* a substance made of cement, sand and water used in the construction of buildings, roads, etc. ○ *Rock, sand and concrete reflect only 10–20% of radiation.*

condensation /ˌkɒnden'seɪʃ(ə)n/ *noun* the process by which vapour changes into liquid ○ *If the air becomes saturated, further cooling results in condensation.* Opposite **evaporation**

condensation trail /ˌkɒnden 'seɪʃ(ə)n treɪl/ *noun* same as **vapour trail**

condense /kən'dens/ *verb* **1.** to change from vapour to liquid form ○ *The most common type of hygrometer is one in which a surface in contact with*

the atmosphere is cooled until moisture begins to condense on the surface. Opposite **evaporate 2.** to remove unnecessary parts from a text to make it shorter ○ *The synoptic code condenses information without loss of sense.*

condenser /kən'densə/ *noun* an electrical capacitor ○ *The condenser prevents spark plugs from arcing.*

condition /kən'dɪʃ(ə)n/ *noun* **1.** the present state of something □ **although the aircraft is old, it is in good condition** the aircraft is old but well cared for **2.** the state of the surrounding atmosphere ○ *In a high relative humidity condition, the evaporation rate is low.* □ **abnormal weather conditions** unusual or unfavourable weather □ **adverse weather conditions** bad weather **3.** circumstances **4.** something on which another thing depends □ **on condition that** only if □ **the flight will depart on condition that the weather improves** the flight will depart only if the weather improves

conducive /kən'djuːsɪv/ *adjective* favourable, which allows something to happen more easily ○ *Atmospheric conditions conducive to the formation of ice are detected and these operate a warning system.*

'…when refuelling, ensure the aircraft is properly earthed. The very low humidity on a crisp, cold day can be conducive to a build-up of static electricity' [*Civil Aviation Authority, General Aviation Safety Sense Leaflet*]

conduct /kən'dʌkt/ *noun* /'kɒndʌkt/ **1.** a manner or way of doing something ○ *The captain is responsible for the safe conduct of the flight.* **2.** behaviour ○ *The investigation found that the flight attendant's conduct was unacceptable.* ■ *verb* **1.** to organise and do something; to carry out ○ *Crew will conduct area checks.* ○ *Security conducted a search of the building.* **2.** to allow something such as electricity, heat etc. to pass through ○ *Water conducts electricity.*

conduction /kən'dʌkʃən/ *noun* the process by which heat or electricity passes through a substance ○ *Heat is transferred to the layer of air next to the Earth's surface by conduction.*

conductive /kən'dʌktɪv/ *adjective* referring to the ability of a substance to allow heat or electricity to pass through ○ *Steel is a conductive material.* ○ *Land masses are less conductive than water.*

conductivity /ˌkɒndʌk'tɪvɪti/ *noun* the ability of a material to allow heat or electricity to pass through ○ *Because of the poor conductivity of air, heat is transferred from the Earth's surface upwards by convection.*

conductor /kən'dʌktə/ *noun* a substance through which heat or electricity can pass ○ *Water and steel are good conductors.*

cone /kəʊn/ *noun* a solid body with a base in the shape of a circle, and with sides which narrow to a point, or any object which has that shape

configuration /kənˌfɪgjə'reɪʃ(ə)n/ *noun* the pattern or way in which things are arranged □ **configuration of an aircraft's fuel tank system** the way in which the tanks are laid out

confine /kən'faɪn/ *verb* **1.** to limit to a particular area ○ *Cooling is confined to the air in contact with the ground.* ○ *The damage was confined to a small area.* **2.** to limit to a given subject □ **the report confines itself to the incident of 3rd January** the report deliberately does not mention anything other than the incident of the 3rd January

confined /kən'faɪnd/ *adjective* limited, small □ **a confined space** a small defined space which does not allow free movement

confirm /kən'fɜːm/ *verb* to agree that something is correct, or to repeat it to remove any uncertainty ○ *The attitude indicator shows that the aircraft is in a nose down attitude and the increasing airspeed confirms that the aircraft is not in level flight.* ○ *Can you confirm that the instructor was flying the aircraft at the time of the collision?* ○ *VHF and/or UHF radio aids confirm ADF bearings.*

COMMENT: Cross-checking of certain flight instruments is used to confirm readings from other instruments, e.g. the airspeed indicator and vertical speed indicator confirm pitch information from the attitude indicator.

conform /kən'fɔːm/ *verb* to correspond to required standards ○ *Fuels must conform to strict requirements.* □ **to conform to regulations** to do what is required by rules and regulations

conformal /kən'fɔːm(ə)l/ *adjective* representing angles, bearings, etc., correctly ○ *Lambert's conformal projection*

congestion /kən'dʒestʃən/ *noun* a situation where there are too many people or vehicles in a confined space for them to be able to move freely ○ *When leaving the aircraft in an emergency, to avoid congestion, passengers should be directed to move away from exits quickly.*

conic /'kɒnɪk/ *adjective* based on the shape of a cone □ **conic projection** the standard two-dimensional representation of the earth

conical /'kɒnɪk(ə)l/ *adjective* shaped like a cone ○ *The nose of Concorde has a conical shape.*

conjunction /kən'dʒʌŋkʃən/ *noun* □ **in conjunction with** working or operating together with ○ *Built-up areas, used in conjunction with other features such as rivers, railways and coastlines which are near them, are more easily identified.*

connect /kə'nekt/ *verb* to join ○ *Batteries are sometimes connected in series.* ○ *A cockpit lever is connected to a needle valve in the float chamber.*

connecting flight /kəˌnektɪŋ 'flaɪt/ *noun* a second aircraft which a passenger should arrive on time to catch, and which will take him or her to the final destination ○ *Instead of flying direct to London, take the flight to Amsterdam and then take a connecting flight to London Heathrow.*

connecting rod /kə'nektɪŋ rɒd/ *noun* an engine part that connects the piston to the crankshaft

connection /kə'nekʃən/ *noun* **1.** the point at which things are joined ○ *There is an electrical connection to the battery.* **2.** a link or feature that makes things interdependent ○ *There is a connection between temperature change and altitude.* **3.** the process of catching a second aircraft to arrive at a final destination ○ *Follow the 'Flight Connection' signs.*

connector /kə'nektə/ *noun* a device which connects two or more things ○ *A connector is used to connect two lengths of wire together.* ○ *Standard connectors consist of a metal coupling with a rubber sandwich joint.*

consecutive /kən'sekjʊtɪv/ *adjective* following one another without a break ○ *4, 5 and 6 are three consecutive numbers.* □ **a period of 28 consecutive days** 28 days following immediately one after the other

consequence /'kɒnsɪkwəns/ *noun* the result of an action ○ *The accident was a consequence of the pilot's actions.* □ **as a consequence** as a result

consequent /'kɒnsɪkwənt/ *adjective* resulting ○ *As temperature rises, there will be a consequent increase in the volume of the gas.*

consequently /'kɒnsɪkwəntli/ *adverb* therefore, as a result ○ *She was late, consequently she missed the start of the examination.*

conserve /kən'sɜːv/ *verb* to avoid using unnecessarily ○ *Release the brakes when necessary and conserve main system pressure.* □ **to conserve energy** to use only as much energy as you really need □ **to conserve fuel** to use as little fuel as possible

consider /kən'sɪdə/ *verb* to think carefully about something ○ *If the aircraft is low on fuel, the commander should consider diverting to the nearest suitable airport.*

'…many purchasers of flight simulators would argue that, when considering the major manufacturers, there is little to choose between them' [*Civil Aviation Training*]

considerable /kən'sɪd(ə)rəb(ə)l/ *adjective* a lot of, quite large ○ *The required range of trim change is considerable.* (NOTE: **Considerable** does not mean that something should be thought about, as the meaning for the verb *consider* might suggest.) □ **a considerable amount of fuel** a lot of fuel, a large amount of fuel □ **a considerable**

distance a long distance □ **considerable force** a lot of force

consideration /kən,sɪdə'reɪʃ(ə)n/ *noun* **1.** something important to remember and to think carefully about □ **to take into consideration** to remember to include when thinking about something, solving a problem or making a calculation **2.** thoughtfulness, respect □ **to show consideration for other people and property** to show respect for what belongs to other people

consist /kən'sɪst/ *verb* □ **to consist of** to be made up of ○ *Layer cloud names consist of a prefix, according to height of base, and a suffix according to shape.* □ **to consist in** to mean, to be

consistent /kən'sɪstənt/ *adjective* always reacting or behaving in the same way ○ *Human hair responds in a consistent manner to changes in the relative humidity.* □ **consistent performance** performance which maintains a particular standard

consolidate /kən'sɒlɪdeɪt/ *verb* to make more solid or strong □ **revision of the subject helps to consolidate it** revision of the subject helps to set it more firmly in the memory

consolidation /kən,sɒlɪ'deɪʃ(ə)n/ *noun* **1.** a process by which something is made more solid or strong **2.** the grouping of goods together for shipment

constant /'kɒnstənt/ *adjective* unchanging □ **the temperature of the gas remains constant** the temperature of the gas stays the same □ **constant pressure** pressure which stays the same

constant speed drive unit /,kɒnstənt spiːd 'draɪv ,juːnɪt/ *noun* a device fitted to aircraft with constant speed propellers. Abbreviation **CSDU**

constant speed propeller /,kɒnstənt spiːd prə'pelə/ *noun* a propeller with a control system which automatically adjusts pitch to maintain selected rpm

constant speed unit /,kɒnstənt 'spiːd ,juːnɪt/ *noun* a device that automatically keeps a propeller at a speed set by the pilot. Abbreviation **CSU**

constituent /kən'stɪtjʊənt/ *noun* any one of the various parts that make up a whole ○ *Water, whether in the form of vapour, liquid or ice, is a very important constituent of the atmosphere.*

constitute /'kɒnstɪtjuːt/ *verb* to make up, to form ○ *Oxygen and nitrogen together constitute most of the atmosphere.*

constrain /kən'streɪn/ *verb* **1.** to prevent somebody from being completely free or from doing something they want to do ○ *The airline was constrained in its purchase of new aircraft by lack of financial resources.* **2.** to force somebody to do something ○ *Lack of financial resources constrained the airline to cancel the purchase of new aircraft.*

constraint /kən'streɪnt/ *noun* something that reduces freedom of action ○ *The number of landings per 24-hour period is subject to constraint.*

constrict /kən'strɪkt/ *verb* to make something narrower, especially to make the flow of gas or liquid more difficult by narrowing the passage through which it flows ○ *In the carburettor venturi, the flow of air is constricted.*

constriction /kən'strɪkʃən/ *noun* the act of constricting, or a place where something is particularly narrow ○ *A thermometer has a constriction in the base of the tube between the bulb and the beginning of the scale.*

construct /kən'strʌkt/ *verb* **1.** to put together ○ *The table on page 4 can be used to construct the low level forecast for the route.* **2.** to build □ **to construct an aircraft** to manufacture or build an aircraft ○ *Wings are constructed of light alloy pressed ribs and an outer skin.*

construction /kən'strʌkʃən/ *noun* **1.** the act of putting things together, or the way in which something is put together ○ *The basic construction of the lead-acid cell consists of a positive electrode and negative electrode.* **2.** a building ○ *The construction of the home-built aircraft took two years.*

consume /kən'sjuːm/ *verb* **1.** to use up in a given time ○ *Drag must be overcome with thrust, which requires engines, which in turn consume fuel.* **2.** to eat

consumption /kən'sʌmpʃ(ə)n/ *noun* **1.** the amount used up in a given time ○ *Fuel consumption is higher in bigger, more powerful engines.* **2.** the process of using up fuel or other resources **3.** the amount eaten **4.** the act of eating

contact /'kɒntækt/ *noun* **1.** touch □ **in contact with** touching ○ *The air in contact with the Earth's surface cools.* **2.** □ **to be in contact with** to communicate with e.g. by telephone or radio □ **to be in visual contact** to see □ **to make contact** to communicate □ **to lose contact** to stop communicating ○ *ATC lost contact with the aircraft.* **3.** a person who can be contacted in order to get something done □ **I have a contact in Madrid who can help** I know somebody in Madrid who can help **4.** an electrical connection ○ *Dirty contacts were the cause of the problem.* ■ *verb* to get in touch with somebody e.g. by radio or telephone ○ *The captain couldn't contact ATC.*

contact breaker /'kɒntækt ˌbreɪkə/ *noun* a mechanically operated switch which is timed to break the primary circuit when maximum current is flowing

contact flight /'kɒntækt flaɪt/ *noun* a method of navigation for aircraft in which the pilot or crew use no navigational aids, but find their way by observing visible features of the ground

contact number /'kɒntækt ˌnʌmbə/ *noun* a telephone number where information can be obtained

contain /kən'teɪn/ *verb* to hold, to have inside ○ *Most clouds contain some super-cooled water droplets.* ○ *The booklet contains details of the airline's flight schedule.*

container /kən'teɪnə/ *noun* a box, bottle, etc., which holds something else ○ *A smouldering fire in a waste container could become very active due to pressure changes during ascent.*

contaminate /kən'tæmɪneɪt/ *verb* to make something impure, harmful or dangerous ○ *If contaminated air enters* *the cabin, the dump valve can be opened.*

contaminated fuel /kən,tæmɪneɪtɪd 'fjuːəl/ *noun* fuel which contains an unwanted substance, such as water, and is therefore dangerous to use

contamination /kən,tæmɪ'neɪʃ(ə)n/ *noun* a process by which a liquid, gas or object is made unusable because impurities or foreign matter are allowed into or onto it □ **contamination of air** air pollution □ **fuel contamination** a situation in which fuel becomes unusable because an unwanted substance such as water gets into it □ **nuclear contamination** damage done to an object, person or substance because of contact with nuclear radiation

content /'kɒntent/ *noun* the amount of a substance that is contained within something, often expressed as a percentage ○ *The stratosphere is a layer in which the water vapour content is low.* □ **the moisture content of the atmosphere** the amount of water vapour in the air

continent /'kɒntɪnənt/ *noun* one of the seven great land masses of the Earth ○ *the continent of Europe*

COMMENT: The seven continents are: Asia, Africa, North America, South America, Australia, Europe and Antarctica.

continental /,kɒntɪ'nent(ə)l/ *adjective* referring to a continent

continental climate /,kɒntɪnent(ə)l 'klaɪmət/ *noun* the type of climate found in areas where there is no effect from the sea

contingency /kən'tɪndʒənsi/ *noun* something which might happen in the future and therefore must be planned for

contingency reserve fuel /kən,tɪndʒənsi rɪ,zɜːv 'fjuːəl/ *noun* fuel which would only be used in an unusual situation such as a diversion

continuity /,kɒntɪ'njuːɪti/ *noun* continuing □ **continuity of precipitation** continuing rain, snow or hail

contour /'kɒntʊə/ *noun* the shape of something

contour chart /'kɒntʊə tʃɑːt/ *noun* chart which shows areas of high and low ground

contour gradient /'kɒntʊə ,greɪdiənt/ *noun* steepness of change in elevation

contour line /'kɒntʊə laɪn/ *noun* a line on a map or chart joining points of equal elevation

contract /kən'trækt/ *verb* to become smaller in volume ○ *Liquids will expand or contract as a result of temperature changes.* Opposite **expand**

contraction /kən'trækʃən/ *noun* the decrease in volume of a substance brought about by cooling ○ *Due to contraction, the length of a mercury column shortens.* Opposite **expansion**

contrail /'kɒntreɪl/ *noun* same as **vapour trail**

contrast /'kɒntrɑːst/ *noun* **1.** the amount of light and dark in something seen ○ *Contrast and colour enable a pilot to identify ground features.* **2.** the difference between two things ○ *There is an enormous contrast between the performance of the two aircraft.* □ **in contrast to** when compared with ○ *Air at altitude is cold in contrast to air at the surface.*

contribute /kən'trɪbjuːt/ *verb* to give or provide as part of the whole ○ *Exhaust gases contribute to engine power.* □ **although the weather was bad, pilot error contributed to the accident** pilot error was partly responsible for the accident

contribution /,kɒntrɪ'bjuːʃ(ə)n/ *noun* **1.** the part that something plays in making or causing something ○ *The differences in the effect of solar radiation on land and sea make the biggest contribution to weather and climate.* **2.** the act of contributing or something, especially money, that is given or provided

contributor /kən'trɪbjʊtə/ *noun* a person or thing that contributes to something ○ *There are other factors which cause the division of the lower atmosphere into two layers but the ozone effect is a major contributor.*

control /kən'trəʊl/ *noun* **1.** the authority or ability to direct somebody or something **2.** □ **crowd control** the management of the movements of large numbers of people **3.** checking or examining ■ *verb* to direct, to manage or to make a machine, system, procedure, etc., work in the correct way ○ *The purpose of the centrifugal switch is to control the starting and ignition circuits.* (NOTE: The word **control** in English is used in a different way to similar words in other languages. In English, the verb **check** is more often used to mean 'look at and verify' while **control** is used in the sense of 'to make something work in a particular way': *the yoke and rudder pedals are used to control the movement of the aircraft.* Note also: **controlling – controlled**.)

control area /kən'trəʊl ˌeəriə/ *noun* the airspace above a particular area on the ground, which is controlled by a particular authority. Abbreviation **CTA**

control column /kən'trəʊl ˌkɒləm/ *noun* the main hand control used by the pilot to control the aircraft in roll and pitch

controlled airspace /kən'trəʊld 'eəspeɪs/ *noun* airspace which is governed by rules and regulations which pilots must comply with. Abbreviation **CAS**

controller /kən'trəʊlə/ *noun* **1.** a device which ensures that something operates in the correct way ○ *the propeller speed controller* **2.** a person who manages systems to ensure the smooth operation of procedures

controls /kən'trəʊlz/ *plural noun* manual or automatic devices that are used to control a machine, a system, etc., or to make a machine, a system, etc., work in a correct way □ **the pilot at the controls of the aircraft** the pilot who is operating the flying controls

control surfaces /kən'trəʊl ˌsɜːfɪsɪz/ *plural noun* moveable aerofoils, usually on the wings and tailplane, which can be operated from the cockpit by the pilot, thus changing aircraft attitude

control tower /kən'trəʊl ˌtaʊə/ *noun* a tall building on an airfield from which air-traffic controllers organise incoming and outgoing aircraft by speaking to their pilots by radio

control zone /kən'trəʊl zəʊn/ *noun* a designated ATC area. Abbreviation **CTR**

convection /kən'vekʃ(ə)n/ *noun* the process by which hot air rises and cool air descends ○ *Heat is transferred from the Earth's surface upwards largely by convection.*

convective /kən'vektɪv/ *adjective* referring to convection, or something which is affected by the vertical circulation of air □ **convective movement** movement caused by warm air rising and cool air descending

convective clouds /kənˌvektɪv 'klaʊdz/ *plural noun* clouds formed as a result of warm moist air rising and condensing at altitude

convenience /kən'viːniəns/ *noun* **1.** personal comfort and benefit ○ *Reading lights are provided for passengers' convenience.* □ **at your convenience** when it is least troublesome for you **2.** ease of understanding ○ *For convenience we will assume that the Earth is round.* **3.** usefulness, or easiness to use

convenient /kən'viːniənt/ *adjective* **1.** useful ○ *The circular slide rule has a convenient scale for converting weights and volumes.* **2.** suitable and unlikely to cause problems ○ *We must arrange a convenient time and place for the meeting.*

convention /kən'venʃən/ *noun* **1.** an idea which because of long usage has become normal and accepted ○ *By convention, wind direction is the direction from which the wind blows.* **2.** a meeting involving large numbers of people and long discussions in order to arrive at an agreed course of action often outlined in a public statement ○ *the Tokyo Convention*

conventional /kən'venʃ(ə)n(ə)l/ *adjective* usual or familiar to most people ○ *Every pilot must know the conventional symbols used for depicting the various ground features on charts.*

converge /kən'vɜːdʒ/ *verb* to come together at a particular point ○ *Meridians converge towards the poles.* □ **aircraft on converging courses** aircraft on courses which may eventually be too close to each other if no corrective action is taken. Opposite **diverge**

convergence /kən'vɜːdʒəns/ *noun* the fact of coming together at a particular point ○ *The inter-tropical convergence zone is the zone in which the trade winds from the two hemispheres approach each other.* ○ *There is convergence of meridians of longitude at the north and south poles.* Opposite **divergence**

converse /'kɒnvɜːs/ *noun* the opposite ○ *The converse of port is starboard.* □ **warm air rises – the converse is also true** in other words, cool air descends

conversion /kən'vɜːʃ(ə)n/ *noun* **1.** a change to a different system or set of rules ○ *The conversion of km into nm is not difficult.* **2.** □ **conversion course** flying training which enables and qualifies a pilot to fly a different aircraft type

convert /kən'vɜːt/ *verb* to change to a different system or set of rules ○ *to convert km into nm* ○ *How do you convert degrees C into degrees F?*

converter /kən'vɜːtə/ *noun* a device which alters the form of something ○ *A backup converter converts the alternating current power into direct current.*

convertible /kən'vɜːtəb(ə)l/ *adjective* possible to change easily, e.g. to fit in with a new system or set of standards ○ *The statute mile, unlike the nautical mile, is not readily convertible into terms of angular measurements.*

convey /kən'veɪ/ *verb* to carry or move from one place to another ○ *A large number of tubes convey the cooling medium through the matrix.* ○ *Buses are used to convey passengers from the aircraft to the terminal building.* □ **to convey information** to pass information from one person to another, or from one place to another

cool /kuːl/ *adjective* a little cold □ **cool weather** weather which is not hot, warm nor very cold ■ *verb* to become or

cause to become less hot ○ *The airflow is used to cool the oil.* ◊ **air-cooled**

coolant /'kuːlənt/ *noun* a substance, usually liquid, used to cool something such as an engine ○ *radiator coolant* ○ *The coolant is sprayed into the combustion chamber inlet.*

cooler /'kuːlə/ *noun* a device for cooling ○ *A self-contained system, consisting of an oil tank, pump, filter, cooler, and oil jets, lubricates the auxiliary power unit.*

cooling /'kuːlɪŋ/ *noun* the action of making something cool ○ *the cooling of the oil by the airflow* ■ *adjective* reducing the temperature of something □ **cooling medium** a substance which reduces the temperature of another substance or material

coordinate /kəʊ'ɔːdɪnət/ *verb* **1.** to bring together the various parts of a procedure or plan to ensure that the operation works correctly ○ *It is the task of air traffic controllers to coordinate the movement of traffic in and out of a terminal.* **2.** to make different parts of the body work well together ○ *During a hover, helicopter pilots must be able to coordinate movements of both hands and feet.*

coordinated flight /kəʊ'ɔːdɪneɪtɪd 'flaɪt/ *noun* flight, especially during turns, in which the horizontal and vertical forces acting on the aircraft are in balance ○ *In coordinated flight, the ball in the turn coordinator will be in the centre.*

COMMENT: The ball in the balance indicator of the turn coordinator shows the pilot if the aircraft is in coordinated flight or if it is slipping or skidding. When the ball moves to the left the pilot should apply left rudder pedal pressure, if the ball moves to the right, the pilot should apply right rudder pedal pressure.

Coordinated Universal Time /kəʊˌɔːdɪneɪtɪd ˌjuːnɪ'vɜːs(ə)l taɪm/ *noun* time used in aviation based on the 24-hour clock format. ◊ **GMT**

coordinates /kəʊ'ɔːdɪnəts/ *plural noun* values used to locate a point on a graph or a map ○ *The airfield can be seen on the map at coordinates B:12.*

coordination /kəʊˌɔːdɪˈneɪʃ(ə)n/ noun **1.** the process of bringing together the various parts of a procedure or plan to ensure that it works correctly ○ *A rescue coordination centre is set up to control the emergency.* **2.** the ability to use different parts of the body together well ○ *A pilot must have good hand/eye coordination.*

cope /kəʊp/ verb to manage to do something, often with some difficulty ○ *In heavy rainstorms, the windscreen wipers may not be able to cope.* ○ *The aircraft structure must be able to cope with increased loads caused by turning movement.*

copilot /ˈkəʊpaɪlət/, **co-pilot** noun a licensed pilot who is second in command to the captain of an aircraft ○ *The copilot landed the aircraft.*

copter /ˈkɒptə/ noun same as **helicopter** (*informal*)

cord /kɔːd/ noun a strong thread, usually of nylon ○ *Tyres are of pure rubber and are either cord-strengthened or reinforced.* (NOTE: Cord is used to reinforce tyres.)

core /kɔː/ noun the central part, the heart of something ○ *The primary windings consist of heavy gauge wire mounted on a soft iron core.* □ **the core of a problem** the central, most fundamental part of a problem

Coriolis force /ˌkɒriˈəʊlɪs ˌfɔːs/ noun force which accelerates the movement of a rotating mass perpendicular to its motion and towards the axis of rotation ○ *The Coriolis force explains why wind patterns are clockwise in the northern hemisphere and anti-clockwise in the southern hemisphere.*

COMMENT: The Coriolis force acts at a right angle to wind direction and is directly proportional to wind speed. It is named after G. G. Coriolis, a French engineer who died in 1843.

correct /kəˈrekt/ adjective right □ **correct tyre pressure** the pressure at which the tyres should be maintained ■ verb **1.** to adjust in order to make right ○ *A servo-motor fitted in the elevator trim system will automatically correct for loads.* ○ *Calibrated airspeed or rec-*tified airspeed is indicated airspeed corrected for instrumentation and installation error. **2.** to mark answers right or wrong, as in an examination ○ *The instructor has corrected the students' examination papers.*

correction /kəˈrekʃ(ə)n/ noun **1.** an adjustment or change made to something to make it correct **2.** the use of a mathematical formula for adjusting a known inaccuracy of calculation ○ *In applying this correction the reading is converted to that which would occur at mean sea level.* **3.** an alteration on, e.g. a test answer, which provides the right answer in place of the wrong answer given ○ *I made several corrections to the text.*

corrective /kəˈrektɪv/ adjective referring to something designed to correct

corrective action /kəˌrektɪv ˈækʃən/ noun action taken to put a situation right ○ *If the pilot realises that the plane is too high on the approach, he or she should take corrective action immediately.*

correlate /ˈkɒrəleɪt/ verb to measure something against something else in order to form a relationship between the two ○ *Power is measured not by the amount of work done, but by units of accomplishment correlated with time.*

correlation /ˌkɒrəˈleɪʃ(ə)n/ noun a measurable and predictable relationship ○ *At a given speed, there is a correlation between time and distance.*

correspond /ˌkɒrɪˈspɒnd/ verb **1.** to fit with or have a direct relationship with ○ *Movements of the control surfaces correspond to movements of the pilots flying controls.* **2.** to be similar to ○ *In the interests of passenger comfort, the ideal cabin conditions to maintain would be those corresponding to sea level.*

corridor /ˈkɒrɪdɔː/ noun same as **air corridor**

corrode /kəˈrəʊd/ verb **1.** to destroy by a slow chemical process such as rust ○ *The sulphur and water content of turbine fuels tend to corrode the components of the fuel and combustion sys-*

tems. **2.** to be destroyed by a slow chemical process such a rust ○ *Aluminium will not corrode easily.*

corrosion /kəˈrəʊʒ(ə)n/ *noun* the destruction of a material by chemical processes ○ *Aluminium has a high resistance to corrosion.* ◊ **anti-corrosion**

corrosion protection /kəˈrəʊʒ(ə)n prəˌtekʃən/ *noun* action and/or measures taken to prevent corrosion such as rust

corrosive /kəˈrəʊsɪv/ *adjective* causing corrosion ○ *Sulphuric acid is very corrosive.*

cosine /ˈkəʊˌsaɪn/ *noun* a trigonometric function defined as the length of the side adjacent to an angle in a right-angled triangle divided by the length of the hypotenuse. Abbreviation **cos**

counter /ˈkaʊntə/ *verb* to act against something so as to remove or reduce its effect ○ *For level flight, lift must counter the force of gravity.* ○ *Some people find that swallowing hard counters the effects of changes in pressure.*

counter- /ˈkaʊntə/ *prefix* against

counterclockwise /ˌkaʊntə ˈklɒkwaɪz/ *adjective, adverb US* same as **anticlockwise**

counter-rotating propellers /ˌkaʊntə rəʊˌteɪtɪŋ prəˈpeləz/ *plural noun* propellers which turn in opposite directions (NOTE: They are also called **contra-rotating propellers**.)

couple /ˈkʌp(ə)l/ *noun* two of something □ **a couple of minutes** two or three minutes ■ *verb* **1.** to connect or to join, often mechanically ○ *The auxiliary power unit is a self-contained unit which normally consists of a small gas turbine engine which is coupled to a gearbox.* **2.** to combine ○ *Pilot error, coupled with poor weather conditions, resulted in an accident.*

coupling /ˈkʌplɪŋ/ *noun* a joining or connecting component ○ *When not in use, the coupling is sealed by a dust cap.*

course /kɔːs/ *noun* **1.** an imaginary line across the surface of the Earth which must be followed in order to arrive at the destination □ **to alter course** to change direction or to follow a different route **2.** a formal period of study ○ *a meteorology course* **3.** continuing time □ **in the course of the briefing** during the briefing

course correction /ˈkɔːs kə ˌrekʃ(ə)n/ *noun* same as **heading correction**

course deviation indicator /ˌkɔːs ˌdiːviˈeɪʃ(ə)n ˌɪndɪkeɪtə/ *noun* a needle in an **omni-bearing indicator** which indicates if an aircraft is on a selected course. Abbreviation **CDI**

cover /ˈkʌvə/ *verb* **1.** to include e.g. the complete extent of a period of time or the whole of a particular area ○ *The restriction covers the period from 4th-8th July.* □ **the area covered by the forecast** the area which the forecast deals with **2.** to deal with a subject, as in a text ○ *The subject of central warning systems is covered in the systems book.* **3.** to be completely over something so as to hide what is underneath ○ *The area is covered in snow.* ■ *noun* something which goes over something else completely □ **cloud cover** the amount of cloud □ **snow cover** a situation in which there is a layer of snow on top of the earth so that the earth cannot be seen

coverage /ˈkʌv(ə)rɪdʒ/ *noun* **1.** the amount of space or time given to a subject, an event, etc. ○ *More complete coverage of the one-in-sixty rule is given in the plotting section of these notes.* **2.** the area within which a radar unit can detect objects ○ *glidepath coverage* ○ *localiser coverage*

cowl /kaʊl/ *noun* a covering usually made up of hinged or removable panels □ **cowl flap** a removable or hinged panel of a cowl ○ *Further cooling can be obtained by the use of controllable cowl flaps which regulate the amount of air flowing across the cylinders.*

cowling /ˈkaʊlɪŋ/ *noun* a covering usually made up of hinged or removable panels ○ *Access to the engine compartment is normally via hinged cowling panels.*

CPL *abbreviation* Commercial Pilot's Licence

crab /kræb/ *noun* a manoeuvre in which an aircraft is steered slightly into a crosswind to compensate for flying slightly off course ■ *verb* to steer an aircraft slightly into a crosswind to compensate for flying slightly off course

craft /krɑːft/ *noun* **1.** a boat, etc., for carrying people or goods on water **2.** an aircraft or spacecraft for carrying people or goods in the air or in space ○ *An airship is classified as a lighter-than-air craft.*

crankcase /ˈkræŋkkeɪs/ *noun* the part of the engine that houses the crankshaft and also usually the oil pump ○ *Oil passages in the crankcase allow lubricating oil to pass through.*

crankshaft /ˈkræŋkʃɑːft/ *noun* the part of a piston engine connecting the pistons, via the connecting rods, to the flywheel and gearbox ○ *Rpm is the number of revolutions per minute that the engine crankshaft is making.*

crash /kræʃ/ *noun* an accident that causes damage ■ *verb* to have an accident or collision that causes damage ○ *The aircraft crashed into the sea.*

crash-dive /ˈkræʃ daɪv/ *verb* to move downwards quickly through the air front first and crash, or cause an aircraft to do this

crash-land /ˌkræʃ ˈlænd/ *verb* to land heavily without using the undercarriage, so that the aircraft is damaged ○ *The aircraft crash-landed short of the runway.*

crash-landing /ˌkræʃ ˈlændɪŋ/ *noun* an act of landing an aircraft heavily, sometimes without the undercarriage ○ *The crash-landing did not damage the aircraft as much as the pilot expected.*

create /kriˈeɪt/ *verb* to make, to produce ○ *The velocity and pressure of the exhaust gas create the thrust in the turbojet engine.*

creep /kriːp/ *noun* **1.** a process of weakening and slow damage to something ○ *Creep is a particular feature of components which are subjected to operation at high temperatures.* **2.** a slight movement of a tyre on a wheel caused by landing ○ *Aligned white marks on the wheel and tyre indicate that there is no creep.*

crest /krest/ *noun* the top of a mountain or wave ○ *Wind speeds increase with height, the speed of the wind at the crest of a mountain or wave being the greatest.*

crew /kruː/ *noun* two or more people who have responsibility for flight operations

criteria /kraɪˈtɪəriə/ ♦ criterion

criterion /kraɪˈtɪəriən/ *noun* a standard by which you define, decide or judge something (NOTE: The plural form is **criteria**.) □ **the criterion for promotion is seniority** senior staff will be promoted first

critical /ˈkrɪtɪk(ə)l/ *adjective* **1.** extremely important, essential ○ *Temperature and oil pressure are critical to any type of system.* **2.** at which an important change occurs ○ *As the angle of attack is increased, it reaches the critical point when the airflow over the upper surface of the wing begins to break down.*

cross /krɒs/ *verb* **1.** to get from one side of an area to another □ **to cross the Atlantic** to go from one side of the Atlantic to the other **2.** to go across each other at an angle ○ *Meridians intersect at the poles and cross the equator at right angles.*

cross-check /ˈkrɒs tʃek/ *noun* verification, making certain ■ *verb* to verify or make certain ○ *Cross-check doors closed and locked and escape slides armed.* (NOTE: This word is often used in brief messages from one crew member to another, as from the pilot to cabin staff, to confirm that an action has been carried out.)

cross-country /ˌkrɒs ˈkʌntri/ *noun* a flight during which the student pilot must demonstrate navigation skills ○ *the qualifying cross-country flight for the PPL*

cross-pointer indicator /ˌkrɒs ˌpɔɪntə ˈɪndɪkeɪtə/ *noun* a display with crossing horizontal and vertical bars to indicate aircraft position in relation to the glideslope

cross-section /'krɒs ˌsekʃən/ *noun* a view of an object seen as if cut through ○ *The diagram is a cross-section of a turbojet engine.*

crosswind /'krɒswɪnd/ *noun* a surface wind which blows at an angle to the landing or take-off heading ○ *On some aircraft, crosswind take-offs should be made with full aileron deflection in the direction from which the wind is blowing.*

COMMENT: A crosswind landing is one of the most difficult exercises for a student pilot. The final approach is usually made with the aircraft yawed into wind, while tracking the extended runway centreline. Just before touchdown, the pilot aligns the aircraft with the direction of flight using the rudder pedals. Correct timing for the alignment and accurate airspeed are required to achieve positive contact with the runway surface otherwise the aircraft may depart the runway to one side.

crosswind component /ˌkrɒs ˌwɪnd kəm'pəʊnənt/ *noun* that part of the wind force acting at an angle to the direction of flight

crosswind leg /'krɒswɪnd leg/ *noun* part of the airfield traffic circuit flown at approximately 90° to the direction of take off and climb out, followed by the downwind leg

CRT /ˌsiː ɑː 'tiː/ *abbreviation* cathode ray tube

cruise /kruːz/ *noun* the main part of the flight between top of climb after take-off and descent for landing ■ *verb* to fly the main part of the flight between top of climb after take-off and descent for landing ○ *We are cruising at 500 kt.* ○ *Cruising speed, cruising power and cruising altitude are selected to give maximum engine efficiency and prolong engine life.*

cruising altitude /'kruːzɪŋ ˌæltɪtjuːd/, **cruising level** *noun* the altitude at which most of a flight is flown en route to a destination, from top of climb to top of descent ○ *Our cruising altitude will be 35,000 feet.*

cruising power /'kruːzɪŋ ˌpaʊə/ *noun* engine power used to give required speed from top of climb to top of descent usually giving fuel economy and long engine life ○ *Cruising power is about 2,300 rpm.*

cruising speed /'kruːzɪŋ spiːd/, **cruise speed** *noun* the speed selected from top of climb to top of descent, usually giving fuel economy and long engine life ○ *The cruising speed is 110 knots.*

cruising weight /'kruːzɪŋ weɪt/ *noun* the weight of an aircraft in flight, consisting of its weight when empty, the weight of its payload, and the weight of the fuel that it has left

crush /krʌʃ/ *verb* to damage by pressure ○ *Excessive load on the beam may crush the core.*

crystal /'krɪstəl/ *noun* a regular geometric shape formed by minerals, or as water freezes

CSDU *abbreviation* constant speed drive unit

CSU *abbreviation* constant speed unit

CTA *abbreviation* control area

CTOT *abbreviation* calculated take-off time

CTR /kən'trəʊl/ *abbreviation* control zone

cubic /'kjuːbɪk/ *adjective* measured in volume, by multiplying length, depth and width □ **cubic centimetres (cc)** the usual unit used to measure the capacity of an internal-combustion engine ○ *The engine has a capacity of 2,000cc.* Abbreviation **cc** □ **cubic foot, cubic inch, cubic metre, cubic yard** the volume of a cube whose edge measures one foot, inch, metre or yard, respectively

cumuliform /'kjuːməlɪfɔːm/ *adjective* which develop vertically ○ *cumuliform clouds such as cumulonimbus*

cumulonimbus /ˌkjuːmjʊləʊ 'nɪmbəs/ *noun* a dark, low cumulus – type of cloud associated with thunderstorms ○ *A cumulonimbus has a characteristic anvil shape.* Abbreviation **CB**

cumulus /'kjuːmjʊləs/ *noun* big, fluffy, white or grey cloud heaped or piled up, which develops at low altitude ○ *Cumulus clouds may develop because* *of thermal activity resulting from the warming of the surface.* ○ *Grey cumulus often develop into cumulonimbus.* ◊ **altocumulus, stratocumulus**

cumulus cloud /ˈkjuːmjʊləs klaʊd/ *noun* clouds which form only in an unstable atmosphere and, as the name suggests, often build vertically for great distances. Also called **heap cloud**

current /ˈkʌrənt/ *adjective* present, actual, happening at the moment □ **current weather conditions** present weather conditions □ **current position** the position now ■ *noun* **1.** an electrical supply ○ *alternating current* ○ *direct current* **2.** flow

curvature /ˈkɜːvətʃə/ *noun* a curved shape □ **curvature of the earth** the curving of the Earth's surface due to the spherical form of the Earth

customary /ˈkʌstəməri/ *adjective* normal or usual ○ *It is customary for the senior cabin supervisor to introduce herself to passengers at the start of a flight.*

customs /ˈkʌstəmz/ *noun* an official department of government concerned with movement of people and freight across national borders □ **customs aerodrome** an aerodrome, usually near a border or coast, with customs facilities

customs duty /ˈkʌstəmz ˌdjuːti/ *noun* same as **import duty** ○ *the duty payable on a carton of cigarettes*

cycle /ˈsaɪk(ə)l/ *noun* a series of actions which end at the same point as they begin ○ *With the piston engine, the cycle is intermittent, whereas in the gas turbine, each process is continuous.* □ **life cycle of the thunderstorm cell** the

process of formation, development and decay of a thunderstorm

cyclic /ˈsɪklɪk, ˈsaɪklɪk/, **cyclical** /ˈsɪklɪk(ə)l/ *adjective* referring to or happening in a cycle ○ *Off-shore and on-shore wind patterns are cyclic.*

cyclone /ˈsaɪkləʊn/ *noun* a system of winds rotating inwards to an area of low barometric pressure ○ *These areas of low pressure are called hurricanes in the Atlantic Ocean, cyclones in the Indian Ocean and Bay of Bengal, and typhoons in the China Sea.* Also called **low, depression**

cyclonic /saɪˈklɒnɪk/ *adjective* referring to air movement, which turns in the same direction as the Earth and which, when seen from above, is anticlockwise in the northern hemisphere and clockwise in the southern hemisphere ○ *In winter the sub-tropical high retreats and gives way to cyclonic pressure patterns which produce cool unsettled conditions with rain at times.*

cylinder /ˈsɪlɪndə/ *noun* a device shaped like a tube, in which a piston moves ○ *Smaller aircraft have a static hydraulic system similar to a car, with a master cylinder and individual brake cylinders at each wheel.* □ **cylinder block** the casing containing the cylinders in a internal combustion engine □ **cylinder head** the removable top part of a piston engine cylinder containing plugs, inlet and exhaust connections and valves

cylindrical /sɪˈlɪndrɪk(ə)l/ *adjective* with the shape of a cylinder ○ *The modern jet engine is basically cylindrical in shape.*

D

D *abbreviation* danger area

DA *abbreviation* danger area

DAAIS *abbreviation* danger area activity information service

DACS *abbreviation* danger area crossing service

DADC *abbreviation* digital air data computer

DADS *abbreviation* digital air data system

DALR *abbreviation* dry adiabatic lapse rate

damage /'dæmɪdʒ/ *noun* harm that is caused to something ○ *If the temperature rises it can cause serious damage to the engine.* ■ *verb* to cause harm to something ○ *Small stones around the run-up area may damage propellers.*

damage tolerance /'dæmɪdʒ ˌtɒlərəns/ *noun* the ability of a material or structure to withstand or resist damage ○ *The structural efficiency of bonded and machined structure is not achieved at the expense of damage tolerance.*

dampen /'dæmpən/ *verb* **1.** to decrease or reduce ○ *An accumulator is fitted to store hydraulic fluid under pressure and dampen pressure fluctuations.* **2.** to make slightly wet

damper /'dæmpə/ *noun* a device to decrease or reduce something ○ *A yaw damper is used for rudder control.*

D & D *abbreviation* distress and diversion cell

danger area /'deɪndʒə ˌeəriə/ *noun* airspace of a particular length, width and depth, within which at particular times there may be activities which are dangerous to the flight of the aircraft. Abbreviation **D, DA**

danger zone /'deɪndʒə zəʊn/ *noun* an area where danger exists

data /'deɪtə/ *noun* **1.** information made up of numbers, characters and symbols often stored on a computer in such a way that it can be processed ○ *Airspeed information is supplied from an air data computer.* □ **meteorological data** information about weather conditions stored on a computer **2.** information. ◊ **recorder**

datum /'deɪtəm/ *noun* a reference or base point of a scale or measurement, e.g. mean sea level

datum shift trim system /ˌdeɪtəm ʃɪft 'trɪm ˌsɪstəm/ *noun* a trim system which varies the incidence of an all-moving tailplane without moving the cockpit controls ○ *In some aircraft, the datum shift is operated automatically.*

dB *abbreviation* decibel

DC *abbreviation* direct current

DCL *abbreviation* departure clearance

de- /diː/ *prefix* undo, remove or stop ○ *deactivate* ○ *depressurise*

deactivate /diːˈæktɪveɪt/ *verb* to turn off a system or a piece of equipment thus stopping it being ready to operate ○ *On some aircraft nose wheel steering must be deactivated prior to retraction.*

dead reckoning /ˌded 'rekənɪŋ/, **ded reckoning** *noun* navigation using calculations based on airspeed, course, heading, wind direction and speed, ground speed, and time ○ *In the early stages of practical navigation, the student pilot navigates by using dead reck-*

oning. Abbreviation **DR** (NOTE: The term comes from 'deduced' reckoning or 'ded' reckoning.)

de-aerate /ˌdiː ˈeərəeɪt/ *verb* to remove gas, especially carbon dioxide or air, from a liquid such as fuel ○ *The pump helps to de-aerate the fuel before it enters the engine.*

de-aeration /ˌdiː eəˈreɪʃ(ə)n/ *noun* the process of removing gas from a liquid such as fuel ○ *Partial de-aeration of fuel takes place in the pump.*

de-aerator /ˌdiː eəˈreɪtə/ *noun* a device to remove gas from a liquid

de-aerator tray /ˌdiː eəˈreɪtə ˌtreɪ/ *noun* a device in the lubrication system to remove air bubbles from oil

deal /diːl/ *noun* □ **a great deal** a large amount of, a lot of ○ *A great deal of damage was done to the aircraft as a result of the fire.* ■ *verb* to handle or manage ○ *A computer can deal with the constant inputs required to control an unstable aircraft.*

debris /ˈdebriː/ *noun* scattered broken pieces ○ *Before running up the engine, check that the aircraft is on firm ground and that the area is free of stones and other debris.* ○ *The aircraft exploded in mid-air, spreading debris over a wide area of the countryside.*

decal /dɪˈkæl/ *noun* picture, letters or digits printed on adhesive paper, which is transferred onto a surface and may be peeled away ○ *A red decal with AVGAS 100LL in white letters indicates the type of fuel to be used.*

decelerate /diːˈseləreɪt/ *verb* to slow down ○ *Reverse thrust and brakes help to decelerate the aircraft after landing.* Opposite **accelerate**

deceleration /diːˌseləˈreɪʃ(ə)n/ *noun* slowing down ○ *Anti-skid braking systems units are designed to prevent the brakes locking the wheels during landing, thus reducing the possibility of wheel skid caused by the sudden deceleration of the wheel.* Opposite **acceleration**

decibel /ˈdesɪbel/ *noun* a unit for measuring the loudness of a sound. Abbreviation **dB**

decimal /ˈdesɪm(ə)l/ *noun* a decimal fraction ■ *adjective* □ **decimal fraction** a fraction as expressed in the decimal system ○ *0.50 is a decimal fraction that is equal to 1/2.* □ **correct to three places of decimal** *or* **to three decimal places** correct to three figures after the decimal point ○ *2.754 is correct to three decimal places, 2.7 is correct to one decimal place.*

decimal notation /ˌdesɪm(ə)l nəʊ ˈteɪʃ(ə)n/ *noun* the method of writing a number in the decimal system ○ *The fraction 3/4 can be written as 0.75 in decimal notation.* ○ *Prices and number are normally written using decimal notation.* ○ *He finds it difficult to understand how the computer works because it uses binary not decimal notation.*

decimal place /ˌdesɪm(ə)l ˈpleɪs/ *noun* the position of a number to the right of the decimal point

decimal point /ˌdesɪm(ə)l ˈpɔɪnt/ *noun* the dot (.) used to separate a whole number from a decimal fraction

COMMENT: The decimal point is used in the USA and Britain. In most European countries a comma (,) is used to show the decimal, so 4,75% in Germany is written 4.75% in Britain.

decimal system /ˈdesɪm(ə)l ˌsɪstəm/ *noun* system of counting based on the number 10 and using the digits 0 – 9

decision /dɪˈsɪʒ(ə)n/ *noun* the act of deciding or of making up one's mind □ **to make a decision** to choose a course of action ○ *The decision to evacuate the aircraft was made by the captain.*

decision height /dɪˈsɪʒ(ə)n haɪt/ *noun* the altitude at which, during an ILS landing approach, a pilot must decide whether to land or carry out a missed approach ○ *The pilot waited until she was at decision height before initiating the missed approach procedure.* Abbreviation **DH**

COMMENT: An ILS approach generally has a decision height of 200 ft (60 m) above ground level.

deck /dek/ *noun* the floor of a ship or aircraft

decode /diːˈkəʊd/ *verb* to change coded information into readable form ○ *Incorrectly spaced information pulses can result in failure by the ground station to decode the aircraft information.*

decoder /diːˈkəʊdə/ *noun* a device used to decode signals from the air traffic control radar beacon system ○ *The aircraft receiver is set to the required frequency and linked to a selective call system decoder which has a 4-letter code.*

decrease *noun* /ˈdiːkriːs/ a lessening or reduction ○ *A decrease in power results in the aircraft descending.* ■ *verb* /dɪˈkriːs/ to become less, to fall ○ *Air density and pressure decrease with an increase in altitude.* ▸ opposite (all senses) **increase**

deduce /dɪˈdjuːs/ *verb* to work something out in the mind using information provided ○ *Sometimes, it is possible to estimate the depth of the layer of mist or fog from the ground observations and hence to deduce the ground range from any height.*

defect /ˈdiːfekt/ *noun* a fault or error ○ *Low oil pressure or excessive temperature indicate the development of a possible defect.*

defective /dɪˈfektɪv/ *adjective* faulty or not operating correctly ○ *Loss of supply pressure is caused by either a defective booster pump or lack of fuel.*

define /dɪˈfaɪn/ *verb* **1.** to give an exact explanation, as in a dictionary □ **it is not easy to define the word** it is difficult to say exactly what the word means **2.** to set the limits of something ○ *Cloud tops are very difficult to define.*

definite /ˈdef(ə)nət/ *adjective* referring to something which is not in doubt, which is certain ○ *Using a time scale on the track, the pilot should be prepared to look for a definite feature at a definite time.* Opposite **indefinite**

definition /ˌdefɪˈnɪʃ(ə)n/ *noun* an exact explanation of what a word or expression means ○ *The definition of a year is the time taken for a planet to describe one orbit around the sun.* □ **by definition** understood by the use of the word itself ○ *A sphere is, by definition, round.*

deflate /diːˈfleɪt/ *verb* to allow air to escape from something, so that it becomes smaller or collapses. Opposite **inflate** □ **to deflate a tyre** to allow the air to escape from a tyre

deflation /diːˈfleɪʃ(ə)n/ *noun* the act of allowing air to escape from something, so that it becomes smaller or collapses ○ *Deflation of a tyre is done by depressing the valve.*

deflect /dɪˈflekt/ *verb* **1.** to cause an object to move away from a neutral or central position ○ *During an out-of-balance turn, the ball in the slip indicator will be deflected to the left or right.* **2.** to move a moving object, gas or liquid away from its intended path ○ *In an open-cockpit aircraft, the windshield deflects the airflow over the pilot's head.*

deflection /dɪˈflekʃ(ə)n/ *noun* **1.** movement away from a central or neutral position ○ *Full deflection of the ailerons is sometimes needed on take-off to counteract a crosswind.* **2.** the movement of a moving object, gas or liquid away from its intended path ○ *In the southern hemisphere the deflection of wind at the equator is to the left.*

deformation /ˌdiːfɔːˈmeɪʃ(ə)n/ *noun* a change of the correct shape caused by stress ○ *Deformation of wing panels may be an indication of serious structural damage.*

deg *abbreviation* degree

degradation /ˌdegrəˈdeɪʃ(ə)n/ *noun* a decrease in quality ○ *Degradation of the radio signal sometimes makes it impossible to understand the message.*

degrade /dɪˈgreɪd/ *verb* to decrease the quality of something ○ *Interfering signals degrade VOR performance.*

degree /dɪˈgriː/ *noun* **1.** a level, amount or quantity □ **the degree of compression** the amount of compression □ **a high degree of safety** a high level of safety □ **to a greater degree** more than □ **to a lesser degree** less than **2.** a unit of temperature ○ *twenty degrees Celsius (20°C)* ○ *twenty degrees Centigrade (20°C)* ○ *seventy* *degrees Fahrenheit (70°F)* **3.** a unit of measurement of an angle equal to 1/360th of a circle – each degree is divided into 60 minutes and each minutes into 60 seconds ○ *Make a turn to the right at a bank angle of 30°.* □ **an angle of 90°** a right angle **4.** a unit of direction as measured on a compass ○ *east = 090°* ○ *west = 270°*

degrees true /dɪˌɡriːz 'truː/ *noun* degrees of direction measured from true north, not magnetic north. Also called **true degrees**. Symbol °**T**

dehydration /ˌdiːhaɪ'dreɪʃ(ə)n/ *noun* an unwanted and sometimes dangerous loss of water from the body ○ *Dehydration can be avoided by drinking plenty of water.*

de-ice /ˌdiː'aɪs/ *verb* to remove ice ○ *The ground crew de-iced the aircraft prior to take-off.*

de-icer /ˌdiː'aɪsə/ *noun* a device or substance used to remove ice ○ *De-icer spray should be checked to make sure it is not harmful to light aircraft windscreens.*

de-icing /ˌdiː'aɪsɪŋ/ *noun* the removal of ice ■ *adjective* referring to the removal of ice ○ *de-icing fluid* ◊ **anti-icing, icing**

delay /dɪ'leɪ/ *noun* a period after the expected time that you have to wait before something happens, the length of time by which something is late ○ *By day, the presence of cloud can cause a delay in clearance of fog.* ■ *verb* **1.** to make late, to cause to be late ○ *Take-off was delayed because of fog.* **2.** to put something off until later ○ *He delayed telling her the news until they had landed.*

delayed-action /dɪˌleɪd 'ækʃən/ *adjective* in which there is an unusual passing of time between stimulus and response ○ *The door is fitted with a delayed-action lock which operates one minute after the power has been switched off.*

deliver /dɪ'lɪvə/ *verb* to provide, to give ○ *The motor will continue to run but will deliver only one-third the rated power.* ○ *The pump can deliver fuel at the rate of 2,000 gph.*

delivery /dɪ'lɪv(ə)ri/ *noun* the act of providing or giving ○ *On some pumps, a depressurising valve is used to block delivery to the system.*

delivery pressure /dɪ'lɪv(ə)ri ˌpreʃə/ *noun* the pressure normally expected when fuel is being pumped

deluge /'deljuːdʒ/ *noun* ♦ **fire deluge system**

demand /dɪ'mɑːnd/ *noun* **1.** a need or use caused by necessity □ **high current demand on a generator** a situation requiring the generator to produce a lot of electricity **2.** a request which is made firmly □ **on demand** when asked for or ordered ○ *A computer will produce, on demand, a flight plan giving the optimum route, levels and fuel.* ■ *verb* **1.** to require as a necessity ○ *Higher operating weights of modern aircraft demand an increase in the number of wheels fitted to the landing gear.* **2.** to ask firmly ○ *He demanded an explanation.*

demonstrate /'demənstreɪt/ *verb* to show by clear example or explanation ○ *Torricelli first demonstrated that the atmosphere has weight.* ○ *It will be demonstrated in chapter 12 that turbulence is associated with strong winds.*

demonstration /ˌdemən'streɪʃ(ə)n/ *noun* a clear, often visual, description or explanation ○ *Your instructor will give a demonstration of the stall-recovery technique.*

dense /dens/ *adjective* **1.** referring to a substance which is closely compacted □ **dense fog** thick fog **2.** referring to the amount of mass of a substance for a given unit of volume ○ *Air which contains water vapour is less dense than air which does not.*

density /'densɪti/ *noun* a quantity of mass for a given unit of volume ○ *air density*

density altitude /ˌdensəti 'æltɪtjuːd/ *noun* the pressure altitude corrected for non-ISA temperature

COMMENT: Density altitude is a very important factor in calculating aircraft performance because of its effect on engine performance, time to reach takeoff speed (and therefore length of take-off run) and rate of climb.

density error /'densəti ˌerə/ *noun* a correction to airspeed to give true airspeed

DEP *abbreviation* departure message

depart /dɪ'pɑːt/ *verb* to leave ○ *The flight departs at 0200 GMT.* Opposite **arrive**

department /dɪ'pɑːtmənt/ *noun* a separate part of a complex whole, especially of an organisation

departure /dɪ'pɑːtʃə/ *noun* **1.** the act of leaving □ **departure time** the time when an aircraft becomes airborne **2.** the distance between two meridians at any given latitude

departure lounge /dɪ'pɑːtʃə laʊndʒ/ *noun* a room at an airport where passengers wait to board their aircraft

departure point /dɪ'pɑːtʃə pɔɪnt/ *noun* a place on the map representing the place from which a flight begins

departures /dɪ'pɑːtʃəz/ *noun* the part of an airport that deals with passengers who are leaving

depend /dɪ'pend/ *verb* **1.** to be controlled or affected entirely by something ○ *Whether or not an object can be seen by aircrew at a given distance will depend on factors such as size, shape and colour of the object.* ○ *If an aircraft ditches in the sea, early rescue depends on rapid location of survivors.* **2.** to rely on ○ *Pilots depend on air traffic controllers to help them conduct a safe flight.*

dependable /dɪ'pendəb(ə)l/ *adjective* reliable, trustworthy ○ *Mercury barometers have largely been replaced by precision aneroid barometers which are smaller, simpler to use, and more dependable.*

dependent /dɪ'pendənt/ *adjective* relying on or unable to do without something ○ *The height indicated by an altimeter is dependent on the pressure which is set on the sub-scale.*

deploy /dɪ'plɔɪ/ *verb* to come into action, to become ready to be used ○ *Slide rafts are door-mounted and automatically deploy and inflate when the door is opened in the armed position.*

deposit /dɪ'pɒzɪt/ *noun* a layer of collected matter on a surface ○ *A deposit of ice crystals causes the aircraft surfaces to change their aerodynamic characteristics.* ○ *Wheel brakes should be inspected for snow or ice deposits.*

depreciate /dɪ'priːʃieɪt/ *verb* to decrease in value ○ *The aircraft depreciated by 100% over the 5 year period.* Opposite **appreciate**

depreciation /dɪˌpriːʃi'eɪʃ(ə)n/ *noun* a decrease in value ○ *There was a depreciation of 100% in the value of the aircraft over the 5 year period.* Opposite **appreciation**

depress /dɪ'pres/ *verb* to push down ○ *Switches on the control columns instantly disengage the autopilot when depressed.*

depression /dɪ'preʃ(ə)n/ *noun* **1.** an area of low atmospheric pressure ○ *In the northern hemisphere, the wind blows anticlockwise round a depression and clockwise round an anticyclone and vice versa in the southern hemisphere.* □ **deep depression** area of very low relative atmospheric pressure **2.** a lower area on a surface, which is often difficult to see ○ *A depression on the wing surface must be investigated in case it is an indication of more serious structural damage.*

depressurisation /diːˌpreʃəraɪ'zeɪʃ(ə)n/, **depressurization** *noun* a loss, especially sudden, of cabin pressure ○ *Emergency oxygen must be available in the event of depressurisation.*

depressurise /diː'preʃəraɪz/, **depressurize** *verb* to lose pressure suddenly, or to cause to lose pressure ○ *The aircraft began to depressurise at 20,000 feet.*

depth /depθ/ *noun* the distance from the top surface of something to the bottom ○ *The troposphere's depth is variable in temperate latitudes.*

derive /dɪ'raɪv/ *verb* to get or to obtain ○ *Performance data is derived from flight tests.* ○ *Kepler derived the laws which relate to the motion of planets in their orbits.*

descend /dɪ'send/ *verb* to lose altitude, usually in a planned manoeuvre □ **the aircraft descended to 10,000 feet** the pilot reduced altitude until the aircraft was at 10,000 feet. Opposite **climb, ascend**

descent /dɪ'sent/ *noun* a planned loss of altitude ○ *The descent from cruise altitude took 40 minutes.* □ **in the descent** during planned loss of altitude, usually in preparation for landing

'...a search of radar recordings showed that a DC-10 had tracked within a few hundred metres of the house while passing 9,500 feet in the descent to Gatwick' [*Pilot*]

describe /dɪ'skraɪb/ *verb* **1.** to give the particular features of something □ **to describe what happened** put into words exactly what happened **2.** to draw a geometric figure or to move in a line that forms a geometric figure ○ *The definition of a year is the time taken for a planet to describe one orbit around the sun.* □ **to describe an arc** to draw or move in an arc

description /dɪ'skrɪpʃən/ *noun* **1.** the act of giving the particular features of something ○ *a detailed description of world climate* **2.** the drawing or making of a geometric figure □ **the description of a triangle** the drawing of a triangle

desert /'dezət/ *noun* a large area of dry often sandy country ○ *Over desert areas the lack of water vapour produces cold nights.*

design /dɪ'zaɪn/ *noun* a plan or drawing of something before it is made ○ *The design and testing of aircraft are important stages in the development programme.* ■ *verb* to draw plans using accurate information in preparation for constructing something □ **to design an aircraft** to have the idea, make drawings, calculate data, etc., with the intention of producing an aircraft

designate /'dezɪgneɪt/ *verb* to choose for a special purpose ○ *This region is designated as a fire zone.*

designator /'dezɪgneɪtə/ *noun* a group of letters and/or numbers that identify something

designer /dɪ'zaɪnə/ *noun* a person who has the idea for, and makes plans to produce, something ○ *Rutan is a designer of unusual-looking aircraft.*

'...test-pilot's tip for a safe first flight – take the designer with you' [*Flight International 9–15 Oct. 1996*]

desirable /dɪ'zaɪərəb(ə)l/ *adjective* preferred or wanted ○ *Equalisation of the air pressure across the eardrum is more difficult to achieve during descents than ascents, and a minimum rate of pressure change is desirable.*

despite /dɪ'spaɪt/ *preposition* in spite of ○ *Many beacons and aids which are provided for low operations are left out to keep the chart clear – despite this, the charts still look very difficult to understand.* □ **despite the weather, we took off** although the weather was bad, we took off

DEST *abbreviation* destination

destination /ˌdestɪ'neɪʃ(ə)n/ *noun* the place to which somebody or something is going ○ *Aerodrome forecasts are normally given in code form for destination and alternates.*

destroy /dɪ'strɔɪ/ *verb* to damage so much as to make useless ○ *The aircraft was destroyed in the accident.*

destruction /dɪ'strʌkʃən/ *noun* an act or instance of making completely useless by breaking ○ *By testing selected parts to destruction, a safe life can be assessed for all structures and components.*

destructive /dɪ'strʌktɪv/ *adjective* referring to something which destroys □ **the winds of a tornado are extremely destructive** tornadoes cause a lot of serious damage

detach /dɪ'tætʃ/ *verb* to remove a part from something, or to be removed ○ *A fuselage panel became detached and had to be replaced.* ○ *The parachute flare is a device which is fired to a height of 1,200 ft where a red flare and parachute detach.*

detachable /dɪ'tætʃəb(ə)l/ *adjective* referring to something which can be unfixed and removed

detachable wheel spats /dɪ ˌtætʃəb(ə)l 'wiːl ˌspæts/ *plural noun* streamlined coverings for the wheels of light aircraft which can be taken off to allow inspection and repairs of tyres

detail /'diːteɪl/ *noun* the important and less important facts about something ○ *The amount of detail which appears on a topographical chart depends upon the scale.*

detect /dɪ'tekt/ *verb* to discover the presence of something ○ *Apart from sensing the abnormal rate of descent of a false glide slope, the pilot can detect an error by comparing height with distance to go.*

detection /dɪ'tekʃən/ *noun* the discovery of the presence of something

detector /dɪ'tektə/ *noun* a device for discovering the existence of something □ **ice detector** a device for detecting the presence of ice on the airframe ○ *When ice forms on the vibrating rod ice detector head, the probe frequency decreases.*

deteriorate /dɪ'tɪəriəreɪt/ *verb* to become or make bad or worse ○ *The electrolyte in the cells of a nickel-cadmium battery does not chemically react with the plates and so the plates do not deteriorate.* □ **deteriorating weather** worsening weather

deterioration /dɪˌtɪəriə'reɪʃ(ə)n/ *noun* worsening □ **a deterioration in the situation** a worsening of the situation

determination /dɪˌtɜːmɪ'neɪʃ(ə)n/ *noun* **1.** the act of finding out by calculation ○ *Structure design for a given safe life has led to the determination of the minimum number of flying hours which should pass before major failure occurs.* **2.** the strength of mind to do what is required ○ *Determination was a major factor in the trainee passing his exams.*

determine /dɪ'tɜːmɪn/ *verb* **1.** to find out by calculation ○ *To determine the average age, divide the total number of years by the number of people.* ○ *When we wish to fly from one place to another, it is first necessary to determine the direction of the destination from the departure point.* **2.** to set or to fix precisely ○ *On a large transport aircraft,*

the safety of hundreds of passengers is involved, and regulations determine the minimum crew that must be carried.

detonation /ˌdetə'neɪʃ(ə)n/ *noun* a sudden, explosive burning of the air/fuel mixture ○ *Prior to the accident, engine detonation could be heard by people on the ground.*

COMMENT: Detonation imposes excessive loads on the pistons and other engine components, possibly causing engine damage and resulting in engine failure.

develop /dɪ'veləp/ *verb* **1.** to come into being ○ *Carburettor icing may develop in any type of carburettor in relatively warm air temperatures.* ○ *Vertical motion and therefore turbulence suggest that thunderstorms may develop.* **2.** to get bigger, to grow and change ○ *During the day, light breezes may develop into strong winds.*

development /dɪ'veləpmənt/ *noun* **1.** something new, made as an improvement on something older ○ *Satellite navigation aids for light aircraft are a recent development.* **2.** growth and change ○ *To study weather and its development, the meteorologist has to be aware of the horizontal changes in atmospheric pressure both in space and time.*

deviate /'diːvieɪt/ *verb* to move away from the normal position or path ○ *If the aircraft deviates beyond the normal ILS glide slope, the flight crew are alerted.*

deviation /ˌdiːvi'eɪʃ(ə)n/ *noun* **1.** the process of moving away from the normal position or path ○ *On final approach, any deviation from the extended centreline of the runway should be corrected immediately.* **2.** a magnetic compass error in a particular aircraft caused by magnetic influences in the structure and equipment of the aircraft itself ○ *Deviation is not a constant value but varies from one aircraft to another.*

device /dɪ'vaɪs/ *noun* an object, especially mechanical or electrical, which has been made for a particular purpose ○ *A capacitor is a device with the ability to temporarily store an electric charge.*

dew /djuː/ *noun* drops of condensed moisture left on the ground overnight in cool places

dew point /'djuː pɔɪnt/ *noun* the temperature at which air is saturated with water vapour and condensation begins

COMMENT: Weather reports usually include the air temperature and dew point temperature. When the difference between temperature and dew point is small, there is a strong possibility of fog, clouds, or precipitation.

DF *abbreviation* direction finding

DFDR *abbreviation* digital flight data recorder

DFR *abbreviation* departure flow regulation

DFTI *abbreviation* Distance from touchdown indicator

DH *abbreviation* decision height

DI *abbreviation* direction indicator

diagonal /daɪˈæɡən(ə)l/ *adjective* 1. joining two opposite corners of a rectangle 2. sloping halfway between the vertical and horizontal ○ *Early aircraft were of the wire braced type of construction, the wire being superseded by tubular diagonal struts.* ■ *noun* a line joining two opposite corners of a rectangle

diagram /'daɪəɡræm/ *noun* an often simplified drawing showing the structure or workings of something ○ *The diagram shows a simple open-circuit system.*

diagrammatic /ˌdaɪəɡrəˈmætɪk/ *adjective* referring to something which is shown as a drawing of a system or structure □ **diagrammatic format** in the form of a diagram

dial /'daɪəl/ *noun* the face of an instrument showing a scale ○ *A cup anemometer is connected to an instrument with a dial showing wind speed in knots.*

diameter /daɪˈæmɪtə/ *noun* the distance from one side of a circle to the other, passing through the centre □ **equatorial diameter** the distance from the equator, through the centre of the Earth to the equator on the opposite side of the globe

diaphragm /'daɪəfræm/ *noun* a thin sheet of material used to separate parts or chambers ○ *Some switches are operated by a diaphragm which flexes under fluid or air pressure.*

differ /'dɪfə/ *verb* to be unlike ○ *Track and heading differ by the amount of drift.* ○ *Because the chart time and the departure/arrival times differ, it is necessary to consider the movement of any weather system which might affect the route.*

differential /ˌdɪfəˈrenʃəl/ *adjective* referring to things which react differently when measured against a norm or standard □ **differential heating of the atmosphere** the heating of the atmosphere to varying temperatures depending on the relative warmth of the land at the equator and the poles

differential expansion switch /ˌdɪfərenʃəl ɪkˈspænʃ(ə)n ˌswɪtʃ/ *noun* a switch which operates on the principle that the coefficients of expansion of dissimilar metals are different

differentiate /ˌdɪfəˈrenʃɪeɪt/ *verb* to recognise the difference between two things; to show two things to be different ○ *Some types of colour blindness make the sufferer unable to differentiate between blue and red.*

diffraction /dɪˈfrækʃ(ə)n/ *noun* the breaking down of a beam of radiation ○ *Diffraction produces a surface wave which follows the curvature of the earth.*

diffuse /dɪˈfjuːs/ *adjective* spread out in every direction ○ *Glare caused by diffuse reflection of sunlight from the top of a layer of fog or haze can seriously reduce air-to-ground visibility.* ■ *verb* to spread out in every direction ○ *Light diffuses as it passes through fog.*

diffuser /dɪˈfjuːzə/ *noun* a device in a jet engine that alters the direction of flow of the air entering the engine as part of the process of compressing it before it reaches the combustion chamber

diffusion /dɪˈfjuːʒ(ə)n/ *noun* the process of spreading out ○ *Gas from the turbine enters the exhaust system at high velocities but, because of high fric-*

tion losses, the speed of flow is decreased by diffusion.

digit /'dɪdʒɪt/ *noun* any number from 0 to 9 ○ *Information is provided in a four-digit group.*

digital /'dɪdʒɪt(ə)l/ *adjective* referring to a system or device which uses signals or information in the form of numbers

dihedral /daɪ'hedr(ə)l/ *noun* the angle between an upward sloping aircraft wing and a horizontal line

diluted /daɪ'luːtɪd/ *adjective* made weaker by adding water or some other fluid ○ *Spillage from a lead acid battery may be neutralised by washing with a diluted solution of sodium bicarbonate.*

diluter /daɪ'luːtə/ *noun* a device for decreasing the strength or concentration of a liquid or gas ○ *Most flight decks use the diluter demand system in which the oxygen is diluted with cabin air.*

dimension /daɪ'menʃən/ *noun* a measurable distance such as height, length, etc., or a measurement of height, length, etc. ○ *Variations of atmospheric pressure produce changes in the dimension of the capsule chamber.*

diminish /dɪ'mɪnɪʃ/ *verb* to decrease or to reduce in size or importance ○ *Friction is greatest near the ground and diminishes with height.* ○ *At higher altitudes, ground objects are less easily seen because of diminished size.*

diode /'daɪəʊd/ *noun* an electronic component that allows an electrical current to pass in one direction and not the other

dioxide /daɪ'ɒksaɪd/ *noun* an oxide containing two atoms of oxygen. ◊ **carbon dioxide**

dip to move e.g. the wing or nose of an aircraft so that it points downwards

direct /daɪ'rekt/ *adjective* **1.** in a straight line; by the shortest route ○ *a direct flight* **2.** complete ○ *the direct opposite* ■ *verb* to guide or control the movement of something ○ *Clamshell doors are hydraulically or pneumatically opened, and direct the exhaust gases forwards to produce reverse thrust.*

direct current /daɪ'rekt 'kʌrənt/ *noun* an electric current flowing in one direction only ○ *An electric starter is usually a direct current electric motor coupled to the engine, which automatically disengages after the engine starts.* Abbreviation **DC**

direction /daɪ'rekʃən/ *noun* the course taken by somebody or something ○ *The Earth rotates about its own axis in an anticlockwise direction.*

directional /daɪ'rekʃən(ə)l/ *adjective* referring to the course taken by somebody or something

directional gyro /daɪˌrekʃ(ə)n(ə)l 'dʒaɪrəʊ/ *noun* a gyroscopic instrument which indicates direction but does not have a north-seeking magnet ○ *The directional gyro should be set to correspond with the magnetic compass.* ◊ **heading indicator**

directional radar beam /daɪˌrekʃ(ə)n(ə)l 'reɪdɑː ˌbiːm/ *noun* a signal from a directional beacon enabling the pilot to determine a bearing from the beacon with a communications receiver

direction indicator /daɪ'rekʃən ˌɪndɪkeɪtə/ *noun* an instrument which gives direction information. Abbreviation **DI**

directive /daɪ'rektɪv/ *adjective* referring to the ability of a device to send or receive signals in straight lines ○ *The antenna is highly directive in transmission and reception.* ■ *noun* general or detailed instructions from management to staff to guide them in their work ○ *According to the management directive, all late arrivals should be logged.*

director /daɪ'rektə/ *noun* **1.** a device with a central controlling function ○ *EFIS is a highly sophisticated type of flight director system.* **2.** a person who is a member of the board that controls the activities of a company ○ *managing director*

disadvantage /ˌdɪsəd'vɑːntɪdʒ/ *noun* an unwanted situation or condition, or a factor which makes somebody or something less likely to succeed ○ *The disadvantage of a booster pump is that the output is constant so that when engine demand is high, fuel pressure* *tends to be low and vice versa.* Opposite **advantage**

disadvantaged /ˌdɪsəd'vɑːntɪdʒd/ *adjective* □ **physically disadvantaged (person)** a person who has a physical disability

COMMENT: The word 'disadvantaged' may be regarded by some people as a politically correct term for 'disabled'. With the help of specially-adapted controls, more and more disabled people are learning to fly.

disappear /ˌdɪsə'pɪə/ *verb* **1.** to vanish ○ *If air blew at right angles to isobars, the horizontal pressure differences would eventually disappear.* **2.** to pass out of sight ○ *The aircraft took off, climbed out and soon disappeared from view.*

disarm /dɪs'ɑːm/ *verb* **1.** to switch off an active or live system ○ *On the ground approaching the terminal, the flight deck will instruct the cabin crew to disarm the escape devices.* **2.** to forcibly remove a weapon from somebody ○ *The hijacker was disarmed by security forces.*

disc /dɪsk/ *noun* a circular flat plate ○ *A turbine consists of a disc on which is mounted a number of blades.*

discharge /dɪs'tʃɑːdʒ/ *noun* a release of power from a source such as a battery ○ *A lightning flash is a large-scale example of an electrical spark, or discharge.* □ **battery discharge** the loss or release of electrical supply from a battery ■ *verb* to release electrical supply from a source such as a battery ○ *The battery discharged overnight.*

disconnect /ˌdɪskə'nekt/ *verb* to separate two things attached to one another ○ *The electrical supply can be disconnected by pulling out the plug.*

discrimination /dɪˌskrɪmɪ'neɪʃ(ə)n/ *noun* the ability to know or see the difference between two similar things ○ *Targets on the same bearing which are separated radially by less than half a pulse length distance will appear at the receiver as one echo, so good target discrimination requires short pulses.*

discuss /dɪ'skʌs/ *verb* to write about or talk about a subject ○ *This chapter will discuss HF and VHF voice communications.*

disembark /ˌdɪsɪm'bɑːk/ *verb* to leave the aircraft after landing ○ *The passengers finally disembarked at 20.00 hours.*

disembarkation /ˌdɪsɪmbɑː'keɪʃ(ə)n/ *noun* the act of leaving the aircraft after landing ○ *The exits are used as conventional doors for disembarkation.*

disengage /ˌdɪsɪn'geɪdʒ/ *verb* to switch off a system or device ○ *Switches on the control columns instantly disengage the autopilot when depressed.*

dish /dɪʃ/ *noun* a shallow container for food

dish antenna /'dɪʃ ænˌtenə/ *noun* a circular antenna with a shape like a shallow bowl

disintegration /dɪsˌɪntɪ'greɪʃ(ə)n/ *noun* the falling apart or destruction of something ○ *Electromagnetic radiations resulting from the disintegration of radioactive materials are known as gamma rays.*

dismantle /dɪs'mænt(ə)l/ *verb* to take apart into single components ○ *One type of inspection is able to reveal fatigue cracks, corrosion, internal damage, the presence of loose articles and mercury spillage without the need to dismantle the aircraft.* Opposite **assemble** (NOTE: The verb 'mantle' is not used.)

disorientation /ˌdɪsɔːriən'teɪʃ(ə)n/ *noun* a state of confusion in which there is loss of understanding of where one is or which direction one is facing, etc. ○ *When the cabin is rapidly and completely filled by smoke and fumes passengers will suffer from disorientation.*

dispensation /ˌdɪspen'seɪʃ(ə)n/ *noun* permission not to have to do something ○ *At very high altitudes the flying pilot must be on oxygen at all times, unless an aircraft dispensation has been obtained.*

dispense /dɪ'spens/, **dispense with** *verb* not to include or not to use something ○ *In some cases the rivets are dis-*

pensed with and the skin is fixed to the internal members by the redux process.

dispersal /dɪˈspɜːs(ə)l/ *noun* **1.** the act of leaving an area and going in different directions □ **the dispersal of a crowd** the disappearance of a crowd **2.** the clearing away of something such as mist, e.g. by the wind ○ *the dispersal of hill fog* ○ *Dispersal of cloud takes place when surface heating lifts the cloud base or drier air is advected.*

disperse /dɪˈspɜːs/ *verb* **1.** to leave an area going in different directions □ **the crowd dispersed** the people in the crowd left the area, going in different directions, so that eventually the crowd disappeared **2.** to clear away ○ *The fluorescent green dye will disperse slowly in a calm sea but quickly in a moderate to rough sea.*

displace /dɪsˈpleɪs/ *verb* to move something out of its normal position ○ *The atmosphere is said to be stable if, when a parcel of air is displaced vertically, it tends to return to its original level.*

displacement /dɪsˈpleɪsmənt/ *noun* movement away from the normal position ○ *The ILS is a cross-pointer indicator which shows the aircraft horizontal displacement from the localiser and vertical displacement from the glide path.*

display /dɪˈspleɪ/ *noun* **1.** the appearance of information on a monitor screen or on the panel of an instrument or of an indicator ○ *There are three different types of electronic display systems: EFIS, EICAS and ECAM.* □ **digital display** information shown as numbers ○ *The clock uses a digital display to show the time of 12:33.* **2.** a show or demonstration ■ *verb* to show, e.g. on a panel or a screen ○ *Alerting and warning information is displayed.*

disseminate /dɪˈsemɪneɪt/ *verb* to send out or spread ○ *Meteorological stations make routine weather observations at fixed intervals and disseminate this information locally.*

dissimilar /dɪˈsɪmɪlə/ *adjective* referring to something which is not the same as, or is unlike, something else ○ *Differ-*

ential expansion switches operate on the principle that the coefficients of expansion of dissimilar metals are different.

dissipate /ˈdɪsɪpeɪt/ *verb* to spread out and lose power or strength, or to cause something to do this ○ *Tropical storms often dissipate as they pass from sea to land.*

dissipation /ˌdɪsɪˈpeɪʃ(ə)n/ *noun* the process of spreading out and losing power or strength ○ *The rubber used on nose or tail wheels is usually constructed to form a good electrical conductor for the safe dissipation of static electricity.*

dissolve /dɪˈzɒlv/ *verb* to become or to cause to become part of a liquid and form a solution ○ *Sugar dissolves in water.* ○ *There is a possibility that in some types of accumulator, gas may be dissolved into the fluid and thus introduced into the system.*

dissolved /dɪˈzɒlvd/ *adjective* that has melted and become of a liquid □ **dissolved water** water in solution in fuel

distance /ˈdɪstəns/ *noun* a space between two places or points, or the measurement of such a space ○ *The distance from point A to point B is 100 nm.* ○ *The distance from point A to point B on the diagram is 2 cm.* ○ *The height of the aircraft is the vertical distance, measured in feet, of the aircraft above the surface of the Earth.*

distance measuring equipment /ˈdɪstəns ˌmeʒ(ə)rɪŋ ɪˌkwɪpmənt/ *noun* an airborne secondary radar whose signal is converted into distance ○ *It is quite common to find a VOR located together with DME (Distance Measuring Equipment) to give simultaneous range and bearing from the same point on the ground.* Abbreviation **DME**

COMMENT: DME equipment is usually located in a VOR station. Other equipment in the aircraft transmits a signal to the VOR station, which replies. The equipment in the aircraft converts the signal into distance and also calculates ground speed and the time needed to reach the station.

distillation /ˌdɪstɪˈleɪʃ(ə)n/ *noun* the process by which a liquid is heated and the resulting vapour is then condensed and collected ○ *With kerosene-type fuels, the volatility is controlled by distillation.*

distinct /dɪˈstɪŋkt/ *adjective* clear and easily seen or understood ○ *When a lead-acid battery is fully charged, each cell displays three distinct indications.*

distinction /dɪˈstɪŋkʃən/ *noun* something which makes one thing different from another ○ *A clear distinction is made between showers and general precipitation.*

distinctive /dɪˈstɪŋktɪv/ *adjective* easily recognised because of particular features or characteristics ○ *Concorde is a very distinctive-looking aeroplane.*

distinguish /dɪˈstɪŋgwɪʃ/ *verb* to know or to see the difference between things ○ *A receiver antenna would be unable to distinguish between signals unless they had some differing characteristics.*

distinguishable /dɪˈstɪŋgwɪʃəb(ə)l/ *adjective* easily recognised as different from ○ *Useful ground features must be easily distinguishable from their surroundings.*

distort /dɪˈstɔːt/ *verb* **1.** to put out of shape ○ *Stress could cause the body of the aircraft to distort or change its shape.* **2.** to produce a bad radio signal ○ *The sound of the transmission is distorted if the volume is set too high.*

distortion /dɪˈstɔːʃ(ə)n/ *noun* **1.** the bending or twisting of something so that it is out of shape ○ *Difficulty in closing a door may be caused by distortion of the airframe.* **2.** alteration of the electrical signal that makes a transmission unclear ○ *Distortion of the signal made it difficult for the controller to understand what the pilot said.*

distress /dɪˈstres/ *noun* **1.** serious danger or difficulty **2.** a personal worry or anxiety ○ *Some passengers were in distress after the incident.*

distress and diversion cell /dɪˌstres ənd daɪˈvɜːʒ(ə)n ˌsel/ *noun* a unit at an air traffic control centre that provides immediate assistance to aircraft in difficulty

distress signal /dɪˌstres ˈsɪgn(ə)l/ *noun* a signal transmitted by an aircraft in danger

distribute /dɪˈstrɪbjuːt/ *verb* **1.** to give or send out ○ *There are two basic configurations which are used to distribute electrical power, the parallel system and the split bus system.* **2.** to spread over a wide area ○ *Multiple wheel undercarriage units distribute the weight of the aircraft.*

distribution /ˌdɪstrɪˈbjuːʃ(ə)n/ *noun* **1.** the act of giving or sending out ○ *Parallel AC and DC power distribution systems are found on commercial aircraft containing three or more engines.* **2.** the fact of being spread over an area ○ *There is a high distribution of used and disused airfields in the south of England.*

distributor /dɪˈstrɪbjutə/ *noun* a device which sends an electrical charge to each spark plug in turn ○ *The distributor directs the high voltage impulses to the cylinders in turn as they reach their ignition point.*

disturb /dɪˈstɜːb/ *verb* to upset the normal condition of something ○ *Small hills can disturb the flow of air.*

disturbance /dɪˈstɜːbəns/ *noun* something that upsets the normal condition of something ○ *In general, the higher the mountain and the faster the air flow the greater is the resulting disturbance.*

ditch /dɪtʃ/ *verb* to land a plane in the sea, in an emergency ○ *Even though aircraft have ditched successfully, lives have been lost because life rafts were not launched in time.*

ditching /ˈdɪtʃɪŋ/ *noun* the act of landing a plane in the sea, in an emergency ○ *After all four engines stopped, the captain had to seriously consider the possibility of a ditching in the Indian Ocean.*

diurnal /daɪˈɜːn(ə)l/ *adjective* referring to the 24-hour cycle of day and night ○ *Diurnal changes in surface temperature over the sea are small.*

dive /daɪv/ *noun* a steep nose-down attitude of an aircraft □ **to pull out of** *or* **from a dive** to return the aircraft to level flight after a nose-down flight path ○ *During manoeuvring of an aircraft, when banking, turning and pulling out from a dive, stresses on the airframe are increased.* ■ *verb* to put the aircraft into a steep nose-down attitude ○ *The aircraft dived to avoid the other aircraft.* (NOTE: **diving – dived**)

diverge /daɪˈvɜːdʒ/ *verb* to move further apart from something else ○ *Air diverges at low levels and converges at high levels, causing a sinking or subsiding effect in the atmosphere.* Opposite **converge**

divergence /daɪˈvɜːdʒəns/ *noun* the act of moving apart ○ *Divergence of air at high levels leads to rising air at low levels with a consequent pressure fall.* Opposite **convergence**

divergent /daɪˈvɜːdʒənt/ *adjective* referring to something which moves further apart from something else

divergent duct /daɪˈvɜːdʒənt dʌkt/ *noun* a duct which has an inlet area which is smaller than the outlet area

diversion /daɪˈvɜːʃ(ə)n/ *noun* a change in route or destination caused by bad weather, technical problem, etc. ○ *The aircraft had to make a diversion to another airport due to fog.*

divert /daɪˈvɜːt/ *verb* to turn away from a course or a destination ○ *An automatic cut-out valve is fitted to divert pump output to the reservoir when pressure has built up to normal operating pressure.* ○ *The aircraft was diverted to Manchester airport because of fog.*

divide /dɪˈvaɪd/ *verb* **1.** to separate into parts ○ *Air masses are divided into two types according to source region and these are known as polar and tropical air masses.* **2.** to calculate how many times a number is contained in another number ○ *Eight divided by four equals two (8 ÷ 4 = 2).*

division /dɪˈvɪʒ(ə)n/ *noun* **1.** separation into parts □ **the division of the lower atmosphere** the separation of the atmosphere into its component layers **2.** the calculation of how may times a number is contained in another number ○ *The division sign is ÷.*

DME *abbreviation* distance measuring equipment

document /ˈdɒkjumənt/ *noun* a piece of writing, e.g. a memo, letter or report ○ *The flight crew route flight plan is a composite document which also serves as a navigation log.*

documentation /ˌdɒkjumen ˈteɪʃ(ə)n/ *noun* a collection of letters, memos, reports, etc. ○ *Flight crews are provided with a full meteorological briefing, backed by documentation, a short time before ETD.*

domestic /dəˈmestɪk/ *adjective* referring or belonging to inside a country ○ *Domestic flights usually leave from Terminal 1.*

dominant /ˈdɒmɪnənt/ *adjective* main or most influential ○ *Both pressure and temperature decrease with height but the pressure change is the dominant one and so, as pressure decreases with height, so does density.*

dominate /ˈdɒmɪneɪt/ *verb* to have the most effect or influence on ○ *Because the chart time and the departure/arrival times differ, it is necessary to consider the movement of any weather system which will dominate the route.*

Doppler radar /ˈdɒplə ˌreɪdɑː/ *noun* radar which can distinguish between fixed and moving targets or provide ground speed and track information from an airborne installation

Doppler VOR /ˌdɒplə viː əʊ ˈɑː/ *noun* an adaptation of VOR to reduce errors caused by location

dot /dɒt/ *noun* a small circular mark on paper ○ *The highest point in a locality is marked by a dot with the elevation marked alongside.*

downdraught /ˈdaʊndrɑːft/ *noun* **1.** cool air which flows downwards as a rainstorm approaches. Opposite **updraught 2.** air which flows rapidly down the lee side of a building, mountain, etc. (NOTE: It is also written **downdraft** in US English.)

downstream /ˌdaʊnˈstriːm/ *adverb* in the direction of flow, or further along the line of flow ○ *Internally driven superchargers are generally used on medium and high powered engines and are fitted downstream of the throttle valve.*

downward /ˈdaʊnwəd/ *adjective* moving to a lower level ○ *When flying in turbulent air conditions, an aircraft is subjected to upward and downward gust loads.*

downwards /ˈdaʊnwədz/ *adverb* to a lower level, towards the bottom ○ *Pull the toggles downwards to inflate the life jacket.* Opposite **upwards** (NOTE: In US English, **downward** is used as an adverb and as an adjective.)

downwind /daʊnˈwɪnd/ *adjective, adverb* in the same direction as the wind is blowing □ **turn downwind** turn the aircraft so that it is flying in the same direction as the wind is blowing. Opposite **upwind**

downwind leg /ˈdaʊnwɪnd leg/ *noun* part of the airfield traffic circuit which runs parallel to, but in the opposite direction to, the approach to land which is made into wind

DR *abbreviation* dead reckoning

draft /drɑːft/ *noun US* same as **draught** ○ *a down draft or an updraft*

drag /dræg/ *noun* the resistance of the air created by moving the aircraft through the air ○ *To reduce the effect of drag on an aircraft by the fixed undercarriage a retractable type was introduced.* ○ *If an engine failure occurs, the windmilling propeller may cause considerable drag.*

COMMENT: There are two basic types of drag called parasite drag and induced drag. Parasite drag is caused by friction between the air and the aircraft surface, aerials, landing gear, etc. Induced drag is produced by lift.

drain /dreɪn/ *noun* a device to allow fluid to escape from its container ○ *When the cabin is pressurised the drains close, preventing loss of pressure.* ■ *verb* to allow fluid to escape by providing a hole or tube, etc., through which it can pass ○ *The moisture drains in the lower skin of the cabin are open when the cabin is unpressurised, allowing moisture to drain.*

drainage /ˈdreɪnɪdʒ/ *noun* **1.** the act of allowing a fluid to escape from its container ○ *Drainage of water from the fuel system should be carried out before the first flight of the day.* **2.** a system of outlets for fluid such as water or fuel to pass out of a closed area

draught /drɑːft/ *noun* a local current of air ○ *a down draught or an updraught* (NOTE: This word is written **draft** in US English.)

draw /drɔː/ *verb* **1.** to make a picture as with a pencil, on paper, etc. ○ *Because there is a temperature gradient across each front it is possible to draw isotherms which reduce in value from warm to cold air.* **2.** to pull or to take ○ *Fluid is drawn into the pump body.* **3.** to pull towards oneself (NOTE: **drawing – drew – drawn**)

drift /drɪft/ *noun* movement away from the desired course, created by wind blowing at an angle to the intended direction of flight ○ *If the wind direction is not the same as the aircraft track or its reciprocal, then the aircraft will experience drift.* ■ *verb* to move away from the desired course ○ *When landing, a cross-wind from the right will cause the aircraft to drift to the left.*

drill /drɪl/ *noun* **1.** a short series of actions carried out in a particular sequence ○ *The starting drill varies between different aircraft types and a starting check procedure is normally used.* **2.** a tool, often electrically powered, for making holes in metal, wood, etc.

drive /draɪv/ *noun* a series of connected devices that transmit power to the wheels, propellers, etc. ○ *Rotation of the engine for starting is done by an electric starter motor connected to a drive shaft in the accessories gearbox.* ■ *verb* **1.** to make something move or turn □ **shaft-driven** using a rotating shaft as a means of transmitting power from one part to another, e.g. from a turbine engine to a helicopter rotor **2.** to control

and guide ○ *He's learning to drive.*
(NOTE: **driving – drove – driven**)

driven /'drɪv(ə)n/ ♦ **drive**

drizzle /'drɪz(ə)l/ *noun* precipitation, often persistent, in the form of very small drops of water ○ *Drizzle is the lightest form of precipitation consisting of fine water droplets.*

COMMENT: In weather reports and forecasts, drizzle is abbreviated to DZ.

drogue parachute /'drəʊg ˌpærəʃuːt/ *noun* a small parachute used in releasing a larger parachute from its pack

drone /drəʊn/ *noun* an aircraft whose flight is controlled from the ground

drop /drɒp/ *noun* **1.** a small amount of liquid that falls ○ *a drop of water* ○ *a few drops of rain* **2.** a sudden lowering ○ *The passage of a cold front is usually followed by a drop in temperature.* ○ *A sudden drop in oil pressure is normally an indication of serious engine trouble.* ■ *verb* to become lower or to decrease suddenly ○ *The temperature dropped by several degrees.*

droplet /'drɒplət/ *noun* a small drop of liquid ○ *Experiments show that smaller droplets of rain can remain super cooled to much lower temperatures than large droplets.*

drove /drəʊv/ ♦ **drive**

drum /drʌm/ *noun* a cylindrical device, often with closed ends

dry /draɪ/ *adjective* containing no water or no moisture ○ *dry air* ◊ **lapse rate**

dry ice /ˌdraɪ 'aɪs/ *noun* solidified carbon dioxide

dual /'djuːəl/ *adjective* double, in pair ○ *Most light aircraft with side-by-side seating have dual controls.*

duct /dʌkt/ *noun* a channel or tube through which fluids or cables can pass ○ *The modern jet engine is basically a duct into which the necessary parts are fitted.*

due /djuː/ *adjective* **1.** expected to arrive □ **the flight is due at 10 o'clock** the flight should arrive at 10 o'clock **2.** □ **due to** because of ○ *Due to daytime heating, the stability decreases and the*

wind speed increases. ■ *adverb* exactly and directly ○ *The aircraft flew due east.*

dump /dʌmp/ *verb* to offload quickly ○ *Normal operating cabin pressure can be reduced rapidly in the event of emergency landings, by dumping air.* ○ *The aircraft flew out to sea in order to dump fuel before landing.*

duplication /ˌdjuːplɪ'keɪʃ(ə)n/ *noun* the act of copying or doubling ○ *Control surfaces are divided into sections operated by a separate control unit, thus providing duplication to guard against failure of a unit.*

durability /ˌdjʊərə'bɪlɪti/ *noun* the ability of a substance or device to last a long time ○ *High quality components have good durability.*

duration /djʊ'reɪʃ(ə)n/ *noun* the length of time for which something continues ○ *The duration of the examination is two hours.* ○ *The duration of the flight was three hours.*

dust /dʌst/ *noun* a fine powdery substance blown by the wind and found on surfaces ○ *Solid particles in the air include dust, sand, volcanic ash and atmospheric pollution.*

duty /'djuːti/ *noun* **1.** a period of work □ **on duty** at work □ **off duty** not at work **2.** same as **import duty** ○ *the duty payable on a carton of cigarettes*

dye /daɪ/ *noun* a material used to change the colour of something ○ *Minute surface cracks which are difficult to detect by visual means may be highlighted by using penetrant dyes.*

dynamic /daɪ'næmɪk/ *adjective* referring to something in motion □ **dynamic pressure** pressure created by the forward movement of the aircraft ○ *If the dynamic pressure increases due to an increase in forward speed, the force required to move the control column will increase.* Opposite **static pressure**

dynamic seal /daɪˌnæmɪk 'siːl/ *noun* a seal which is part of a moving component, e.g. in a hydraulic system ○ *dynamic seals require lubrication to remain effective*

DZ /ˌdiː 'zed/ *abbreviation* drizzle

E

E *abbreviation* east

ear /ɪə/ *noun* the hearing organ

ear defenders /ˈɪə dɪˌfendəz/ *plural noun* same as **acoustic ear muffs**

eardrum /ˈɪədrʌm/ *noun* a membrane inside the ear which vibrates with sound and passes the vibrations to the inner ear ○ *Equalisation of the air pressure across the eardrum is more difficult to achieve during descents than ascents.*

ear muffs /ˈɪə mʌfs/ *plural noun* ♦ **acoustic ear muffs**

ear protectors /ˈɪə prəˌtektəz/ *plural noun* same as **acoustic ear muffs**

earth /ɜːθ/ *noun* **1.** □ **(the planet) Earth** the planet where we live **2.** ground or soil ■ *verb* to connect an electrical appliance to a position of zero potential ○ *When refuelling a light aircraft, ensure that the aircraft is properly earthed.* (NOTE: The US expression is **to ground**.)

east /iːst/ *noun* **1.** a compass point on the mariner's compass 90° clockwise from due north and directly opposite west ○ *London is east of New York.* **2.** the direction in which the Earth rotates, the direction of the rising sun ■ *adjective* **1.** referring to areas or regions lying in the east ○ *the east coast of Canada* **2.** the eastern part of a region ○ *East Africa* ■ *adverb* towards the east ○ *The aircraft was flying east.*

eastbound /ˈiːstbaʊnd/ *adjective* travelling towards the east ○ *an eastbound flight*

easterly /ˈiːstəli/ *adjective* **1.** situated towards the east **2.** □ **easterly component** one part of the wind direction coming from the east **3.** □ **to move in an**

easterly direction to move towards the east ■ *noun* a wind which blows from the east

eastern /ˈiːst(ə)n/ *adjective* situated in the east ○ *one of the eastern provinces of Canada*

Eastern Standard Time /ˈiːstən ˈstændəd ˈtaɪm/ *noun* the time zone of the eastern USA and Canada, 5 hours behind GMT. Abbreviation **EST**

eastward /ˈiːstwəd/ *adjective* going towards the east ■ *adverb US* same as **eastwards**

eastwards /ˈiːstwədz/ *adverb* towards the east ○ *Flying eastwards or westwards for long periods of time affects sleep patterns.*

east wind /iːst wɪnd/ *noun* a wind blowing from or coming from the east (NOTE: A wind is named after the direction it comes from.)

EAT *abbreviation* expected approach time

EATMP *abbreviation* European air traffic management programme

ECAC *abbreviation* European civil aviation conference

ECAM *abbreviation* electronic centralised aircraft monitor

echo /ˈekəʊ/ *noun* **1.** the repetition of a sound by reflection of sound waves from a surface **2.** the return of a signal back to the source from which it was transmitted ○ *The strength of the returning echo from a radar transmission depends on a number of factors.*

economic /ˌiːkəˈnɒmɪk/ *adjective* financially rewarding ○ *It was no longer* *economic to keep the maintenance operation going.*

economical /ˌiːkəˈnɒmɪk(ə)l/ *adjective* referring to a substance or device for which input is minimised and output maximised (thereby saving costs) □ **economical engine** an engine which uses less fuel to produce the same power as comparable engines ○ *Jet engines are more efficient and economical when operated at high altitudes.*

ECS *abbreviation* environmental control system

EDDUS *abbreviation* electronic data display and update system

eddy /ˈedi/ *noun* a current of air moving in the opposite direction to the main current, especially in a circular motion ○ *When wind flows over an obstruction such as a building, an eddy is formed on the lee, or downwind side.*

edge /edʒ/ *noun* a line of intersection or joining of two surfaces

EET *abbreviation* estimated elapsed time

effect /ɪˈfekt/ *noun* **1.** something which results from a cause ○ *Ultra-violet radiation has the effect of warming the atmosphere.* ○ *Pressure patterns have an effect on weather.* **2.** the condition of being in full force □ **in effect** in operation □ **to take effect**, **to come into effect** to start to operate ○ *A new regulation comes into effect tomorrow.* □ **with effect from** starting from ■ *verb* to cause or carry out □ **to effect a change** to make a change □ **modifications were effected** modifications were carried out. Compare **affect**

effective /ɪˈfektɪv/ *adjective* **1.** having an expected and satisfactory result □ **the new cleaning fluid was very effective** it cleaned well **2.** operative, in effect ○ *The regulation is effective immediately.*

effectiveness /ɪˈfektɪvnəs/ *noun* how well something works ○ *Ice covering reduces the effectiveness of an aerial.*

effective pitch /ɪˌfektɪv ˈpɪtʃ/ *noun* the distance the aircraft moves forward in flight for one 360° rotation of the propeller

efficiency /ɪˈfɪʃ(ə)nsi/ *noun* **1.** the fact of being able to act or produce something with a minimum of waste, expense, or unnecessary effort ○ *Efficiency is a key component of a successful business.* **2.** the ratio of the energy delivered by a machine to the energy supplied for its operation ○ *mechanical efficiency* ○ *propeller efficiency* □ **thermal efficiency** the efficiency of conversion of fuel energy to kinetic energy

efficient /ɪˈfɪʃ(ə)nt/ *adjective* able to act or produce something with a minimum of waste, expense, or unnecessary effort ○ *At some speeds and altitudes the pure jet engine is less efficient than a piston engine.* □ **efficient combustion** combustion in which fuel energy is used to its maximum capability

effort /ˈefət/ *noun* **1.** the use of physical or mental energy to do something ○ *In order to qualify for a licence, it is necessary to put some effort into the training course.* ○ *Flying a high performance aerobatic light aircraft to its limits requires a lot of physical effort on the part of the pilot.* **2.** force applied against inertia ○ *Actuators are capable of exerting low-speed turning effort.*

EFIS *abbreviation* electronic flight instrument system

eggbeater /ˈegbiːtə/ *noun* a rotary-wing aircraft (*informal*)

EGNOS *noun* a European system that improves the quality of data from existing satellite navigation systems to make the data suitable for use by aircraft. Full form **European Geostationary Navigation Overlay Service** (NOTE: The US equivalent is **WAAS**.)

EICAS *noun* a cockpit display for monitoring the engines and warning of malfunction. Full form **engine indicating and crew alerting system**

eject /ɪˈdʒekt/ *verb* to throw out forcefully ○ *On depressurisation the oxygen mask is ejected automatically from the service panel.*

ejection /ɪˈdʒekʃən/ *noun* an act of throwing out forcefully ○ *ejection seat*

ejection seat /ɪˈdʒekʃən siːt/, **ejector seat** /ɪˈdʒektə siːt/ *noun* an emergency escape seat in military aircraft which is fired out of the aircraft while the crew-member is still in it

ejector /ɪ'dʒektə/ *noun* **1.** a device to throw something out forcefully **2.** a device using a jet of water, air, or steam to withdraw a fluid or gas from a space ○ *A jet transfer pump or fuel ejector is used to transfer fuel.*

elapse /ɪ'læps/ *verb* to pass ○ *The radio altimeter works on the principle that, if the path followed by the radio wave is straight down and up, then the elapsed time between the outgoing and incoming signal is a function of the aircraft's height.*

elastic /ɪ'læstɪk/ *adjective* flexible, easily returning to its original shape after being stretched or expanded ○ *At low values of stress, if the plot of stress and strain is a straight line, this indicates that the material is elastic within this range.*

elasticity /ˌɪlæ'stɪsɪti/ *noun* the property of returning to an original form or state following deformation ○ *Titanium falls between aluminium and stainless steel in terms of elasticity, density and elevated temperature strength.*

electric /ɪ'lektrɪk/ *adjective* powered or worked by electricity

electrical /ɪ'lektrɪk(ə)l/ *adjective* **1.** referring to electricity ○ *an electrical fault* **2.** powered or worked by electricity ○ *Activation may be mechanical or electrical.*

electric current /ɪˌlektrɪk 'kʌrənt/ *noun* the mass movement of electric charge in a conductor

electricity /ɪˌlek'trɪsɪti/ *noun* an electric current used to provide light, heat, power

electric power /ɪˌlektrɪk 'paʊə/ *noun* electricity used to drive machines or devices

electro- /ɪ'lektrəʊ/ *prefix* electricity

electrode /ɪ'lektrəʊd/ *noun* a solid electrical conductor through which an electric current enters or leaves an electrolytic cell ○ *A battery has a positive and a negative electrode.*

electrolyte /ɪ'lektrəlaɪt/ *noun* a chemical compound that becomes con-

ductive when dissolved or molten ○ *The electrolyte in a lead-acid battery consists of sulphuric acid diluted with distilled water.*

electrolytic /ɪˌlektrə'lɪtɪk/ *adjective* ◻ **electrolytic cell** a cell consisting of electrodes in an electrolyte solution

electro-magnet /ɪˌlektrəʊ 'mægnɪt/ *noun* a magnet consisting of a coil of insulated wire wrapped around a soft iron core that is magnetised only when current flows through the wire

electro-magnetism /ɪˌlektrəʊ ˌmægnə'tɪz(ə)m/ *noun* a force exerted by a magnetic field found around any conductor carrying current, the strength of which will depend on the amount of current flow

electromotive force /ɪ ˌlektrəʊməʊtɪv 'fɔːs/ *noun* a source of electrical energy required to produce an electric current, produced by devices such as batteries or generators and measured in volts. Abbreviation **emf**

electron /ɪ'lektrɒn/ *noun* a subatomic particle that has a negative electrical charge ○ *Electrons in the outer orbits of an atom may not be strongly attracted to the nucleus and may be lost.*

electronic /ˌelek'trɒnɪk/ *adjective* referring to, based on, operated by, or involving the controlled conduction of electrons especially in a vacuum, gas, or semi-conducting material ○ *Lightning does not often seriously damage aircraft but it may affect sensitive electronic equipment.*

electronic centralised aircraft monitor /ˌelektrɒnɪk ˌsentrəlaɪzd 'eəkrɑːft ˌmɒnɪtə/ *noun* a display on two cathode ray tubes giving pilots engine and systems information. Abbreviation **ECAM**

electronic flight instrument system /ˌelektrɒnɪk 'flaɪt ˌɪnstrʊmənt ˌsɪstəm/ *noun* primary flight and navigation information on a cathode ray tube. Abbreviation **EFIS**

COMMENT: The electronic flight instrument system can show basic flight information and engine performance information, as well as moving maps and checklists.

element /'elɪmənt/ *noun* **1.** a substance composed of atoms with an identical number of protons in each nucleus ○ *Elements cannot be reduced to simpler substances by normal chemical methods.* **2.** the resistance coil in an electrical device such as a heater **3.** a removable component or removable part, such as in an air filter or oil filter

elevate /'elɪveɪt/ *verb* to move something to a higher place or position from a lower one; to lift ○ *In some light aircraft the magnetic compass is elevated to a position as far away from the interfering effect of other components as possible.*

elevated /'elə,veɪtɪd/ *adjective* □ **elevated temperature** increased or raised temperature

elevation /,elə'veɪʃ(ə)n/ *noun* the height at which something is above a point of reference such as the ground or sea level ○ *The highest point in a locality is marked by a dot with the elevation marked alongside.* □ **aerodrome elevation** distance in feet of the aerodrome above sea level ○ *Elevation is indicated on charts by means of contour lines, spot heights, etc.*

elevator /'elɪveɪtə/ *noun* **1.** a movable control surface, usually attached to the horizontal stabiliser of an aircraft, used to produce the nose up/down motion of an aircraft in level flight known as pitch ○ *Elevators should be checked for full and free movement immediately prior to take-off.* **2.** US same as **lift** *noun* 2

COMMENT: Some aircraft have an all-moving tailplane called a 'stabilator' (a combination of the words stabiliser and elevator).

eliminate /ɪ'lɪmɪneɪt/ *verb* to get rid of or remove ○ *Air dryers are provided to eliminate the possibility of ice forming.* ○ *To eliminate the need for complex mechanical linkage, the selector is operated electrically.* □ **to eliminate a danger** to remove a danger

ellipse /ɪ'lɪps/ *noun* an oval-shaped line ○ *Each planet moves in an ellipse and the sun is at one of the foci.*

elliptical /ɪ'lɪptɪk(ə)l/ *adjective* having an oval shape ○ *the elliptical path of the Earth around the sun*

ELR *abbreviation* **1.** environmental lapse rate **2.** extra long range (*ICAO*)

embarkation /,embɑː'keɪʃ(ə)n/ *noun* the act of going onto an aircraft ○ *Embarkation will start in ten minutes.* (NOTE: **Boarding** is usually preferred.) □ **embarkation time** the time at which passengers will be asked to go onto the aircraft

embed /ɪm'bed/ *verb* to fix firmly in a surrounding mass ○ *A temperature probe is embedded into the stator of the generator.* ○ *Water outlets have heater elements embedded in rubber seals in the outlet pipe.*

emergency /ɪ'mɜːdʒənsi/ *noun* a serious situation that happens unexpectedly and demands immediate action ○ *to deal with* or *to handle an emergency*

emergency descent /ɪ,mɜːdʒənsi dɪ'sent/ *noun* a planned rapid losing of altitude because of a serious situation

emergency equipment *noun* devices for use only in serious situations

emergency exit /ɪ,mɜːdʒənsi 'egzɪt/ *noun* a way out only to be used in case of an emergency ○ *How many emergency exits are there in the aircraft?*

emergency frequency /ɪ,mɜːdʒənsi 'friːkwənsi/ *noun* 121.5 MHz, the frequency on which aeronautical emergency radio calls are made

emergency landing /ɪ,mɜːdʒənsi 'lændɪŋ/ *noun* a landing made as a result of an in-flight emergency

emergency procedures *plural noun* a set of actions pre-planned and followed in the event of a serious situation

emergency services /ɪ'mɜːdʒənsi ,sɜːvɪsɪz/ *plural noun* the fire, ambulance and police services ○ *The alarm will activate the emergency services.*

emf *abbreviation* electromotive force

emission /ɪ'mɪʃ(ə)n/ *noun* **1.** the process of sending out e.g. matter, energy or signals ○ *light emissions* ○

radio emission ○ *One factor on which the operational range of a radio emission depends is the transmitted power.* **2.** a substance discharged into the air, as by an internal combustion engine ○ *Exhaust emissions contain pollutants.*

emit /ɪ'mɪt/ *verb* to send out e.g. matter, energy or radiation ○ *radiation emitted by the sun* ○ *An X-ray tube emits radiation.* ○ *Latent heat is emitted when condensation takes place.* (NOTE: **emitting – emitted**)

empennage /em'penɪdʒ/ *noun* the tail assembly of an aircraft ○ *The empennage usually includes the fin, rudder, horizontal stabiliser (or tailplane), and elevator.*

emphasis /'emfəsɪs/ *noun* force of expression that gives importance to something ○ *It is only in recent years that much emphasis has been placed on determining the causes of metal fatigue.*

emphasise /'emfəsaɪz/, **emphasize** *verb* to give importance to something ○ *On some maps, different elevations are emphasised by colouring.*

employ /ɪm'plɔɪ/ *verb* **1.** to use ○ *There are two methods employed to cool the cylinders down.* ○ *In some aircraft, particularly those employing nickel-cadmium batteries, temperature sensing devices are located within the batteries to provide a warning of high battery temperatures.* **2.** to give somebody regular paid work

empty weight /'empti weɪt/ the weight of a plane without fuel, people or freight

enable /ɪn'eɪb(ə)l/ *verb* to make something possible or easier ○ *Isolation valves are fitted to enable servicing and maintenance to be carried out.*

enclose /ɪn'kləʊz/ *verb* to surround on all sides ○ *The housing encloses the various mechanical parts.* ○ *Fuses form a weak link in a circuit and are usually made of a strip of tinned copper enclosed in a glass tube.*

encode /ɪn'kəʊd/ *verb* to put into code ○ *Weather information is encoded to allow large amounts of information to be given in a short space of time.*

encounter /ɪn'kaʊntə/ *verb* to meet something unexpected or unwanted ○ *Severe icing can be encountered in wave cloud.*

endurance /ɪn'djʊərəns/ *noun* the length of time an aircraft can stay in the air without refuelling ○ *The flight time to the PNR and back will equal the endurance of the aircraft.*

energy /'enədʒi/ *noun* **1.** the ability of a physical system to do work **2.** power from electricity, petrol, heat, etc. ○ *The engine converts heat energy into mechanical energy.* ○ *The generator converts mechanical energy into electrical energy.*

engage /ɪn'geɪdʒ/ *verb* **1.** to switch on and use ○ *The autopilot may be engaged during climb or descent.* Opposite **disengage 2.** □ **engaged in** working on a particular job or task ○ *Personnel engaged in ground running must ensure that any detachable clothing is securely fastened and they should wear acoustic ear muffs.*

engine /'endʒɪn/ *noun* a machine that converts energy into mechanical force or motion, different from an electric or hydraulic motor because of its use of a fuel ○ *jet engine* ○ *piston engine* ○ *internal combustion engine* ◊ **combustion, jet, piston** □ **engine-driven** referring to equipment and devices which take their power from the engine when it is running ○ *engine-driven generator* ○ *engine-driven pump* □ **engine running** engine operating or working □ **the engine is running** the engine is working ○ *The accident investigation demonstrated that the engine was running at full power when the aircraft hit the ground.*

COMMENT: In British usage, there is a clear distinction between the terms 'engine' and 'motor', the term 'motor' only being used for electric power units. In American usage, however, 'motor' is used for all types of power unit including the internal-combustion engine.

engine block /'endʒɪn blɒk/ *noun* a cylinder block with integral crankcase

engine capacity /'endʒɪn kə,'pæsɪtɪ/ *noun* the swept volume of an engine

engine compartment /'endʒɪn kəm,pɑːtmənt/ *noun* a space in the airframe where the engine is located

engineer /,endʒɪ'nɪə/ *noun* a person who is qualified to design, build and repair machines □ **aircraft engineer** an engineer who specialises in the maintenance and repair of aircraft

engineering /,endʒɪ'nɪərɪŋ/ *noun* the use of scientific and mathematical principles for practical reasons such as the design, manufacture, and operation of machines and systems, etc. □ **aircraft engineering** the branch of aviation concerned with the maintenance and repair of aircraft ○ *Reinforced plastics or composites are being used in aircraft engineering instead of metals because they are much lighter.*

engine failure /'endʒɪn ,feɪljə/ *noun* a situation in which an engine stops during running

engine indicating and crew alerting system /,endʒɪn ,ɪndɪkeɪtɪŋ ən 'kruː ə,lɜːtɪŋ ,sɪstəm/ *noun* full form of **EICAS**

engine instruments /'endʒɪn ,ɪnstrʊmənts/ *plural noun* instruments which give the pilot information about engine temperature, speed, etc.

engine intake /'endʒɪn ,ɪnteɪk/ *noun* the front part of the engine where air enters the engine

engine malfunction /'endʒɪn mæl,fʌŋkʃən/ *noun* a situation in which the engine does not work as it should

engine oil /'endʒɪn ɔɪl/ *noun* oil used especially to lubricate engines

engine performance /'endʒɪn pə'fɔːməns/ *noun* a description of how well the engine works or detailed statistical information about the capabilities of the engine

enhance /ɪn'hɑːns/ *verb* to make greater or better or clearer ○ *Chances of survival are enhanced if passengers know where the emergency exits are.*

'...any automation must be designed to enhance the decision making abilities of

the crew, not replace them' [*INTER PILOT*]

enhancement /ɪn'hɑːnsmənt/ *noun* the process of making greater, better or clearer □ **enhancement of an image on a screen** the improvement of an image on a screen

enlarge /ɪn'lɑːdʒ/ *verb* to make bigger or larger □ **enlarge the hole** make the hole bigger

enplane /en'pleɪn/ *verb* to board or allow somebody to board an aircraft

en route /,ɒn 'ruːt/ *adverb, adjective* on or along the way □ **en route from New York to London** on the way from New York to London □ **en route alternate** an airfield where it is possible to land if there is an in-flight problem □ **en route weather conditions** a description of the weather along the path of flight

ensure /ɪn'ʃʊə/ *verb* to make certain, to make sure ○ *The generator cut-out ensures that the battery cannot discharge.* ○ *Before the engine is stopped, it should normally be allowed to run for a short period at idling speed, to ensure gradual cooling.*

enter /'entə/ *verb* **1.** to come or go into ○ *Air enters at the front of the cabin and leaves at the rear.* **2.** to write down e.g. information ○ *Enter the rectified airspeed in the log.* ○ *Enter your name in the correct place in the form.* **3.** to put data into a computer, especially by using the keyboard to type it in ○ *Enter the data into the computer.*

entire /ɪn'taɪə/ *adjective* whole, having no part excluded or left out □ **the entire life of a thunderstorm** the complete life of a thunderstorm

entry /'entri/ *noun* **1.** the act or instance of going in ○ *the flow of traffic at entry points to the airfield.* **2.** the writing in of an item, as in a record or log ○ *An entry should be made in the technical log.*

entry point /'entri pɔɪnt/ *noun* a position on the ground above which an aircraft entering a control zone crosses the boundary

envelop /ɪn'veləp/ *verb* to surround and cover ○ *The atmosphere envelops the earth.*

envelope /ˈenvələʊp/ *noun* **1.** the set of limitations within which a technological system, especially an aircraft, can perform safely and effectively ○ *The boundaries of flight envelopes vary between aircraft categories and performance groups but in each case, there is a speed which must not be exceeded which is called the Vne (never-exceed speed).* **2.** a cover ○ *The atmosphere is the gaseous envelope surrounding the earth.*

environment /ɪnˈvaɪrənmənt/ *noun* **1.** nearby conditions or circumstances ○ *A body of air warmer than its environment will rise.* □ **a non-computer environment** a computer-free working situation **2.** the natural world in which people, animals and plants live ○ *People are interested in issues to do with the environment, such as global warming.*

environmental /ɪnˌvaɪrən ˈment(ə)l/ *adjective* referring to the immediate surroundings ○ *environmental conditions*

environmental control system /ɪnˌvaɪrənmənt(ə)l kənˈtrəʊl ˌsɪstəm/ *noun* an air-conditioning system for the aircraft. Abbreviation **ECS**

environmental lapse rate /ˌɪnvaɪrənmənt(ə)l ˈlæps ˌreɪt/ *noun* the rate at which the temperature of the air falls as one rises above the earth ○ *Although there is an average ELR of 1.98°C per 1,000 feet, in practice the ELR varies considerably with space and time.* Abbreviation **ELR**

epoxy-based primer /ɪˌpɒksi beɪst ˈpraɪmə/ *noun* a primer containing epoxy resin, a substance which, with the addition of hardeners, becomes very strong and hard after a time at normal temperatures

equal /ˈiːkwəl/ *adjective* having the same quantity, measure, or value as another ○ *For every action, there is an equal and opposite reaction.* ■ *verb* to be the same in value as ○ *Two plus two equals four (2 + 2 = 4).*

equalise /ˈiːkwəlaɪz/, **equalize** *verb* to become the same in quantity, measure or value ○ *Fluid pressure and gas pressure equalise at normal system pressure.*

equate /ɪˈkweɪt/ *verb* to be the same as ○ *In an electrical circuit, an increase in length equates to an increase in resistance.*

equation /ɪˈkweɪʒ(ə)n/ *noun* a statement, usually in symbols, that two quantities or mathematical expressions are equal ○ *X2 + Y2 = Z2.* ○ *The equation Vg = P can be used to find the geostrophic wind.*

equator /ɪˈkweɪtə/ *noun* the imaginary great circle around the Earth's surface, equidistant from the poles and perpendicular to the Earth's axis of rotation which divides the Earth into the northern hemisphere and the southern hemisphere ○ *Every point on the equator is equidistant from the poles.*

equatorial /ˌekwəˈtɔːriəl/ *adjective* referring to the equator or to conditions that exist at the Earth's equator ○ *equatorial heat* ○ *equatorial climate*

equilibrium /ˌiːkwɪˈlɪbriəm/ *noun* a state of physical balance ○ *When an aircraft is in unaccelerated straight and level flight at a constant speed, the forces of lift, thrust, weight and drag are in equilibrium.*

equipment /ɪˈkwɪpmənt/ *noun* devices, systems, machines, etc., that are needed for a particular purpose (NOTE: **Equipment** has no plural form; for one item say: *a piece of equipment.*) □ **electrical equipment** devices, components, systems, etc., which use electricity

equivalent /ɪˈkwɪvələnt/ *adjective* having the same purpose or value as something else ○ *The function of a logic gate is equivalent to that of a switch.* ○ *A metal part could be as much as 25 times heavier than an equivalent plastic part.*

equivalent shaft horsepower /ɪ ˌkwɪvələnt ʃɑːft ˈhɔːspaʊə/ *noun* the unit used for stating the total power of a turboprop engine, consisting of the **shaft horsepower** of the engine plus the thrust from the engine. Abbreviation **ESHP**

error /'erə/ *noun* **1.** a mistake or incorrect calculation ○ *an error in somebody's work* ○ *errors caused by location* **2.** the known inaccuracy of an instrument or system which has to be corrected by calculating the true value

escape /ɪ'skeɪp/ *noun* the act of getting away from or out of a place after being held □ **escape of fuel or oil** unwanted loss of fuel or oil □ **escape from danger** getting to a safe place ▪ *verb* to get away from or out of after being held ○ *If there is a hole in the fuselage of a pressurised aircraft, air escapes from the cabin to the atmosphere.*

escape hatch /ɪ'skeɪp hætʃ/ *noun* a small doorway only used in emergencies

escape route /ɪ'skeɪp ruːt/ *noun* the passengers' way out of an aircraft after an emergency landing

escape slide /ɪ'skeɪp slaɪd/ *noun* a device which allows passengers to exit the aircraft safely in an emergency, when no steps are available

ESHP *abbreviation* equivalent shaft horsepower

essential /ɪ'senʃəl/ *adjective* absolutely necessary ○ *Teamwork within the crew is essential.* ○ *A knowledge of the tropopause is essential.* □ **non-essential** not necessary

EST *abbreviation* **1.** Eastern Standard Time **2.** estimate (*ICAO*) **3.** estimated (*ICAO*)

establish /ɪ'stæblɪʃ/ *verb* **1.** to be confirmed as stable in a particular flight condition, such as a flight level or glideslope, etc. ○ *Once established on the downwind leg, the pilot should perform the checks.* **2.** to work out or to calculate □ **establish your position** find out where you are **3.** to position ○ *Low-power NDBs (Non-Directional Radio Beacons) are often established at the outer or middle marker sites.* **4.** □ **to establish communication** to make contact with □ **to establish control** to get control

estimate /'estɪmeɪt/ *verb* **1.** to calculate approximately the cost, value or size of something ○ *I estimate that it will take about two hours for us to reach our destination.* ○ *Cloud heights may be measured or estimated.* **2.** to form a judgement about □ **to estimate the chances of something** to weigh the possibilities and form an opinion

estimated take-off time /ˌestɪmeɪtɪd 'teɪk ɒf ˌtaɪm/ *noun* the time when an aircraft is expected to take off. Abbreviation **ETOT**

estimated time of arrival /ˌestɪmeɪtɪd ˌtaɪm əv ə'raɪv(ə)l/ *noun* the time when an aircraft is expected to arrive. Abbreviation **ETA**

estimated time of departure /ˌestɪmətɪd ˌtaɪm əv dɪ'pɑːtʃə/ *noun* the time when an aircraft is expected to take off. Abbreviation **ETD**

estimation /ˌestɪ'meɪʃ(ə)n/ *noun* **1.** an approximate calculation ○ *an estimation of ground speed* ○ *Estimation of visibility is achieved by noting the distances at which lights of known candle power can be observed and relating these distances to visibility-by-day values.* **2.** an opinion □ **in my estimation** in my opinion

ETA *abbreviation* estimated time of arrival

ETD *abbreviation* estimated time of departure

ETOT *abbreviation* estimated take-off time

Eurocontrol /'jʊərəʊkən,trəʊl/ *noun* the European organisation for the safety of air navigation (NOTE: Eurocontrol operates the ATC centre at Maastricht in the Netherlands and the Central Flow Management Unit in Brussels.)

European Geostationary Navigation Overlay Service /ˌjʊərəpiən ˌdʒiːəʊsteɪʃ(ə)n(ə)ri ˌnævɪgeɪʃ(ə)n 'əʊvələɪ ˌsɜːvɪs/ *noun* full form of **EGNOS**

evacuate /ɪ'vækjueɪt/ *verb* **1.** to remove all the people from somewhere in the event of an emergency ○ *to evacuate all passengers from the airport* **2.** to empty somewhere of all people in it because of an emergency ○ *to evacuate the aircraft* **3.** to create a vacuum □

evacuate a glass jar remove all the air from a glass jar

evacuation /ɪˌvækjuˈeɪʃ(ə)n/ *noun* **1.** the act of removing all people from somewhere in the event of an emergency ○ *The evacuation of the passengers from the airport was not ordered.* **2.** an act of emptying somewhere of all people in it because of an emergency ○ *The evacuation of the aircraft did not take long.* □ **evacuation command** an evacuation order from the captain □ **ditching evacuation** an evacuation after the aircraft has force-landed on water

evaluate /ɪˈvæljueɪt/ *verb* to examine and judge carefully ○ *Deposits of ice are detected and continuously evaluated to operate a warning system.*

evaluation /ɪˌvæljuˈeɪʃ(ə)n/ *noun* the examination and judgement of something ○ *The ice detector system provides continuous evaluation of conditions conducive to the formation of ice.*

evaporate /ɪˈvæpəreɪt/ *verb* to convert or change a liquid into a vapour ○ *In the heat of the day, water evaporates from the surface of the earth.* Opposite **condense**

evaporation /ɪˌvæpəˈreɪʃ(ə)n/ *noun* the changing of a liquid into vapour, vaporisation ○ *Carburettor icing can be caused by the expansion of gases in the carburettor and the evaporation of liquid fuel.*

even /ˈiːv(ə)n/ *adjective* **1.** flat or smooth, with no bumps or dents **2.** the same in all parts of an area or over a whole surface ○ *an even distribution of passengers* ○ *an even application of paint* **3.** □ **even numbers** exactly divisible by 2, e.g. 4, 6, 20 ■ *adverb* **1.** yet more ○ *It will be even higher than the new building.* □ **even faster** not just as fast as, but more **2.** □ **even if** whether or not ○ *Stop at the holding point even if there are no other aircraft on the approach.* □ **even though** in spite of the fact that ○ *He gained his private pilot's licence even though he was 73 years old.*

event /ɪˈvent/ *noun* a happening ○ *The Paris air show is a major event.* □ **in the event of** if something should happen ○ *Passengers should fasten their seat belts in the event of turbulence.* □ **in the event of main pump failure** if there should be a failure of the main pump □ **in the event of fire** if there should be a fire

eventual /ɪˈventʃuəl/ *adjective* happening at an unspecified time in the future ○ *Water in the fuel may lead to eventual engine stoppage.*

eventually /ɪˈventʃuəli/ *adverb* at an unspecified time in the future ○ *Vapour cools and eventually condenses.*

evidence /ˈevɪd(ə)ns/ *noun* an outward sign □ **external evidence of cracks** something which can be seen on the surface which suggests that there is a deeper structural problem ○ *Deformed wing panels may be evidence of an over-stressed airframe.*

evident /ˈevɪd(ə)nt/ *adjective* obvious, easily seen or understood ○ *It is evident from the information available that language problems played a part in the cause of the accident.* □ **self-evident** clear in itself, without further explanation

exact /ɪɡˈzækt/ *adjective* completely accurate or correct ○ *The exact fuel flow and pressure is adjusted.* □ **the calculation is not exact** the calculation is not 100% correct

exactly /ɪɡˈzæktli/ *adverb* **1.** accurately, correctly ○ *Measure the quantity exactly.* **2.** absolutely, completely ○ *A fuel injection system performs exactly the same function as a carburettor.*

examination /ɪɡˌzæmɪˈneɪʃ(ə)n/ *noun* **1.** a set of questions or exercises testing knowledge or skill ○ *The examination includes a flight plan.* **2.** □ **medical examination** medical check-up **3.** a careful observation or inspection ○ *the examination of a faulty component*

'…the pilot of a Grumman Cheetah refused to be breathalysed, and was taken to a police station for examination by a police surgeon, who confirmed that he had been drinking' [*Pilot*]

examine /ɪgˈzæmɪn/ *verb* **1.** to find out how much knowledge or skill somebody possesses by means of questions or exercises ○ *Students will be examined in four subjects.* **2.** to test or check the condition or health of somebody ○ *to examine a patient* **3.** to study or analyse something ○ *to examine charts*

exceed /ɪkˈsiːd/ *verb* to be greater than ○ *Vertical velocity of updraughts can exceed 50 kt.*

exception /ɪkˈsepʃən/ *noun* something or somebody not included □ **an exception to the rule** an example which does not conform to a general rule □ **with the exception of** not including □ **with the exception of Smith, all the students passed their exams** Smith did not pass, but the other students did

exceptional /ɪkˈsepʃən(ə)l/ *adjective* **1.** being an exception, uncommon □ **in exceptional circumstances** in unusual circumstances **2.** well above average, extraordinary □ **an exceptional pilot** a very good pilot

excess /ɪkˈses/ *noun* an amount or quantity beyond what is normal or sufficient □ **excess power** the difference between horsepower available and horsepower required □ **in excess of** more than □ **a height in excess of 50,000 feet** a height greater than 50,000 feet

excess baggage /ˌekses ˈbæɡɪdʒ/ *noun* an amount, usually expressed as weight, of baggage which exceeds the airline's limit per passenger

excessive /ɪkˈsesɪv/ *adjective* more than the normal, usual, reasonable, or proper limit ○ *Excessive use of power when taxiing will require excessive use of brakes.*

exchange /ɪksˈtʃeɪndʒ/ *verb* to give in return for something received ○ *Meteorological stations exchange information with other meteorological stations.*

excitation /ˌeksɪˈteɪʃ(ə)n/ *noun* the act of supplying a small current to the windings of larger electrical motors, etc. ○ *Pilot excitation consists of a pilot exciter and a main exciter, to provide*

the direct current for the motor of the alternating current generator.

exciter /ɪkˈsaɪtə/ *noun* the source of a small current to supply electrical current to the windings of larger electrical motors, etc., e.g. a battery ○ *Pilot excitation consists of a pilot exciter and a main exciter, to provide the direct current for the motor of the alternating current generator.*

exclude /ɪkˈskluːd/ *verb* to keep out, to prevent from entering ○ *Joints and interfaces should exclude moisture and improve fatigue life.*

exercise /ˈeksəsaɪz/ *noun* an activity that requires physical or mental effort or practice ○ *a classroom exercise* ○ *Swimming is good physical exercise for people such as pilots who spend a lot of time sitting down.* ■ *verb* to use or to put into play or operation ○ *Student pilots must exercise special care when landing in a strong crosswind.*

exert /ɪgˈzɜːt/ *verb* □ **to exert a force** to put a force on something ○ *Pressure is the force per unit area exerted by the atmosphere on a given surface area.* □ **to exert an influence** to have an influence □ **to exert pressure** to put pressure onto something

exhaust /ɪgˈzɔːst/ *noun* **1.** the escape or release of vaporous waste material from an engine **2.** a pipe through which waste gases pass out of the engine ○ *The exhaust valve opens to allow for the exit of exhaust gases.* ■ *verb* to consume or use up all of something ○ *Supplies of fuel are exhausted.* (NOTE: **To run out** is less formal.)

exhaust gas /ɪgˈzɔːst ɡæs/ *noun* gas which is the product of the combustion process and which is passed out through the exhaust system ○ *Exhaust gases contain carbon monoxide.*

exhaust system /ɪgˈzɔːst ˌsɪstəm/ *noun* a system of pipes, silencers, etc., which carry exhaust gases from the engine to a point where they are released into the atmosphere

exhaust valve /ɪgˈzɔːst vælv/ *noun* a valve in a piston engine which allows exhaust gases to leave the cylinder

exhibit /ɪgˈzɪbɪt/ *verb* to have or to display ○ *Composites, due to their construction, exhibit good fatigue behaviour.* ○ *Altocumulus are (usually) white layers or patches of cloud frequently exhibiting a waved appearance.*

exist /ɪgˈzɪst/ *verb* to be present under particular circumstances or in a specified place ○ *Water can exist in the atmosphere in three forms.* ○ *A fire risk may exist following failure or leakage of any component.*

existence /ɪgˈzɪstəns/ *noun* the fact or state of being ○ *Warning systems are provided to give an indication of a possible failure or the existence of a dangerous condition.*

exit /ˈegzɪt/ *noun* **1.** the act of going out of a place ○ *The exhaust valve opens to allow for the exit of exhaust gases.* □ **exit velocity** the velocity of exhaust gases from a jet engine **2.** a way out

exit nozzle /ˈeksɪt ˌnɒz(ə)l/ *noun* a pipe or opening through which exhaust gases leave a jet engine

exit point /ˈeksɪt pɔɪnt/ *noun* a position on the ground above which an aircraft leaving a control zone crosses the boundary

expand /ɪkˈspænd/ *verb* to increase in size, volume or quantity, to enlarge ○ *Air expands when heated and contracts when cooled.*

expansion /ɪkˈspænʃən/ *noun* an increase in size, volume or quantity ○ *There is an expansion of the gas when it is heated.*

expansion chamber /ɪkˈspænʃən ˌtʃeɪmbə/ *noun* a container which allows for expansion of a fluid caused by increase in temperature, etc.

expect /ɪkˈspekt/ *verb* to hope or to assume that something is going to happen ○ *the weather to be expected along a route* ○ *We expect flight AC 309 within ten minutes.* □ **as might be expected** as people think would happen

'...by 1959 there were some 40 pilots past age 60 flying the line with the number expected to rise to 250 within the next few years' [*INTER PILOT*]

expected /ɪkˈspektɪd/ *adjective* being thought or hoped to be taking place ○ *the expected number of passengers*

expected approach time /ɪk ˌspektɪd əˈprəʊtʃ ˌtaɪm/ the time at which air traffic control expects an arriving aircraft to complete its approach for landing, following a delay. Abbreviation **EAT**

expedite /ˈekspɪdaɪt/ *verb* to speed up the progress of □ **to expedite the evacuation** to speed up the evacuation □ **to expedite the disembarkation** to get the passengers off the aircraft quickly

expel /ɪkˈspel/ *verb* to force out, to drive out ○ *Exhaust gases are expelled from the cylinder by the upward movement of the piston.* ○ *The piston draws fluid into the cylinders on the outward stroke and expels fluid into the system on the inward stroke.*

experience /ɪkˈspɪəriəns/ *noun* **1.** the building up of knowledge or skill over a period of time by an active participation in events or activities ○ *a pilot with 20 years' experience* **2.** an event or incident ○ *The first solo is an experience most pilots never forget.* ■ *verb* to undergo, participate in or find oneself in a particular situation ○ *It is not unusual to experience traffic delays on the ground prior to departure.* ○ *Turbulence can be experienced when flying through a trough.*

experiment *noun* /ɪkˈsperɪmənt/ a scientific test, carried out under controlled conditions, that is made to demonstrate or discover something ○ *Experiments have shown that left-handed people often have better hand/eye coordination than right handed people.* □ **to conduct an experiment** to perform an experiment ■ *verb* /ɪkˈsperɪment/ □ **to experiment (with)** to carry out a scientific test under controlled conditions in order to demonstrate or discover something

experimental /ɪkˌsperɪˈment(ə)l/ *adjective* referring to something still at an early stage of development, not tried and tested ○ *the experimental and testing stages of a new type of aircraft.* □ **an experimental aircraft** an aircraft designed to be used for experimental purposes ○ *The experimental aircraft were used to investigate high-speed flight.*

explanatory /ɪkˈsplænət(ə)ri/ *adjective* referring to something which explains □ **explanatory paragraph** a paragraph of text which explains something □ **self-explanatory** something which does not need any further explanation

explosion /ɪkˈspləʊʒ(ə)n/ *noun* **1.** a release of energy in a sudden and often violent way ○ *an explosion caused by a bomb* **2.** an act of bursting as a result of internal pressure ○ *tyre explosion due to overheating* **3.** the loud sound made as a result of an explosion ○ *The passengers heard an explosion.*

explosive /ɪkˈspləʊsɪv/ *adjective* referring to something having the nature of an explosion □ **an explosive effect** having the effect of an explosion ■ *noun* a substance, especially a prepared chemical, that explodes or causes explosions, e.g. Semtex

expose /ɪkˈspəʊz/ *verb* to uncover something or leave something uncovered so that it is not protected from something such as rain or sunlight ○ *When the slope of a hill is exposed to solar radiation, wind currents are set up.* □ **exposed to the sun** in sunlight without covering □ **exposed surface** a surface without paint or covering of any sort

exposure /ɪkˈspəʊʒə/ *noun* **1.** the fact of being exposed, especially to severe weather or other forces of nature ○ *After 24 hours in the sea, she was suffering from the effects of exposure and was taken to hospital.* **2.** the fact of being subjected to something ○ *Exposure to radio-active substances may cause cancer.*

express /ɪkˈspres/ *verb* to put into words, symbols or signs ○ *Bearings may be expressed as true or relative.* ○ *An angle may be expressed in degrees, minutes and seconds.* ○ *Pressure altitudes are expressed in hundreds of feet.*

extend /ɪkˈstend/ *verb* to stretch or spread from one point to another in space or time ○ *Air from the Gulf of Mexico can extend into Canada.* ○ *Cumulonimbus clouds may extend to over 50,000 ft.* □ **to extend the duration of something** to prolong the time ○ *The visit was extended to allow time for more discussions.*

extensive /ɪkˈstensɪv/ *adjective* large in range or amount □ **an extensive area** a large area □ **extensive cloud** a lot of cloud □ **extensive use is made of** much use is made of

extent /ɪkˈstent/ *noun* a range or amount of something ○ *The horizontal extent of the cloud averages about 50 km.* ○ *Clouds of great vertical extent are not uncommon.* □ **to a certain extent, to some extent** partly ○ *The accident was caused, to a certain extent, by the poor weather.* □ **to a lesser extent** not as much as something previously stated ○ *The cloud types which are most likely to affect flying conditions in terms of icing, precipitation and turbulence are cumulus, cumulonimbus and, to a lesser extent, nimbostratus.*

external /ɪkˈstɜːn(ə)l/ *adjective* referring to, existing on, or connected with the outside or an outer part ○ *The only external force acting on air is gravity.* Opposite **internal** □ **external appearance** the appearance of something from the outside

external ambient pressure /ɪkˌstɜːn(ə)l ˌæmbiənt ˈpreʃə/ *noun* pressure outside the aircraft

extinguish /ɪkˈstɪŋgwɪʃ/ *verb* to put out ○ *The fire services extinguished the fire.*

extinguisher /ɪkˈstɪŋgwɪʃə/ *noun* a portable mechanical device for spraying and putting out a fire with chemicals ○ *Hand-operated fire extinguishers are provided to combat any outbreaks of fire in the flight crew compartment and passengers' cabins.*

extract *noun* /ˈekstrækt/ a part taken from a longer text ○ *The following paragraph is an extract from a flight manual.* ■ *verb* /ɪkˈstrækt/ **1.** to obtain from a substance by chemical or mechanical action ○ *A dehumidifier extracts moisture from the atmosphere.* **2.** to take out or to obtain information from something ○ *Extract the important information from a text.*

extrapolate /ɪkˈstræpəleɪt/ *verb* to estimate by using known facts ○ *Information given on a synoptic chart can be extrapolated, by the use of some simple guidelines.*

extreme /ɪkˈstriːm/ *adjective* **1.** most distant in any direction, the outermost or farthest ○ *the most extreme point on the map* **2.** to the greatest or highest degree, very great □ **extreme care must be taken** the greatest care must be taken □ **extreme difficulty** great difficulty ■ *noun* either of the two things, values, situations, etc., situated at opposite ends of a range ○ *the extremes of boiling and freezing* ○ *The region experiences extremes of temperature.*

eye /aɪ/ *noun* an organ in the head which lets you see. ◊ **coordination**, **vision**

F

F *symbol* **1.** Fahrenheit **2.** farad

FAA *abbreviation US* Federal Aviation Administration

fabric /ˈfæbrɪk/ *noun* material or cloth produced especially by knitting or weaving ○ *A breathing mask has a fabric carrying bag.*

fabricate /ˈfæbrɪkeɪt/ *verb* to make or manufacture ○ *Selected wing panels are fabricated entirely from magnesium alloys.* ○ *The ease with which aluminium can be fabricated into any form is one of its most important qualities.*

face /feɪs/ *noun* **1.** the surface of an object ○ *the face of the earth* ○ *The exhaust cone prevents the hot gases from flowing across the rear face of the turbine disc.* □ **the north face of the mountain** the vertical or near-vertical side facing north **2.** the front part with dial, indicators, etc. ○ *the face of an instrument* □ **the face of a clock** the front part of the clock with numbers **3.** the front of the head, including the eyes, nose, mouth □ **full face smoke mask** a protective mask for fighting fires which covers the whole face ■ *verb* to be turned towards a particular direction ○ *Hills and mountains which face the sun receive more intense radiation.* □ **the building faces north** the building has its front towards the north

facilitate /fəˈsɪlɪteɪt/ *verb* to enable something to happen more easily or quickly ○ *A ramp is used to facilitate access to the wing.* ○ *Clearly marked exits facilitate rapid evacuation of passengers.*

facility /fəˈsɪlɪti/ *noun* **1.** ability or ease in moving, acting, or doing something □ **a facility in learning to fly** a good natural ability for flying **2.** an installation or building which provides specific operating assistance ○ *DME (Distance Measuring Equipment) ground facility* **3.** a mode of operation which allows the user of equipment to do something ○ *The printer has a self-test facility.* **4.** □ **facilities** things, especially buildings or equipment, that people can use □ **a clubhouse with good facilities** a clubhouse with a number of features which can be used by members and guests, e.g. restaurant, bar, reading room, swimming pool □ **medical facilities** hospitals, clinics, etc.

facsimile /fækˈsɪmɪli/ *noun* same as **fax**

fact /fækt/ *noun* information presented as real ○ *Temperature changes are an important fact in meteorology.* □ **in (point of) fact** in reality, in truth

factor /ˈfæktə/ *noun* **1.** an important part of a result, a process, etc. ○ *Visibility remains a very important factor in aviation.* □ **critical factor** extremely important factor □ **dominant factor** most important factor □ **safety factor** something which plays an important part in safety **2.** □ **by a factor of** quantity by which a stated quantity is multiplied or divided, so as to indicate an increase or decrease in a measurement □ **by a factor of ten** ten times ○ *The rate is increased by a factor of 10.* □ **conversion factor** a formula or figure used for conversion of temperatures, distances, etc., from one system to another ○ *The conversion factor for converting UK gallons to litres is: x 4.546.*

fade /feɪd/ *noun* **1.** a periodic reduction in the received strength of a radio transmission ○ *Surface wave at night causes fade of the signal.* **2.** a periodic reduction in braking power ○ *Hard braking can cause fade and tyre burst through overheating.* ■ *verb* to lose strength, brightness, loudness, or brilliance gradually □ **the lights faded** the lights became less and less bright, the lights dimmed □ **the radio signal faded** the radio signal became weaker and weaker

Fahrenheit /ˈfærənhaɪt/ *noun* a scale of temperatures where the freezing and boiling points of water are 32° and 212° respectively. Compare **Celsius, centigrade** (NOTE: Used in the USA but now less common in the UK; usually written as an **F** after the degree sign: **32° F.**)

fail /feɪl/ *verb* **1.** to stop working properly □ **the brakes failed** the brakes did not work □ **the wing failed during a high-speed turn** the wing broke during a high-speed turn **2.** to receive an academic grade below the acceptable minimum in an examination or a course of study □ **the trainee failed his navigation examination** the trainee did not pass her navigation exam □ **without fail** certainly, definitely ○ *Be here at 8 o'clock without fail.*

fail safe /ˈfeɪl seɪf/ *noun* the principle of designing a structure so that the failure of one part does not affect the safety of the whole

fail safe system /ˈfeɪl seɪf ˌsɪstəm/ *noun* a system or device which has in-built safeguards against total failure ○ *The term fail safe means that the structure, though damaged, is capable of supporting a reasonable percentage of its design load.*

failure /ˈfeɪljə/ *noun* **1.** a stoppage or a breakdown ○ *bearing failure* ○ *Engine failure is sometimes accompanied by fire.* □ **power failure** loss of engine power, or loss of electrical power supply **2.** the fact of not achieving the desired goal or result ○ *the failure of an experiment* □ **failure to do something** not doing something ○ *The steward's failure to remain at his station made the*

emergency situation worse. **3.** the fact of not passing a course, a test, or an examination ○ *His failure in the GFT (General Flying Test) meant that he didn't finish the course.*

fair /feə/ *adjective* **1.** free of clouds or storms, clear and sunny □ **fair weather** good weather **2.** just, reasonable, free of favouritism or bias □ **a fair exam** an exam which tested students on what they had been taught, was of reasonable difficulty and duration and which did not trick the candidates □ **it is fair to say that he should have done better** it is reasonable to say that he should have done better ■ *verb* to join pieces so as to be smooth, even, or regular ○ *The aircraft's wing is faired into the fuselage.*

fairing /ˈfeərɪŋ/ *noun* a device to improve the flow of air over a surface ○ *There is a dorsal fairing at the base of the fin or vertical stabiliser.* ○ *Wheel fairings, called spats, are fitted to light aircraft to reduce drag.* ◊ **spat, nacelle**

fairly /ˈfeəli/ *adverb* moderately, rather, quite □ **fairly high levels** moderately high levels □ **fairly simple** moderately simple

fall /fɔːl/ *noun* **1.** a drop or lessening in amount □ **fall in pressure** a drop in pressure **2.** the amount of rain or snow which comes down at any one time ○ *an overnight fall of snow* **3.** *US* autumn ■ *verb* **1.** to become less in amount □ **atmospheric pressure is falling** atmospheric pressure is decreasing **2.** to be included within the range of something ○ *Aircraft fall into a number of type categories.* ○ *Design methods fall into four groups.* ○ *Long-range high-frequency communications fall in the frequency bracket 2–25 MHz.* **3.** to drop or come down freely because of gravity ○ *Light rain may fall occasionally.* **4.** to occur at a particular time ○ *New Year's Day falls on a Thursday this year.* (NOTE: **falling – fell – fallen**)

false /fɔːls/ *adjective* not true, incorrect ○ *Lightning may cause false readings from sensitive instruments.* □ **false glide path information** incorrect glide path information

familiar /fəˈmɪliə/ *adjective* **1.** often seen, common ○ *Clouds are the most familiar visible meteorological feature.* **2.** known ○ *Symbols and abbreviations which are strange at present become familiar after a time.* □ **to be familiar with** to have some knowledge of something ○ *He is familiar with the procedure.*

familiarise /fəˈmɪliəraɪz/, **familiarize** *verb* □ **to familiarise yourself with** to get to know something well

fan /fæn/ *noun* a circular device with rotating blades, powered by an engine or motor, for moving a gas such as air ○ *The compressor has large rotating fan blades and stator blades.*

fanjet /ˈtɜːbəʊfæn/ *noun* US same as **turbofan**

FANS *abbreviation* future air navigation systems

FAR *abbreviation* US Federal Aviation Regulation

farad /ˈfæræd/ *noun* the SI unit of capacitance. Symbol **F**

fasten /ˈfɑːs(ə)n/ *verb* to secure or to close, as by fixing firmly in place □ **fasten your seat belt** put on and attach your seat belt ○ *If in-flight conditions require the captain to activate the fasten seat belt sign, all cabin service ceases and cabin crew take up their assigned seats and strap in.*

fatigue /fəˈtiːg/ *noun* **1.** physical or mental tiredness resulting from exertion ○ *Pilot fatigue was a contributing factor in the accident.* **2.** the weakening or failure of a material such as metal, resulting from stress ○ *Fan blades must be resistant to fatigue and thermal shock.* ○ *Titanium has good fatigue resistance.* □ **fatigue crack** crack due to material fatigue

fault /fɔːlt/ *noun* a defect in a circuit or wiring caused by bad connections, etc. ○ *A fault in the automatic boost control unit was repaired.*

faulty /ˈfɔːlti/ *adjective* containing a fault or defect, imperfect ○ *The faulty component was replaced.*

fax /fæks/ *noun* **1.** an exact copy of a document, drawing, etc., transmitted and received by a fax machine connected to a telephone link **2.** an electronic apparatus linked to a telephone used to send and receive a fax ○ *Charts are transmitted by fax to meteorological offices.* ◊ **CAMFAX** ■ *verb* to send a fax ○ *Charts are faxed to meteorological offices.*

FDPS *abbreviation* flight data processing system

FDR *abbreviation* flight data recorder

FDS *abbreviation* flight director system

feather /ˈfeðə/ *verb* □ **to feather a propeller** to turn the blades of a stopped propeller edge on to the airflow in order to reduce drag or wind resistance ○ *The feathered position not only reduces drag, but also minimises engine rotation, thus preventing any additional damage to the engine.*

feathering /ˈfeðərɪŋ/ *noun* the act of turning the blades of a stopped propeller edge on to the airflow in order to reduce drag ○ *Feathering is accomplished by moving the pilot's control lever.*

feathering gate /ˈfeðərɪŋ geɪt/ *noun* a device on the propeller pitch control to prevent unwanted selection of the feathering position

feathering position /ˈfeðərɪŋ pə ˌzɪʃ(ə)n/ *noun* a position of the propeller pitch control in which the blades are feathered

feature /ˈfiːtʃə/ *noun* **1.** an important, noticeable or distinctive aspect, quality, or characteristic ○ *Sea breeze is a regular feature of coastal climates.* **2.** □ **ground features** noticeable, important objects in the landscape which are useful aids to navigation, e.g. bridges, rivers, railway lines, etc. ■ *verb* to have as a particular characteristic ○ *Many Rutan designs feature a canard wing.*

Federal Aviation Administration /ˌfed(ə)rəl ˌeɪviˈeɪʃ(ə)n ˌædmɪnɪstreɪʃ(ə)n/ *noun* the body responsible for the regulation of aviation in the United States ○ *The FAA issues licenses.* Abbreviation **FAA**

Federal Aviation Regulation /ˌfed(ə)rəl ˌeɪvieɪʃ(ə)n ˌregjʊ

'leɪʃ(ə)n/ *noun* a regulation governing aviation in the United States. Abbreviation **FAR**

feed /fiːd/ *noun* a supply of fuel, energy, etc. provided for use

feedback /'fiːdbæk/ *noun* **1.** the return of part of the output of a process or system to the input, especially when used to maintain performance or to control a system ○ *The LC ensures that a feedback signal of the monitored output frequency is sent back to the CSDU.* **2.** a feedback mechanism

ferry /'feri/ *verb* to make a delivery of an aircraft by flying it to its operator

fibre /'faɪbə/ *noun* a natural or synthetic filament like cotton or nylon (NOTE: The US English is **fiber.**)

FIC *abbreviation* flight information centre

field /fiːld/ *noun* **1.** an area of grass on farmland, in the countryside ○ *In the event of a power failure, it is important to select the most suitable field for a forced landing.* **2.** an imaginary area

field of vision /ˌfiːld əv 'vɪʒ(ə)n/ *noun* the area in which something can be seen without moving the head or the eyes

fighter /'faɪtə/ *noun* small, single-seat or two-seat aircraft for use in military conflict ○ *The F16 is an American-built fighter.*

figure /'fɪgə/ *noun* **1.** a diagram or drawing ○ *Figure 1 shows a cross-section of an internal combustion engine.* **2.** a number, especially in mathematical calculations □ **a head for figures** good at figures, arithmetic, accounting, etc. □ **a two-figure code** a code with two numbers between 0 and 9 **3.** a form consisting of any combination of points or lines, e.g. a triangle

film /fɪlm/ *noun* **1.** a thin skin or layer ○ *An electrical element made of gold film is sandwiched between the layers of glass.* **2.** a thin covering or coating ○ *There is a film of oil between the piston and cylinder wall.*

filter /'fɪltə/ *noun* **1.** a material or device through which a liquid or a gas is passed in order to separate the fluid from solid matter or to remove

unwanted substances ○ *fuel filter* ○ *oil filter* **2.** an electric, electronic, acoustic, or optical device used to reject signals, vibrations, or radiations of particular frequencies while passing others ○ *The tuner is a band pass filter which confines the bandwidth passed to the receiver to that required.* ■ *verb* to pass a liquid or gas through a filter in order to remove unwanted substances ○ *Fuel is filtered before entering the carburettor.*

filter cartridge /'fɪltə ˌkɑːtrɪdʒ/ *noun* same as **filter element**

filter element /'fɪltə ˌelɪmənt/ *noun* a removable paper or metal component in a filter housing which must be replaced periodically ○ *From time to time the filter element must be removed and cleaned or replaced.* Also called **filter cartridge**

fin /fɪn/ *noun* a fixed vertical aerofoil at the rear of a plane, the vertical stabiliser ○ *The fin provides directional stability about the vertical axis.* Also called **vertical stabiliser**

final /'faɪn(ə)l/ *noun* the end part of a series or process ■ *adjective* coming at the end □ **final assembly** the last in a series of stages of construction of an aircraft when all the pre-assembled parts are put together

final approach /ˌfaɪn(ə)l ə'prəʊtʃ/ *noun* **1.** a flight path in a direction along the extended centre line of the runway on which a plane is about to land ○ *The aspect of the runway on final approach helps the pilot to judge height and progress.* **2.** the last stage of an aircraft's descent before landing, from when it turns into line with the runway to the procedures immediately before it lands

fine /faɪn/ *adjective* **1.** of superior quality, skill, or appearance □ **a fine day** a day when the weather is good □ **fine weather** good weather **2.** very small in size, thickness or weight ○ *Cirrus cloud has a fine, hair-like appearance.* □ **fine powder** powder consisting of very small particles □ **fine spray** a spray consisting of very small drops of liquid **3.** □ **fine wire** very thin wire **4.** referring to the pitch or blade angle setting of the propeller ○ *Fine pitch enables full engine speed to be used on take-off and coarse pitch allows an economical engine speed to be used for cruising.*

FIR *abbreviation* flight information region

fire /faɪə/ *noun* an area of burning ○ *To guard against the risk of fire, passengers are requested not to smoke in the toilets.* □ **an engine fire** a fire in an engine ■ *verb* to shoot a gun, or to launch something such as a flare or a rocket

fire deluge system /ˌfaɪə ˈdeljuːdʒ ˌsɪstəm/ *noun* a system which extinguishes fire by spraying large quantities of water on it ○ *A lever actuates the fire deluge system.*

fire detection system /ˌfaɪə dɪˈtekʃən ˌsɪstəm/ *noun* a system to detect the presence of fire in an aircraft

fire extinguisher /ˈfaɪər ɪkˌstɪŋgwɪʃə/ *noun* a portable device full of foam, water, powder, etc., for putting out fires

fireproof /ˈfaɪəpruːf/ *adjective* designed to resist the effect of fire ○ *A fireproof bulkhead is provided to separate the cool area of the engine from the hot area.*

fire triangle /ˈfaɪə ˌtraɪæŋgəl/ *noun* the illustration of the chemistry of fire as the three sides of a triangle representing fuel, oxygen and heat ○ *If fuel, oxygen or heat is removed from the fire triangle, combustion will cease.*

first aid kit /ˌfɜːst ˈeɪd ˌkɪt/ *noun* a small pack containing plasters, bandages, antiseptic cream, etc., to be used in case of an emergency

first officer /ˌfɜːst ˈɒfɪsə/ *noun* the officer who is second-in-command to the captain of an aircraft

FIS *abbreviation* flight information service

fishtail /ˈfɪʃteɪl/ *verb* to move the tail of an aircraft from side to side as a way of reducing speed

FISO *abbreviation* flight information service operator

fit /fɪt/ *adjective* in good physical condition, healthy ○ *Keep fit with diet and exercise.* ■ *noun* the exactness with which surfaces are adjusted to each other in a machine ○ *There should be a loose fit between the cylinder and the piston, the difference being taken up by the piston rings.* ■ *verb* **1.** to be the correct size and shape for ○ *Oxygen masks should fit the wearer properly.* **2.** to put on or attach ○ *Wheel fairings, called spats, are fitted to some light aircraft to reduce drag.* (NOTE: **fitting – fitted**)

fitment /ˈfɪtmənt/ *noun* an act of attaching or fixing ○ *Attachment points are supplied for the fitment of heavy equipment.*

fitness /ˈfɪtnəs/ *noun* the state or condition of being physically fit, especially as the result of exercise and proper eating habits ○ *The age and physical fitness of some passengers can be a limiting factor in an evacuation.* □ **fitness to fly** description of the physical or mental capabilities a person needs to fly an aircraft

fixed-wing /ˌfɪkst ˈwɪŋ/ *adjective* referring to an aircraft that has wings that do not move, rather than rotor blades

FL *abbreviation* flight level

flag /flæg/ *noun* **1.** a usually square or rectangular piece of cloth with a symbolic design or colour ○ *Flags are flown from the signal mast.* **2.** a small visual warning or indicating device on the face of an instrument ○ *There is a warning flag on the instrument if there is a problem.*

flame /fleɪm/ *noun* the usually yellow area of burning gases seen when something is burning ○ *Flames were seen coming from number 2 engine.*

flame arrester /ˈfleɪm əˌrestə/ *noun* a device to prevent flame from an external source from entering a fuel tank

flame out /ˌfleɪm ˈaʊt/ *verb* to cease from some cause other than the shutting off of fuel ○ *Air in the fuel line can cause an engine to flame out or stop.*

flame-out /ˈfleɪm aʊt/ *noun* the ceasing of combustion in a gas turbine engine from some cause other than the shutting off of fuel (NOTE: The word is also written **flameout**.)

flammable /'flæməb(ə)l/ *adjective* easily ignited and capable of burning fiercely and rapidly, and therefore hazardous ○ *Aviation gasoline is a flammable liquid.* (NOTE: **Flammable** and **inflammable** mean the same thing.)

flange /flændʒ/ *noun* the outside edge or rim of a part such as a beam or wheel ○ *The web connects the upper and lower flanges of a beam.*

flap /flæp/ *noun* a movable control surface on the trailing edge of an aircraft wing, used primarily to increase lift and drag during final approach and landing ○ *Flaps should be retracted immediately after landing to decrease lift and therefore increase brake effectiveness.* ◊ **cowl**

COMMENT: Flaps are not usually used for take-offs in light aircraft except when a short take-off run is required. Flaps are not primary control surfaces of an aircraft.

flare /fleə/ *noun* **1.** a stage of the flight immediately before touchdown when the nose of the aircraft is raised into the landing attitude ○ *The approach, flare and landing can be carried out by automatic systems.* **2.** a small rocket-like device with a bright light, for attracting attention

flash /flæʃ/ *noun* giving off light in sudden or periodic bursts ○ *Lightning is accompanied by a brilliant flash.* ○ *Loss of vision may occur due to lightning flashes especially at night.* ■ *verb* **1.** to give off light in regular bursts □ **warning lights flash** warning lights go on and off rapidly **2.** to appear or to happen suddenly ○ *The image flashed onto the screen.*

flash point /flæʃ pɔɪnt/ *noun* temperature at which fuel vapour or oil vapour will burst into flame

flat /flæt/ *adjective* **1.** having a horizontal surface without a slope, tilt or curvature ○ *It has been shown that the flat chart misrepresents the globe-shaped earth.* □ **flat country** country with no hills or mountains **2.** having no air inside ○ *The flat tyre had to be changed because it had a puncture.* **3.** electrically discharged or with no elec-

trical charge left in it ○ *The engine wouldn't start because the battery was flat.*

flat spin /ˌflæt 'spɪn/ *noun* a descent in small circles by an aircraft flying in a nearly horizontal position

flatten /'flæt(ə)n/, **flatten out** *verb* to make flat ○ *As altitude increases, the countryside appears to flatten out.* ○ *The Earth is spherical in shape but it is flattened at the poles.*

flaw /flɔː/ *noun* an imperfection in a material, often hidden, that may be an indication of future structural failure □ **flaw detection** a process or system by which small weaknesses in metal structures are found

flew /fluː/ ◆ **fly**

flexibility /ˌfleksɪ'bɪlɪti/ *noun* **1.** the amount or extent to which something can be bent or flexed ○ *Wing structures must have flexibility in order to absorb sudden changes in loading.* **2.** the extent to which a system or device can change or respond to a variety of conditions or situations ○ *The more reliable and quick fly-by-wire system allows a much greater degree of flexibility with aircraft stability.* Opposite **rigidity**

flexible /'fleksɪb(ə)l/ *adjective* **1.** not rigid, not stiff □ **flexible pipes** pipes made of soft material such as rubber or plastic **2.** capable of responding to a variety of conditions or situations; adaptable ○ *AC electrical energy is more flexible and more efficient than DC.* Opposite **rigid**

flier /'flaɪə/ *noun* **1.** the pilot of an aircraft **2.** a passenger on an aircraft

flight /flaɪt/ *noun* **1.** the motion of an object in or through the Earth's atmosphere or through space **2.** the distance covered by a body, e.g. an aircraft, as it flies through the atmosphere ○ *The flight from London to Paris took 55 minutes.* **3.** a scheduled airline journey ○ *Passengers for flight GF 008 to Amman should proceed to gate number 4.*

flight attendant /'flaɪt əˌtendənt/ *noun* a member of the flight crew who looks after passengers, serves food, etc. ○ *If you need something, press the call button and a cabin attendant will* *respond within a few minutes.* Also called **cabin attendant**

flight bag /'flaɪt bæg/ *noun* a bag used by flight crew to carry manuals, documents, headset, etc.

flight-briefing room /'flaɪt ˌbriːfɪŋ ruːm/ *noun* a room where instructors talk to trainees immediately before a training flight or where a pilot talks to his or her crew immediately before boarding the aircraft

flight crew /'flaɪt kruː/ *noun* airline staff responsible for flying the aircraft

flight data recorder /'flaɪt ˌdeɪtə rɪ ˌkɔːdə/ *noun* an electronic device located in the tail section of an aircraft that picks up and stores data about a flight. Abbreviation **FDR**. Also called **black box** (NOTE: It is often called the **black box**, although it is not black.)

flight deck /'flaɪt dek/ *noun* a place where the flight crew of an airliner sit while flying the aircraft

flight deck instruments *plural noun* instruments used by the flight crew when flying an aircraft

flight engineer /'flaɪt ˌendʒɪnɪə/ *noun* the member of the crew of a plane who is responsible for checking that its systems, including the engines, perform properly

flight envelope /'flaɪt ˌenvələʊp/ *noun* same as **envelope**

flight information region /ˌflaɪt ˌɪnfəˈmeɪʃ(ə)n ˌriːʒən/ *noun* airspace with defined limits which has an air traffic control information and alerting service. Abbreviation **FIR**

flight level /'flaɪt ˌlev(ə)l/ *noun* **1.** the level of constant atmospheric pressure related to a reference datum of 1013.25 mb ○ *FL 250 = 25,000 ft.* Abbreviation **FL 2.** the height at which a particular aircraft is allowed to fly at a particular time

flight line /'flaɪt laɪn/ *noun* the area of an airfield, especially a military airfield, where aircraft are parked, serviced, and loaded or unloaded

Flight Manual /'flaɪt ˌmænjʊəl/ *noun* same as **Pilot's Operating Handbook**

flight operations /'flaɪt ˌɒpəreɪʃ(ə)nz/ *plural noun* the use of aircraft

flight path /'flaɪt pɑːθ/ *noun* a line, course or track along which an aircraft flies

flight plan /'flaɪt plan/ *noun* a written statement that gives details of the flight that a pilot intends to make

flight progress strip /ˌflaɪt 'prəʊgres ˌstrɪp/ *noun* a thin cardboard strip with information on it about a flight, which is updated by air traffic controllers as the flight progresses

flight simulator /'flaɪt ˌsɪmjʊleɪtə/ *noun* a device or computer program which allows a user to pilot an aircraft, showing a realistic control panel and moving scenes, used as training programme

flight-test /'flaɪt test/ *verb* to test the performance of an aircraft or component in flight

float /fləʊt/ *noun* **1.** a floating ball attached to a lever to regulate the level of a liquid in a tank, etc. □ **float-operated switch** a shut-off valve operated by a float **2.** a hollow structure fixed below an aircraft that allows it to float on water. Also called **pontoon** ■ *verb* to remain on the surface of a fluid without sinking ○ *Because of the air-tight nature of the fuselage, most large aircraft will float for some time before sinking.*

float chamber /'fləʊt ˌtʃeɪmbə/ *noun* the part of a carburettor which houses the float

floatplane /'fləʊtpleɪn/ *noun* a seaplane that has hollow structures attached underneath its wings and sometimes its fuselage on which it floats so that the main body of the plane is not in contact with the water. Compare **flying boat**

flow /fləʊ/ *verb* **1.** to move or run smoothly with continuity, as a fluid ○ *Air flows over the wing surfaces and lift is produced.* **2.** to circulate ○ *Liquid coolant flows around the engine.* ■ *noun* continuous movement in a particular direction ○ *The flow of fuel from the fuel tanks to the engines.*

flowmeter /'fləʊmiːtə/ *noun* a device for measuring the flow of a liquid or gas ○ *The oxygen flowmeter should blink once for each breath.*

fluctuate /'flʌktʃueɪt/ *verb* to vary or change irregularly ○ *The magnetic field will fluctuate at the supply frequency.*

fluid /'fluːɪd/ *noun* a substance which is not solid, whose molecules move freely past one another and that takes the shape of its container □ **de-icing fluid** a liquid for removing ice

fluorescent /fluə'res(ə)nt/ *adjective* referring to the emission of electromagnetic radiation of visible light ○ *The fluorescent penetrant process of flaw detection uses a penetrant containing a fluorescent dye which fluoresces in ultra-violet light.*

fly /flaɪ/ *verb* to move through the air or to cause an aircraft to move through the air in a controlled manner ○ *An aeroplane may not fly over a city below such a height as would allow it to alight in the event of an engine failure.* ○ *He's learning to fly.* (NOTE: **flying – flew – flown**) □ **to fly in formation** to fly as a group which maintains a particular pattern or arrangement in the air

fly-by-wire /'flaɪ baɪ ˌwaɪə/ *noun* technology which interprets movements of the pilot's controls and, with the aid of computerised electronics, moves the control surfaces accordingly ○ *Using fly-by-wire technology, the stalling angle cannot be exceeded regardless of stick input.* ○ *The more reliable and quick fly-by-wire system allows a much greater degree of flexibility with aircraft stability.*

COMMENT: Fighters like the General Dynamics F16 and large transport aircraft such as the Boeing 777 and Airbus A320 have fly-by-wire systems.

flying /'flaɪɪŋ/ *noun* the act of making an aircraft move through the air in a controlled manner

flying boat /'flaɪɪŋ bəʊt/ *noun* a seaplane with a body that acts like a boat's hull and allows the plane to float on water. Compare **floatplane**

flying conditions /'flaɪɪŋ kən,dɪʃ(ə)nz/ *plural noun* the weather and its suitability for flying

flying controls /'flaɪɪŋ kən,trəʊlz/ *plural noun* the yoke or control column, rudder pedals and other devices used by the pilot in order to manoeuvre the aircraft

flying field /'flaɪɪŋ fiːld/ *noun* a small airfield from which light aircraft can operate

flying instructor /'flaɪɪŋ ɪn,strʌktə/ *noun* a trained person, a pilot, who teaches people how to fly an aircraft

fly-past /'flaɪ pɑːst/ *noun* the flight of an aircraft or group of aircraft over a place as a spectacle for people on the ground

FMS /ˌef em 'es/ *abbreviation* flight management system

foam /fəʊm/ *noun* **1.** a mass of bubbles of air or gas in a liquid film ○ *foam fire extinguishers* ○ *Airport fire crews covered the fuselage with foam to control the fire.* **2.** any of various light, porous, semi-rigid or spongy materials used for thermal insulation or shock absorption ○ *Polyurethane foam is used in packaging.*

focal point /'fəʊk(ə)l pɔɪnt/ *noun* same as **focus**

focus /'fəʊkəs/ *noun* the point at which rays of light or other radiation converge ○ *The focus of a lens is also called the focal point.* (NOTE: The plural form is **foci**. /'fəʊsaɪ/) □ **to come into focus** to become clearer as through the viewfinder of a camera ■ *verb* **1.** to make things such as light rays converge on a central point ○ *A parabolic reflector focuses the transmission into a narrow beam.* **2.** to give an object or image a clear outline or detail by adjustment of an optical device ○ *Focus the microscope in order to make the image easier to see.* **3.** to direct toward a particular point or purpose ○ *The crew focused all their attention on finding a solution to the problem.*

fog /fɒg/ *noun* condensed water vapour in cloud-like masses lying close to the ground and limiting visibility ○

When visibility is less than 1,000 m owing to suspended water droplets in the atmosphere, the condition is known as fog. □ **evaporation fog** steam fog ○ *Evaporation fog is usually confined to water surfaces and adjacent areas of land.*

föhn /fɜn/ *noun* a warm dry wind that blows down the lee side of a mountain, particularly in the Alps (NOTE: The word is also written **foehn**.)

foil /fɔɪl/ *noun* same as **aerofoil**

foot /fʊt/ *noun* a unit of length in the US and British Imperial Systems equal to 12 inches or 30.48 centimetres. Symbol **ft** (NOTE: The plural form is **feet;** foot is usually written **ft** or ' after figures: **10ft** or **10'**.)

foot-pound /fʊt paʊnd/ *noun* the ability to lift a one pound weight a distance of one foot. Abbreviation **ft-lb**

force /fɔːs/ *noun* **1.** the capacity to do work or cause physical change ○ *the force of an explosion* **2.** power used against a resistance ○ *In small aerobatic aircraft, considerable force is needed on the control column when performing high-speed manoeuvres.* **3.** a vector quantity that produces an acceleration of a body in the direction of its application (NOTE: We say **centrifugal force,** but **the force of gravity.**) □ **the force of gravity** the natural force of attraction which pulls bodies towards each other and which pulls objects on Earth towards its centre ■ *verb* **1.** to use power against resistance ○ *Because of distortion to the airframe, the pilot had to force the door open in order to exit the aircraft.* **2.** □ **to force someone to do something** to use physical or psychological power to make somebody do something they otherwise would not do ○ *The hijackers forced the crew to fly to Athens.*

forced landing /ˌfɔːst ˈlændɪŋ/ *noun* an unexpected landing that a pilot of an aircraft has to make because of an emergency situation

force down /ˌfɔːs ˈdaʊn/ *verb* to force an aircraft to land, usually because of an emergency situation

force-land /ˌfɔːs ˈlænd/ *verb* to land an aircraft before it gets to its destination because of an emergency situation, or land in these circumstances

forces of flight /ˌfɔːsɪz əv ˈflaɪt/ *plural noun* the aerodynamic forces, lift, drag, weight and thrust, which act on an object that is travelling though the air

fore /fɔː/ *adjective* located at or towards the front □ **the fore and aft axis of the aircraft** the longitudinal axis of the aircraft □ **to come to the fore** to become important or to start to play a leading role ○ *The jet engine came to the fore in the late forties.* ◊ **aft**

forecast /ˈfɔːkɑːst/ *noun* a statement of what is likely to happen in the future or describing expected events or conditions ○ *weather forecast* □ **forecast weather charts** charts with information about the weather coming to a particular area ■ *verb* to estimate or calculate weather conditions by studying meteorological information ○ *Rain is forecast for this afternoon.* (NOTE: **forecasting—forecast** or **forecasted**)

forecast chart /ˈfɔːkɑːst tʃɑːt/ *noun* same as **prognostic chart** ○ *Prognostic or forecast charts are prepared, by the central meteorological office of each region, normally for periods up to 24 hours ahead.*

form /fɔːm/ *noun* **1.** a document with blanks for the insertion of details or information ○ *insurance form* ○ *application form* **2.** a kind or type ○ *The ground automatic relief valve is a form of discharge valve.* ○ *Drizzle is the lightest form of precipitation.* **3.** the shape of an object ○ *Fluids take on the form of the container in which they are found.* □ **in the form of a triangle** in the shape of a triangle **4.** the way in which a thing exists, acts, or shows itself ○ *water in the form of ice* ○ *fuel in the form of a spray* ■ *verb* **1.** to come into being ○ *In some conditions, ice forms on the leading edge of the wing.* ○ *Cumulus clouds only form in an unstable atmosphere.* **2.** to make a shape ○ *Three points on the chart form a triangle.* **3.** to make up or constitute ○ *The* *classroom and accommodation building form the main part of the college.*

formation /fɔːˈmeɪʃ(ə)n/ *noun* **1.** the process of coming into being or forming □ **cloud formation** the natural production and development of clouds □ **ice formation** the natural production and development of ice **2.** □ **to fly in formation** to fly in a group which maintains a particular pattern or arrangement in the air

former /ˈfɔːmə/ *adjective* having been in the past □ **a former military pilot** a pilot who used to be a military pilot ■ *noun* **1.** the first of two things mentioned **2.** a light secondary structure of the airframe which gives improved shape

'...much has changed in the former Eastern European States, especially in terms of aviation operations and training' [*Civil Aviation Training*]

formula /ˈfɔːmjʊlə/ *noun* a mathematical rule expressed in symbols ○ *The formula for calculating speed is D ÷ T = S (where D = distance, T = time and S = speed).* (NOTE: The plural form is **formulas** or **formulae**.)

forward /ˈfɔːwəd/ *adjective* at, near, or belonging to the front ○ *the forward section of the aircraft* ○ *forward and aft exits*

forwards /ˈfɔːwədz/ *adverb* towards a position in front ○ *The throttles are moved forwards for take-off.* (NOTE: The US English is **forward**.)

fouling /ˈfaʊlɪŋ/ *noun* contamination of the spark plugs with oil or petrol so that they do not fire correctly ○ *The engine should be run at a positive idling speed to prevent spark plug fouling.*

four-digit group /ˌfɔː ˌdɪdʒɪt ˈɡruːp/ *noun* four single numbers found together

four-stroke combustion engine /ˌfɔː strəʊk kəmˈbʌstʃ(ə)n ˌendʒɪn/ *noun* an engine which operates in accordance with the four-stroke cycle ○ *Induction, compression, power and exhaust are the four phases of the four-stroke combustion engine.*

fpm *abbreviation* feet per minute

FPPS *abbreviation* flight plan processing system

frame /freɪm/ *noun* **1.** a structure that gives shape or support ○ *Early aircraft fuselages were made of a frame covered by a fabric.* **2.** an open structure for holding, or bordering ○ *a door or window frame*

FREDA ♦ mnemonic

freeze /friːz/ *verb* to pass from the liquid to the solid state by loss of heat ○ *In some conditions, rain droplets freeze rapidly on striking the aircraft.* (NOTE: **freezing – froze – frozen**)

freight /freɪt/ *noun* anything other than people transported by a vessel or vehicle, especially by a commercial carrier ○ *Freight holds are usually located beneath the passenger cabins.*

freighter /ˈfreɪtə/ *noun* an aircraft designed to carry freight

frequency /ˈfriːkwənsi/ *noun* **1.** the number of times or the rate at which something happens in a given period of time ○ *The frequency of flights to holiday destinations increases during the summer time.* **2.** the number of repetitions per unit time of a complete waveform, as of an electric current frequency

'...a Baltimore man adjusted a baby alarm to improve its performance and found his youngster's squawks were being picked up by incoming aircraft tuned to the local NDB frequency' [*Pilot*]

frequency bracket /ˈfriːkwənsi ˌbrækɪt/ *noun* a range of frequencies ○ *VHF communications are allocated the frequency bracket 118–137 MHz.*

frequent /ˈfriːkwənt/ *adjective* happening or appearing often ○ *frequent inspection*

friction /ˈfrɪkʃ(ə)n/ *noun* a force that resists the relative motion or tendency to such motion of two bodies in contact ○ *Energy is converted to heat through friction.*

front /frʌnt/ *noun* **1.** the forward part or surface ○ *The entrance is at the front.* **2.** the area, location, or position directly before or ahead □ **in front** in a forward position relative to something else ○ *Row 23 is in front of row 24.* **3.** the mixed area between air masses of different temperatures or densities

frontal /'frʌnt(ə)l/ *adjective* **1.** referring to the forward part or surface area of something ○ *the frontal area* □ **frontal surface** the boundary between two air masses **2.** of or relating to a meteorological weather front ○ *a frontal storm*

frontal depression /ˌfrʌnt(ə)l dɪ'preʃ(ə)n/ *noun* an area of low pressure found together with a weather front

frontal system /'frʌnt(ə)l ˌsɪstəm/ *noun* a series of rain-bearing changes in the weather

frost /frɒst/ *noun* a deposit of very small ice crystals formed when water vapour condenses at a temperature below freezing ○ *Frost had to be cleared from training aircraft which had been parked outside overnight.* ◊ **hoar**

ft /fʊt/ *abbreviation* foot

fuel /'fjuːəl/ *noun* a substance such as gas, oil, petrol, etc., which is burnt to produce heat or power ○ *Each wing tank holds 20 gallons of fuel.* ○ *A fuel system includes tanks, fuel lines, fuel pumps, fuel filters and a carburettor or fuel injection system.*

fuel/air mixture /ˌfjuːəl eə 'mɪkstʃə/ *noun* a combination of fuel and air which is ignited in a piston engine to provide power

COMMENT: Aircraft engines operate at different altitudes and the pilot must adjust the mixture to produce the most efficient fuel/air mixture for the atmospheric density.

fuel gauge /'fjuːəl geɪdʒ/ *noun* an instrument indicating fuel contents

fuel injection /'fjuːəl ɪnˌdʒekʃ(ə)n/, **fuel injection system** *noun* system in which fuel is sprayed under pressure into the combustion chamber of an engine

fuel injector /'fjuːəl ɪnˌdʒektə/ *noun* an injector that sprays fuel into the combustion chamber of an engine

fuel pump /'fjuːəl pʌmp/ *noun* a device which moves fuel along pipes from the tanks to the engine

fumes /fjuːmz/ *plural noun* smoke, gas or vapour given off by a substance, often unpleasant or harmful ○ *When the cabin is rapidly and completely filled by smoke and fumes, passengers will suffer from disorientation.*

function /'fʌŋkʃən/ *noun* **1.** a specific occupation or role ○ *Rota planning is one of the functions of the chief instructor.* **2.** purpose ○ *Seals perform a very important function in a hydraulic system.* ○ *The function of the flaps is to increase lift and drag.* ■ *verb* **1.** to act as, or to serve the purpose of ○ *The escape slide also functions as a life raft.* **2.** to operate or to work ○ *The system functions well.*

fundamental /ˌfʌndə'ment(ə)l/ *adjective* **1.** of or relating to the foundation or base ○ *the fundamental laws of aerodynamics* **2.** central, forming or serving as an essential component of a system or structure ○ *Electricity is one of the fundamental types of energy that exist in nature.*

fungal growth /'fʌŋgəl 'grəʊθ/ *noun* a type of organism which lives and multiplies in particular fuels ○ *Fuel contains chemicals for the inhibition of fungal growth.*

fuse /fjuːz/ *noun* a safety device that protects an electric circuit from an excessive current ○ *Circuit breakers perform the same function as a fuse.*

fuselage /'fjuːzəlɑːʒ/ *noun* the central body of a plane, to which the wings and tail assembly are attached and which accommodates the crew, passengers, and cargo ○ *The fire started in the wing but soon spread to the fuselage.*

G

g /dʒiː/ *symbol* the acceleration due to Earth's gravity ▪ *abbreviation* gram

G /dʒiː/ *abbreviation* giga-

GA *abbreviation* general aviation

gain /geɪn/ *noun* **1.** an increase ○ *There is a gain of heat by the Earth due to solar radiation.* □ **a gain in altitude** an increase in altitude **2.** an increase in signal power, voltage, or current ○ *The amplifier boosts the gain of the incoming signal.* **3.** a benefit or advantage ▪ *verb* **1.** to increase ○ *He failed the test because the aircraft gained 100 ft in the 360° level turn.* **2.** to get or obtain ○ *She gained a pass in her meteorology exam.*

gale /geɪl/ *noun* a very strong wind usually blowing from a single direction ○ *Gales are forecast for the area.*

gallon /ˈɡælən/ *noun* **1.** □ **imperial gallon** unit of volume in the British Imperial System, used in liquid measure and sometimes in dry measure, equal to 4.546 litres ○ *The system delivers fuel at the rate of 100 to 2,000 gallons per hour.* Abbreviation **gal 2.** a unit of volume in the US Customary System, used in liquid measure, equal to 3.785 litres

GAMA *abbreviation* General Aviation Manufacturers Association

gamma rays /ˈɡæmə reɪz/ *plural noun* electromagnetic radiation given off by some radioactive substances ○ *Gamma rays are given off when radioactive material breaks down.*

gap /ɡæp/ *noun* **1.** a space between objects or points **2.** the difference ○ *Micro switches have a very small gap between make and break.* **3.** an opening ○ *The pilot could see the airfield through a gap in the clouds.*

gas /ɡæs/ *noun* a state of matter other than solid and liquid ○ *Oxygen and nitrogen are gases.* □ **gas turbine engine** an engine with a turbine which is rotated by expanding hot gases

gaseous /ˈɡæsiəs/ *adjective* relating to, or existing as a gas ○ *The atmosphere is the gaseous envelope surrounding the earth.*

gasket /ˈɡæskɪt/ *noun* any of a wide variety of seals or packings used between matched machine parts or around pipe joints to prevent the escape of a gas or fluid ○ *Seals, gaskets and packing make a seal by being squeezed between two surfaces.*

gasoline /ˈɡæsəliːn/ *noun* US a liquid made from petroleum, used as a fuel in an internal combustion engine

GAT *abbreviation* general air traffic

gate /ɡeɪt/ *noun* **1.** a device for controlling the passage of water or gas through a pipe ○ *The waste gate may be controlled manually by the pilot.* ○ *During a descent from altitude, with low power set, the turbocharger waste gate is fully closed.* **2.** a circuit with many inputs and one output that works only when a particular input is received ○ *A logic gate is almost the same as a switch.* **3.** a device to prevent a lever from being moved to an incorrect setting ○ *It is necessary to move the rpm control lever through a feathering gate to the feathering position.*

gauge /ɡeɪdʒ/ *noun* **1.** an instrument for measuring or testing ○ *temperature gauge* ○ *pressure gauge* **2.** a unit of diameter or width □ **heavy gauge wire** thick wire ■ *verb* calculate approximately by using the senses ○ *In fog, it is difficult to gauge horizontal distances.* (NOTE: **gauging – gauged**)

GCA *abbreviation* ground-control approach

gear /gɪə/ *noun* **1.** a toothed wheel that turns with another toothed part to transmit motion or change speed or direction **2.** □ **valve gear** the mechanism for opening and closing valves **3.** equipment and/or clothing

'…as pilots, we understand the need for a convenient way to transport flight gear. That's why we custom-designed this line of soft-sided flight bags in a variety of styles' [*Advertisement in Pilot*]

gearbox /'gɪəbɒks/ *noun* a device to allow changes in the ratio of engine speed to final drive speed ○ *The auxiliary power unit (APU) is a small gas turbine engine which is connected to a gearbox.*

GEM *abbreviation* ground-effect machine

genera /'dʒenərə/ plural of **genus**

general /'dʒen(ə)rəl/ *adjective* concerned with or applicable to a whole group of people or things □ **general description** not a detailed description □ **general principles** main ideas □ **general purpose switches** all-purpose switches □ **general weather situation** the overall weather picture without the detail □ **as a general rule** usually □ **in general use** used a lot

general aviation /ˌdʒen(ə)rəl ˌeɪvi'eɪʃ(ə)n/ *noun* all aviation other than commercial airlines or the military ○ *The number of GA aircraft stolen is down sharply since the general aviation community has taken steps to enhance security.* Abbreviation **GA**

general flying test /ˌdʒen(ə)rəl 'flaɪɪŋ ˌtest/ *noun* a test of aircraft-handling skills for student pilots. Abbreviation **GFT**

generate /'dʒenəreɪt/ *verb* **1.** to bring into being ○ *In an emergency, it may be necessary for crew to generate a little panic in passengers to motivate them to move.* **2.** to produce something

such as heat or electricity as a result of a chemical or physical process ○ *The passage of air around the wing generates lift.*

generation /ˌdʒenə'reɪʃ(ə)n/ *noun* **1.** the act or process of creating or making □ **generation of ideas** the process of producing or getting ideas □ **generation of electricity** the production of electricity **2.** a class of objects derived from an earlier class □ **a new generation of computers** computers which share a recent development in computer technology which separates them as a class from earlier computers

generator /'dʒenəreɪtə/ *noun* a power-operated device for making electricity ○ *Starter generators are a combination of a generator and a starter housed in one unit.*

genus /'dʒiːnəs/ *noun* a class, group, or family ○ *Various types of cloud are grouped into ten basic cloud genera.* (NOTE: The plural form is **genera**.)

geographic /dʒiːə'græfɪk/, **geographical** /ˌdʒiːə'græfɪk(ə)l/ *adjective* referring to geography ○ *a specific geographical area* ○ *the north geographic pole*

geography /dʒi'ɒgrəfi/ *noun* □ **physical geography** the study of the Earth's surface and its features

geometric /ˌdʒiːə'metrɪk/ *adjective* referring to geometry ○ *A triangle is a geometric figure.* ○ *Geometric pitch (US) is the distance which a propeller should move forward in one revolution.*

geometry /dʒi'ɒmətri/ *noun* **1.** the study of the properties, measurement, and relationships of points, lines, angles, surfaces, and solids ○ *An understanding of geometry is essential to the student of navigation.* **2.** a configuration or arrangement ○ *the geometry of the engine nacelle*

geostationary /ˌdʒiːəʊ 'steɪʃ(ə)n(ə)ri/ *adjective* referring to an object, such as a satellite in space, which rotates round the Earth at the same speed as the Earth and is therefore stationary with reference to a point on the Earth ○ *There are two main types of satellite that are used for collection and* *transmission of meteorological data, polar and geostationary.*

geostrophic wind /ˌdʒiːəʊstrɒfɪk 'wɪnd/ *noun* a wind which blows horizontally along the isobars, across the surface of the earth

GFT *abbreviation* general flying test

GHz *abbreviation* gigahertz

giga- /ɡɪɡə/ *prefix* one thousand million. Symbol **G**

gigahertz /'ɡɪɡəhɜːts/ *noun* a frequency of 10^9 Hertz. Abbreviation **GHz**

given /'ɡɪv(ə)n/ *adjective* **1.** particular, specified, fixed ○ *At high altitudes, less fuel is consumed for a given airspeed than for the same airspeed at a lower altitude.* **2.** □ **given (that)** taking into account, considering ○ *Given the condition of the engine, it is surprising that it starts.*

glare /gleə/ *noun* a strong blinding light ○ *Glare can be caused by diffuse reflection of sunlight from the top of a layer of fog.*

glass fibre reinforced plastic *noun* a composite material made of plastic which is strengthened by glass fibres, used in the manufacture of airframes and other aircraft components. Abbreviation **GRP**

glide /glaɪd/ *verb* to fly without power ○ *In the event of an engine failure, it is important to have enough altitude to be able to glide clear of houses, people, etc.*

glidepath /'glaɪdpɑːθ/, **glide path** *noun* a path followed by the aircraft down the glide slope □ **glidepath coverage** the vertical and horizontal dimensions of the glide slope radio beam

glider /'glaɪdə/ *noun* a fixed wing aeroplane, normally with no power plant propulsion ○ *Nowadays, gliders are often made of composite materials.*

glideslope /'glaɪdsləʊp/, **glide slope** *noun* the part of the ILS which provides a radio beam at an angle of approximately 3° to the point of touchdown from the outer marker thus giving the pilot information about the height of the aircraft on final approach

gliding /'glaɪdɪŋ/ *noun* **1.** flying in a glider □ **gliding club** association of members who fly gliders as a pastime **2.** flying in a powered aircraft with the engine either switched off or idling ○ *The best gliding speed for the aircraft is 75 knots.*

COMMENT: On June 24th 1982, a British Airways 747 flying from Kuala Lumpur to Perth lost all power from all four engines for 13 minutes, yet landed safely in Jakarta: proof that even a large aircraft is capable of gliding.

global /'ɡləʊb(ə)l/ *adjective* worldwide, referring to something related to the whole Earth □ **global pressure patterns** the pressure patterns of the whole planet

global positioning system /ˌɡləʊb(ə)l pə'zɪʃ(ə)nɪŋ ˌsɪstəm/ *noun* a satellite-based navigation system. Abbreviation **GPS**

globe /gləʊb/ *noun* an object shaped like a ball ○ *If the Earth were a uniform globe, the average temperature would vary only with latitude.*

GLONASS *noun* a system of satellite navigation operated by Russia. Full form **Global Orbiting Navigation Satellite System**

GMT *abbreviation* Greenwich Mean Time

GNSS *abbreviation* global navigation satellite system

go-around /'gəʊ əˌraʊnd/ *noun* a climb into the circuit and manoeuvring into position for a new approach and landing ○ *Because the plane was too high on the approach, the pilot executed a go-around.*

govern /'ɡʌv(ə)n/ *verb* to control or limit the speed, size or amount of something ○ *The size and number of valves required for a particular type of aircraft is governed by the amount of air necessary for pressurisation and air conditioning.* ○ *The type of undercarriage fitted to an aircraft is governed by the operating weight.*

governor /'ɡʌv(ə)nə/ *noun* a device for controlling or limiting the speed size or amount of something ○ *Overspeed-*

ing of the engine is prevented by a governor in the fuel system. ◊ **valve**

gph /'dʒiː 'piː 'eɪtʃ/ *abbreviation* gallons per hour

GPS *abbreviation* global positioning system

GPWS *abbreviation* ground proximity warning system

GR *abbreviation* hail

grade /greɪd/ *noun* **1.** a position in a scale of size or quality ○ *Kevlar 49 is the grade used in aircraft composites.* **2.** a mark indicating a student's level of accomplishment ○ *Students who scored below a particular grade in the examinations were not allowed to continue the course.*

gradient /'greɪdiənt/ *noun* the rate at which a quantity such as temperature or pressure changes relative to change in a given variable, especially distance ○ *Because there is a temperature gradient across each front it is possible to draw isotherms which reduce in value from warm to cold air.* ○ *A pressure gradient occurs aloft from land to sea.*

gradual /'grædʒuəl/ *adjective* happening slowly but continuously ○ *Loss of cabin pressure may be gradual rather than sudden.* □ **gradual change** a change which takes place over a period of time

graduate /'grædʒuˌeɪt/ *verb* **1.** to be granted an academic degree or diploma ○ *She graduated from Oxford University with a first class honours degree.* **2.** to advance to a new level of skill, achievement, or activity ○ *After 50 hours of flying the single engine trainer, the student pilots graduate to flying the twin engine aircraft.* **3.** to divide into marked intervals, especially for use in measurement ○ *A thermometer has a scale graduated in degrees Celsius.*

gram /græm/ *noun* a unit of measurement of weight, equal to one thousandth of a kilogram. Symbol **g**

graph /grɑːf/ *noun* a diagram that shows a relationship between two sets of numbers as a series of points often joined by a line ○ *The graph shows the relationship between lift and drag at various airspeeds.*

graphic /'græfɪk/ *adjective* **1.** □ **graphic solution** a technique of using geometric constructions to solve problems ○ *One side of the calculator has a moveable slide which is used for the graphic solution of triangle of velocities problems.* **2.** described in vivid detail ○ *The eye witness provided a graphic description of the events leading to the accident.* ■ *noun* a picture used in a computer application ○ *The instructor's worksheets were greatly improved by the incorporation of graphics to aid comprehension of the subject matter.*

grasshopper /'grɑːshɒpə/ *noun* a light, unarmed military aeroplane used for reconnaissance

graticule /'grætɪkjuːl/ *noun* **1.** a series of fine lines in an optical instrument such as a telescope, used for measuring **2.** the network of lines formed by the meridians and parallels of longitude and latitude of the Earth on a flat sheet of paper ○ *A graticule of lines of latitude and longitude is imagined to cover the Earth.*

gravity /'grævɪti/ *noun* **1.** a natural force of attraction which pulls bodies towards each other and which pulls objects on Earth towards its centre ○ *In order for an aeroplane to fly, lift must overcome the force of gravity.* **2.** seriousness ○ *Throughout the crisis caused by the engine failure, the passengers were unaware of the gravity of the situation.*

gravity feed /'grævəti fiːd/ *noun* a feed which uses the force of gravity to move the fuel from the tank to the carburettor

great /greɪt/ *adjective* **1.** large in size, quantity, number, etc. □ **great distances** long distances □ **a great deal of money** a large sum of money □ **great importance** enormous importance **2.** very good, enjoyable or exciting

Greenwich Mean Time /ˌgrenɪtʃ 'miːn ˌtaɪm/ *noun* local time on the Greenwich Meridian. Abbreviation **GMT**

COMMENT: GMT is now called Coordinated Universal Time (UTC) and is also known as Zulu time. UTC is expressed in 24-hour format; for example, 7:00 P.M. is 1900 hours (say: nineteen hundred hours).

grid /grɪd/ *noun* **1.** a pattern of equally spaced vertical and horizontal lines, sometimes used on a map ○ *Grid lines facilitate the quick location of a point of reference.* **2.** a metal cylinder in a cathode ray tube **3.** a pattern of equally spaced vertical and horizontal metal rods or bars ○ *Lead-antimony alloy grid plates are components in a lead-acid battery.*

ground /graʊnd/ *noun* the solid surface of the earth ○ *Hail being much denser and heavier than snow, falls at a much faster rate and can reach the ground even with the 0° isotherm at 10,000 ft.* ■ *verb* **1.** to prohibit an aircraft or member of an aircrew from flying ○ *The pilot was grounded after failing a medical examination.* **2.** *US* to connect an electrical circuit to a position of zero potential ○ *While refuelling a light aircraft it is important to ground the airframe to prevent sparking caused by static electricity.* (NOTE: **To earth** is preferred in British English.)

ground crew /graʊnd kruː/ *noun* a team of employees who service and maintain the aircraft while it is on the ground

ground-effect machine /graʊnd ɪ ˌfekt məˌʃiːn/ *noun* a hovercraft. Abbreviation **GEM**

ground elevation /graʊnd ˌeləveɪʃ(ə)n/ *noun* the vertical distance, in feet, of the ground above sea level

ground instructor /graʊnd ɪn ˌstrʌktə/ *noun* a trained person who teaches support subjects such as meteorology in a classroom

groundling /graʊndlɪŋ/ *noun* a member of the ground crew at an airport or air force base

ground loop /graʊnd luːp/ *noun* a sharp unplanned turn made by an aircraft that is taxiing, taking off, or landing, caused by unbalanced drag

ground movement /graʊnd ˌmuːvmənt/ *noun* a manoeuvre such as taxiing carried out by an aircraft while on the ground, or any movement on an airfield by people or surface vehicles

ground position /graʊnd pə ˌzɪʃ(ə)n/ *noun* the point on the surface of the Earth immediately beneath the aircraft

ground proximity warning system /ˌgraʊnd prɒkˌsɪmɪti ˈwɔːnɪŋ ˌsɪstəm/ *noun* a system in aircraft which warns pilot, by means of an audible signal, that the aircraft is below a preset height. Abbreviation **GPWS**

ground-running operation /ˌgraʊnd ˌrʌnɪŋ ˌɒpəˈreɪʃ(ə)n/ *noun* a procedure of running the engine while the aircraft is stationary on the ground to check engine performance

ground signal /graʊnd ˌsɪgn(ə)l/ *noun* a visual signal displayed on an airfield to give information about local traffic rules to aircraft in the air

ground speed /graʊnd spiːd/ *noun* the speed of the aircraft in relation to the ground over which it is flying. Abbreviation **GS, G/S**

ground temperature /graʊnd ˌtemprɪtʃə/ *noun* the temperature recorded by a thermometer placed at ground level

ground visibility /graʊnd ˌvɪzɪbɪliti/ *noun* horizontal visibility near the surface of the earth

group /gruːp/ *noun* **1.** a number of individual items or people brought together because of similarities **2.** a collection of letters, numbers or symbols used in weather forecasting, etc.

growth /grəʊθ/ *noun* an increase in size, number, amount, etc. ○ *the growth of ice crystals* ○ *the growth of air travel*

GRP *abbreviation* glass fibre reinforced plastic

GS, G/S *abbreviation* ground speed

guard /gɑːd/ *noun* **1.** a device to prevent injury or loss, etc. ○ *The thermocouple probes consist of two wires of dissimilar metal that are joined together inside a metal guard tube.* **2.** a person who protects or keeps watch ○ *a security guard* ■ *verb* to protect from harm by watching over □ **to guard against** to take steps to ensure that something does not happen ○ *To guard against the risk of fire, passengers are requested not to smoke in the toilets.*

guidance /'gaɪd(ə)ns/ *noun* **1.** helpful advice ○ *Guidance is provided to assist people in filling in the form.* ○ *The booklet contains guidance on the advisability of flying with a cold.* **2.** the action of giving directions to an aircraft

guidance system /'gaɪd(ə)ns ˌsɪstəm/ *noun* a system which provides signals to the flight control system for steering the aircraft

guide /gaɪd/ *noun* something that directs or indicates □ **rough guide** a simple explanation to help a person to find his or her own way through more complex information ■ *verb* to direct or to indicate ○ *If there is smoke in the cabin, clear commands from the crew will help to guide passengers to the emergency exits.*

gust /gʌst/ *noun* a strong, sudden rush of wind ○ *a gust of 30 feet per second* ○ *On final approach, the pilot must be prepared to counteract the effect of gusts in order to maintain a smooth descent along the extended centreline of the runway.* □ **gust load** an increased load to the airframe caused by a sudden increase in wind strength ■ *verb* to increase in strength suddenly ○ *Wind is at 10 knots gusting to 20 knots.*

gyro /'dʒaɪrəʊ/ *noun* same as **gyroscope**

gyro- /'dʒaɪrəʊ/ *prefix* gyroscopic

gyrocompass /'dʒaɪrəʊˌkʌmpəs/ *noun* a compass which uses gyroscopic directional stability rather than magnetism to indicate direction ○ *The gyrocompass should be checked against the*

magnetic compass and reset if necessary.

gyroplane /'dʒaɪrəʊpleɪn/ *noun* an aircraft fitted with an unpowered rotor for producing lift

gyroscope /'dʒaɪrəskəʊp/ *noun* a device consisting of a spinning wheel, mounted on a base so that its axis can turn freely in one or more directions and thereby maintain its own direction even when the base is moved ○ *The traditional attitude indicator, heading indicator and turn-coordinator contain gyroscopes.* ◊ **directional** (NOTE: The word is often shortened to **gyro**.)

COMMENT: A spinning gyro maintains its position even when an aircraft banks, climbs, or dives. Gyros drive the attitude indicator, direction indicator and turn coordinator to help pilots control an aircraft while flying in cloud or in poor visibility.

gyroscopic /ˌdʒaɪrə'skɒpɪk/ *adjective* referring to a gyroscope or using the properties of a gyroscope

gyroscopic compass /ˌdʒaɪrəskɒpɪk 'kʌmpəs/ *noun* a compass which uses gyroscopic directional stability rather than magnetism to indicate directions. Also called **gyrocompass**

gyroscopic precession /ˌdʒaɪrəskɒpɪk pri'seʃ(ə)n/ *noun* a characteristic of a gyroscope, that the force applied to a spinning gyroscope will act at a point 90° in the direction of rotation, not at the point where the force is applied ○ *Forces of gyroscopic precession act on the direction indicator to keep it aligned vertically and horizontally.*

H

hail /heɪl/ *noun* precipitation as small pellets of ice ○ *Precipitation is the falling of water, as rain, sleet, snow or hail onto the surface of the earth.* ○ *Although hail, and in particular, heavy hail is rare and of short duration, damage to an aircraft may be severe.*

COMMENT: In weather reports and forecasts, hail is indicated by the abbreviation 'GR'.

hailstone /ˈheɪlstəʊn/ *noun* a small pellet of ice which falls from clouds ○ *A hailstone starts as a small ice particle in the upper portion of a cumulonimbus cloud.*

hailstorm /ˈheɪlstɔːm/ *noun* a storm, where the precipitation is hail instead of rain or snow ○ *Flying through the hailstorm damaged the leading edges.*

hand flying /ˌhænd ˈflaɪɪŋ/ *noun* flying an aircraft by moving the flight controls with the hands rather than by using the autopilot

hand-held /ˈhænd held/ *adjective* possible to hold in the hand ○ *Nowadays, headsets are usually used in preference to hand-held microphones.* ◊ **hold**

handle /ˈhænd(ə)l/ *noun* a device for holding, or being operated, by the hand ○ *a door handle* ○ *a fire control handle* ■ *verb* **1.** to touch with the hands ○ *Cabin staff should not handle unwrapped food which is to be served to passengers.* **2.** to move or operate by hand ○ *The student pilot handled the aircraft well in the turbulent conditions.* **3.** to deal with, or to manage ○ *Flight crew must be able to handle any emergency when it occurs.*

handling /ˈhændlɪŋ/ *noun* **1.** the act of touching with the hands **2.** the use of the hands to move or operate something □ **aircraft handling** the act of manoeuvring the aircraft in the desired manner **3.** the act of dealing with or managing something ○ *Her handling of a difficult situation won the admiration of the whole crew.*

hand luggage /ˈhænd ˌlʌɡɪdʒ/ *noun* small bags that passengers can take with them into the cabin of an aircraft ○ *The amount of hand luggage is limited to one bag.*

hand signals /ˈhænd ˌsɪɡn(ə)lz/ *plural noun* same as **marshalling signals**

hands off /ˌhændz ˈɒf/ *adjective, adverb* where the operator does not control the operation, which is automatic ○ *Automatic flight control system capable of landing an aircraft hands off.*

hangar /ˈhæŋə/ *noun* a large shelter for housing and maintaining aircraft ○ *Light aircraft should be left with parking brakes off so that they can be moved quickly in the event of a fire in the hangar.*

hard landing /ˌhɑːd ˈlændɪŋ/ *noun* an uncontrolled landing by an aircraft that results in its being damaged or destroyed

HASELL ♦ **mnemonic**

haul /hɔːl/ *noun* ♦ **long-haul, short-haul**

hazard /ˈhæzəd/ *noun* a possible danger ○ *Thunderclouds are of special interest to aircrew because of the hazards they may pose to aircraft in flight.*

hazardous /'hæzədəs/ *adjective* possibly risky or dangerous ○ *Flying over mountainous terrain can be hazardous.* ○ *Structural icing is a hazardous phenomenon for rotary wing as well as fixed wing aircraft.*

haze /heɪz/ *noun* dust or smoke in the atmosphere ○ *Haze can seriously reduce air-to-ground visibility.*

head /hed/ *noun* **1.** the top part of the body above the shoulders **2.** a person □ **head count** an easy way of counting large numbers of people **3.** a main end part or top of something **4.** a leader, chief or director □ **head of department** the most senior person in the department ■ *verb* to fly in a particular direction □ **head north** to fly towards the north

heading /'hedɪŋ/ *noun* the direction in which the longitudinal axis of the aircraft is pointing, expressed in degrees from north

COMMENT: Wind affects an aircraft in flight, therefore heading does not always coincide with the aircraft's track. The pilot must head the aircraft slightly into the wind to correct for drift.

heading bug /'hedɪŋ bʌg/ *noun* a movable plastic marker on the horizontal situation indicator

heading correction /'hedɪŋ kə,rekʃ(ə)n/ *noun* a change of heading in order to deal with a new situation. Also called **course correction**

heading indicator /'hedɪŋ ,ɪndɪkeɪtə/ *noun* an instrument which gives course or direction information e.g. a horizontal situation indicator (HSI) or direction indicator (DI)

COMMENT: The heading indicator is driven by a gyro and provides steady, exact indications of heading.

heading to steer /,hedɪŋ tə 'stɪə/ *noun* a gyro-compass point in which to direct the aircraft

head-on /,hed 'ɒn/ *adjective, adverb* □ **to approach head-on** to approach from opposite directions

head-on collision /,hed ɒn kə'lɪʒ(ə)n/ *noun* a collision between two things or vehicles coming from opposite directions

headphones /'hedfəʊnz/ *noun* small speakers with padding, worn over a person's ears, used for private listening ○ *Headphones are used to monitor the signal.*

headset /'hedset/ *noun* headphones with a microphone attached, used for RT communications ○ *Headsets are usually used in preference to hand-held microphones.*

head-up display *noun* a cockpit system where data from flight instruments is projected onto a screen or the windscreen so that the pilot can see it without having to look down. Abbreviation **HUD**

headwind /'hedwɪnd/ *noun* a wind which is blowing in the opposite direction to the direction of movement or flight. Compare **tailwind** (NOTE: The word is also written **head wind**.)

headwind component /'hedwɪnd kəm,pəʊnənt/ *noun* one of the three possible components of a wind, the other two being crosswind and tailwind

heap /hiːp/ *noun* a group of things piled or thrown one on top of another

heap cloud /'hiːp klaʊd/ *noun* same as **cumulus cloud**

heat /hiːt/ *noun* warmth, being hot ○ *The heat generated by combustion is considerable.* ■ *verb* to make warm or warmer ○ *The air leaving the turbocharger is very warm and can be used to heat the cabin.*

heater /'hiːtə/ *noun* a device for heating ○ *Pitot heads contain heater elements to prevent icing.*

heating /'hiːtɪŋ/ *noun* the process of making something warmer ○ *the heating action of the sun* ◊ **kinetic**

heavier-than-air /,heviə θən 'eə/ *adjective* weighing more than the air it displaces, and so needing power to fly

heavy /'hevi/ *adjective* having a lot of weight □ **a heavy load** a load of great weight □ **heavy rain** rain which is dense and distributes a lot of water over the surface of the Earth in a relatively short time

heavy-duty /,hevi 'djuːti/ *adjective* referring to something designed for hard wear or use ○ *a heavy-duty battery* ○ *Longerons are heavy-duty steel members.*

heavy landing /ˌhevi ˈlændɪŋ/ *noun* a routine landing in which the aircraft makes contact with the surface with more force than usual, thereby possibly causing damage to the undercarriage ○ *The pilot reported a heavy landing.*

hedgehop /ˈhedʒhɒp/ *verb* to fly at very low height above the ground

height /haɪt/ *noun* the vertical distance of a point, level or object measured from a particular point, e.g. sea level ○ *Pressure decreases with increasing height.* □ **height of the aircraft** the vertical distance, measured in feet, of the aircraft above the surface of the earth

held /held/ ♦ **hold**

heli /ˈheli/ *noun* a rotary-wing aircraft

heliborne /ˈhelibɔːn/ *adjective* transported by helicopter

helicopter /ˈhelikɒptə/ *noun* an aircraft with one or more rotors rotating around vertical axes which provide lift and control ○ *Helicopter operations are carried out at the airport.*

helicopter rotor /ˈhelikɒptə ˌrəutə/ *noun* two or more rotating blades, known as the main rotor, which provide lift and thrust for a helicopter;

helideck /ˈhelidek/ *noun* a deck on something such as a ship or offshore oil platform that is used as a landing area for helicopters

heliograph /ˈhiːlɪəˌɡrɑːf/ *noun* an instrument with a mirror to send messages by reflecting the sun ○ *Heliographs enable reflected sunlight to be directed to a ship or aircraft in periods of direct sunlight.*

helipad /ˈhelipæd/ *noun* an area where helicopters take off and land

heliport /ˈhelipɔːt/ *noun* an airport designed for helicopters

helistop /ˈhelistɒp/ *noun* a place where helicopters can take off and land, but usually one that does not have the support facilities found at a heliport

helo /ˈhiːləʊ/ *noun* **1.** a rotary-winged aircraft **2.** same as **heliport**

hemisphere /ˈhemɪsfɪə/ *noun* half a sphere

Hertz /hɜːts/ *noun* the SI unit of frequency, defined as the number of cycles per second of time. Abbreviation **Hz**

HF *abbreviation* high frequency

high /haɪ/ *adjective* **1.** having great vertical distance ○ *a high mountain* **2.** great, large, a lot □ **high engine rpm** fast engine speed □ **high pressure** a lot of pressure □ **high reliability** good reliability □ **high speed** a fast speed □ **high temperature** a hot temperature ■ *noun* an area of high atmospheric pressure ○ *There is a high over the British Isles.*

high frequency /ˌhaɪ ˈfriːkwənsi/, **high frequency band** /ˌhaɪ ˈfriːkwənsi ˌbænd/ *noun* a radio communications range of frequencies between 3–30 MHz. Abbreviation **HF**

high-performance /ˌhaɪ pəˈfɔːməns/ *adjective* a system which provides better-than-usual output ○ *an engine with a high performance* ○ *Some high-performance engines have coolant and oil system thermostats which aid warming-up.*

high performance aircraft /ˌhaɪ pəˌfɔːməns ˈeəkrɑːft/ *noun* an aircraft capable of flying faster, higher or with more manoeuvrability than normal aircraft

hijack /ˈhaɪdʒæk/ *verb* to take over control of an aircraft by one or several unauthorised person or persons with the intention of forcing the crew to fly it to a different destination ○ *The airliner was hijacked on its way to Paris.*

hijacker /ˈhaɪdʒækə/ *noun* a person who hijacks an aircraft or other vehicle

hijacking /ˈhaɪdʒækɪŋ/ *noun* the act of taking over control of an aircraft by one or several unauthorised person or persons with the intention of forcing the crew to fly it to a different destination ○ *The crew must be alert at all times to the possibility of hijacking, bombs and stowaways.*

hill /hɪl/ *noun* an easily-seen, natural elevation, smaller than a mountain ○ *Slopes on the side of a hill or mountain facing away from the sun receive less intense radiation.* ○ *Hill shading is pro-*

duced by assuming that bright light is shining across the chart sheet so that shadows are cast by the high ground.

hinder /'hɪndə/ *verb* to make it difficult for something to happen ○ *Free flow of fuel may be hindered by a blockage in the fuel line.* ○ *Her illness hindered his progress on the course.*

hinge /hɪndʒ/ *noun* a device which allows a door, flap or lid to open and close on a stationary frame ○ *Flying control hinges should be inspected before flight.* ■ *verb* to move against a stationary frame ○ *Access to the engine compartment is normally via hinged cowling panels.*

HIRF *abbreviation* high-intensity radiated fields

HMR *abbreviation* helicopter main route

hoar /'hɔː/, **hoar frost** *noun* a frozen dew which forms on outside surfaces when the temperature falls below freezing point ○ *Rapid descent from cold altitudes into warm moist air may produce hoar frost on the aircraft.*

hold /həʊld/ *noun* an area or compartment within the aircraft for carrying freight ○ *Carry-on baggage is limited by regulations as to size and weight and items in excess of this should be stowed in the luggage hold.* ■ *verb* **1.** to keep and prevent from moving ○ *The function of the autopilot system is to hold the aircraft on a desired flight path by means of gyroscopes and/or accelerometers.* ○ *If the operating pressure falls or fails, a mechanical lock holds the reverser in the forward thrust position.* **2.** to keep an aircraft in a particular position on the ground or in the air while waiting for further clearance from air traffic control ○ *It is normal practice for ATC to hold taxiing aircraft well clear of the glide path and localiser antenna when visibility is poor.* **3.** to have and keep in the hand ○ *Hold the microphone in your right hand.* □ **hand-held** possible to hold in the hand ○ *Nowadays, headsets are usually used in preference to hand-held microphones.* **4.** to have (NOTE: **holding – held**) □ he

holds an IMC rating he has an IMC rating

holder /'həʊldə/ *noun* **1.** a device for holding something ○ *a holder for a fire extinguisher* **2.** a person who has a particular title or qualification ○ *a holder of two awards for distinguished service*

holding fuel /'həʊldɪŋ ˌfjuːəl/ *noun* extra fuel carried by an aircraft to allow for time spent in the hold waiting for air traffic control clearance

holding pattern *noun* a racetrack-shaped flight pattern with two parallel sides and two turns, flown usually while an aircraft is waiting for clearance to land

holding point /'həʊldɪŋ pɔɪnt/ *noun* **1.** a particular location, in the air or on the ground where aircraft spend time, waiting for further clearance from air traffic control **2.** a place, often designated Alpha, Bravo, Charlie, etc., where aircraft wait before entering the runway, as instructed by air traffic control

holding stack /'həʊldɪŋ stæk/ an area of airspace where planes are instructed to wait before landing if there are delays (NOTE: Aircraft circle and descend according to the controller's instructions until they are released from the lowest height in the stack for their final approach to the airport.)

hollow /'hɒləʊ/ *adjective* having a space within, not solid ○ *a hollow drive shaft* Opposite **solid**

home /həʊm/ *noun* the home airfield □ **home airfield** the airfield which one returns to after a two-leg flight

homeward /'həʊmwəd/ *adjective* going towards home ○ *homeward journey* ■ *adverb* □ **homeward bound** heading towards home

homewards /'həʊmwədz/ *adverb* towards home ○ *They were heading homewards when the accident happened.*

homing /'həʊmɪŋ/ *noun* a flight towards or away from a radio station while using direction finding equipment ○ *Where an RBI is fitted, homing to an NDB can be made by initially turning the aircraft until the relative bearing is zero.*

homogeneous /ˌhəʊməʊˈdʒiːniəs/ *adjective* of the same kind ○ *If the air over a large region were homogeneous, there would be no horizontal differences in surface temperature.* ○ *The atmosphere is not homogeneous – pressure, temperature and humidity can all change with height.*

hop /hɒp/ *noun* a flight or section of a flight in an aircraft (*informal*)

horizon /həˈraɪz(ə)n/ *noun* the line where the sky and the ground appear to join □ **visual horizon** a horizon which can be seen

horizontal /ˌhɒrɪˈzɒnt(ə)l/ *adjective* parallel to the horizon, or at right angles to the vertical ○ *The horizontal motion of air is known as wind.*

horizontal axis /ˌhɒrɪzɒnt(ə)l ˈæksɪs/ *noun* a horizontal reference line of a graph ○ *The plot shows the effect of airspeed on lift with airspeed shown on the horizontal axis and lift on the vertical axis.*

horizontal situation indicator /ˌhɒrɪzɒnt(ə)l ˌsɪtʃuˈeɪʃ(ə)n ˌɪndɪkeɪtə/ *noun* a cockpit instrument which gives the pilot information about the direction of the aircraft's flight path ○ *On the aircraft, the horizontal situation indicator is located on the instrument panel below the attitude indicator.* Abbreviation **HSI**

COMMENT: The horizontal situation indicator combines the function of the heading indicator and a VOR/ILS display.

horizontal stabiliser /ˌhɒrɪzɒnt(ə)l ˈsteɪbəlaɪzə/ *noun* a tailplane ○ *The horizontal stabiliser provides stability about the lateral axis of the aircraft.*

horn /hɔːn/ *noun* a device for projecting sound □ **warning horn** device which emits a loud warning noise

horn balance /ˈhɔːn ˌbæl(ə)ns/ *noun* part of a control surface forward of the hinge line which reduces the force needed by the pilot to move the surface

horsepower /ˈhɔːspaʊə/ *noun* the accepted unit for measuring the rate of doing work ○ *Horsepower is defined as 33,000 foot-pounds of work done in one minute.* Abbreviation **h.p.**, **HP**

hose /həʊz/ *noun* a long, flexible pipe usually made of fabric, plastic or rubber for pumping gases or liquids □ **refuelling hose** a flexible pipe used to pump fuel from the bowser to the aircraft

hot /hɒt/ *adjective* very warm, having a high temperature ○ *hot weather* □ **hot air** air introduced to melt ice forming in the carburettor in a piston engine aircraft

hour /aʊə/ *noun* **1.** a period of time which lasts sixty minutes ○ *It's a three-hour flight to Greece from London.* **2.** a method of indicating time ○ *Flight BA 321 landed at Heathrow at 10.30 hours.*

house /haʊz/ *verb* to contain or accommodate ○ *The areas between the ribs in the wings are utilised to house fuel tanks.* ○ *The wing tips house the navigation lights.*

housing /ˈhaʊzɪŋ/ *noun* a compartment or container ○ *The crankcase is the housing that encloses the various mechanical parts surrounding the crankshaft.* □ **engine housing** engine compartment

hover /ˈhɒvə/ *verb* to remain stationary, relative to the earth, while in the air ■ *noun* a period of stationary flight ○ *During a hover, helicopter pilots must be able to coordinate movements of both hands and feet.*

hovercraft /ˈhɒvəkrɑːft/ *noun* a vehicle that can travel over land and water supported on a cushion of air that is produced by a powerful engine that blows air downwards. Also called **air cushion vehicle**, **ground effect machine**

however /haʊˈevə/ *adverb* but ○ *The wind was gusty, however the landing was good.* ○ *The incident was serious, however she escaped with only a warning.*

hrs *abbreviation* hours

HSI *abbreviation* horizontal situation indicator

hub /hʌb/ *noun* a major airport where international or long-distance flights take off and land

hub airport /'hʌb ˌeəpɔːt/ *noun* same as **hub**

HUD *abbreviation* head-up display

human factors /ˌhjuːmən 'fæktəz/ *noun* the study of the way in which humans handle, and react to, things in their environment. It is used in aviation to develop safer systems and procedures. (NOTE: Human factors is followed by a verb in the singular.)

humid /'hjuːmɪd/ *adjective* containing a lot of water vapour □ **humid weather** weather which, although warm, feels damp and uncomfortable

humidity /hjuː'mɪdɪti/ *noun* a measurement of how much water vapour is contained in the air □ **the humidity is high** there is a lot of moisture or water vapour in the air

hydraulic /haɪ'drɔːlɪk/ *adjective* referring to any system or device which uses fluids such as oil to transmit a force from one place to another using pipes ○ *a hydraulic pump*

hydraulic fluid /haɪˌdrɒlɪk 'fluːɪd/ *noun* thin oil used in hydraulic braking systems, etc.

hydraulic pressure /haɪ'drɔːlɪk 'preʃə/ *noun* the pressure exerted by hydraulic fluid

hydraulic tubing /haɪ'drɔːlɪk 'tjuːbɪŋ/ *noun* system of tubes or thin pipes connecting the main components of a hydraulic system

hydro- /haɪdrəʊ/ *prefix* water ○ *a hydro-mechanical governor*

hygrometer /haɪ'grɒmɪtə/ *noun* an instrument used for the measurement of humidity ○ *The most common type of hygrometer is the wet and dry bulb thermometer arrangement.*

hypoxia /haɪ'pɒksiə/ *noun* a medical condition in which not enough oxygen is supplied to the body ○ *The symptoms of hypoxia are sometimes difficult to detect.*

COMMENT: Cabin pressurisation or oxygen equipment is usually required for flying at altitudes at or above about 10,000 ft (3,048 m).

Hz *abbreviation* Hertz

I

IAS /ˌaɪ eɪ 'es/ *abbreviation* indicated airspeed

IATA *abbreviation* International Air Transport Association

I-beam /'aɪ biːm/ a large bar of metal or some other strong substance with a cross-section shaped like the letter 'I'

ICAO /aɪ'keɪəʊ/ *abbreviation* International Civil Aviation Organization

ice /aɪs/ *noun* frozen water

ice crystal /'aɪs ˌkrɪst(ə)l/ *noun* a type of precipitation composed of crystals in the form of needles, plates or columns

icing /'aɪsɪŋ/ *noun* a process by which part of the aircraft becomes covered in ice while in flight ○ *Engine icing can be extremely hazardous to flight.* ○ *Airframe icing can be encountered in wave cloud.* ◊ **anti-icing, de-icing**

ideal /aɪ'dɪəl/ *adjective* perfect, as good as can be expected or the best possible □ **an ideal situation** a very good situation □ **ideal flying conditions** very good flying conditions

ident /'aɪdent/ *noun* a function on the transponder panel which helps a controller to identify the aircraft ○ *The ident is suppressed until the standby VOR is fully run-up and has passed its monitor checks.* Full form **identity**

identical /aɪ'dentɪk(ə)l/ *adjective* exactly the same □ **identical computers** computers which are exactly the same

identification /aɪˌdentɪfɪ'keɪʃ(ə)n/ *noun* the process by which a person, aircraft, etc., is recognised □ **identification of ground features** means by which particular features on a chart,

such as railway lines or bridges, are matched with the real feature on the ground

identification beacon /aɪˌdentɪfɪ'keɪʃ(ə)n ˌbiːkən/ *noun* an aeronautical beacon which gives out a Morse signal which enables a pilot to establish their location in relation to the beacon ○ *Civil and military aerodrome identification beacons can be distinguished by colour.*

identifier /aɪ'dentɪfaɪə/ *noun* a grouped number/letter code by which a weather station or beacon can be recognised ○ *When a TAF requires amendment, the amended forecast is indicated by inserting AMD (amended) after TAF in the identifier and this new forecast covers the remaining validity period of the original TAF.*

identify /aɪ'dentɪfaɪ/ *verb* to recognise ○ *Crew members can be identified by their uniforms.* ○ *In conditions of poor visibility, it is sometimes difficult to identify ground features.*

identity /aɪ'dentɪti/ *noun* the name and details of a person, aircraft, etc. ○ *The air traffic controllers are trying to establish the identity of the aircraft.* ◊ **ident**

idle /'aɪd(ə)l/ *noun* the state of an engine when it is running but not delivering power to move the vehicle or aircraft ■ *verb* to turn over slowly without providing enough power to move the vehicle or aircraft ○ *After starting a piston engine from cold, it is good practice to allow it to idle for a short time before opening the throttle wide.*

idle cut-off /ˌaɪd(ə)l 'kʌt ˌɒf/ *noun* a position on the mixture control of a light aircraft which allows the engine to be shut down without leaving a combustible fuel/air mixture in the engine

idle rpm /ˌaɪd(ə)l ˌɑː piː ˈem/ *noun* the speed at which a piston engine turns when it is not running fast enough to move the vehicle or aircraft, i.e. on a light aircraft when the throttle is almost closed

idling /ˈaɪd(ə)lɪŋ/ *noun* a state in which the engine is turning over slowly without providing enough power to move the vehicle or aircraft

idling speed /ˈaɪd(ə)lɪŋ spiːd/ *noun* the rpm of the engine when it is idling ○ *After start-up, the engine accelerates up to idling speed.* ○ *Before the engine is stopped, it should normally be allowed to run for a short period at idling speed to ensure gradual cooling.*

IF *abbreviation* **1.** instrument flying **2.** intermediate frequency

IFR *abbreviation* instrument flight rules

ignite /ɪgˈnaɪt/ *verb* to burn or cause to burn ○ *The spark plug ignites the fuel/air mixture.* ○ *The air/fuel mixture ignites.*

igniter /ɪgˈnaɪtə/ *noun* a device for starting gas turbine engines ○ *An electric spark from the igniter plug starts combustion.*

ignition /ɪgˈnɪʃ(ə)n/ *noun* **1.** the starting of burning of a substance ○ *Satisfactory ignition depends on the quality of the fuel.* **2.** the moment, in an internal combustion engine, when a spark from the spark plug causes the fuel/air mixture to burn ○ *Ignition should occur just before top-dead-centre.* **3.** an electrical system, usually powered by a battery or magneto, that provides the spark to ignite the fuel mixture in an internal-combustion engine ○ *Ignition problems are a source of many engine failures.* **4.** a switch that activates the ignition system □ **the key is in the ignition** the key is in its position in the ignition lock

ignition key /ɪgˈnɪʃ(ə)n kiː/ *noun* a key used to switch on the ignition

ignition lock /ɪgˈnɪʃ(ə)n lɒk/ *noun* a key-operated switch for activating the ignition circuit of an aircraft or a vehicle

illuminate /ɪˈluːmɪneɪt/ *verb* **1.** to give light to an otherwise dark area ○ *A flare illuminates the ground below it.* **2.** to show a light or become bright ○ *When the aircraft is 5 knots above stalling speed, a warning lamp illuminates.*

illumination /ɪˌluːmɪˈneɪʃ(ə)n/ *noun* light ○ *Batteries provide about 20 minutes illumination for the lamp.* □ **daylight illumination** the amount of light in normal daytime conditions

illustrate /ˈɪləstreɪt/ *verb* **1.** to demonstrate or explain clearly, often by using pictures ○ *Contour charts illustrate the horizontal distribution of height above mean sea level.* **2.** to show as an example ○ *A number of aviation disasters have illustrated the importance of clear, correct use of language in R/T (Radiotelephony) communications.*

illustration /ˌɪləˈstreɪʃ(ə)n/ *noun* **1.** a picture which explains something ○ *The illustration on page 23 shows a cross section of a typical gas-turbine engine.* **2.** an example ○ *The mechanics of the föhn wind provide a good illustration of the adiabatic process in action.*

ILS *abbreviation* instrument landing system

ILS glideslope /ˌaɪ el es ˈglaɪdsləʊp/ *noun* a radio beam in an ILS which gives vertical guidance ○ *The angle of the glide slope is usually about three degrees to the horizontal.* ◊ **glideslope**

ILS locator beacon /ˌaɪ el es ləʊ ˈkeɪtə ˌbiːk(ə)n/ *noun* a non-directional beacon used for final approach ○ *Power output can be as little as 15 watts for an ILS locator beacon.*

IM *abbreviation* inner marker

image /ˈɪmɪdʒ/ *noun* a reproduction of the form of an object or person ○ *Although difficult to see, the photograph shows the image of the aircraft with part of the fin missing.* (NOTE: It suggests that the image has no detail and that it is the shape which is important.)

imaginary /ɪ'mædʒɪn(ə)ri/ *adjective* not real ○ *The equator is an imaginary line around the earth.*

IMC *abbreviation* instrument meteorological conditions

immediate /ɪ'miːdiət/ *adjective* **1.** happening at once or instantly ○ *Fire extinguishers should be ready for immediate use in the event of an emergency.* □ **in the immediate future** in the very near future **2.** nearby, close at hand ○ *The immediate area surrounding the Earth is known as the atmosphere.*

immerse /ɪ'mɜːs/ *verb* to cover completely in liquid, to submerge ○ *Fuel is pumped from the main tanks via fully immersed booster pumps mounted on the base of the fuel tank.*

imminent /'ɪmɪnənt/ *adjective* due to happen in a very short time ○ *The transmission made it clear that the aircraft was in imminent danger.* ○ *A message from the flight deck informs cabin staff that take-off is imminent.*

impact /'ɪmpækt/ *noun* the striking of one body against another, a collision □ **on impact** as soon as it hit something ○ *One of the tyres burst on impact (with the ground).* ○ *Super-cooled water droplets start to freeze on impact with an aircraft surface.*

impact resistance /'ɪmpækt rɪ ˌzɪstəns/ *noun* the ability of a material to withstand an impact

impair /ɪm'peə/ *verb* to cause to become less effective ○ *Constant exposure to very loud noise impairs the hearing.* ○ *The pilot's vision may be temporarily impaired by lightning flashes.* ○ *An incorrect grade of fuel impairs engine performance.*

impairment /ɪm'peəmənt/ *noun* a lessening of effectiveness ○ *De-icing equipment is used to prevent impairment of the lifting surfaces through ice formation.*

impart /ɪm'pɑːt/ *verb* to give, to pass on ○ *A rotating propeller imparts rearward motion to a mass of air.*

impedance /ɪm'piːd(ə)ns/ *noun* total electrical resistance to current flow in an alternating current circuit ○ *Imped-*

ance will vary with changes in frequency.

impede /ɪm'piːd/ *verb* to hinder or obstruct progress ○ *Hills and mountains impede the horizontal flow of air.*

impeller /ɪm'pelə/ *noun* a rotor used to force a fluid in a particular direction

importance /ɪm'pɔːt(ə)ns/ *noun* significance, strong effect or influence ○ *Upper winds are of great importance in meteorology.* (NOTE: The expressions **of fundamental importance, of great importance, of prime importance, of utmost importance, of vital importance** all mean **very important**.)

import duty /'ɪmpɔːt ˌdjuːti/ *noun* payment made to a government on particular goods imported or exported ○ *the duty payable on a carton of cigarettes* Also called **customs duty, duty**

impose /ɪm'pəʊz/ *verb* **1.** to force something upon a person or thing ○ *The trimmer is used to ease the loads imposed on the flying controls during flight.* **2.** □ **to impose a fine** to require somebody to pay a sum of money as punishment □ **to impose restrictions** to place limitations on somebody's actions

improve /ɪm'pruːv/ *verb* to make or become better ○ *Turbochargers improve aircraft performance.* ○ *The trainee's flying skills improved a lot in a short period of time.*

improvement /ɪm'pruːvmənt/ *noun* the process of becoming better, or something that makes a thing better ○ *An improvement in weather conditions enabled the flight to depart.*

impulse /'ɪmpʌls/ *noun* a force of short duration ○ *A magneto is designed to produce electrical impulses one after another at precise intervals, so that each separate impulse can be used to provide a spark at a spark plug.*

impulse magneto /'ɪmpʌls mæg ˌniːtəʊ/ *noun* a magneto with a mechanism to give a sudden rotation and thus produce a strong spark

inability /ˌɪnə'bɪlɪti/ *noun* the fact of being unable to do something

inactive /ɪn'æktɪv/ *adjective* not switched on, in a passive state ○ *At the* *time of the accident the autopilot was inactive.*

inadvertent /ˌɪnəd'vɜːt(ə)nt/ *adjective* not intended, not meant, accidental ○ *A safety mechanism prevents inadvertent retraction of the undercarriage while the aircraft is on the ground.*

inboard /'ɪnbɔːd/ *adverb* closer to the centre of an aircraft rather than the sides or edges

inbound /'ɪnbaʊnd/ *adverb, adjective* towards a destination ○ *The aircraft flies outbound from the beacon along the airway and inbound to the facility at the other end of the leg.* □ **inbound traffic** aircraft flying towards an airfield

incapacity /ˌɪnkə'pæsɪti/ *noun* the inability to do what is needed, not having the necessary power to do something □ **crew incapacity** an injury to a crew member which prevents him or her from performing his or her normal duties ○ *Accident research has shown that crew incapacity greatly increases the risk to passengers' safety.*

inch /ɪnʃ/ *noun* a British Imperial System unit of length, also used in the US, equal to 25.4 millimetres or 2.54 centimetres or 1/12 of a foot. Abbreviation **in** (NOTE: The plural form is **inches**, usually written **in** or " with numbers, **5ft 6in** or **5' 6"**. Say five foot six inches.)

incidence /'ɪnsɪd(ə)ns/ *noun* the frequency of occurrence ○ *The incidence of structural failure has decreased with the introduction of modern construction materials and techniques.*

incident /'ɪnsɪd(ə)nt/ *noun* an event or happening which interrupts normal procedure ○ *A violent passenger had to be removed from the aircraft before departure, and details of the incident were reported in the local newspapers.*

'…in 1995, a pilot flying above Las Vegas was struck by a laser beam and incapacitated for more than two hours. It was one of over fifty incidents involving lasers and aircraft reported in the area that year' [*Pilot*]

inclination /ˌɪnklɪ'neɪʃ(ə)n/ *noun* a slope or slant from the horizontal or vertical

incline /ɪn'klaɪn/ *verb* to slope or slant from the horizontal or vertical, to tilt ○ *The runway inclines slightly upwards.* ■ *noun* /'ɪnklaɪn/ a slope or slant ○ *There is a steep incline at the end of the runway.*

inclinometer /ˌɪnklɪ'nɒmɪtə/ *noun* the lower part of a **turn coordinator**, in which a ball in a sealed curved tube indicates if a turn is coordinated. Also called **rudder ball**. ◊ **ball**

include /ɪn'kluːd/ *verb* to take in as a part, to count along with others ○ *Solid particles in the atmosphere include dust, sand, volcanic ash and atmospheric pollution.* ○ *A fuel system includes tanks, fuel lines, fuel pumps, fuel filters and a carburettor or fuel injection system.* Opposite **exclude**

inclusive /ɪn'kluːsɪv/ *adjective* taking in the extremes in addition to the part in between □ **bearings 180° to 270° inclusive** bearings 180° and 270° are part of the range of bearings mentioned

incoming /'ɪnkʌmɪŋ/ *adjective* something which is being received, e.g. radio waves or solar radiation ○ *incoming transmissions* ○ *incoming signal* ○ *There is a fall of temperature until about one hour after dawn when incoming solar radiation balances outgoing terrestrial radiation.* Opposite **outgoing**

incorporate /ɪn'kɔːpəreɪt/ *verb* to include as part of something which already exists ○ *Some types of outflow valve incorporate safety valves.* ○ *Warning lamps often incorporate a press-to-test facility.*

'…the instrument panel on the Mooney Encore has been re-engineered to incorporate improvements' [*Civil Aviation Training*]

incorrect /ˌɪnkə'rekt/ *adjective* not correct, not right ○ *If the trim position is incorrect, a warning horn will sound when number three thrust lever is advanced.*

increase *noun* /'ɪnkriːs/ a rise to a greater number or degree ○ *Decreasing engine rpm results in an increase in the rate of descent.* Opposite **reduction** ■

verb /ɪn'kriːs/ to become greater or more, to rise ○ *As you increase height, the countryside below you appears to flatten out.* Opposite **reduce** ▸ opposite (all senses) **decrease**

increment /'ɪŋkrɪmənt/ *noun* something added ○ *The minimum detection range of a pulse radar system is equal to half the pulse length plus a small increment.*

incur /ɪn'kɜː/ *verb* to acquire or to receive something, often something unwanted ○ *Fuel penalties can be incurred if fuel surplus to requirements is carried.* ○ *In some aircraft, the datum shift is operated automatically to cater for any large trim changes incurred by operating undercarriage, flaps, etc.* (NOTE: **incurring – incurred**) □ **to incur a financial loss** to lose money, in a business or commercial sense

indefinite /ɪn'def(ə)nət/ *adjective* without limits □ **an indefinite period of time** a period of time which, in reality, may have no end

independent /ˌɪndɪ'pendənt/ *adjective* free from the influence or effects of other people or things ○ *Airspeed is independent of wind and is the same regardless whether the aircraft is flying upwind, downwind or at any angle to the wind.* □ **independent system** a system which can operate by itself

index /'ɪndeks/ *noun* an alphabetical list of references to page numbers found at the end of a book or long document (NOTE: The plural form is **indexes** or **indices** /'ɪndɪsiːz/ .)

index letter /'ɪndeks ˌletə/, **index number** /'ɪndeks ˌnʌmbə/ *noun* a letter or number which makes it easier to reference or look up information ○ *Each observing meteorological station is shown on the chart as a small circle, identified by its own index number.*

indicate /'ɪndɪkeɪt/ *verb* **1.** to show or point out ○ *A lamp on the instrument panel will indicate when the pump is operating.* ○ *The needle indicated to zero.* **2.** to serve as a sign or symptom ○ *Black smoke from the exhaust may indicate a rich mixture or worn piston rings.*

indicated airspeed /ˌɪndɪkeɪtɪd 'eəspiːd/ *noun* the airspeed shown by the cockpit or flight-deck instrument ○ *The aircraft stalls at an indicated airspeed of 50 knots.* Abbreviation **IAS**

indication /ˌɪndɪ'keɪʃ(ə)n/ *noun* **1.** pointing out ○ *Indication of altitude is given on the altimeter.* **2.** a sign or symptom ○ *A drop in engine rpm is an indication of ice forming in the carburettor.* □ **audible indication** a sound which serves as a warning, e.g. a bleep

indicator /'ɪndɪkeɪtə/ *noun* something which shows information

individual /ˌɪndɪ'vɪdʒuəl/ *adjective* existing as a separate thing ○ *The hydraulic braking system consists of a master cylinder with individual brake cylinders at each wheel.* ○ *There is a maintenance manual for each individual engine.* ■ *noun* a separate human being considered as one rather than as a member of a larger group ○ *The instructor regards her trainees as a number of individuals rather than a group.*

induce /ɪn'djuːs/ *verb* to bring about, to cause to happen ○ *If a coil carrying a changing current is placed near another coil, the changing magnetic field cuts the other coil and induces a voltage in it.* ○ *Unequal deposits on moving parts can induce severe vibration especially on propellers and helicopter rotors.*

induced drag /ɪn,djuːst 'dræg/ *noun* part of total drag, created by lift ○ *There are two basic types of drag, induced drag and parasite drag.*

COMMENT: Induced drag is created when high-pressure air below a wing rotates around the tip to the low-pressure area above and increases as airspeed decreases and angle of attack increases.

inductance /ɪn'dʌktəns/ *noun* a measure of a conductor's ability to bring a voltage into itself when carrying a changing current, e.g. during short times when the circuit is switched on or off ○ *At low frequencies, the rate of collapse of the magnetic field will be slow and the inductance will be low.*

induction /ɪn'dʌkʃən/ *noun* **1.** the process by which the fuel/air mixture is drawn into the cylinders of an internal combustion engine ○ *The four strokes of the engine are induction, compression, combustion and exhaust.* **2.** the production of electrical current in a conductor by a change of magnetic field ○ *A transformer is a static device that changes the amplitude or phase of an alternating voltage or current by electro-magnetic induction.*

inductive /ɪn'dʌktɪv/ *adjective* referring to the production of electrical current in a conductor by a change of magnetic field ○ *One side effect of low frequency in an inductive circuit is that excess heat may be produced.*

inductor /ɪn'dʌktə/ *noun* a component in the ignition system that produces electrical current in itself by a change of magnetic field

inert /ɪ'nɜːt/ *adjective* not reacting with other substance

inert gas /ɪ'nɜːt gæs/ *noun* a gas that does not react with other substances ○ *Inert gases, dust, smoke, salt, volcanic ash, oxygen and nitrogen together constitute 99% of the atmosphere.* (NOTE: The inert gases include helium, neon, argon, krypton and xenon.)

inertia /ɪ'nɜːʃə/ *noun* the tendency of a body at rest to stay at rest or of a moving body to continue moving in a straight line unless acted on by an outside force ○ *Inertia switches operate automatically when a particular g (acceleration due to Earth's gravity) loading occurs.*

inertial /ɪ'nɜːʃ(ə)l/ *adjective* referring to inertia

inertial navigation system /ɪˌnɜːʃ(ə)l ˌnævɪ'geɪʃ(ə)n ˌsɪstəm/ *noun* a navigation system which calculates aircraft position by comparing measurements of acceleration with stored data, using gyros rather than radios. Abbreviation **INS**

inferential /ˌɪnfə'renʃ(ə)l/ *adjective* obtained by deduction ○ *The inferential method of ice detection is used in flight trials for aircraft certification.*

inflammable /ɪn'flæməb(ə)l/ *adjective* easily set on fire ○ *Petrol is an inflammable liquid.* (NOTE: **Flammable** and **inflammable** mean the same thing.) □ **highly inflammable** very easily set on fire, and therefore hazardous

inflate /ɪn'fleɪt/ *verb* to blow air into something and thereby increase its size ○ *A sharp pull on the cord will discharge the gas bottle and inflate the life jacket.* Opposite **deflate**

inflation /ɪn'fleɪʃ(ə)n/ *noun* **1.** the act of blowing air into something, e.g. a balloon or a tyre, and so increasing its size ○ *Tyre inflation pressures should be maintained within 4% limits.* **2.** a continuing increase in the price of things and a decrease in the buying power of money ○ *Annual inflation is 4%.* Opposite **deflation**

in-flight /'ɪn flaɪt/ *adjective* taking place during a flight ○ *in-flight emergency* ○ *in-flight oil loss*

influence /'ɪnfluəns/ *noun* a power which affects people or things ○ *The Atlantic Ocean has a great influence on the climate of the British Isles.* ■ *verb* to have an effect on, to change ○ *In an emergency, a crew member's power of command will influence the reaction of passengers.*

inform /ɪn'fɔːm/ *verb* to tell somebody something ○ *After a particularly heavy landing, the pilot should inform an engineer so that checks can be made to the aircraft structure.*

information /ˌɪnfə'meɪʃ(ə)n/ *noun* a collection of facts or data ○ *Meteorological visibility gives information on the transparency of the atmosphere to a stationary ground observer.* (NOTE: **Information** has no plural form.)

infra- /ɪnfrə/ *prefix* below or beneath

infrared /ˌɪnfrə'red/, **infra-red** *adjective* referring to the range of invisible radiation wavelengths from about 750 nanometres to 1 millimetre ○ *Solar radiation is short wave and of high intensity while terrestrial radiation is infra-red.*

infrequent /ɪn'friːkwənt/ *adjective* not often ○ *In northern Europe, thunderstorms are infrequent in winter time.*

ingest /ɪn'dʒest/ *verb* to take in, or to absorb into, something such as a jet engine through the intake ○ *Jet engines may be damaged by ingested chunks of ice.*

ingestion /ɪn'dʒestʃən/ *noun* the act of taking something into something such as a jet engine through the intake ○ *Ingestion of birds may seriously damage the blades of turbo-fan engines.*

inherent /ɪn'hɪərənt/ *adjective* existing as a basic or fundamental characteristic ○ *A boiling point of 100°C is an inherent characteristic of water.*

in hg *noun* the unit for measuring absolute pressure. Full form **inch(es) of mercury**

inhibit /ɪn'hɪbɪt/ *verb* to prevent or to limit the effect of something ○ *Cloud cover inhibits cooling of the Earth's surface at night.*

inhibition /ˌɪnhɪ'bɪʃ(ə)n/ *noun* the prevention or limitation of the effect of something ○ *Fuel contains chemicals for the inhibition of fungal growth.*

inhibitor /ɪn'hɪbɪtə/ *noun* a device or substance which prevents or limits the effect of something □ **icing inhibitor** a substance added to fuel to prevent fuel system icing

initial /ɪ'nɪʃ(ə)l/ *adjective* relating to or occurring at the beginning, the first □ **initial climb** the period of climb immediately after take-off □ **initial letter** the first letter of a word □ **initial stage** first stage ■ *noun* the first letter of a word

initials /ɪ'nɪʃ(ə)lz/ *plural noun* the first letters of a name ○ *His name is John Smith, his initials are JS.*

initiate /ɪ'nɪʃieɪt/ *verb* to get something going by taking the first step, to start ○ *In a serious emergency, a member of the cabin crew may initiate an evacuation of the aircraft.*

initiation /ɪˌnɪʃi'eɪʃ(ə)n/ *noun* the act of getting something going by taking the first step, starting ○ *Normally speaking, the captain is responsible for the initiation of emergency procedures.*

initiative /ɪ'nɪʃətɪv/ *noun* the power or ability to begin or to follow through competently with a plan or task ○ *Crew members must be able to act collectively and with initiative in unusual situations.*

inject /ɪn'dʒekt/ *verb* to force or drive a fluid into something ○ *An accelerator pump, operated by the movement of the throttle lever, injects fuel into the choke tube.*

injection /ɪn'dʒekʃən/ *noun* the forcing of fluid into something ○ *Power output can be boosted to a value over 100% maximum power, by the injection of a water methanol mixture at the compressor inlet or at the combustion chamber inlet.*

injector /ɪn'dʒektə/ *noun* a device that will force or drive a fluid into something

injury /'ɪndʒəri/ *noun* damage or harm done to a person ○ *Escape slides are designed to minimise the risk of injury to passengers when leaving the aircraft.*

inland /'ɪnlənd/ *adjective, adverb* referring to the interior of a country or land mass ○ *Sea fog can extend for considerable distances inland.*

inlet /'ɪnlet/ *noun* **1.** an opening which allows an intake of something ○ *turbine inlet* ○ *combustion chamber inlet* ○ *Air enters the cabin through an inlet.* **2.** a coastal feature such as at the mouth of a river

inlet valve /'ɪnlət vælv/ *noun* the valve in a piston engine which allows fuel to enter the cylinder

inner /'ɪnə/ *adjective* positioned farther inside □ **inner wing** the part of the wing near the fuselage

inner marker /ˌɪnə 'mɑːkə/ *noun* an ILS marker beacon placed between the middle marker and the end of the ILS runway

inoperative /ɪn'ɒpərətɪv/ *adjective* not functioning ○ *To prevent accidental retraction of the undercarriage, a safety switch is fitted in such a way to the oleo, that when it is compressed on the ground, the 'undercarriage up' selection is inoperative.*

input /'ɪnpʊt/ *noun* something such as energy, electrical power or information, put into a system to achieve output or a result ○ *Pumps require high input cur-*

rent. ○ *If the number of turns on the secondary winding is greater than the number of turns on the primary, the output voltage from the secondary will be greater than the input voltage to the primary.* □ **pilot control input** movements on the flying controls made by the pilot

INS *abbreviation* inertial navigation system

insert /ɪn'sɜːt/ *verb* to put in or into ○ *To prevent tyre explosion due to overheating, fusible plugs are inserted into the wheel assemblies.* ○ *Insert your telephone number in the space provided on the form.* ○ *Insert the key in the lock and turn it.*

insertion /ɪn'sɜːʃ(ə)n/ *noun* the act of putting in or into ○ *There is a space on the form for the insertion of a postal address.* ○ *When the contours for a particular pressure level have been drawn in, the chart is completed by insertion of spot temperatures and wind speed information.*

insignificant /ˌɪnsɪg'nɪfɪkənt/ *adjective* not important, of no consequence ○ *Minor changes in wind speed or direction are insignificant.*

inspect /ɪn'spekt/ *verb* to look at something closely and to check for problems or defects ○ *Propellers should be inspected prior to flight.*

inspection /ɪn'spekʃ(ə)n/ *noun* a careful check for problems ○ *Before flight, the pilot should carry out a careful inspection of the aircraft.*

instability /ˌɪnstə'bɪlɪti/ *noun* a condition in which a body or mass moves easily, and with increasing speed, away from its original position ○ *Atmospheric instability often results in strong vertical currents of air.* ○ *The built-in instability of some modern fighter aircraft makes them highly manoeuvrable but difficult to control without fly-by-wire technology.*

install /ɪn'stɔːl/ *verb* to put in position, connect and make ready for use ○ *Most carburettors are installed in a warm position to help against icing.* □ **installed battery** a battery in position in the aircraft

installation /ˌɪnstə'leɪʃ(ə)n/ *noun* **1.** the act of putting equipment or devices into position and connecting them for use ○ *The installation of the computer took three hours.* **2.** equipment or devices which are installed ○ *In some auxiliary-power-unit installations the air intake area is protected against ice formation by bleeding a supply of hot air from the compressor over the intake surfaces.*

instance /'ɪnstəns/ *noun* an example which is used to provide evidence of something ○ *Failure to check fuel levels before take-off is an instance of bad airmanship.* □ **for instance** e.g.

instant /'ɪnstənt/ *adjective* immediate, happening immediately ■ *noun* a very short period of time ○ *The pilot has to act in an instant to counteract the severe downdraughts of a microburst.*

instinctive /ɪn'stɪŋktɪv/ *adjective* natural, rather than thought-out ○ *In most modern light aircraft, use of the trim wheel is instinctive, i.e. forwards for nose down and backwards for nose up.*

instruct /ɪn'strʌkt/ *verb* to give information or knowledge, usually in a formal setting such as a lesson or briefing ○ *The safety officer instructs employees on the use of the breathing equipment.* ○ *The training captain instructs trainee pilots in the simulator.*

instruction /ɪn'strʌkʃən/ *noun* **1.** the act of giving information or knowledge, usually in a formal setting such as a lesson or briefing ○ *Trainees receive first-aid instruction.* **2.** information on how something should be operated or used ○ *You must follow the instructions.*

instruction manual /ɪn'strʌkʃən ˌmænjuəl/ *noun* a book containing information on how something should be operated or used

instructor /ɪn'strʌktə/ *noun* a person who gives information or knowledge, usually in a formal setting such as a lesson or briefing

instrument /'ɪnstrʊmənt/ *noun* a device for recording, measuring or controlling, especially functioning as part of a control system ○ *Airspeed is given* *on an instrument called the airspeed indicator.*

instrument approach procedure /ˌɪnstrʊmənt əˈprəʊtʃ prəˌsiːdʒə/ *noun* a set of procedures which a pilot must follow when approaching an airport under **instrument flight rules**

instrumentation /ˌɪnstrʊmenˈteɪʃ(ə)n/ *noun* a set of specialised instruments on an aircraft ○ *Instrumentation in some basic light aircraft is restricted to a few instruments only.* ○ *Some modern light aircraft have very sophisticated instrumentation.*

instrument error /ˈɪnstrʊmənt ˌerə/ *noun* the difference between indicated instrument value and true value

instrument flight rules /ˌɪnstrʊmənt ˈflaɪt ˌruːlz/ *plural noun* regulations which must be followed when weather conditions do not meet the minima for visual flight ○ *The flight from Manchester to Prestwick was conducted under instrument flight rules.* Abbreviation **IFR**

instrument flying /ˈɪnstrʊmənt ˌflaɪɪŋ/ *noun* flying using no references other than the flight instruments ○ *Some conditions require instrument flying.* ○ *When in cloud, instrument flying is required.* Abbreviation **IF**

instrument landing /ˈɪnstrʊmənt ˌlændɪŋ/ *noun* the landing of an aircraft when a pilot is relying on information obtained from instruments rather than from what can be seen outside the aircraft

instrument landing system /ˌɪnstrʊmənt ˈlændɪŋ ˌsɪstəm/ *noun* aids for an instrument landing approach to an airfield, consisting of a localiser, glide slope, marker beacons and approach lights ○ *The instrument landing system provides both horizontal and vertical guidance to aircraft approaching a runway.* Abbreviation **ILS**

COMMENT: The ILS is the most used precision approach system in the world.

instrument meteorological conditions /ˌɪnstrʊmənt ˌmiːtiərəlɒdʒɪk(ə)l kənˈdɪʃ(ə)nz/ *plural noun* meteorological conditions of visibility and distance from cloud ceiling which are less than those for visual meteorological conditions ○ *The basic licence does not permit the pilot to fly in instrument meteorological conditions.* Abbreviation **IMC**

instrument rating /ˈɪnstrʊmənt ˌreɪtɪŋ/ *noun* an additional qualification added to a licence, such as PPL, allowing a pilot to fly in instrument meteorological conditions ○ *He gained his instrument rating in 1992.* Abbreviation **I/R**

COMMENT: An instrument rating is required for operating in clouds or when the ceiling and visibility are less than those required for flight under visual flight rules (VFR).

insufficient /ˌɪnsəˈfɪʃ(ə)nt/ *adjective* not enough ○ *Insufficient height resulted in the pilot landing short of the runway.*

insulate /ˈɪnsjʊleɪt/ *verb* **1.** to prevent the passing of heat, cold or sound into or out of an area **2.** to prevent the passing of electricity to where it is not required, especially by using a non-conducting material ○ *Bus bars are insulated from the main structure and are normally provided with some form of protective covering.*

insulating /ˈɪnsjʊleɪtɪŋ/ *adjective* preventing the unwanted passage of heat, cold, sound or electricity

insulating tape /ˈɪnsjʊleɪtɪŋ ˌteɪp/ *noun* special adhesive tape which is used to insulate electrical wires ○ *Insulating tape was used to prevent the electrical wires from touching.*

insulation /ˌɪnsjʊˈleɪʃ(ə)n/ *noun* an act of or state of preventing the passing of heat, cold, sound or electricity from one area to another ○ *For continuous supersonic flight, fuel tank insulation is necessary to reduce the effect of kinetic heating.*

insulator /ˈɪnsjʊleɪtə/ *noun* a substance which will insulate, especially which will not conduct electricity ○ *Wood is a good insulator.*

intake /ˈɪnteɪk/ *noun* an opening through which a fluid is allowed into a container or tube

intake guide vane /'inteik gaid ˌvein/ *noun* a device to direct the flow of air at the air-intake

intake lip /'inteik lip/ *noun* the rim or edge of the air intake of a jet engine ○ *As sonic speed is approached, the efficiency of the intake begins to fall because of shock waves at the intake lip.*

intake temperature gauge /ˌinteik 'tempritʃə ˌgeidʒ/ *noun* an instrument to indicate the temperature of air entering an engine

integral /'intigrəl/ *adjective* which completes the whole or which belongs to a whole ○ *Meteorology is an integral part of a flying training course.* □ **integral fuel tanks** tanks which are located within the structure of the aircraft

integrity /in'tegriti/ *noun* the state of being complete and in good working condition ○ *The engine fire warning system is checked to test its integrity.* ○ *The integrity of an aid used to conduct procedural approaches must be high.*

intend /in'tend/ *verb* to have a particular plan, aim or purpose ○ *A battery is intended to supply only limited amounts of power.* □ **intended track** desired course of flight

intense /in'tens/ *adjective* **1.** extreme in amount □ **intense heat** very high heat □ **intense wind** very strong wind **2.** □ **intense concentration** very hard or deep concentration

intensity /in'tensiti/ *noun* the amount or strength of heat, light, radiation ○ *Surface air temperatures depend mostly on the intensity and duration of solar radiation.*

intention /in'tenʃən/ *noun* the course of action one means or plans to follow ○ *It is not the intention of this chapter to give a detailed description of world weather.* ○ *Our intention is to provide safe, cost-effective flying.*

inter- /intə/ *prefix* between

interact /ˌintər'ækt/ *verb* to act on each other ○ *Angle of attack and the profile of the wing section interact to produce lift.* ○ *Direct and reflected path signals can interact to cause bending of the localiser and/or generation of a false glidepath.*

intercept /ˌintə'sept/ *verb* to stop or interrupt the intended path of something ○ *When a radio transmission is made from a moving platform, there will be a shift in frequency between the transmitted and intercepted radio signals.*

interconnect /ˌintəkə'nekt/ *verb* to connect together ○ *The fire extinguishers for each engine are interconnected, so allowing two extinguishers to be used on either engine.*

inter-crew /ˌintə 'kruː/ *adjective* □ **inter-crew communications** communications between members of the crew ○ *The lack of inter-crew communication contributed to the accident.*

interfere /ˌintə'fiə/ *verb* □ **to interfere with** to get in the way of something or come between things and thus create a problem ○ *An engine intake close to another surface, such as the fuselage tail section, must be separated from that surface so that the slower boundary layer air does not interfere with the regular intake flow.*

interference /ˌintə'fiərəns/ *noun* the prevention of reception of a clear radio signal ○ *Some equipment, such as generators and ignition systems, will cause unwanted radio frequency interference.* □ **precipitation interference** interference caused by rain, snow or hail

interlock /ˌintə'lɒk/ *noun* a series of switches and/or relays ○ *Interlocks operate in a specific sequence to ensure satisfactory engagement of the autopilot.* ■ *verb* to connect together parts of a mechanism, so that the movement or operation of individual parts affects each other ○ *The two parts interlock to create a solid structure.*

intermediate /ˌintə'miːdiət/ *adjective* **1.** in a position between two others **2.** between beginners and advanced □ **he is at an intermediate stage in his studies** he is in the middle of his course of study □ **an intermediate level language student** a second language learner who has reached a level between elementary and advanced level

intermediate approach /ˌintəmiːdiət ə'prəutʃ/ *noun* the part of the approach from arriving at the first navigational fix to the beginning of the final approach

intermediate frequency /ˌɪntəmiːdiət ˈfriːkwənsi/ *noun* the frequency in a radio receiver to which the incoming received signal is transformed. Abbreviation **IF**

intermittent /ˌɪntəˈmɪt(ə)nt/ *adjective* stopping and starting at intervals ○ *The cycle of induction, compression, combustion and exhaust in the piston engine is intermittent, whereas in the gas turbine, each process is continuous.*

internal /ɪnˈtɜːn(ə)l/ *adjective* referring to the inside or interior of something ○ *internal damage* Opposite **external**

internal combustion engine /ɪn ˌtɜːn(ə)l kʌmˈbʌstʃən ˌendʒɪn/ *noun* type of engine in which the fuel is burnt within the cylinders of the engine, as opposed to the steam engine

international /ˌɪntəˈnæʃ(ə)nəl/ *adjective* between countries □ **international call** a telephone call between people in two different countries

International Air Transport Association /ˌɪntənæʃ(ə)nəl eə ˈtrænspɔːt əˌsəʊsieɪʃ(ə)n/ *noun* an international organisation that supervises and coordinates air transport and to which most major airlines belong. Abbreviation **IATA**

International Calling Frequency /ˌɪntənæʃ(ə)nəl ˈkɔːlɪŋ ˌfriːkwənsi/, **International Distress Frequency** /ˌɪntənæʃ(ə)nəl dɪsˈtres ˌfriːkwənsi/ *noun* 2182 kHz or 500 kHz

International Civil Aviation Organization /ˌɪntənæʃ(ə)nəl ˌsɪvɪl ˌeɪviˈeɪʃ(ə)n ˌɔːgənaɪzeɪʃ(ə)n/ *noun* an organisation established in 1947 by governments that 'agreed on particular principles and arrangements in order that international civil aviation may be developed in a safe and orderly manner…' ○ *Air navigation obstructions in the United Kingdom are shown on ICAO aeronautical charts.* Abbreviation **ICAO**

COMMENT: ICAO is based in Montreal (Canada).

international standard atmosphere /ˌɪntənæʃ(ə)nəl ˌstændəd ˈætməsfɪə/ *noun* an internationally agreed unit of pressure used in the calibration of instruments and the measurement of aircraft performance ○ *For en route weather the datum chosen is international standard atmosphere at mean sea level.* Abbreviation **ISA**

interphone /ˈɪntəfəʊn/ an internal telephone communications system within an aircraft that enables members of the crew to speak to one another

interpolation /ɪnˌtɜːpəˈleɪʃ(ə)n/ *noun* the estimation of a middle value by reference to known values each side ○ *Spot temperatures at positions other than those printed are obtained by interpolation.*

interpret /ɪnˈtɜːprɪt/ *verb* to understand something presented in code or symbolic form ○ *Aircrew must be able to interpret information printed on a contour chart.*

interpretation /ɪnˌtɜːprɪˈteɪʃ(ə)n/ *noun* an understanding of something presented in code or symbolic form ○ *Synoptic charts require interpretation in order to understand the information given.*

interrogate /ɪnˈterəgeɪt/ *verb* to transmit SSR or ATC signals to activate a transponder ○ *Secondary surveillance radar interrogates the aircraft equipment which responds with identification and height information.*

interrogation /ɪnˌterəˈgeɪʃ(ə)n/ *noun* the transmission of a SSR or ATC signal to activate a transponder ○ *A transponder replies to interrogation by passing a four-digit code.*

interrogator /ɪnˈterəgeɪtə/ *noun* a ground-based surveillance radar beacon transmitter/receiver ○ *The questioner, better known as the interrogator, is fitted on the ground, while the responder, also known as the transponder, is an airborne installation.*

interrupt /ˌɪntəˈrʌpt/ *verb* to break the continuity of something ○ *The conversation was interrupted by a telephone call.* ○ *In the northern hemisphere, the westerly flow of air is* *interrupted by variations which occur in pressure patterns.*

interruption /ˌɪntəˈrʌpʃən/ *noun* a break in the continuity of something ○ *Because of the summer holiday, there was an interruption in the flying training course.*

intersect /ˌɪntəˈsekt/ *verb* to cut across each other ○ *Meridians intersect at the poles and cross the equator at right angles.*

intersection /ˈɪntəˌsekʃən/ *noun* the point at which two lines cross each other ○ *The aircraft came to a stop at the intersection between runways 09 and 16.* ○ *The intersection of the drift line and the wind vector gives the drift point.*

intertropical convergence zone /ˌɪntətrɒpɪk(ə)l kənˈvɜːdʒəns ˌzəʊn/ *noun* the boundary between the trade winds and tropical air masses from the northern and southern hemispheres ○ *The intertropical convergence zone is the zone in which the trade winds from the two hemispheres approach each other.* Abbreviation **ITCZ**

interval /ˈɪntəv(ə)l/ *noun* **1.** the amount of space between places or points ○ *The intervals at which contours are drawn depends on the scale of the chart and this interval, known as the vertical interval, is noted on the chart.* **2.** the period of time between two events ○ *A precise interval is essential to obtain correct ignition timing on all cylinders.*

introduction /ˌɪntrəˈdʌkʃ(ə)n/ *noun* **1.** something written which comes at the beginning of a report, chapter, etc., or something spoken which comes at the beginning of a talk ○ *In his introduction, the chief executive praised the efforts of the workforce over the previous 12 months.* **2.** the act of bringing into use ○ *The introduction of fly-by-wire technology has made the pilot's task easier.*

inverse /ɪnˈvɜːs/ *adjective* reversed in order or effect ○ *There is an inverse relationship between altitude and temperature, i.e. temperature decreases as altitude increases.*

inversion /ɪnˈvɜːʃ(ə)n/ *noun* **1.** an atmospheric phenomenon where cold air is nearer the ground than warm air ○ *Smog is smoke or pollution trapped on the surface by an inversion of temperature with little or no wind.* **2.** turning something upside down ○ *Inversion of the aircraft in flight may result in fuel stoppage.*

inversion layer /ɪnˈvɜːʃ(ə)n ˌleɪə/ *noun* a layer of the atmosphere in which the temperature increases as altitude increases

invert /ɪnˈvɜːt/ *verb* to turn upside down ○ *A glass tube is sealed at one end, filled with mercury and then inverted so that the open end is immersed in a bowl containing mercury.*

investigate /ɪnˈvestɪgeɪt/ *verb* to examine or look into something in great detail ○ *If the starter engaged light stays on after starting, it means that power is still connected to the starter and, if it is still on after 30 seconds, the cause must be investigated.*

investigation /ɪnˌvestɪˈgeɪʃ(ə)n/ *noun* a detailed inquiry or close examination of a matter □ **accident investigation** process of discovering the cause of accidents

'…accident investigation by the FAA and the German LBA revealed that the crashed aircraft had been completely repainted in an unauthorized paint shop' [*Pilot*]

investigator /ɪnˈvestɪgeɪtə/ *noun* a person who investigates ○ *Accident investigators found poor coordination between controllers.*

invisible /ɪnˈvɪzɪb(ə)l/ *adjective* impossible to see ○ *Oxygen is an invisible gas.*

involve /ɪnˈvɒlv/ *verb* to include ○ *In large transport aircraft, because of the distance and numbers of people involved, effective and rapid communications are required between flight crew and cabin crew and between cabin crew and passengers.* ○ *Two aircraft were involved in an accident.*

involved /ɪnˈvɒlvd/ *adjective* overcomplex, difficult ○ *The procedure for* *replacing a lost passport is very involved.*

inward /ˈɪnwəd/ *adjective* directed to or moving towards the inside or interior ○ *To provide protection against smoke and other harmful gases, a flow of 100% oxygen is supplied at a positive pressure to avoid any inward leakage of poisonous gases at the mask.*

inwards /ˈɪnwədz/ *adverb* towards the inside or the interior ○ *The door opens inwards.* Opposite **outwards**

ion /ˈaɪən/ *noun* an atom or a group of atoms that has obtained an electric charge by gaining or losing one or more electrons ○ *negative ion* ○ *positive ion* ○ *Ultra-violet light from the sun can cause electrons to become separated from their parent atoms of the gases in the atmosphere, the atoms left with resultant positive charges being known as ions.*

ionisation /ˌaɪənaɪˈzeɪʃ(ə)n/, **ionization** *noun* the process of producing ions by heat or radiation ○ *The intensity of ionisation depends on the strength of the ultra-violet radiation and the density of the air.*

ionosphere /aɪˈɒnəsfɪə/ *noun* the part of the atmosphere 50 km above the surface of the earth ○ *Since the strength of the sun's radiation varies with latitude, the structure of the ionosphere varies over the surface of the earth.*

ionospheric /aɪˌɒnəˈsferɪk/ *adjective* referring to the ionosphere

ionospheric attenuation /aɪˌɒnəsferɪk əˌtenjuˈeɪʃ(ə)n/ *noun* loss of signal strength to the ionosphere

ionospheric refraction /aɪˌɒnəsferɪk rɪˈfrækʃən/ *noun* a change in direction as the wave passes through an ionised layer

I/R *abbreviation* instrument rating

irregular /ɪˈregjʊlə/ *adjective* not regular ○ *Pilots of long-haul flights are subject to an irregular sleep pattern.*

irrespective /ˌɪrɪˈspektɪv/, **irrespective of** *preposition* taking no account of, regardless of ○ *Rescue flights continue their work irrespective of the weather conditions.*

ISA /ˈaɪsə/ *abbreviation* international standard atmosphere

isobar /ˈaɪsəʊbɑː/ *noun* a line on a weather chart joining points of equal atmospheric pressure ○ *Isobars are analogous to contour lines.*

isobaric /aɪsəˈbærɪk/ *adjective* referring to or showing isobars ○ *isobaric charts*

isolate /ˈaɪsəleɪt/ *verb* to separate something from other things or somebody from other people ○ *The low-pressure fuel cock isolates the airframe fuel system from the engine fuel system to enable maintenance and engine removals to be carried out.*

isolated /ˈaɪsəleɪtɪd/ *adjective* separate □ **isolated rain showers** well spaced out rain showers

isolation /ˌaɪsəˈleɪʃ(ə)n/ *noun* the state of being separated from something or somebody ○ *Isolation of the aircraft's passengers and crew from the reduced atmospheric pressure at altitude is achieved by pressurisation of the cabin.*

isotach /ˌaɪsəʊˈtæʃ/ *noun* a line of equal wind speed on charts (NOTE: Wind speed is normally given in the form of isotachs.)

isotherm /ˈaɪsəʊθɜːm/ *noun* a line of equal temperature on charts ○ *Ascent of stable air over high ground may result in a lowering of the 0°C isotherm.*

issue /ˈɪʃuː/ *noun* a number or copy ○ *The article was in last month's issue of the magazine.* ■ *verb* **1.** to give out ○ *The captain issued the evacuate command.* **2.** to publish ○ *The magazine is issued monthly.* **3.** to give out, to grant ○ *The Civil Aviation Authority issue licences.*

ITCZ *abbreviation* intertropical convergence zone

item /ˈaɪtəm/ *noun* a single article or unit in a collection, on a list, etc. ○ *Before practising stalls, the pilot should secure all loose items in the cockpit.*

J

J *symbol* joule

JAA *abbreviation* Joint Aviation Authorities

jack /dʒæk/ *noun* a powered device to move heavy components, such as control surfaces of large aircraft

jacket /'dʒækɪt/ *noun* **1.** a short coat with long sleeves worn with trousers or skirt **2.** an outer covering or casing ○ *Liquid cooling of a piston engine is achieved by circulating a liquid around the cylinder barrels, through a passage formed by a jacket on the outside.*

jam /dʒæm/ *verb* to cause moving parts to become locked and unable to be moved □ **a jammed door** a door which has become fixed and unmovable ○ *The investigation revealed that the accident had been caused by the controls being jammed due to a spanner caught in the control cables.*

JAR *abbreviation* Joint Aviation Requirements

jato /'dʒeɪtəʊ/ *noun* an auxiliary jet or rocket designed to aid the combined thrust of aircraft jet engines during take-off

jeopardise /'dʒepədaɪz/, **jeopardize** *verb* to put in doubt or danger ○ *Injury to a crew member will seriously jeopardise the successful evacuation of the aircraft.*

Jeppesen chart /'dʒepəs(ə)n tʃɑːt/ *noun* a type of aeronautical chart produced by a US company and widely used in aviation

jet /dʒet/ *noun* **1.** a strong fast stream of fluid forced out of an opening ○ *a jet of water from a pipe* **2.** a type of engine used to power modern aircraft which takes in air at the front, mixes it with fuel, burns the mixture and the resulting expansion of gases provides thrust ○ *The turbo jet engine was invented by Frank Whittle in 1941.* **3.** a type of aircraft which has jet engines ○ *The de Havilland Comet was the first commercial jet.*

jetbridge /'dʒetbrɪdʒ/ *noun* same as **loading bridge**

jet fighter /'dʒet ˌfaɪtə/ *noun* a fighter plane that is powered by a jet engine or engines

jet lag /'dʒet læg/ *noun* the temporary disturbance of body rhythms such as sleep and eating habits, caused by high-speed travel across several time zones ○ *When I fly to Canada, it always takes me a couple of days to recover from jet lag.*

jetliner /'dʒetlaɪnə/ *noun* a large passenger aircraft powered by jet engines

jet plane /'dʒet pleɪn/ *noun* an aircraft powered by jet engines

jet-propelled aircraft /ˌdʒet prə ˌpeld 'eəkrɑːft/ *noun* aircraft powered by jet engines

jet propulsion /ˌdʒet prə'pʌlʃ(ə)n/ *noun* jet power which provides thrust for an aircraft ○ *The first known example of jet propulsion was when Hero, a Greek engineer, made a machine as a toy in the year 120 BC.*

jet stream /dʒet striːm/ *noun* **1.** a band of strong winds at high altitude ○ *The occurrence of the equatorial jet stream is due to a temperature gradient with colder air to the south.* **2.** the flow of gases from a jet engine

jettison /'dʒetɪs(ə)n/ *verb* to throw off or release from a moving aircraft ○ *The undercarriage failed to retract and the captain had to jettison the fuel over the sea before landing the aircraft.*

join /dʒɔɪn/ *verb* **1.** to connect ○ *Join the two wires.* ○ *With a pencil and ruler, join point A to point B.* **2.** to bring together to make one whole part ○ *Wing panels are joined by rivets.* **3.** to become a member of a club, etc. ○ *She had to pay a membership fee to join the gliding club.*

joint /dʒɔɪnt/ *noun* the place at which two or more things are joined together ○ *Fuselage frame rings are formed with only one joint.* ■ *adjective* combined, with two or more things linked together or shared by two or more people ○ *a joint effort*

Joint Aviation Authorities /ˌdʒɔɪnt ˌeɪviˈeɪʃ(ə)n ɔːˌθɒrətiz/ *noun* a body, consisting of European representatives, set up to control and regulate aspects of civil aviation in Europe ○ *The Joint Aviation Authorities is an arrangement between European countries which has developed since the 1970s.* Abbreviation **JAA**

COMMENT: The Joint Aviation Authorities currently has 37 member states, including all the countries of the European Union.

Joint Aviation Requirement /ˌdʒɔɪnt ˌeɪviˈeɪʃ(ə)n rɪˈkwaɪəmənt/ *noun* a JAA requirement concerning design, manufacture, maintenance and operation of aircraft. Abbreviation **JAR** (NOTE: JARs of relevance to maintenance staff are JAR-145, JAR-OPS 1 and JAR-OPS 3.)

joule /dʒuːl/ *noun* an International System unit of electrical, mechanical, and thermal energy ○ *Ignition units are measured in joules (1 joule = 1 watt per second).* (NOTE: It is usually written **J** with figures: *25J.*)

jumbo /'dʒʌmbəʊ/ *noun* same as **jumbo jet** (*informal*)

jumbo jet /'dʒʌmbəʊ dʒet/ *noun* a large wide-bodied aircraft capable of carrying several hundred passengers

jump jet /'dʒʌmp dʒet/ *noun* a jet aircraft with fixed wings that can take off and lands vertically

junction /'dʒʌŋkʃən/ *noun* a place where two things meet ○ *the junction of two wires*

junction box /'dʒʌŋkʃən bɒks/ *noun* electrical unit where a number of wires can be connected together

K

K *symbol* kelvin

katabatic /ˌkætəˈbætɪk/ *adjective* referring to a cold flow of air travelling down hillsides or mountainsides ○ *Due to katabatic effects, cold air flows downwards and accumulates over low ground.* Compare **anabatic**

katabatic wind /ˌkætəˈbætɪk ˈwɪnd/ *noun* a wind which occurs when the air in contact with the slope of a hill is cooled to a temperature lower than that in the free atmosphere, causing it to sink. Compare **anabatic wind**

kelvin /ˈkelvɪn/ *noun* the base SI unit of measurement of thermodynamic temperature. Symbol **K** (NOTE: Temperatures are shown in kelvin without a degree sign: *20K*. Note also that 0°C is equal to 273.15K.)

kerosene /ˈkerəsiːn/, **kerosine** *noun* a thin fuel oil made from petroleum ○ *Kerosene will only burn efficiently at, or close to, a ratio of 15:1.*

Kevlar /ˈkevlə/ *noun* a trademark for a light and very strong composite material ○ *Kevlar and carbon fibre account for a large percentage of a modern jet airliner's structure.*

key /kiː/ *noun* a piece of metal used to open a lock

kg *symbol* kilogram

kHz *symbol* kilohertz

kick-back /ˈkɪkbæk/ *noun* the tendency of the engine to suddenly reverse the rotation of the propeller momentarily when being started ○ *On most modern engines the spark is retarded to top-dead-centre, to ensure easier starting and prevent kick-back.*

kilo /ˈkiːləʊ/ *noun* same as **kilogram** ○ *This piece of luggage weighs 15 kilos.*

kilo- /kɪləʊ/ *prefix* one thousand

kilogram /ˈkɪləgræm/ *noun* a measure of weight equal to one thousand grams ○ *This piece of luggage weighs 15 kg.* Abbreviation **kg** (NOTE: It is written **kg** after figures.)

kilohertz /ˈkɪləhɜːts/ *noun* a unit of frequency measurement equal to one thousand Hertz. Abbreviation **kHz**

kilometre /kɪˈlɒmɪtə/ *noun* a measure of length equal to one thousand metres (NOTE: It is written **km** with figures: *150 km*. The US spelling is **kilometer**.)

kilowatt /ˈkɪləwɒt/ *a* unit of measurement of electricity equal to 1000 watts. Abbreviation **kW**

kilowatt-hour /ˈkɪləˌwɒt aʊə/ *noun* a unit of 1000 watts of electricity used for one hour. Abbreviation **kW-hr**

kinetic /kɪˈnetɪk, kaɪˈnetɪk/ *adjective* referring to motion or something produced by motion □ **kinetic heating** the heating of aircraft skin by friction with the air as it moves through it

kinetic energy /kaɪˌnetɪk ˈenədʒi/ *noun* energy of motion

kit /kɪt/ *noun* a set of items used for a specific purpose ○ *A physician's kit containing surgical equipment would be available to a qualified doctor assisting crew with major medical problems.*

knob /nɒb/ *noun* **1.** a rounded handle ○ *door knob* **2.** a rounded control switch or dial ○ *When the control knob is moved from the central position, the* *ailerons are moved.* **3.** a round button such as on a receiver ○ *Turn the knob to increase the volume.*

knot /nɒt/ *noun* a unit of speed equal to one nautical mile per hour, approximately 1.85 kilometres or 1.15 statute miles per hour. Abbreviation **kt** (NOTE: Wind speeds in aviation are usually given in knots.)

COMMENT: American light aircraft manufactured prior to 1976 had airspeed indicators marked in statute miles per hour. Knot means 'nautical miles per hour'. It is therefore incorrect to say 'knots per hour'.

knowledge /'nɒlɪdʒ/ *noun* familiarity, awareness or understanding gained through experience or study ○ *A knowledge of the factors which affect surface temperatures will contribute a great deal to the understanding of meteorology.*

kt *abbreviation* knot

L

label /'leɪb(ə)l/ *noun* a small piece of paper or cloth attached to an article with details of its owner, contents, use, destination, etc. ○ *Hydraulic tubing has a label with the word HYDRAULIC.* ■ *verb* **1.** to identify by using a label ○ *Parts are labelled with the manufacturer's name.* **2.** to add identifying words and numbers to a diagram ○ *There is a standard way of labelling the navigation vector.*

lack /læk/ *noun* the absence of something or a need for something ○ *The engine stopped because of a lack of fuel.*

lag /læg/ *noun* a delay, especially the time interval between an input and the resultant output ○ *There is a time lag between the piston moving down and the mixture flowing into the cylinder.* ◊ **jet lag**

Lambert's projection /'læmbəts prə,dʒekʃ(ə)n/ a map projection of the earth based around two standard parallels of latitude. ◊ **Mercator's projection**

laminate /'læmɪnət/ *noun* a sheet of man-made material made up of bonded layers ○ *Direction of the fibres and types of cloth used in the laminate are all very important factors.* ■ *verb* /'læmɪneɪt/ to make by using bonded layers of material ○ *laminated windscreens*

lamp /læmp/ *noun* a small light □ **warning lamp** a small light, often red, which informs of a possible danger by lighting up ○ *The switch is connected to a warning lamp on the instrument panel which will illuminate if the oil pressure falls below an acceptable minimum.*

land /lænd/ *noun* solid ground, as opposed to the sea ○ *a large land mass such as Greenland* ■ *verb* **1.** to set an aircraft onto the ground or another surface such as ice or water, after a flight □ **to force land the aircraft** to land the aircraft when it can no longer be kept in the air for any particular reason **2.** to arrive on the ground after a flight ○ *Flight BA321 landed at London Heathrow at 1030 hours.* ◊ **crash-land**. Opposite **take off**

landing /'lændɪŋ/ *noun* the act of setting an aircraft onto the ground or another surface such as ice or water after flight ○ *Take-off and landing are normally made into wind in order to reduce the length of the take-off and landing run.* ○ *In order to achieve a safe landing in a cross wind, the correct techniques must be used.*

landing beacon /'lændɪŋ ,biːkən/ *noun* a radio transmitter at an airfield that sends a beam to guide aircraft that are landing

landing beam /'lændɪŋ biːm/ *noun* a radio beam from a beacon at a landing field that helps incoming aircraft to make a landing

landing charges /'lændɪŋ ,tʃɑːdʒɪz/ *plural noun* money paid to an airport authority by an operator or private pilot for landing an aircraft

landing field /'lændɪŋ fiːld/ *noun* a place where aircraft can land and take off

landing gear /'lændɪŋ gɪə/ *noun* same as **undercarriage**

landing pad /'lændɪŋ pæd/ *noun* same as **helipad**

landing run /ˈlændɪŋ rʌn/ *noun* the distance on the runway from the touchdown point to the stopping point or taxiing speed

landing speed /ˈlændɪŋ spiːd/ *noun* the lowest speed at which an aircraft must be flying in order to land safely

landing strip /ˈlændɪŋ strɪp/ *noun* a specially prepared area of land for an aircraft to land on

landing weight /ˈlændɪŋ weɪt/ *noun* the weight of an aircraft when it lands, which is made up of its empty weight, the weight of its payload, and the weight of its remaining fuel

landmark /ˈlændmɑːk/ *noun* something on the ground which enables the pilot to know where he/she is, e.g. a noticeable building, bridge, coastal feature, etc. ○ *Railway lines are usually useful landmarks.*

landside /ˈlændsaɪd/ *noun* the part of an airport farthest from the aircraft

lane /leɪn/ *noun* same as **air lane**

lapse rate /ˈlæps reɪt/ *noun* the rate at which temperature changes according to altitude □ **adiabatic lapse rate** the rate at which air temperature decreases as it rises above the Earth's surface. As the height increases, the temperature decreases.

COMMENT: It has been found that when dry or unsaturated air rises, its rate of fall of temperature with height (i.e. lapse rate) is constant at 3°C per 1,000 feet. Similarly, descending air warms by compression at that rate. This dry adiabatic lapse rate is normally referred to as the DALR. Air rising and cooling often reaches its dew point temperature, becomes saturated and any further cooling results in condensation and the release of latent heat. Release of latent heat delays the cooling process and the lapse rate at low levels is reduced to 1.5°C per 1,000 feet. This temperature change is called the saturated adiabatic lapse rate and is normally referred to as the SALR.

largely /ˈlɑːdʒli/ *adverb* mainly, mostly ○ *Heat is transferred from the Earth's surface upwards largely by convection.* ○ *The southern hemisphere consists largely of oceans.*

laser ring gyro /ˌleɪzə rɪŋ ˈdʒaɪrəʊ/ *noun* an instrument that uses beams of laser light in a closed circuit to detect whether something is level or not

last /lɑːst/ *adjective* coming or placed after all the others ■ *verb* **1.** to continue for a period of time ○ *A gust is a sudden increase in wind speed above the average speed lasting only a few seconds.* **2.** to stay in good or usable condition ○ *A piston engine lasts longer if it is handled carefully and serviced regularly.* ◇ **the last chapter 1.** the final chapter in a book **2.** the chapter before the one being read

latent heat /ˌleɪt(ə)nt ˈhiːt/ *noun* heat taken in or given out when a solid changes into a liquid or vapour, or when a liquid changes into a vapour at a constant temperature and pressure □ **latent heat of fusion** the quantity of heat required to convert ice, at its melting point, into liquid at the same temperature □ **latent heat of vaporization** the quantity of heat required to convert liquid to vapour at the same temperature □ **latent heat of sublimation** the quantity of heat required to convert ice to vapour at the same temperature

lateral /ˈlæt(ə)rəl/ *adjective* referring to the side ○ *Drift is the lateral movement of the aircraft caused by the wind.*

lateral axis /ˌlæt(ə)rəl ˈæksɪs/ *noun* the axis of the aircraft from wing tip to wing tip about which the aircraft pitches up and down. ◊ **axis, pitch**

latitude /ˈlætɪtjuːd/ *noun* the angular distance north or south of the Earth's equator, measured in degrees, minutes and seconds, along a meridian, as on a map or chart, etc. ○ *Parallels of latitude are imaginary circles on the surface of the Earth, their planes being parallel to the plane of the equator.* ○ *The centre of London is latitude 51°30'N, longitude 0°5'W.* Compare **longitude**

latter /ˈlætə/ *adjective* referring to something coming at the end or finish □ **the latter part of the take-off run** the part of the take-off run immediately before the aircraft leaves the ground ■ *noun* the second of two things mentioned earlier. Opposite **former** □ **of the**

Airbus A320 and A340, the latter is the larger aircraft the A340 is the larger of the two

launch /lɔːntʃ/ *noun* a small boat often used to transport people from a larger boat or ship to the shore ■ *verb* **1.** to slide or drop a boat into the water to make it ready for use ○ *While passengers are fitting life jackets, crew will open exits and launch the life-rafts.* **2.** to force something into motion ○ *to launch a rocket*

lavatory /ˈlævətri/ *noun* same as **toilet 2**

law /lɔː/ *noun* **1.** a basic principle describing a relationship observed to be unchanging between things while particular conditions are met ○ *the law of gravity* **2.** a set of agreed rules ○ *aviation law*

layer /ˈleɪə/ *noun* **1.** one horizontal part ○ *The lowest layer of the atmosphere is called the troposphere.* **2.** a thickness of something ○ *Layers of fluid next to the surface over which it is flowing travels more slowly than layers further from the surface.*

layer cloud /ˈleɪə klaʊd/ *noun* same as **stratus**

layout /ˈleɪaʊt/ *noun* the way in which things are arranged □ **cockpit layout** the design of the cockpit and the particular placement of controls, instruments, etc.

LC *abbreviation* load controller

LCD /ˌel siː ˈdiː/ *abbreviation* liquid crystal display

LDA *abbreviation* landing distance available

LDR *abbreviation* landing distance required

lead¹ /led/ *noun* a very heavy soft metallic element. Symbol **Pb** □ **lead-free** not containing lead ○ *Low-lead or lead-free fuel is used in most modern piston engines.*

lead² /liːd/ *noun* **1.** an electrical wire or narrow cable ○ *A lead connects the monitor to the computer.* **2.** □ **to take the lead** to take control of a situation ○ *It is vital in any emergency situation that a crew member should take the lead.* ■ *verb* **1.** to guide or show the way

by going first ○ *In an emergency situation the aircraft commander may lead his passengers to safety.* ○ *In a smoke-filled cabin, floor lighting leads passengers to the emergency exit.* **2.** to cause ○ *In winter, the cold conditions often lead to frost and fog.* ○ *Contraction of metal parts and seals can lead to fluid leakage.* (NOTE: **leading – led**)

lead-acid battery /ˌled ˌæsɪd ˈbat(ə)ri/ *noun* a system of lead plates and dilute sulphuric acid, used as a starter battery or traction battery

leading edge /ˈliːdɪŋ edʒ/ *noun* the front part of the wing which meets the oncoming air first ○ *In icing conditions, ice may build up on the leading edges.*

leak /liːk/ *noun* the escape of liquid or gas from a sealed container, or the amount of liquid or gas that has escaped ○ *Any failure of the aircraft structure may cause a leak of pressurised air which might be very difficult to cure.* □ **exhaust leak** an escape of exhaust gases ■ *verb* to escape from a sealed container ○ *Fuel may leak from a fuel tank if the drain plug is not seated correctly.*

leakage /ˈliːkɪdʒ/ *noun* the escape of liquid or gas from a sealed container ○ *Any internal or external leakage of fuel will cause a reduction in the operating period.* (NOTE: **Leak** is normally used for an individual instance while **leakage** is used more generally: *There is a fuel leak from the central tank*; *Fuel leakage is a safety hazard.*)

lean /liːn/ *adjective* referring to a mixture in which the ratio of air to fuel is greater than usual ○ *Moving the mixture control lever aft to the lean position reduces the amount of fuel mixing with the air.*

lean mixture /ˌliːn ˈmɪkstʃə/ *noun* a fuel/air mixture in which the ratio of air to fuel is greater than usual

LED /ˌel iː ˈdiː/ *noun* a semiconductor diode that emits light when current is applied. LEDs are used in cockpit displays. Full form **light-emitting diode**

lee /liː/ *adjective, noun* which is protected from the wind ○ *The air on the lee side is drier than that on the wind-*

ward side. ○ *The flow of air over and to the lee of hills and mountains may cause particularly severe turbulence.* Opposite **windward**

leg /leg/ *noun* part of a flight pattern that is between two stops, positions, or changes in direction ○ *An airfield traffic pattern is divided into take-off, crosswind leg, downwind leg, base leg and final approach.*

'...their route was across the States to Canada, Greenland and the North Pole, into Norway, through Europe, back to Iceland, then two long legs across the Atlantic via South Greenland and back to Seattle' [*Pilot*]

legal /'liːg(ə)l/ *adjective* lawful or within the law ○ *Alcohol concentrations of 40 milligrams per 100 millilitres, i.e. half the legal driving limit in the UK, are associated with substantial increases in errors committed by pilots.*

legend /'ledʒənd/ *noun* a list explaining the symbols on a chart or a map ○ *A legend is usually to be found at the edge or on the reverse side of most topographical charts.*

length /leŋθ/ *noun* **1.** a measurement along something's greatest dimension ○ *the length of the aircraft* ○ *The runway length is 3 kilometres.* **2.** a piece of something that is normally measured along its greatest dimension ○ *a length of pipe* **3.** the extent from beginning to end ○ *the length of a book* **4.** extent or duration, the distance between two points in space or time □ **the length of a briefing** how much time the briefing takes □ **the length of the working life of components** how long the components last ◇ **the length of a flight 1.** the time it takes to complete a flight ○ *The length of the flight meant that there was no time for a meal to be served to the passengers.* **2.** the distance of the flight in nautical miles or kilometres ○ *The length of the flight is 100nm.*

lengthen /'leŋθən/ *verb* to make long or longer ○ *The mercury column shortens when cooled and, due to expansion, lengthens when heated.* Opposite **shorten**

lengthwise /'leŋθwaɪz/ *adjective, adverb* along the length of something ○ *in a lengthwise direction*

lengthy /'leŋθi/ *adjective* **1.** long, extensive ○ *He wrote a lengthy report.* **2.** long, which lasts for a long time (NOTE: **Lengthy** often suggests a meeting or explanation which is longer than necessary and therefore uninteresting.) □ **lengthy meeting** a long meeting □ **lengthy explanation** a long explanation

lens /lenz/ *noun* a normally round piece of glass with curved surfaces found in microscopes, telescopes, cameras, spectacles, etc.

lens-shaped cloud /ˌlenz ʃeɪpt 'klaʊd/, **lenticular cloud** /lenˌtɪkjʊlə 'klaʊd/ *noun* cloud with slightly outwardly-curved upper and lower surfaces

lessen /'les(ə)n/ *verb* to make less ○ *Reverse thrust is used to lessen the loads on brakes and tyres.* ○ *Clean filters lessen the possibility of blockage.*

letdown /'letdaʊn/ *noun* the descent of an aircraft in preparation for landing, before the actual landing approach

level /'lev(ə)l/ *adjective* **1.** □ **level with** at the same height or position as something else ○ *In most light aircraft, the aeroplane will be in a climb if the engine cowling is level with the horizon.* **2.** having a flat, smooth surface □ **a level runway** a runway without bumps, etc. **3.** on a horizontal plane **4.** steady, referring to something with no sudden changes □ **speak in a level voice** do not raise and lower the sound of your voice □ **the level tone of an engine** the unchanging sound of an engine □ **level head** clear thinking ○ *It is essential that the crew keeps a level head in an emergency.* ■ *noun* **1.** a position along a vertical axis ○ *ground level* ○ *reference level* ○ *The tropopause is the level at which the lapse rate ceases to be so important.* □ **the fluid level in the reservoir** the point where the surface of the fluid reaches up to □ **high-level cloud** high-altitude cloud **2.** a position on a scale ○ *an advanced level of study* **3.** a relative amount, intensity, or concentration ○ *an unsafe level of contamination* ○ *a reduced level of noise* ○ *A gas turbine engine has an extremely low vibration level.*

level off /ˌlev(ə)l ˈɒf/ *verb* to start to fly level with the ground after climbing or descending, or make an aircraft do this

lever /ˈliːvə/ *noun* **1.** a device with a rigid bar balanced on a fixed point and used to transmit force, as in raising a weight at one end by pushing down on the other ○ *Push the lever fully up to activate the brake mechanism.* ○ *Push the button to release the lever.* **2.** a handle used to adjust or operate a mechanism ○ *throttle lever* ○ *undercarriage selector lever* ○ *Feathering is accomplished by moving the pilot's control lever.* ■ *verb* to move as with a lever ○ *The door would not open so the emergency services had to lever it open with specialised equipment.*

LF *abbreviation* low frequency

licence /ˈlaɪs(ə)ns/ *noun* a document which is proof of official permission to do or to own something

COMMENT: Each licence has its own specific requirements and privileges. In the UK, one of the fundamental differences between a Private Pilot's Licence and other types of licence is that the holder of a PPL is not allowed to fly for 'hire or reward', i.e. the pilot cannot receive payment for flying.

licence holder /ˈlaɪs(ə)ns ˌhəʊldə/ *noun* **1.** a person who has a licence **2.** a leather case, etc., in which to keep the licence document

license /ˈlaɪs(ə)ns/ *noun US* same as **licence** ■ *verb* to give somebody a licence or official permission to do or to own something

lie /laɪ/ *verb* **1.** to be in a flat position, often horizontal ○ *Seat rails are attached to the floor beams and lie level with the flooring.* **2.** to be situated ○ *Great circles are represented by curves which lie on the polar side of the rhumb line.* (NOTE: Care should be taken with the verbs to lie, as defined here: **lie – lay – lain**; **to lie** meaning 'not to tell the truth': **lie – lied – lied** and **lay,** meaning

'to put down' as in **'lay the book on the table': lay – laid – laid.**)

life jacket /ˈlaɪf ˌdʒækɪt/ *noun* an inflatable device, sometimes resembling a sleeveless jacket, to keep a person afloat in water ○ *Pull down the toggles to inflate the life jacket.*

life raft /ˈlaɪf rɑːft/ *noun* a small boat-like vessel for use on an emergency over water

life vest /ˈlaɪf vest/ *noun* same as **life jacket** ○ *You will find a life vest under your seat.*

lift /lɪft/ *noun* **1.** a component of the total aerodynamic force acting on an aerofoil which causes an aeroplane to fly ○ *In level flight, a lift force equal to the weight must be produced.* ○ *The pilot can achieve maximum lift by pulling hard back on the controls.* **2.** an electrically operated machine for moving people or goods between the floors of a building (NOTE: The US English is **elevator.**) ■ *verb* to move to a higher position ○ *A foot-pound is the ability to lift a one pound weight a distance of one foot.*

COMMENT: Bernoulli's principle states that if the speed of a fluid increases, its pressure decreases; if its speed decreases, its pressure increases. Wings are shaped so that the high-speed flow of air that passes over the curved upper surface results in a decrease in pressure. Lift is created because of the pressure differential between upper and lower surfaces of the wing. Lift is also created because the angle of attack allows the airflow to strike the underside of the wing. Daniel Bernoulli (1700–82) was a Swiss scientist.

light /laɪt/ *noun* **1.** brightness produced by the sun, the moon, a lamp, etc. **2.** electromagnetic radiation which can be sensed by the eyes □ **artificial light** light made by using electrical, gas, etc., power **3.** a source of light such as a lamp ○ *Switch off the navigation lights.* ■ *adjective* **1.** without much weight, not heavy ○ *Aluminium is a light metal.* **2.** of little force or requiring little force □ **a light wind** a gentle wind □ **light controls** flying controls which do not need much pilot effort to move them **3.** of little quantity ○ *light rain* ○ *light snow* **4.** of thin consistency □ **light oil** oil which pours easily

light aircraft /ˌlaɪt ˈeəkrɑːft/ *noun* a small, single engine aircraft generally for private not commercial use

lighting /ˈlaɪtɪŋ/ *noun* lights or a system of lights ○ *Cabin lighting is switched off for take-off and initial climb.* ○ *Emergency floor lighting guides passengers to the emergency exits.*

lightning /ˈlaɪtnɪŋ/ *noun* a powerful and sudden electrical discharge from a cloud ○ *Lightning is the most visible indication of thunderstorm activity.*

lightning activity /ˈlaɪtnɪŋ æk ˌtɪvɪti/ *noun* a period of time when there are a lot of lightning flashes

lightning strike /ˈlaɪtnɪŋ straɪk/ *noun* the hitting of something by a discharge of lightning

light plane /ˌlaɪt ˈpleɪn/ *noun* US same as **light aircraft**

likely /ˈlaɪkli/ *adjective* probable □ **rain is likely** rain will probably fall □ **icing is likely to occur in cumulonimbus clouds** icing is often a problem if flying in cumulonimbus clouds

limit /ˈlɪmɪt/ *noun* a point or line past which something should not go ○ *There is a time limit of one hour for the examination.* ○ *The minimum age limit for holding a PPL in the UK is 17.* □ **the upper limit of cloud** the highest point at which there is cloud ■ *verb* to restrict or to prevent from going past a particular point ○ *The amount of cabin baggage is limited to one bag per passenger.*

limitation /ˌlɪmɪˈteɪʃ(ə)n/ *noun* the act of limiting or the state of being limited ○ *Limitation of the maximum engine rpm to a little above maximum engine cruise rpm prevents compressor stall at the higher rpm range.*

line /laɪn/ *noun* **1.** a thin continuous mark as made by a pencil, pen, etc. or printed ○ *Draw a line from point A to point B.* **2.** a real or imaginary mark placed in relation to points of reference ○ *An isobar is a line joining points of equal pressure.* **3.** a long row of people,

etc. ○ *a line of people* ○ *a line of cumulus clouds* **4.** a row of written or printed words ○ *Look at line 4 on page 26.* **5.** a telephone connection to another telephone or system ○ *Dial 9 to get an outside line.* **6.** an electrical cable or wire □ **telephone line** cable supported on pylons from one telephone exchange to another ○ *On final approach to an unfamiliar airfield, pilots of light aircraft should keep a sharp lookout for power lines and telephone lines.* **7.** a system of pipes ○ *a fuel line* **8.** a company which owns and manages a system of transportation routes ○ *a shipping line* ○ *an airline such as KLM or QANTAS*

linear /ˈlɪniə/ *adjective* referring to a line, straight ○ *Although air may appear to be still or calm it is, in fact, moving west to east in space, the linear velocity being zero at the poles and approximately 1,000 mph at the equator.* □ **linear scale** a horizontal or vertical straight-line, rather than circular, scale on an instrument

linear actuator /ˌlɪniə ˈæktjueɪtə/ *noun* an actuator which operates in a straight back and forth manner, e.g. to open undercarriage doors

line feature /ˈlaɪn ˌfiːtʃə/ *noun* a useful navigational landmark, e.g. a railway line, road or river

line of position /ˌlaɪn əv pə ˈzɪʃ(ə)n/ *noun* same as **position line**

line of sight /ˌlaɪn əv ˈsaɪt/ *noun* a clear path between sending and receiving antennas. Abbreviation **LOS**

line up /ˌlaɪn ˈʌp/ *verb* to move aircraft into position ready for departure ○ *Line up with the nosewheel on the runway centre line.*

link /lɪŋk/ *noun* **1.** a connection ○ *Light aircraft can be steered while taxiing via a direct link from rudder pedals to nosewheel.* **2.** a relationship ○ *There is a link between alcohol abuse and pilot error resulting in accidents.* ■ *verb* **1.** to make a connection, to join ○ *The connecting rod links the piston to the crankshaft.* **2.** to establish a relationship between two situations ○ *They link alcohol abuse and pilot error.*

linkage /'lɪŋkɪdʒ/ *noun* a system or series of mechanical connections such as rods, levers, springs, etc. ○ *throttle linkage* ○ *rudder linkage* ○ *The linkage from the control column to the control surfaces should allow full and free movement.*

liquid /'lɪkwɪd/ *adjective* having a consistency like that of water ○ *Liquid oxygen is stored in cylinders.* ■ *noun* a substance with a consistency like water ○ *Water is a liquid, ice is a solid.*

liquid crystal display /ˌlɪkwɪd ˌkrɪst(ə)l dɪsˈpleɪ/ *noun* liquid crystals that reflect light when a voltage is applied, used in many watch, calculator and digital displays. Abbreviation **LCD**

liquid fire /ˌlɪkwɪd 'faɪə/ *noun* oil or petrol fire

list /lɪst/ *noun* a series of names, words, things to do, etc., arranged one after the other in a vertical column ■ *verb* to write a series of names, words, etc. one after the other in a vertical column ○ *List the advantages of a stressed-skin construction.*

liter /'liːtə/ *noun US* same as **litre**

lithium /'lɪθiəm/ *noun* a soft silvery metallic element, the lightest known metal, often used in batteries ○ *an alloy of aluminium and lithium*

litmus /'lɪtməs/ *noun* a substance which turns red in acid, and blue in alkali

litmus paper /'lɪtməs ˌpeɪpə/ *noun* small piece of paper impregnated with litmus to test for acidity or alkalinity

litre /'liːtə/ *noun* the volume of one kilogram of water at 4°C (= 1,000cc or 1.76 pints) (NOTE: It is written **l** after a figure: **10l**; also written **liter** in US English.)

live /laɪv/ *adjective* carrying electricity ○ *live wire*

livery /'lɪvəri/ *noun* the colour scheme and markings on the outside of an aircraft that identify it as belonging to a particular airline

LMT *abbreviation* local mean time

load /ləʊd/ *noun* **1.** the weight or mass which is supported ○ *The load on the undercarriage decreases as lift* increases and, when the aircraft rises into the air, the aircraft is supported by the wings. □ **load bearing** supporting some weight **2.** a force which a structure is subjected to when resisting externally applied forces ○ *The load on the control column is increased when the aircraft is flown out of trim.* **3.** something that is carried in the aircraft ○ *fuel load* □ **passenger load** the number of passengers on board **4.** the power output of a generator or power plant **5.** the resistance of a device or of a line to which electrical power is provided ■ *verb* **1.** to put something into a container, often for the purpose of transportation ○ *The aircraft is loaded with fuel before take-off.* **2.** to transfer data from disk into a computer main memory ○ *She loaded the software onto the computer.*

load-bearing structure /ˌləʊd ˌbeərɪŋ 'strʌktʃə/ *noun* a structure which supports the weight of the aircraft in flight or on the ground

load controller /'ləʊd kənˌtrəʊlə/ *noun* a device which monitors the output of a generator

load factor /'ləʊd ˌfæktə/ *noun* the stress applied to a structure as a multiple of stress applied in 1g flight ○ *The higher the angle of bank, the greater the load factor.*

COMMENT: In straight and level, unaccelerated flight, the load factor is 1. When an aircraft turns or pulls up out of a dive, the load factor increases. An aircraft in a level turn at a bank angle of 60 degrees has a load factor of 2. In such a turn, the aircraft's structure must support twice the aircraft's weight.

loading /'ləʊdɪŋ/ *noun* **1.** the act or process of adding a load to an aircraft □ **loading is in progress** passengers, baggage, freight, etc., are being put on the aircraft **2.** the total aircraft weight or mass divided by wing area ○ *Inertia switches operate automatically when a particular g (acceleration due to Earth's gravity) loading occurs.* **3.** a force or stress acting on an object □ **centrifugal loading** centrifugal force acting on something ○ *Centrifugal loading* *moves the valve towards the closed position.* **4.** the act of transferring data from disk to memory ○ *Loading can be a long process.*

loading bridge /ˈləʊdɪŋ brɪdʒ/ *noun* a covered walkway from an airport departure gate that connects to the door of an aircraft, used by passengers and crew getting on and off the aircraft

load manifest /ˈləʊd ˌmænɪfest/ *noun* a detailed list of the cargo on a flight. Also called **load sheet**

loadmaster /ˈləʊdmɑːstə/ *noun* the person who is in charge of the work of loading cargo onto a military or commercial transport aircraft

load sheet /ˈləʊd ʃiːt/ *noun* same as **load manifest**

lobe /ləʊb/ *noun* one of two, four or more sub-beams that form a directional radar beam ○ *Any system employing beam sharpening is vulnerable to side lobe generation at the transmitter.*

LOC *abbreviation* localiser

local /ˈləʊk(ə)l/ *adjective* not broad or widespread □ **local meteorological conditions** weather conditions in the restricted area of a particular place

local authority /ˌləʊk(ə)l ɔːˈθɒrɪti/ *noun* a government body responsible for the various services of an area

localised /ˈləʊkəlaɪzd/, **localized** *adjective* restricted in area or influence □ **a localized fire** a fire which has not spread

localiser /ˈləʊkəˈlaɪzə/, **localizer** *noun* a component of the instrument landing system that provides horizontal course guidance to the runway ○ *If, during the approach, the aircraft deviates beyond the normal ILS glideslope and/or localiser limits, the flight crew are alerted.* Abbreviation **LOC**

locality /ləʊˈkælɪti/ *noun* a small geographical area ○ *The highest point in a locality is marked by a dot with the elevation marked alongside.*

local mean time /ˌləʊk(ə)l ˈmiːn ˌtaɪm/ *noun* the time according to the mean sun. Abbreviation **LMT**

local time /ˈləʊk(ə)l ˌtaɪm/ *noun* the time in the country you are talking about

locate /ləʊˈkeɪt/ *verb* **1.** to find the position of ○ *Survival beacons transmit a signal which enables search aircraft/vessels to rapidly locate accident survivors still in the sea.* **2.** to position ○ *The digital flight data recorder is located in the tail section.*

location /ləʊˈkeɪʃ(ə)n/ *noun* **1.** a place where something can be found ○ *Before take-off, cabin staff brief passengers on the location of emergency exits and life jackets.* **2.** finding where something is ○ *Rapid location of survivors is important.*

locator /ləʊˈkeɪtə/ *noun* a non-directional beacon used as an aid to final approach ○ *Terminal control areas require charts which show detail on a large scale – terminal VORs, locator beacons, ILS installations, holding patterns, arrival/departure and transit routes.*

lock /lɒk/ *noun* a device operated by a key for securing a door, etc. ■ *verb* **1.** to secure a door by turning a key in the lock ○ *Lock the door before leaving the building.* **2.** to be in or to move into a secure position **3.** to block or prevent moving ○ *Anti-skid braking systems units are designed to prevent the brakes locking the wheels during landing.* **4.** □ **to lock on** to search for, find and follow a target with a thin radar beam

locking pin /ˈlɒkɪŋ pɪn/ *noun* a short metal device to prevent a nut from turning

log /lɒg/ *noun* a written record of a flight, flying hours, maintenance checks, etc., for an aircraft, engine or propeller ■ *verb* to write an entry in a log book or on a log sheet ○ *He calculates headings to steer for each flight stage and logs them.*

logic /ˈlɒdʒɪk/ *noun* electronic circuits which obey mathematical laws ○ *Circuit packs consist of basic decision-making elements, referred to as logic gates, each performing operations on their inputs and so determining the state of their outputs.*

logical /'lɒdʒɪk(ə)l/ *adjective* referring to something which, because of previous experience or knowledge, is natural or expected ○ *Pre-flight checks on light aircraft are made in a logical manner from one side of the aircraft to the other.*

longeron /'lɒndʒ(ə)rən/ *noun* the main structural part of an aircraft fuselage extending from nose to tail ○ *Longerons are normally used in aircraft which require longitudinal strength for holds underneath the floor.*

long-haul /ˌlɒŋ 'hɔːl/ *adjective* travelling over a long distance ○ *Crew flying long-haul routes have to adapt to time changes.* Opposite **short-haul**

longitude /'lɒŋgɪtjuːd/ *noun* the angular distance on the Earth's surface, measured east or west from the prime meridian at Greenwich, UK, to the meridian passing through a position, expressed in degrees, minutes, and seconds ○ *The centre of London is latitude 51°30′N, longitude 0°5′W.* Compare **latitude**

longitudinal /ˌlɒŋgɪ'tjuːdɪn(ə)l/ *adjective* in a lengthwise direction

longitudinal axis /ˌlɒŋgɪtjuːdɪn(ə)l 'æksɪs/ *noun* the axis of the aircraft which extends from the nose to the tail. ◊ **axis**, **roll**

long-range /ˌlɒŋ 'reɪndʒ/ *adjective* **1.** covering a long distance ○ *long-range radar* **2.** □ **long-range weather forecast** covering a period more than 5 days ahead

lookout /'lʊkaʊt/ *noun* a careful watch ○ *Keep a careful lookout for other aircraft.* □ **to be on the lookout for** to watch carefully for something

loop /luːp/ *noun* a flight manoeuvre in which the aircraft rotates, nose up, through 360° while holding its lateral position

loop antenna /'luːp ænˌtenə/ *noun* circular-shaped conductive coil which rotates to give a bearing to a ground station

LORAN *abbreviation* long-range air navigation system

lose /luːz/ *verb* not to have something any longer (NOTE: **losing – lost**) □ **to lose altitude** to descend from higher to lower altitude

loss /lɒs/ *noun* no longer having something ○ *The pilot reported loss of engine power.* □ **loss of control** no longer being able to control □ **loss of life** death in an accident □ **loss of a signal** disappearance of a signal ○ *The term attenuation means the loss of strength of a radio signal.*

loudspeaker /ˌlaʊd'spiːkə/ *noun* an electromagnetic device that converts electrical signals into audible noise. Also called **speaker**

lounge /laʊndʒ/ *noun* □ **VIP lounge** a special room at an airport for VIPs. ◊ **departure lounge**

louvre /'luːvə/ *noun* thin, horizontal openings for air cooling ○ *Cold air can be let into the cabin through adjustable louvres.* (NOTE: The US spelling is **louver**.)

low /ləʊ/ *adjective* **1.** not high, not tall ○ *a low building* □ **low cloud** cloud relatively near the surface of the earth □ **low ground** an area of land which is not high, as opposed to mountains **2.** not high, or below normal ○ *an area of low pressure* □ **low temperature** a temperature which shows that it is cold **3.** quiet, not loud ■ *noun* an area of low atmospheric pressure □ **polar low** an area of low atmospheric pressure over polar regions

lower /'ləʊə/ *adjective* **1.** referring to something that is at a low level or towards the bottom ○ *the lower layers of the atmosphere* □ **the lower surface of the wing** the underneath surface of the wing **2.** referring to something which is below something else of the same sort ○ *Air is cooler high up than at lower levels.* Opposite **upper** ■ *verb* **1.** to let down to a lower position □ **lower the undercarriage** move the undercarriage into position ready for landing □ **lower the flaps** set the flaps to a down position **2.** to reduce in amount or intensity □ **to lower the temperature** to reduce the temperature □ **to lower the pressure** to decrease the pressure □ **to lower**

the volume (of sound) to make something such as a radio quieter or less loud

lower airspace /ˌləʊə 'eəspeɪs/ *noun* the airspace below FL245 (approximately 24,500 ft)

lower atmosphere /ˌləʊə 'ætməsfɪə/ *noun* the layer of the atmosphere in which changes in the weather take place. Also called **troposphere**

low frequency /ˌləʊ 'friːkwənsi/, **low frequency band** /ˌləʊ 'friːkwənsi ˌbænd/ *noun* a radio communications range of frequencies between 30–300 kHz. Abbreviation **LF**

lubricate /'luːbrɪkeɪt/ *verb* to oil or to grease moving parts in order to reduce friction ○ *Oil passes through the hollow crankshaft to lubricate the big-end bearings.* ○ *Turbo chargers are lubricated by the engine oil system.*

lubrication /ˌluːbrɪ'keɪʃ(ə)n/ *noun* the act or process of covering moving surfaces with oil or grease in order to reduce friction □ **lubrication system** the tank, pipes, pumps, filters, etc., which together supply oil to moving parts of the engine

luggage /'lʌɡɪdʒ/ *noun* baggage, i.e. cases and bags that somebody takes when travelling

M

m¹ *abbreviation* metre

m² *abbreviation* minute

Mach /mæk/ *noun* the ratio of the speed of an object to the speed of sound in the same atmospheric conditions ○ *Mach 2 equals twice the speed of sound.*

COMMENT: Named after E. Mach, the Austrian physicist who died in 1916.

machine /məˈʃiːn/ *noun* a device with fixed and moving parts that takes mechanical energy and uses it to do useful work ○ *A drill is a machine for making holes in things.* ○ *An electrical circuit is designed to carry energy to a particular device or machine which can then perform useful work.*

Machmeter /ˈmækmiːtə/ *noun* an instrument for measuring the Mach number of an aircraft

Mach number /mæk/ *noun* a number that expresses the ratio of the speed of an object to the speed of sound

magnesium /mægˈniːziəm/ *noun* a light, silvery-white metallic element that burns with a brilliant white flame. Symbol **Mg** (NOTE: The atomic number of magnesium is **12**.)

magnesium flare /mægˈniːziəm fleə/ *noun* a device for distress signalling at night ○ *to send off magnesium flares*

magnet /ˈmægnɪt/ *noun* an object that produces a magnetic field, and attracts iron and steel ○ *Magnetism in a magnet appears to be concentrated at two points called the poles.*

magnetic /mægˈnetɪk/ *adjective* referring to or having the power of a magnet or something with a magnetic field ○ *A freely suspended magnet – not influenced by outside forces – will align itself with the Earth's magnetic lines of force which run from the north magnetic pole to the south magnetic pole.*

magnetic bearing /mægˌnetɪk ˈbeərɪŋ/ *noun* the angle measured in a clockwise direction of a distant point, relative to magnetic north

magnetic declination /mægˌnetɪk ˌdeklɪˈneɪʃ(ə)n/ *noun* same as **magnetic variation** ○ *To convert magnetic bearing into true bearing it is necessary to apply magnetic variation at the point at which the bearing was taken.*

magnetic field /mægˌnetɪk ˈfiːld/ *noun* area of magnetic influence

magnetic north /mægˌnetɪk ˈnɔːθ/ *noun* the direction of the Earth's magnetic pole, to which the north-seeking pole of a magnetic needle points if unaffected by nearby influences

magnetic pole /mægˌnetɪk ˈpəʊl/ *noun* one of the two poles which are the centres of the Earth's magnetic field

magnetic variation /mægˌnetɪk ˌveərɪˈeɪʃ(ə)n/ *noun* differences in the Earth's magnetic field in time and place ○ *To convert magnetic bearing into true bearing it is necessary to apply magnetic variation at the point at which the bearing was taken.* Also called **magnetic declination**

magnetise /ˈmægnətaɪz/, **magnetize** *verb* to convert an object or material into a magnet ○ *Ferro-magnetic materials are easily magnetised.*

magnetism /ˈmægnətɪz(ə)m/ *noun* a force exerted by a magnetic field ○ *An electric current produces magnetism,* *and movement of a magnet can produce electricity.*

magneto /mæg'ni:təʊ/ *noun* a device that produces electrical current for distribution to the spark plugs of piston aero-engines

COMMENT: The crankshaft turns the magnetos, which provide the electrical energy to create a spark from the spark plugs. This ensures that the spark plugs work even if the aircraft's battery and electrical system fail. Most aircraft have two magnetos per engine in case one fails.

magnify /'mægnɪfaɪ/ *verb* **1.** to increase the size of, especially by using a lens, microscope, etc. ○ *It was only after the image was magnified that it was possible to see the flaw.* **2.** to increase the effect of something ○ *The stress level is magnified at times of high work load, for example, preparation for landing.* (NOTE: **magnifying – magnified**)

magnitude /'mægnɪtju:d/ *noun* greatness in size or extent ○ *The magnitude of the pressure gradient force is inversely proportional to the distance apart of the isobars.* ○ *When the surface wind speed reaches a particular magnitude the term gale is used.*

maiden flight /ˌmeɪd(ə)n 'flaɪt/ *noun* the first flight of a new aircraft ○ *The maiden flight of the A340 was in October 1991.*

main /meɪn/ *adjective* most important; principal □ **main disadvantages** principal negative points

main gear /ˌmeɪn 'gɪə/ *noun* two main landing wheel assemblies

mainplane /'meɪnpleɪn/ *noun* an aircraft wing, compared with the tailplane ○ *The region between the mainplane front and rear spars is commonly sealed off and used as tanks.*

maintain /meɪn'teɪn/ *verb* **1.** to keep up, to carry on or continue □ **to maintain the present heading** to continue on the same heading □ **to maintain a constant selected engine speed** not to change the engine speed **2.** to keep in good mechanical or working order ○

Aero-engines must be maintained regularly to maximise engine life.

maintenance /'meɪntənəns/ *noun* a regular periodic inspection, overhaul, repair and replacement of parts of an aircraft and/or engine ○ *The gas turbine is a very simple engine with few moving parts when compared with a piston engine, giving it a high reliability factor with less maintenance.* □ **maintenance manual** the manufacturer's instruction book of maintenance procedures

'...poor maintenance training is expensive for the airline who notices the problem in late departures, longer than necessary maintenance periods and worst of all, crashes' [*Civil Aviation Training*]

maintenance crew /'meɪntənəns ˌkru:/ *noun* ground staff whose responsibility it is to keep the aircraft serviceable ○ *The maintenance crew worked through the night to complete the work.*

major /'meɪdʒə/ *adjective* important ○ *There are two major cloud groups, stratus and cumulus.* Opposite **minor** □ **major airport** a large, important or international airport □ **major problem** a serious problem. Opposite **minor**

majority /mə'dʒɒrɪti/ *noun* the greater number or larger part – anything more than 50% ○ *The majority of passengers prefer to sit in a non-smoking area of the cabin.*

malfunction /mæl'fʌŋkʃən/ *noun* a failure to work or to function correctly ○ *The oil pressure and temperature of the CSDU can be monitored by the pilot and if a malfunction occurs, the pilot can then choose to disconnect the CSDU from the engine.* ■ *verb* to function incorrectly or fail to function ○ *Oscillating outputs from the alternators could cause sensitive equipment to malfunction.*

mandatory /'mændət(ə)ri/ *adjective* compulsory, required or ordered by an official organisation or authority ○ *Fire detection systems in toilets are mandatory.*

maneuver /mə'nu:və/ *noun US* same as **manoeuvre**

maneuverability /mə,nuːv(ə)rə'bılıti/ *noun US* same as **manoeuvrability**

maneuvering area /mə'nuːv(ə)rıŋ ,eəriə/ *noun US* same as **manoeuvring area**

manifold /'mænıfəʊld/ *noun* a system of pipes for a fluid from single input to multiple output or multiple input to single output ○ *inlet and exhaust manifolds of a piston engine*

manifold pressure /,mænı,fəʊld 'preʃə/ *noun* absolute pressure in the induction system of a piston engine measured in inches of mercury

manner /'mænə/ *noun* a way of doing something ○ *Wind is said to be veering when it changes direction in a clockwise manner.* ○ *Pre-flight checks should be done in the correct manner.*

manoeuvrability /mə,nuːv(ə)rə'bılıti/ *noun* the ability and speed with which an aircraft can turn away from its previous path ○ *Light training aircraft do not have great manoeuvrability but they are stable and therefore easier to fly.* (NOTE: The US spelling is **maneuverability**.)

manoeuvre /mə'nuːvə/ *noun* any deliberate or intended departure from the existing flight or ground path (NOTE: It is also written **maneuver** in US English.) □ **flight manoeuvre** turns, loops, climbs and descents □ **ground manoeuvre** taxiing and turning onto runways and taxiways, etc.

manoeuvring area /mə'nuːv(ə)rıŋ ,eəriə/ *noun* the part of the aerodrome used for the take-off, landing and taxiing of aircraft

manual /'mænjuəl/ *adjective* referring to the hands, or done or worked by hand ○ *The electronic flight instrument system has two self-test facilities – automatic and manual.* ■ *noun* a reference book giving instructions on how to operate equipment, machinery, etc. ○ *maintenance manual* ○ *aircraft operating manual*

manual control /,mænjuəl kən'trəʊl/ *noun* hand-flying an aircraft equipped with an autopilot or automatic flight control system

manually /'mænjuəli/ *adverb* by hand ○ *The system is switched on manually.*

manufacture /,mænjʊ'fæktʃə/ *verb* to make a product for sale using industrial machines ○ *The centrifugal compressor is usually more robust than the axial flow type and also easier to develop and manufacture.*

map /mæp/ *noun* a representation of the Earth's surface on a flat surface such as a sheet of paper ○ *a map of Africa* ■ *verb* to make measurements and calculations of part of the Earth's surface in order to produce a map

MAP *abbreviation* missed approach point

margin /'maːdʒın/ *noun* **1.** a blank space bordering the written or printed area on a page ○ *Write notes in the margin of the book.* **2.** an amount allowed in addition to what is needed ○ *safety margin* ○ *In some configurations, it is possible for the buffet speed to be less than the required 7% margin ahead of the stall.*

maritime /'mærıtaım/ *adjective* referring to the sea □ **maritime wind** a wind blowing from the sea ○ *The Rocky Mountains of North America act as a barrier to the cool maritime winds from the Pacific Ocean.*

mark /maːk/ *noun* **1.** a visible trace on a surface, e.g. a dot or a line ○ *There are marks on tyres and wheel rims which are aligned and indicate the extent of tyre creep.* **2.** the number of points or a percentage given for academic work ■ *verb* **1.** to make a visible line, dot, etc., on a surface ○ *Mark the departure point on the chart.* **2.** to show or indicate ○ *The weather front marks the boundary between the two air masses.* **3.** to correct or check academic work done by a student ○ *The instructor marked the exam papers.*

marked /maːkt/ *adjective* very noticeable, clear and definite □ **a marked increase** a noticeable, therefore possibly large, increase □ **a marked change in the weather** a significant change in the weather

marker /'mɑːkə/ *noun* **1.** something which acts as an indicator of something such as distance or position **2.** a radio beacon that is part of the ILS

COMMENT: The outer marker (OM) is indicated on the instrument panel, by a blue light. The middle marker (MM) is indicated by an amber light and the inner marker (IM) by a white light.

marker dye /'mɑːkə daɪ/ *noun* a brightly coloured substance used by people adrift at sea to draw the attention of flight crews to their position

marshal /'mɑːʃ(ə)l/ *verb* to direct aircraft into their parking positions on the apron by means of hand signals ○ *After taxiing, a marshaller marshals the aircraft to the disembarkation and unloading point.*

marshaller /'mɑːʃ(ə)lə/ *noun* a member of ground staff whose job is to direct aircraft into parking positions by means of hand signals

'…when under a marshaller's control, reduce speed to a walking pace' [*Civil Aviation Authority, General Aviation Safety Sense Leaflet*]

marshalling signals /'mɑːʃlɪŋ ˌsɪgnəlz/ *plural noun* hand signals used by a marshaller ○ *Marshalling signals are used to direct aircraft on the ground.*

MAS *abbreviation* middle airspace service

mask /mɑːsk/ *noun* a device to cover the face □ **oxygen mask** a device to cover the nose and mouth which is connected to an oxygen supply ○ *Anoxia at high altitudes can be overcome by breathing through an oxygen mask.* ■ *verb* to hide or cover up ○ *When practising instrument flying, the aircraft windows are masked to prevent the (student) pilot from seeing out of the aircraft.*

MASPS *abbreviation* minimum aircraft system performance specifications

mass /mæs/ *noun* **1.** the physical volume of a solid body ○ *Mass is a basic property of matter and is called weight when it is in a field of gravity such as that of the Earth.* **2.** a large body of something with no particular shape ○ *a*

land mass such as the continent of Africa ■ *adjective* involving a large number of people or things □ **mass exit** the departure of everybody, or nearly everybody, from a place

mass ascent /ˌmæs ə'sent/ *noun* a slow ascent of a large body of air in regions of low pressure and of warm air rising over a cold air mass

mast /mɑːst/ *noun* **1.** a vertical pole for a flag or antenna ○ *Ice accretes on the leading edge of the detector mast.* **2.** a tube projecting from the underside of the aircraft from which liquid can drain well away from the airframe

master /'mɑːstə/ *adjective* main or principal □ **master cylinder** a hydraulic cylinder from which pressure is transmitted to smaller slave cylinders ■ *verb* to overcome the difficulty of something ○ *It takes practice to master crosswind landings in light aircraft.*

master key /'mɑːstə kiː/ *noun* a key which can open a number of doors, etc.

master switch /'mɑːstə swɪtʃ/ *noun* the most important of a number of switches operating a system

match /mætʃ/ *verb* **1.** to go well together ○ *The most important factor when matching a propeller to an engine is tip velocity.* **2.** to be equal to ○ *The polarisation of the antenna must match that of the transmitter.*

material /mə'tɪəriəl/ *noun* a substance out of which something can be made ○ *Wood, fabric and paper are all free-burning materials.*

MATO *abbreviation* military air traffic operations

matrix /'meɪtrɪks/ *noun* a grid-like arrangement of circuit elements ○ *Oil coolers consist of a matrix, divided into sections by baffle plates.*

matter /'mætə/ *noun* **1.** a physical substance ○ *Mass is a basic property of matter.* □ **foreign matter** something unwanted which is found in a substance or a device (such as sand or water in fuel) ○ *Turbine blades can be damaged by foreign matter such as stones entering through the engine intake on take-off.* □ **solid matter** solid substances **2.** a subject for discussion, concern or action ○ *Safety is a matter of great importance.* **3.** trouble or difficulty □ **what's the matter?** what's the problem? □ **it doesn't matter** it isn't important, so don't worry

MATZ *abbreviation* military aerodrome traffic zone

maximum /'mæksɪməm/ *adjective* greatest possible ○ *The maximum daily temperature is 35°C.* ○ *The maximum speed of the aircraft is 200 kt.* ■ *noun* the greatest possible quantity, amount, etc. ○ *There is a net gain of heat by the Earth until terrestrial radiation balances solar radiation when the daily temperature is at its maximum.*

maximum total weight authorised /ˌmæksɪməm ˌtəʊt(ə)l weɪt 'ɔːθəraɪzd/ *noun* the maximum authorised weight of aircraft fuel, payload, etc., given in the Certificate of Airworthiness. Abbreviation **MTWA**

mb *abbreviation* millibar

MDA /ˌem diː 'eɪ/ *abbreviation* minimum descent altitude

mean /miːn/ *adjective* referring to something average, midway between two extremes □ **mean daily temperature** average daily temperature □ **mean wind** the average speed of a wind ■ *noun* something having a medium or average position, midway between two extremes □ **arithmetic mean** the average value of a set of numbers ■ *verb* **1.** to signify or to have something as an explanation ○ *Airspeed means the speed of the aircraft in relation to the air around it.* **2.** to intend to do something ○ *I meant to telephone the reservations desk this morning but I forgot.* **3.** to result in ○ *Installing a new computer network means a lot of problems for everybody.* (NOTE: **meaning – meant**)

mean effective pressure /ˌmiːn ɪ ˌfektɪv 'preʃə/ *noun* the average pressure exerted on the piston during the power stroke. Abbreviation **MEP**

means /miːnz/ *noun* a way of doing something which brings a result ○ *A clear window fitted in the reservoir provides a means of checking hydraulic fluid level during servicing.* (NOTE: **Means** has no plural form.) □ **by means**

of by using ○ *Fuel is transferred from the tanks to the carburettor by means of pipes.* □ **there are various means for navigation** there are various different methods used for the purposes of navigation

mean sea level /ˌmiːn 'siː ˌlev(ə)l/ *noun* the average level of the sea taking tidal variations into account ○ *Below FL50 cloud heights are referred to a datum of mean sea level.* Abbreviation **MSL**

mean sun /ˌmiːn 'sʌn/ *noun* the position of an imaginary sun in a solar day of exactly 24 hours, behind the real sun in February and in advance of the real sun in November ○ *Local mean time (LMT) is the time according to the mean sun.*

mean time between failures /ˌmiːn taɪm bɪˌtwiːn 'feɪljəz/ *noun* full form of **MTBF**

mean time to repair /ˌmiːn 'taɪm tə, tʊ/ *noun* full form of **MTTR**

measure /'meʒə/ *noun* **1.** an indication or way of assessing ○ *The way he dealt with the in-flight emergency is a measure of his skill as a pilot.* **2.** a reference for discovering the dimensions or amount of something ○ *The litre is a measure of capacity.* **3.** a device used for measuring □ **a 1-metre measure** a ruler that is 1 metre long **4.** an action taken to get a result ○ *Stricter safety measures were introduced.* **5.** an amount of something ○ *To be a good pilot, you need a measure of self-confidence.* ■ *verb* **1.** to find the dimensions or amount of something ○ *to measure a distance* ○ *to measure an angle* ○ *to measure the speed of an aircraft* ○ *Wind directions are measured from magnetic north.* **2.** to be of a particular size, length, quantity, etc. ○ *How much does the pipe measure?*

measurement /'meʒəmənt/ *noun* **1.** an act of measuring ○ *Measurement of relative humidity is done using an instrument called a hygrometer.* **2.** the result of measuring ○ *The measurements of the room are: height = 4 metres, length = 10 metres, width = 4 metres.*

mechanical /mɪˈkænɪk(ə)l/ *adjective* referring to machines ○ *Activation may be electrical or mechanical.* □ **mechanical pump** a pump operated by the engine rather than by electrical power

mechanical advantage /mɪ ˌkænɪk(ə)l ədˈvɑːntɪdʒ/ *noun* the ratio of the output force produced by a machine to the input force

mechanical engineering /mɪ ˌkænɪk(ə)l ˌendʒɪˈnɪərɪŋ/ *noun* the study of design, construction, and use of machinery or mechanical structures ○ *She gained a degree in mechanical engineering from university.*

mechanical linkage /mɪˌkænɪk(ə)l ˈlɪŋkɪdʒ/ *noun* a system of rods, cables and levers in a light aircraft, which connect the control column in the cockpit to the control surfaces on the wings, tailplane and fin

mechanics /mɪˈkænɪks/ *noun* **1.** the study of the action of forces on matter or material systems **2.** the way something works ○ *The mechanics of the föhn wind provide a good illustration of the adiabatic process.*

mechanism /ˈmekənɪz(ə)m/ *noun* **1.** the arrangement of connected parts in a machine or system ○ *the landing gear mechanism* ○ *the nose wheel steering mechanism* **2.** a physical process ○ *the mechanism by which thunderstorms develop*

MEDA *abbreviation* military emergency division aerodrome

medical certificate /ˈmedɪk(ə)l sə ˌtɪfɪkət/ *noun* a document which confirms that the named person has been medically examined and declared to be in good physical condition

medical emergency *noun* a situation when somebody is unwell and quickly needs medical care

medium /ˈmiːdiəm/ *adjective* referring to something that has a position or represents a condition midway between extremes ○ *high, medium and low frequencies* ○ *medium level cloud* ■ *noun* a substance through which something else is transmitted or carried ○ *Tubes convey the cooling medium.* ○ *The cool-*

ing medium for cooling oil can be ram-air or fuel.

medium frequency /ˌmiːdiəm ˈfriːkwənsi/, **medium frequency band** /ˌmiːdiəm ˈfriːkwənsi ˌbænd/ *noun* radio frequency range between 300 kHz and 3000 kHz – often referred to as medium wave (MW). Abbreviation **MF**

mega- /megə/ *prefix* large. Opposite **micro-** (NOTE: The prefix **mega-** is used in front of SI units to indicate one million: **megahertz =** one million hertz.)

megahertz /ˈmegəhɜːts/ *noun* a measure of frequency equal to one million cycles per second. Abbreviation **MHz**

melt /melt/ *verb* to become liquid by heating ○ *Ice melts at temperatures above freezing.* □ **melting point** temperature at which a solid turns to liquid ○ *Magnesium has a melting point of 1204°F.*

member /ˈmembə/ *noun* **1.** a large, important structural unit ○ *The skin in bonded to the internal members.* ○ *A beam is a member which is designed to withstand loading applied at an angle to it, often perpendicular.* **2.** a person who joins a club or organisation ○ *He is a member of the gliding club.* **3.** a person in a team or crew ○ *Most large passenger aircraft are now operated by two crew members.*

memorise /ˈmeməraɪz/, **memorize** *verb* to fix in the memory, to learn by heart ○ *It is helpful if a student pilot can memorise certain items, such as downwind checks, early in his training.*

memory /ˈmem(ə)ri/ *noun* **1.** the mental ability of remembering and recalling past events or information □ **he has a good memory** he remembers things easily **2.** part of a computer which is used for the fast recall of information ○ *The computer cannot run many programs at the same time because it doesn't have enough memory.*

mental /ˈment(ə)l/ *adjective* referring to the mind or brain ○ *Anoxia severely limits physical and mental performance.* □ **mental calculation** a calculation done in your head, without using aids such as pen, paper or calculator

mention /ˈmenʃ(ə)n/ *verb* to refer to something briefly ○ *as mentioned in chapter 4* ○ *as I mentioned yesterday* ○ *No one mentioned the incident.*

MEP *abbreviation* mean effective pressure

Mercator's projection /mɜːˈkeɪtəz prəˌdʒekʃ(ə)n/ *noun* a map projection of the Earth onto a cylinder so that all the parallels of latitude are the same length as the equator ○ *Since meridians on this projection are represented by parallel straight lines, it is impossible to represent the poles on Mercator's projection.* ◊ **Lambert's projection**

COMMENT: Named after the Latinised name of G. Kremer, the Flemish-born geographer who died in 1594.

mercury /ˈmɜːkjʊri/ *noun* a silver-coloured metallic element, liquid at room temperature, used in thermometers ○ *Manifold pressure gauges are calibrated in inches of mercury.*

mercury barometer /ˌmɜːkjʊri bə ˈrɒmɪtə/ *noun* type of barometer where the atmospheric pressure is balanced against a column of mercury ○ *The principle of a mercury barometer has not changed since 1643 when Torricelli demonstrated that the atmosphere can support a column of liquid.*

meridian /məˈrɪdiən/ *noun* an imaginary great circle on the Earth's surface passing through the north and south geographic poles

mesh /meʃ/ *noun* a net-like structure ■ *verb* (*of gears*) to link together with cogs on another wheel

message /ˈmesɪdʒ/ *noun* a short written, coded or verbal communication ○ *The crew can use the public address system to broadcast messages to the passengers.* ○ *There's a message from Mr. Jones on your desk.*

met /met/ *abbreviation* meteorology

metal /ˈmet(ə)l/ *noun* one of the metallic elements e.g. iron, gold, mercury, copper, aluminium

metallic /meˈtælɪk/ *adjective* referring to or like metal □ **metallic materi-**als metals such as aluminium, titanium, steel, etc. ○ *Some fire extinguishers do not harm metallic, wooden, plastic or fabric materials.* □ **non-metallic materials** wood, plastics, fabrics, etc., which are not made of metal

METAR /ˈmiːtɑː/ *abbreviation* aviation routine weather report

meteorological /ˌmiːtiərə ˈlɒdʒɪk(ə)l/ *adjective* referring to meteorology □ **meteorological forecast** a prediction of the weather to come □ **meteorological visibility** the greatest horizontal distance at which objects can be seen and recognised by an observer on the ground with normal eyesight and under conditions of normal daylight illumination ○ *Meteorological visibility is given in metres up to 5,000 metres, and thereafter in kilometres.* ◊ **MOTNE**

meteorological chart /ˌmiːtiərə ˈlɒdʒɪk(ə)l tʃɑːt/ *noun* a chart of part of the Earth's surface with information about weather conditions

meteorological conditions /ˌmiːtiərəlɒdʒɪk(ə)l kənˈdɪʃ(ə)nz/ *plural noun* a description of the weather in a given area

meteorologist /ˌmiːtiəˈrɒlədʒɪst/ *noun* a person who studies, reports and forecasts the weather ○ *The analysis of the surface chart is the procedure in which the meteorologist completes the chart by inserting the fronts and isobars in their correct positions.*

meteorology /ˌmiːtiəˈrɒlədʒi/ *noun* a science which studies weather and weather conditions ○ *Terrestrial radiation plays an important part in meteorology.*

meter /ˈmiːtə/ *noun* **1.** *US* same as **metre 2.** a device to measure current, rate of flow, vertical distance, speed, etc. ○ *a gas meter* ◊ **altimeter, ammeter, flowmeter**

methanol /ˈmeθənɒl/ *noun* a colourless, toxic, flammable liquid, CH_3OH, used as an antifreeze, a general solvent, and a fuel, also called methyl alcohol or wood alcohol ○ *Power output can be restored, or can be boosted to a value over 100% maximum power, by the injection of a water/methanol mixture* *at the compressor inlet or at the combustion chamber inlet.*

method /ˈmeθəd/ *noun* a particular way of doing something, especially if it is well thought out and systematic ○ *The most common method of displaying radar information is on a cathode ray tube.*

metre /ˈmiːtə/ *noun* an international standard unit of length, approximately equivalent to 39.37 inches. Abbreviation **m** (NOTE: It is also written **meter** in US English.)

MF *abbreviation* medium frequency

MFD *abbreviation* multi-function display

MHz *symbol* megahertz

micro- /maɪkrəʊ/ *prefix* small. Opposite **mega-** (NOTE: The prefix **micro-** is used in front of SI units to indicate a one millionth part: **microsecond** = one millionth of a second.)

microburst /ˈmaɪkrəʊbɜːst/ *noun* a particularly strong wind-shear especially associated with thunderstorms ○ *The investigation revealed that the crew lost control of the aircraft as it flew through the microburst.*

microlight /ˈmaɪkrəlaɪt/ *noun* a small light aircraft, often with an open fuselage, that can carry one or two people at low speeds and is used for flying for pleasure or reconnaissance

micro-switch /ˈmaɪkrəʊswɪtʃ/ *noun* a miniature switch used to govern systems automatically ○ *Operation of an aircraft may also be seriously affected by the freezing of moisture in controls, hinges and micro-switches.* (NOTE: The plural form is **micro-switches**.)

microwave landing system /ˌmaɪkrəweɪv ˈlændɪŋ ˌsɪstəm/ *noun* an extremely accurate guidance system for landing aircraft that uses microwaves. Abbreviation **MLS**

mid- /mɪd/ *prefix* middle □ **mid-summer** the middle of the summer

mid-air /ˌmɪd ˈeə/ *adjective* □ **mid-air collision** collision between aircraft in the air rather than on the ground

middle /ˈmɪd(ə)l/ *adjective* in the centre ○ *middle marker* ■ *noun* the centre ○ *the seat in the middle of the row*

middle airspace service /ˌmɪd(ə)l ˈeəspeɪs ˌsɜːvɪs/ a radar service provided by an air traffic control area radar unit in the airspace between FL100 and FL245. Abbreviation **MAS**

middle marker /ˈmɪd(ə)l ˌmɑːkə/ *noun* an ILS marker beacon on extended runway centre line, usually 3500 feet from the runway threshold

MIL *abbreviation* military

mile /maɪl/ *noun* ♦ statute mile

military /ˈmɪlɪt(ə)ri/ *adjective* relating to war or to the armed services

milk run /ˈmɪlk rʌn/ *noun* a routine trip, especially an airline's regular flight

millibar /ˈmɪlibɑː/ *noun* a unit of atmospheric pressure equal to 1 thousandth of a bar. Symbol **mb**

milligramme /ˈmɪligræm/ *noun* one thousandth of a gramme

millilitre /ˈmɪliliːtə/ *noun* one thousandth of a litre (NOTE: It is usually written **ml** after figures: *35ml*. Also written **milliliter** in US English.)

millimetre /ˈmɪlimiːtə/ *noun* one thousandth of a metre (NOTE: It is usually written **mm** after figures: *35mm*. Also written **millimeter** in US English.)

min *abbreviation* minimum

minima /ˈmɪnɪmə/ ♦ minimum

minimal /ˈmɪnɪm(ə)l/ *adjective* very small in amount, importance or degree ○ *Safety equipment carried on some light aircraft may be as minimal as a portable fire extinguisher.* ○ *Any attempt to increase range by applying power is of minimal benefit.*

minimise /ˈmɪnɪmaɪz/, **minimize** *verb* to reduce or decrease to the smallest amount possible

minimum /ˈmɪnɪməm/ *adjective* smallest possible ○ *the minimum amount required* ○ *Minimum weather requirements for a particular operation such as runway visual range (RVR).* ■ *noun* the smallest or least possible quantity or amount ○ *Fires should be tackled with the minimum of delay.* ○ *To keep the weight of the fuselage structure* *to a minimum, the difference between cabin pressures and the external atmospheric pressures should be kept to a minimum.* (NOTE: The plural form is **minima** or **minimums**.)

minimum flying speed /ˌmɪnɪməm ˈflaɪɪŋ ˌspiːd/ *noun* the lowest true air speed at which an aircraft can maintain height

minimum fuel /ˌmɪnɪməm ˈfjuːəl/ *noun* the amount of fuel required to reach destination and land without delay

minimum sector altitude /ˌmɪnɪməm ˈsektə ˌæltɪtjuːd/ *noun* the lowest altitude at which an aircraft may fly under emergency conditions and which will provide a minimum clearance of 1000 ft above all obstacles located within a particular sector

minimum separation /ˌmɪnɪməm ˌsepəˈreɪʃ(ə)n/ *noun* the minimum vertical or horizontal distance allowed between two aircraft

minor /ˈmaɪnə/ *noun* a person under the age of legal adulthood ■ *adjective* small in size or amount and therefore relatively unimportant. Opposite **major** □ **minor repairs** repairs which can be made quickly and with the minimum amount of equipment

minus /ˈmaɪnəs/ *preposition* reduced by ○ *6 minus 2 equals 4 (6 − 2 = 4).* ■ *noun* a minus sign (-) ○ *minus forty degrees Celsius (- 40° Celsius)*

minute *noun* /ˈmɪnɪt/ **1.** a time period of 60 seconds ○ *There are 60 minutes in one hour.* □ **wait a minute** wait a while or a short period of time **2.** a unit of angular measurement equal to one sixtieth of a degree ○ *20 degrees and 20 minutes east (20° 20'E).* ■ *adjective* /maɪˈnjuːt/ very small indeed ○ *Metal fatigue begins as minute cracks, too small to be seen, at the point of maximum stress.*

miscellaneous /ˌmɪsəˈleɪniəs/ *adjective* various, mixed, not all the same ○ *The first aid box contains miscellaneous items for use in a medical emergency.*

miss /mɪs/ *verb* not to get or catch ○ *Two passengers arrived so late that they missed the flight.*

missed approach /ˌmɪst əˈprəʊtʃ/ *noun* an approach that does not result in a landing and is followed by a go-around

missed approach point /ˌmɪst ə ˈprəʊtʃ ˌpɔɪnt/ *noun* the point at which a pilot must carry out a **missed approach procedure** if a particular visual reference has not been made

missed approach procedure /ˌmɪst əˈprəʊtʃ prəˌsiːdʒə/ *noun* the action and flight path to be followed after a missed approach at a particular aerodrome

mist /mɪst/ *noun* **1.** visible water vapour, in the form of very fine droplets, in the atmosphere ○ *Mist is thinner than fog.* **2.** liquid in spray form ○ *an air/oil mist* ■ *verb* □ **to mist up** to become covered in tiny water droplets and therefore prevent clear vision through a surface ○ *The windscreen misted up.*

mix /mɪks/ *verb* to put together in order to form one mass ○ *It is a fact of nature that different air masses do not mix together.*

mixture /ˈmɪkstʃə/ *noun* something which is the result of a number of things mixed together

mixture control /ˈmɪkstʃə kən ˌtrəʊl/ *noun* a device for controlling the ratio of fuel to air entering an engine's carburettor or fuel injection system. The mixture control is a knob or lever marked in red usually to the right of the throttle lever. ○ *In order to stop the engine, the mixture control should be moved fully aft.*

MLS *abbreviation* microwave landing system

mm *abbreviation* millimetre

MM *abbreviation* middle marker

MMR /ˌem em ˈɑː/ *abbreviation* multi-mode receiver

mnemonic /nɪˈmɒnɪk/ *noun* something such as a word, sentence or little poem which helps the memory

COMMENT: Some of the well known mnemonics are: **ARROW**= Airworthiness Certificate, Registration Document, Radio Station Licence, Operating Handbook, Weight and Balance document – documents to be carried in (light) aircraft (U5); **BUMF checks**= Brakes, Undercarriage, Mixture, Fuel – downwind checks in a light, single engine aircraft with a fixed-pitch propeller; **FREDA**= Fuel, Radio, Engine, Direction indicator, Altimeter – airfield approach checks; **HASELL**= Height, Airframe, Security, Engine, Location, Lookout – pre-stall checks; **variation east, magnetic least: variation west, magnetic best**= a mnemonic to help remember whether to add or subtract variation.

MOA *abbreviation* military operations area

mode /məʊd/ *noun* **1.** a particular selected setting for the operation or functioning of equipment ○ *automatic mode* ○ *manual mode* **2.** a letter or number given to the various pulse spacings of airborne transponders and ground interrogators ○ *Mode A and mode C for altitude reporting, are used in air traffic control.*

model /ˈmɒd(ə)l/ *noun* a simplified description of a system, often in mathematical form, designed to make calculation simpler ○ *The description of the weather patterns is a model only which, in reality, is modified greatly by a number of factors.*

moderate *adjective* /ˈmɒd(ə)rət/ **1.** referring to something well within limits, not extreme □ **a moderate climate** a climate which is not too hot, not too cold **2.** the middle of three descriptions of intensity or amount, i.e. light, moderate, severe □ **moderate humidity** humidity which is not light or severe □ **light to moderate** varying between light and moderate ○ *light to moderate icing* □ **moderate to severe** varying between moderate and severe ○ *moderate to severe turbulence* ■ *verb* /ˈmɒdəreɪt/ to become or cause to become less extreme ○ *The south west wind moderates the climate of the UK* ○ *As the wind moderated, the aircraft was allowed to take off.*

modern /ˈmɒd(ə)n/ *adjective* up to date, referring to the present day ○ *Modern engines are far more powerful than engines used in the past.*

modification /ˌmɒdɪfɪˈkeɪʃ(ə)n/ *noun* an alteration or change in character or form which is normally an improvement ○ *There have been many modifications to the simple carburettor over the years.* ○ *As a result of the crash, modifications were made to the rudder linkage.*

modify /ˈmɒdɪfaɪ/ *verb* to change or alter in order to improve ○ *The landing gear was modified to provide greater strength.* (NOTE: **modifying – modified**)

modulate /ˈmɒdjʊˌleɪt/ *verb* to change the frequency, amplitude, phase, or other characteristic of an electromagnetic wave ○ *The ground station transmits a code in two short bursts, each of which is modulated with two tones.*

modulation /ˌmɒdjuˈleɪʃ(ə)n/ *noun* a change in a property of an electromagnetic wave or signal, such as its amplitude, frequency, or phase ○ *Pulse modulation is a series of quick, short bursts of energy which are radiated from an antenna which serves both the transmitter and the receiver.*

module /ˈmɒdjuːl/ *noun* a replaceable detachable unit

moist /mɔɪst/ *adjective* a little wet, damp or humid ○ *Warm moist air from the Gulf of Mexico can extend into Canada.*

moisture /ˈmɔɪstʃə/ *noun* water or other liquid ○ *When the air passing through the carburettor is reduced below 0°C (Celsius), any moisture in the air changes into ice.*

moisture content /ˈmɔɪstʃə ˌkɒntent/ *noun* the amount of water in the atmosphere or as seen when it condenses onto cold surfaces

mold /məʊld/ *noun, verb US* same as **mould**

molecule /ˈmɒlɪkjuːl/ *noun* the smallest particle into which an element or a compound can be divided without changing its chemical and physical properties ○ *The molecules of a gas* *move more quickly than the molecules of a liquid.*

moment /'məʊmənt/ *noun* **1.** a short period of time ○ *It only takes a moment to fill in the log book.* **2.** a point in time □ **at the moment** at this particular time ○ *He's not in the office at the moment.* **3.** the product of a quantity and its perpendicular distance from a reference point ○ *A load on the end of a beam creates a bending moment.* **4.** the tendency to cause rotation about a point or an axis ○ *The tailplane provides a pitching moment to keep the aircraft level.*

momentum /məʊ'mentəm/ *noun* a measure of the motion of a body equal to the product of its mass and velocity ○ *In rain, the faster an aircraft travels the more water it meets and the greater the relative momentum of the water droplets.*

monitor /'mɒnɪtə/ *noun* a visual display unit for a computer ■ *verb* to check, on a continuing basis ○ *Flowmeters are fitted which allow crew to monitor the flow of fuel to each engine.*

monitor system /'mɒnɪtə 'sɪstəm/ *noun* system for checking and warning

monocoque /'mɒnəkɒk/ *noun* a three-dimensional body with all the strength in the skin and immediately underlying framework ○ *In monocoque construction there is no internal stiffening, as the thickness of the skin gives the strength and stability.*

monoplane /'mɒnəʊpleɪn/ *noun* an aircraft that has only one pair of wings

monsoon /mɒn'suːn/ *noun* a wind from the south-west or south that brings heavy rainfall to southern Asia in the summer ○ *Although the monsoon winds are thought of as being Asiatic phenomena, they do occur over Africa and parts of North America, especially the Gulf of Mexico.* □ **monsoon season** a season of wind and heavy rainfall in tropical countries

morning mist /ˌmɔːnɪŋ 'mɪst/ *noun* a mist which usually disappears before midday, as the result of warming from the sun

Morse /mɔːs/ *noun* a code used for transmitting messages in which letters of the alphabet and numbers are represented by dots and dashes or short and long signals ○ *VOR (very high frequency omni-directional radio range) stations transmit a 2 or 3-letter aural Morse callsign on the reference signal at least every 30 seconds.* (NOTE: Morse is still used for identifying some radio beacons.)

COMMENT: Named after S. F. B. Morse, the American electrician who died in 1872.

motion /'məʊʃ(ə)n/ *noun* movement, the act of changing position or place □ **horizontal motion** movement from side to side □ **rotary motion** circular movement □ **vertical motion** up and down movement

MOTNE *noun* a network for the exchange of meteorological information needed by meteorological offices, VOLMET broadcasting stations, air traffic service units, operators and other aeronautical users. Full form **Meteorological Operational Telecommunications Network Europe**

motor /'məʊtə/ *noun* a machine which provides power for moving a vehicle or device with moving parts ○ *an electric motor* ○ *a hydraulic motor* (NOTE: Piston or jet power plants for aircraft are referred to as **engines** not motors.)

mould /məʊld/ *noun* a hollow shape for forming plastics, etc. ○ *Moulds are used in the manufacture of plastic components.* ■ *verb* to shape, often using a mould ○ *Thermo-plastic material become soft when heated and can be moulded again and again.* (NOTE: It is also written **mold** in US English.)

mount /maʊnt/ *verb* to fix to a support ○ *A propeller consists of a number of separate blades mounted in a hub.*

mountain /'maʊntɪn/ *noun* a mass of rock rising above ground level, higher than a hill ○ *They flew over mountains in the south of the country.*

Mountain Standard Time /ˌmaʊntɪn 'stændəd ˌtaɪm/ *noun* a time zone of the west-central part of the USA and Canada, 7 hours behind GMT

mounted /'maʊntɪd/ *adjective* fixed to a support □ **rear-mounted** mounted at the rear of the aircraft ○ *Some aircraft such as the Boeing 727 have rear-mounted engines.*

mounting /'maʊntɪŋ/ *noun* a supporting component or attachment point ○ *Airbus aircraft have engine mountings under the wings.*

movement /'muːvmənt/ *noun* a change in place or position ○ *The upward movement of the piston compresses the fuel/air mixture.* □ **movement of the crankshaft** the rotation of the crankshaft □ **the downward movement of cool air** the downward flow of cool air

mph *abbreviation* miles per hour

MSL *abbreviation* mean sea level

MTA /ˌem tiː 'eɪ/ *abbreviation* military training area

MTBF /ˌem tiː biː 'ef/ *noun* the average period of time that a piece of equipment will operate between problems. Full form **mean time between failures**

MTTR /ˌem tiː tiː 'ɑː/ *noun* the average period of time required to repair a faulty piece of equipment. Full form **mean time to repair**

MTWA *abbreviation* maximum total weight authorised

muff /mʌf/ *noun* ♦ acoustic ear muffs

multi- /mʌlti/ *prefix* multiple or many

multi-engine /ˌmʌlti 'endʒɪn/, **multi-engined** /ˌmʌlti 'endʒɪnd/ *adjective* □ **multi-engine(d) aircraft** aircraft with more than two engines

multi-function display /ˌmʌlti ˌfʌŋkʃ(ə)n dɪ'spleɪ/ *noun* an electronic cockpit instrument which displays information such as weather radar or navigation data. Abbreviation **MFD**

multi-mode receiver /ˌmʌlti məʊd rɪ'siːvə/ *noun* a type of radio receiver used in navigation and landing that can receive signals from a variety of different transmission systems

multiplane /'mʌltipleɪn/ *noun* an aircraft with more than one pair of wings

multiple /'mʌltɪp(ə)l/ *adjective* many ○ *Autoland system redundancy employs multiple systems operating in such a manner that a single failure within a system will have little effect on the aircraft's performance during the approach and landing operation.*

multiplication /ˌmʌltɪplɪ'keɪʃ(ə)n/ *noun* a mathematical operation to work out a specified number of times the value of a number (NOTE: The multiplication sign is x.)

multiply /'mʌltɪplaɪ/ *verb* to work out a specified number of times the value of a number ○ *To multiply 20 by 6 is to calculate what is 6 times 20 (6 x 20).* ○ *4 multiplied by 2 is 8 (4 x 2 = 8).* ○ *To calculate fuel required, multiply the duration of the flight by the consumption of the engine at the required power.*

multi-purpose /ˌmʌlti 'pɜːpəs/ *adjective* suitable for many different uses □ **multi-purpose tool** a tool which can be used in many different ways

multi-wheel combinations /ˌmʌlti ˌwiːl ˌkɒmbɪ'neɪʃ(ə)nz/ *plural noun* undercarriages consisting of a number of wheels on each unit

mutual /'mjuːtʃuəl/ *adjective* directed and received in equal amount

mutual inductance /ˌmjuːtʃuəl ɪn 'dʌktəns/ *noun* electro-magnetic field in one circuit caused by a quickly changing magnetic field in another circuit

N

N *abbreviation* north

nacelle /nə'sel/ *noun* a streamlined housing for an engine ○ *The ram air intake is located in a wing leading edge or an engine nacelle fairing.*

narrow /'nærəʊ/ *adjective* not wide ○ *narrow band of cloud* ○ *a narrow beam of electrons* ○ *The narrow aisles of passenger aircraft makes it difficult to evacuate an aircraft quickly.* Opposite **wide**, **broad**

NAS *abbreviation* national airspace system

NASA /'næsə/ *abbreviation* National Aeronautics and Space Administration

national /'næʃ(ə)nəl/ *adjective* belonging to a country ○ *KLM is the national airline of the Netherlands.*

National Aeronautics and Space Administration /,næʃ(ə)nəl ,eərənɔːtɪks ən 'speɪs əd,mɪnɪstreɪʃ(ə)n/ *noun* a US organisation for flight and space exploration. Abbreviation **NASA**

national airspace system /,næʃ(ə)nəl 'eəspeɪs ,sɪstəm/ *noun* an integrated system of control and communications facilities that is responsible for ensuring the safe and efficient movement of aircraft through the national airspace of the US. Abbreviation **NAS**

National Air Traffic Services /,næʃ(ə)nəl eə 'træfɪk ,sɜːvɪsɪz/ *plural noun* the organisation that is responsible for air traffic control at most UK airports. Abbreviation **NATS**

NATS *abbreviation* National Air Traffic Services

nature /'neɪtʃə/ *noun* **1.** the world, especially plants, animals and their environment in general ○ *Electricity is one of the fundamental forces of nature.* **2.** sort or type ○ *Action taken by the crew will depend on the nature of the emergency.* **3.** the essential qualities of something ○ *the convective nature of thunderstorms* ○ *Magnesium is a fire hazard of unpredictable nature.*

nautical /'nɔːtɪk(ə)l/ *adjective* referring to the sea ○ *The terms pitch, roll and yaw are nautical in origin.*

nautical mile /'nɔːtɪk(ə)l maɪl/ *noun* 1.852 kilometres ○ *One knot is equal to one nautical mile per hour.* Abbreviation **nm**. Compare **statute mile** (NOTE: A nautical mile is precisely defined as the length of an arc on the Earth's surface subtended by an angle of one minute at the centre of the Earth.)

NAVAID /'næveɪd/ *abbreviation* navigational aid

navigation /,nævɪ'geɪʃ(ə)n/ *noun* the theory and practice of planning, controlling and recording the direction of an aircraft ○ *The basis of air navigation is the triangle of velocities.*

navigational /,nævɪ'geɪʃ(ə)nəl/ *adjective* referring to navigation ○ *The accuracy of modern navigational equipment is much greater than older systems.*

navigational aid /,nævɪ'geɪʃ(ə)nəl eɪd/ *noun* a mechanical or electronic device designed to help a pilot navigate ○ *Any type of navigational aid but particularly electronic aids, for example ADF (automatic direction finding) and*

NDBs (non-directional beacons). Abbreviation **NAVAID**

navigational line /ˌnævɪˈɡeɪʃ(ə)nəl laɪn/ *noun* same as **position line**

navigation lights /ˌnævɪˈɡeɪʃ(ə)n laɪts/ *plural noun* lights on an aircraft consisting of a red light on the left wing tip, a green light on the right wing tip and a white light on the tail

COMMENT: Navigation lights must be used between sunset and sunrise.

navigation log /ˌnævɪˈɡeɪʃ(ə)n lɒɡ/ *noun* written details of headings and times for a flight ○ *The flight crew route flight plan is a composite document which also serves as a navigation log.*

NDB *abbreviation* non-directional beacon

necessary /ˈnesɪs(ə)ri/ *adjective* needed or essential ○ *A rich mixture is necessary at slow running.* □ **as necessary** when needed ○ *Warnings, cautions and advisory messages are displayed only when necessary.*

necessity /nəˈsesɪti/ *noun* something that is necessary or very important ○ *Student pilots should understand the necessity for treating thunderstorms with great respect.*

needle /ˈniːd(ə)l/ *noun* a thin metal pointer in an instrument ○ *The needle indicated to zero.*

needle valve /ˈniːd(ə)l vælv/ *noun* a valve formed of a tapered needle projecting into a small opening in a tube, etc., usually connected to a float, which provides fine adjustment of fluid flow ○ *Atmospheric pressure will allow the capsule to expand, causing the needle valve to move into the opening thus reducing the flow of fuel.*

negative /ˈneɡətɪv/ *adjective* **1.** a value of less than 0 ○ *In a reversing propeller, the propeller mechanism includes a removable ground fine pitch stop which enables the propeller to be set to a negative pitch.* **2.** referring to an electric charge of the same sign as that of an electron □ **the negative terminal of a battery** the terminal of a battery marked with the symbol – and normally coloured black rather than red **3.** show-

ing refusal □ **a negative answer** no **4.** showing resistance or non-co-operation ○ *a negative attitude*

negligible /ˈneɡlɪdʒɪb(ə)l/ *adjective* small or unimportant to the extent that it is not worth considering ○ *Atmospheric attenuation is negligible until the upper end of the UHF (ultra high frequency) band when it increases rapidly.* □ **negligible risk** almost no risk

neoprene /ˈniːəʊpriːn/ *noun* a type of synthetic rubber

net /net/ *adjective* after all necessary deductions

net dry weight /ˌnet draɪ ˈweɪt/ *noun* the basic weight of an engine without fluids and without accessories not essential for the engine to function

network /ˈnetwɜːk/ *noun* **1.** a complex interconnected group or system ○ *A network of meteorological stations around the world exchange information.* **2.** a system of lines or channels which cross each other ○ *On a map, meridians of longitude and parallels of latitude form a network of lines called a graticule.* **3.** a system of computers interconnected in order to share information

neutral /ˈnjuːtrəl/ *adjective, noun* **1.** indicating an electrical charge which is neither positive nor negative **2.** indicating the position of a switch or lever which leaves a system active but not engaged, e.g. an engine gear lever position in which the engine is disconnected from the driven parts **3.** indicating the middle position of a control surface providing no aerodynamic effect other than that as part of the wing ○ *After a turn, the auto-control will return the ailerons to neutral as the aircraft returns to straight flight.*

neutralise /ˈnjuːtrəlaɪz/, **neutralize** *verb* to cancel the effect of ○ *Spillage from a lead acid battery may be neutralised by washing with a diluted solution of sodium bicarbonate.*

never-exceed speed /ˌnevər ɪk ˈsiːd ˌspiːd/ *noun* a speed which must not be exceeded. Also called **Vne (Velocity Never Exceeded)**

night rating /'naɪt ˌreɪtɪŋ/ *noun* an additional qualification gained from a course of training for night flying

nil /nɪl/ *noun* nothing, zero □ **nil drizzle** no drizzle

nimbostratus /ˌnɪmbəʊ'streɪtəs/ *noun* a cloud forming a low dense grey layer from which rain or drizzle often falls

nitrogen /'naɪtrədʒən/ *noun* a colourless, odourless gas which makes up four fifths of the Earth's atmosphere ○ *Some aircraft have high pressure air or nitrogen bottles provided in the undercarriage and flap circuits for emergency lowering.* (NOTE: The atomic number of nitrogen is **7**.)

nm *abbreviation* nautical mile

nocturnal /nɒk'tɜːn(ə)l/ *adjective* happening or appearing during the night ○ *Because there is a requirement for a cold ground, a katabatic wind tends to be nocturnal, but if the slope is snow-covered, it can also occur during the day.*

no-fly zone /ˌnəʊ 'flaɪ ˌzəʊn/ *noun* an area over which aircraft, especially those of another country, are forbidden to fly

nominal /'nɒmɪn(ə)l/ *adjective* **1.** not significant or not important □ **a nominal increase** a very small increase **2.** named, specific ○ *As an installed battery becomes fully charged by the aircraft generator, the battery voltage nears its nominal level and the charging current decreases.*

non- /nɒn/ *prefix* not or no

non-directional beacon /ˌnɒn daɪ ˌrekʃ(ə)nəl 'biːkən/ *noun* a radio beacon transmitting a signal by which the pilot can determine his or her bearing. Abbreviation **NDB**

non-essential /ˌnɒn ɪ'senʃ(ə)l/ *adjective* not necessary ○ *In order to ensure the shortest possible take-off run, all non-essential equipment was removed.*

non-return valve /ˌnɒn rɪˌtɜːn 'vælv/ *noun* a valve which allows a fluid to pass in one direction only ○ *As the piston moves upwards in the cylinder, fluid is drawn in through a non-return valve.*

non-smoking area /ˌnɒn 'sməʊkɪŋ ˌeəriə/ *noun* an area where smoking is not allowed

normal /'nɔːm(ə)l/ *adjective* referring to something which is usual and is to be expected □ **under normal conditions** when everything is as it usually is

normal room temperature /ˌnɔːm(ə)l ˌruːm 'temprɪtʃə/ *noun* the temperature regarded as comfortable for usual daily activity

north /nɔːθ/ *noun* compass point 360°, the direction towards which the magnetic needle points on a compass ○ *Fly towards the north.* ○ *The wind is blowing from the north.* □ **north facing mountain side** the face of the mountain which looks towards the north ■ *adjective* **1.** referring to areas or regions lying in the north, referring to the compass point 360° ○ *the north coast of France* **2.** the northern part of a region or country ○ *North America* ■ *adverb* towards the north ○ *The aircraft was heading north.* ◊ **compass**, **magnetic**, **true**

northbound /'nɔːθbaʊnd/ *adjective* travelling towards the north ○ *a northbound flight*

north-east /ˌnɔːθ 'iːst/ *noun* the direction between north and east ○ *After take-off, the aircraft turned to the north-east.* ■ *adjective* **1.** situated in the north-east ○ *the north-east coast of England* **2.** blowing from or coming from the north-east ○ *a north-east wind* ■ *adverb* towards the north-east ○ *We are heading north-east.*

north-easterly /ˌnɔːθ 'iːstəli/ *adjective* **1.** blowing from or coming from the north-east ○ *A north-easterly wind was blowing.* **2.** moving towards the north-east ○ *Follow a north-easterly direction.*

north-eastern /ˌnɔːθ 'iːstən/ *adjective* referring to or situated in the north-east ○ *the north-eastern part of the United States*

northerly /'nɔːðəli/ *adjective* **1.** situated towards the north ○ *the most northerly point of a country* **2.** blowing from or coming from the north □ **northerly airflow** airflow coming from the north

○ *a northerly airflow from the polar regions* **3.** moving towards the north ○ *We are flying in a northerly direction.* ■ *noun* a wind which blows from the north

northern /'nɔːð(ə)n/ *adjective* referring to or situated in the north ○ *the northern hemisphere*

northern hemisphere /ˌnɔːð(ə)n ˌhemɪ'sfɪə/ *noun* the area of the Earth to the north of the equator

North Pole /ˌnɔːθ 'pəʊl/ *noun* the point which is furthest north on the earth ○ *From the UK the aircraft flew over the North Pole to Vancouver.*

northward /'nɔːθwəd/ *adjective* going towards the north ■ *adverb US* same as **northwards**

northwards /'nɔːθwədz/ *adverb* towards the north ○ *One of the aircraft was flying northwards.*

north-west /ˌnɔːθ 'west/ *noun* the direction between north and west ○ *The aircraft turned towards the north-west.* ■ *adjective* **1.** situated in the north-west ○ *the north-west coast of England* **2.** blowing from or coming from the north-west ○ *a north-west wind* ■ *adverb* towards the north-west ○ *We are heading north-west.*

north-westerly /ˌnɔːθ 'westəli/ *adjective* **1.** blowing from or coming from the north-west ○ *A north-westerly wind was blowing.* **2.** moving towards or to the north-west ○ *Follow a north-westerly direction.*

north-western /ˌnɔːθ 'westən/ *adjective* referring to or situated in the north-west ○ *the north-western part of the United States*

north wind /nɔːθ wɪnd/ *noun* a wind blowing from or coming from the north (NOTE: A wind is named after the direction it comes from.)

nose /nəʊz/ *noun* the extreme forward end of the aircraft

nose cone /'nəʊz kəʊn/ *noun* the foremost part of the nose of a multi-engine aircraft which may house electronic equipment, but not an engine

nose dive /'nəʊz daɪv/ *noun* an extremely steep descent by an aircraft front first

nose-dive /'nəʊz daɪv/ *verb* to fall steeply with the front end pointing downwards

nose gear /'nəʊz ɡɪə/ *noun* the nose wheel and supporting struts and linkages

nosewheel /'nəʊzwiːl/ *noun* the undercarriage wheel at the front of the aircraft. Compare **tailwheel**

no-smoking sign /ˌnəʊ 'sməʊkɪŋ ˌsaɪn/ *noun* a sign, usually lit-up, warning passengers and crew that smoking is not allowed

note /nəʊt/ *noun* **1.** a brief message on a piece of paper ○ *There's a note on your desk.* **2.** a brief comment made on paper about something that you are reading, listening to, or watching ○ *Make notes while you watch the video recording.* **3.** a short comment or explanation in a text, often at the end of a book or at the bottom of a page **4.** a piece of paper money ○ *a £10 note* (NOTE: The US English is **bill**.) **5.** a musical tone of definite pitch ○ *The note of the engine changes as rpm (revolutions per minute) is increased.* ■ *verb* **1.** to observe carefully, to take notice ○ *Note that true north is always along a meridian.* **2.** to write down ○ *Note the time of departure on the log sheet.* ○ *Note the time of any incident.*

'…immediately you become unsure of your position, note the time and, if you are in touch with an ATC unit, especially a radar unit, you should request assistance' [*Civil Aviation Authority, General Aviation Safety Sense Leaflet*]

notice /'nəʊtɪs/ *noun* **1.** a written or spoken announcement **2.** a formal warning or notification □ **to give notice** to inform an employee or employer in advance and in writing, of a termination to a period of employment ○ *As a result of the accident, the instructor was given three months' notice.* □ **the student pilot is grounded until further notice** the student pilot cannot fly again until told by those in authority that he or she can continue ■ *verb* to observe ○ *While* *doing the pre-flight checks, Captain Smith noticed that there was a leak of hydraulic fluid from one of the brake cylinders.*

noticeable /'nəʊtɪsəb(ə)l/ *adjective* catching the attention, easily noticed □ **a noticeable increase** an increase which is important enough to be observed ○ *There was a noticeable improvement in the trainee's recent exam results.*

notice board /'nəʊtɪs bɔːd/ *noun* a usually wooden board in a corridor or classroom, etc., where information on paper can be displayed

notification /ˌnəʊtɪfɪ'keɪʃ(ə)n/ *noun* the act of informing somebody about something ○ *Notification of the new procedures will follow in a few days.* ○ *She received notification that she had been accepted for the job.*

notify /'nəʊtɪfaɪ/ *verb* to inform ○ *Students were notified of their exam results by post.* ○ *The authorities must be notified of all in-flight incidents.*

nozzle /'nɒz(ə)l/ *noun* a projecting part with an opening at the end of a pipe, for regulating and directing a flow of fluid ○ *The nozzle of a portable fire*

extinguisher should be pointed at the base of the fire.

nucleus /'njuːkliəs/ *noun* the central part around which other parts are grouped ○ *An atom consists of a nucleus with orbiting electrons.* ○ *Condensation occurs on very small particles suspended in the air which are known as condensation nuclei.* (NOTE: The plural form is **nuclei**.)

null /nʌl/ *noun* an instrument reading of zero □ **the null position** the zero position ○ *Nulls are used for direction sensing because they are better defined than the maxima.*

numerical /njuː'merɪk(ə)l/ *adjective* referring to numbers or digits

numerical value /njuːˌmerɪk(ə)l 'væljuː/ *noun* a number

numerous /'njuːm(ə)rəs/ *adjective* very many, a lot ○ *Large transport aircraft have numerous clearly-marked exits to facilitate rapid evacuation of passengers.* ○ *Numerous refinements to the simple actuator will be found in use.*

nut /nʌt/ *noun* a metal ring which screws on a bolt to hold it tight ○ *Turn the nut anticlockwise to loosen it.*

O

OAT *abbreviation* **1.** operational air traffic **2.** outside air temperature

obey /əˈbeɪ/ *verb* **1.** to carry out or comply with a command ○ *Pilots must obey landing instructions.* **2.** to follow a physical law ○ *Winds obey Buys Ballot's Law.*

OBI *abbreviation* omni-bearing indicator

object /ˈɒbdʒekt/ *noun* **1.** something that you can touch and see and that has a particular form and dimensions ○ *Any given object will collect more ice when travelling at high speed than at low speed.* **2.** intention or aim ○ *The object of the briefing is to inform all aircrew of the new procedures.* ■ *verb* /əbˈdʒekt/ to raise or voice opposition ○ *Staff objected to the introduction of longer working hours.*

oblong /ˈɒblɒŋ/ *adjective* rectangular ○ *an oblong piece of aluminium* ■ *noun* a rectangle

OBS *abbreviation* omni-bearing selector

obscure /əbˈskjʊə/ *adjective* not clearly understood □ **the explanation was obscure** the explanation was difficult to understand because it wasn't clear ■ *verb* to make difficult to see ○ *Deposits of ice crystals on the windscreen will obscure vision.*

obscured /əbˈskjʊəd/ *adjective* □ **sky obscured** a meteorological term to mean that fog or mist prevents sight of the sky

observation /ˌɒbzəˈveɪʃ(ə)n/ *noun* careful watching ○ *The type of cloud is established by observation and comparison with cloud photographs.*

observe /əbˈzɜːv/ *verb* to watch carefully ○ *Local wave action can be observed from a height of 200 feet.* ○ *Wing deflection can be observed from the passenger cabin.*

observer /əbˈzɜːvə/ *noun* a person working in a meteorological station who assesses weather conditions by visual means ○ *Meteorological visibility is the greatest horizontal distance at which objects can be seen and recognised by an observer on the ground with normal eyesight and under conditions of normal daylight illumination.*

obstacle /ˈɒbstək(ə)l/ *noun* something which blocks a path or prevents progress ○ *Low frequency transmissions can penetrate obstacles such as mountains.* ○ *Knowing the heights of obstacles en route, it must be ensured that in the event of an emergency, the flight may be continued in safety.*

obstacle clearance /ˈɒbstək(ə)l ˌklɪərəns/ *noun* the fact of being at a sufficient height to be able to fly over any obstacles in the area

obstruct /əbˈstrʌkt/ *verb* to block a path or to prevent the progress of something ○ *Bags and luggage must not obstruct the aisles.* ○ *A safety valve is normally provided, in case the water separator assembly becomes obstructed by ice.*

obstruction /əbˈstrʌkʃən/ *noun* **1.** the act or process of obstructing ○ *The glidepath antenna cannot be placed close to the centre line of the runway because it would cause an obstruction.* **2.** something which blocks a path or prevents progress ○ *Before start-up, the* *air intakes and jet pipes must be inspected, to ensure that they are free from any debris or obstruction.*

'…taxiways and aerodrome obstructions may be hidden by snow, so ask if you are not certain' [*Civil Aviation Authority, General Aviation Safety Sense Leaflet*]

obtain /əb'teɪn/ *verb* to acquire, to get ○ *Telephone the meteorological office in order to obtain the latest weather forecast.* ○ *The probes are positioned in the gas stream in order to obtain an accurate temperature reading.*

obvious /'ɒbvɪəs/ *adjective* clear and easily seen or understood ○ *It is obvious that high ground will disturb the smooth horizontal flow of air.*

occasion /ə'keɪʒ(ə)n/ *noun* the time at which an event or happening occurs ○ *In recent months the aircraft suffered two engine failures, on the first occasion the aircraft force-landed safely.* ○ *The maiden flight of an aircraft is a great occasion.* □ **on occasions** sometimes

occasional /ə'keɪʒ(ə)n(ə)l/ *adjective* happening from time to time □ **occasional rain** periodic rain □ **occasional turbulence** turbulence happening from time to time

occluded front /ə'kluːdɪd frʌnt/ *noun* a weather front created when air is forced upward from the Earth's surface, as when a cold front overtakes and undercuts a warm front ○ *Jet streams are very rare near occluded fronts because of the much smaller temperature gradient across the fronts.*

occlusion /ə'kluːʒ(ə)n/ *noun* the forcing of air upward from the Earth's surface, as when a cold front overtakes and undercuts a warm front ○ *If the air ahead of the warm front is less cold than the air behind the cold front, the cold front will undercut the less cold air and form a cold occlusion.*

occupant /'ɒkjʊpənt/ *noun* a person who has a seat in an aircraft □ **occupants** the crew plus passengers ○ *In-flight emergency procedures are designed to successfully combat airborne emergencies which threaten the safety of the aircraft and its occupants.*

occupy /'ɒkjʊpaɪ/ *verb* **1.** to have a position, to be in a place ○ *The passenger is occupying the wrong seat.* **2.** to busy oneself ○ *Once an evacuation process is under way the crew will be fully occupied carrying out emergency drills.*

occur /ə'kɜː/ *verb* to happen ○ *Heavy rains occur during the monsoon season.* ○ *Tropical revolving storms generally occur from June to October.* ○ *An accident occurred on June 12th.*

occurrence /ə'kʌrəns/ *noun* a happening or event ○ *There were a number of occurrences of hijacking in the eighties.* ○ *The occurrence of the equatorial jet stream is due to a temperature gradient with colder air to the south.*

ocean /'əʊʃ(ə)n/ *noun* **1.** the body of salt water which covers the earth (NOTE: This is a chiefly American usage: British English prefers the word **sea.**) **2.** any of the major sea areas of the world ○ *the Atlantic Ocean*

COMMENT: The five oceans are: the Atlantic, the Pacific, the Indian, the Arctic and the Antarctic (or Southern).

oceanic /ˌəʊʃi'ænɪk/ *adjective* referring to the oceans ○ *The trade winds maintain their direction over the oceanic areas, especially the Pacific, more than over land areas.* □ **an oceanic crossing** a flight across sea or ocean

octa /'ɒktə/ *noun* same as **okta**

octane rating /'ɒkteɪn ˌreɪtɪŋ/ *noun* the ability of the fuel to resist detonation, i.e. the higher the number, the greater is the fuel's resistance to detonation

odd /ɒd/ *adjective* **1.** strange, peculiar ○ *an odd situation* ○ *The fact that moist air is lighter than an equivalent volume of dry air seems odd to many people.* **2.** □ **odd tenth** an odd decimal, e.g. 0.1, 0.3, etc. ○ *Frequency allocation of localisers in the VHF band is 108–112 MHz at odd tenths e.g. 108.1 and 109.3, the even decimals being allocated to VOR facilities.* **3.** indicating a number a little greater than the approximate number given □ **it is 60-odd miles to our destination** it is a little more than 60 miles to our destination

odd number /ˌɒd ˈnʌmbə/ *noun* a number which cannot be exactly divided by two, e.g. 1, 3, 5, 7, etc. ○ *A (battery) cell contains an odd number of plates.*

OEM /ˌəʊ iː ˈem/ *abbreviation* original equipment manufacturer

offer /ˈɒfə/ *noun* something, e.g. a sum of money, that is presented for acceptance or rejection ○ *He made an offer of $85,000 for the aircraft.* ■ *verb* **1.** to show readiness to do something ○ *He offered to pick up the tickets in advance.* **2.** to present for acceptance or rejection ○ *The company offered her a job and she accepted it.* **3.** to provide ○ *The battery offers a short term power capability.*

official /əˈfɪʃ(ə)l/ *adjective* referring to an authority, such as the government or a recognised organisation □ **an official weather report** a weather report produced by a meteorological station ■ *noun* a person employed by a government authority or a corporation ○ *An official of the civil aviation department will be visiting today.*

offshore /ˈɒfʃɔː/ *adjective* at a distance from the shore

offshore wind /ˌɒfˈʃɔː wɪnd/ *noun* a wind which blows from the coast towards the sea. Compare **onshore wind**

ohm /əʊm/ *noun* a unit of measurement of electrical resistance. ◊ **ampere**

COMMENT: Ohm's Law states that the current in a circuit is directly proportional to the voltage causing it and inversely proportional to the resistance of the circuit.

oil /ɔɪl/ *noun* a thick mineral liquid used as a fuel or to make mechanical parts move smoothly

oil pan /ˈɔɪl pæn/ *noun US* same as **sump**

okta /ˈɒktə/, **octa** *noun* a unit of visible sky equal to one eighth of total area visible to the horizon ○ *The amount of cloud cover is given in oktas.*

COMMENT: To measure cloud cover, the sky is divided into imaginary sections, each covering one eighth of the total. A cloudless sky is 'zero

oktas', and a sky which is completely covered with clouds is 'eight oktas' or 'eight eighths'.

oleo /ˈəʊliəʊ/ *noun* a telescopic strut in the undercarriage which absorbs impact loads on landing ○ *A safety switch is fitted in such a way to the oleo, that when the oleo is compressed on the ground, the 'undercarriage up' selection cannot be operated.* Full form **oleo-pneumatic**

OM *abbreviation* outer market

omit /əʊˈmɪt/ *verb* to leave out, not to include ○ *High charts show only information relevant to high altitude flights and many beacons/aids which are provided for low operations are omitted to keep the chart clear.* (NOTE: **omitting – omitted**)

omni-bearing indicator /ˌɒmni ˌbeərɪŋ ˈɪndɪkeɪtə/ *noun* a cockpit instrument that displays VOR information and is used for radio navigation. Abbreviation **OBI**

omni-bearing selector /ˌɒmni ˌbeərɪŋ sɪˈlektə/ *noun* a knob on an **omni-bearing indicator** which the pilot turns to select a radial from a VOR station. Abbreviation **OBS**

omnirange /ˈɒmnireɪndʒ/ *noun* a very-high-frequency radio navigation network that allows pilots to choose and fly on any bearing relative to a transmitter on the ground

one-in-sixty rule /ˌwʌn ɪn ˈsɪksti ˌruːl/ *noun* in navigation, every 1° of track error, and every 60 nautical miles flown, results in the aircraft being 1 nm off track

onshore /ˈɒnʃɔː/ *adjective* towards the coast

onshore wind /ˌɒnʃɔː ˈwɪnd/ *noun* a wind which blows from the sea towards the coast. Compare **offshore wind**

opacity /əʊˈpæsɪti/ *noun* the state of not allowing light to pass through ○ *Sometimes, it is possible to estimate the depth and opacity of the layer of mist or fog from the ground observations.*

opaque /əʊˈpeɪk/ *adjective* not allowing light to penetrate or pass through ○ *Rime ice is an opaque, white, granular ice which forms on leading edges.*

opening /'əʊp(ə)nɪŋ/ noun **1.** a space which acts as a passage through which something or somebody can go ○ *an inlet valve opening* **2.** a formal start of operation ○ *the opening of the new flying school* **3.** a vacancy for a job ○ *There's an opening for a new chief ground instructor.*

open-skies /ˌəʊpən 'skaɪz/ adjective referring to a policy of allowing aircraft belonging to any country to fly over an area, without restrictions on surveillance of military installations

operate /'ɒpəreɪt/ verb **1.** to control the working of ○ *The control column operates the ailerons and elevators.* ○ *The flaps are operated by a switch.* **2.** to use or manage ○ *The airline operates a fleet of Boeing aircraft.* **3.** to perform or function ○ *Jet transports operate at high altitudes.* **4.** to perform a surgical procedure, by cutting into the body ○ *The surgeon operated on the patient.*

operating jack /'ɒpəreɪtɪŋ dʒæk/ noun a device which converts rotary motion into linear or reciprocating motion in order to move heavy control surfaces

operating weight /'ɒpəreɪtɪŋ weɪt/ noun the total mass of aircraft ready for flight but excluding fuel and payload ○ *The type of undercarriage fitted to an aircraft is governed by the operating weight.*

operation /ˌɒpə'reɪʃ(ə)n/ noun **1.** the process of making something work ○ *The operation of the ignition system in a light aircraft is quite simple.* **2.** □ **long-haul operations** flying over long-distance routes **3.** an effect □ **to come into operation** to come into effect ○ *The new procedures come into operation on 1st January.* **4.** a surgical procedure ○ *The doctor performed an operation.* **5.** a procedure such as addition or subtraction

'…periodically check the carburettor heating system and controls for proper condition and operation' [*Civil Aviation Authority, General Aviation Safety Sense Leaflet*]

operational /ˌɒpə'reɪʃ(ə)nəl/ adjective **1.** working or functioning ○ *Air traffic control facilities were not operational at the time of the accident.* □ **the operational life of the aircraft** the expected working life of an aircraft **2.** ready for use, referring to an aircraft in a suitable condition to fly □ **an operational aircraft** an aircraft that can be used for its assigned purpose

operational air traffic /ˌɒpəreɪʃ(ə)nəl 'eə ˌtræfɪk/ noun flights operating in accordance with military air traffic service procedures. Abbreviation **OAT**

operations department /ˌɒpə'reɪʃ(ə)nz dɪˌpɑːtmənt/ noun the part of an airline or airport organisation which deals with flight operations

operative /'ɒp(ə)rətɪv/ adjective functioning or working ○ *The system is now operative after the recent maintenance.*

operator /'ɒpəreɪtə/ noun a person who operates or uses equipment ○ *A ring graticule around the edge of the cathode ray tube enables the operator to read the bearing directly.*

oppose /ə'pəʊz/ verb **1.** to work against ○ *In level flight, the force of lift opposes the force of gravity.* **2.** to reject, be in conflict with or try to prevent ○ *The local people oppose the building of the new runway.* **3.** □ **as opposed to** in contrast with ○ *over sea as opposed to over land*

opposite /'ɒpəzɪt/ adjective **1.** situated or placed directly across from something, facing □ **opposite sides of a building** the back and front of a building **2.** completely different, the reverse ○ *For every action there is an equal and opposite reaction.* ■ noun something completely different, the reverse ○ *The opposite of a katabatic wind is an anabatic wind.* ○ *The opposite of starboard is port.* ◇ **going in opposite directions 1.** moving away from each other **2.** moving towards each other

opposition /ˌɒpə'zɪʃ(ə)n/ noun □ **in opposition** against ○ *Drag acts in opposition to thrust.* ○ *The electromotive force that is produced by all motors is in opposition to supply voltage and is* *directly proportional to motor rpm (revolutions per minute).*

optimum /'ɒptɪməm/ *adjective* referring to the point at which the condition or amount of something is the best ○ *The optimum altitude for jet aircraft is higher than that for piston engine aircraft.* ■ *noun* the point at which the condition or amount of something is the best ○ *Generally speaking, engine output is at its optimum at cruising speed.*

option /'ɒpʃən/ *noun* a choice or alternative ○ *On a bad approach, the pilot of a powered aircraft always has the option of going around.* ○ *He was given the option of buying two aircraft instead of one.*

orbit /'ɔːbɪt/ *noun* the path of a planet, or of a satellite. as it moves around another celestial body. ○ *A year is the time taken for the Earth to complete one orbit round the sun.* □ **to put into orbit**, **to send into orbit** to launch something into space so that it revolves around a celestial body such as the sun ■ *verb* to revolve around ○ *The Earth orbits the sun.* (NOTE: **orbiting – orbited**)

order /'ɔːdə/ *noun* **1.** an instruction given as a command by somebody in authority ○ *The captain gave the order to evacuate the aircraft.* **2.** the sequence of occurrence ○ *The firing order of sparking plugs in a piston engine is 1, 3, 4, 2.* □ **alphabetical order** arrangement in which words beginning with letter A come first, followed by those beginning with letter B, then C, etc. □ **numerical order** arrangement in which the lowest numbers (1, 2, 3, etc.) come first and higher numbers (25, 26, 27, etc.) come later **3.** a condition or state ○ *Although the aircraft is old, it is in good working order.* □ **out of order** not working ○ *The telephone is out or order.* **4.** □ **in the order of** approximately ○ *VOR (very high frequency omni-directional radio range) beacons of 200 watts have a range in the order of 200 nm (nautical miles).* □ **in order to** so as to ○ *Indicated airspeed must be corrected in order to obtain true airspeed.* ■ *verb* **1.** to give a command ○ *Before impact, the captain will order the crew to secure themselves at their assigned emergency stations.* **2.**

to put in a sequence ○ *Order the items in importance from 1 to 10.*

organisation /ˌɔːɡənaɪ'zeɪʃ(ə)n/, **organization** *noun* **1.** an association of people working together for the same cause ○ *The World Meteorological Organization* ○ *The International Civil Aviation Organization* **2.** the act of putting things into a structured and systematic form ○ *The organisation of training materials for the new self-access learning centre is under way.* **3.** planning ○ *Captain Scott is responsible for the organisation of examinations.*

organise /'ɔːɡənaɪz/, **organize** *verb* **1.** to arrange into a system ○ *Organise your notes so that you can find things easily.* **2.** to plan ○ *The trip was well organised and everybody enjoyed themselves.*

orientate /'ɔːriənteɪt/ *verb* to locate in relation to the compass ○ *The first step in map reading is to orientate the chart by relating the direction of land features to their representation on the chart.*

orientation /ˌɔːriən'teɪʃ(ə)n/ *noun* a position in relation to the compass ○ *The horizontal situation indicator (HSI) presents a selectable, dynamic colour display of flight progress and plan view orientation.*

orifice /'ɒrɪfɪs/ *noun* an opening, mouth or vent ○ *The liquid expands and builds up a pressure differential across an orifice which leads to the expansion chamber.*

origin /'ɒrɪdʒɪn/ *noun* **1.** a source, the place where something starts ○ *An air mass takes on the characteristics of its place of origin.* **2.** the base from which a map projection is drawn ○ *The value of convergence used is correct at the parallel of origin.*

original /ə'rɪdʒən(ə)l/ *adjective* before all others, the first ○ *The atmosphere is said to be stable if, when a parcel of air is displaced vertically, it tends to return to its original level.*

originate /ə'rɪdʒɪneɪt/ *verb* to be created or to come into being ○ *Tropical revolving storms originate within 5–15° of the equator.* ○ *Aircraft fires after an* *emergency landing, often originate in the wing area.*

orographic /ˌɒrəˈgræfɪk/ *adjective* referring to mountains □ **orographic uplift** the lifting of air masses in contact with mountain regions

orographic cloud /ˌɒrəʊgræfɪk ˈklaʊd/ *noun* a cloud formed by air being forced upward over mountainous areas

orthomorphic /ˌɔːθəʊˈmɔːfɪk/ *adjective* of the correct shape ○ *An orthomorphic chart is one which has meridians and parallels which intersect at right angles and, at any point on the chart, the scale must be the same in all directions.*

orthomorphism /ˌɔːθəʊˈmɔːfɪz(ə)m/ *noun* a shape representation on a map ○ *Orthomorphism means that bearings may be measured correctly at any point on a chart.*

oscillate /ˈɒsɪleɪt/ *verb* **1.** to move regularly between extremes **2.** to increase or decrease regularly so as to produce oscillations ○ *Instability protection is incorporated to guard against oscillating outputs from the alternators.*

oscillation /ˌɒsɪˈleɪʃ(ə)n/ *noun* **1.** a regular movement between extremes ○ *Ridge waves can be thought of as oscillations about the stable state of the undisturbed air flow with the range of hills providing the disturbance.* **2.** a regular increase and decrease of electrical current ○ *The supply is subject to oscillation.*

oscillator /ˈɒsɪleɪtə/ *noun* an electronic circuit that produces a pulse or a signal at a particular frequency ○ *The local oscillator replicates the radio frequency of the frequency generator at the transmitter.*

out /aʊt/ *adverb* □ **out of** away from, no longer in

outboard /ˈaʊtbɔːd/ *adverb* in a direction away from the centre of an aircraft ■ *adjective* situated away from the main body of an aircraft and towards the wing tips

outbound /ˈaʊtbaʊnd/ *adjective, adverb* towards a destination away from a VOR ○ *The aircraft flies outbound from the beacon along the airway and inbound to the facility at the other end of the leg.* □ **outbound traffic** aircraft flying away from an airfield

outbreak /ˈaʊtbreɪk/ *noun* a sudden start ○ *Showers are local outbreaks of precipitation from detached cumulus or cumulonimbus.* ○ *Hand operated fire extinguishers are provided to combat any outbreaks of fire in the flight crew compartment and passengers cabins.*

outer /ˈaʊtə/ *adjective* **1.** external ○ *Pneumatic de-icer boots are made from vulcanised rubber fabric with an outer covering of neoprene.* **2.** positioned away from the centre ○ *Winds near anticyclones are normally light near the centre, but tend to be stronger towards the outer edges.* **3.** □ **outer wing** the part of the wing nearest the tip

outer marker /ˌaʊtə ˈmɑːkə/ *noun* an ILS marker beacon, usually on centre line of approach at about 4.5 nm from the runway threshold

outflow /ˈaʊtfləʊ/ *noun* flow in an outward direction ○ *The outflow valve is controlled by the cabin pressure controller.*

outgoing /aʊtˈgəʊɪŋ/ *adjective* going out ○ *There is a fall of temperature until about one hour after dawn when incoming solar radiation balances outgoing terrestrial radiation.* Opposite **incoming**

outlet /ˈaʊtlət/ *noun* a passage for exit or escape ○ *The air leaves the compressor outlet and passes through a matrix assembly of the secondary heat exchanger.* ○ *When the controlling super-charger outlet pressure is reached, the capsule is compressed sufficiently to open its bleed valve.*

outline /ˈaʊtlaɪn/ *noun* **1.** a line around the shape of something ○ *Warning labels have a solid red outline.* **2.** a shape ○ *At low level, features are most easily recognised from their outline in elevation.* ○ *Cumulus cloud has detached domes or towers which are generally dense and have sharp outlines.* ■ *verb* to explain simply and briefly ○ *The changes in conditions outlined in the next paragraph.*

out-of-balance turn /ˌaʊt əv ˌbæləns 'tɜːn/ *noun* a turn in which the aircraft 'skids' upwards and outwards from the turn or 'slips' inwards and downward ○ *During an out-of-balance turn, the ball in the slip indicator will be deflected to the left or right.*

out of trim /ˌaʊt əv 'trɪm/ *adjective* referring to a situation in which the aircraft is not in static balance in pitch, so that if the pilot releases the yoke or control stick, the aircraft will start to climb or descend

output /'aʊtpʊt/ *noun* the product of a process ○ *Air density will affect the output of the engine.* ○ *The function of the supercharger is to increase the power output.* ○ *The power output of an engine depends on the weight of mixture which can be burnt in the cylinders in a given time.*

outrigger /'aʊtrɪɡə/ *noun* a projection attached to an aircraft to stabilise it or to support something

outward /'aʊtwəd/ *adjective* moving away from the centre or starting point ○ *The piston draws fluid into the cylinders on the outward stroke and expels fluid into the system on the inward stroke.* ◊ **bound**

outwards /'aʊtwədz/ *adverb* away from the centre or starting point, towards the outside ○ *The door opens outwards.* (NOTE: The US English is **outward**.)

overall /ˌəʊvər'ɔːl/ *adjective* including everything ○ *The total aerodynamic losses result in an overall turbine efficiency of 92%.* ○ *Although the student failed in one of the five exams, her overall result was a pass.* ■ *adverb* generally ○ *Overall, the test flight was a success.* ■ *noun* /'əʊvərɔːl/ a one-piece item of protective clothing ○ *The engineer was wearing an overall to prevent his clothes from getting dirty.*

overalls /'əʊvərɔːlz/ *plural noun* protective trousers with a bib and straps over the shoulders ○ *Wear overalls to protect your clothes.*

overcome /ˌəʊvə'kʌm/ *verb* to beat, to conquer, to win against ○ *The effects of anoxia at high altitudes can be over-* come by breathing through a mask. ○ *Drag must be overcome with thrust in order for an aircraft to increase speed.*

overflew /ˌəʊvə'fluː/ ♦ **overfly**

overflight /'əʊvəflaɪt/ *noun* the flight of an aircraft over an area

overfly /ˌəʊvə'flaɪ/ *verb* to fly over an area (NOTE: **overflew – overflown**)

overhang /'əʊvəhæŋ/ *noun* **1.** the distance from the last outer strut to the end of a monoplane's wing **2.** a distance equivalent to half of the difference in the spans of the two wings of a biplane

overhaul *verb* /ˌəʊvə'hɔːl/ to take apart and examine carefully in order to repair and clean, etc. ○ *To overhaul the system will take a couple of days.* ■ *noun* /'əʊvəhɔːl/ the act of taking apart in order to repair and clean ○ *Other than the oil pump and the generator rotor, there are no other moving parts in the system to wear or which require periodic overhaul.*

overhead /ˌəʊvə'hed/ *adjective* **1.** vertically above the point where a course is measured or timed ○ *The aircraft started from overhead A at 1000 hours on a heading of 230°T.* **2.** above the level of people's heads ○ *Overhead baggage lockers must be secured immediately prior to take-off.* ■ *adverb* above one's head ○ *She noticed a plane flying overhead.*

overheat /ˌəʊvə'hiːt/ *verb* to get too hot ○ *An acceleration/deceleration control is fitted to prevent the turbine assembly from overheating during acceleration, and to prevent flame-out during deceleration.*

overlap *noun* /'əʊvəlæp/ part of one thing covering something else ■ *verb* /ˌəʊvə'læp/ to have an area or range in common with something else, or to cover part of something else ○ *The maps overlap each other at the edges by three centimetres.* (NOTE: **overlapping – overlapped**)

overload *noun* /'əʊvələʊd/ an excessive amount of work or electricity ○ *Resettable circuit protective devices should be designed so that when an overload or circuit fault exists, they will open the circuit.* ■ *verb* /ˌəʊvə'ləʊd/ **1.**

to load a device or system, such as an electrical circuit, with too much work; to demand more than a system is capable of ○ *Operating pressure is maintained in that part of the system which leads to the selector valves, and some method is used to prevent overloading the pumps.* **2.** to load too heavily ○ *The aircraft failed to gain height after take-off because it was overloaded.*

overload operations /ˈəʊvələʊd ˌɒpəreɪʃ(ə)nz/ *noun* operation of aircraft in unusual situations when take-off weight exceeds the permitted maximum

override /ˌəʊvəˈraɪd/ *verb* to take over control of the operation of an automatic device or system ○ *A circuit-protective device must not be of a type which can be overridden manually.* (NOTE: **overriding – overrode – overridden**)

overrun /ˈəʊvərʌn/ *noun* a cleared level area at the end of a runway, available in case a plane does not stop quickly enough

overshoot /ˌəʊvəˈʃuːt/ *verb* to fly past a target ○ *The pilot tried to land but the aircraft overshot the runway.* (NOTE: **overshooting – overshot**)

overspeed *verb* /ˌəʊvəˈspiːd/ to go too fast ○ *A fault in the constant speed drive unit causes the generator to overspeed.* ■ *noun* /ˈəʊvəspiːd/ a speed that is too fast ○ *Overspeed is usually a fault in the constant speed drive unit which causes the generator to overspeed.*

overspeeding /ˌəʊvəˈspiːdɪŋ/ *noun* the act of going too fast ○ *Overspeeding of the engine is prevented by a governor in the fuel system.*

overstress /əʊvəˈstres/ *verb* to subject to too much force ○ *It takes less g force to overstress a heavy aircraft than a light one.*

owing to /ˈəʊɪŋ tuː/ *preposition* because of ○ *Integral tanks are now favoured for aircraft owing to the very high utilisation of space and saving of weight.* ○ *Owing to the aerodrome being unserviceable, the landing was made at another aerodrome some distance away.*

oxidation /ˌɒksɪˈdeɪʃ(ə)n/ *noun* the combination of a substance with oxygen, with loss of electrons ○ *When aluminium surfaces are exposed to the atmosphere, a thin invisible oxide skin forms immediately that protects the metal from further oxidation.*

oxide /ˈɒksaɪd/ *noun* a compound of an element with oxygen ○ *When aluminium surfaces are exposed to the atmosphere, a thin invisible oxide skin forms immediately that protects the metal from further oxidation.*

oxidise /ˈɒksɪdaɪz/, **oxidize** *verb* to form an oxide by the reaction of oxygen with another chemical substance ○ *Over a period of time, the metal is oxidised by contact with air.*

oxygen /ˈɒksɪdʒən/ *noun* a colourless, odourless gas, which is essential to human life, constituting 21% by volume of the Earth's atmosphere ○ *Our bodies can get oxygen through the lungs.* ○ *At very high altitudes the flying pilot must be on oxygen at all times, unless an aircraft dispensation has been obtained.* (NOTE: The atomic number of oxygen is 8.)

ozone /ˈəʊzəʊn/ *noun* a poisonous form of oxygen found naturally in the atmosphere which is toxic to humans at concentrations above 0.1 parts per million ○ *The maximum concentration of ozone is between 20 and 25 km above the Earth's surface.* Symbol O_3

P

PA *abbreviation* public address

Pacific Standard Time /pə'sɪfɪk 'stændəd 'taɪm/ *noun* the time zone of the west coast area of the USA and Canada, 8 hours behind Greenwich Mean Time

pack /pæk/ *noun* **1.** a detachable system ○ *Circuit packs consist of basic decision-making elements, referred to as logic gates, each performing combinational operations.* ○ *A power pack system is one in which most of the major components, with the exception of the actuators and, in some systems, the pumps, are included in a self-contained unit.* **2.** a small package containing a set number of items ○ *The survival pack includes heliographs, sea marker dyes, day/night distress flares and parachute flares.*

pad /pæd/ *noun* same as **helipad**

pair /peə/ *noun* two matched items, similar in appearance and function ○ *A brake control valve usually contains four elements, one pair for the brakes on each side of the aircraft, to provide duplicated control.*

pancake /'pænkeɪk/ (*informal*) *noun* same as **pancake landing** ■ *verb* to make a pancake landing, or cause an aircraft to make a pancake landing

pancake landing /'pænkeɪk ˌlændɪŋ/ *noun* a landing in which an aircraft drops suddenly straight to the ground from a low altitude, usually because of engine failure

panel /'pæn(ə)l/ *noun* **1.** a flat, often rectangular piece of the skin of the aircraft ○ *Access to the engine compartment is normally via hinged cowling panels.* **2.** a board with switches, dials, control knobs, etc. ○ *The pilot is trained to scan an instrument panel.*

panic /'pænɪk/ *noun* a sudden overpowering fear or terror ○ *In order to prevent mass panic amongst passengers in an emergency situation, crew may have to use force.*

PAPI *abbreviation* precision approach path indicator

PAR *abbreviation* precision approach radar

parachute /'pærəʃuːt/ *noun* a device used to slow down free fall from an aircraft, consisting of a light piece of fabric attached by cords to a harness and worn or stored folded until used in descent

parachute flare /'pærəʃuːt fleə/ *noun* a distress signal, suspended from a parachute to allow more time for the flare to be seen, which is fired to a height of 1200 ft

parachutist /'pærəʃuːtɪst/ *noun* a person who returns to the ground from an aircraft using a parachute

parallel /'pærəlel/ *adjective* **1.** side by side and having the same distance between them at every point ○ *As one aircraft flew round to attempt another landing, a Boeing 757 was taking off on the parallel runway.* ○ *The runway is parallel to the main road.* **2.** □ **in parallel** arranged so as to join at common points at each end ○ *When batteries are connected in parallel, voltage remains constant but capacity increase.* ■ *noun* a line which is parallel to another □ **parallels of latitude** imaginary lines of constant latitude around the Earth's surface

parameter /pə'ræmɪtə/ *noun* a set of measurable values such as temperature which define a system and determine its behaviour ○ *Parameters required by the crew to set and monitor engine thrust are permanently displayed on the screen.*

parasite drag /'pærəsaɪt dræg/ *noun* a component of total lift, caused by friction between the airflow and the structure of the aircraft ○ *Parasite drag increases as speed increases.*

parcel /'pɑːs(ə)l/ *noun* a small package □ **parcel of air** small body of air ○ *When a parcel of air is heated, its volume increases and its density decreases thus there is a fall in pressure.*

park /pɑːk/ *verb* to leave a vehicle such as a car or an aircraft in a particular place when no one is using it ○ *Park beside the Cessna 150.*

parking brake /'pɑːkɪŋ breɪk/ *noun* a brake that is set, often by hand, when the aircraft is stationary for a period of time ○ *Make certain that the parking brake is on before doing engine run-up checks.* ○ *Light aircraft should be left with parking brakes off so that they can be moved quickly in the event of a fire in the hangar.*

partial /'pɑːʃ(ə)l/ *adjective* in part, not fully □ **partial closing of an undercarriage door** not full closing of the doors □ **partial filter blockage** incomplete blockage of a filter

particle /'pɑːtɪk(ə)l/ *noun* a very small piece or part ○ *Solid particles in the atmosphere include sand, dust, volcanic ash and atmospheric pollution.* ○ *Hailstones start as ice particles in the upper part of a cumulonimbus cloud.*

particular /pə'tɪkjʊlə/ *adjective* special, given, distinct, not general ○ *a particular time* ○ *a particular speed* ○ *The size and number of valves required for a particular type of aircraft is governed by the amount of air necessary for pressurisation and air conditioning.*

pass /pɑːs/ *noun* 1. a badge or document which allows one to enter a restricted or prohibited area ○ *a security*

pass 2. a successful result in an exam ■ *verb* 1. to move ○ *Tropical storms dissipate as they pass from sea to land.* ○ *The air leaves the compressor outlet and passes through a matrix assembly.* 2. □ **to pass information** to give information □ **pass your message** an instruction to a pilot to give information via radio to an air traffic control facility 3. □ **pass an exam** to be successful in an exam 4. □ **to pass a book to someone** to pick up and give a book to somebody nearby 5. □ **to pass another aircraft** to move past another aircraft

passage /'pæsɪdʒ/ *noun* 1. movement over, along, or through something ○ *The passage of air over a turbine is used to power a small emergency generator.* ○ *The passage of a trough is marked by a sharp veer in the wind.* 2. a channel through which something can pass ○ *Liquid cooling is achieved by circulating a liquid around the cylinder barrels, through a passage formed by a jacket on the outside.* 3. part of a book or speech, etc. ○ *a passage from a training manual*

passenger /'pæsɪndʒə/ *noun* a person who travels in an aircraft, car, train, etc., and has no part in the operation of it ○ *The Piper Archer has seating for a pilot and three passengers.*

passenger aircraft /'pæsɪndʒə ˌeəkrɑːft/ *noun* an aircraft specially designed for carrying people

passive /'pæsɪv/ *adjective* receiving an action but taking no action ○ *In primary radar systems, the target is passive.* □ **passive state** referring to a system or device which may be switched on or 'live' but not reacting to any input. Opposite **active**

pass-mark /'pɑːs mɑːk/ *noun* the mark which separates those who fail and those who pass an examination

passport control /'pɑːspɔːt kən ˌtrəʊl/ *noun* 1. the action of checking passports of people arriving in or leaving a country ○ *We now have to go through passport control.* 2. the place where passports are checked when people arrive in or leave a country ○ *At* *passport control, a customs official checks passports.*

patch /pætʃ/ *noun* a small area ○ *a patch of fog* ○ *a patch of cloud* ○ *Patches of early morning fog made identification of ground features difficult.*

path /pɑːθ/ *noun* a route or course along which something moves ○ *Projection of the path of the aircraft over the ground is called its track.*

pattern /'pæt(ə)n/ *noun* a form or method which shows particular, consistent characteristics □ **pressure pattern** changes in pressure areas which take place regularly, e.g. every year

pavement /'peɪvmənt/ *noun* a prepared concrete or tarmac surface for ground manoeuvring of aircraft, including taxiways and runways (NOTE: The bearing strengths of pavements intended for aircraft of 5,700 kg MTWA (maximum total weight authorised) or less are reported as the maximum allowable weight and maximum allowable tyre pressure.)

pavement classification number /,peɪvmənt ,klæsɪfɪ 'keɪʃ(ə)n ,nʌmbə/ *noun* a number expressing the bearing strength of a pavement for unrestricted operations. Abbreviation **PCN**

PAX *abbreviation* passengers

payload /'peɪləʊd/ *noun* the money-earning load carried by the aircraft including the passengers, baggage and freight ○ *The shape of an aircraft is determined by the requirement to provide an aerodynamic lift force great enough to support the weight of the aircraft and payload whilst in flight.*

PCN *abbreviation* pavement classification number

PDC *abbreviation* pre-departure clearance

peak /piːk/ *noun* the highest point ○ *The intensity of solar radiation reaches a peak around noon.* □ **peak value** maximum value

PED *abbreviation* portable electronic device

pedal /'ped(ə)l/ *noun* a foot-operated lever

penalty /'pen(ə)lti/ *noun* **1.** an unwanted result of an action ○ *The penalty of using a circular polarisation transmission may be some loss of definition.* **2.** a punishment or fine ○ *Fuel penalties can be incurred if fuel surplus to requirements is carried.*

penetrant /'penətrənt/ *noun* something which forces or gets entry into an area or substance ○ *Penetrant dye inspection is a non-destructive test used mainly for the detection of defects open to the surface.* ○ *Penetrant oil can be used to loosen rusty bolts, etc.*

penetrate /'penɪtreɪt/ *verb* to force a way into ○ *Cool air from the Atlantic can sometimes penetrate far into Europe.* ○ *Occasionally, thunder cloud will penetrate through the tropopause.*

penetration /,penɪ'treɪʃ(ə)n/ *noun* the act of forcing a way into or through ○ *Long-range radars are little affected by weather interference and have good cloud penetration characteristics.*

per /pɜː, pə/ *preposition* for each, for every ○ *feet per minute (fpm)* ○ *gallons per hour (gph)*

per cent /pə 'sent/ *noun* the number out of each hundred □ **fifty per cent (50%)** half or ½ or 50 out of 100 □ **twenty-five per cent (25%)** one quarter or ¼ or 25 out of 100

percentage /pə'sentɪdʒ/ *noun* **1.** a fraction with 100 as the understood denominator ○ *Volumetric efficiency is usually expressed as a percentage.* **2.** part of the total ○ *Only a small percentage of passengers take in the pre-departure safety briefing.*

perform /pə'fɔːm/ *verb* to do ○ *Circuit breakers perform the same function as a fuse.* ○ *The pilot performed a loop to conclude his flying display.*

performance /pə'fɔːməns/ *noun* the ability of a system such as an aircraft or an engine to function as required ○ *The performance of the turbojet engine is measured in thrust produced at the propelling nozzle or nozzles.*

period /'pɪəriəd/ *noun* a length of time ○ *a 24 hour period* ○ *a period of 3 minutes*

periodic /ˌpɪəriˈɒdɪk/ *adjective* happening from time to time or at regular intervals, occasional □ **periodic maintenance** maintenance made at a particular time interval ○ *Periodic calibration of ILS (instrument landing system) installations is recommended.*

peritrack /ˈperitræk/ *noun* same as **taxiway**

permanent /ˈpɜːmənənt/ *adjective* lasting or remaining without change □ **permanent deformation** damage to a structure which must be repaired by replacing the damaged part □ **permanent magnet** a metal component which always has a magnetic influence. Opposite **temporary**

permissible /pəˈmɪsɪb(ə)l/ *adjective* allowable, not prohibited ○ *Great care must be taken to ensure that the aircraft operates within regulated or permissible weight limits.*

permission /pəˈmɪʃ(ə)n/ *noun* consent or authorisation ○ *A passenger who is drunk can be refused permission to board the aircraft.*

permit *noun* /ˈpɜːmɪt/ a document or pass that is proof of official permission to do or have something ○ *You need a permit to enter the restricted area.* ■ *verb* /pəˈmɪt/ to allow ○ *When oxygen mask are pulled down to the usable position, valves are opened which permit oxygen to flow.* ○ *Information passed to the operations department will be sufficient to permit the flight to be planned.*

Permit to Fly /ˌpɜːmɪt tə ˈflaɪ/ *noun* a certificate issued by the Civil Aviation Authority in the UK for aircraft which do not qualify for a Certificate of Airworthiness

perpendicular /ˌpɜːpənˈdɪkjʊlə/ *adjective* at right angles or 90° to a base or a line ○ *The vertical grid lines are perpendicular to the horizontal ones.* ○ *The air is acted upon by a force perpendicular to the isobars in the direction of low pressure.*

persist /pəˈsɪst/ *verb* 1. to continue to exist ○ *Snow cover tends to persist on north-facing slopes of mountains.* 2. to continue without giving up ○ *She per-* sisted with her request until it was granted.

persistence /pəˈsɪstəns/ *noun* 1. the fact of continuing to exist and not disappearing ○ *The persistence and movement of cols is governed by the movement of the adjacent pressure systems.* 2. the act of continuing to do something and not giving up ○ *He managed to overcome his difficulties through persistence and hard work.*

personnel /ˌpɜːsəˈnel/ *noun* a body of people involved in a common purpose such as work ○ *Smoke masks are available for use by personnel within the aircraft.*

PFCU *abbreviation* power flying control unit

PFD *abbreviation* primary flight display

phase /feɪz/ *noun* 1. a stage or part ○ *An emergency situation may occur during any phase of the flight.* 2. the relationship between voltage and current ○ *The CSDU (constant speed drive unit) drive shaft turns the permanent magnet generator and single phase AC (alternating current) is induced in the winding on the stator.*

phase angle /ˈfeɪz ˌæŋg(ə)l/ *noun* the difference between two periodic phenomena expressed as an angle

phase difference /ˈfeɪz ˌdɪf(ə)rəns/ *noun* a measure of phase angle from any VOR radial related to that on bearing 360°

phenomenon /fəˈnɒmɪnən/ *noun* an occurrence or circumstance which can be perceived by the senses ○ *Metal fatigue is not a modern phenomenon.* ○ *Of all meteorological phenomena, thunderstorms present the greatest hazard to aviation.* (NOTE: The plural form is **phenomena**.)

photographic film /ˌfəʊtəgræfɪk ˈfɪlm/ *noun* a celluloid material usually contained in a small metal cylindrical casing for use in cameras

physical /ˈfɪzɪk(ə)l/ *adjective* 1. referring to matter and energy or the sciences dealing with them, especially physics ○ *Oxygen and nitrogen together constitute 99% of the atmosphere and*

obey the physical laws as any other gas.
2. referring to the human body ○ *In some aircraft operating for long periods at high altitudes, physical discomfort may arise from low relative humidity.* □ **physical fitness** the state of health of the body

PIC *abbreviation* pilot in command

piece /piːs/ *noun* a bit, portion or part ○ *The upper and lower skin panel of each wing can be made in one piece.* (NOTE: **Piece** is often used to show one item of something which has no plural: *a piece of equipment; a piece of information.*) □ **piece of equipment** an item of equipment ○ *Early rescue depends on rapid location of survivors and the survival beacon is the most important piece of equipment in this regard.*

pilot /ˈpaɪlət/ *noun* **1.** a person who operates an aircraft in flight **2.** the part of a system or device that leads the whole ■ *verb* to operate or guide ○ *to pilot an aircraft*

COMMENT: A pilot holding a private or commercial pilot's licence may log as pilot-in-command time only the flight time during which he or she is the only operator of the aircraft's flying controls.

pilot in command /ˌpaɪlət ɪn kə ˈmɑːnd/ *noun* the pilot who has responsibility for the operation and safety of the aircraft during flight time. Abbreviation **PIC**

Pilot's Operating Handbook /ˌpaɪləts ˈɒpəreɪtɪŋ ˌhændbʊk/ *noun* a book giving details of an aircraft with recommendations and instructions regarding its use. Abbreviation **POH**

pin /pɪn/ *noun* a short, usually cylindrical metal rod

pinpoint /ˈpɪnpɔɪnt/ *noun* a visual observation of the precise position of an aircraft ○ *The pinpoint is a very positive means of establishing position, as long as the feature is properly identified.* ■ *verb* to draw attention to ○ *to pinpoint a problem*

pipe /paɪp/ *noun* a hollow cylinder or tube to convey a fluid ○ *a delivery pipe* ○ *an exhaust pipe*

pipeline /ˈpaɪplaɪn/ *noun* a long hollow cylinder or tube to convey a fluid such as oil or natural gas ○ *The incompressibility of liquids enables force to be transmitted long distances through pipelines.*

piston /ˈpɪstən/ *noun* a solid cylinder that fits into a larger cylinder and moves under fluid pressure, as in petrol and diesel engines or compresses fluids, as in pumps and compressors

piston engine /ˈpɪstən ˌendʒɪn/ *noun* a petrol or diesel engine in which pistons are moved by combustion of fuel, this reciprocating movement producing rotating movement

piston ring /ˈpɪstən rɪŋ/ *noun* one of the metal rings which seals the space between the piston and the cylinder wall ○ *There should be a loose fit between the cylinder and the piston, the difference being taken up by the piston rings.*

pitch /pɪtʃ/ *noun* **1.** a nose up/down movement of the aircraft about its lateral axis ○ *If the control column is moved forward or aft, the pitch attitude of the aircraft changes.* **2.** the distance a propeller would advance in one rotation if there was no slip □ **fine pitch setting and coarse pitch setting** angular propeller-blade settings ○ *Variable pitch propellers were originally produced with two blade-angle settings – fine pitch to enable full engine speed to be used on take off and coarse pitch to allow an economical engine speed to be used for cruising.* ■ *verb* to move about the lateral axis ○ *Move the yoke fore and aft to pitch down and up.*

pitch angle /ˈpɪtʃ ˌæŋg(ə)l/ *noun* the angle between the blade element chord line and the plane of rotation of the propeller

pitch lock /ˈpɪtʃ lɒk/ *noun* a means of holding the fine pitch stop in a prescribed position (NOTE: Some manufacturers use the term to describe a device which locks the blades at whatever angle they are at if there is a failure of the pitch change mechanism.)

pitch trim /ˈpɪtʃ trɪm/ *noun* the trim of the aircraft in the lateral axis so that there are no forward/aft forces on the control stick or yoke

pitot head /'pi:təʊ hed/ *noun* an externally mounted device which senses and sends airspeed information to the airspeed indicator in the cockpit

pitot-static system /,pi:təʊ 'stætɪk ,sɪstəm/ *noun* a pressure system for the airspeed indicator, altimeter and vertical speed indicator

pitot tube /'pi:təʊ tju:b/, **Pitot tube** *noun* an open-ended tube used to measure the speed of flow of a fluid ○ *device to sense pitot pressure created by the movement of air over the aircraft*

pivot /'pɪvət/ *noun* a short rod on which another part rotates ■ *verb* to turn on a point ○ *The rocker arm pivots on a bearing and opens the valve.*

place /pleɪs/ *noun* **1.** a space or area ○ *Greenwich is a place on the 0° meridian.* **2.** a position ○ *decimal place* **3.** □ **in place of** instead of □ **to take place** to happen ○ *The explosion took place just before the aircraft landed.* ■ *verb* to put ○ *Place the chart on the seat next to you.* ○ *Rotate the grid to place the wind direction under true.*

plain /pleɪn/ *adjective* without pattern or marking or writing □ **a plain sheet of paper** a sheet of paper with nothing on it

plan /plæn/ *noun* **1.** a drawing or diagram of a place viewed from above ○ *The horizontal situation indicator presents a selectable dynamic colour display of flight progress and plan view orientation.* **2.** a scheme or programme worked out in advance of putting something into operation ■ *verb* to organise a scheme or programme ○ *Jeppesen charts are used to plan and fly a safe route to a destination.*

plane /pleɪn/ *noun* **1.** an imaginary surface containing all the straight lines that connect any two points on it ○ *The planes of parallels of latitude are parallel to the plane of the equator.* ○ *The pitch angle is the angle between the blade element chord line and the plane of rotation of the propeller.* **2.** an aeroplane (NOTE: Because of possible confusion with meaning 1, **plane** as in

meaning 2 is considered bad usage by some. The word **aircraft** is preferred in that case.)

planning /'plænɪŋ/ *noun* making plans ○ *The instructor gave a talk on flight planning.*

plan position indicator /,plæn pə'zɪʃ(ə)n ,ɪndɪkeɪtə/ *noun* the normal type of display for a radar signal, which resembles a map with the radar site at the centre

plant /plɑːnt/ *noun* large and usually heavy equipment or tools used for doing something

plate /pleɪt/ *noun* a smooth, flat rigid object with the same thickness all over ○ *The basic construction of a lead-acid cell consists of a positive electrode and negative electrode, each of which is made up of lead-antimony alloy grid plates.*

play /pleɪ/ *noun* a slightly loose fitting of engineering parts which allows them to move freely ○ *Some play should be felt in the aileron actuator rod linkage.* ■ *verb* □ **to play a part** to be part of a whole which has an effect on something ○ *Contrast and colour play a part in identifying coastlines.*

plot /plɒt/ *noun* a graph or diagram that shows a relationship between two sets of numbers as a series of points joined by a line ○ *a plot of applied stress and resulting strain* ■ *verb* to calculate and mark a line on a graph or chart, etc. □ **to plot a course** to calculate and draw the desired route of an aircraft on a chart

plug /plʌg/ *noun* **1.** a device for making an electrical connection ○ *Alternating current ground power can be fitted to an aircraft via a six-pin ground power plug.* □ **a 3-pin plug** an electrical supply plug with three electrodes: live, neutral and earth **2.** a device for igniting fuel in an engine ○ *An electric spark from an igniter plug starts combustion.* ○ *The fuel/air mixture is ignited by a spark plug.* **3.** a device to prevent liquid flowing out of a container ○ *oil drain plug* ◊ **spark plug** ■ *verb* **1.** □ **to plug a hole** to fill a hole so that fluid cannot escape **2.** □ **to plug something in** to make an electrical connection, often by inserting the plug on an electrical device such as a computer into an electrical supply socket

plunger /'plʌndʒə/ *noun* a machine part that operates with a thrusting or plunging movement, e.g. a piston ○ *A flow indicator valve comprises a body, a spring-loaded plunger connected to an actuator arm, and a micro-switch.*

plus /plʌs/ *preposition* increased, added to ○ *At the selected decision height plus 50 feet, an aural alert chime sounds.* ○ *Four plus four equals eight (4 + 4 = 8).*

PMS /ˌpiː em 'es/ *abbreviation* performance management system

pneumatic /njuː'mætɪk/ *adjective* operating by means of air under pressure or compressed air ○ *High-pressure pneumatic systems are generally fitted on the older types of piston-engine aircraft to operate the landing gear, wing flaps, wheel brakes.*

pneumatically /njuː'mætɪkli/ *adverb* by using air under pressure or compressed air ○ *Clamshell doors are hydraulically or pneumatically opened.*

PNR *abbreviation* point of no return

POB *abbreviation* persons on board

pocket /'pɒkɪt/ *noun* same as **air pocket**

pod /pɒd/ *noun* a streamlined casing or housing ○ *The engine bay or pod is usually cooled by atmospheric air.*

POH *abbreviation* Pilot's Operating Handbook

point /pɔɪnt/ *noun* **1.** a particular figure on a scale ○ *The melting point of ice is 0°C (Celsius).* **2.** a particular place □ **a point on a map** a particular place on a map **3.** the sharp end of something ○ *a pencil point* ■ *verb* **1.** to direct towards ○ *Point the aircraft towards the airfield.* **2.** to indicate direction, often with a finger ○ *point to the east* **3.** □ **to point out** to draw attention to ○ *The instructor pointed out the dangers of not keeping a good lookout.*

pointer /'pɔɪntə/ *noun* an indicating device on an instrument, e.g. a needle ○ *The pointer centralises to indicate that the aircraft is aligned with the runway centre line.*

point of no return /ˌpɔɪnt əv nəʊ rɪ'tɜːn/ *noun* a place on the route where the aircraft does not have enough fuel to return to the starting place ○ *The point of no return is calculated before departure to cover the chance that both the terminal airfield and its alternate become unavailable during flight.* Abbreviation **PNR**

polar /'pəʊlə/ *adjective* **1.** located in or coming from the region around the north or south pole ○ *polar air* ○ *a polar region* ○ *The greatest horizontal gradients of mean temperatures of a layer are found at the boundaries between cold polar and warm tropical air masses.* **2.** referring to the pole or poles of an electrical device or of a magnet ○ *Bar magnets attract each other because of polar differences.*

polar diameter /ˌpəʊlə daɪ'æmɪtə/ *noun* the distance from one pole, passing through the centre of the Earth, to the other pole ○ *The Earth's polar diameter is shorter than its average equatorial diameter.*

polar ice cap /ˌpəʊlə 'aɪs ˌkæp/ *noun* the permanent area of ice at north or south pole

polarisation /ˌpəʊləraɪ'zeɪʃ(ə)n/, **polarization** *noun* **1.** a characteristic of light or radio or other electromagnetic waves in which the waves are aligned in one direction and show different properties in different directions ○ *The antenna must have the same effective length and the same polarisation as the transmitter.* **2.** partial or complete polar separation of positive and negative electric charge

polarise /'pəʊləraɪz/, **polarize** *verb* **1.** to align in one plane ○ *The frequency allocation for VOR (very high frequency omni-directional radio range) is 108–117.975 MHz (megahertz) and transmissions are horizontally polarised.* **2.** to separate positive and negative electric charges

polarity /pəʊ'lærɪti/ *noun* the direction of flow of flux or current in an object ○ *During discharge, when the* *polarity of the supply changes, the stored energy is returned to the supply.* □ **polarity test** a test to see which terminal is positive and which is negative

pole /pəʊl/ *noun* **1.** the north or south point of the Earth's axis ○ *A meridian is a line joining pole to pole.* **2.** a terminal, e.g. of a battery ○ *negative pole* ○ *positive pole* **3.** a long, rounded piece of wood or metal ○ *a flag pole*

pollution /pə'luːʃ(ə)n/ *noun* the presence of unusually high concentrations of harmful substances in the environment

pontoon /pɒn'tuːn/ *noun* same as **float**

poor /pɔː/ *adjective* bad ○ *poor weather conditions* ○ *poor visibility* ○ *Air is a poor conductor.*

poppet valve /'pɒpɪt vælv/ *noun* an intake or exhaust valve of a piston engine, operated by springs and cams

porous /'pɔːrəs/ *adjective* referring to substances which allow fluid to pass through them ○ *The de-icing fluid passes through a porous plastic sheet.*

port /pɔːt/ *noun* **1.** an entrance which is opened periodically ○ *inlet port* ○ *As a piston in the pump moves outwards into its cylinder, it covers the inlet port and forces fluid out of the top of the cylinder.* **2.** the left-hand side of an aircraft when facing forwards when inside the aircraft ○ *Unless an aircraft is flying in the same or exactly opposite direction to the wind, it will experience either port or starboard drift.* Opposite **starboard**

portable /'pɔːtəb(ə)l/ *adjective* capable of being carried in the hands ○ *a portable fire extinguisher* ○ *The aneroid barometer is a more portable device than a mercury barometer.*

portable electronic device /ˌpɔːtəb(ə)l ˌɪlektrɒnɪk dɪ'vaɪs/ *noun* a piece of electronic equipment such as a mobile phone or laptop which is small enough to be carried onboard an aircraft, and which may cause problems with the aircraft's systems during flight. Abbreviation **PED**

portion /'pɔːʃ(ə)n/ *noun* a part or section ○ *A hailstone starts as a small ice*

particle in the upper portion of a cumulus cloud.

position /pə'zɪʃ(ə)n/ *noun* **1.** a place or location where something is ○ *The Greenwich or prime meridian and the equator are the axes of the system called latitude and longitude which is used for expressing position on the Earth.* **2.** the setting of a control, etc. ○ *the neutral position* **3.** □ **in a sitting position** seated ■ *verb* to place something in a special location ○ *The magnetic compass is positioned away from magnetic sources.*

position line /pə'zɪʃ(ə)n laɪn/ *noun* a line along which an aircraft is known to be at a particular time, usually by taking a VOR bearing. Also called **line of position, navigational line**

position report /pə'zɪʃ(ə)n rɪˌpɔːt/ *noun* a report over a known location as transmitted by an aircraft to an air traffic control station

positive /'pɒzɪtɪv/ *adjective* **1.** definite, without doubt ○ *The pinpoint is a very positive means of establishing aircraft position.* **2.** referring to a number greater than zero ○ *Oil is ducted to the front of the pitch change piston and the blades move to a positive angle.* **3.** referring to the + symbol □ **positive terminal** the terminal of a battery marked +

positive idling speed /ˌpɒzɪtɪv 'aɪd(ə)lɪŋ ˌspiːd/ *noun* idling speed selected with the throttle to ensure that the engine runs correctly without spark plug fouling ○ *An adjustable stop on the throttle control ensures a positive idling speed.*

possibility /ˌpɒsɪ'bɪlɪti/ *noun* a chance occurrence ○ *Anti-braking systems are designed to prevent the wheels from locking during landing thus reducing the possibility of wheel skid.*

possible /'pɒsɪb(ə)l/ *adjective* capable of happening ○ *If possible, control surfaces should be moved by hand.* ○ *There will be a possible delay.* ○ *Fire in a toilet could present difficulties due to the confined space and possible smoke accumulation.*

potential /pə'tenʃəl/ *adjective* capable of being, but not yet in existence ○ *A designated fire zone is a region where a potential fire risk may exist.* □ **potential danger** possible future danger ■ *noun* voltage ○ *Precipitation static develops due to friction between the aircraft surface and precipitation causing the aircraft to become charged to a high potential.*

pound /paʊnd/ *noun* a unit of weight equal to 16 ounces or 453.592 grams. Abbreviation **lb**

powder /'paʊdə/ *noun* a substance made of ground or otherwise finely dispersed solid particles ○ *Dry chemical fire-extinguishers contain a non-toxic powder.*

power /'paʊə/ *noun* energy or force

power-assisted /ˌpaʊə ə'sɪstɪd/ *adjective* □ **power-assisted controls** controls which require less human effort to move

power dive /'paʊə daɪv/ *noun* a steep dive made by an aircraft with its engines at high power to increase the speed

powered /'paʊəd/ *adjective* driven by something such as a type of energy or motor ○ *system powered by electricity*

power line /'paʊə laɪn/ *noun* a thick cable, supported by pylons, which carries electricity for long distances

powerplant /'paʊəplɑːnt/ *noun* an engine used to move a vehicle or aircraft ○ *Additional strength is required for the powerplant attachment point.* (NOTE: The word also written **power plant**.)

'...by replacing the Rotax engine with a four-stroke Jabiru powerplant, the aircraft designers claim the aircraft will be provided with more power and increased all-round performance' [*Flight International 16–22 July 1997*]

power supply /ˌpaʊə sə'plaɪ/ *noun* an electrical circuit that provides particular direct current voltage and current levels from an alternating current source for use in other electrical circuits ○ *If the power supply from the amplifier to the gauge fails, the needle slowly falls to zero.*

PPI *abbreviation* plan position indicator

PPL *abbreviation* Private Pilot's Licence

PPR *abbreviation* prior permission required

PR *abbreviation* public relations

practicable /'præktɪkəb(ə)l/ *adjective* capable of being put into practice or effect ○ *Some military aircraft use braking parachutes but this is not practicable on civil aircraft.*

practical /'præktɪk(ə)l/ *adjective* referring to practice or action rather than theory ○ *For practical purposes, any straight line drawn on a Lambert's conformal projection represents a great circle.*

practice /'præktɪs/ *noun* **1.** habitual or customary behaviour ○ *It is common practice for pilots to take turns to sleep on long-haul flights.* **2.** a performance or operation □ **in practice** when actually done, in reality ○ *Frequency modulation (FM) in theory has a limitless number of sidebands, but in practice only the first eight pairs are significant.* ■ *verb US* same as **practise**

'...if the aircraft has been standing overnight or longer, check the drains for water. This should, of course, be normal practice' [*Civil Aviation Authority, General Aviation Safety Sense Leaflet*]

practise /'præktɪs/ *verb* to do something repeatedly in order to improve ○ *In order to improve flying skills, a trainee pilot must practise regularly.* (NOTE: This word is also written **practice** in US English.)

pre- /priː/ *prefix* before

pre-arrange /ˌpriː ə'reɪnʒ/ *verb* to decide or to plan in advance, to predetermine ○ *Selective calling uses the four-letter code pre-arranged with the controlling authorities.*

precaution /prɪ'kɔːʃ(ə)n/ *noun* an action taken to prevent or avoid a dangerous situation or failure ○ *Personnel concerned with fuelling should take every precaution to prevent outbreaks of fire.*

precede /prɪ'siːd/ *verb* to take place or to come before something else ○ *A period of calm often precedes a storm.* ○ *When the RVR (runway visual range) is greater than the maximum value which can be assessed, the group will be preceded by the letter indicator P followed by the highest value which can be assessed.*

precedence /'presɪd(ə)ns/ *noun* the quality of being more important or urgent than something else □ **to take precedence over** to have priority over, to be more important than ○ *Emergency landings take precedence over all others.*

preceding /prɪ'siːdɪŋ/ *adjective* taking place or coming before something else □ **as mentioned in the preceding paragraph** as written in the paragraph before the one being read

precipitation /prɪ,sɪpɪ'teɪʃ(ə)n/ *noun* water falling as rain, drizzle, hail, sleet and snow from the atmosphere onto the surface of the Earth ○ *Cloud droplets are small and light at first, but when the droplets grow and become heavier, they fall as precipitation.* ○ *Precipitation is classified as light, moderate or heavy according to its rate of fall.*

precise /prɪ'saɪs/ *adjective* exact or accurate ○ *A pinpoint is an indication of the precise position of the aircraft.* ○ *A precise interval is essential to obtain correct ignition timing on all cylinders during engine running.*

precision /prɪ'sɪʒ(ə)n/ *noun* exactness or accuracy ○ *Precision flying is only achieved by constant practice.* □ **with precision** with exactness

precision approach path indicator /prɪ,sɪʒ(ə)n ə'prəʊtʃ pɑːθ ,ɪndɪkeɪtə/ *noun* a set of lights that enables pilots to judge whether their glide slope is correct on the final approach to landing

precision approach radar /prɪ ,sɪʒ(ə)n ə,prəʊtʃ 'reɪdɑː/ *noun* a ground-based primary radar system to give vertical and lateral information about an aircraft's final approach path. Abbreviation **PAR**

precision area navigation /prɪ ,sɪʒ(ə)n ,eəriə ,nævɪ'geɪʃ(ə)n/ *noun* a standard of performance for navigation that requires an aircraft to remain within 1 nautical mile of the centreline of its course for 95% of the time. Abbreviation **PRNAV**

pre-departure /,priː dɪ'pɑːtʃə/ *adjective* taking place before a departure ○ *Only a few passengers absorb the pre-departure safety information.*

pre-departure clearance /,priː dɪ ,pɑːtʃə 'klɪərəns/ *noun* a message that the pilot must receive from air traffic control before the plane is allowed to take off

predetermine /,priːdɪ'tɜːmɪn/ *verb* to decide and set or fix beforehand

predetermined /,priːdɪ'tɜːmɪnd/ *adjective* decided and set beforehand ○ *When the roll control knob is returned to the central position, the aircraft rolls out on to a predetermined heading.*

predict /prɪ'dɪkt/ *verb* to foretell or to say beforehand ○ *Rain is predicted within the next hour.* ○ *Dead reckoning position is the position of the aircraft as predicted by calculation.*

predictable /prɪ'dɪktəb(ə)l/ *adjective* **1.** reliably regular and therefore foreseeable ○ *Only the high frequency band has predictable, reliable sky wave propagation by day and by night.* **2.** capable of being foreseen, expected or anticipated □ **the accident was predictable** it was possible to know that the accident would happen before it happened

prediction /prɪ'dɪkʃən/ *noun* the act of saying what will happen in the future ○ *The map display combines current ground speed and lateral acceleration into a prediction of the path over the ground to be followed over the next 30, 60 and 90 seconds.*

predominance /prɪ'dɒmɪnəns/ *noun* greatest importance or influence ○ *The predominance of a cold northerly airstream during the winter months.*

predominant /prɪ'dɒmɪnənt/ *adjective* most important or influential, more powerful than others ○ *The ocean surface usually consists of a predominant* *swell three or four feet high and 500 to 1,000 feet between crests.*

predominate /prɪˈdɒmɪneɪt/ *verb* to have greater number or importance, or to be more powerful than others ○ *A cold northerly airstream predominates during the winter months.*

prefer /prɪˈfɜː/ *verb* to like more, to favour ○ *Of the two basic types of fuel pump, where lower pressures are required at the burners, the gear-type pump is preferred because of its lightness.* (NOTE: **preferring – preferred**)

preferable /ˈpref(ə)rəb(ə)l/ *adjective* better than, more desirable ○ *Three position lines are preferable to two.* ○ *If there is a choice between two courses of action, the safest is the most preferable.*

preference /ˈpref(ə)rəns/ *noun* □ **in preference to** by choice, rather than ○ *For some applications, e.g. landing gear and flaps, hydraulic systems are used in preference to mechanical or electrical systems.*

prefix /ˈpriːfɪks/ *noun* part of a word added at the beginning of a word to alter the meaning ○ *Pre- is a prefix meaning 'before'.* (NOTE: The plural form is **prefixes**.)

COMMENT: The prefixes for cloud types are: **alto-** medium level cloud (6,500 feet to 23,000 feet); **cirro-** high cloud (16,500 feet and above); **nimbo-** any height, but rain-bearing as for example **nimbostratus**: rain carrying, low-level cloud; **strato-** low cloud (up to 6,500 feet).

pre-flight /ˌpriː ˈflaɪt/ *adjective* taking place before a flight □ **pre-flight briefing** a short instructional talk before a flight □ **pre-flight checks** checks made on the aircraft structure and systems before taking off ○ *During pre-flight checks, control surfaces should be moved by hand to ascertain that they have full and free movement.* ■ *noun* the set of procedures and checks that pilots and ground crew must carry out before an aircraft takes off ■ *verb* to inspect an aircraft before it takes off to ensure that it is airworthy

pre-ignition /ˌpriːɪɡˈnɪʃ(ə)n/ *noun* the ignition of the fuel/air mixture in the combustion chamber, occurring before the spark ○ *Pre-ignition is often caused by a hot spot in the combustion chamber which ignites the mixture.*

preparation /ˌprepəˈreɪʃ(ə)n/ *noun* a state of readiness or act of making something ready for use beforehand ○ *Normal aircraft preparation are actions and precautions taken by the cabin crew on every flight to ready the aircraft for any abnormal or emergency situation which may occur during any phase of the flight.*

prepare /prɪˈpeə/ *verb* **1.** to make ready beforehand for a particular purpose, as for an event or occasion ○ *The instructor prepared the students for the exams.* □ **prepare for take-off** to get ready for take-off **2.** to make by putting various elements or ingredients together ○ *Regional area forecasting centres use information about upper wind speeds and temperatures to prepare specific forecasts and significant weather charts.*

prescribe /prɪˈskraɪb/ *verb* to set down as a rule or a guide □ **prescribed procedures** a set or fixed pattern of doing something ○ *A means of holding the fine pitch stop in a prescribed position is also called 'pitch lock'.*

pre-select /ˌpriːsɪˈlekt/ *verb* to select or to choose in advance

pre-selected /ˌpriːsɪˈlektɪd/ *adjective* selected or chosen in advance ○ *The CSU (constant speed unit) maintains the pre-selected propeller speed.*

presence /ˈprez(ə)ns/ *noun* existence ○ *The presence of cloud by day decreases the value of the maximum temperatures.* ○ *A fuel sample hazy or cloudy in appearance would indicate the presence of water.*

present /ˈprez(ə)nt/ *adjective* **1.** in place, existing ○ *Fuel, oxygen and heat must all be present for fire to exist.* **2.** the period in time through which we are now living, between the past and the future □ **at the present time** at this time, now □ **present day aircraft** modern aircraft □ **present weather** the weather at the moment of speaking ■ *verb* /prɪˈzent/ **1.** to create or to make ○ *A fire in a toilet could present difficul-*

ties. ○ *Learning to fly presents a challenge.* □ **to present an opportunity** to create or to give an opportunity **2.** to give a prize or award ○ *Charter passengers on Concorde were presented with a certificate as a souvenir of their flight.*

presentation /ˌprez(ə)n'teɪʃ(ə)n/ *noun* showing, a display ○ *The most widely acceptable presentation of flight fuel data is in a tabular form.*

presently /'prez(ə)ntli/ *adverb* **1.** soon ○ *I'll be there presently.* **2.** *US* now, at the present time □ **he's presently in France** at the present time, he is in France □ **a number of methods are presently in use** a number of methods are currently in use

preset /'priː'set/ *verb* to set in advance ○ *Radios allow the user to preset a number of different frequencies.* (NOTE: **presetting – preset**) ■ *adjective* set in advance

press /pres/ *verb* to push or exert pressure on ○ *press to test/talk (PTT) button* ○ *Press the button.*

pressure /'preʃə/ *noun* force applied uniformly over a surface, measured as force per unit of area □ **fuel pressure** pressure exerted by fuel as it is pumped from the tanks to the engine □ **pressure switch** a switch which is activated when a preset pressure is attained ○ *On some engines a fuel differential pressure switch fitted to the fuel filter senses the pressure difference across the filter element.* ◊ **absolute pressure**

pressure altimeter /ˌpreʃə ˌæltɪ'miːtə/ *noun* a conventional altimeter which operates using atmospheric pressure

pressure altitude /'preʃə ˌæltɪtjuːd/ *noun* the altitude indicated when the altimeter is set to 1013.2 millibars ○ *When using flight levels, the altimeter should be set to 1013.2 mb to give the pressure altitude.*

COMMENT: Pressure altitude is used in determining density altitude, true altitude and true airspeed.

pressure bulkhead /'preʃə ˌbʌlkhed/ *noun* a partition inside the aircraft which separates pressurised from non-pressurised areas

pressure gauge /'preʃə geɪdʒ/ *noun* an instrument for measuring pressure

pressure relay /'preʃə ˌriːleɪ/ *noun* a component which transmits fluid pressure to a direct reading pressure gauge, or to a pressure transmitter which electrically indicates pressure on an instrument on the hydraulic panel

pressurisation /ˌpreʃərai'zeɪʃ(ə)n/, **pressurization** *noun* the act of increasing the air pressure inside a space, e.g. an aircraft cabin, so that it feels normal for the occupants when the outside air pressure decreases

pressurise /'preʃəraɪz/, **pressurize** *verb* to increase the pressure of ○ *When air pressure is used to transfer fuel, it will be necessary to pressurise the fuel tanks.*

prevail /prɪ'veɪl/ *verb* to be most common or frequent ○ *Hot dry conditions prevail in the Middle East in summertime.* □ **the prevailing wind is from the south-west** the wind blows from the south west more often than from any other direction

prevent /prɪ'vent/ *verb* to stop from happening ○ *Heated air provides sufficient heat in the outer skin to melt ice already formed and prevent any further ice formation.*

previous /'priːviəs/ *adjective* coming before, earlier □ **the previous chapter** the chapter before the one being read or referred to □ **previous reports** earlier reports

primarily /praɪ'mer(ə)li/ *adverb* most often, mainly ○ *Dry chemical fire extinguishers are primarily used for electrical fires.*

primary /'praɪməri/ *adjective* first or most important □ **of primary importance** of greatest importance □ **primary coil** an induction coil

primary flight display *noun* same as **primary flight instruments**

primary flight instruments /ˌpraɪməri 'flaɪt ˌɪnstrʊmənts/ *plural noun* the six instruments displayed on the instrument panel immediately in front of the pilot: airspeed indicator, attitude indicator, altimeter, turn coordinator, heading indicator, and vertical speed indicator ○ *When practising instrument flying, the attitude indicator is the most important of the primary flight instruments.*

primary radar /ˌpraɪməri 'reɪdɑː/ *noun* a radar system which uses reflected radio signals

prime /praɪm/ *adjective* first □ **prime importance** greatest importance ■ *verb* to pump fuel spray into the piston engine inlet manifold to make starting from cold easier ○ *During the summer, after the first flight of the day, it is not normally necessary to prime the engine.*

prime number /ˌpraɪm 'nʌmbə/ *noun* a number, which, if there is to be no remainder, is only divisible by itself and 1, e.g. 13, 17, 19, 23, 29

primer /'praɪmə/ *noun* **1.** a protective substance which is applied to a metal or wood surface before painting ○ *Interior metal finishing is done with dust shedding gloss-paint over a primer.* **2.** a small hand-operated pump, operated from the cockpit, to spray fuel into the piston engine inlet manifold to make starting from cold easier

principal /'prɪnsɪp(ə)l/ *adjective* main ○ *Four principal control modes can be selected on the EFIS (electronic flight instrument system) control panel.*

principle /'prɪnsɪp(ə)l/ *noun* a basic truth or law ○ *Fire extinguishing is based on the principle of removing one of the three components necessary for fire to exist – fuel, oxygen and heat.* (NOTE: Do not confuse with **principal**.)

prior /'praɪə/ *adjective* earlier, previous ○ *prior approval* ○ *prior permission* □ **prior to** before ○ *prior to our departure* □ **prior to take-off** before take-off

'…the pilot remembered hearing the stall warning immediately prior to impact' [*Pilot*]

priority /praɪ'ɒrɪti/ *noun* the order of importance or urgency □ **high priority** important or urgent in the circumstances □ **low priority** not important or urgent in the circumstances

Private Pilot's Licence /ˌpraɪvət 'paɪləts ˌlaɪs(ə)ns/ *noun* the basic licence for flying light aircraft. Abbreviation **PPL**

PRNAV *abbreviation* precision area navigation

probability /ˌprɒbə'bɪlɪti/ *noun* likelihood, the chance of occurrence ○ *The probability of aquaplaning increases as the depth of tyre tread decreases.*

probable /'prɒbəb(ə)l/ *adjective* likely, most possible ○ *Pilot error was the probable cause of the accident.*

probe /prəʊb/ *noun* a metal sensing device ○ *Ice is allowed to accumulate on a probe which projects into the airstream.*

procedural /prə'siːdʒərəl/ *adjective* referring to procedure

procedural approach /prə 'siːdʒərəl əˌprəʊtʃ/ *noun* a specific approach made often after procedure turns as part of timed, accurately flown flight pattern to prepare for a landing at a particular aerodrome ○ *It is important that the integrity of an aid used to conduct procedural approaches is high.*

procedure /prə'siːdʒə/ *noun* **1.** a series of actions taken to achieve something ○ *an emergency procedure* **2.** the process by which aircraft are brought into position for an instrument approach and landing

procedure turn /prə'siːdʒə tɜːn/ *noun* a turn made at 3° per second to align the aircraft with the runway

process /'prəʊses/ *noun* a series of actions or changes which achieve a particular result ○ *adiabatic process* ○ *combustion process* ○ *cooling process*

produce /prə'djuːs/ *verb* **1.** to create ○ *Low altostratus clouds often produce rain.* **2.** to make or to manufacture ○ *Most light aircraft are produced in the United States.* **3.** to show ○ *The pilot must produce her licence to the authorities within two weeks.*

product /'prɒdʌkt/ *noun* **1.** something created or made by human or natural methods ○ *Carbon monoxide is a product of the combustion process.* **2.** a number obtained by multiplying two other numbers together ○ *The amount of power produced in a purely resistive* *circuit is a product of voltage and current (P = VI watts).*

production /prə'dʌkʃən/ *noun* **1.** creation ○ *The movement of air over the aerofoil is necessary for the production of lift.* **2.** the process of manufacturing something ○ *Production of aircraft in the factory came to a stop in 1974.* **3.** the act of showing ○ *An authorised person may require the production of a certificate of airworthiness.*

profile /'prəʊfaɪl/ *noun* **1.** an outline or shape of something, seen from a side view ○ *The de-icing panels are formed to the profiles of the wing and tail unit leading edges into which they are fitted.* **2.** a short description ○ *The handbook gives a short profile of the different aircraft types.*

prognostic /prɒg'nɒstɪk/ *adjective* referring to foretelling or foreseeing events such as the weather

prognostic chart /prɒg͵nɒstɪk 'tʃɑːt/ *noun* a chart which predicts the weather for a given area ○ *Prognostic or forecast charts are prepared, by the central meteorological office of each region, normally for periods up to 24 hours ahead.* Also called **forecast chart**

programme /'prəʊdʒekt/ *noun* the schedule of events to take place or procedures to be followed ○ *Every part of the aircraft must be designed to carry the load imposed on it and in order to determine such loads a programme of stress analysis is always carried out.* (NOTE: The word is also written **program** in US English.)

progress /'prəʊgres/ *noun* movement towards an end or aim ○ *the progress of an aircraft in flight* □ **in progress** taking place □ **embarkation is in progress** passengers are boarding the aircraft

progression /prəʊ'greʃ(ə)n/ *noun* a continuous series or sequence ○ *The instruments are checked in logical progression from left to right.*

progressive /prə'gresɪv/ *adjective* gradual, in stages ○ *Throttle movements should be kept to a minimum and be smooth and progressive.*

prohibit /prəʊ'hɪbɪt/ *verb* to disallow or forbid ○ *Smoking is prohibited in toilets.*

project *noun* /'prɒdʒekt/ a large-scale plan or scheme ○ *a project to modernise the airport* ■ *verb* /prə'dʒekt/ **1.** to protrude or jut out ○ *Ice is allowed to accumulate on a probe which projects into the airstream.* **2.** to produce an image on a screen with a film or slide projector ○ *The instructor projected a diagram of the fuel system onto the screen.*

projection /prə'dʒekʃən/ *noun* the production of an image on a surface

prolong /prə'lɒŋ/ *verb* to increase the duration or time, often unnecessarily ○ *to prolong the life of an engine* ○ *Prolonged idling at low rpm (revolutions per minute) could cause spark plug fouling.*

promulgate /'prɒmədʒeɪt/ *verb* to make known through official means ○ *The range promulgated for NDBs (non-directional radio beacons) in the United Kingdom is based on a daytime protection ratio between wanted and unwanted signals.*

prone /prəʊn/ *noun* □ **prone to** likely to do something, or more than usually affected by something ○ *Wing leading edges and engine intakes and propellers are prone to icing.*

pronounced /prə'naʊnst/ *adjective* noticeable or marked ○ *Turbulence caused by convection is more pronounced over paved surfaces than over forest or grassy terrain.*

propagation /͵prɒpə'geɪʃ(ə)n/ *noun* transmission ○ *The speed of propagation of radio waves is slower over land than sea.*

propel /prə'pel/ *verb* to cause to move ○ *Fronts are propelled by the wind behind them.*

propeller /prə'pelə/ *noun* a rotating shaft with blades which, together with the engine, moves an aircraft through the air

propeller blade /prə'pelə bleɪd/ *noun* one of the elements of a propeller which generate lift when the unit is turning

propeller pitch /prə'pelə pɪtʃ/ *noun* the distance a propeller would advance in one rotation if there was no slip

propeller tip /prə'pelə tɪp/ *noun* the part of the blade of a propeller furthest from the central hub

propelling nozzle /prə,pelɪŋ 'nɒz(ə)l/ *noun* the extreme rear part of the jet engine where the jet exhaust enters the atmosphere

properly /'prɒpəli/ *adverb* correctly ○ *When the chart is properly orientated, it is easier to compare distance between landmarks.* ○ *The pinpoint is a very positive means of establishing position, as long as the feature is properly identified.*

property /'prɒpəti/ *noun* **1.** a characteristic or quality ○ *Mass is a basic property of matter.* ○ *One of the properties of mercury is that it is liquid at room temperature.* **2.** the things that somebody owns, possessions □ **personal property** things belonging to a particular person

propjet /'prɒpdʒet/ *noun* same as **turboprop**

proportion /prə'pɔːʃ(ə)n/ *noun* **1.** part of the whole compared with another part ○ *Only a small proportion of passengers absorb the pre-departure safety information.* **2.** □ **in proportion to** directly related to ○ *The force required to move the control column is in proportion to the force being exerted by the control surface.*

proportional /prə'pɔːʃ(ə)n(ə)l/ *adjective* **1.** comparable **2.** related □ **(directly) proportional** directly related ○ *The wind blows along contours with low values on the left, and the speed is directly proportional to the contour gradient.* □ **inversely proportional** so that as one thing increases and another decreases by the same amount ○ *Temperature is inversely proportional to altitude.* ○ *The magnitude of the pressure gradient force is inversely proportional to the distance apart from the isobars.*

propulsion /prə'pʌlʃən/ *noun* an act or instance of pushing or driving forwards (NOTE: The verb is **to propel**.)

propulsive /prə'pʌlsɪv/ *adjective* pushing or driving ○ *The propeller is a means of converting engine power into a propulsive force called thrust.* (NOTE: The verb is **to propel**.)

propulsive power /prə,pʌlsɪv 'paʊə/ *noun* the power needed to produce thrust

protect /prə'tekt/ *verb* to keep from harm, injury or damage ○ *Gloves are worn to protect the hands in the event of a fire.*

protection /prə'tekʃən/ *noun* the act of keeping something from harm, injury or damage □ **fire protection** action or measures taken to prevent fire

protective /prə'tektɪv/ *adjective* referring to something which keeps something else from harm, injury or damage ○ *Busbars are insulated from the main structure and are normally provided with some form of protective covering.*

protrude /prə'truːd/ *verb* to extend above a surface ○ *Prominent mountains frequently protrude above low-lying cloud and mist.*

protrusion /prə'truːʒ(ə)n/ *noun* something which protrudes or extends above a surface ○ *When it has been necessary to physically remove a layer of snow, all protrusions and vents should be examined for signs of damage.*

prove /pruːv/ *verb* **1.** to show that something is true ○ *The pilot proved that she was not at fault.* **2.** to be found to be, to be discovered to be (NOTE: **proving – proved – has proved** or **has proven**) □ **to prove useful** to be discovered as useful by experience □ **dry chemical extinguishers are used primarily for electrical fires and have also proved effective on liquid fires** it was discovered that, although these extinguishers were designed for electrical fires, they were good at putting out liquid fires such as petrol fires

provide /prə'vaɪd/ *verb* to supply or to give ○ *Radio altimeters provide a continuous indication of height above the surface immediately below the aircraft up to a maximum of 5,000 feet.* ○ *Flight crews are frequently provided*

with a full meteorological briefing. ○
*Each tank is provided with a shut off
valve.* ○ *When aquaplaning, a tyre is not
capable of providing directional control
or effective braking.* □ **provided that** on
condition that, if ○ *The flight will take
off on schedule provided that the
weather improves.*

provision /prə'vɪʒ(ə)n/ *noun* **1.** providing something, or what is provided ○
*The provision of fresh air is important
for passengers' comfort.* ○ *Catering
companies are responsible for the provision of food.* ○ *There is a generator for
the provision of emergency power.* ○
*The oil tank has provision for filling and
draining.* **2.** a legal statement which
provides for something such as particular circumstances

proximity /prɒk'sɪmɪti/ *noun* near-
ness in space or time ○ *The two aircraft
were in close proximity.*

psychological   **stress**
/ˌsaɪkəlɒdʒɪk(ə)l 'stres/ *noun* a mentally or emotionally upsetting condition
which affects one's health

PTT *abbreviation* press to test/talk

public /'pʌblɪk/ *noun* people in general ■ *adjective* referring to the people
in general

public address system /ˌpʌblɪk ə
'dres ˌsɪstəm/ *noun* a microphone,
amplifier and loudspeaker set up to
allow one person to be heard by a group
of people ○ *The captain made a public
address (PA) system announcement
asking passengers to remain seated.*
Abbreviation **PA system**

publication /ˌpʌblɪ'keɪʃ(ə)n/ *noun*
1. the act of making something public,
publishing ○ *the publication of the latest figures* **2.** a book, magazine, chart,
etc., which has been published ○ *The
book is a Civil Aviation Authority publication.*

public relations /ˌpʌblɪk rɪ
'leɪʃ(ə)nz/ *noun* the task of maintaining
good relations with the public. Public
relations may also involve putting
across a point of view or publicising a
product. ○ *The arrangements for the
VIPs are being handled by the public
relations department.* Abbreviation **PR**

publish /'pʌblɪʃ/ *verb* to prepare and
issue a book, magazine, chart, etc., and
sell or distribute it to the public ○ *All
known air navigation obstructions in
the UK are published in the Air Pilot.*

pull out /ˌpʊl 'aʊt/ *verb* to stop a dive
in an aircraft and return to level flight

pullout /'pʊlaʊt/ *noun* a manoeuvre
in which an aircraft changes from a dive
to level flight

pulse /pʌls/ *noun* a single vibration of
electric current

pulse   modulation   /'pʌls
ˌmɒdjuleɪʃ(ə)n/ *noun* the use of a
series of short pulses, which are modified by an input signal, to carry information

pump /pʌmp/ *noun* a device with
rotary or reciprocating action which is
used to move fluids along pipes or for
compressing fluids ■ *verb* to move or
compress a fluid by means of a pump ○
*Fuel is pumped from the tanks to the
carburettor.*

COMMENT: Most modern aircraft are
fitted with hydraulic pumps driven from
the engine. Other types of pumps may
be found, but these are usually used to
power emergency systems. Pumps
can be driven directly from the engine
gearbox, by an electric motor, or by air.

pure /pjʊə/ *adjective* not mixed with
something else ○ *Inner tubes for tyres
are made of pure rubber.* ○ *Magnesium
does not possess sufficient strength in
its pure state for structural uses.* □ **pure
aluminium** aluminium which has not
been combined with any other metal to
create an aluminium alloy

purple airway /ˌpɜːp(ə)l 'eəweɪ/
noun an area of temporarily controlled
airspace, established to provide special
protection to Royal flights in fixed-
wing aircraft, in which additional rules
for air traffic apply at all times and in all
weathers

purpose /'pɜːpəs/ *noun* **1.** function ○
*The purpose of the engine is to convert
heat energy to mechanical energy.* **2.** a
use ○ *For practical purposes, any
straight line drawn on a Lambert's
chart represents a great circle.* □ **gen-**

eral purpose for all-round or general use

push-back /'pʊʃ bæk/ *noun* the process of pushing a plane out from its parked position using a special vehicle

pushrod /'pʊʃrɒd/ *noun* a steel or aluminium rod which moves the rocker arm ○ *The camshaft operates the pushrod.* (NOTE: The **pushrod** is part of the valve mechanism.)

pylon /'paɪlən/ *noun* **1.** a structure on the wing of an aircraft to support an engine (NOTE: Most modern jet passenger transport aircraft have pylon-mounted engines.) **2.** a tall metal structure built to support electricity or telephone cables ○ *Electricity pylons are difficult to see from the air so pilots of light aircraft should be particularly careful to note their positions.*

pyrotechnic /ˌpaɪrə'teknɪk/ *adjective* of or relating to fireworks □ **pyrotechnic lights** lights created by rockets or flares

Q

Q-code /'kju: kəʊd/ *noun* an international telegraph code which is now used in RTF operations

QDM *noun* in the Q-code system, the magnetic bearing to a direction-finding station

QFE *noun* in the Q-code system, the atmospheric pressure at aerodrome level

QFI *abbreviation* qualified flying instructor

QNE *noun* in the Q-code system, the altimeter setting for flight level reading, 1013.25 mb

QNH *noun* in the Q-code system, the atmospheric pressure at mean sea level

QNH datum /ˌkju: en 'eɪtʃ ˌdeɪtəm/ *noun* the barometric level from which altitude is measured

QTE *noun* in the Q-code system, the true bearing from a direction-finding station

quadrant /'kwɒdrənt/ *noun* **1.** a device shaped like a quarter of a circle □ **gated quadrant** a quadrant with a device preventing a lever from being moved to an incorrect setting ○ *The throttles, usually known as power levers, operate in a gated quadrant.* **2.** □ **compass quadrant** the quarter part of a circle centred on a navigational aid

COMMENT: **NE** quadrant = 000° – 089°; **SE** quadrant = 090° – 179°; **SW** quadrant = 180° – 269°; **NW** quadrant = 270° – 359°.

quadrantal /kwɒ'drænt(ə)l/ *adjective* referring to a quadrant or to a quarter of a circle □ **quadrantal error** a radio signal error caused by the metal structure of the receiving aircraft □ **quadrantal height** flight levels in each of the compass quadrants designed to provide safe separation for aircraft heading towards each other

qualified /'kwɒlɪfaɪd/ *adjective* having gained a certificate after having completed a specialised course of study

qualified flying instructor /ˌkwɒlɪfaɪd 'flaɪɪŋ ɪnˌstrʌktə/ *noun* a pilot with an instructor's rating. Abbreviation **QFI**

qualify /'kwɒlɪfaɪ/ *verb* **1.** to add reservations or modify an earlier statement to make it less absolute ○ *Fire in the wing may cause the captain to qualify the evacuation command, informing cabin crew of these conditions and allowing them to adjust the evacuation plan accordingly.* **2.** to study for and obtain a diploma which allows to do a particular type of work ○ *He qualified as an engineer in 1996.*

quality /'kwɒlɪti/ *noun* the amount of excellence of something ○ *Satisfactory ignition depends on the quality of the fuel.*

quantity /'kwɒntɪti/ *noun* the size, extent, weight, amount or number of something ○ *A small quantity of illegal drug was found in the passenger's bag.*

quarter /'kwɔːtə/ *noun* one fourth of something ○ *The fuel tank is only a quarter full.*

QUJ *noun* in the Q-code system, the true track to reach a destination

R

radar /'reɪdɑ:/ *noun* a method of detecting distant objects and establishing their position, velocity, or other characteristics by analysis of very high frequency radio waves reflected from their surfaces

radar advisory service /ˌreɪdɑ: əd 'vaɪz(ə)ri ˌsɜːvɪs/ *noun* an air traffic radar service which gives pilots advice on actions necessary to ensure that they remain at a standard distance from other aircraft that are also receiving the service. Abbreviation **RAS**

radar beam /'reɪdɑ: biːm/ *noun* a shaft of radar waves directed towards a distant point

radar information service /ˌreɪdɑ: ˌɪnfə'meɪʃ(ə)n ˌsɜːvɪs/ an air traffic radar service which gives pilots details of the positions, distances and levels of other aircraft to enable them to decide on any avoiding action which may be appropriate. Abbreviation **RIS** (NOTE: An RIS is often provided when it is not possible or practical to provide an RAS.)

radar screen /'reɪdɑ: skriːn/ *noun* a cathode ray tube screen on which radar information is displayed

radar vectoring /ˌreɪdɑ: 'vektərɪŋ/ *noun* the provision of navigational guidance to aircraft in the form of specific headings, based on the use of radar

radial /'reɪdɪəl/ *adjective* referring to lines of radius having a common centre □ **radial engine** engine in which the pistons are arranged like the spokes of a wheel ■ *noun* a line of radio bearing from a VOR beacon ○ *To get to a facility*

you must track the reciprocal of the VOR radial.

radiate /'reɪdɪeɪt/ *verb* to send out rays or waves ○ *The Earth radiates low intensity infrared waves.* ○ *Short bursts of energy are radiated from an antenna.*

radiation /ˌreɪdi'eɪʃ(ə)n/ *noun* the act or process of sending out rays or waves □ **terrestrial radiation** radiation from the Earth

radiation fog /ˌreɪdi'eɪʃ(ə)n ˌfɒg/ *noun* fog caused by the cooling of the Earth to below the dew point, combined with saturation and condensation and a light mixing wind ○ *Radiation fog cannot form over the sea.*

radiator /'reɪdɪeɪtə/ *noun* a liquid-to-air heat exchanger that transfers engine heat to the outside air ○ *Anti-icing additives are used in radiator coolants.* ◊ **coolant**

radio /'reɪdɪəʊ/ *noun* wireless transmission through space of electromagnetic waves in the approximate frequency range from 10 kHz to 300,000 MHz □ **radio waves** electromagnetic radiation waves ○ *The atmosphere absorbs radio waves.*

radio aid /'reɪdɪəʊ eɪd/ *noun* a navigation aid utilising radio waves

radio altimeter /ˌreɪdɪəʊ ˌæltɪ 'miːtə/ *noun* a device for measuring the height of the aircraft above the Earth using reflected radio waves

radio horizon /'reɪdɪəʊ hə,raɪz(ə)n/ *noun* a line along which direct rays from a radio frequency transmitter become tangential to the Earth's surface

radio magnetic indicator /ˌreɪdɪəʊ mæg,netɪk 'ɪndɪkeɪtə/ *noun* a cockpit navigation instrument which combines a bearing indicator and a heading indicator and can be used with ADF or VOR. Abbreviation **RMI**

radiotelephony /ˌreɪdiəʊtəˈlefəni/ *noun* the transmission of speech by radio ○ *Correct use of R/T phraseology avoids ambiguity.* Abbreviation **R/T**

radius /ˈreɪdiəs/ *noun* □ **the radius of a circle** a line drawn from a point on the circumference of a circle to the centre point (NOTE: The plural form is **radii**. /ˈreɪdiaɪ/)

radome /ˈreɪdəʊm/ *noun* a dome that protects a radar antenna, made from materials that do not interfere with the transmission and reception of radio waves

RAF *abbreviation* Royal Air Force

raft /rɑːft/ *noun* a flat-bottomed inflatable rubber craft for floating on water

railway line /ˈreɪlweɪ laɪn/ *noun* a railway track or train track ○ *A railway line is a useful landmark.*

rain /reɪn/ *noun* precipitation or water which falls from clouds in small drops ○ *Rain is falling heavily.* ○ *Rain and weather present fewer problems for area radar compared to the other types.* ■ *verb* to fall as drops of water from clouds ○ *It is raining.* ○ *I don't think it will rain.*

rainstorm /ˈreɪnstɔːm/ *noun* heavy rain accompanied by wind ○ *In heavy rainstorm, the windscreen wipers may not be able to cope.*

raise /reɪz/ *verb* **1.** to lift □ **raise the landing gear** retract the undercarriage **2.** to increase ○ *to raise the temperature* ○ *to raise the pressure* **3.** to cause problems ○ *Fuel vaporisation can raise problems when starting the engine.* (NOTE: Do not confuse with the verb **to rise**. Grammatically, the verb **raise** takes an object whereas the verb **rise** does not: *temperature rises*; *The sun's rays raise the temperature of the surface.*)

rake /reɪk/ *noun* the angle between a wing or propeller blade of an aircraft and a perpendicular or line of symmetry

ram /ræm/ *noun* an increase in air pressure caused by the forward speed of the aircraft ○ *Due to ram effect from aircraft forward speed, extra air is taken into the engine.*

ram air /ˈræm eə/ *noun* airflow created by the movement of the aircraft which is used to cool, ventilate or drive turbines ○ *Oil cooling is often achieved by using ram air or fuel.*

ramjet /ˈræmdʒet/ *noun* a type of jet engine in which fuel is burned in a duct with air compressed by the forward motion of the aircraft

ramp /ræmp/ *noun* **1.** an inclined track for loading and unloading ○ *The height of the cabin floor to the ground on large jet transports means that injuries can occur by exiting through the doors when steps or ramps are not available.* **2.** *US* same as **apron**

range /reɪndʒ/ *noun* **1.** the amount or extent of variation ○ *range of frequencies* ○ *range of temperatures* **2.** a row or chain of mountains or hills ○ *the Rocky Mountain range* ○ *Valley winds require at least a reasonable pressure gradient, preferably along a range of hills which will produce a wind at right angles to the hills.* **3.** the maximum distance an aircraft can fly on a given amount of fuel ○ *Cruise level is selected to give the greatest fuel economy, i.e. the greatest range for least fuel.* **4.** the maximum effective distance of operation ○ *Precision approach radar (PAR) is subject to weather interference and has a limited range.* ■ *verb* □ **to range from … to …** to vary from … to … ○ *Temperatures range from 0°C (Celsius) at night to 40°C (Celsius) at midday.*

rapid /ˈræpɪd/ *adjective* fast, with great speed ○ *Hoar frost is a light crystalline deposit which can form on the aircraft as a result of rapid descent from cold altitudes into warm moist air.* □ **rapid changes** fast changes

rapidity /rəˈpɪdɪti/ *noun* great speed ○ *Spontaneous combustion occurs with such rapidity that there is an audible explosion.*

rapidly /ˈræpɪdli/ *adverb* with great speed, quickly ○ *Rime ice is formed when individual droplets of water freeze rapidly on striking the aircraft surface.*

rare /reə/ *adjective* uncommon, not often occurring ○ *Smog or smoke fog is now rare because of pollution controls.*

RAS *abbreviation* **1.** radar advisory service **2.** rectified air speed

rate /reɪt/ *noun* a quantity measured in relation to another measured quantity □ **rate of climb** speed of ascent measured in feet per minute □ **rate of descent** speed of descent measured in feet per minute □ **flow rate** the amount of movement of a fluid through a system in a given time, e.g. gallons per minute

rather /'rɑːðə/ *adverb* **1.** to some extent, somewhat □ **rather cold weather** weather which is quite cold, but not very cold **2.** □ **rather than** instead of, preferably ○ *Air tends to flow around hills rather than rise over them.*

rating /'reɪtɪŋ/ *noun* **1.** an authorisation on a licence, and forming part of the licence, giving special conditions or privileges **2.** a classification according to a scale

ratio /'reɪʃiəʊ/ *noun* a relationship between two quantities expressed as the quotient of one divided by the other ○ *The air/fuel ratio is 15:1.* ○ *Chart scale is the ratio of the chart distance to Earth distance.* (NOTE: The ratio of 7 to 4 is written 7:4 or 7/4.)

ray /reɪ/ *noun* a thin or narrow beam of light or other radiant energy ○ *cathode ray* ○ *The Earth is heated by the rays of the sun.* ◊ **X-ray**

RBI *abbreviation* relative bearing indicator

RCC *abbreviation* rescue co-ordination centre

RCL *abbreviation* runway centreline

re- /riː/ *prefix* again ○ *reassemble* ○ *rewrite* (NOTE: Not all verbs beginning with **re-** have the meaning 'again', e.g. **remember**.)

reach /riːtʃ/ *verb* **1.** to arrive at a place ○ *The aircraft reached its destination on time.* **2.** to get to a particular level ○ *Up-currents in thunderstorms can reach 3,000 feet per minute.* ○ *Temperatures can reach 49°C (Celsius) in summertime in the Gulf region.* **3.** to extend ○

The tops of thunderstorm clouds can reach through the tropopause.

react /ri'ækt/ *verb* **1.** to act in response to an action ○ *Because the rotors and stators of a compressor are of aerofoil shape, the airflow reacts in a similar way to the airflow over a wing.* **2.** to do or to say something in response to words or to an event ○ *The cabin crew reacted swiftly when the fire broke out.* **3.** □ **to react with something** to change chemical composition because of another substance ○ *The electrolyte in the cells of a lead-acid battery reacts chemically with the plates.*

reactance /ri'æktəns/ *noun* a component of impedance in an alternating current circuit ○ *Reactance is a form of resistance which varies as the frequency changes.*

reaction /ri'ækʃən/ *noun* a response to an action or stimulus ○ *For every action there is an equal and opposite reaction.* ○ *Passenger reaction may be slower than usual in an emergency situation.* ○ *Quick reactions are needed in an emergency.*

reaction thrust principle /ri ˌækʃən 'θrʌst ˌprɪnsɪp(ə)l/ the process by which exhaust gases coming of the back of an object cause a reaction force to act on the object and push it forwards

readback /'riːdbæk/ *noun* the action of repeating an ATC message to the controller to enable him or her to check that it was correctly received

readily /'redɪli/ *adverb* **1.** promptly, immediately ○ *Fire extinguishers must be readily available for use.* ○ *Ice melts very readily at 0°C (Celsius).* **2.** □ **it can readily be seen** it can be easily understood ○ *It can readily be seen from the preceding paragraph that density and pressure are linked.*

reading /'riːdɪŋ/ *noun* **1.** information indicated by an instrument or gauge □ **altimeter reading** the altitude indicated by the altimeter □ **barometer reading** the barometric pressure indicated by the barometer **2.** □ **map reading** the act of interpreting information on a map

readout /'ri:daʊt/ *noun* a display or presentation of data from calculations or storage ○ *The rotating beam cloud base recorder/indicator operates continuously, day and night and produces an automatic readout of cloud base height.*

rear /rɪə/ *noun* the aft part, the part furthest from the front ○ *the rear of the aircraft* ■ *adjective* at the back, or referring to the back ○ *The rear part of the aircraft is called the aft section.*

rearward /'rɪəwəd/ *adjective* towards the aft or the rear ○ *The expanding gas travels in a rearward direction.*

reason /'ri:z(ə)n/ *noun* the basis or motive for an action ○ *A rough surface is more susceptible to fatigue cracking than a smooth one and for this reason highly stressed members are often polished.*

reasonable /'ri:z(ə)nəb(ə)l/ *adjective* 1. acceptable or fair □ **a reasonable sum of money** a sum of money which is not too high or which is acceptable 2. within the boundaries of common sense ○ *It would be reasonable to expect that radio frequencies would travel through the air in straight lines as a direct wave, but they bend, or refract.*

receive /rɪ'si:v/ *verb* to get, to obtain ○ *The sides of the hills and mountains which face the sun receive more intense radiation than flat surfaces because of the angle of exposure to the sun.*

receiver /rɪ'si:və/ *noun* a device that receives incoming radio signals and converts them to sound or light ○ *The transponder in the aircraft consists of a transmitter and a receiver.*

recent /'ri:s(ə)nt/ *adjective* referring to a time immediately before the present ○ *Recent engine designs include variable angle stator blades.* ○ *A more recent development is the barograph which utilises the electrical output of the digital display barometer.* □ **recent weather** significant weather observed in the period since the previous observation, but not now

reception /rɪ'sepʃən/ *noun* an act or instance of receiving radio signals ○

The antenna is highly directive in transmission and reception.

reciprocal /rɪ'sɪprək(ə)l/ *adjective* □ **reciprocal heading** an opposite heading, 180° from a given heading ○ *The reciprocal heading of 090° is 270°.* ■ *noun* the exactly opposite direction ○ *A wave transmitted vertically returns to Earth on its reciprocal.*

reciprocating /rɪ'sɪprəkeɪtɪŋ/ *adjective* moving backwards and forwards or up and down

recognise /'rekəgnaɪz/, **recognize** *verb* to identify, or to know to be something that has been seen, heard, etc. before ○ *It may be difficult to recognise a particular stretch of coastline simply by its appearance.*

recognition /ˌrekəg'nɪʃ(ə)n/ *noun* the process of seeing or hearing something or somebody and knowing what it is or who he or she is ○ *Hydraulic fluids are coloured for recognition purposes.*

recommend /ˌrekə'mend/ *verb* to say that something is worthy, desirable or suitable ○ *Dry chemical extinguishers are recommended for use on aircraft brake fires.* ○ *Aircraft should be operated to the manufacturers recommended limits.*

record *noun* /'rekɔːd/ 1. a written account of facts and information for future reference 2. a set of electronically stored data ■ *verb* /rɪ'kɔːd/ 1. to write down something such as information or data ○ *Measure track angles and distances and record them in a log.* 2. to capture and store electronically ○ *Details of wind speed, direction, visibility and cloud cover are recorded onto a cassette.*

recorder /rɪ'kɔːdə/ *noun* a device for capturing sound onto cassette or magnetic tape ○ *cockpit voice recorder*

recording /rɪ'kɔːdɪŋ/ *noun* the act of writing or of picking up and storing information ○ *An anemograph is an instrument which maintains a continuous recording of wind direction and speed on a graph.*

recover /rɪ'kʌvə/ *verb* 1. to return to an earlier, normal condition or attitude □ **recover from a stall** to return the aircraft to straight and level flight **2.** to rescue and remove from a particular area, often the sea ○ *Emergency services recovered two bodies from the wreckage of the helicopter.*

recovery /rɪˈkʌv(ə)ri/ *noun* **1.** a return to an earlier, normal condition or attitude □ **recovery from unusual attitudes** a flight exercise requiring the student pilot to return the aircraft to its previous, normal, that is, straight and level attitude, after it has been in an unusual attitude **2.** rescue and removal from a particular area ○ *The recovery of survivors from the sea was carried out by helicopters.*

rectangle /ˈrektæŋɡəl/ *noun* a 4-sided plane figure with 4 right angles, and with opposite sides of equal length ○ *The colour identification of refuelling equipment for AVGAS is: blue rectangle, red decal with AVGAS 100LL in white letters.*

rectangular /rekˈtæŋɡjʊlə/ *adjective* referring to something with the shape of a rectangle ○ *a rectangular wing panel*

rectification /ˌrektɪfɪˈkeɪʃ(ə)n/ *noun* the process of changing an alternating current into direct current ○ *Part of the generator alternating current (AC) is passed through a rectification circuit.*

rectified airspeed /ˌrektɪfaɪd ˈeə ˌspiːd/ *noun* indicated airspeed corrected for instrument error and pressure error ○ *When rectified airspeed (RAS) is corrected for density error the resultant is known as the true airspeed.*

rectifier /ˈrektɪfaɪə/ *noun* an electronic circuit that converts an alternating current supply into a direct current supply ○ *The ignition unit receives an alternating current which is passed through a transformer and rectifier.*

rectify /ˈrektɪfaɪ/ *verb* **1.** to change alternating current into direct current ○ *Alternating current output is rectified and regulated externally and returned as direct current to the stator field winding.* **2.** to correct □ **to rectify a mistake** to put right a mistake

redeye /ˈredaɪ/ *noun* a late night or overnight airline service

reduce /rɪˈdjuːs/ *verb* to decrease, to make less. Opposite **increase** □ **reduce altitude** to descend □ **reduce temperature** to make cooler

reduced separation /rɪˌdjuːst ˌsepəˈreɪʃ(ə)n/ *noun* a revised minimum separation which is smaller than the previous minimum separation

reduction /rɪˈdʌkʃən/ *noun* a decrease ○ *reduction in temperature, pressure, speed*

reduction gear /rɪˈdʌkʃən ˌɡɪə/ *noun* gears in an engine which allow the propeller to turn at a slower speed than the engine

redundancy /rɪˈdʌndənsi/ *noun* the duplication of component parts of a system to enable the system to function even if one component fails ○ *With system redundancy, a single failure within a system will have little effect on the aircraft's performance during the approach and landing operation.*

redundant /rɪˈdʌndənt/ *adjective* referring to a system which provides extra component parts to enable the system to function even if one component fails ○ *Redundant structure design is composed of a large number of members, all of which share a load, so that if one of the members is lost, the load carried by the member is divided between all the others in such a way that the total load-carrying ability is reduced only slightly.*

redux /ˈredʌks/ *noun* a method of fixing components together using adhesives and glues

re-enter /ˌriː ˈentə/ *verb* to enter again ○ *For engine checks the aircraft should be headed into wind to prevent hot exhaust gases re-entering the engine.*

refer /rɪˈfɜː/ *verb* **1.** to describe or give a name to ○ *The term wind is used to refer to the horizontal motion of air.* **2.** to direct someone to a source of help or information (NOTE: **referring** – **referred**) □ **refer to chapter 10 for more details** look at or read chapter 10 for more information

reference /'ref(ə)rəns/ *noun* something used as a basis for further calculation or investigation □ **visual reference** anything seen and used as a guide to something else ○ *Use the large building as a visual reference for the turn onto final approach.* □ **reference book** a book in which you can look for information, e.g. a dictionary □ **by reference to** by looking at and comparing

reference datum /'ref(ə)rəns ˌdeɪtəm/ *noun* a line fixed by the designer from which measurements are made when checking or adjusting wing angles, etc.

reference point /'ref(ə)rəns pɔɪnt/ *noun* a fixed datum near the centre of the airfield landing area

reference signal /'ref(ə)rəns ˌsɪɡn(ə)l/ *noun* a signal against which telemetry data signals are compared

refinement /rɪ'faɪnmənt/ *noun* an improvement ○ *An internal locking device is one of the numerous refinements to the simple actuator.*

reflect /rɪ'flekt/ *verb* to throw back something such as radio waves or light ○ *Snow surfaces reflect up to 90% of radiation while rock, sand and concrete reflect only 10–20%.*

reflection /rɪ'flekʃən/ *noun* the process of throwing back of something such as radio waves or light ○ *Glare caused by reflection of sunlight from the top of a layer of fog or haze can seriously reduce the air-to-ground visibility.*

reflective /rɪ'flektɪv/ *adjective* able to throw back something such as radio waves or light ○ *Reflective power means that at low angles of elevation of the sun, water reflects a great amount of solar radiation thus slowing down the rise in sea surface temperatures.*

reflector /rɪ'flektə/ *noun* a device which throws back something such as light ○ *The shape of a water droplet makes it a good reflector, so water in the atmosphere absorbs and scatters radio waves.*

refract /rɪ'frækt/ *verb* to cause a wave, such as light or sound, to change direction or turn as it passes from one medium into another of different den-

sity ○ *A sky wave starts life as a direct wave and, on reaching the ionosphere, the direct wave is refracted and returns to the Earth's surface.*

refraction /rɪ'frækʃən/ *noun* the change in direction or turning of a wave, such as light or sound, as it passes from one medium into another of different density

refrigerant /rɪ'frɪdʒərənt/ *noun* a substance to provide cooling either as the working substance of a refrigerator or by direct absorption of heat ○ *Heated air from the main air supply system passes through the evaporator matrix and by induction releases heat into the liquid refrigerant.*

refuel /riː'fjuːəl/, **re-fuel** *verb* to fill with fuel again ○ *Fire risk is always present when you defuel and refuel.*

regain /rɪ'ɡeɪn/ *verb* to obtain again or to acquire again ○ *The omni-bearing selector/course deviation indicator is a demand instrument which indicates which way to turn to regain the required bearing.*

regard /rɪ'ɡɑːd/ *noun* a particular point or aspect □ **in this regard** concerning this or with reference to this □ **with regard to** concerning or with reference to ○ *With regard to the turbo-propeller engine, changes in propeller speed and pitch have to be taken into account.* ■ *verb* to look upon or consider in a particular way ○ *Thoughtful concern for others is regarded as an essential component of good airmanship.*

regardless /rɪ'ɡɑːdləs/ *preposition* in spite of, despite, with no thought of □ **with fly-by-wire technology, the aircraft's stalling angle of attack cannot be exceeded regardless of control stick input** the stalling angle of attack cannot be exceeded, despite or no matter what the pilot does with the flying controls

region /'riːdʒən/ *noun* **1.** an area, usually a large geographical area ○ *The troposphere is deepest in equatorial regions and shallowest near the poles.* **2.** □ **in the region of** about or approximately ○ *The burning temperature of* *the fuel is in the region of 2,000°C (Celsius).*

register /'redʒɪstə/ *noun* an official list or record ○ *The student's name was not on the register.* ▪ *verb* **1.** to record or to indicate on an instrument ○ *During ground running checks, if oil pressure does not register within a few seconds, the engine should be stopped and the cause investigated.* ○ *Electrically operated pressure gauges register main and emergency system pressure.* **2.** to enter details on an official list ○ *to register an aircraft*

registration /ˌredʒɪ'streɪʃ(ə)n/ *noun* the entry of civil aircraft into records of national certification authority with details of letter and number code displayed on aircraft □ **certificate of registration** a document issued as proof of registration

regular /'regjʊlə/ *adjective* **1.** occurring at fixed time intervals ○ *a regular flight* □ **regular inspections** inspections taking place at equal intervals of time **2.** ordinary or standard ○ *part of the regular menu*

regulate /'regjʊleɪt/ *verb* to control, to adjust to a specific requirement ○ *Controllable cowl flaps regulate the amount of air flowing across the cylinders.*

regulation /ˌregjʊ'leɪʃ(ə)n/ *noun* an act or instance of controlling or adjusting to a specific requirement ○ *Regulation of cabin temperature is controlled by the manual setting of a mechanically controlled switch.*

regulations /ˌregjʊ'leɪʃ(ə)nz/ *plural noun* rules or laws

regulator /'regjʊleɪtə/ *noun* a device used to control the flow of fluids or electric current □ **voltage regulator** a device to control the level of voltage

Reid vapour pressure test /ˌriːd 'veɪpə ˌpreʃə test/ *noun* a test to determine the pressure required above a liquid to hold the vapours in the liquid at a given temperature

reinforce /ˌriːɪn'fɔːs/ *verb* to make stronger or to strengthen ○ *Typical skin materials used in aircraft are made from epoxy resins which are reinforced with glass, carbon or Kevlar fibres.*

reinforced /ˌriːɪn'fɔːst/ *adjective* made stronger or strengthened

reinforced plastics /ˌriːɪnfɔːst 'plæstɪks/ *plural noun* plastic materials used with glass fibres to repair some types of aircraft structure

reinforcement /ˌriːɪn'fɔːsmənt/ *noun* the act of strengthening, or a material or structure used to strengthen something ○ *There is reinforcement around each opening in the pressure cabin, such as the cabin door, escape hatch and windows.*

relate /rɪ'leɪt/ *verb* **1.** to make a connection or link, to associate ○ *Orientating the chart relates the direction of land features to their representation on the chart and aids recognition.* **2.** □ **to relate to** to concern or to be about ○ *Kepler derived the laws which relate to the motion of planets in their orbits.*

relation /rɪ'leɪʃ(ə)n/ *noun* **1.** a natural or logical association between things ○ *the relation between thrust and drag* □ **this bears no relation to that** this is not connected with that in any way **2.** □ **in relation to** with reference to ○ *The range at which objects can be recognised is affected by the direction of viewing in relation to the position of the sun or the moon.* ○ *The VOR station on the ground does the calculation and, depending on where the aircraft is in relation to the VOR station, it will receive signals which define the bearing of the aircraft from the VOR.*

relationship /rɪ'leɪʃ(ə)nʃɪp/ *noun* a natural or logical association between things ○ *There is a close relationship between altitude and pressure.*

relative /'relətɪv/ *adjective* □ **relative to** compared to, with reference to ○ *Ground-speed is the speed of the aircraft relative to the ground.*

relative airflow /ˌrelətɪv 'eəfləʊ/ *noun* airflow over an aerofoil, often related to the chord line of the aerofoil. Also called **relative wind**

relative bearing /ˌrelətɪv 'beərɪŋ/ *noun* the bearing of a radio station or object with reference to the aircraft's heading

relative density /ˌrelətɪv 'densɪti/ *noun* the ratio of density of a liquid with reference to water, or of a gas with reference to air

relative humidity /ˌrelətɪv hjuː'mɪdɪti/ *noun* the ratio between the amount of water vapour in the air and the amount which would be present if the air was saturated, at the same temperature and the same pressure

relative wind /ˌrelətɪv 'wɪnd/ *noun* same as **relative airflow**

relay /'riːleɪ/ *noun* a device which responds to a small current or voltage change by activating switches or other devices in an electric circuit ○ *Thermocouple detectors operate a sensitive relay or electronic circuit when a predetermined temperature is exceeded.* ■ *verb* to pass an ATC message to an aircraft via another aircraft that is on the same frequency and within radio range (NOTE: Messages may have to be relayed when atmospheric conditions make a direct transmission impossible)

release /rɪ'liːs/ *noun* the act of freeing something from something that holds it ○ *Air rising and cooling often reaches its dew point temperature, becomes saturated and any further cooling results in condensation and the consequent release of latent heat.* ■ *verb* to free from something that holds it ○ *Push the button to release the lever.* □ **release the brakes** let the brakes off □ **to release the pressure** to allow pressure to reduce

relevant /'reləv(ə)nt/ *adjective* having a connection with the matter in hand ○ *High charts show only information relevant to high altitude flights and many beacons and aids which are provided for low operations are omitted to keep the chart clear.* □ **relevant information** useful information which is related to the matter in question

reliability /rɪˌlaɪə'bɪlɪti/ *noun* dependability, trustworthiness ○ *The gas turbine is a very simple engine with few moving parts, giving it high reliability with less maintenance.*

'…where a State introduces drug testing, high standards of medical reliability must be maintained' [*INTER PILOT*]

reliable /rɪ'laɪəb(ə)l/ *adjective* dependable, trustworthy ○ *The gas turbine is a very simple and reliable engine.*

relief /rɪ'liːf/ *noun* **1.** variations in elevation of the surface of the earth ○ *Relief is usually represented on aeronautical charts by contours, gradient tints or hill shading.* **2.** a lessening of pressure

relief valve /rɪ'liːf vælv/ *noun* a valve which opens at maximum safe pressure and closes again upon return to normal operating conditions

relieve /rɪ'liːv/ *verb* to cause a lessening in, or to remove, excess pressure or tension ○ *Safety valves relieve excess cabin pressure.* ○ *A trim tab on the elevator relieves the forward and aft forces on the control stick or yoke.*

relight /riː'laɪt/ *verb* to ignite again ○ *The ability of the engine to relight will vary according to the altitude and the forward speed of the aircraft.*

rely /rɪ'laɪ/ *verb* to be dependent on ○ *Pressure carburettors do not rely on venturi suction to discharge fuel into the airstream.*

remain /rɪ'meɪn/ *verb* to stay, to continue to be ○ *During the evacuation, crew must remain at their assigned stations and redirect passengers.* ○ *The fuel/air ratio does not remain constant, but, as the speed increases, the mixture gets richer.* ○ *The audible fire warnings may be cancelled but the red warning light will remain on.*

remainder /rɪ'meɪndə/ *noun* **1.** something left after excluding other parts, the rest ○ *The auxiliary power unit is usually found in the tail section, separated from the remainder of the fuselage by a firewall.* **2.** the number left over when one number is divided by another

remote /rɪ'məʊt/ *adjective* **1.** far away, and not near anything else ○ *a remote area* ○ *When the destination is a remote island, the calculation of the point of no return (PNR) becomes* *essential.* **2.** operated or controlled from a distance ○ *remote cabin pressure controllers* **3.** □ **a remote chance** a small but unlikely possibility

removal /rɪˈmuːv(ə)l/ *noun* the act of taking something away, or of moving something from the position it occupies ○ *The repair to the aircraft required the removal of the engine.*

remove /rɪˈmuːv/ *verb* to take something away or move it from the position it occupies ○ *Filters are fitted in lines in a hydraulic system, in order to remove foreign particles from the fluid.* ○ *The engine will have to be removed for repair.*

render /ˈrendə/ *verb* **1.** to cause to become ○ *The failure of any component in the fire detection system will render the system inoperative.* ○ *Tropical air moving northwards is subjected to surface cooling and rendered increasingly stable in its lower layers.* **2.** to give □ **to render assistance** to provide help ○ *Only when all possible assistance has been rendered inside the cabin will crew themselves evacuate.*

repair /rɪˈpeə/ *noun* an action designed to return something to good condition after damage ○ *The repair to the nosewheel took three hours.* ■ *verb* to mend or otherwise return to good condition after damage ○ *After the wheels-up landing, the flaps had to be repaired.*

'Mr Pike elected to await repairs instead of taking up the offer of alternative flights, and found himself the only passenger aboard the Jumbo as it flew back to Heathrow four hours late' [*Pilot*]

repeat /rɪˈpiːt/ *verb* **1.** to do again ○ *The first officer repeated the transmission.* ○ *The trainee had to repeat her navigation examination.* **2.** to occur again ○ *Metal fatigue is induced by repeated stress cycling.* **3.** to say again ○ *Could you repeat that please? I didn't hear.* ○ *The message was repeated a few minutes later.*

repel /rɪˈpel/ *verb* to push away by a force ○ *Like poles (i.e., north and north, or south and south) of a magnet repel*

each other. (NOTE: **repelling** – **repelled**)

repellent /rɪˈpelənt/ *noun* a substance used to resist the effect of something ○ *Rain repellent is sprayed onto the windscreen and spread by the wipers.*

replace /rɪˈpleɪs/ *verb* to take the place or to fill the place of ○ *As warm air rises, cold air moves in to replace it.* ○ *The term Greenwich Mean Time (GMT) is being replaced by the term Coordinated Universal Time (UTC).*

replacement /rɪˈpleɪsmənt/ *noun* **1.** the act of replacing something with something else ○ *The replacement of moist air by dry air is the only sure way of dispersing advection fog.* **2.** something or somebody that replaces something or somebody else ○ *She was hired as a replacement for a manager who had recently retired.*

reply /rɪˈplaɪ/ *noun* an answer or response ○ *Secondary surveillance interrogation is made on 1030 MHz (megahertz) and the reply on 1090 MHz (megahertz).* ■ *verb* to answer, to respond ○ *He replied to the letter.* (NOTE: **replying** – **replied**)

report /rɪˈpɔːt/ *noun* an official account of an occurrence ○ *incident report* ○ *weather report* ■ *verb* to write or tell information in an official manner ○ *The observer measures this distance in a number of directions and reports the minimum value as the meteorological visibility.* ○ *An accident must be reported.*

reporting point /rɪˈpɔːtɪŋ pɔɪnt/ *noun* a specified geographical location on an aircraft's route at which the crew must report to air traffic control

represent /ˌreprɪˈzent/ *verb* to indicate or to show, using signs or symbols ○ *On a Mercator projection, meridians are represented as parallel straight lines.*

representation /ˌreprɪzenˈteɪʃ(ə)n/ *noun* a way of showing something, using signs or symbols ○ *The synoptic chart provides a representation of the weather over a large area at a particular time.*

representative /ˌreprɪˈzentətɪv/ *adjective* □ **representative of** which is a typical example of what all others are like ○ *Surface air temperatures are taken in such a way as to be representative of the air temperature near the surface yet unaffected by the direct surface heating or cooling effects.* ■ *noun* a person who acts or speaks for another person or for an organisation such as a company

request /rɪˈkwest/ *noun* a polite demand, or what is asked for ○ *ATC (air traffic control) received a request from the pilot for departure clearance.* □ **on request** when asked for ○ *A personal flying log book must be retained for production on request by an authorised person.* ■ *verb* to ask for something ○ *The pilot requested vectors to enable him to locate the airfield.*

require /rɪˈkwaɪə/ *verb* **1.** to need ○ *Dynamic seals require lubrication to remain effective.* **2.** to impose an obligation, to compel by law ○ *Transport operations over water require the carriage of life rafts, life jackets, survival beacons and pyrotechnics.*

requirement /rɪˈkwaɪəmənt/ *noun* **1.** what is necessary ○ *Planning for an in-flight emergency is a standard requirement of pre-departure preparation.* **2.** □ **legal requirement** an obligation by law **3.** something which is demanded or required ○ *The airframe had to be built to very specific requirements.*

re-register /ˌriː ˈredʒɪstə/ *verb* to register again ○ *The aircraft had to be re-registered because of an administrative error.*

rescue /ˈreskjuː/ *noun* the act of freeing from danger ○ *Early rescue depends on the rapid location of survivors.* ■ *verb* to free from danger ○ *Passengers were rescued from the burning aircraft.*

reserve /rɪˈzɜːv/ *noun* something kept back for possible future use ■ *verb* to keep something such as a seat for somebody ○ *Seats 23A and 23B are reserved for Mr and Mrs Smith.*

reserve fuel /rɪˌzɜːv ˈfjuːəl/ *noun* fuel used only in a situation when the aircraft has to be in the air for a longer time than expected, as because of a go-around or diversion

reservoir /ˈrezəvwɑː/ *noun* a container for holding a store of fluid ○ *A reservoir provides both storage space for the system fluid, and sufficient air space to allow for any variations in the volume of the fluid in the system.*

reset /riːˈset/ *verb* to set again ○ *Instruments which need resetting in flight must be accessible to the crew.* (NOTE: **resetting – reset**)

resettable /riːˈsetəb(ə)l/ *adjective* possible to reset ○ *Circuit breakers are resettable protective devices.*

residual /rɪˈzɪdjuəl/ *adjective* referring to the residue of something

residue /ˈrezɪdjuː/ *noun* the remainder of something after the removal of the main part ○ *The leaking oil left a sticky residue on the ground.*

resin /ˈrezɪn/ *noun* materials which are used with fillers and other components to form plastics, e.g. polyesters, epoxies and silicones ○ *To make a composite it is necessary to combine the reinforcing glass fibres with some form of special glue or resin.*

resist /rɪˈzɪst/ *verb* to fight off the effects of something ○ *A tube resists bending in any direction but beams are designed usually to resist bending in one or two directions only.* ○ *In order for an aeroplane to fly, lift and thrust must resist and overcome the forces of gravity and drag.*

resistance /rɪˈzɪstəns/ *noun* **1.** a force that opposes **2.** the opposition of a body or substance to current passing through it ○ *The shunt coil is made of fine wire which gives a high resistance and small current flow.*

resistant /rɪˈzɪst(ə)nt/ *adjective* referring to something which is unaffected by a force, process or substance ○ *crash resistant and heat resistant materials* ○ *Some alloys are less resistant to corrosion than others.*

resistive /rɪˈzɪstɪv/ *adjective* referring to resistance ○ *Windscreen heating and electrical de-icing systems are resistive load circuits.*

resistor /rɪˈzɪstə/ *noun* a device used to control current in an electric circuit by providing a resistance ○ *Components such as resistors, rectifiers and internal switches are all embedded in micro-size sections of semi-conductor material.*

respect /rɪˈspekt/ *noun* □ **in some respect** in some way ○ *The flat chart inevitably misrepresents the Earth's surface in some respect.* □ **with respect to** concerning or with reference to ○ *Frost point is the temperature to which air must be cooled at constant pressure in order to reach a state of saturation with respect to ice.*

respective /rɪˈspektɪv/ *adjective* referring to two or more persons or things regarded individually ○ *The passengers returned to their respective seats.* ○ *The temperature and pressure of the fuel supply are electrically transmitted to their respective indicators, i.e. temperature to the temperature gauge and pressure to the pressure gauge.*

respond /rɪˈspɒnd/ *verb* **1.** to reply or to answer **2.** to react, to act in return □ **the aircraft responds to the controls** the aircraft attitude changes as a result of the pilot's movements of the flying controls

responder /rɪˈspɒndə/ *noun* same as **transponder**

response /rɪˈspɒns/ *noun* **1.** an answer or reply ○ *transponder response* ○ *Despite repeated air traffic control transmissions, there was no response from the pilot.* **2.** a reaction □ **in response to** as a reaction to ○ *The primary function of the outflow valves is to regulate the discharge of cabin air in response to the pressure signals received from the controller.*

responsibility /rɪˌspɒnsɪˈbɪlɪti/ *noun* the condition of being responsible ○ *It is the responsibility of the captain to order an evacuation.*

responsible /rɪˈspɒnsɪb(ə)l/ *adjective* **1.** being a source or cause ○ *Frontal systems are responsible for much of the weather and clouds which occur in temperate latitudes.* **2.** directing or being in charge, and open to blame if something goes wrong ○ *Cabin crew are responsible for the well-being of passengers.* □ **responsible to someone** answerable for one's actions to somebody highly placed

restore /rɪˈstɔː/ *verb* to return something to its original or normal condition ○ *Loss of engine power should be fully restored when the control is returned to the cold air position.*

restrict /rɪˈstrɪkt/ *verb* **1.** to make free movement limited or difficult ○ *The narrow aisles of the aircraft restrict the rapid movement of people.* **2.** to limit □ **during the bomb-scare, entry to the airport was restricted to authorised people only** only authorised people could enter the airport

restricted area /rɪˌstrɪktɪd ˈeəriə/ *noun* airspace of a particular length, width and depth, within which the flight of an aircraft must be carried out in accordance with particular conditions

restriction /rɪˈstrɪkʃ(ə)n/ *noun* **1.** a narrowing or partial blockage ○ *Any restriction in a pipeline will increase liquid velocity and produce turbulence.* **2.** a limitation ○ *There are restrictions on the taking of photographs in the vicinity of the airport.*

restrictor valve /rɪˈstrɪktə vælv/ *noun* a valve designed to permit limited flow in one direction and full flow in the other direction ○ *The extent to which the oil pressure will fall depends on the size of the restrictor valve.*

result /rɪˈzʌlt/ *noun* a consequence or outcome ○ *Engine oil and cylinder temperature will also increase as a result of higher combustion temperatures.* ■ *verb* □ **to result from** to happen as a consequence ○ *The structural weakness resulted from a minor collision while taxiing two years previously.* □ **to result in** to produce as an effect ○ *Failure to secure seat belts could result in serious injury.*

resultant /rɪˈzʌltənt/ *adjective* that happens as a result of something ○ *The temperature of the land rises, causing the layer of air in contact with it to warm up and expand with a resultant decrease in density.* ■ *noun* one vector that is the equivalent of a set of vectors

○ *When two or more velocities act simultaneously on a body, the aircraft movement is called the resultant velocity due to the two or more component velocities.*

retain /rɪ'teɪn/ *verb* to keep or to hold ○ *Retentivity is the ability of a material has to retain magnetism.* ○ *When fuel-dumping, sufficient fuel must be retained for landing.*

retard /rɪ'tɑːd/ *verb* **1.** to cause to occur later, or to delay ○ *On most modern engines the spark is retarded to top dead centre, to ensure easier starting and prevent kick-back.* **2.** to move backwards ○ *When reducing power, always retard the throttles before reducing RPM (revolutions per minute) with the propeller levers.*

retentivity /ˌrɪten'tɪvɪti/ *noun* the ability to remain magnetised after the magnetising force has gone ○ *Steel has high retentivity, but soft iron has low retentivity.*

retract /rɪ'trækt/ *verb* to move back, or to raise ○ *Mechanically operated sequence valves ensure that the landing gear does not extend until the doors are open and that the landing gear is retracted before the doors close.*

retractable /rɪ'træktəb(ə)l/ *adjective* possible to pull back or raise □ **retractable undercarriage** an undercarriage which can be raised into the fuselage or wings after use ○ *Early aircraft had non-retractable undercarriages.*

retraction /rɪ'trækʃən/ *noun* the act of pulling back or raising □ **retraction of the undercarriage** the raising of the undercarriage into the fuselage after use

return /rɪ'tɜːn/ *noun* the act of coming back or going back to a place ○ *We're waiting for the return of the aircraft.* □ **radar return** radar echo ■ *adjective* □ **return flight** a flight back to the point of departure ■ *verb* to cause to come back or to go back to an earlier position or place ○ *Fly from A to B and return.* ○ *The auto-control will return the ailerons to neutral as the aircraft returns to level flight.*

return valve /rɪ'tɜːn vælv/ *noun* a valve which allows flow of fluid in both directions

reveal /rɪ'viːl/ *verb* to allow to be seen ○ *Radiographic inspection of the aircraft structure is able to reveal fatigue cracks without the need to dismantle the aircraft.*

reversal /rɪ'vɜːs(ə)l/ *noun* a change to the opposite position, direction, or order ○ *Stationary eddies can be hazardous, not only because of the down currents but also because an aircraft encountering the reversal of direction might have its airspeed momentarily reduced below stalling speed.*

reverse /rɪ'vɜːs/ *noun* the opposite ○ *One would expect a unit of humid air to be heavier than a similar unit of dry air but, in fact, the reverse is true.* ■ *adjective* going backwards or in the opposite direction □ **reverse flow** the flow of a fluid in the opposite direction to normal ■ *verb* to go backwards or in the opposite direction □ **to reverse a vehicle** to make a vehicle go backwards

reverse panic /rɪˌvɜːs 'pænɪk/ *noun* a form of shock which makes passengers unable to comprehend the need for urgency

reverser /rɪ'vɜːsə/ *noun* □ **thrust reverser** a device to change the direction of thrust so that it operates in the opposite direction to the normal direction ○ *In many turbo-jet thrust reversers, clamshell doors direct the exhaust gases forward.*

reverse thrust /rɪˌvɜːs 'θrʌst/ *noun* thrust in the opposite direction to normal in order to decelerate the aircraft after landing

reversible /rɪ'vɜːsɪb(ə)l/ *adjective* that can be made to go backwards or to change direction ○ *a reversible electric motor*

reversible pitch propeller /rɪˌvɜːsəb(ə)l ˌpɪtʃ prə'pelə/ *noun* a propeller which allows the aircraft to be propelled backwards when taxiing

reversion /rɪ'vɜːʃ(ə)n/ *noun* a return to an earlier condition or state ○ *In smaller aircraft, reversion to manual* *control is possible if complete loss of hydraulic power occurs.*

revert /rɪ'vɜːt/ *verb* to return to an earlier condition or state ○ *The elevator system has the ability to revert to manual control after a hydraulic failure.*

revolution /ˌrevə'luːʃ(ə)n/ *noun* a rotation or turn about an axis □ **a revolution of the crankshaft** a 360° turn of the crankshaft

revolutions per minute /ˌrevəluːʃ(ə)nz pə 'mɪnɪt/ *noun* the speed of an engine or the number of rotations of the crankshaft per minute ○ *Rpm is the number of revolutions per minute that the engine crankshaft is making.* ○ *The actuator control is sensitive to engine rpm.* Abbreviation **rpm**, **r.p.m.**

revolve /rɪ'vɒlv/ *verb* to turn about an axis ○ *The Earth revolves around the sun.*

revolving /rɪ'vɒlvɪŋ/ *adjective* □ **tropical revolving storm** an intense depression of a kind that can develop over tropical oceans ○ *Tropical revolving storms originate within 5–15° of the equator.* ○ *Tropical revolving storms generally occur from June to October.*

rhumb /rʌm/ *noun* one of the points of a compass

rhumb line /'rʌm laɪn/ *noun* **1.** a regularly curved line on the surface of the Earth which cuts all meridians at the same angle **2.** a steady course taken by aircraft along one compass bearing

rhumb line direction /'rʌm laɪn daɪ,rekʃ(ə)n/ *noun* the average of all the great circle directions between the two points ○ *Because the great circle direction between two points on the surface of the Earth is not constant, it is often more convenient to consider the rhumb line direction.*

rib /rɪb/ *noun* one of many cross pieces of the airframe that provide an aircraft wing with shape and strength ○ *Additional strength is required for the rib sections which are placed in the area of the undercarriage mountings, flaps and power plant attachment point.*

rich /rɪtʃ/ *adjective* referring to a mixture in which the ratio of fuel to air is greater than usual ○ *Moving the mixture control lever forward to the rich position increases the amount of fuel mixing with the air.*

rich mixture /ˌrɪtʃ 'mɪkstʃə/ *noun* a fuel/air mixture in which the proportion of fuel is greater than normal

ridge /rɪdʒ/ *noun* **1.** a long narrow hill with a crest ○ *The mountain ridge stretches for miles.* **2.** a long zone of relatively high atmospheric pressure ○ *a ridge of high pressure* ○ *On average, the wind backs with the passage of a ridge.*

ridge waves /'rɪdʒ weɪvz/ *plural noun* oscillations about the stable state of the undisturbed air flow with the range of hills providing the disturbance

rigging position /'rɪgɪŋ pə,zɪʃ(ə)n/ *noun* an attitude of the aircraft in which the lateral axis and usually the longitudinal axis are horizontal ○ *The aircraft was put into the rigging position.*

rigid /'rɪdʒɪd/ *adjective* unbending, inflexible ○ *The areas between the ribs are utilised to house fuel tanks which can be either rigid or flexible.* Opposite **flexible** □ **rigid pipes** pipes that do not bend easily □ **a rigid structure** a firm unbendable structure

rigidity /rɪ'dʒɪdɪti/ *noun* inflexibility, stiffness ○ *Extra strength and rigidity must be provided in the tail section for aircraft with a tail wheel unit.* Opposite **flexibility**

rim /rɪm/ *noun* the outer edge of something circular, e.g. a wheel ○ *Creep marks are painted on the tyre and the wheel rim.* ○ *The rim of the air intake is prone to icing.*

rime ice /'raɪm aɪs/ *noun* ice formed when individual droplets of water freeze rapidly on striking the aircraft surface

ring /rɪŋ/ *noun* a circle ○ *Around the impeller is a ring of stationary vanes called a diffuser ring.*

ripcord /'rɪpkɔːd/ *noun* a cord that is pulled to release a parachute from its pack and open it

RIS *abbreviation* radar information service

rise /raɪz/ *noun* **1.** an increase ○ *a rise in temperature* **2.** □ **to give rise to** to cause ○ *Hills and mountains may give rise to particularly severe turbulence.* ■ *verb* **1.** to move upwards ○ *air rises* **2.** to increase ○ *The temperature is rising.* ◊ **raise**

risk /rɪsk/ *noun* the possibility of suffering harm or injury, danger ○ *When starting an engine, it is bad practice to pump the throttle lever as there is a risk of fire in the carburettor air intake.* ■ *verb* to take a dangerous chance □ **to risk the lives of passengers** to put the lives of passengers in danger by taking a particular course of action

rivet /ˈrɪvɪt/ *noun* a type of metal bolt or pin with a head on one end, inserted through one of the aligned holes in the parts to be joined and then compressed on the plain end to form a second head ○ *Tensile or compressive loading makes the joined materials tend to slide and break the rivet or bolt.* ■ *verb* to join with rivets ○ *The skin is riveted to both stringers and frames.*

RMI *abbreviation* radio magnetic indicator

RNAV *abbreviation* area navigation

robot pilot /ˌrəʊbɒt ˈpaɪlət/ *noun* same as **autopilot**

rocker arm /ˈrɒkə ɑːm/ *noun* part of the valve mechanism in an internal combustion engine, which transmits the movement of the pushrod to the valve

rod /rɒd/ *noun* a thin straight piece of metal ○ *Aluminium rods and bars can readily be employed in the high-speed manufacture of parts.*

rogallo /rɒˈgæləʊ/ *noun* a fabric-covered delta-shaped wing that can be folded compactly, used on ultralight aircraft

role /rəʊl/ *noun* function ○ *Movement of air plays a major role in the development of weather patterns.* □ **the role of the aircraft** the type of operation the aircraft is required to perform

roll /rəʊl/ *noun* **1.** a rotation about the longitudinal axis of the aircraft, created by movement of the ailerons ○ *Roll is produced by moving the stick to the left or right.* ◊ **bank 2.** a flight manoeuvre

with 360° rotation about the longitudinal axis of the aircraft ○ *Loops and rolls are aerobatic manoeuvres.* ■ *verb* to rotate the aircraft around its longitudinal axis ○ *Move the control column to the left to roll the aircraft to the left.* □ **to roll into a turn** to roll or bank the aircraft so that it turns left or right ○ *By rotating the yoke the ailerons are moved and the aircraft rolls into a turn.*

COMMENT: The difference between **roll** and **bank** is that roll is movement whereas bank suggests a fixed attitude of the aircraft. Consequently, a turn might be expressed in angles of bank: *turn at a bank angle of 30°*, and the movement to obtain the bank might be expressed as roll: *roll the aircraft to the left.*

roll cloud /ˈrəʊl klaʊd/ *noun* cloud created in the rotor zone on the downwind side of mountain ranges

roller /ˈrəʊlə/ *noun* a cylindrical metal device which rotates ○ *The most common bearings used in gas turbine engine are the ball or roller type.*

RON *abbreviation* remain overnight

root /ruːt/ *noun* □ **the root of the problem** the cause of the problem

rose /rəʊz/ *noun* □ **compass rose** the compass card or its marking of 32 points on a map ○ *An arc of the compass scale, or rose, covering 30° on either side of the instantaneous track, is at the upper part of the display.*

rotary /ˈrəʊtəri/ *adjective* rotating □ **rotary motion** rotating movement

rotary actuator /ˌrəʊtəri ˈæktjueɪtə/ *noun* an actuator which rotates and operates a screw jack, e.g. to extend flaps

rotary inverter /ˈrəʊtəri ɪnˌvɜːtə/ *noun* a DC motor driving an AC generator, the output of which must be regulated to give constant voltage and frequency

rotary wing aircraft /ˌrəʊtəri wɪŋ ˈeəkrɑːft/ *noun* an aircraft with a rotor which provides lift, such as a helicopter

rotate /rəʊˈteɪt/ *verb* to turn around on an axis or centre ○ *In the event of flame extinction in flight, the engine will continue to rotate, due to the air-*

flow through it caused by the forward speed of the aircraft. ○ *The aircraft should be rotated to the recommended nose-up attitude for touch down.* ○ *Counter-rotating propellers rotate in opposite directions.* ◊ **rotation**

rotation /rəʊˈteɪʃ(ə)n/ *noun* **1.** the act of moving the control yoke or stick aft to raise the nose of an aircraft during the take-off run to facilitate the aircraft becoming airborne ○ *Rotation should begin at about 60 knots.* **2.** the act of turning around an axis or centre ○ *the rotation of the earth* ○ *crankshaft rotation* ○ *The speed of rotation determines the frequency of the generator output.*

COMMENT: The aircraft rotates around three axes: **pitch** = rotation around the lateral axis; **roll** = rotation around the longitudinal axis; **yaw** = rotation around the vertical axis.

rotational /rəʊˈteɪʃ(ə)nəl/ *adjective* rotating ○ *rotational movement of the camshaft* ○ *The rotational movement of the propeller blades creates lift at right angles to the blade.*

rotor /ˈrəʊtə/ *noun* a device which turns about an axis or centre ○ *The rotor blade of a compressor.*

rotor blade /ˈrəʊtə bleɪd/ *noun* a long thin aerofoil on a helicopter rotor

rotorcraft /ˈrəʊtəkrɑːft/ *noun* same as **rotary wing aircraft**

rough /rʌf/ *adjective* **1.** not smooth, having an irregular surface. Opposite **smooth** □ **rough air** turbulent air □ **rough running** referring to a piston engine which is not operating correctly **2.** not fully detailed □ **a rough estimate** an approximate calculation, good enough for a given purpose □ **a rough drawing** a quick drawing usually used to illustrate or explain

roughness /ˈrʌfnəs/ *noun* unevenness of a surface ○ *The strength of turbulence near the Earth's surface depends largely on the surface temperature, the surface wind, and the roughness of the surface.*

rough terrain /ˌrʌf təˈreɪn/ *noun* uneven ground

round /raʊnd/ *adjective* circular ○ *a round life raft* ■ *adverb* in a circular movement ○ *The pointer swings round.*

route /ruːt/ *noun* a course of travel ○ *The purpose of charts is to plan and fly a safe route to a destination.* ◊ **en route** ■ *verb* to plan to send an aircraft, passengers or freight to a place along a particular route

route flight plan /ˌruːt ˈflaɪt ˌplæn/ *noun* detailed information concerning an intended flight, provided to an air traffic control facility in written or oral form

routine /ruːˈtiːn/ *noun* a standard procedure ○ *Meteorological information for scheduled flights will be passed to the operations department as a matter of routine.* ■ *adjective* standard and regular □ **routine servicing** servicing carried out in the normal way at regular, scheduled intervals

row /rəʊ/ *noun* **1.** a series of objects in a line ○ *Each row of rotating rotor blades is followed by a row of stationary stator blades.* **2.** a series of seats in an aircraft ○ *There are no empty seats in Row 8.*

rpm, r.p.m. *abbreviation* revolutions per minute ○ *Rpm is the number of revolutions per minute that the engine crankshaft is making.* ○ *The actuator control is sensitive to engine rpm.*

R/T *abbreviation* radiotelephony (NOTE: **R/T** is frequently used in spoken language, whereas **RTF** is the ICAO abbreviation.)

RTF *abbreviation* radiotelephony (*ICAO*)

rudder /ˈrʌdə/ *noun* a control surface on the fin which rotates the aircraft about its vertical axis to produce yaw ○ *The A320 retains a backup mechanical linkage for elevator trim and rudder to allow control in the unlikely event of complete electrical failure.*

COMMENT: The rudder does not turn the aircraft. It is used, together with aileron deflection, to initiate turns, to balance forces in turns and to counteract yawing motions created by the propeller during flight. The rudder pedals are mounted on the floor of the cockpit.

rudder ball /'rʌdə bɔːl/ *noun* same as **inclinometer**

rudder pedal /'rʌdə ˌped(ə)l/ *noun* a foot-operated lever which moves the rudder ○ *Just before take-off, the pilot should make sure that his or her feet are correctly positioned on the rudder pedals.*

rule /ruːl/ *noun* **1.** a standard and authoritative instruction or guide ○ *According to the rules, your ticket must be paid for two weeks in advance.* □ **as a rule** usually ○ *As a general rule, radio signals travel in straight lines.* **2.** an instrument for determining length

rule of thumb /ˌruːl əv 'θʌm/ *noun* easily remembered, useful guide to a more complex principle

run /rʌn/ *noun* a route or distance ■ *verb* **1.** to extend ○ *Magnetic lines of force run from the north magnetic pole to the south magnetic pole.* **2.** to operate an engine ○ *An engine should be run at low r.p.m. (revolutions per minute) after flight to allow engine components to cool to a more uniform temperature.*

run up /ˌrʌn 'ʌp/ *noun* □ **engine run-up** the testing of a piston engine at high power, in a light aircraft, just before take-off ○ *Make certain that the parking brake is on before doing engine run-up checks.*

runway /'rʌnweɪ/ *noun* a strip of level, usually paved ground on which aircraft take off and land ○ *Heathrow airport has four terminals and two main runways.* ○ *To achieve a safe landing, an aircraft has to be controlled so that its wheels make contact with the runway smoothly.* ○ *The aircraft lined up perfectly on the runway extended centre line.* Abbreviation **R/W**

COMMENT: Large airports often have more than one runway, arranged to cope with varying wind directions. Some busy airports have parallel runways which can be used simultaneously.

runway visual range /ˌrʌnweɪ 'vɪʒuəl ˌreɪndʒ/ *noun* the distance along a runway at which selected lights can be seen, adjusted to simulate approach visibility ○ *Runway visual range is obtained by an observer standing at the side of the runway in the vicinity of the threshold counting the number of markers or lights visible along the side of the runway.* Abbreviation **RVR**

rupture /'rʌptʃə/ *noun* the process of breaking open or bursting ○ *Pressure in the fuel tanks must be controlled to prevent rupture or collapse.* ■ *verb* to break open or burst ○ *The impact ruptured the fuel tank.*

RVR *abbreviation* runway visual range

R/W, RWY *abbreviation* runway

S

S *abbreviation* south

safe /seɪf/ *adjective* free from danger ○ *Approach to land must be made at a safe speed.* □ **safe landing** a landing which does not endanger people or damage the aircraft. ◊ **fail safe**

safeguard /'seɪfɡɑːd/ *noun* something done as a precaution ○ *A propeller is feathered after engine failure, or as a safeguard when low oil pressure or excessive temperature have indicated the development of a possible defect.* ■ *verb* to take action to make sure that something is protected from harm ○ *A pressure maintaining valve is generally used to safeguard operation of important services, such as flying controls and wheel brakes.*

safe life /seɪf laɪf/ *noun* the principle of putting the least load or force on each component, so that it will last well beyond a plane's expected life

safety /'seɪfti/ *noun* freedom from danger, injury or risk ○ *Turbulence can have serious effects on aircraft safety and performance and makes air travel uncomfortable.* □ **safety conscious** the state of being aware at all times of the importance of safety and the means by which it is achieved and maintained

safety pilot /'seɪfti ˌpaɪlət/ *noun* a pilot present in the cockpit to ensure the safety of the flight, e.g. when a student is practising instrument flying

safety regulations /'seɪfti ˌreɡjʊleɪʃ(ə)nz/ *plural noun* rules or laws which must be followed to make a place safe ○ *Equipment and furnishings on modern jet transports must comply*

with safety regulations concerning fire resistance.

safety straps /'seɪfti stræps/ *plural noun* device to keep a person in position in a seat

sailplane /'seɪlpleɪn/ *noun* a light glider particularly well adapted to making use of rising air currents

St Elmo's Fire /sənt ˌelməʊz 'faɪə/ *noun* a luminous electrical discharge sometimes seen on aircraft during storms

SALR *abbreviation* saturated adiabatic lapse rate

salvage /'sælvɪdʒ/ *verb* to save items of property which may be in danger of being lost ○ *In the event of a crash landing in a remote area on land, an attempt should be made to salvage all items of survival equipment from the wreckage including beacons, rafts and raft equipment.*

sample /'sɑːmpəl/ *noun* a small amount which is representative of the whole ○ *If a sample of fuel taken from a tank was found to be hazy or cloudy in appearance, this would indicate the presence of water in suspension.* ○ *If fuel contamination by water is suspected, a sample of fuel should be drained from the tank for inspection.*

sandwich /'sænwɪdʒ/ *noun* a construction of three layers, the material of the one in the middle being different from the two on each side ○ *Standard connectors consist of a metal coupling with a rubber sandwich joint.*

SAR *abbreviation* **1.** special aerodrome report **2.** search and rescue (*ICAO*)

SAS *abbreviation* stability augmentation system

satellite /'sætəlaɪt/ *noun* an object launched to orbit the earth, usually receiving and transmitting signals, pictures and data ○ *Satellite communications improve the effective distribution of world area forecasts.*

satellite navigation /ˌsæt(ə)laɪt ˌnævɪ'ɡeɪʃ(ə)n/, **satellite navigation system** *noun* a system of navigation which uses orbiting satellites to determine the position of an aircraft or point, in relation to the Earth's surface. Abbreviation **SATNAV**

satisfactory /ˌsætɪs'fækt(ə)ri/ *adjective* adequate, good enough ○ *For satisfactory operation, an engine requires an adequate supply of oil.*

'...during the engine run-up, check that the use of carburettor heat gives a satisfactory drop in rpm or manifold pressure' [*Civil Aviation Authority, General Aviation Safety Sense Leaflet*]

satisfy /'sætɪsfaɪ/ *verb* **1.** to meet a particular prescribed standard ○ *Shell Avgas 100LL satisfies British specification.* **2.** to meet the needs or requirements of something ○ *To satisfy the requirements of aviation there are three types of meteorological offices for aviation, each with a specific role to fulfil.*

SATNAV /'sætnæv/ *abbreviation* satellite navigation

saturate /'sætʃəreɪt/ *verb* to cause a substance to combine with the greatest possible amount of another substance ○ *When a sample of air contains the maximum amount of water vapour for its particular temperature, it is said to be saturated.* ◊ **lapse rate**

saturation /ˌsætʃə'reɪʃ(ə)n/ *noun* the state of being filled with the maximum amount of something which can be absorbed, e.g. a sample of air which contains the maximum amount of water vapour for its temperature ○ *The various types of fog are classified by the manner in which saturation is reached.* □ **the moisture in the air reached saturation point and fell as rain** the air could absorb no more water

saturation point /ˌsætʃə'reɪʃ(ə)n pɔɪnt/ *noun* the level at which no more of a substance can be absorbed

save /seɪv/ *verb* to prevent unnecessary use of ○ *Electro-magnetic switches are generally used to control high-current devices by means of a small current thus saving heavy duty cable and therefore weight.*

SB *abbreviation* service bulletin

scale /skeɪl/ *noun* **1.** marks at fixed intervals used as a reference standard in measurement ○ *This ruler has scales in inches and centimetres.* **2.** a graded system of classification **3.** a proportion used in determining distance on charts ○ *Many aeronautical charts use a scale of 1:500,000.*

scan /skæn/ *verb* **1.** to look at quickly and systematically ○ *The pilot is trained to scan the instrument panel.* **2.** to move a radar beam in a systematic pattern in search of a target ○ *Some radars scan in azimuth and glideslope.*

scatter /'skætə/ *noun* deflection of radiation ○ *High frequencies are freer of ionospheric scatter and are relatively free of noise.*

schedule /'ʃedjuːl/ *noun* **1.** a list of times of departures and arrivals ○ *an airline schedule* **2.** a printed or written list of items in the form of a table ○ *inspection schedule* ○ *maintenance schedule* ■ *verb* **1.** to plan for a particular time or date ○ *The meeting is scheduled for 3 o'clock.* **2.** to enter on a schedule ○ *Calculate and schedule each item on the proper form.*

scheduled /'ʃedʒuːld/ *adjective* □ **scheduled landing** an arrival at a time-tabled destination

scheduled flights /ˌʃedʒuːld 'flaɪts/ *plural noun* flights that are listed in the airline timetable, as opposed to charter flights

schematic /skiː'mætɪk/ *adjective* showing the function of a device or system without trying to create a realistic image ○ *Figure 3 shows a schematic diagram of the autopilot.*

scramjet /'skræmdʒet/ *noun* a ramjet aircraft in which fuel is burned in air that is moving at supersonic speeds

screen /skriːn/ *noun* the surface of a TV or computer monitor on which the image is seen ○ *The airborne weather radar (AWR) allows the range of cloud to be estimated from range markers displayed on the screen.*

screw /skruː/ *noun* a type of threaded connector used to fix things together by rotating it

screw jack /ˈskruː dʒæk/, **screw-jack** /ˈskruːdʒæk/ *noun* a lifting device working with rotary input ○ *Pitch trim is achieved by lowering or raising the tailplane leading edge with a screw jack powered by two hydraulic motors.*

sea /siː/ *noun* **1.** a body of salt water between land masses ○ *Swissair flight 111 crashed into the sea.* □ **mean sea level** the average level of the sea taking tidal variations into account ○ *Altitude is the vertical distance between an aircraft – or a point or a level – and mean sea level.* **2.** a particular area of a body of salt water ○ *the North Sea* ○ *the South China Sea* ◊ **ocean**

sea-anchor /ˈsiː ˌæŋkə/ *noun* a device under a raft to provide stability ○ *Each life raft is equipped with a flame orange coloured canopy and a sea-anchor.*

seaboard /ˈsiːbɔːd/ *noun US* a coast ○ *the eastern seaboard of the USA*

seal /siːl/ *noun* **1.** a device that joins two parts and prevents leakage ○ *An oil seal reduces the clearance between the rotating and static members.* □ **static seal** a seal which is part of a non-moving component ○ *Static seals, gaskets and packing are used in many locations.* **2.** a way in which a liquid or a gas may be prevented from escaping ○ *Static seals, gaskets and packing effect a seal by being squeezed between two surfaces.* ■ *verb* to join two parts in such a way as to prevent leakage ○ *In pressurised aircraft, bulkheads are provided at the front and rear ends of the fuselage to seal off the crew compartment and the passenger cabin.*

sealant /ˈsiːlənt/ *noun* a substance painted or sprayed onto a surface to prevent the escape of a liquid or gas ○ *The integral fuel tank may be completely coated on the inside with a layer of sealant.*

sea level /ˈsiː ˌlev(ə)l/ *noun* the average level of the surface of the sea, used for measuring barometric pressure

sealing compound /ˈsiːlɪŋ ˌkɒmpaʊnd/ *noun* same as **sealant**

seaplane /ˈsiːpleɪn/ *noun* a plane that can take off from and land on water

search /sɜːtʃ/ *noun* an act of looking for something in order to find it ○ *The aircraft reduced altitude and carried out a visual search for survivors.* ■ *verb* to look for in order to find something ○ *The investigators searched the scene of the crash for the flight data recorder.*

season /ˈsiːz(ə)n/ *noun* one of the four natural divisions of the year, spring, summer, autumn, or winter ○ *The amount of solar radiation received by the Earth depends on the season.*

seasonal /ˈsiːz(ə)n(ə)l/ *adjective* **1.** referring to the four natural divisions of the year, or characteristic of a particular time of the year ○ *seasonal temperatures* ○ *seasonal winds* **2.** only lasting for a season ○ *seasonal work*

seasonal variation /ˌsiːz(ə)n(ə)l ˌveəriˈeɪʃ(ə)n/ *noun* a change occurring according to the season

seat /siːt/ *noun* a place for sitting ○ *pilot's seat* □ **window seat** a seat next to a window

seated /ˈsiːtɪd/ *adjective* sitting, on your seat ○ *Passengers should remain seated.* ◊ **sit**

seating capacity /ˈsiːtɪŋ kəˌpæsɪti/ *noun* the maximum number of people an aircraft, bus, etc., can seat

secondary /ˈsekənd(ə)ri/ *adjective* **1.** of the second rank in importance, etc., not primary **2.** an induced current that is generated by a primary source

secondary radar /ˌsekənd(ə)ri ˈreɪdɑː/ *noun* a radar system in which the active target replies to the interrogation unit

secondary surveillance radar /ˌsekənd(ə)ri səˈveɪləns ˌreɪdɑː/ *noun* a radar which uses ground equipment called **interrogators** and airborne equipment called **transponders** to identify aircraft, determine altitude and range, etc. ○ *Secondary surveillance radar (SSR) is normally used to supplement data from primary systems.* Abbreviation **SSR**

section /'sekʃən/ *noun* **1.** a component or part of a structure ○ *tail section and nose section of the aircraft* ○ *the non-smoking section of the aircraft* **2.** part of a text ○ *The book is divided into four sections, and the first four chapters form the first section.* **3.** a diagram of a solid object as it would appear if cut, so that the internal structure is displayed. ◊ **cross-section**

sectional /'sekʃən(ə)l/ *adjective* **1.** referring to a section or composed of sections **2.** showing a solid object as it would appear if it were cut

sector /'sektə/ *noun* **1.** part of the flight between an aircraft moving under its own power until it next stops after landing in its allocated parking position ○ *On some sectors, because of fuel costs at the destination, it can be economical to carry excess fuel.* **2.** the portion of a circle inside two radii and the included arc **3.** a segment of airspace with its own team of air traffic controllers

secure /sɪ'kjʊə/ *adjective* fastened or locked, safe ○ *Overhead baggage lockers must be secure.* ■ *verb* to attach firmly, to fasten or to make safe ○ *If the onset of turbulence is sudden, crew must immediately secure themselves in the nearest available seats.*

security /sɪ'kjʊərɪti/ *noun* **1.** safety **2.** people whose job is to protect buildings or other people against crime

SELCAL *noun* a high-frequency radio system which alerts the crew of an aircraft to the fact that air traffic control is trying to contact them. Full form **selective call**

seldom /'seldəm/ *adverb* not often, rarely ○ *Aircraft are seldom hit by lightning.* ○ *The wet sump system of lubrication is seldom used on modern aircraft.*

select /sɪ'lekt/ *verb* to choose something such as a particular instrument or system setting ○ *A reverse thrust lever in the crew compartment is used to select reverse thrust.* ○ *The cabin pressure controller is used to select cabin altitude.*

selection /sɪ'lekʃən/ *noun* **1.** a choice of something such as a particular instrument or system setting ○ *By manual selection of the heating switch, the formed ice can be dispersed.* **2.** a collection of carefully chosen things ○ *a selection of photographs*

selector /sɪ'lektə/ *noun* a manually operated device like a switch, which offers a choice of settings ○ *Turn the selector control.* ○ *The purpose of this selector is to direct fluid to the appropriate side of an actuator.*

self-contained /,self kən'teɪnd/ *adjective* independent ○ *The auxiliary power unit is a self-contained unit.*

self-positioning /,self pə'zɪʃ(ə)nɪŋ/ *noun* the positioning of the aircraft on the extended centreline of the runway using the on-board navigation system. Also called **centre fix**

semi- /semi/ *prefix* half

semicircle /'semi,sɜːk(ə)l/ *noun* half a circle ○ *Most mathematical protractors are made of plastic in the shape of a semicircle.*

semicircular /,semi'sɜːkjʊlə/ *adjective* in the shape of half a circle ○ *Most mathematical protractors are semicircular in shape.*

semiconductor /,semikən'dʌktə/ *noun* a solid crystalline substance with electrical conductivity greater than insulators but less than good conductors ○ *Semiconductor material is used to make many electronic devices.*

senior /'siːniə/ *adjective* older or more important in rank ○ *senior cabin supervisor*

sense /sens/ *noun* **1.** manner, way ○ *After turning the aircraft, the auto-control will operate in the opposite sense and return the ailerons to neutral as the aircraft returns to level flight.* **2.** any of the physiological means by which we experience our surroundings: sight, hearing, smell, taste and touch ○ *When flying in cloud, pilots must rely on the instruments and not on their senses.* **3.** wisdom or natural intelligence ○ *He has a lot of (common) sense.* **4.** the meaning of a word ○ *The word 'bearing' is used in a lot of different senses.* ■ *verb* to detect automatically ○ *The fire warning system is designed to sense two levels of temperature – overheat and fire.* ◊ **sensor**

sensitive /'sensɪtɪv/ *adjective* able to register very small differences or changes in conditions ○ *Oscillating outputs from the alternators could cause sensitive equipment to malfunction or trip off.* ○ *The actuator is sensitive to engine rpm.*

sensitivity /ˌsensɪ'tɪvɪti/ *noun* the quality or state of being able to register very small differences or changes in conditions ○ *Monitors detect disturbances which are below the sensitivity level of the gyros.*

sensor /'sensə/ *noun* a device which receives and responds to a signal or stimulus ○ *pressure sensor* ○ *temperature sensor* ○ *The inlet pressure is sensed by a single pitot-type sensor probe which is situated just in front of the compressor.*

separate *adjective* /'sep(ə)rət/ existing as an independent thing ○ *Propellers consist of a number of separate blades mounted in a hub.* ■ *verb* /'sepəreɪt/ to set or keep apart ○ *Dry chemical extinguishants separate the oxygen element from the fire thus retarding combustion.*

separation /ˌsepə'reɪʃ(ə)n/ *noun* **1.** the condition of being spaced apart **2.** the removal of something from a mixture or combination ○ *The oil and air mixture flows over the de-aerator tray in the oil tank, where partial separation takes place.*

separation standards /ˌsepə'reɪʃ(ə)n ˌstændədz/ *plural noun* internationally agreed minimum separation limits for aircraft in flight

separator /'sepəreɪtə/ *noun* a device which removes something from a mixture or combination ○ *The water separator will extract a percentage of free moisture from the air.*

sequence /'siːkwəns/ *noun* a series of things or events which follow one another, an order ○ *The ignition system* provides a rapid series of sparks timed to fire in each cylinder in the correct sequence.

sequence valves /'siːkwəns vælvz/ *plural noun* a fluid flow controller which performs a number of actions in a particular order ○ *Sequence valves are often fitted in a landing gear circuit to ensure correct operation of the landing gear doors and actuators.*

series /'sɪəriːz/ *noun* a number of things or events which come one after the other in a particular order ○ *a series of photographs* ○ *a series of switches*

series circuit /'sɪəriːz ˌsɜːkɪt/ *noun* an electric circuit connected so that current passes through each component of the circuit in turn without branching

serious /'sɪəriəs/ *adjective* important, or giving cause for great concern or worry □ **serious damage** very bad damage □ **serious injury** very bad injury

serve /sɜːv/ *verb* **1.** to act or to function as ○ *In some aircraft, pressure gauges also serve as a maintenance check on leakage.* **2.** to be used for a purpose ○ *Different colour-coded warning lights serve to alert the observer that something is wrong with the system.*

'...a recent incident in Argentina serves to highlight some of the many safety problems in Latin America' [*INTER PILOT*]

service /'sɜːvɪs/ *noun* **1.** a facility ○ *A pressure reducing valve is often used to reduce main system pressure to a value suitable for operation of a service such as the wheel brakes.* **2.** work done for others as a profession ○ *Automatic Terminal Information Service (ATIS)* ○ *Cabin crew provide a commercial service to passengers.* **3.** maintenance or repairs carried out ■ *verb* to do maintenance or repairs on ○ *Jet engines are simpler to dismantle and service than piston engines.*

serviceability /ˌsɜːvɪsə'bɪlɪti/ *noun* the ability to function as required ○ *When carrying out engine checks, it is usual to turn off the magnetos in turn to check their serviceability.*

serviceable /'sɜːvɪsəb(ə)l/ *adjective* able to function as required ○ *The pilot must make sure that the radio equipment is serviceable prior to take-off.*

service area /'sɜːvɪs ˌeəriə/ *noun* area where maintenance and repairs are carried out

service bay /'sɜːvɪs beɪ/ *noun* a space in the structure of an aeroplane where equipment can be located for maintenance or repairs ○ *In most modern aircraft a number of the major components are grouped together in a hydraulic service bay which is easily accessible for routine servicing operations.*

service bulletin /'sɜːvɪs ˌbʊlɪtɪn/ *noun* a notice issued by the manufacturer of an aircraft, engine or other equipment to alert people to problems with that equipment. Abbreviation **SB**

servicing /'sɜːvɪsɪŋ/ *noun* the action of carrying out maintenance and repairs ○ *Accessibility of components and equipment during servicing enables work to be done more quickly.*

servo /'sɜːvəʊ/ *abbreviation* servomechanism

servo-assisted /ˌsɜːvəʊ ə'sɪstɪd/ *adjective* partially operated by a servomechanism ○ *servo-assisted brakes* ○ *servo-assisted steering*

servo-control unit /ˌsɜːvəʊ kən'trəʊl ˌjuːnɪt/ *noun* a unit, a combined selector valve and actuator, which moves a control surface ○ *A servo-control unit is part of the system which relieves the effects of aerodynamic forces on the flight controls.*

servomechanism /ˌsɜːvəʊ 'mekənɪz(ə)m/ *noun* a device to convert input forces into much larger output forces ○ *Two phase motors are normally used for very small or miniature motors in servomechanisms.*

set /set/ *noun* a group of things which belong together ○ *a set of instruments* ○ *a set of figures* ■ *adjective* fixed or established ○ *a set procedure* ■ *verb* **1.** to adjust to a particular point or figure ○ *The aircraft receiver is set to the required frequency.* **2.** to put in a particular position ○ *Set the throttle fully*

closed. **3.** to harden ○ *The resin sets.* (NOTE: **setting – set**) □ **cold setting materials** materials which do not need heat to harden

set down /ˌset 'daʊn/ *verb* to land an aircraft, or land somewhere in an aircraft

setting /'setɪŋ/ *noun* **1.** a particular figure or position which a device is adjusted to □ **altimeter setting** adjustment of the sub-scale of the altimeter to read QFE, QNH, etc. **2.** the action of adjusting a device to a particular position, etc. ○ *The setting of the altimeter is done prior to take-off.*

settle /'set(ə)l/ *verb* to move into a final position ○ *When wheels are first fitted to an aircraft, the tyres tend to move slightly as they settle down on the rims.*

several /'sev(ə)rəl/ *adjective* a number of but not many, more than a few ○ *There are several types of instrument landing systems (ILS) in use.* □ **several minutes** a number of minutes

severe /sɪ'vɪə/ *adjective* extreme or intense (NOTE: Generally speaking, weather conditions can be described as light, moderate or severe, depending on the amount or intensity of the condition.) □ **severe icing** bad icing □ **severe turbulence** violent turbulence

severity /sɪ'verɪti/ *noun* the amount, intensity or seriousness of a condition ○ *When the wind is strong the vertical currents become quite vigorous with the resultant increase in the severity of turbulence.*

SFAR *abbreviation* Special Federal Aviation Regulation

shade /ʃeɪd/ *noun* **1.** intensity or richness of colour ○ *Shades of colour of the landscape become lighter in misty conditions.* **2.** cover or shelter from the sun ○ *Surface air temperature is the temperature recorded in the shade at a height just above ground level.*

shadow /'ʃædəʊ/ *noun* an area which is not affected by full radiation because of partial or full blocking of rays by something between the area and the source of the radiation ○ *Solar radiation does not exist at night when the rotation* *of the Earth creates a shadow zone from the sun.* ○ *Line-of-sight transmission path means that obstacles and terrain can create shadow zones.*

shaft /ʃɑːft/ *noun* a long, generally cylindrical bar, especially one that rotates and transmits power ○ *engine drive shaft* ○ *propeller shaft*

shaft horsepower /ˌʃɑːft ˈhɔːspaʊə/ *noun* the unit used for stating the power delivered to the shaft of a turboshaft or turboprop engine. Abbreviation **SHP**

shaker /ˈʃeɪkə/ *noun* a device which shakes or vibrates violently ○ *Large aircraft use a stick shaker to supplement the natural stall warning of buffet.*

shallow /ˈʃæləʊ/ *adjective* not deep □ **shallow angle** small angle

shallow depression /ˌʃæləʊ dɪˈpreʃ(ə)n/ *noun* an area of slightly low relative atmospheric pressure

shape /ʃeɪp/ *noun* form ○ *The shape of an aircraft is determined by the requirement to provide an aerodynamic lift force great enough to support the weight of the aircraft and payload whilst in flight.*

sharp /ʃɑːp/ *adjective* **1.** thin and capable of cutting or piercing ○ *If a piece of thermosetting plastic is hit hard enough, it breaks into pieces with straight sharp edges.* **2.** clear ○ *The sharp setting means the bandwidth is reduced to 1kHz (kilohertz) to minimise noise or interference.* **3.** clear and distinct ○ *Cumulus clouds have sharp outlines.* **4.** sudden and acute □ **a sharp increase** a sudden large increase

shatter /ˈʃætə/ *verb* to break into a number of pieces when hit ○ *Clear ice is hard to shatter and break off.*

shear /ʃɪə/ *verb* to break by lateral movement

shearing load /ˈʃɪərɪŋ ləʊd/ *noun* load caused by sliding apart the layers of a structure

shear stress /ˈʃɪə stres/ *noun* stress that occurs in riveted and bolted joints when a force causes one layer of material to slide over an adjacent layer

shed /ʃed/ *verb* to get rid of ○ *Non-essential loads may need to be shed in order to reduce weight.*

sheet /ʃiːt/ *noun* **1.** a large, thin, flat piece of material ○ *aluminium sheet* **2.** a relatively large piece of paper □ **instruction sheet** a piece of paper on which special instructions are written or printed

shell /ʃel/ *noun* the outer covering of something such as an aircraft fuselage

shield /ʃiːld/ *noun* a protective covering ○ *heat shield* ■ *verb* to protect by covering ○ *The beacon should be sited on the highest ground to prevent the transmitted signal from being shielded.*

shift /ʃɪft/ *noun* **1.** movement from one place to another ○ *a shift in position* **2.** a change ○ *When a radio transmission is made from a moving platform, there will be a shift in frequency between the transmitted and intercepted radio signals.* ■ *verb* to change the position of something ○ *to shift a load*

shock /ʃɒk/ *noun* **1.** a sudden violent impact ○ *On all undercarriages some form of accepting the shock of landing must be included.* **2.** disturbance of mental functions caused by a terrible experience or injury ○ *Crew should be aware of reverse panic, a form of shock which makes passengers unable to comprehend the need for urgency.*

shock absorber /ˈʃɒk əbˌzɔːbə/ *noun* device to minimise the shock to the main structure of the aircraft when it lands

shock wave /ˈʃɒk weɪv/ *noun* compression wave caused by supersonic motion ○ *As sonic speed is approached, the efficiency of the intake begins to fall, because of the formation of shock waves at the intake lip.*

shore /ʃɔː/ *noun* a stretch of land at the edge of the sea or a lake, etc. ○ *At a height of 3,000 feet it was possible to see the shore.* ◊ **offshore, onshore**

shorten /ˈʃɔːt(ə)n/ *verb* to make short or shorter in length or duration ○ *Mishandling of aero-engines during operation can cause considerable damage and wear which can shorten the life of the engine.* ○ *The length of the mercury* *column shortens when cooled.* Opposite **lengthen**

short-haul /ˈʃɔːt hɔːl/ *adjective* travelling over a short distance

short-haul flight /ˌʃɔːt hɔːl ˈflaɪt/ *noun* a flight over a short distance, up to 1,000km ○ *On short-haul flights, passengers are usually offered only light meals.*

short-term conflict alert /ˌʃɔːt tɜːm ˈkɒnflɪkt əˌlɜːt/ *noun* a warning that an aircraft may soon be flying too close to another aircraft

shot /ʃɒt/ *noun* a discharge ○ *Extinguishing of a fire in an auxiliary power unit (APU) compartment is normally done by a single-shot fire extinguisher.*

shower /ˈʃaʊə/ *noun* a short period of rain or snow ○ *Showers are forecast for the evening.* ○ *Snow showers are expected in the area.*

SHP *abbreviation* shaft horsepower

shroud /ʃraʊd/ *noun* **1.** an extension of a fixed surface of a wing towards the rear, which covers the leading edge of a movable surface hinged to it **2.** any one of the lines by which the harness of a parachute is attached to the canopy

shunt /ʃʌnt/ *noun* a low-resistance connection between two points in an electric circuit that forms an alternative path for a portion of the current ○ *The shunt-wound generator, used in conjunction with a voltage regulator, is the most common type of DC (direct current) generator system for aircraft.* Also called **bypass**

shutter /ˈʃʌtə/ *noun* a hinged door which controls the flow of air ○ *oil cooler shutters* ○ *radiator shutters*

SID *abbreviation* standard instrument departure

sidestick controller /ˈsaɪdstɪk kənˌtrəʊlə/ *noun* a small side-mounted control column used on aircraft such as the Airbus A340

sight /saɪt/ *noun* **1.** view ○ *The fog cleared and the mountain came into sight.* **2.** □ **with the airfield in sight** a transmission to air traffic control to confirm that the pilot can see the landing airfield **3.** the ability to see using the eyes ■ *verb* to see something when it is a long way away ○ *Sea marker dyes can only be used once and should only be used when a search aircraft is sighted.*

sight glass /ˈsaɪt glɑːs/ *noun* a simple fluid-level gauge

SIGMET /ˈsɪgmet/ *abbreviation* significant meteorological information

sign /saɪn/ *noun* **1.** a small quantity or amount of a something which may suggest the existence of a much larger quantity ○ *Any sign of smoke or fire outside a wing exit means it cannot be used.* **2.** a display with letters and/or numbers, sometimes lit up ○ *the 'fasten seat belt' sign* ○ *'no-smoking' sign* **3.** a symbol such as: -, +, x or ÷, which represents an operation ■ *verb* to put one's signature on a document, a letter, etc. ○ *Remember to sign the letter.*

signal /ˈsɪgn(ə)l/ *noun* **1.** a device, action or sound which passes information **2.** a radio wave transmitted or received ○ *As a general rule, radio signals travel in straight lines.*

signals area /ˈsɪgn(ə)lz ˌeəriə/ *noun* an area on an aerodrome used for displaying ground signals

signals mast /ˈsɪgn(ə)lz mɑːst/ *noun* a vertical pole on an airfield from which signal flags are flown

signals square /ˈsɪgn(ə)lz skweə/ *noun* an area on an aerodrome from which ground signals are displayed

signature /ˈsɪgnɪtʃə/ *noun* the name of a person written in a special way to show that a document has been authorised or to show who is the author of a letter, etc. ○ *Look at the signature to see who wrote the letter.*

significance /sɪgˈnɪfɪkəns/ *noun* importance ○ *Except near a coastline where the sea breeze may augment the upslope motion, anabatic winds are of little significance.*

significant /sɪgˈnɪfɪkənt/ *adjective* important and therefore noticeable ○ *a significant change in temperature* ○ *The vertical currents and eddies formed by the flow of air over hills and mountains have a significant effect on aircraft encountering them.*

significant meteorological information /sɪgˌnɪfɪkənt ˌmiːtiərəlɒdʒɪk(ə)l ˌɪnfəˈmeɪʃ(ə)n/ *noun* a weather advisory concerning weather conditions important to the safety of all aircraft, such as severe or extreme turbulence. Abbreviation **SIGMET**

significant points /ˌsɪgnɪfɪkənt ˈpɔɪnts/ *plural noun* geographical positions used in air navigation, which are defined by latitude and longitude and have names consisting of five letters

significant weather chart /sɪg ˌnɪfɪkənt ˈweðə ˌtʃɑːt/ *noun* a weather chart with important weather information marked on it

signify /ˈsɪgnɪfaɪ/ *verb* to indicate, to suggest, to mean ○ *Buffet signifies the approach of a stall.* (NOTE: **signifies – signifying – signified**)

silence /ˈsaɪləns/ *noun* the absence of sound □ **total silence** the complete absence of sound ■ *verb* to stop, or stop something, making a noise ○ *When an engine fire warning is received on the flight deck, the first action should be to silence the warning bell.*

silencer /ˈsaɪlənsə/ *noun* a device to reduce noise ○ *In order to reduce the level of noise from the blower, silencers are incorporated in the main supply ducting.*

similar /ˈsɪmɪlə/ *adjective* nearly the same ○ *Turbo-shaft engines are similar to turboprop engines.*

similarity /ˌsɪmɪˈlærɪti/ *noun* the fact of having features that are nearly the same ○ *There are points of difference and similarity between the two aircraft.*

simple /ˈsɪmpəl/ *adjective* **1.** basic, not complex ○ *A simple fuel system consists of a gravity feed tank, a filter, a shut-off valve and pipes.* **2.** easy ○ *a simple question*

simplicity /sɪmˈplɪsɪti/ *noun* the quality of having a basic, uncomplicated design or concept ○ *Because of its lightness, cheapness and simplicity, a fixed pitch propeller is often fitted to single-engine aircraft.*

simplify /ˈsɪmplɪfaɪ/ *verb* to make easy, to make less complex or complicated ○ *Repair procedures are being further simplified by increasing use of cold setting resins.*

simulate /ˈsɪmjʊleɪt/ *verb* to imitate the conditions or behaviour of something ○ *The computer program simulates the action of an aircraft.*

simulated instrument flight /ˌsɪmjʊleɪtɪd ˌɪnstrʊmənt ˈflaɪt/ *noun* an instrument flight carried out in a simulator on the ground or in a specially prepared aircraft with screens on the windows

simulation /ˌsɪmjʊˈleɪʃ(ə)n/ *noun* an imitation of a real situation, created often for training purposes ○ *a simulation of an engine fire* ○ *The computer animation showed a simulation of the events which followed the explosion on board the aircraft.*

simulator /ˈsɪmjʊleɪtə/ *noun* a machine that is constructed to look like an aircraft cockpit with a full set of instruments, in which people can be trained to fly a particular type of aircraft

simultaneous /ˌsɪm(ə)lˈteɪniəs/ *adjective* happening at the same time ○ *Most aircraft are now fitted with remote magnetic indicator displays which can be selected to show two simultaneous bearings from different radio navaids.*

sine /saɪn/ *noun* a trigonometric function defined as the length of the side opposite to an angle in a right-angled triangle divided by the length of the hypotenuse. Abbreviation **sin**

single /ˈsɪŋg(ə)l/ *adjective* one only

single-engined aircraft /ˌsɪŋg(ə)l ˌendʒɪn ˈeəkrɑːft/, **single-engine aircraft** *noun* an aircraft with one engine only

sink /sɪŋk/ *noun* a downdraught of air □ **rate of sink** the rate of descent of a glider ○ *In order to achieve a safe landing, a glider has to be controlled so that it makes contact with the runway smoothly at a very low rate of sink.* ■ *verb* to move downwards as in a fluid ○ *If water enters the fuel tank, it will sink to the bottom of the tank where it can be drained off.*

sit /sɪt/ *verb* to be resting with your behind on a seat such as a chair ○ *The* *pilot sits in the cockpit.* (NOTE: **sitting – sat**)

site /saɪt/ *noun* a selected area of land ○ *landing site* ■ *verb* to position or to put in a particular place ○ *Where it is impossible or inadvisable to site the localiser antenna on the runway centreline, it may be positioned to one side.*

sitting /ˈsɪtɪŋ/ *adjective* □ **sitting position** the position of a person who is on a seat ○ *The correct technique of using the escape slides is to assume a sitting position.*

situate /ˈsɪtʃueɪt/ *verb* to put in a particular place, to locate ○ *The inlet pressure is sensed by a single pitot-type probe which is situated just in front of the compressor.*

situation /ˌsɪtʃuˈeɪʃ(ə)n/ *noun* **1.** a location, the place where something is ○ *The situation of the flight controls is important.* **2.** the conditions or circumstances in a particular place or at a particular time ○ *The synoptic chart is a graphical representation of the general weather situation over a given area at a given time.*

six character group /ˌsɪks ˌkærɪktə ˈɡruːp/ *noun* a group of six letters and/or numbers

six degrees of freedom of motion /ˌsɪks dɪˌɡriːz əv ˌfriːdəm əv ˈməʊʃ(ə)n/ *plural noun* the six types of movement that an aircraft must be able to make: forward, upward and downward, and roll, yaw and pitch

size /saɪz/ *noun* the extent of a thing, how big something is ○ *Whether or not an object can be seen by aircrew at a given distance will depend on factors such as the size, shape and colour of the object.*

skid /skɪd/ *noun* **1.** a slide on slippery ground ○ *Anti-skid braking systems units are designed to prevent the brakes locking the wheels during landing, thus reducing the possibility of wheel skid.* **2.** a condition of uncoordinated flight then the aircraft moves away from the centre of a turn ○ *Deflection of the ball in the turn coordinator indicates a slip or a skid.* ◊ **anti-skid** (NOTE: To correct a skid, the pilot should increase the bank,

or increase rudder pressure on the same side as the ball has moved to in the **turn coordinator**.) ■ *verb* **1.** to slide on slippery ground ○ *If you brake too hard on a wet surface, you might skid.* (NOTE: **skidding – skidded**) □ **to skid to a halt** to slide or skid until you stop **2.** to move sideways towards the outside of a turning manoeuvre

skill /skɪl/ *noun* expertise, an excellent ability in something ○ *Skill in accurate flying can only be achieved by constant practice.*

skin /skɪn/ *noun* the outer layer of a body, or the outer layer of an aircraft ○ *The aircraft skin is riveted to stringers and frames.*

skip distance /ˈskɪp ˌdɪstəns/ *noun* the shortest distance at which a sky wave can be received ○ *The higher the layer in which a direct wave signal is totally refracted and returns as a sky wave, the greater the skip distance.*

skiplane /ˈskiːpleɪn/ *noun* an aircraft equipped with skis for taking off from and landing on snow

sky /skaɪ/ *noun* the atmosphere and outer space as seen from the earth ○ *The higher the sun is in the sky, the more intense is the radiation per unit area.*

skyjack /ˈskaɪdʒæk/ *verb* to use force to take illegal control of an aircraft, especially a commercial aircraft, when it is in the air

sky wave /ˈskaɪ weɪv/ *noun* part of a radiated wave which is returned to Earth by refraction from the ionosphere

skyway /ˈskaɪweɪ/ *noun* a route used by aircraft

skywriting /ˈskaɪraɪtɪŋ/ *noun* **1.** the use of an aircraft releasing coloured smoke to form letters in the sky **2.** letters or a message formed in the sky by coloured smoke released from an aircraft

slack /slæk/ *adjective* **1.** not tight □ **a slack cable** a loose cable **2.** not busy ○ *Early afternoon is a slack period of the day.* **3.** widely spaced ○ *Throughout the tropics and sub-tropics, where pressure gradients are normally slack, the sea breeze is a regular feature.* ○ *Land and* *sea breezes occur in coastal areas when there is a slack pressure gradient.*

slant /slɑːnt/ *noun* a slope or inclination ○ *Distance Measuring Equipment (DME) is a radio aid which measures aircraft slant range to a ground beacon.* ■ *verb* to slope ○ *The wing slants upwards from the root to the tip.*

slat /slæt/ *noun* a movable device on the leading edge of a wing which, when extended, creates a gap that allows air to pass smoothly over the top of the wing thus reducing the possibility of a stall ○ *The Socata Rallye is one of the few light aircraft with leading edge slats.*

sleet /sliːt/ *noun* **1.** melting snow or a mixture of rain and snow falling together **2.** *US* frozen rain in the form of clear drops of ice or glaze ice covering surface objects (NOTE: Care should be taken to avoid any ambiguity.) ■ *verb* to fall in the form of sleet ○ *It is sleeting.*

slide /slaɪd/ *noun* a device which allows continuous movement over a smooth surface ■ *verb* to move continuously over a smooth surface ○ *Shear stress is the stress that resists the force tending to cause one layer of a material to slide over an adjacent layer.* (NOTE: **sliding – slid**)

slide raft /ˈslaɪd rɑːft/ *noun* an escape slide which, when detached from the aircraft, can be used as a life-raft

slide rule /ˈslaɪd ruːl/ *noun* a graduated device with sliding parts for performing complex mathematical operations

slight /slaɪt/ *adjective* small, minor □ **a slight increase** a small increase □ **a slight drop in temperature** a small decrease in temperature

slip /slɪp/ *noun* a condition of uncoordinated flight when the aircraft moves towards the inside of a turn ○ *Slip is indicated by deflection of the ball in the turn and slip indicator.* ■ *verb* to move sideways towards the inside of a turning manoeuvre as a result of excessive bank (NOTE: **slipping – slipped**)

COMMENT: To correct a slip, the pilot should decrease the bank, or increase rudder pressure on the same side as the deflected ball in the turn coordinator. Slips are often used in aircraft with no flaps to increase the rate of descent without increasing the airspeed.

slippery /ˈslɪp(ə)ri/ *adjective* which is difficult to grip firmly because of wetness, smoothness, etc. ○ *a slippery surface such as a wet or snow-covered runway*

slipring /ˈslɪprɪŋ/ a metal ring in a generator to which current is delivered by the brushes

slipstream /ˈslɪpstriːm/ *noun* the flow of air sent backwards by an aircraft's propeller

slope /sləʊp/ *noun* **1.** a slanting surface or slanting piece of ground, an incline ○ *A slope of the runway may increase or decrease the take-off and landing runs.* **2.** a state in which one end of an aircraft is higher than the other ■ *verb* to be inclined, to be at an angle ○ *When the runway slopes upwards, away from the aircraft, the approach may appear to be higher than it actually is.*

slot /slɒt/ *noun* **1.** a groove or channel into which something can be fitted ○ *The float engages with a slot cut in the tube, so that, as the fuel level changes, the float moves up and down.* **2.** the particular time at which an aircraft is scheduled to depart ○ *Flight GF 506 missed its slot and will have to wait 45 minutes for another.*

sm *abbreviation* statute mile

smog /smɒg/ *noun* a mixture of smoke and fog ○ *Smog is now rare because of pollution control.*

smoke /sməʊk/ *noun* a white, grey or black product formed of small particles given off by something which is burning ○ *The weather associated with visibility reductions by particles suspended in the atmosphere is classified either as fog, mist, haze or smoke.* ■ *verb* **1.** to give off smoke ○ *Somebody noticed that one of the engines was smoking.* **2.** to breathe in smoke from a cigarette, cigar, etc. ○ *Passengers are not allowed to smoke in the toilets.*

smoke alarm /ˈsməʊk əˌlɑːm/ *noun* a warning system that will ring or light up if there is smoke somewhere ○ *Wash-rooms are fitted with smoke alarms.*

smoking /'sməʊkɪŋ/ *noun* the act of breathing in smoke from a cigarette, cigar, etc. □ **the airline has a no-smoking policy** the airline does not allow passengers to smoke during a flight

smooth /smuːð/ *adjective* **1.** even and without lumps or dents ○ *a smooth surface* **2.** not rough or turbulent ○ *High ground will disturb the smooth, horizontal flow of air.* Opposite **rough** □ **a smooth running engine** an engine which is operating well

SMR *abbreviation* surface movement radar

snap roll /'snæp rəʊl/ *noun* a manoeuvre in which an aircraft turns a complete circle longitudinally while maintaining altitude and direction of flight

snow /snəʊ/ *noun* atmospheric water vapour frozen into ice crystals and falling to Earth as white flakes ○ *Snow cover tends to persist on north-facing slopes of mountainous regions after it has melted on south-facing slopes.*

snowfall /'snəʊfɔːl/ *noun* a quantity of snow which comes down at any one time ○ *a heavy snowfall*

snowflake /'snəʊfleɪk/ *noun* a small piece of snow formed from a number of ice crystals ○ *The size of a snowflake depends on the temperature.*

snow plough /'snəʊ plaʊ/ *noun* a vehicle built to push the snow from roads, tarmac, etc.

snowstorm /'snəʊstɔːm/ *noun* a heavy fall of snow accompanied by wind ○ *The airport is closed because of the snowstorm.*

soft /sɒft/ *adjective* not hard ○ *Thermoplastic materials become soft when heated.*

soften /'sɒf(ə)n/ *verb* to make soft ○ *Thermoplastic materials are softened by many aircraft fluids.*

solar /'səʊlə/ *adjective* referring to the sun

solar-powered /'səʊlə ˌpaʊəd/ *adjective* powered by energy derived from the suns rays

'...a 210–240-foot wingspan solar-powered aircraft for flight at 100,000 feet, is being designed in California' [*Pilot*]

solar radiation /ˌsəʊlə ˌreɪdi'eɪʃ(ə)n/ *noun* the total electromagnetic radiation given off by the sun

solar system /'səʊlə ˌsɪstəm/ *noun* the sun and the planets governed by the sun

sole /səʊl/ *adjective* only ○ *the sole survivor of the air crash*

solenoid /'sɒlənɔɪd/ *noun* a cylindrical coil of wire acting as a magnet when carrying electric current ○ *Fuel is metered from the aircraft fuel system by a solenoid-operated control valve.*

solid /'sɒlɪd/ *adjective* **1.** referring to something which is not liquid or gaseous ○ *Visibility is reduced by the presence of solid particles such as dust or sand in the atmosphere.* **2.** □ **solid line** unbroken line ■ *noun* a substance which is not a liquid or a gas ○ *Ice is a solid, water is a liquid and vapour is a gas.*

solid-state /'sɒlɪd steɪt/ *adjective* referring to semiconductor devices

solid-state device /ˌsɒlɪd steɪt dɪ'vaɪs/ *noun* an electronic device that operates by using the effects of electrical or magnetic signals in a solid semiconductor material

solid-state technology /ˌsɒlɪd steɪt tek'nɒlədʒi/ *noun* technology using the electronic properties of solids to replace those of valves

solo /'səʊləʊ/ *adverb* done by one person alone ○ *to go solo or to fly solo* ○ *He flew solo across the Atlantic.*

solution /sə'luːʃ(ə)n/ *noun* **1.** an answer to or means of solving a problem or difficulty ○ *The navigation computer or slide rule is suitable for the solution of many different types of mathematical problem.* **2.** a liquid made by dissolving a solid or gas in water or some other fluid ○ *Spillage from a lead acid battery may be neutralised by washing with a dilute solution of sodium bicarbonate.*

solve /sɒlv/ *verb* to find the answer to, or a way of removing, a difficulty or problem ○ *The triangle of velocities is used to solve navigation problems.*

somewhat /'sʌmwɒt/ *adverb* to some extent, a bit ○ *The usefulness of pure aluminium as a structural material is somewhat limited.*

sonic /'sɒnɪk/ *adjective* **1.** referring to sound **2.** within the human hearing range □ **sonic speed** the speed of sound

sonic boom /ˌsɒnɪk 'buːm/ *noun* a noise, due to shock waves, produced when an aircraft travels through the air faster than the speed of sound

sophisticated /sə'fɪstɪkeɪtɪd/ *adjective* highly developed and complex ○ *The electronic flight instrument system, commonly known as EFIS, is a highly sophisticated type of flight director system.* ○ *The A340 is a sophisticated aeroplane.*

sortie /'sɔːti/ *noun* an operational flight by one aircraft ○ *The test programme has accumulated 1,146 sorties.*

sound /saʊnd/ *adjective* strong ○ *A stressed skin structure is used on modern aircraft which gives a sound structure with relatively low weight.* ■ *noun* something that can be heard and is caused by vibration of the surrounding air ○ *FM (frequency modulation) gives a wide range of sounds or a very high data rate.* ■ *verb* **1.** to make a noise ○ *If the trim position is incorrect, a warning horn will sound when number three thrust lever is advanced for take off.* ◊ **sonic 2.** to seem ○ *It sounds as if the pilot is having trouble.*

source /sɔːs/ *noun* a supply ○ *Under emergency conditions, the battery may be the only source of electrical power.* ○ *Jet aircraft have a ready source of compressed air from the compressor sections of their engines.*

south /saʊθ/ *noun* a compass point on the mariner's compass 180° clockwise from due north and directly opposite north ○ *Fly towards the south.* □ **south facing mountain side** the face of a mountain which looks towards the south ■ *adjective* **1.** referring to areas or regions lying in the south, referring to the compass point 180° from north ○ *the south side of the river* **2.** the southern part of a region or country ○ *South America* ○ *South Dakota* ■ *adverb*

towards the south ○ *The aircraft is flying south.*

southbound /'saʊθbaʊnd/ *adjective* travelling towards the south ○ *a southbound flight*

south-east /ˌsaʊθ 'iːst/ *noun* the direction between south and east ○ *a region in the south-east of Canada* ■ *adjective* **1.** situated in the south-east ○ *the south-east coast of England* **2.** blowing from or coming from the south-east ■ *adverb* towards the south-east ○ *We were heading south-east.*

south-easterly /ˌsaʊθ 'iːstəli/ *adjective* **1.** blowing from or coming from the south-east ○ *a south-easterly wind* **2.** moving towards the south-east ○ *We were following a south-easterly direction.*

south-eastern /ˌsaʊθ 'iːstən/ *adjective* referring to or situated in the south-east ○ *the south-eastern coast of Spain*

southerly /'sʌðəli/ *adjective* **1.** situated towards the south ○ *the most southerly point of a country* **2.** coming from the south ○ *A southerly wind was blowing.* **3.** moving to or towards the south ○ *We were flying in a southerly direction.* ■ *noun* a wind which blows from the south

southern /'sʌð(ə)n/ *adjective* situated in the south ○ *the southern hemisphere* ○ *the southern Atlantic*

southern hemisphere /ˌsʌð(ə)n 'hemɪsfɪə/ *noun* the area of the Earth to the south of the equator

South Pole /ˌsaʊθ 'pəʊl/ *noun* the point which is furthest south on the earth ○ *to fly over the South Pole*

southward /'saʊθwəd/ *adjective* going towards the south ○ *to go in a southward direction* ■ *adverb US* same as **southwards**

southwards /'saʊθwədz/ *adverb* towards the south ○ *The aircraft was flying southwards.*

south-west /ˌsaʊθ 'west/ *noun* the direction between south and west ○ *a region in the south-west of France* ■ *adjective* **1.** situated in the south-west ○ *the south-west tip of England* **2.** blowing from or coming from the south-west

■ *adverb* towards the south-west ○ *We were heading south-west.*

south-westerly /ˌsaʊθ ˈwestəli/ *adjective* **1.** blowing from or coming from the south-west ○ *a south-westerly wind* **2.** moving towards the south-west ○ *We were following a south-westerly direction.*

south-western /ˌsaʊθ ˈwestən/ *adjective* referring to or situated in the south-west ○ *The south-western corner of England includes Cornwall and Devon.*

south wind /ˌsaʊθ ˈwɪnd/ *noun* a wind blowing from or coming from the south (NOTE: A wind is named after the direction it comes from.)

space /speɪs/ *noun* **1.** an empty area ○ *A major problem with fuel storage is finding space within the airframe.* **2.** the physical universe outside the Earth's atmosphere ○ *VHF (very high frequency) waves tend to pass through the layers of the ionosphere into space.*

span /spæn/ *noun* the distance between two points

spar /spɑː/ *noun* the main longitudinal beam of an aircraft wing ○ *Designing a wing skin, a rib or a spar as a single big item rather than assembling it from many smaller components minimises the number of structural parts.*

spark /spɑːk/ *noun* a light produced by a sudden electrical discharge ■ *verb* to suddenly start a process or action ○ *Crew must quickly establish control to ensure panic does not spark a premature evacuation.*

spark plug /ˈspɑːk plʌg/, **sparking plug** /ˈspɑːkɪŋ ˈplʌg/ *noun* a device screwed into each cylinder head in spark ignition engines, which initiates fuel combustion by an electric spark. ◊ **air gap.** Also called **sparking plug**

spat /spæt/ *noun* a streamlined covering for a wheel fitted on a light aircraft to reduce drag. Also called **wheel fairing**

spatial disorientation *noun* a situation of bad visibility and/or unusual manoeuvres which result in the pilot not knowing what attitude the aircraft is in

speaker /ˈspiːkə/ *noun* ♦ **loudspeaker**

special /ˈspeʃ(ə)l/ *adjective* particular, specific, or not ordinary ○ *To make a composite, it is necessary to combine the reinforcing glass fibres with some form of special glue.* ■ *noun* a special meteorological report

special aerodrome report /ˌspeʃ(ə)l ˈeərədrəʊm rɪˌpɔːt/ *noun* report used if there are significant weather changes since the last meteorological aerodrome report. Abbreviation **SAR**

special VFR flight *noun* a controlled VFR flight permitted by air traffic control to fly within a control zone in meteorological conditions below visual meteorological conditions

specific /spəˈsɪfɪk/ *adjective* clearly defined and definite ○ *Flight levels are specific pressure altitudes.* ○ *The airframe has to be built to very specific requirements.*

specification /ˌspesɪfɪˈkeɪʃ(ə)n/ *noun* a detailed description that sets out what something consists of, what is needed, what is involved, etc. ○ *Fluids are coloured for recognition purposes and fluids of different specifications must never be mixed.*

specific gravity /spəˌsɪfɪk ˈgrævɪti/ *noun* the density of a substance compared with that of water, which is 1.00 (NOTE: This is the old name for **relative density**.)

specify /ˈspesɪfaɪ/ *verb* to name in detail ○ *The minimum values for decision heights are specified by the national licensing authorities for various types of aircraft and for various airports.* ○ *Pressure must be maintained within specified limits during all phases of flight.*

specimen /ˈspesɪmɪn/ *noun* a part taken as an example of the whole ○ *By testing specimen structures and components to destruction a safe life can be assessed for all such structures and components.*

speed /spiːd/ *noun* the rate of motion over a distance in time

sphere /sfɪə/ *noun* an object in the shape of a ball ○ *The Earth is not a perfect sphere.* ○ *A circle drawn on the surface of a sphere, whose plane passes through the centre of the sphere is called a great circle.*

spherical /'sferɪk(ə)l/ *adjective* shaped like a sphere ○ *The Earth is almost spherical in shape.* ○ *Drain cocks are generally simple, manually operated spherical valves.*

spill /spɪl/ *noun* the running out of a liquid from a container, especially when it is unintentional ○ *an oil spill* ○ *a fuel spill* ■ *verb* to cause liquid to run out of a container, usually unintentionally ○ *If fuel is spilt, it creates a fire hazard.* (NOTE: **spilling – spilled** or **spilt**)

spillage /'spɪlɪdʒ/ *noun* the spilling of a liquid ○ *Any fuel spillage must be cleaned up immediately.* (NOTE: The word **spillage** is used in a more general sense than the word **spill**.)

spin /spɪn/ *noun* **1.** fast rotation ○ *the spin axis of the earth* **2.** the continued spiral descent of an aircraft where the angle of attack of one wing is greater than the stalling angle ■ *verb* **1.** to rotate rapidly ○ *The Earth is spinning on its axis.* **2.** to put an aircraft into a continued spiral descent with the angle of attack of the mainplane greater than the stalling angle ○ *It is prohibited to spin general-purpose light aircraft which are not equipped with a suitable harness.*

COMMENT: The Moroccan aerobatic team 'La Marche Verte' perform a formation manoeuvre with three aircraft spinning through multiple rotations while inverted.

spindle /'spɪnd(ə)l/ *noun* a pin or bar which rotates or on which something rotates ○ *A cup anemometer has three cups, mounted on a spindle, that are driven by the wind causing the spindle to rotate.*

spine /spaɪn/ *noun* the longitudinal central part of an engine ○ *Annular inner and outer air casings form a tunnel around the spine of the engine.*

spinner /'spɪnə/ *noun* a cap that fits over the hub of the propeller of an aircraft

spiral /'spaɪrəl/ *adjective* winding continuously in circles as it ascends or descends

spiral dive /ˌspaɪrəl 'daɪv/ *noun* a dangerous uncontrolled turning descent of an aircraft in which rate of descent and speed increase

spline /splaɪn/ *noun* a groove in a shaft for meshing or engaging with another component

split /splɪt/ *noun* **1.** a division **2.** a break along a line, especially in wood, plastic or rubber ○ *a split in a tyre* ■ *verb* **1.** to divide ○ *Retractable undercarriages can be split into three groups.* **2.** to break along a line ○ *One of the tyres split on impact.* (NOTE: **splitting – split**) ■ *adjective* divided or broken along a line

split bus system /ˌsplɪt 'bʌs ˌsɪstəm/ *noun* an electrical system in which there are two separate power generation systems ○ *The parallel system and the split bus system are both used to distribute electrical power.*

spoiler /'spɔɪlə/ *noun* a hinged surface on the upper wing which, when opened, decreases lift and increases drag ○ *If a problem occurs in the spoiler system a master caution light illuminates.*

COMMENT: Spoilers are sometimes called 'speed brakes'. They are used during the descent prior to landing and immediately after landing to decrease lift and increase braking effect.

sponson /'spɒnsən/ *noun* an air-filled structure or small wing projecting from the lower hull of a seaplane to keep it steady on water

spontaneous /spɒn'teɪniəs/ *adjective* happening without external cause ○ *Spontaneous ignition may occur if oxygen is allowed to come into contact with oil or grease.*

spool /spuːl/ *noun* one complete axial-compressor rotor ○ *The single spool compressor consists of one rotor assembly and stators.* ■ *verb* □ **to spool down** to allow the revolutions of a turbofan engine to decrease □ **to spool up** to increase the revolutions per minute of a turbofan engine

spot /spɒt/ *noun* **1.** a special or small place ○ *Charts should be kept in a convenient spot in the cockpit.* **2.** a small roundish mark or piece ○ *a spot of oil on a shirt* □ **spot height** the height of a particular place, e.g. a mountain peak, marked on a chart

spotlight /'spɒtlaɪt/ *noun* a powerful, often moveable light which illuminates a small area ○ *A spotlight is mounted on the roof.*

spray /spreɪ/ *noun* **1.** a body of liquid in fine drops ○ *The generator is cooled by oil spray delivered by the constant speed drive section.* **2.** a container that sends out liquid in fine drops ■ *verb* to apply or to send out liquid in the form of fine drops ○ *Some engines have the coolant sprayed directly into the compressor inlet, but for axial flow compressor engines, it is more suitable to spray the coolant into the combustion chamber inlet.*

spread /spred/ *noun* an extension of the area covered or affected by something ○ *Measures are taken to prevent the spread of fire.* ■ *verb* to extend the area of something ○ *Strong jets of water should not be used on a liquid fire as this may cause the fire to spread.* ○ *The system sprays a quantity of fluid onto the windscreen, which is then spread by the wipers.* (NOTE: **spreading** – **spread**)

spring /sprɪŋ/ *noun* **1.** a metal device which, when under tension, tries to resume its previous position ○ *The pitch lock piston is held in the forward position by a spring.* **2.** the season between winter and summer

squall /skwɔːl/ *noun* a sudden increase in wind speed lasting for several minutes ○ *Surface squalls are due to the spreading out of strong down draughts at the surface.* ○ *Even with a light mean wind speed, squalls of 50 kt (knots) or more can occur with sudden changes in direction.*

square /skweə/ *noun* a shape with 4 equal sides and 4 right angles ■ *adjec-*

tive shaped like a square ○ *a square panel*

square foot /ˌskweə 'fʊt/ *noun* a unit of measurement of area, which is one foot long by one foot wide

square metre /ˌskweə 'miːtə/ *noun* a unit of measurement of area, which is one metre long by one metre wide ○ *The room is 5m x 9m so the area is 45 square metres (45m²).*

square root /ˌskweə 'ruːt/ *noun* divider of a quantity that, when multiplied by itself, gives the quantity ○ *3 is the square root of 9.*

squawk /skwɔːk/ *noun* an identification code. ◊ **transponder** ■ *verb* to activate specific modes, codes or functions on a transponder ○ *Garbling occurs when two signals are received simultaneously and can be resolved either technically or by making one of the aircraft squawk.*

squeeze /skwiːz/ *verb* to press hard from opposite directions ○ *Static seals, gaskets and packing are used in many locations, and these effect a seal by being squeezed between two surfaces.*

SR *abbreviation* sunrise

SS *abbreviation* sunset

SSR *abbreviation* secondary surveillance radar

stabilise /'steɪbəlaɪz/, **stabilize** *verb* to become steady and unchanging ○ *After the engine has been started, engine speed is increased to 1,000 r.p.m. (revolutions per minute) until cylinder head and oil temperatures have stabilised at normal operating temperatures.*

stabiliser /'steɪbɪlaɪzə/, **stabilizer** *noun* a device to improve the tendency of an aircraft to return to its original attitude after being deflected

COMMENT: Some aircraft have an all-moving tailplane called a 'stabilator' (a combination of the words **stabiliser** and **elevator**).

stabilitator /stə'bɪlɪteɪtə/ *noun* ♦ **stabiliser**

stability /stə'bɪlɪti/ *noun* **1.** being stable or steady ○ *The stability of the Cessna 150 makes it an ideal training air-*

craft. **2.** a state of the atmosphere in which air will resist vertical displacement ○ *When air moves away from its source region, the stability of the lower atmosphere changes.*

COMMENT: Stability can be classified as three types. **Positive stability** is the tendency of a body to return to its original state after being displaced. Light training aircraft have positive stability. **Neutral stability** is the tendency of a body to remain in the new position after displacement. **Negative stability** is the tendency of a body to continue moving away from its original position after displacement.

stability augmentation system
/stə,bɪlɪti ,ɔːgmən'teɪʃ(ə)n ,sɪstəm/ *noun* a flight control system which automatically adjusts pitch and yaw to improve an aircraft's stability. Abbreviation **SAS**

stable /'steɪb(ə)l/ *adjective* **1.** steady **2.** referring to an atmosphere in which there is little or no vertical movement ○ *Layer cloud occurs in a stable atmosphere.*

stack /stæk/ *verb* **1.** to put one on top of the other ○ *By stacking rows of horizontal dipoles one above the other, a well-defined electronic glide path can be transmitted.* **2.** to keep aircraft circling at different heights while they are waiting to land at an airport ■ *noun* a number of aircraft waiting to land at an airport that are circling at different heights

stacked /stækt/ *adjective* circling at different heights prior to landing

stackup /'stækʌp/ *noun* same as **stack**

stage /steɪdʒ/ *noun* **1.** one of several sections, steps, or levels into which a process can be divided ○ *There are three stages in the life cycle of a thunderstorm: process of formation, development and decay.* ○ *Calculate headings to steer for each stage of the flight.* □ **cruise stage of the flight** the section of a flight between top of climb after take-off and start of descent to land □ **at a later stage** at a later time **2.** a group components forming part of an electrical or electronic system ○ *In the axial*

flow compressor, many stages of moving and stationary blades are needed, each row of rotors and a row of stators forming a stage.

stagger /'stægə/ *noun* a design in which the leading edge of one wing of a biplane projects beyond that of the other wing ■ *verb* to make the leading edge of one wing of a biplane project beyond the leading edge of the other wing

stall /stɔːl/ *noun* **1.** a loss of lift caused by the breakdown of airflow over the wing when the angle of attack passes a critical point ○ *In some configurations it is possible for the buffet speed to be less than the required 7% margin ahead of the stall.* **2.** a situation in which an engine or machine stops suddenly because an opposing force overcomes its driving power ○ *Compressor stall can be caused by ice formation in the air intake.* ◊ **recovery** ■ *verb* to lose lift by the breakdown of airflow over the wing when the angle of attack passes a critical point ○ *Many light aircraft stall when the angle of attack exceeds 15°.* ◊ **recover**

COMMENT: A stall has nothing to do with the engine stopping. An aircraft can stall at any airspeed and in any attitude.

stalling angle /'stɔːlɪŋ ,æŋg(ə)l/ *noun* the angle relative to the horizontal at which the flow of air around an aerofoil changes abruptly, resulting in significant changes in the lift and drag of an aircraft

stalling speed /'stɔːlɪŋ spiːd/ *noun* the speed at which the angle of attack is such that lift over the wing surface breaks down

COMMENT: Traditionally, an aircraft can stall at any airspeed, providing the angle of attack is great enough. Stalling speed is often used to refer to the speed below which the aircraft cannot remain airborne.

stall warning system /,stɔːl 'wɔːnɪŋ ,sɪstəm/ *noun* a system to warn the pilot that the aircraft is about to stall

standard /'stændəd/ *noun* something, e.g. a quality or measure, that is officially recognised as an example that others must conform with ○ *Water is the standard for determining relative density.* □ **a high standard of skill** a high level of skill ∎ *adjective* normal, officially or generally accepted □ **standard procedure** normal procedure

standard atmosphere /ˌstændəd 'ætməsfɪə/ *noun* a unit of pressure defined as the pressure that will support a 760 mm column of mercury at 0°C at sea level, equal to 1.01325×10^5 newtons per square metre

standard instrument departure /ˌstændən ˌɪnstrʊmənt dɪ'pɑːtʃə/ *noun* a published navigational chart showing the route an aircraft must take as it takes off and climbs away from an airport. Abbreviation **SID**

standard parallels /ˌstændəd 'pærəlelz/ *plural noun* (*in a conical projection*) the parallels of latitude where the cone cuts the surface

standard pressure setting /ˌstændəd 'preʃə ˌsetɪŋ/ *noun* 1013.25 millibars. Abbreviation **SPS**

standard rate turn /ˌstændəd reɪt 'tɜːn/ *noun* a turn made at a precise number of compass degrees per second

COMMENT: Rate 1 turn = 180 ° in 1 minute, Rate 2 turn = 360 ° in 1 minute, Rate 3 turn = 540 ° in 1 minute, Rate 4 turn = 720 ° in 1 minute. Standard rate turns are made using particular angles of bank for specific airspeeds and are used while flying under Instrument Flight Rules (IFR). The pilot can make accurate turns to given headings by banking at the standard rate and timing the turn.

standard time /'stændəd taɪm/ *noun* a universally adopted time for all countries based on zone time

standby /'stændbaɪ/ *adjective* secondary, able to be used as a back-up ○ *Some aircraft use a ram air turbine that can be very useful as a standby power source in the event of failure of a complete main AC (alternating current) generating system.*

standby ticket /'stændbaɪ ˌtɪkɪt/ *noun* a cheaper air ticket bought just before departure time ○ *There are no standby tickets to Montreal.*

standing agreement /ˌstændɪŋ ə'griːmənt/ *noun* an agreement between controlling units in different flight information regions to allow the transfer of control from one sector to the next without individual coordination, provided agreed parameters are met

standing wave /'stændɪŋ weɪv/ *noun* the motion of air downwind of a steep hill or mountain in which the high and low points of the wave do not move

STAR *abbreviation* standard arrival route

starboard /'stɑːbəd/ *noun, adjective* the right-hand side of an aircraft when facing forwards when inside the aircraft ○ *The angle between heading and track of an aircraft is called drift and is expressed in degrees to the port or starboard side of aircraft heading.* Opposite **port**

starter /'stɑːtə/ *noun* a device to start an engine

starter motor /'stɑːtə ˌməʊtə/ *noun* in a piston engine, a small electrically operated device to turn the engine until ignition starts

start-up /'stɑːt ʌp/ *noun* a procedure to start an engine ○ *After start-up, the engine accelerates up to idling speed.*

state /steɪt/ *noun* the existing condition of something ○ *a state of equilibrium* ○ *Ice in a liquid state is called water.* ○ *Water in a gaseous state is known as vapour.* ○ *A logic gate is a two-state device i.e. on/off.* □ **in a poor state** in a bad condition ∎ *verb* to say or to mention, or to give information clearly ○ *It states in the information that you must not open the can near a flame.* ○ *Please state your name and address.*

statement /'steɪtmənt/ *noun* something formally expressed in words ○ *After the crash, the president and chief executive of the company made a brief statement to the waiting news reporters.*

static /'stætɪk/ *adjective* not acting, not changing, passive or not moving ∎ *noun* the background noise during radio transmission

static display /ˈstætɪk dɪˌspleɪ/
noun a display of parked aircraft on the
ground

static electricity /ˌstætɪk ˌɪlek
ˈtrɪsɪti/ *noun* electricity not flowing as
a current ○ *When the aircraft travels
through the air, friction causes a charge
of static electricity to be built up on the
airframe.*

static ground running /ˌstætɪk
ˈɡraʊnd ˌrʌnɪŋ/ *noun* the running of
the engine while the aircraft is stationary on the ground

static line /ˌstætɪk ˈlaɪn/ *noun* a rope
attached to an aircraft and a parachute
that automatically opens the parachute
when the parachutist jumps

static port /ˈstætɪk pɔːt/ *noun* a
small hole in the side of the aircraft
which senses static pressure and is used
in the operation of the altimeter, vertical
speed indicator and airspeed indicator ○
Ensure that the static port is clear.

static pressure /ˌstætɪk ˈpreʃə/
noun the pressure of a fluid acting on
and moving with a body

station /ˈsteɪʃ(ə)n/ *noun* **1.** a particular assigned location ○ *The interphone
system allows the flight deck to communicate with cabin crew stations.* **2.** the
location of a radio transmitter ○ *a VOR
station*

stationary /ˈsteɪʃ(ə)n(ə)ri/ *adjective*
not moving ○ *The aircraft was stationary on the ground with engine running.*

stator /ˈsteɪtə/ *noun* a fixed part of a
rotary machine ○ *The low-pressure
compressor has large rotor blades and
stator blades and is designed to handle
a far larger airflow than the other two
compressors.* ○ *A temperature probe is
embedded into the stator of the generator and a meter is provided, so that generator stator temperature can be monitored.*

status /ˈsteɪtəs/ *noun* condition ○ *The
centre-zero ammeter tells the pilot the
status of the aircraft battery.*

statute mile /ˈstætʃuːt maɪl/ *noun* a
non-SI unit of length equalling 1.609
kilometres ○ *It is 20 statute miles to the
airport.* Abbreviation **sm**

STC *abbreviation* supplemental type
certificate

STCA *abbreviation* short-term conflict
alert

steady /ˈstedi/ *adjective* constant and
unchanging ○ *The manual test will give
a steady red light.* □ **a steady wind** a
wind of constant speed and direction

steam fog /ˈstiːm fɒɡ/ *noun* fog
formed when cold air moves over relatively warm water ○ *Visibility was
impaired because of steam fog.*

steel /stiːl/ *noun* a metal alloy of iron,
carbon and other compounds □ **stainless steel** steel containing chromium
and nickel that is highly resistant to corrosion ○ *Tubing in parts of the system
containing fluid at high pressure are
usually made from stainless steel.*

steep /stiːp/ *adjective* **1.** sloping
sharply □ **a steep angle of approach**
the angle formed by the aircraft
approach flight path and the horizontal
is greater than usual **2.** closely spaced **3.**
referring to marked changes in pressure
or temperature in a relatively short horizontal distance ○ *Cooling of the air in
contact with the ground at night can
cause a very steep inversion of temperature at the surface.* ○ *Pressure gradients in anti-cyclonic curvature tend not
to be steep.*

steer /stɪə/ *verb* to direct by using a
wheel or control stick ○ *The aircraft is
steered on the ground by using the rudder pedals.*

steering /ˈstɪərɪŋ/ *noun* **1.** guiding or
directing ○ *Steering is controlled by
rudder pedals.* **2.** a system for guiding
or directing a car, aircraft, etc. ○ *Most
modern light aircraft have nose-wheel
steering but older tail-draggers are
steered on the ground by using differential braking.*

step /step/ *noun* **1.** a stage ○ *The first
step in map reading is to orientate the
chart.* **2.** one stair ○ *Mind the step!*

steward /ˈstjuːəd/ *noun* a male member of airline staff who look after passengers during the flight. ◊ **cabin crew,
flight attendant, stewardess** (NOTE:
Different airlines use different terminology for their staff.)

stewardess /ˌstjuːəˈdes/ *noun* a female member of airline staff who look after passengers during the flight. ◇ **cabin crew**, **flight attendant**, **steward** (NOTE: Different airlines use different terminology for their staff.)

stick /stɪk/ *noun* the main hand control used by the pilot to control the aircraft roll and pitch ○ *Using fly-by-wire technology, the stalling angle cannot be exceeded regardless of stick input.* ■ *verb* to become fixed, as if with glue ○ *Ice crystals and snowflakes do not stick to airframes, and so icing is a problem only when super-cooled water droplets are present.*

stiff /stɪf/ *adjective* **1.** rigid or inflexible ○ *Kevlar 49 is stiffer than glass, but only about half as stiff as carbon fibres.* **2.** not easily bent or turned □ **control surfaces may become stiff as a result of icing** control surfaces may become difficult to move **3.** □ **a stiff wind** a fairly strong wind

stiffen /ˈstɪf(ə)n/ *verb* **1.** to make rigid or inflexible, to make stiff ○ *Beams can be additionally stiffened in a downward direction by vertical and diagonal members.* **2.** to become stronger

STOL /stɒl/ *noun* **1.** a flying system that allows an aircraft to take off and land on a very short runway **2.** an aircraft fitted with the STOL system. Full form **short takeoff and landing**

stop /stɒp/ *noun* **1.** the end of a movement □ **to come to a stop** to stop moving **2.** a component which limits the distance that a moving part can move ○ *An adjustable stop on the throttle control ensures a positive idling speed.*

storage /ˈstɔːrɪdʒ/ *noun* the act of storing something ○ *A reservoir provides storage space for the system fluid.*

store /stɔː/ *noun* **1.** a supply ○ *The maintenance section keeps a store of spare components.* **2.** *US* a shop ■ *verb* to put away for future use ○ *A capacitor is a device with the ability to temporarily store an electric charge.*

stores /stɔːz/ *plural noun* goods ○ *Freight carrying aircraft have supporting members of greater strength to allow for the carriage of heavy stores.*

storm /stɔːm/ *noun* a violent weather disturbance with high winds and rain or snow ○ *Storms produced by daytime heating are most frequently encountered in the afternoon and early evening.*

stow /stəʊ/ *verb* to place something in its correct position in the aircraft ○ *Make sure the fire-extinguisher is stowed.*

stowage /ˈstəʊɪdʒ/ *noun* a space for stowing things ○ *A multi-wheel combination has the advantage of smaller and lighter undercarriage structures, and wing stowage problems can be overcome by suitable mechanisms.*

stowaway /ˈstəʊəˌweɪ/ *noun* a person who travels secretly by hiding in an aircraft, or a ship, not paying the fare ○ *The crew must be alert at all times to the possibility of hijacking, bombs and stowaways.*

strain /streɪn/ *noun* deformation caused by stress

strap /stræp/ *noun* a long narrow strip of fabric with a buckle ■ *verb* □ **to strap in** to fasten a seat or safety belt around somebody

stratocumulus /ˌstrætəʊˈkjuːmjʊləs/ *noun* a layer of small cumulus clouds lower than altocumulus, i.e. below 3,000 m ○ *Light rain may fall occasionally from stratocumulus.*

stratosphere /ˈstrætəsfɪə/ *noun* the layer of the atmosphere which extends from the tropopause to about 50 km above mean sea level ○ *A cumulonimbus cloud may extend vertically, into the stratosphere.*

stratus /ˈstreɪtəs/ *noun* a low-altitude layer cloud ○ *Drizzle falls from shallow layer cloud such as stratus.*

stream /striːm/ *noun* a steady current of a fluid ○ *Thermocouple probes are positioned in the gas stream, so as to obtain a good average temperature reading.*

strength /streŋθ/ *noun* **1.** the ability of a material to take pressure or support a load ○ *Aircraft wheels require great strength and are constructed in two halves which are bolted together after the tyre is fitted.* ○ *Magnesium does not* possess sufficient strength in its pure state for structural uses, but when mixed with zinc, aluminium, and manganese it produces an alloy having the highest strength-to-weight ratio of any of the commonly used metals. □ **high-strength materials** materials which are very strong **2.** the degree of clarity and volume of a signal ○ A radio wave loses strength as range increases. **3.** the degree of dilution of a liquid ○ Incorrect mixture strength may cause detonation. **4.** intensity of radiation ○ The strength of the sun's radiation varies with latitude. **5.** the speed and force of a wind ○ High ground will disturb the smooth horizontal flow of air, with the degree of disturbance depending upon the strength of the wind and the roughness of the terrain.

strengthen /ˈstreŋθ(ə)n/ verb to make strong or stronger ○ Some alloys are hardened and strengthened by heat treatment. □ **the wind is strengthening** the wind is increasing in speed

strengthening /ˈstreŋθ(ə)nɪŋ/ noun **1.** the act of making stronger ○ Aircraft which require large apertures in the fuselage for freight doors, etc., need increased strengthening around these areas. **2.** the fact of becoming stronger ○ strengthening of the wind

stress /stres/ noun **1.** the load per unit area to which a body that resists distortion or change of shape is subjected by internal forces ○ Turbine blades in the average jet engine vibrate at frequencies of 1 million per minute, and in each cycle experience stress. **2.** a worried, anxious and tired state brought on e.g. by overwork ○ He gave stress as the reason for wanting a week off work. **3.** emphasis ■ verb to emphasise ○ It must be stressed that the description is a model and departures from it often occur.

stretch /stretʃ/ noun a continuous unbroken length ○ a stretch of coast ■ verb to extend or enlarge beyond the proper limits ○ Tensile stress or tension is the resistance of a material to being stretched.

stretching /ˈstretʃɪŋ/ noun extending or enlarging beyond the proper lim-

its ○ Tensile stress is the resistance to pulling apart, or stretching, produced when two forces in opposition act along the same straight line.

strict /strɪkt/ adjective precise, exact ○ Fuels for aircraft must conform to strict requirements. ○ All generator voltages, frequencies and their phase sequence must be within very strict limits to ensure proper system operation.

strike /straɪk/ noun an impact or collision ■ verb to hit (NOTE: **striking – struck**)

stringer /ˈstrɪŋə/ noun a thin metal or wood strip which goes from one end of the fuselage to the other ○ Stringers are made of a light alloy material.

strip /strɪp/ noun a long narrow piece, usually of the same width from end to end ○ a strip of paper ■ verb to dismantle ○ After the collision, the engine was stripped down to its component parts.

stroke /strəʊk/ noun any of a series of movements of a piston from one end of the limit of its movement to another ○ The connecting rod links the piston to the crankshaft and transmits the force of the power stroke from the piston to the crankshaft.

structural /ˈstrʌktʃ(ə)rəl/ adjective referring to the structure of something such as an aircraft ○ As laid down in the flight manual, the structural limitations must never be exceeded. □ **structural failure** a breaking of part of the aircraft structure

structure /ˈstrʌktʃə/ noun **1.** something constructed ○ Aircraft structure serves the same purpose for an aircraft as the skeleton for a human body. **2.** framework

strut /strʌt/ noun a bar or rod used to strengthen a structure against forces from the side ○ A strut is designed to withstand compressive loads.

stub /stʌb/ noun a short rectangular extension ○ The plan-form of a military air traffic zone is in the shape of a circle with a stub.

sub- /sʌb/ prefix **1.** of less importance in rank **2.** below

sub-beam /ˈsʌb biːm/ noun a less important or minor beam ○ A lobe is one *of two, four or more sub-beams that form a directional radar beam.*

subject /'sʌbdʒɪkt/ *noun* a topic or matter for discussion or study ○ *A knowledge and understanding of the subject of ice accretion is essential in order that the hazard can be minimised.*

subjected /səb'dʒektɪd/ *adjective* □ **subjected to** affected by or made to experience something ○ *To maintain the pressure difference between two internal engine sections, which are subjected to air pressures of different value, a multi-air seal is used.* (NOTE: There is an important difference between **subject to** and **subjected to**.)

subject to /sʌb'dʒekt tuː/ *adjective* likely to be affected by, liable to ○ *The airspeed indicator is subject to error.* ○ *Turbine engines are subject to icing during flight through super-cooled droplet cloud.* ■ *verb* □ **to subject to** to make something or somebody experience something, often something unpleasant ○ *The aircraft was subjected to rigorous tests.*

sublimate /'sʌblɪmeɪt/ *verb* to transform directly from the solid to the gaseous state or from the gaseous to the solid state without becoming a liquid ○ *For hoar frost to form on an aircraft the airframe temperature must be below 0°C (Celsius), so that the surrounding air is cooled to below its dew point and water vapour in contact with the aircraft skin is directly sublimated into ice crystals.*

sublimation /ˌsʌblɪ'meɪʃ(ə)n/ *noun* transformation directly from the solid to the gaseous state or from the gaseous to the solid state without becoming a liquid ○ *In sub-zero conditions sublimation will occur when air is cooled below the frost point, producing a deposit of ice crystals.*

sub-scale /'sʌb skeɪl/ *noun* a secondary, not main, scale on an instrument ○ *The barometric pressure is set on the sub-scale and the altimeter main scale displays height or altitude.*

subsequent /'sʌbsɪkwənt/ *adjective* following in time or order ○ *A structural prototype is put through cycles of stressing far more severe than can be expected during the aircraft's subsequent operational life.* □ **a subsequent occasion** a following occasion

subside /səb'saɪd/ *verb* **1.** to sink to a lower level ○ *Cool air subsides.* **2.** to become less active or strong □ **the storm subsided** the storm grew quiet

subsidence /'sʌbsɪd(ə)ns/ *noun* the act of sinking to a lower level ○ *Descending air occurs because of subsidence in the high pressure belts of the sub-tropics and poles.*

subsonic /sʌb'sɒnɪk/ *adjective* flying at speeds slower than the speed of sound, or not designed to fly above the speed of sound

substance /'sʌbstəns/ *noun* a material of a particular sort ○ *Specific heat is the amount of heat required to raise the temperature of a substance by 1°C (Celsius) compared to the amount of heat required to raise the temperature of water by 1°C.*

substantial /səb'stænʃəl/ *adjective* considerable, important □ **substantial damage** a lot of damage □ **substantial increase** a big increase

subtend /səb'tend/ *verb* to be opposite to and delimit ○ *The angle subtended by an arc equal to one 360th part of the circumference of a circle is called 1° (degree).*

subtract /səb'trækt/ *verb* to deduct or to take away ○ *6 subtracted from 10 equals 4 (10 − 6 = 4).*

subtraction /səb'trækʃən/ *noun* the operation of taking away or deducting ○ *The major arithmetic operations are addition, subtraction, multiplication and division.*

subtropical /sʌb'trɒpɪk(ə)l/ *adjective* referring to the areas between the tropics and the temperate zone ○ *In winter, the subtropical high retreats and gives way to cyclonic pressure patterns.*

sub-zero /ˌsʌb 'zɪərəʊ/ *adjective* below zero degrees ○ *In sub-zero conditions sublimation will occur when air is cooled below the frost point, producing a deposit of ice crystals.*

success /sək'ses/ *noun* the achievement of something wanted ○ *The key to* *success in navigation is pre-flight planning.*

successful /sək'sesf(ə)l/ *adjective* satisfactory, as wanted ○ *His second attempt at landing was successful.*

succession /sək'seʃ(ə)n/ *noun* the process of following in a particular order ○ *A succession of minor incidents created a more serious situation.*

successive /sək'sesɪv/ *adjective* following one after the other without interruption ○ *All aircraft remained grounded for three successive days because of fog.* ○ *A day is the period between successive transits of a meridian by the sun.*

such /sʌtʃ/ *adjective* **1.** of this kind ○ *An example of such a chart is shown on page 3.* **2.** of a large enough extent or amount ○ *The height of the cabin floor to the ground on large jet transports is such that serious injuries can occur by exiting through the doors when steps or ramps are not available.*

suction /'sʌkʃən/ *noun* a force that causes a fluid or solid to be drawn into a space because of the difference between the external and internal pressures ○ *In a fuel injection system, fuel is induced into the inlet port or combustion chamber by a pump rather than the suction caused by the venturi of a carburettor.*

sudden /'sʌd(ə)n/ *adjective* immediate and without warning ○ *a sudden change* or *sudden drop in temperature*

suffer /'sʌfə/, **suffer from** *verb* to be affected by, to experience ○ *Piston engines suffer from icing in moist air when the ambient air temperature is well above 0°C (Celsius).*

sufficient /sə'fɪʃ(ə)nt/ *adjective* enough ○ *During pre-flight checks, the pilot must ensure that there is sufficient fuel for the flight.*

suffix /'sʌfɪks/ *noun* an addition to the end of a word creating a new word ○ *Apart from cirrus and stratus, which are complete names, all layer cloud names consist of a prefix according to height of base, and a suffix according to shape.* (NOTE: In the word **cloudless**, **-less** is the suffix meaning *without*.)

suggest /sə'dʒest/ *verb* **1.** to indicate a possibility ○ *A strong cloud echo on radar suggests that hailstones are present.* **2.** to mean, to imply ○ *Heap clouds, as the name suggests, often have great vertical extent.*

suit /suːt/ *verb* to meet the requirements of ○ *On some engines, the ignition can be varied as the engine is running and is moved to suit the engine speed and load.*

suitable /'suːtəb(ə)l/ *adjective* appropriate or right for a particular purpose ○ *Taking into account the limits imposed by aircraft performance, a suitable route must be chosen.*

sulfur /'sʌlfə/ *noun US* same as **sulphur**

sulphur /'sʌlfə/ *noun* a yellow nonmetallic chemical element ○ *Turbine fuels tend to corrode the components of the fuel and combustion systems mainly as a result of the sulphur and water content of the fuel.* (NOTE: The atomic number of sulphur is **16**.)

sum /sʌm/ *noun* the result of two or more numbers added together ○ *When the component velocities act in the same direction, the resultant velocity is equal to the sum of their speeds in that direction.*

summarise /'sʌməraɪz/, **summarize** *verb* to present something in a shortened, concise form ○ *The effects of ice deposits on aircraft can be summarised as follows ....*

summary /'sʌməri/ *noun* a brief account of something more detailed ○ *At the end of each chapter there is a summary.*

sump /sʌmp/ *noun* the oil reservoir of a piston engine situated at its base ○ *The oil level in the sump or tank is normally checked after the engine has been stopped for a particular length of time.*

sun /sʌn/ *noun* a very bright star around which the Earth travels and which gives light and heat ○ *The sun was just rising when we landed.* ○ *The sun and the planets governed by the sun form the solar system.* ○ **solar**

sunrise /'sʌnraɪz/ *noun* the time when the upper edge of the sun appears on the visible horizon. Abbreviation **SR**

sunset /'sʌnset/ *noun* the time when the upper edge of the sun just disappears over the horizon. Abbreviation **SS**

super- /suːpə/ *prefix* more than normal

supercharge /'suːpətʃɑːdʒ/ *verb* to increase the power of an engine by using a supercharger ○ *A supercharged engine delivers greater power than a non-supercharged engine of the same size.*

supercharger /'suːpətʃɑːdʒə/ *noun* a blower or compressor, usually driven by the engine, for supplying air under high pressure to the cylinders of an internal combustion engine ○ *The function of the supercharger is to increase the power output and maintain sealevel conditions at altitude.*

super-cooled /ˌsuːpə 'kuːld/, **supercooled** /'suːpəkuːld/ *adjective* cooled below freezing point without solidification ○ *supercooled fog* ○ *Nimbostratus cloud is composed of liquid water droplets some of which are supercooled.*

superimpose /ˌsuːpərɪm'pəʊz/ *verb* to lay or to place something over the top of something else ○ *The computer utilises a technique in which each successive atmospheric layer is analysed and superimposed on the previous ones.*

superjet /'suːpədʒet/ *noun* a large supersonic jet aircraft

supersonic /ˌsuːpə'sɒnɪk/ *adjective* faster than the speed of sound ○ *For sustained supersonic flight, tank insulation is necessary to reduce the effect of kinetic heating.*

supervisor /'suːpəvaɪzə/ *noun* a person in charge ○ *senior cabin supervisor*

supplement *noun* /'sʌplɪmənt/ an angle or arc that, when added to a given angle or arc, makes 180° or a semicircle ■ *verb* /'sʌplɪment/ to add to in order to make more complete ○ *The main power plant fire detection system should con-*tain an audible warning device to supplement the visual indication.*

supplemental type certificate /ˌsʌplɪment(ə)l 'taɪp sɜːˌtɪfɪkət/ *noun* a certificate issued by an airworthiness authority to indicate that a modification to an aircraft or engine design has been approved. Abbreviation **STC**

supplementary /ˌsʌplɪ'ment(ə)ri/ *adjective* extra or additional ○ *supplementary information*

supplementary angle /ˌsʌplɪment(ə)ri 'æŋg(ə)l/ *noun* an angle that, when added to a given angle, makes 180°

supply /sə'plaɪ/ *noun* the amount of something available for use ○ *An engine requires an adequate supply of oil.* ■ *verb* to make available for use, to provide ○ *A battery is designed to supply limited amounts of electrical power.* (NOTE: **supplies – supplying – supplied**)

support /sə'pɔːt/ *noun* **1.** a device to hold something in position ○ *Direct-reading indicators consist of a float contained within a metal support tube.* **2.** practical assistance ■ *verb* to bear the weight of ○ *The wings support the aircraft in flight.*

support facilities /sə'pɔːt fə ˌsɪlɪtiz/ *plural noun* equipment and buildings used by ground staff when working on aircraft at an airport

support services /sə'pɔːt ˌsɜːvɪsɪz/ *plural noun* services provided to an aircraft while it is at an airport

suppress /sə'pres/ *verb* **1.** to prevent the development or spreading of something □ **the fire crew suppressed the fire** the fire crew brought the fire under control **2.** to prevent electrical interference from affecting a radio signal ○ *R/T noise interference can be suppressed.*

suppressed antenna /sə,prest æn 'tenə/ *noun* an antenna which is mounted under the airframe skin ○ *Static interference can be reduced by installing suppressed antennas.*

suppression /sə'preʃ(ə)n/ *noun* **1.** the prevention of the development or spreading of something ○ *a fire suppres-*

sion system **2.** the prevention of electrical interference of a radio signal

suppressor /sə'presə/ *noun* a device used in an electrical or electronic system to reduce unwanted currents, e.g. a resistor or grid ○ *A suppressor improves the quality of the signal.*

surface /'sɜːfɪs/ *noun* **1.** an outer covering of something, or the top part of something ○ *the surface of the wing* **2.** the Earth's surface or ground

surface air temperature /ˌsɜːfɪs 'eə ˌtemprɪtʃə/ *noun* the temperature recorded in the shade at a height just above ground level

surface front /'sɜːfɪs frʌnt/ *noun* a weather front at the surface of the earth ○ *The cirrus cloud can be 900 miles ahead of the surface front with a rain belt as wide as 200 miles.*

surface heating /'sɜːfɪs ˌhiːtɪŋ/ *noun* the heating of the ground by the sun

surface movement radar *noun* a type of radar used at airports to monitor aircraft traffic on the ground. Abbreviation **SMR**

surface synoptic chart /ˌsɜːfɪs sɪ ˌnɒptɪk 'tʃɑːt/ *noun* a chart of a geographical area with symbols, fronts and isobars giving a representation of the weather over the area at a particular time

surface tension /'sɜːfɪs ˌtenʃ(ə)n/ *noun* the tension of the surface film of a liquid

surface wind /'sɜːfɪs wɪnd/ *noun* a wind which blows across the land surface

surge /sɜːdʒ/ *noun* a sudden increase in something such as electrical power □ **engine surge** instability in the power output of an engine ■ *verb* to move with force like a wave ○ *If combustion pressure increases above compressor outlet pressure, the airflow will reverse in direction and surge forward through the compressor.*

surplus /'sɜːpləs/ *adjective* excess, more than is needed ○ *Fuel penalties can be incurred if fuel surplus to requirements is carried.*

surround /sə'raʊnd/ *noun* something which encloses or borders ○ *The design of windows, hatches or door surrounds is very critical.* ■ *verb* to encircle or to enclose ○ *The Earth is surrounded by the atmosphere.*

surveillance /sə'veɪləns/ *noun* the act of watching or monitoring

surveillance radar /sə'veɪləns ˌreɪdɑː/ *noun* primary radar scanning, often through 360°

survey *noun* /'sɜːveɪ/ a detailed examination ○ *An aerodrome meteorological office maintains a continuous survey of meteorological conditions over the aerodromes for which it is designated to prepare forecasts.* ■ *verb* /sə 'veɪ/ to determine the boundaries, area, or elevations of land by means of measuring angles and distances ○ *Take care when using wooded areas to fix position because the cutting down of trees may have led to a change in shape since the map was made.*

survival /sə'vaɪv(ə)l/ *noun* the fact of remaining alive after an accident ○ *The survival of passengers in the sea depends on rapid location and rescue.*

'…survival training is a vital element of all aircrew knowledge. Just because modern aircraft are more reliable than their predecessors, the need for such training does not diminish' [*Civil Aviation Training*]

survival beacon /sə'vaɪv(ə)l ˌbiːkən/ *noun* a beacon which transmits a signal which enables search aircraft to locate survivors in the water ○ *VHF and/or UHF survival beacons are carried on all jet transports.*

survivor /sə'vaɪvə/ *noun* a person who continues to live after an accident ○ *Whilst awaiting rescue on land or at sea, survivors should avoid exposure and conserve energy.* ○ *The aircraft crashed into the sea and there were no survivors.*

susceptible /sə'septɪb(ə)l/ *adjective* prone to, likely to be affected by ○ *A rough surface is more susceptible to fatigue cracking than a smooth one, and for this reason highly stressed members are often polished.*

suspect *adjective* /'sʌspekt/ referring to something believed to be causing problems ○ *The magnetic flaw detection technique is to induce a magnetic field in the suspect part and then to brush over it an ink containing a magnetic powder.* ■ *verb* /sə'spekt/ to believe to be the case ○ *If fuel contamination by water is suspected, a sample of fuel should be drained from the tank for inspection.*

suspend /sə'spend/ *verb* **1.** to hang freely from a point ○ *When it is freely suspended, a magnet will turn until one pole is towards the Earth's magnetic north pole.* **2.** to float freely in the air or in a liquid ○ *The weather associated with visibility reductions by particles suspended in the atmosphere is classified as fog, mist, haze or smoke.*

suspension /sə'spenʃən/ *noun* **1.** the act of state of hanging freely from a point **2.** the dispersion of particles in a liquid or gas ○ *If a sample of fuel taken from a tank is hazy or cloudy in appearance, this indicates the presence of water in suspension.*

sustain /sə'steɪn/ *verb* **1.** to continue, to maintain ○ *For sustained supersonic flight, some measure of tank insulation is necessary to reduce the effect of kinetic heating.* **2.** to receive, experience or suffer ○ *The aircraft sustained major damage in the crash.* ○ *The pilot sustained minor injuries.*

sweep /swiːp/ *verb* to move across quickly and with force ○ *Cold arctic air sweeps over North America in winter.*

sweepback /'swiːpbæk/ *noun* an aircraft wing that slopes backwards towards the tail, forming an acute angle with the body of the aircraft

swell /swel/ *noun* a long wave on water that moves continuously without breaking ○ *When ditching an aircraft the selection of a landing direction which will result in the minimum relative speed between the aircraft and sea swell will reduce impact forces and minimise structural damage.*

sweptback /'sweptbæk/ *adjective* referring to a wing that slopes backwards towards the tail of the aircraft

sweptwing /'sweptwɪŋ/ *adjective* referring to an aircraft that has swept-back wings

swing /swɪŋ/ *verb* **1.** to move from side to side with some force ○ *There is often a tendency for a propeller driven aircraft to swing or yaw on take-off.* **2.** □ **to swing a compass** to calibrate compass deviation by recording its value on a compass base while rotating the aircraft through 360° **3.** □ **to swing a propeller** to turn a propeller by hand to start the engine

swirl /swɜːl/ *noun* a movement with a twisting motion ○ *Swirls of smoke came out of the engine.*

swirl chamber /swɜːl 'tʃeɪmbə/ *noun* a small chamber in the cylinder head to promote swirl ○ *The usual method of atomising the fuel is to pass it through a swirl chamber, so converting its pressure energy to kinetic energy.*

switch /swɪtʃ/ *noun* a device to open or break an electric current ○ *There is an on/off switch on the front panel.* □ **centrifugal switch** a switch operated by centrifugal force ■ *verb* to connect or disconnect two lines by activating a switch □ **to switch on** to start to provide power to a system by using a switch ○ *Switch on the light.* □ **to switch off** to disconnect the power supply to a device or system ○ *Switch off the navigation lights.*

symbol /'sɪmbəl/ *noun* a printed or written sign used to represent something ○ *The work done by an electrical circuit or the power consumed is measured in watts and is given the symbol P.*

symbolic /sɪm'bɒlɪk/ *adjective* referring to symbols ○ *A symbolic code is used for synoptic charts.*

symmetric /sɪ'metrɪk/, **symmetrical** /sɪ'metrɪk(ə)l/ *adjective* referring to something which has an exact likeness of form on opposite sides of a central dividing line ○ *The area covered by the forecast is divided into a series of grid or reference points at approximately 300 km (kilometres) symmetrical spacing.*

symptom /'sɪmptəm/ *noun* a sign or indication of something, possibly a problem ○ *Buffet caused by turbulent airflow acting on the tailplane is one of the first symptoms of the approaching stall.*

synchronisation /ˌsɪŋkrənaɪ'zeɪʃ(ə)n/, **synchronization** *noun* occurrence at the same time or rate ○ *Prior to engagement, when the aircraft is being flown manually, the autopilot system will be following the aircraft flight attitude, thus ensuring that synchronisation is achieved.*

synchronise /'sɪŋkrənaɪz/, **synchronize** *verb* to cause to occur or operate at the same time or rate ○ *The aircraft must be trimmed for the desired flight attitude before engaging the autopilot, which must be synchronised to maintain that attitude when it is engaged.*

synchronous /'sɪŋkrənəs/ *adjective* referring to something operating at the same time or rate ○ *Synchronous motors will run at constant speed and are small and light in weight.*

synoptic /sɪ'nɒptɪk/ *adjective* referring to something which gives a brief outline or general view of something more complex ○ *With the addition of fronts and isobars, the synoptic chart provides a representation of the weather over a large area, at a particular time.*

synthetic /sɪn'θetɪk/ *adjective* not natural, artificial ○ *Mineral-based fluids are normally coloured red, and must be used with synthetic rubber seals and hoses.*

system /'sɪstəm/ *noun* a group of interdependent parts forming and operating as a whole ○ *a braking system* ○ *an electrical system*

T

tab /tæb/ *noun* the hinged rear part of flight control surface used for trimming ○ *Trim tabs remove the pilot's control loads by aerodynamically holding the control surface in the required position.*

table /'teɪb(ə)l/ *noun* a set of facts or figures displayed in columns and rows ○ *Charts are issued at UK meteorological offices and show, for selected locations, a table of winds and temperatures at selected flight levels.*

tabular /'tæbjʊlə/ *adjective* □ **in tabular form** arranged in a table ○ *The most widely acceptable presentation of fuel data is in tabular form but graphical presentations may also be used.*

Tacan /'tækən/ *noun* an aircraft navigation system that uses UHF signals from a transmitting station for distance and bearing. Full form **Tactical area navigation aid**

tachometer /tæ'kɒmɪtə/ *noun* an instrument for the measurement of revolutions per minute of a rotating shaft ○ *The pilot checks the tachometer and notes the resulting drop in r.p.m. for each magneto.*

TAF *abbreviation* **1.** terminal aerodrome forecast **2.** aerodrome forecast (*ICAO*)

tail /teɪl/ *noun* the rear part of the aircraft ○ *The tail section is the aft part of the fuselage to which is fitted the tail unit, comprising the tailplane, elevators, fins and rudders.*

tail assembly /'teɪl ə,sembli/ *noun* the aft part of the fuselage with the fin and rudder, tailplane and elevators attached

tail-dragger /'teɪl ,drægə/ *noun* same as **tailwheel aircraft** (*informal*)

tailplane /'teɪlpleɪn/ *noun* a horizontal stabiliser, a horizontal aerofoil at the rear of the aircraft ○ *On most high performance aircraft the incidence of the horizontal stabiliser (or tailplane) can be varied in flight.*

tail rotor /'teɪl ,rəʊtə/ *noun* a small rotor on the tail of a helicopter that prevents the helicopter from spinning in the direction opposite to the rotation of the main rotor

tailskid /'teɪlskɪd/ *noun* a support or runner on the underside of the tail of an aircraft

tailspin /'teɪlspɪn/ *noun* a rapid and uncontrolled spiral descent of an aircraft

tail unit /'teɪl ,juːnɪt/ *noun* the rear part of the aircraft, usually consisting of the fin and tailplane

tailwheel /'teɪlwiːl/ *noun* a small wheel under the tail of an aircraft. Compare **nosewheel**

tailwheel aircraft /,teɪlwiːl 'eəkrɑːft/ *noun* aircraft with a small wheel at the tail instead of a nosewheel. Also called **tail-dragger**

tailwheel conversion course /,teɪlwiːl kən'vɜːʃ(ə)n ,kɔːs/ *noun* a course which familiarises qualified pilots with the differences in handling characteristics between nosewheel and tailwheel aircraft

tailwind /'teɪlwɪnd/ *noun* a wind which is blowing in the same direction as the direction of movement or flight ○ *Because of the tailwind, the flight took only six hours.* Compare **headwind**

take off /ˌteɪk ˈɒf/ *verb* to leave the ground ○ *When flying speed is reached the aeroplane takes off.*

take-off /ˈteɪk ɒf/, **takeoff** /ˈteɪkɒf/ *noun* the procedure when an aircraft leaves the ground ○ *The aircraft has to accelerate before take-off.* ○ *There is a tendency for propeller driven aircraft to swing or yaw on take-off.* Abbreviation **TO, T/O**

take-off run /ˈteɪk ɒf ˌrʌn/ *noun* the distance from the start of take-off to the point where the wheels leave the ground ○ *Acceleration forces can be felt as the aircraft begins its take-off run.*

take-off weight /ˈteɪk ɒf ˌweɪt/ *noun* the weight of an aircraft at take-off, made up of its empty weight, plus the weight of its passengers, freight and fuel

talk down /ˌtɔːlk ˈdaʊn/ *verb* to give advice to a pilot by radio on how to land an aircraft

tan *abbreviation* tangent

tangent /ˈtændʒənt/ *noun* a straight line, curve or surface which meets another curve or curved surface at a point, but which, if extended, does not cut through at that point ○ *The glide path is at a tangent to the runway.* Abbreviation **tan**

tangential /tænˈdʒenʃ(ə)l/ *adjective* positioned at a tangent to something else

tank /tæŋk/ *noun* a large container for storing fluid ○ *An aluminium alloy fuel tank is housed in each wing.*

taper /ˈteɪpə/ *verb* to reduce in thickness towards one end ○ *Fuel flowing from the float chamber passes through a jet, in which is positioned a tapered needle valve.*

tapered wing /ˈteɪpəd wɪŋ/ *noun* a wing which becomes narrower in width from root to tip

target /ˈtɑːgɪt/ *noun* the indication shown on a radar screen resulting from a primary radar return or a radar beacon reply ○ *In a secondary radar system, the target is active.*

tarmac /ˈtɑːmæk/ *noun* the runway and taxiways of an airport ○ *They were working fast to clear the snow from the tarmac.*

TAS *abbreviation* true airspeed

task /tɑːsk/ *noun* a function or duty ○ *Present day transport aircraft are required to fly accurately, in all weather, for long distances or long periods of time and, in order to carry out this task efficiently, an autopilot is used.*

taxi /ˈtæksi/ *verb* to move an aircraft along the ground under its own power before take-off or after landing ○ *Light aircraft can be steered while taxiing via a direct link from rudder pedals to the nosewheel.* (NOTE: **taxies – taxiing – taxied**; the US English is **taxying**.)

taxiing /ˈtæksiɪŋ/ *noun* the movement of an aircraft along the ground under its own power before take-off or after landing ○ *the landing and taxiing of an aircraft* ○ *The taxiing of tail-wheel aircraft is more difficult than nosewheel aircraft.* (NOTE: The US spelling is also **taxying**.)

taxiway /ˈtæksiweɪ/ *noun* a tarmac surface connecting the ramp or apron with the runway ○ *an airfield, i.e. an area given over to runways, taxiways and aprons*

TCA *abbreviation* terminal control area

TCAS *abbreviation* traffic alert and collision avoidance system

TCDS *abbreviation* type certificate data sheet

technical /ˈteknɪk(ə)l/ *adjective* **1.** referring to mechanical subjects or applied sciences ○ *a technical education* **2.** referring to the mechanical, electrical, hydraulic or pneumatic systems of an aircraft ○ *A technical problem with the aircraft prevented it from taking off on time.*

technique /tekˈniːk/ *noun* a special method for doing something ○ *The preparation of charts is done by computer using numerical forecasting techniques.*

technology /tekˈnɒlədʒi/ *noun* the study and use of the mechanical arts or applied sciences □ **new technology** new electronic equipment ○ *The use of fly-by-wire in airliners was delayed to allow thorough development and* *encourage universal acceptance of the new technology.*

TEHP *abbreviation* total equivalent horsepower

telemetry /tə'lemɪtri/ *noun* the work of recording and transmitting data about an object situated at a distance from the observer

TEMP /temp/ *abbreviation* temperature

temperate /'temp(ə)rət/ *adjective* mild, not extreme ○ *Cold air in temperate latitudes is usually unstable.*

temperature /'temprɪtʃə/ *noun* a measurement, in degrees, of the intensity of heat of a body ○ *Ground temperature is the temperature recorded by a thermometer placed at ground level.* ○ *The altitude and temperature of the tropopause are of concern to aircrew.*

temperature error /'temprɪtʃə ˌerə/ *noun* the variation in pressure altitude caused by a deviation of temperature from ISA

tempo /'tempəʊ/ *noun* the speed of an activity ○ *The flow of passengers to exits and tempo of evacuation will be influenced by the number of exits available.*

TEMPO /'tempəʊ/ *abbreviation* temporary (*ICAO*)

temporary /'temp(ə)rəri/ *adjective* lasting for a short time, not permanent ○ *The indicator 'tempo', followed by a 4-figure time group indicates a period of temporary fluctuations to the forecast meteorological conditions which may occur at any time during the period given.* Opposite **permanent**

tend /tend/ *verb* to be apt or inclined to do something more often than not ○ *Depressions tend to move around large anticyclones following the circulation of wind.* □ **the weather tends to be wet in the UK in the winter** the weather is often, but not always, wet

tendency /'tendənsi/ *noun* an inclination, situation or condition which occurs more often than not ○ *There is a tendency for propeller-driven aircraft to swing or yaw on take-off.* □ **he has a**

tendency to be late he is often late □ **he has a tendency to forget things** he is forgetful

tensile /'tensaɪl/ *adjective* referring to stretching or pulling out ○ *Reinforced plastic may have to support a tensile load, a compressive load or a bending load.*

tensile load /'tensaɪl ləʊd/ *noun* the load caused by forces acting in opposite directions away from each other

tensile strength /'tensaɪl strenθ/ *noun* the strength of a structure to resist forces pulling it apart from opposite directions

tensile stress /'tensaɪl stres/ *noun* the forces that try to pull a structure apart from opposite directions

tension /'tenʃən/ *noun* a strained condition resulting from forces acting in opposition to each other ○ *A rod which is bent is shortened or in compression on the inside of the bend and is stretched or in tension on the outside of the bend.*

term /tɜːm/ *noun* **1.** a word or expression ○ *The term 'payload' includes passengers, baggage and freight.* **2.** a limited period of time □ **a 5 year term** a period of 5 years □ **in the long term** when considering a long period of time □ **short term forecast** a weather forecast for the next few hours only

terminal /'tɜːmɪn(ə)l/ *adjective* referring to a limit or to a final point ■ *noun* **1.** the departure and/or arrival building at an airport ○ *The flight leaves from terminal three at Heathrow airport.* **2.** an electrical connection point ○ *The negative terminal of the battery is marked -.*

terminal aerodrome forecast /ˌtɜːmɪnəl ˌeərədrəʊm 'fɔːkɑːst/ *noun* the weather forecast for the area around an aerodrome ○ *In terminal aerodrome forecasts, the height of the cloud base forecast is above airfield level unless otherwise stated.* Abbreviation **TAF**

COMMENT: TAFs are scheduled four times daily for 24-hour periods beginning at 0000Z, 0600Z, 1200Z, and 1800Z.

terminal airfield /ˌtɜːmɪn(ə)l 'eəfiːld/ *noun* the airfield at which a flight finishes

terminal area forecast /ˌtɜːmɪn(ə)l ˌeəriə 'fɔːkɑːst/ *noun* the weather forecast for the area around an airport. Abbreviation **TAF**

terminal control area /ˌtɜːmɪn(ə)l kən'trəʊl ˌeəriə/ *noun* an air traffic control area established at the meeting place of a number of routes near one or more major airports ○ *In some areas where there is a local concentration of traffic, terminal control areas are set up.* Abbreviation **TCA**, **TMA**

terminate /'tɜːmɪneɪt/ *verb* to end, or to bring to a close ○ *The flight terminates in New York.* □ **the transmission terminated abruptly** the transmission stopped suddenly and unexpectedly

terminology /ˌtɜːmɪ'nɒlədʒi/ *noun* a set of words or expressions used for a particular subject ○ *It is necessary to learn some of the terminology associated with aircraft navigation.*

terrain /tə'reɪn/ *noun* land, especially in relation to its physical geography ○ *Special attention should be paid to wind flow when flights are made over hills or mountainous terrain.*

terrestrial /tə'restriəl/ *adjective* referring to the earth ○ *Clear skies allow terrestrial radiation to escape.*

territory /'terɪt(ə)ri/ *noun* the extent of the surface of the Earth governed by a particular country, ruler, state, etc. ○ *All places in the same territory, or part of the same territory, maintain a standard of time as laid down by the government responsible for that territory.*

tertiary /'tɜːʃəri/ *adjective* referring to something which is third in order of rank, behind primary and secondary ○ *Tertiary radar systems are synonymous with long-range navigation aids.* ○ *Tertiary structures, for example fairings, wheel doors and minor component brackets, are essential parts of the airframe.*

tertiary radar /ˌtɜːʃəri 'reɪdɑː/ *noun* long-range navigation aids

test /test/ *noun* **1.** a series of operations to find out if something is working

well ○ *The manual test for the engine fire warning system will give a steady red light on all the fire control handles.* **2.** an examination to assess the knowledge of a person ○ *There is a navigation test for students at 0800 hours.* ■ *verb* **1.** to operate something in order to find out whether it functions correctly ○ *Oxygen under pressure is used to test the oxygen masks and equipment for fit and leakage.* **2.** to examine somebody in order to assess his or her knowledge ○ *The students are tested in five subjects.*

test pilot /'test ˌpaɪlət/ *noun* a pilot who flies new aircraft in order to check their performance

TGT *abbreviation* turbine gas temperature

theory /'θɪəri/ *noun* a system of ideas or principles explaining something ○ *The theory of navigation must be studied before any practical plotting exercises are done.*

theory of flight /ˌθɪəri əv 'flaɪt/ *noun* the ideas and principles which contribute to our understanding of how things fly

thereafter /ðeər'ɑːftə/ *adverb* after that, beyond that ○ *Meteorological visibility is given in metres up to 5,000 metres and thereafter in km (kilometres).*

thereby /ðeə'baɪ/ *adverb* by that means or in that way ○ *The evacuation was carried out at a slower rate, thereby minimising the risk of injury to passengers.*

therefore /'ðeəfɔː/ *adverb* as a result, consequently ○ *At small throttle openings, the depression at the choke is very small and therefore no fuel flows from the main jet.*

thermal /'θɜːm(ə)l/ *adjective* referring to heat ○ *Intense surface heating causes thermal currents to develop and create convection.* ■ *noun* a rising current of relatively warm air in the lower atmosphere ○ *Glider pilots circle in thermals in order to gain height.*

thermal activity /ˌθɜːm(ə)l æk 'tɪvɪti/ *noun* a period of time when there is a lot of vertical movement of air caused by heating ○ *Cumulus clouds* *may develop because of thermal activity resulting from the warming of the surface.*

thermal barrier /ˌθɜːm(ə)l ˈbæriə/ *noun* the heat caused by air friction on an aircraft flying at high speed

thermo- /θɜːməʊ/ *prefix* heat

thermocouple /ˈθɜːməʊkʌp(ə)l/ *noun* a device for measuring temperature ○ *Variation in temperature of the cooling air will give some indication of engine trouble through a thermocouple system to a temperature gauge.*

thermodynamic /ˌθɜːməʊdaɪˈnæmɪk/ *adjective* referring to the conversion of one form of energy into another and how this affects temperature, pressure, volume, mechanical action and work

thermometer /θəˈmɒmɪtə/ *noun* an instrument for measuring temperature ○ *Ground temperature is the temperature recorded by a thermometer placed at ground level.*

thermoplastic /ˌθɜːməʊˈplæstɪk/ *noun* a type of plastic which can be softened by heating then shaped, then softened again by heating

thermosetting plastic /ˌθɜːməʊsetɪŋ ˈplæstɪk/ *noun* a type of plastic which is heated while being shaped but which cannot be softened by reheating ○ *If a piece of thermosetting plastic is hit hard enough, it breaks into pieces with straight sharp edges.*

thick /θɪk/ *adjective* **1.** of great or particular extent between two surfaces ○ *a 1cm thick steel bar* ○ *This sheet of aluminium is not very thick.* **2.** with a large diameter ○ *thick wire* **3.** dense ○ *thick fog* ○ *thick cloud* **4.** of a consistency which does not flow easily ○ *thick oil* Opposite **thin**

thickness /ˈθɪknəs/ *noun* **1.** the extent between two surfaces ○ *In monocoque construction, there is no internal stiffening because the thickness of the skin gives strength and stability.* **2.** the extent of the diameter of a wire **3.** the state or condition of being thick

thin /θɪn/ *adjective* **1.** of small extent between two surfaces ○ *a thin layer of paint* **2.** with a small diameter ○ *thin*

wire **3.** not dense ○ *thin mist* ○ *Altostratus cloud is thin enough for the sun to be dimly visible.* **4.** of a consistency which flows easily ○ *thin oil* Opposite **thick**

thinness /ˈθɪnnəs/ *noun* **1.** a small extent between two surfaces ○ *The thinness of the material makes it unsuitable.* **2.** a small extent of the diameter of a wire **3.** the state or condition of being thin

thorough /ˈθʌrə/ *adjective* complete ○ *All cabin crew must have a thorough knowledge of fire fighting equipment and procedures.* □ **a thorough inspection** a very detailed, comprehensive inspection

THP *abbreviation* thrust horsepower

three-letter group /ˌθriː ˌletə ˈɡruːp/ *noun* three letters of the alphabet found together

three-point landing /ˌθriː ˌpɔɪnt ˈlændɪŋ/ *noun* an aircraft landing in which the two main wheels of the landing gear and the nosewheel or tailwheel touch the ground at the same time

threshold /ˈθreʃhəʊld/ *noun* the beginning of the part of the runway, usable for landing ○ *Runway visual range is obtained by an observer standing at the side of the runway in the vicinity of the threshold counting the number of markers or lights visible along the side of the runway.*

COMMENT: The threshold is marked with a single white line on visual runways or by eight parallel white lines arranged longitudinally in two groups of four each side of the runway centreline for runways with instrument approach/landing facilities.

throttle /ˈθrɒt(ə)l/ *noun* **1.** a throttle lever **2.** a throttle valve ■ *verb* □ **to throttle back** to reduce engine power ○ *Throttle back to increase the rate of descent.*

COMMENT: The verbs 'open' or 'advance' (= to increase engine power) and 'close' or 'throttle back' (= to decrease engine power) are frequently used by instructors to explain the required movement of the throttle lever in the cockpit.

throttle lever /ˈθrɒt(ə)l ˌliːvə/ *noun* a device operating the throttle valve ○

When starting an engine, it is inadvisable to pump the throttle lever because of the risk of fire.

throttle quadrant /'θrɒt(ə)l ˌkwɒdrənt/ *noun* an arc-shaped device in which the throttle levers move

throttle setting /'θrɒt(ə)l ˌsetɪŋ/ *noun* the particular position of the throttle which gives a required revolutions per minute or power

throttle valve /'θrɒt(ə)l vælv/ *noun* a device controlling the flow of fuel in an engine

throughout /θruː'aʊt/ *adverb* from the beginning to the end of a time or place ○ *Emergency lighting is provided throughout the cabin.* ○ *Heavy snow fell throughout the night.* □ **throughout the life of the aircraft** during the entire life of the aircraft □ **throughout the world** all over the world □ **throughout the year** from January 1st to December 31st

thrust /θrʌst/ *noun* a force produced by a propeller, jet or rocket ○ *A propeller is a means of converting engine power into a propulsive force known as thrust.* ○ *In order for the aircraft to increase speed, thrust must overcome drag.* ◊ **reversal, reverser** ■ *verb* to push suddenly with force ○ *A nozzle is an opening at the rear of a jet engine through which exhaust gases are thrust.* (NOTE: **thrusting – thrust**)

thrust horsepower /ˌθrʌst 'hɔːspaʊə/ *noun* the amount of horsepower of an engine that is transformed into thrust. Abbreviation **THP**

thrust reversal /'θrʌst rɪˌvɜːsəl/ *noun* setting of throttle levers to provide thrust in the opposite direction to decelerate the aircraft after landing

thunder /'θʌndə/ *noun* the noise created by the violent expansion and contraction of air momentarily heated by a lightning discharge ○ *Thunder immediately following the flash of lightning usually indicates that the storm is overhead.*

thunderstorm /'θʌndəstɔːm/ *noun* a violent weather condition in which wind speeds increase, rain or hail falls and there is lightning activity ○ *Thun-*

derstorms occur in well-developed cumulonimbus clouds. ○ *The process of formation, development and decay of a thunderstorm.*

thunderstorm activity /'θʌndəstɔːm ækˌtɪvɪti/ *noun* the occurrence of weather conditions associated with thunderstorms, such as rain, thunder, wind or lightning

thus /ðʌs/ *adverb* **1.** in this way ○ *This device fits with the other thus.* **2.** therefore, as a result ○ *The glide slope and localiser beam signals control the aircraft about the pitch and roll axes, thus maintaining alignment with the runway.* ○ *Anti-skid braking systems are designed to prevent the brakes locking the wheels during landing, thus reducing the possibility of wheel skid.*

tie /taɪ/ *noun* a basic structural member which is designed to withstand mainly tensile loads ○ *Diagonal ties can be used to relieve tension and increase the effectiveness of the top boom.*

tight /taɪt/ *adjective* closely or firmly fitting or put together □ **a tight fit** a situation when there is just about enough space to fit ■ *adverb* closely or firmly, with no air leaks ○ *The door must be shut tight.*

tilt /tɪlt/ *noun* a sloping position ○ *Land creates a drag effect on an electro-magnetic wave-front, reducing the velocity of the wave thereby causing a tilt.* ■ *verb* to be at an angle to the vertical or horizontal, to slope ○ *The Earth tilts on its axis.*

timetable /'taɪmteɪb(ə)l/ *noun* a printed list which shows the times of departure from and arrival to various destinations ○ *All the scheduled flights are listed in the airline timetable.*

timetabled /'taɪmteɪb(ə)ld/ *adjective* listed in a timetable ○ *A scheduled landing is an arrival at a timetabled destination.*

time zone /'taɪm zəʊn/ *noun* one of the 24 parts of the Earth in which the same standard time is used

tip /tɪp/ *noun* the end of a small or tapering thing

tire /'taɪə/ *noun US* same as **tyre**

titanium /taɪ'teɪniəm/ *noun* a light metal used to make strong alloys ○ *The fatigue resistance of titanium is greater than that of aluminium or steel.*

TKOF *abbreviation* take off (*ICAO*)

TMA *abbreviation* terminal control area

T/O, TO *abbreviation* take off

toggle /'tɒg(ə)l/ *noun* a short piece of wood or other material, attached with a string to e.g. a life jacket ○ *Pull the toggles downwards to inflate the life jacket.*

toilet /'tɔɪlət/ *noun* **1.** a bowl with a seat on which you sit to get rid of waste from your body **2.** a room or cubicle with a toilet bowl in it ○ *There are two toilets at the rear of the plane and one at the front.*

tolerance /'tɒlərəns/ *noun* an allowable variation in something which can be measured ○ *a tolerance of 2°* ○ *a tolerance of 1mm (millimetre)*

tone /təʊn/ *noun* a sound of one pitch ○ *The ground transmits a code in two short bursts each of which is modulated with two tones.*

tool kit /'tuːl kɪt/ *noun* a set of tools consisting of spanners, screwdrivers, pliers, etc.

top /tɒp/ *noun* the highest point or part ○ *If cumulonimbus clouds cannot be avoided then flight through the top is less hazardous than through the centre or bottom of the cloud.*

top-dead-centre /ˌtɒp ded 'sentə/ *noun* the position of the piston at the extreme top of its stroke in a piston engine ○ *Ignition should occur just before top-dead-centre.*

topic /'tɒpɪk/ *noun* the subject of something heard, said, written or read ○ *The first section in the book deals with the topic of airmanship.*

topographical /ˌtɒpə'græfɪk(ə)l/ *adjective* referring to topography ○ *An advantage of using airfield QNH is that altimeter readings can be compared directly with heights represented on topographical maps.*

topography /tə'pɒgrəfi/ *noun* **1.** a representation of detailed natural and man-made features of the Earth's surface as represented on a map ○ *The chart shows the topography of the area.* **2.** relative elevations of the Earth's surface, or features of a geographical area ○ *The general circulation is complicated because the Earth tilts and its surface is neither level, because of topography, nor uniform due to areas of land and sea.*

tornado /tɔː'neɪdəʊ/ *noun* a violent storm of small extent, with rotating winds ○ *The winds of a tornado are of hurricane force.*

torque /tɔːk/ *noun* a moment of forces causing rotation ○ *Torque forces try to bend the propeller against the direction of rotation.* ○ *High current flows through both the field and armature windings producing the high torque required for engine starting.*

torquemeter /'tɔːkmitə/ *noun* a device for measuring forces (**torque**) causing rotation ○ *Engine torque is used to indicate the power that is developed by a turboprop engine and the indicator is known as a torquemeter.*

torsion /'tɔːʃ(ə)n/ *noun* twisting, especially of one end of a body while the other is fixed ○ *Rivets are subjected to torsion and may break.*

torsion load /'tɔːʃ(ə)n ləʊd/ *noun* the load caused by twisting of a structure

total /'təʊt(ə)l/ *adjective* complete, whole ○ *Of the total amount of radiation emitted by the sun, the Earth receives only a very small part.* □ **total system failure** complete system failure □ **total seating capacity** the maximum number of passengers who can be accommodated on seats

touch down /ˌtʌtʃ 'daʊn/ *verb* to make controlled contact with the landing surface after a flight ○ *If the atmospheric pressure at an airfield is 1,000 millibars (mb) and that pressure is set on the sub-scale of an aircraft altimeter, when the aircraft touches down at the airfield, the altimeter will read zero.*

touchdown /'tʌtʃdaʊn/ *noun* the moment, after a flight, when the aircraft makes controlled contact with the landing surface ○ *One of the aircraft's tyres burst on touchdown.*

touchdown point /'tʌtʃdaʊn pɔɪnt/ *noun* the place on the runway where the aircraft undercarriage first touches the ground on landing

tow /təʊ/ *verb* to pull an aircraft or vehicle using a bar, rope, etc. attached to another aircraft or vehicle ○ *The glider was towed into the air by a Rollason Condor.*

tower /'taʊə/ *noun* a tall airport or airfield air traffic control building ○ *Wait for permission from the tower before crossing an active runway.*

'T' piece adapter /'ti: 'pi:s ə 'dæptə/ *noun* a device for connecting two inputs to one output or vice versa

track /træk/ *noun* a projection on the Earth's surface of the path of an aircraft, which can be expressed in degrees from north ○ *Where an aircraft track and wind direction are the same, there will be a headwind component acting on the aircraft.* ○ *The actual track does not necessarily follow the planned track and is given the name track made good.* ■ *verb* to follow a line of the flight path of an aircraft, as projected on the Earth surface ○ *On final approach, track the imaginary extended centre line of the runway.*

tractor /'træktə/ *noun* **1.** an aircraft that has its propeller in front of its engine **2.** a propeller in front of an aircraft engine, which has the effect of pulling the aircraft through the air

trade winds /'treɪd wɪndz/ *plural noun* steady winds which blow on the side of the sub-tropical highs nearest to the equator ○ *Trade winds maintain their direction over the oceanic areas, especially the Pacific, more than over land areas.*

traffic /'træfɪk/ *noun* the number of aircraft in operation ○ *Standard instrument routes are structured to provide the safest and most efficient flow of traffic from entry and exit points to the airfield.*

traffic pattern /'træfɪk ˌpæt(ə)n/ *noun* **1.** the shape marked out on the ground of an aircraft track in the aero-

drome circuit **2.** the pattern of routes that an aircraft must keep to when approaching or circling an airport

trailing /'treɪlɪŋ/ *adjective* referring to something which comes after something else ○ *The trailing brush is positioned behind the main brush on the rotor arm, thereby giving a retarded spark.*

trailing edge /ˌtreɪlɪŋ 'edʒ/ *noun* aft part of an aerofoil ○ *The trailing edge of the wing is the section behind the rear spar and is of light construction because the aerodynamic loads on this area are relatively low.*

train /treɪn/ *verb* to teach a person a particular skill ○ *The student pilot is trained to scan an instrument panel, whilst at the same time listening to the aircraft radio and flying the aircraft.* ■ *noun* a series of connected parts or wheels in machinery ○ *The turboprop turbine transmits increased power forward through a shaft and a gear train, to drive the propeller.*

trainee /treɪ'ni:/ *noun* a person who is being taught ○ *a trainee pilot*

transducer /trænz'dju:sə/ *noun* a device which converts a non-electrical signal into an electrical one ○ *The manifold is connected into the pressure ratio transmitter, which consists of a transducer, to sense the pressure ratio, and an associated electrical circuit, providing signals to the servo indicator in the cockpit.*

transfer *noun* /'trænsfɜ:/ the act of passing or moving to another place ○ *External cooling of the engine is necessary to prevent the transfer of heat to the aircraft structure.* ■ *verb* /træns'fɜ:/ to pass or to move to another place ○ *It is sometimes necessary to transfer fuel from one tank to another tank.* (NOTE: **transferring – transferred**)

transform /træns'fɔ:m/ *verb* to change completely ○ *The purpose of an actuator is to transform fluid flow into motion, i.e. it converts pressure energy into mechanical energy.* ○ *Friction results in some of the power available from a pump being transformed into heat.*

transformer /træns'fɔːmə/ *noun* a device for changing the voltage or current amplitude of an alternating current signal ○ *Current transformers differ from voltage transformers in that the primary circuit consists of a supply feeder cable rather than a coil connected across a supply.*

transient /'trænziənt/ *adjective* passing or temporary, lasting only a short time ○ *Transient loads can be absorbed by the busbar with a minimum of voltage fluctuations.*

transit /'trænzɪt/ *noun* an act of moving ○ **in transit** moving ○ *A green light indicates the undercarriage is locked down, and a red light is displayed when the undercarriage is in transit.* □ **transit route** a route taken by one aircraft through controlled airspace

transition /træn'zɪʃ(ə)n/ *noun* an act of passing from one place, state or condition to another

transition altitude /træn'zɪʃ(ə)n ˌæltɪtjuːd/ *noun* altitude in the vicinity of an airport, at or below which the vertical position of the aircraft is controlled by reference to altitudes above mean sea level ○ *When a flight takes place above the transition altitude, the standard pressure setting of 1013.25 mb (millibars) is used.*

transition layer /træn'zɪʃ(ə)n ˌleɪə/ *noun* the airspace between the transition altitude and the transition level (NOTE: The depth of this layer will normally be insignificant and will never exceed 500 ft.)

transition level /træn'zɪʃ(ə)n ˌlev(ə)l/ *noun* the lowest flight level above the transition altitude

transit lounge /'trænzɪt laʊndʒ/ *noun* a room where transit passengers wait for connecting flights

transit passenger /'trænzɪt ˌpæsɪndʒə/ *noun* a traveller who is changing from one aircraft to another

translation /træns'leɪʃ(ə)n/ *noun* **1.** the movement of an object in a straight line in which every part of the object follows a parallel course and no rotation takes place **2.** the act of expressing the meaning of words in one language in words from another language

transmission /trænz'mɪʃ(ə)n/ *noun* **1.** the sending of a radio signal ○ *The combination of loop and sense antennae can determine the direction from which a transmission is made.* **2.** a radio signal that is transmitted

transmit /trænz'mɪt/ *verb* **1.** to pass, to convey ○ *As the camshaft rotates, the cam will transmit a lifting force through rods and pivots to open the valve.* ○ *The charts are transmitted from one station to another by fax.* **2.** to send out a radio signal ○ *Survival beacons transmit a signal which enables search aircraft to rapidly locate survivors in the water.* (NOTE: **transmitting – transmitted**)

transmitter /trænz'mɪtə/ *noun* a device for sending out radio signals ○ *Although continuous wave radars operate continuously, separate transmitter and receiver antennae must be used.* ○ *Signal strength is inversely proportional to the distance from the transmitter.*

transparency /træns'pærənsi/ *noun* the condition of being transparent ○ *Meteorological visibility gives information on the transparency of the atmosphere to a stationary ground observer.*

transparent /træns'pærənt/ *adjective* allowing light to pass through so that things can be seen ○ *Aircraft windows and canopies are usually made from transparent acrylic plastic.*

transponder /træn'spɒndə/ *noun* a device in an aircraft for receiving a radio signal and automatically transmitting a different signal so that an air traffic control station can identify the aircraft ○ *The transponder in the aircraft comprises a transmitter and a receiver.*

'…flight trials began recently of a low-cost hand-held IFF transponder' [*Pilot*]

COMMENT: The pilot sets an identification code, or 'squawk', assigned by ATC, on the transponder in the aircraft.

transport /'trænspɔːt/ *noun* a system for moving people, freight and baggage from one place to another ○ *On a large* *transport aircraft, the safety of hundreds of passengers is involved.*

transport aircraft /ˈtrænspɔːt ˌeəkrɑːft/ *noun* an aircraft designed to carry ten or more passengers or the equivalent cargo and having a maximum take-off weight greater than 5,670 kg

trap /træp/ *verb* to catch and prevent from escaping ○ *If there is a failure of the pressurised air supply, the check valve will close and trap pressurised air in the cabin.* ○ *Smog is smoke or pollution trapped on the surface by an inversion of temperature with little or no wind.*

tread /tred/ *noun* a series of patterns moulded into the surface of a tyre to provide grip ○ *The risk of aquaplaning increases as the depth of tyre tread is reduced.*

treat /triːt/ *verb* **1.** to behave or act towards something or somebody in a particular way ○ *Pilots should treat the engine carefully, if they want to prolong its life.* **2.** to apply a process to something in order to get a particular result □ **treated water** water which has been made drinkable □ **heat-treated alloys** alloys which have undergone a process of hardening by using heat

treatment /ˈtriːtmənt/ *noun* subjection to the action of a chemical or physical process ○ *anti-corrosion treatment* ○ *heat treatment*

trembler /ˈtremblə/ *noun* an automatic vibrator for making and breaking an electrical circuit

trend /trend/ *noun* **1.** a general direction or tendency ○ *Continuous VOLMET, which is normally broadcast on a designated VHF (very high frequency) channel, contains current aerodrome reports and trends where available.* **2.** an up-to-date or modern way of doing things ○ *Warning systems can take the form of lights, captions, and aural signals, and the modern trend is to incorporate them into a central warning system.*

triangle /ˈtraɪæŋgəl/ *noun* a plane figure with three sides and three angles ○ *The triangle of velocities is a vector*

solution of what happens to an aircraft when wind causes drift. ◊ **wind¹**

trigger /ˈtrɪgə/ *verb* to cause to operate, to set off ○ *Normally, both the captain's and first officer's airspeed indicator trigger an aural warning if the airspeed limits are exceeded.*

trijet /ˈtraɪdʒet/ *noun* an aircraft powered by three jet engines

trim /trɪm/ *noun* a condition in which an aircraft is in static balance in pitch ○ *Trim indicators have a green band, to show when the trim is correct for take-off.* (NOTE: Some aircraft have rudder and aileron trim.) ■ *verb* to adjust trimmers in order to get the required hands-off pitch attitude ○ *Trim the aircraft for level flight.*

trim wheel /ˈtrɪm wiːl/, **trimmer** /ˈtrɪmə/ *noun* a wheel-shaped device, sometimes situated between the front seats of light aircraft, to trim the aircraft by hand ○ *The trimmer is used to ease the loads imposed on the flying controls during flight.*

trip /trɪp/ *verb* to cause an electrical device to suddenly stop working ○ *Oscillating outputs from alternators could cause sensitive equipment to malfunction or trip.*

triplane /ˈtraɪpleɪn/ *noun* an aircraft with three main wings fixed one above the other

triple /ˈtrɪp(ə)l/ *adjective* consisting of three parts ○ *Probes may be of single, double or triple element construction.*

tropical /ˈtrɒpɪk(ə)l/ *adjective* referring to the area between the parallels of latitude 23° 26' north and south of the equator ○ *Tropical air moving northwards is subjected to surface cooling and becomes increasingly stable in its lower layers.*

tropical storm /ˌtrɒpɪk(ə)l ˈstɔːm/ *noun* a violent wind system which forms over tropical oceans ○ *Tropical storms often dissipate when they pass from sea to land.*

tropics /ˈtrɒpɪks/ *noun* □ **the tropics** the area between the parallels of latitude 23° 26' north and south of the equator ○ *Throughout the tropics and* *sub-tropics, the sea breeze is a regular feature.*

tropopause /'trɒpəpɔ:z/ *noun* the level at which the troposphere and the stratosphere meet ○ *The altitude and temperature of the tropopause are of concern to aircrew because they affect aircraft performance.*

troposphere /'trɒpəsfɪə/ *noun* the lowest region of the atmosphere ○ *The troposphere is at its deepest near the equator and shallowest near the poles.*

trough /trɒf/ *noun* a long area of low barometric pressure ○ *Severe icing and turbulence can be experienced when flying through a trough and the precipitation may be of hail, rain, snow or sleet.*

true /tru:/ *adjective* referring to a calculation or reading which has been corrected for errors

true airspeed /ˌtru: 'eəspi:d/ *noun* airspeed corrected for instrument and position error in addition to altitude, temperature and compressibility errors

true altitude /ˌtru: 'æltɪtju:d/ *noun* real or actual height above sea level

true bearing /ˌtru: 'beərɪŋ/ *noun* bearing with reference to true north, not magnetic north

true degrees /ˌtru: dɪ'gri:z/ *noun* degrees of direction measured from true north, not magnetic north. Also called **degrees true**. Symbol °**T**

true north /ˌtru: 'nɔ:θ/ *noun* the direction towards north pole along a meridian through the observer

tube /tju:b/ *noun* a long, hollow cylindrical device for holding or carrying fluids ○ *A liquid-type fire detector consists of a tube and expansion chamber filled with liquid.*

tubing /'tju:bɪŋ/ *noun* tubes in general ○ *hydraulic tubing*

tubular /'tju:bjʊlə/ *adjective* referring to something which is shaped like a tube ○ *Diagonal members can be of angle section, box spar or tubular in shape.*

tune /tju:n/ *verb* **1.** to set a system at its optimum point by careful adjustment ○ *The engine has not been properly*

tuned. **2.** to adjust to the particular frequency of the required signal ○ *The RBI shows the bearing of the tuned radio beacon with reference to the aircraft's heading.*

tuner /'tju:nə/ *noun* a part which allows the operator to select the particular frequency of the required signal ○ *The tuner reduces interference.*

turbine /'tɜ:baɪn/ *noun* a rotary motor or engine formed of a wheel driven by a flow of air or gas

turbo- /tɜ:bəʊ/ *prefix* turbine

turbocharger /'tɜ:bəʊˌtʃɑ:dʒə/ *noun* a supercharger driven by a turbine powered by exhaust gases ○ *The turbocharger significantly increases engine power.*

turbofan /'tɜ:bəʊfæn/ *noun* a jet engine in which most of the thrust is produced by air, accelerated by a large fan, which does not pass through the combustion chamber of the engine ○ *The Airbus A340 is powered by four CFM56 turbofans.* (NOTE: The US term is **fanjet**.)

COMMENT: Turbofan engines are much quieter than older turbojets and make a characteristic sound when in operation. The fan can be clearly seen in the front part of the engine. Modern airliners use turbofan engines produced by major manufacturers such as Rolls Royce, CFM or Pratt and Whitney.

turbojet /'tɜ:bəʊdʒet/ *noun* a jet engine which includes a turbine-driven compressor for the air taken into the engine ○ *The de Havilland Comet was the world's first turbojet commercial transport aircraft.*

COMMENT: In recent years turbofan engines have taken over from turbojet engines. Frank Whittle (1907–96) was an English engineer and RAF officer who invented the turbojet aircraft engine. Whittle developed a jet aircraft by 1941 and the first military jet aircraft, the Gloster Meteor, became operational in 1944.

turboprop /'tɜ:bəʊprɒp/, **turbopropeller** /'tɜ:bəʊprəˌpelə/ *noun* a turbojet engine in which the turbine also drives a propeller ○ *The turboprop* *engine is often used in transport aircraft.*

COMMENT: Turboprop aircraft are efficient at lower speeds than turbojet aircraft and are often used for short-haul operations.

turboshaft /ˈtɜːbəʊʃɑːft/ *noun* an engine similar to a turboprop engine, except that it is used primarily in helicopters

turbulence /ˈtɜːbjʊləns/ *noun* an irregular motion of the atmosphere

turbulent /ˈtɜːbjʊlənt/ *adjective* referring to the irregular motion of the atmosphere ○ *When flying in turbulent air conditions, an aircraft is subjected to upward and downward gust loads.*

turn /tɜːn/ *noun* **1.** an angular change in track ○ *a 180° turn* ○ *The autopilot may be engaged during a climb or descent but not usually in a turn.* **2.** a section of a wire which is wound 360° around a centre ○ *The voltage in each winding is directly proportional to the number of turns in each winding.* ■ *verb* **1.** to make an angular change in track ○ *turn right* ○ *Turn to the west.* **2.** to rotate ○ *The crankshaft turns through 720° for every cycle of four strokes.* □ **turn the knob** rotate the knob or control **3.** □ **to turn (in)to** to change state ○ *As it descends into warmer air, snow turns into rain.* **4.** to find a page, section, passage, etc., in a book ○ *Turn to page 64.* ◇ **in turn 1.** for its or their part ○ *Drag must be overcome with thrust, which requires engines, which in turn consume fuel.* **2.** one after the other ○ *Turn off the magnetos in turn to check their serviceability.*

turnaround /ˈtɜːnəˌraʊnd/ *noun US* same as **turnround**

turn coordinator /ˈtɜːn kəʊˌɔːdɪneɪtə/ *noun* an instrument that shows the pilot if the aircraft is in **coordinated flight** or if it is slipping or skidding

turn off /ˌtɜːn ˈɒf/ *verb* **1.** to switch an electrical device or system 'off' ○ *When carrying out engine checks, turn off the magnetos in turn to check their serviceability.* **2.** to stop the flow of something by using a valve ○ *Turn off the fuel.*

turn on /ˌtɜːn ˈɒn/ *verb* **1.** to switch an electrical device or system 'on' ○ *Can you turn the light on or turn on the light?* **2.** to start the flow of something by using a valve ○ *Turn on the fuel.*

turnround /ˈtɜːnraʊnd/ *noun* unloading, loading and preparing an aircraft for another flight and the time taken to do this (NOTE: The word **turnaround** is preferred in US English.)

twin engine aircraft /ˌtwɪn ˌendʒɪn ˈeəkrɑːft/, **twin-engined aircraft** /ˌtwɪn ˌendʒɪnd ˈeəkrɑːft/ *noun* an aircraft with two identical engines

twist /twɪst/ *verb* to turn against resistance ○ *Centrifugal, bending and twisting forces act on a propeller during flight.*

TWR *abbreviation* aerodrome control tower

type /taɪp/ *noun* **1.** a sort or kind ○ *Temperature and oil pressure are critical to any type of system.* **2.** a class of things having shared characteristics ○ *The type of undercarriage fitted to an aircraft is governed by the operating weight.* □ **type of aircraft** *or* **aircraft type** all aircraft of the same basic design

type certificate /ˈtaɪp sɜːˌtɪfɪkət/ *noun* a document issued by an aviation authority which indicates that the design of a certain aircraft, engine etc has been approved

type certificate data sheet *noun* a document associated with a type certificate, giving information about why the certificate has been granted and general information about the design which has been approved. Abbreviation **TCDS**

type rating /ˈtaɪp ˌreɪtɪŋ/ *noun* authorisation, usually entered on a licence, which allows the pilot to fly a particular aircraft type

typical /ˈtɪpɪk(ə)l/ *adjective* **1.** normal, standard □ **a typical fuel system** a standard type of fuel system **2.** representative of a particular class of things ○ *The Piper Archer is a typical single-engine light aircraft.*

tyre /ˈtaɪə/ *noun* a rubber covering for a wheel (NOTE: The US spelling is **tire**.)

tyre creep /'taɪə kriːp/ *noun* the gradual rotation of the tyre in relation to the wheel, caused by landing ○ *to convert magnetic bearing into true bearing it is necessary to apply magnetic variation at the point at which the bearing was taken*

COMMENT: Tyre creep can lead to damage to the tyre valve and subsequent unwanted and possibly dangerous deflation of the tyre.

tyre pressure /'taɪə ˌpreʃə/ *noun* the air pressure in a tyre ○ *maximum allowable tyre pressure*

U

UAR *abbreviation* upper air route

UAS *abbreviation* upper air space

UHF *abbreviation* ultra high frequency

UIR *abbreviation* upper air region

UK *abbreviation* United Kingdom

ultimate /ˈʌltɪmət/ *adjective* final, from which no further advance can be made ○ *To determine the ultimate load which a structure must be capable of withstanding, a multiplier, called the ultimate factor of safety is used.* ○ *The ultimate responsibility for safety rests with the crew.*

ultra- /ʌltrə/ *prefix* beyond

ultra high frequency /ˌʌltrə haɪ ˈfriːkwənsi/, **ultra high frequency band** /ˌʌltrə haɪ ˈfriːkwənsi ˌbænd/ *noun* a radio frequency range between 300 MHz and 3000 MHz. Abbreviation **UHF**

ultralight /ˈʌltrəlaɪt/ *noun* a small single-seat or two-seat aircraft constructed of light materials and powered by a small motor, flown mainly for recreation

ultrasonic /ˌʌltrəˈsɒnɪk/ *adjective* referring to frequencies in the range of 20,000 Hz which cannot be heard by the human ear

ultrasonic inspection /ˌʌltrəsɒnɪk ɪnˈspekʃ(ə)n/ *noun* a non-destructive inspection of materials using extremely high frequency vibrations. Also called **ultrasonic detection**

ultraviolet /ˌʌltrəˈvaɪələt/ *adjective* referring to or occurring in the invisible part of the light spectrum beyond violet. Abbreviation **UV** □ **ultraviolet radia-**tion the invisible part of the light spectrum beyond violet

unaccompanied /ˌʌnəˈkʌmpənid/ *adjective* □ **unaccompanied baggage** baggage that travels on a different flight from the passenger who owns it. ◊ **accompanied**

uncontrolled airspace /ˌʌnkəntrəʊld ˈeəspeɪs/ *noun* airspace in which air traffic control does not provide a service and in which an ATC clearance is not required to fly ○ *While first learning to handle an aircraft, student pilots fly in uncontrolled airspace.* (NOTE: Pilots must still follow certain rules when flying through uncontrolled airspace.)

uncoordinated flight *noun* flight, especially during turns, in which the horizontal and vertical forces acting on the aircraft are out of balance. This can result in the aircraft going into a **slip** or a **skid**.

undercarriage /ˈʌndəkærɪdʒ/ *noun* the landing gear of an aircraft ○ *To reduce the effect of drag by fixed undercarriages a retractable type of undercarriage was introduced.* (NOTE: The **undercarriage** is often called the **landing gear** or simply **gear**.)

COMMENT: The main landing gear are nearest the aircraft's centre of gravity. Main landing gear are designed to withstand a greater landing shock than the nose wheel or tail wheel and consequently should make contact with the surface first when landing.

undercarriage assembly /ˌʌndəkærɪdʒ əˈsembli/ *noun* wheels, struts and linkages which make up the complete unit

undercarriage down and locked
/ˌʌndəkærɪdʒ ˌdaʊn ən ˈlɒkd/ *noun*
confirmation that the undercarriage is
secure in preparation for landing

undergo /ˌʌndəˈgəʊ/ *verb* to experience, to pass through a process ○ *When
water changes from vapour to liquid,
energy is released into the atmosphere
which is thus warmed, although the
water itself does not undergo a change
of temperature.* (NOTE: **undergoing –
underwent – has undergone**)

underlying /ˌʌndəˈlaɪɪŋ/ *adjective* **1.**
being under ○ *Thermal modifications
occur when the temperature of the
underlying surface differs from that of
the source region.* **2.** forming the basis
of a theory or principle ○ *The principle
underlying the construction of a mercury barometer has not changed since
1643, when Torricelli first demonstrated that the atmosphere has weight.*

undershoot /ˌʌndəˈʃuːt/ *verb* to
land before, or in front of the intended
target ○ *Because of the strong wind, the
student pilot undershot the runway and
landed before the runway threshold.*

underside /ˈʌndəsaɪd/ *noun* the surface underneath something ○ *The
underside of the wing should be carefully inspected for damage or leaks.*

undertake /ˌʌndəˈteɪk/ *verb* to do ○
*In light aircraft, pilot/passenger com-
munication can be satisfactorily undertaken verbally on a one to one basis.*
(NOTE: **undertaking – undertook –
has undertaken**)

undulating /ˈʌndjʊleɪtɪŋ/ *adjective*
rising and falling in gentle slopes ○
*Flight over undulating terrain will
result in changing indications of aircraft height on the indicator of the radio
altimeter.*

uniform /ˈjuːnɪfɔːm/ *adjective* the
same, not varying in quality, dimensions, etc. ○ *An engine should be run at
low r.p.m. (revolutions per minute) after
flight to allow engine components to
cool to a uniform temperature.*

unique /juːˈniːk/ *adjective* the one
and only of its sort, having no like or
equal ○ *The pulse coded message contains a unique 4-number identification.*

unit /ˈjuːnɪt/ *noun* **1.** a quantity or
amount used as a standard, an accepted
measurement ○ *The internationally
agreed unit of pressure is the millibar.* ○
*The higher the sun is in the sky, the
more intense is the radiation per unit
area.* **2.** a person, group or device, complete in itself ○ *The operation of flying
controls is by means of self-contained
power flying control units (PFCUs).*

universal /ˌjuːnɪˈvɜːs(ə)l/ *adjective*
affecting all or everybody ○ *The use of
fly-by-wire systems in airliners was
delayed to allow thorough development
and encourage universal acceptance of
the new technology.* ◊ **Coordinated
Universal Time**

unload /ʌnˈləʊd/ *verb* to remove a
load from an aircraft ○ *It took three
hours to unload the aircraft.*

unloading point /ʌnˈləʊdɪŋ pɔɪnt/
noun the place where an aircraft is
unloaded ○ *After taxiing, a marshaller
marshals the aircraft to the disembarkation and unloading point.*

unsaturated /ʌnˈsætʃəreɪtɪd/
adjective □ **unsaturated air** air that
does not contain the maximum amount
of water vapour for its temperature

unserviceable /ʌnˈsɜːvɪsəb(ə)l/
adjective not operative ○ *The aircraft
cannot be flown because the radio is
unserviceable.* (NOTE: It is often abbreviated in spoken English as U (you) S
(ess).)

unstick /ʌnˈstɪk/ (*informal*) *verb* to
cause an aircraft to take off, or take off
in an aircraft ■ *noun* a take-off in an aircraft

update /ʌpˈdeɪt/ *verb* to bring up to
date, to add the latest information to
something ○ *Forecasts are updated and
reissued every four hours.*

updraft /ˈʌpdrɑːft/ *noun US* same as
updraught

updraught /ˈʌpdrɑːft/ *noun* a rising
current of air ○ *In cumulonimbus
clouds, there are updraughts of tremen-
dous force.* Opposite **downdraught**
(NOTE: It is written **updraft** in US English.)

uplift /ˈʌplɪft/ *noun* the lifting of air by
surface features ○ *Thunderstorms are*

triggered off by convection and/or oro-graphic uplift.

upper /'ʌpə/ *adjective* **1.** at high altitude ○ *upper air* ○ *upper winds* ○ *In modern meteorological practice, upper air analysis and the construction of contour charts is carried out by computer.* **2.** top. Opposite **lower** □ **the upper surface of the wing** the surface of the wing facing upwards, as opposed to the underside

upper air chart /ˌʌpə 'eə ˌtʃɑːt/ *noun* a chart showing airflow pattern and distribution of temperatures at specific altitudes above about 10,000 feet

upper air route /ˌʌpə 'eə ˌruːt/ *noun* a route above FL245, approximately 24,500 ft. Abbreviation **UAR**

upper airspace /ˌʌpə 'eəspeɪs/ *noun* the airspace above FL245, approximately 24,500 ft. Abbreviation **UAS**

upper information region *noun* airspace which covers the same geographical area as a **flight information region** but above 24,500 ft. Abbreviation **UIR**

upward /'ʌpwəd/ *adjective* moving or directed up ○ *As the aircraft accelerates down the runway, the forces on the wing tips and wing surfaces start reversing direction and instead of being only downward forces of weight, they become upward forces of lift.* (NOTE: In US English, **upward** is used as an adjective and as an adverb.)

upwards /'ʌpwədz/ *adverb* towards the top ○ *Heat is transferred from the Earth's surface upwards by convection.* Opposite **downwards**

upwind /ʌp'wɪnd/ *adverb* against the wind ○ *The glider was released from the aero-tow 3 miles upwind of the airfield.* Opposite **downwind**

urgency /'ɜːdʒənsi/ *noun* importance or need for prompt or fast action ○ *Warnings, cautions and advisory messages are displayed only when necessary and are colour coded to communicate the urgency of the fault to the flight crew.*

USA, US *abbreviation* United States of America

usable /'juːzəb(ə)l/ *adjective* capable of being used ○ *On receiving the evacuate order, cabin crew must assess if their exits are usable.*

usage /'juːsɪdʒ/ *noun* the act of using something, consumption ○ *Fuel flight planning combines navigation data with fuel usage.*

use *noun* /juːs/ the act of using something, or the state of being used ○ *It must be ensured that smoke masks are available for use by employees within the aircraft.* □ **runway in use** runway currently being used for take-offs and landings ■ *verb* /juːz/ to put something to work for a purpose ○ *Gas turbine engines use low viscosity synthetic oil.*

UTC *abbreviation* Coordinated Universal Time

utilisation /ˌjuːtɪlaɪ'zeɪʃ(ə)n/, **utilization** *noun* the act of making use of ○ *Integral tanks are now favoured for aircraft owing to the high utilisation of space and reduction in weight.*

utilise /'juːtɪlaɪz/, **utilize** *verb* to make use of ○ *The most common type of barograph is one which utilises an aneroid capsule mechanically connected to a pen.*

UV *abbreviation* ultraviolet

V

vacuum /'vækjuːm/ *noun* a space completely empty of everything including air ○ *If the fuel tank vent pipe is blocked, a vacuum will form in the tank and fuel flow to the engine will be restricted.*

valid /'vælɪd/ *adjective* **1.** having official force or effect ○ *All passengers should have valid passports.* **2.** worth taking seriously, acceptable because it is true or well-based ○ *Significant weather charts use abbreviations and symbols to illustrate en route weather phenomena and are valid for a specified time.* □ **a valid assumption** a well-based supposition

validity /və'lɪdɪti/ *noun* the state of being valid ○ *the period of validity of a visa* ○ *Aerodrome forecasts included in VOLMET should have a validity period of 9 hours.*

valley /'væli/ *noun* an area of low-lying land between mountains or hills ○ *An example of a valley wind is the Mistral.*

value /'væljuː/ *noun* **1.** a quantity shown as a number ○ *Deviation is not a constant value but varies from one aircraft to another.* **2.** the quality of being useful or desirable □ **the value of doing something** the usefulness or worth of doing something

valve /vælv/ *noun* a mechanical device for controlling the flow of a fluid

valve overlap /'vælv ˌəʊvəlæp/ *noun* the period when both the exhaust and inlet valves are open together, with the exhaust valve closing and the inlet valve opening

valve seat /'vælv siːt/ *noun* an angled ring in the cylinder head on which the poppet valve sits when closed

vane /veɪn/ *noun* a flat surface acted on by the wind or an airflow ○ *A centrifugal compressor consists of a disc on which is formed a number of radially spaced vanes.*

vapor /'veɪpə/ *noun* US same as **vapour**

vaporise /'veɪpəraɪz/, **vaporize** *verb* to turn into vapour ○ *Water vaporises when heated.*

vapour /'veɪpə/ *noun* the gaseous form of a liquid ○ *Over desert areas, the lack of water vapour in the atmosphere produces cold nights.* (NOTE: It is also written **vapor** in US English.)

vapour lock /'veɪpə lɒk/ *noun* a blockage of fuel flow from a tank caused by a bubble of vapour at a high point in the pipeline

vapour trail /'veɪpə treɪl/ *noun* a visible trail of condensed vapour left behind by an aircraft flying at high altitude

variable /'veəriəb(ə)l/ *adjective* changing or changeable ○ *Winds are more variable in the northern hemisphere than in the southern hemisphere.*

variable geometry /ˌveəriəb(ə)l dʒiː'ɒmətri/ *noun* technology which allows the angle between wing and fuselage to be altered to give a more or less swept wing for better high-speed and low-speed flight characteristics

variable-geometry /ˌveəriəb(ə)l dʒi'ɒmətri/ *adjective* referring to an aircraft with hinged wings that can move backwards or forwards during flight (NOTE: The wings are swept back to give low drag in supersonic flight and are moved forwards for takeoff and landing.)

variable pitch propeller /ˌveəriəb(ə)l pɪtʃ prə'pelə/ *noun* a propeller with a mechanism to change the blade angle, to suit flight conditions

variable-sweep /ˌveəriəb(ə)l 'swiːp/ *adjective* same as **variable-geometry**

variation /ˌveəri'eɪʃ(ə)n/ *noun* **1.** a change or the amount of a change **2.** the angular difference between magnetic north and true north, which is measured in degrees and is named east or west according to whether the north-seeking end of a freely suspended magnet lies to the east or to the west of the true meridian at that point □ **variation east, magnetic least: variation west, magnetic best** a mnemonic to help somebody remember whether to add or subtract variation

variety /və'raɪəti/ *noun* a lot of different things ○ *Display units provide a wide variety of information relevant to engine and other automated systems operation.*

variometer /ˌveəri'ɒmɪtə/ *noun* an instrument used for measuring the rate of climb of an aircraft such as a glider

vary /'veəri/ *verb* to change, to be different ○ *The tropopause over the UK can vary between 25,000 feet and 45,000 feet according to whether the country is covered by a polar or tropical air mass.*

VASI *abbreviation* visual approach slope indicator

vast /vɑːst/ *adjective* large, immense, huge □ **the vast majority** most ○ *the vast majority of people*

VCR *abbreviation* visual control room

VDF *abbreviation* very high frequency direction-finding

vector /'vektə/ *noun* **1.** a quantity with magnitude and direction indicated by a line of a given length, representing magnitude and specific direction ○ *The triangle of velocities is a vector solution of what happens to an aircraft when wind causes drift.* **2.** a heading given to

a pilot to provide navigational guidance by radar ○ *Wind velocity is indicated by a vector, identified by a single arrow, pointing in the direction the wind is blowing towards.*

veer /vɪə/ *noun* the shifting of the wind in a clockwise direction in the northern hemisphere ○ *The passing of a weather trough is marked by a sharp veer in the direction of the wind.* ■ *verb* **1.** to change in a clockwise direction in the northern hemisphere ○ *Winds veer and increase with height ahead of a warm front.* Opposite **back 2.** to change direction, especially as in an uncontrolled movement ○ *The aircraft veered off the runway into the grass.*

velocity /və'lɒsɪti/ *noun* the rate of change of position in a given direction which is composed of both speed and direction ○ *wind velocity* ○ *The anemograph gives a continuous recording of wind velocity which is displayed on a chart and reveals gusts, squalls and lulls.* ◊ **triangle**

vent /vent/ *noun* a hole serving as an inlet or outlet for a fluid, usually a gas such as air ○ *During the pre-flight inspection, check that the fuel tank vent pipe is not blocked.* ○ *The vent/pressurisation system must allow for the passage of air whenever a fuel tank is refuelled or defuelled or the aircraft climbs or descends.*

ventilate /'ventɪleɪt/ *verb* to cause air to pass in and out freely ○ *The water separator is installed downstream of the cold air unit to extract a percentage of free moisture from the air, which subsequently ventilates and pressurises the cabin.*

ventilation /ˌventɪ'leɪʃ(ə)n/ *noun* free circulation of air in and out ○ *A constant supply of air for ventilation purposes is always available from the air conditioning system.*

venturi /ven'tjʊəri/, **venturi tube** *noun* a tube which narrows at the centre, a choke tube ○ *When the temperature of the air passing through the carburettor is reduced below 0°C (Celsius), any moisture in the air forms* *into ice and builds up on the venturi and throttle valve.*

verification /ˌverɪfɪˈkeɪʃ(ə)n/ *noun* an act or instance of establishing the truth or validity of something ○ *The document required verification.*

versus /ˈvɜːsəs/ *preposition* against, as compared with ○ *The diagram illustrates typical strength properties by plotting applied stress versus resulting strain.*

vertical /ˈvɜːtɪk(ə)l/ *adjective* at right angles to the Earth's surface or to another line or plane ○ *Beams can be additionally stiffened in a downward direction by vertical and diagonal members.* ○ *Height is defined as the vertical distance of a level, point or object, considered to be a point, from a specified datum.* ■ *noun* a vertical line or plane ○ *The hot rod ice detector head consists of an aluminium alloy oblong base on which is mounted a steel tube detector mast, angled back to approximately 30° from the vertical.*

vertical axis /ˌvɜːtɪk(ə)l ˈæksɪs/ *noun* **1.** an imaginary line running through the fuselage at the centre of gravity from top to bottom, around which the aircraft rotates when it yaws ○ *The rudder is a control surface on the fin which rotates the aircraft about its vertical axis to produce yaw.* ◊ **yaw 2.** a vertical reference line (**Y axis**) of a graph ○ *The vertical axis shows engine power available.*

vertically /ˈvɜːtɪk(ə)li/ *adverb* in a vertical position ○ *The aircraft pitched up vertically.*

vertical speed indicator /ˌvɜːtɪk(ə)l ˈspiːd ˌɪndɪkeɪtə/ *noun* a flight instrument which indicates the rate of climb and descent. Abbreviation **VSI**

vertical stabiliser /ˌvɜːtɪk(ə)l ˈsteɪbɪlaɪzə/ *noun* same as **fin**

very high frequency /ˌveri haɪ ˈfriːkwənsi/, **very high frequency band** /ˌveri haɪ ˈfriːkwənsi ˌbænd/ *noun* the radio frequency range between 30 MHz and 300 MHz. Abbreviation **VHF**

very high frequency omni-directional radio range /ˌveri haɪ ˌfriːkwənsi ˌɒmnidaɪrekʃən(ə)l ˈreɪdiəʊ ˌreɪndʒ/ *noun* full form of **VOR**

vessel /ˈves(ə)l/ *noun* a boat or ship ○ *When flying over the sea you must not fly closer than 500 feet to a vessel.*

VFR *abbreviation* visual flight rules

VHF *abbreviation* very high frequency

via /ˈvaɪə/ *preposition* by way of ○ *The flight is from Cairo to Paris via Rome.* ○ *After heating, the air passes into the cabin via a chamber through which cold air also flows.*

vibrate /vaɪˈbreɪt/ *verb* to move rapidly and continuously backwards and forwards ○ *Turbine blades in the average jet engine vibrate at frequencies of 1 million per minute.*

vibration /vaɪˈbreɪʃ(ə)n/ *noun* a rapid and continuous movement ○ *According to the pilot, engine vibration was detected in engine number one.*

vice versa /ˌvaɪsə ˈvɜːsə/ *adjective* the other way around □ **when engine demand is high, fuel pressure tends to be low and vice versa** when the engine demand is low, fuel pressure tends to be high

vicinity /vəˈsɪnɪti/ *noun* the area nearby ○ *After an emergency evacuation, passengers should be directed to move away from the vicinity of the aircraft quickly.* □ **in the vicinity of the airport** near the airport

view /vjuː/ *noun* **1.** what you are able to see from a particular place ○ *Cabin crew must have a clear view of the aisles from their stations.* **2.** a picture of something presented in a particular way ○ *a cross-sectional view of an aerofoil* **3.** a personal opinion ○ *He expressed strong views on the subject of airport security.* **4.** □ **with a view to** with the intention of ○ *She wrote the report with a view to improving in-flight services.* □ **in view of** because of ○ *In view of the poor weather conditions, the flight will be delayed.*

violate /ˈvaɪəleɪt/ *verb* **1.** to enter without permission ○ *The aircraft violated a danger area.* **2.** to break rules or regulations ○ *By not wearing a cap, the cadet is violating the dress code.*

violent /'vaɪələnt/ *adjective* with great force ○ *Flying through atmospheric dust causes the airframe to build up a static electrical charge and the associated discharges can be violent.*

VIP *abbreviation* very important person

virtually /'vɜːtʃuəli/ *adverb* almost ○ *Resistance to alternating current remains virtually constant and is independent of frequency.*

viscosity /vɪ'skɒsɪti/ *noun* a liquid's internal resistance to flowing ○ *Excessive oil temperatures are dangerous, as the oil viscosity is reduced and inadequate bearing lubrication results.*

visibility /ˌvɪzɪ'bɪlɪti/ *noun* the ability to see unlighted objects by day and lighted objects by night, subject to atmospheric conditions ○ *Measurement of visibility by day is made by direct observation of objects at known distances and is therefore an estimated value.* □ **poor visibility** a situation in which things cannot be seen clearly, e.g. because of fog, mist or smoke

visibility-by-day values /ˌvɪzəbɪlɪti baɪ 'deɪ ˌvæljuːz/ *noun* values which indicate how easily seen an object is in a horizontal line from an observer in daylight conditions

visible /'vɪzɪb(ə)l/ *adjective* that can be seen ○ *When the undercarriage is selected down it may be visible from the crew compartment, but it is not usually possible to tell if it is securely locked.* ○ *If the sun is seen through cumulus cloud it will be clearly visible.*

vision /'vɪʒ(ə)n/ *noun* **1.** the power of seeing, the ability to see ○ *Lightning at night may cause temporary loss of vision.* **2.** what you are able to see ○ *In low wing aircraft, downward vision may be limited by the airframe.*

visual /'vɪʒuəl/ *adjective* referring to seeing ○ *The instrument landing system is to provide guidance in the horizontal and vertical planes to an aircraft on final approach into a position from which a safe visual landing can be made.*

visual approach slope indicator /ˌvɪʒuəl əˌprəʊtʃ 'sləʊp ˌɪndɪkeɪtə/ *noun* an arrangement of red and white lights on each side of the runway touchdown point to give the pilot information about the plane's height on final approach. Abbreviation **VASI**

visual control room /ˌvɪʒuəl kən'trəʊl ˌruːm/ the control room in the tower at an airport. Abbreviation **VCR**

visual examination /ˌvɪʒuəl ɪg ˌzæmɪ'neɪʃ(ə)n/ *noun* a close observation or inspection with the eyes. Also called **visual inspection**

visual flight rules /ˌvɪʒuəl 'flaɪt ˌruːlz/ *plural noun* rules set down by an authority for flight in visual conditions, regarding such things as flight visibility and distance from cloud. Abbreviation **VFR.** ◊ **special VFR flight**

COMMENT: Particular requirements for VFR depend on the type of airspace, time of day, and height above terrain.

visual indication /ˌvɪʒuəl ˌɪndɪ 'keɪʃ(ə)n/ *noun* something which is seen and which suggests a more serious cause, e.g. a warning lamp ○ *Distorted wing panels are often a visual indication of structural damage to the airframe.*

visual meteorological conditions /ˌvɪʒuəl ˌmiːtiərəlɒdʒɪk(ə)l kən'dɪʃ(ə)nz/, **visual meteorological conditions criteria** /ˌʌpə 'eə ˌtʃɑːt/ *plural noun* all the factors which define the limits of flying in visual meteorological conditions. Abbreviation **VMC**

visual warning /ˌvɪʒuəl 'wɔːnɪŋ/ *noun* a warning that can be seen as opposed to a audible warning that can be heard

vital /'vaɪt(ə)l/ *adjective* extremely important ○ *Verbal commands from the crew are vital at all times but particularly so if smoke restricts cabin visibility.* ○ *Accurate measurements of atmospheric pressure and the rate of change of pressure are of vital interest to the meteorological forecaster.*

viz /vɪz/ *adverb* namely, in other words, that is to say ○ *There are two types of inverter, viz rotary and static.*

VMC *abbreviation* visual meteorological conditions

Vne *abbreviation* never-exceed speed

volatile /'vɒlətaɪl/ *adjective* describes a liquid which easily changes into a gas or vapour ○ *To aid starting in cold weather, more volatile fuels can be used*

volatility /ˌvɒlə'tɪlɪti/ *noun* the ease with which a liquid changes into a gas or vapour ○ *With kerosene-type fuels, the volatility is controlled by distillation and flash point, but with the wide-cut fuels it is controlled by distillation and the Reid Vapour Pressure test.*

VOLMET /'vɒlmet/ *noun* a routine ground-to-air broadcast of meteorological information ○ *The meteorological Operational Telecommunications Network Europe (MOTNE) is provided for the exchange of meteorological information needed by meteorological offices, VOLMET broadcasting stations, air traffic service units, operators and other aeronautical users.*

volplane /'vɒlpleɪn/ *noun* a glide towards the ground in an aircraft with the engine turned off ■ *verb* to glide towards the ground in an aeroplane with the engine turned off

volt /vəʊlt/ *noun* the SI unit of electrical potential ○ *The system requires a power supply of either 115 volts AC (alternating current), 28 volts DC (direct current), or both.* Abbreviation **V**

voltage /'vəʊltɪdʒ/ *noun* electrical force measured in volts ○ *As an installed battery becomes fully charged by the aircraft generator, the battery voltage nears its nominal level and the charging current decreases.*

volume /'vɒljuːm/ *noun* **1.** the amount of space occupied by a solid, a liquid or a gas ○ *If the pressure of a given mass of gas is maintained constant, the volume of gas increases as its temperature is increased.* **2.** the loudness of a transmission □ **turn down the volume** to make the sound less loud by adjusting the volume control

volume control /'vɒljuːm kən,trəʊl/ *noun* a knob used to adjust the sound by making it louder or less loud

VOR *noun* a navigational aid based on the ground, to help the pilot establish the bearings of the aircraft. Full form **very high frequency omni-directional radio range**

COMMENT: The VOR projects 360 radials which can be followed to fly a particular path over the ground. VORs operate on VHF frequencies between 108.0 to 177.95 MHz.

VOR bearing /ˌviː əʊ 'ɑː ˌbeərɪŋ/ *noun* the direction of the VOR transmitter relative to the aircraft measured in degrees

VORTAC /'vɔːtæk/ *noun* a system that combines VOR and Tacan

VSI *abbreviation* vertical speed indicator

V/STOL /'viːstɒl/ *noun* **1.** a system used by some aircraft that allows them to take off and land vertically or on a short runway **2.** an aircraft that is able to take off and land vertically or on a short runway. Full form **vertical and short takeoff and landing**

VTOL /'viːtɒl/ *noun* **1.** a system used by some aircraft that allows them to take off and land vertically **2.** an aircraft that is able to take off and land vertically. Full form **vertical takeoff and landing**

vulnerable /'vʌln(ə)rəb(ə)l/ *adjective* unprotected and liable to attack or damage ○ *Some engines still retain the centrifugal type of compressor because it is simple, comparatively cheap to manufacture, robust in construction and less vulnerable to damage.*

W

W *abbreviation* west

WAAS *noun* a US navigation system which processes and improves data from GPS satellites to provide location information. Full form **Wide Area Augmentation System** (NOTE: The European equivalent is **EGNOS**.)

wake turbulence /ˈweɪk ˌtɜːbjʊləns/ *noun* the disturbance of the air remaining after the passage of an aircraft

wall /wɔːl/ *noun* the side ○ *There is a film of oil between the piston and cylinder wall.*

warm front /ˌwɔːm ˈfrʌnt/ *noun* an advancing mass of warm air moving over a mass of cooler air

warn /wɔːn/ *verb* to give notice of possible danger ○ *A light illuminates to warn the crew.*

'…ultrasonic technology which automatically warns pilots of ice build-up on aircraft may soon be approved for general use by carriers' [*Flight International 16–22 July 1997*]

warning /ˈwɔːnɪŋ/ *noun* notice of possible danger ■ *adjective* giving notice of possible danger ○ *The main power plant fire detection system should contain an audible warning device to supplement the visual indication.*

warning indicator /ˈwɔːnɪŋ ˌɪndɪkeɪtə/ *noun* an indicator which gives notice of a possible problem which may require some action. ◊ **VASI**

warning light /ˈwɔːnɪŋ laɪt/ *noun* a small light, often red, which informs of a possible danger by lighting up ○ *At 5 knots above stalling speed, a warning light on the instrument panel will flash.*

washroom /ˈwɒʃruːm/ *noun* same as **toilet 2**

waste /weɪst/ *noun* something which can no longer be used ○ *A smouldering fire in a toilet waste container or waste disposal bin could become very active due to pressure changes during descent.*

water-tight /ˈwɔːtə taɪt/ *adjective* that does not leak water or other fluid

watt /wɒt/ *noun* the SI unit of measurement of electrical power ○ *The work done by an electrical circuit or the power consumed is measured in watts.*

wave /weɪv/ *noun* **1.** the motion by which heat, light, sound or electric current is spread ○ *The speed of propagation of radio waves is faster over sea than over land.* **2.** a mass of water moving across the surface of a lake or the sea, rising higher than the surrounding water as it moves ○ *Wind speeds increase with height, the speed of the wind at the crest of a wave being the greatest.*

waveform /ˈweɪvfɔːm/ *noun* the shape of a repetitive wave ○ *A cycle is one complete sequence of the waveform, from any point, to the same value 360° later.*

wavelength /ˈweɪvleŋθ/ *noun* the distance from the highest point of one wave to the highest point of the next ○ *Short wavelength permits sharper beams for direction finding and more efficient reflections.*

waveoff /ˈweɪvɒf/ *noun* a signal or instruction to an aircraft that it should not land

waypoint /'weɪpɔɪnt/ *noun* a predetermined position on a route, used for monitoring flight progress or for navigating around controlled airspace. Abbreviation **WP**

weak /wiːk/ *adjective* **1.** not strong o *a weak radio signal* **2.** overdiluted with water or air □ **weak mixture** a fuel/air mixture in which there is more air than usual o *Excessive cylinder head temperatures could be caused by prolonged use of a weak mixture, especially at high altitude.* □ **weak solution** a mixture of water and some other substance in which the amount of water is more than usual

weaken /'wiːkən/ *verb* to make weak o *Inflation of the de-icer boot weakens the bond between the ice and de-icer boot surfaces.*

wear /weə/ *noun* damage or loss of quality by use o *Mishandling of aero-engines during operation can cause considerable damage and wear which can shorten the life of the engine.* ∎ *verb* **1.** to become damaged or to lose quality because of use o *The more the brakes are used, the more they wear.* **2.** to have on the body o *The nature of modern jet transport does not require the pilot to wear an oxygen mask.*

weather /'weðə/ *noun* the conditions of atmospheric temperature, pressure, wind, moisture, cloudiness, precipitation and visibility o *Generally speaking, weather conditions can be described as light, moderate or severe depending on the intensity of the conditions.* □ **forecast weather** predicted weather, not actual weather

weathercock /'weθəkɒk/ *verb* to tend to turn in the direction of the wind

weather report /'weðə rɪˌpɔːt/ *noun* an official account of weather conditions

web /web/ *noun* the main vertical member of a beam o *The web connecting the upper and lower flanges of the beams must be rigid enough to withstand direct compressive loads without buckling.*

weigh /weɪ/ *verb* to measure how heavy something is o *A given quantity of lead weighs more than the same quantity of aluminium.*

weight /weɪt/ *noun* the force with which a body is drawn towards the centre of the Earth o *Carry-on baggage is limited by regulations as to size and weight and items in excess of this should be stowed in the hold.*

west /west/ *noun* **1.** a compass point on the mariner's compass 270° clockwise from due north and directly opposite east o *In Europe, snow occurs more frequently in the east than in the west.* **2.** the direction of the setting sun ∎ *adjective* **1.** referring to areas or regions lying in the west **2.** the western part of a country o *West Africa* ∎ *adverb* towards the west o *The aircraft was flying west.*

westbound /'westbaʊnd/ *adjective* travelling towards the west o *a westbound flight*

westerly /'westəli/ *adjective* **1.** situated towards the west **2.** blowing or coming from the west o *A westerly wind is blowing.* **3.** moving to the west or towards the west o *He should fly in a westerly direction.* ∎ *noun* a wind which blows or comes from the west o *Temperate westerlies occur on the side of the sub-tropical anti-cyclonic belts which is remote from the equator.*

western /'westən/ *adjective* situated in the west o *Western Europe*

westward /'westwəd/ *adjective* going towards the west ∎ *adverb US* same as **westwards**

westwards /'westwədz/ *adverb* towards the west o *Flying eastwards or westwards for long periods of time affects sleep patterns.*

west wind /ˌwest 'wɪnd/ *noun* a wind blowing from or coming from the west (NOTE: A wind is named after the direction it comes from.)

wheel /wiːl/ *noun* a circular, rotating, load-carrying part between the tyre and axle, or the whole wheel and tyre assembly on which a vehicle rolls

wheel bay /'wiːl beɪ/ *noun* a space in the fuselage or wing structure in which the wheel is housed after retraction o *To avoid damage to the wheel bay, the nose* *wheel must be aligned in a fore and aft direction during retraction.*

wheel bearing /'wiːl ˌbeərɪŋ/ *noun* a device which allows the wheel to rotate freely around the axle

wheel fairing /'wiːl ˌfeərɪŋ/ *noun* same as **spat**

wheels up /ˌwiːlz 'ʌp/ *adjective* airborne after having taken off from a runway

whereas /weərˈæz/ *conjunction* but in contrast, on the other hand ○ *In the piston engine, the cycle is intermittent, whereas in the gas turbine, each process is continuous.* ○ *Kerosene has a low vapour pressure and boils only at very high altitudes or high temperatures, whereas a wide-cut fuel will boil at a much lower altitude.*

whereby /weəˈbaɪ/ *adverb* according to which ○ *Compression heating relies on the principle whereby the air temperature is increased by compression.* ○ *In ram air supply systems, the cooling method is of the simplest type, whereby the cold air can be directly admitted to the cabin via adjustable louvres.*

whereupon /ˌweərəˈpɒn/ *adverb* at that point, or after which ○ *Pitch changes are achieved using the throttle lever, which is usually taken up and back through a gate in the quadrant whereupon fuel is added to increase power.*

wherever /weərˈevə/ *adverb* □ **wherever possible** in places where it is possible □ **wherever possible, thunderstorms should be avoided by a wide margin** thunderstorms should be avoided by a wide margin in situations or places where it is possible to avoid them

while /waɪl/ *conjunction* **1.** during the time that ○ *The pilot is trained to scan an instrument panel, while at the same time listening to the aircraft radio and flying the aircraft.* **2.** in spite of the fact that ○ *While metal fatigue is not a modern phenomenon, it is only in recent years that much emphasis has been placed upon determining its causes.* (NOTE: **Whilst** is sometimes used in place of **while**.)

whipstall /'wɪpstɔːl/ *noun* a manoeuvre in a small aircraft in which it goes into a vertical climb, pauses briefly, and then drops towards the earth, front first

whole /həʊl/ *adjective* complete ○ *The whole aircraft should be inspected to ensure that it is free from deposits of ice, snow and frost.* □ **whole number** an undivided number, a number which is not a fraction

wide /waɪd/ *adjective* **1.** referring to the distance of something measured from side to side ○ *The localiser antenna array is normally about 80 feet wide and 12 feet high.* **2.** □ **a wide range of temperatures** a large difference between the lowest and the highest temperature □ **a wide variety of information** a lot of different information. ◊ **width**

Wide Area Augmentation System *noun* full form of **WAAS**

wide-bodied /ˌwaɪd 'bɒdiːd/ *adjective US* same as **wide-body**

widebody /'waɪdbɒdi/ *noun* a jet aircraft with a body wide enough to accommodate three rows of seats across the width of the plane, with spaces on each side of the middle set

wide-body /'waɪd ˌbɒdi/ *adjective* referring to a jet aircraft with a body wide enough to have three sets of passenger seats in a row across the width of the plane, with spaces on each side of the middle set

wide-cut fuel /ˌwaɪd kʌt 'fjuːəl/ *noun* a general term for aviation turbine fuels made up of a wider variety of petroleum products than kerosene-type fuels ○ *Kerosene has a low vapour pressure and boils only at very high altitudes or high temperatures, whereas a wide-cut fuel will boil at a much lower altitude.*

widespread /'waɪdspred/ *adjective* found or distributed across a large area ○ *The storm caused widespread damage.* □ **widespread precipitation** rainfall or snowfall covering a large area

width /wɪdθ/ *noun* the distance of something measured from side to side, compared to length ○ *The polar front jet* *stream may have a width of up to 200 nm (nautical miles).* ◊ **wide**

wind¹ /wɪnd/ *noun* horizontal movement of air in relation to the Earth's surface

wind² /waɪnd/ *verb* to move in a curving or twisting manner ○ *If a wire is wound as a coil, the field will be like that of a bar magnet.* (NOTE: **winding – wound**)

windblast /ˈwɪndblɑːst/ *noun* the harmful effect of air flow on a pilot who has ejected from an aircraft travelling at high speed

wind cone /ˈwɪnd kəʊn/ *noun* same as **windsock**

wind currents /ˈwɪnd ˌkʌrənts/ *plural noun* the movement of air in a particular direction through a mass of air which is not moving so much

wind direction /ˈwɪnd daɪˌrekʃən/ *noun* a description of where the wind is blowing from, given as north, south, east, west, etc., or a number of degrees, e.g. a wind coming from the west would be a wind direction of 270° ○ *Wind direction and speed only affect the movement of the aircraft over the ground.*

wind gradient /ˈwɪnd ˌɡreɪdiənt/ *noun* the rate of increase of wind strength with unit increase in height above ground level ○ *After take-off, as the aircraft gains altitude, the ground speed may be affected by the wind gradient.*

winding /ˈwaɪndɪŋ/ *noun* a series of 360° turns of wire ○ *The voltage in each winding is directly proportional to the number of turns in each winding.*

windmill /ˈwɪndmɪl/ *verb* to turn round by wind force only without engine power

windscreen /ˈwɪndskriːn/ *noun* the front window of an aircraft through which the pilot has forward vision ○ *The windscreen is a glass laminated construction with an electrical element, made of gold film, sandwiched between the layers.* ◊ **wiper**

windshear /ˈwɪndʃɪə/ *noun* a change in wind direction and speed between slightly different altitudes ○ *Windshear,*

if strong enough, can produce clear air turbulence. ○ *Fly-by-wire technology can be very useful in windshear situations.*

windshield /ˈwɪndʃiːld/ *noun US* same as **windscreen**

windsock /ˈwɪndsɒk/ *noun* a pole at the top of which is a fabric tube through which the wind blows, showing the wind direction

windspeed /ˈwɪndspiːd/ *noun* the speed of the wind which, if combined with a direction, is called velocity. It is usually measured in knots. ○ *Wind direction is given in degrees true rounded to the nearest 10°, followed by the mean windspeed.*

wind tunnel /ˈwɪnd ˌtʌn(ə)l/ *noun* a tunnel-shaped chamber through which air can be passed at a known speed in order to test the aerodynamic properties of an object such as an aircraft placed inside it

wind velocity /ˈwɪnd vəˌlɒsɪti/ *noun* wind speed and direction

windward /ˈwɪndwəd/ *adjective, adverb* facing the direction from which the wind blows. Opposite **lee** □ **windward of a range of hills** upwind of the range of hills ○ *If precipitation occurs, water will have been removed from the atmosphere thus causing the air on the lee side to be drier than that on the windward side.*

wing /wɪŋ/ *noun* the main horizontal aerofoil or mainplane ○ *The wing supports the weight of the aircraft in flight.*

winglet /ˈwɪŋlət/ *noun* an upturned wing tip or small additional vertical aerofoil on a wing tip ○ *The attachment of winglets improved the handling characteristics of the aeroplane.*

wing loading /ˈwɪŋ ˌləʊdɪŋ/ *noun* the weight of an aircraft per unit wing area

wingman /ˈwɪŋmæn/ *noun* a pilot who flies in a position behind and to the side of the leader of a group of flying aircraft

wingover /ˈwɪndəʊvə/ *noun* a manoeuvre to turn a flying aircraft in which the pilot puts the aircraft into a steep turning climb until it almost stalls and then allows the nose to fall

wing panel /'wɪŋ ˌpæn(ə)l/ *noun* a rectangular aluminium section of the aircraft skin of a wing ○ *Wing panels of light aircraft are normally riveted together.*

wing root /'wɪŋ ruːt/ *noun* the part of the wing where it meets with the fuselage

wingspan /'wɪŋspæn/ *noun* a measurement from the tip of one wing to the tip of the other wing ○ *The wingspan of the aircraft is 7 metres.*

wing tip /'wɪŋ tɪp/ *noun* the outermost part of the wing ○ *As an aircraft takes off, the forces on the wing tip and wing surfaces start reversing direction and instead of being only downward forces of weight, they become upward forces of lift.*

wipe /waɪp/ *verb* to clean or to dry by using a cloth ○ *In the event of hydraulic fluid spillage on paintwork, the affected area should be wiped clean immediately.*

wiper /'waɪpə/ *noun* a device with a rubber blade which clears rain, snow, etc., from a windscreen ○ *In some circumstances, such as heavy rainstorms, the windscreen wipers may not be able to cope and pilot's visibility is impaired.*

wire /'waɪə/ *noun* metal drawn out into the form of a thread or string ○ *While the shunt coil is made of fine wire which gives a high resistance and small current flow, the series coil is made of thick wire, which gives a low resistance and large current flow.*

wire mesh /'waɪə meʃ/ *noun* metal sheeting made of criss-crossed wiring

withdraw /wɪð'drɔː/ *verb* to pull back, to draw back ○ *Instructions are given to the cabin crew to arm the escape devices immediately the boarding steps or airbridges are withdrawn.* (NOTE: **withdrew – withdrawn**)

within /wɪ'ðɪn/ *preposition* in or inside ○ *Great care must be taken to ensure that the aircraft operates within regulated or permissible weight limits.* □ **within two hours** in about two hours or less, but not more

withstand /wɪð'stænd/ *verb* to resist or bear ○ *Wings must be capable of not only withstanding the aircraft weight, but also the stresses and strains which are imposed during flight.*

WMO *abbreviation* World Meteorological Organization

work /wɜːk/ *noun* **1.** the operation of a force to produce movement or some other physical change ○ *1 horsepower is defined as 33,000 foot-pounds of work accomplished in one minute (a foot-pound being the ability to lift a one pound weight a distance of one foot).* **2.** something which has to be done, e.g. maintenance ○ *Work is being carried out on the auxiliary power unit (APU).* **3.** something done to earn a living ○ *She enjoys her work as an airport security officer.* ■ *verb* **1.** to operate, to function □ **the computer doesn't work** the computer doesn't operate as it should do because there is something wrong with it **2.** to do something such as maintenance ○ *Engineers worked on the aircraft all night.* **3.** to do something to earn a living ○ *She works for a large airline.* **4.** □ **to work out** to calculate, to solve a mathematical problem ○ *Aircraft performance is a function of weight and therefore it is important that you can work out weight from volume and vice-versa.*

working conditions /'wɜːkɪŋ kən ˌdɪʃ(ə)nz/ *plural noun* those aspects of working lives which affect the way people feel about their work

work load /'wɜːk ləʊd/ *noun* the share of work done by a person, system or device

WP *abbreviation* waypoint

XYZ

X-ray /'eks reɪ/ *noun* **1.** a ray with a very short wavelength, which is invisible, but can go through soft tissue or material and register as a photograph on a film **2.** a photograph taken using X-rays ■ *verb* to take an X-ray photograph of luggage

yard /jɑːd/ *noun* a unit of length in the US and British Imperial Systems equal to 3 ft or 0.9144 m. Abbreviation **yd**

yaw /jɔː/ *noun* rotation of the aircraft around its vertical axis ○ *Three-axis control of roll, pitch and yaw is effected by ailerons, elevators and rudder.* ■ *verb* to rotate around the vertical axis ○ *Single-engine, propeller-driven aircraft tend to yaw on take-off.*

yoke /jəʊk/ *noun* **1.** a type of aircraft control column by which the pilot controls ailerons by rotating a device on top of the column to the left or right ○ *Rotate the yoke to the left to roll the aircraft to the left.* **2.** a supporting structure like the forked metal mounting for the nosewheel ○ *The yoke was damaged in the incident.*

Z *abbreviation* Zulu time

zero /'zɪərəʊ/ *noun* nought or the figure 0 ○ *If the atmospheric pressure at an airfield is 1,000 millibars (mb) and this pressure is set on the sub-scale of an aircraft altimeter, then when that aircraft touches down at the airfield, the altimeter will read zero.*

zero-zero /ˌzɪərəʊ 'zɪərəʊ/ *adjective* referring to flying conditions of thick, low cloud when a pilot can see nothing ahead and nothing above or below the aircraft

zonal /'zəʊn(ə)l/ *adjective* referring to one of the five parts into which the Earth's surface is divided by imaginary lines parallel to the equator ○ *The circulation of air around the Earth is zonal in character.*

zone /zəʊn/ *noun* **1.** an area with particular features or purpose **2.** an administrative area of airspace ○ *control zone* ○ *aerodrome traffic zone (ATZ)* **3.** one of five divisions into which the Earth's surface is divided by imaginary lines parallel to the equator ○ *temperate zone* ◊ **climatic zone**

zoom /zuːm/ *verb* to make an aircraft climb rapidly at a very steep angle, or move upwards in this way

Zulu time /'zuːluː taɪm/ *noun* ◆ **Greenwich Mean Time**

SUPPLEMENTS

The Phonetic Alphabet
Standard words and phrases used in pilot communications
Aircraft registration codes
Airline codes
Airport codes
Local times around the world
International dialling codes
Standard symbols and abbreviations
Weights and measures
Conversion factors

The Phonetic Alphabet

Certain letters of the alphabet sound very similar, especially when a person is talking on the telephone or radio. The phonetic alphabet is designed to prevent confusion, by using a distinctive word to represent each letter.

Aa	Alpha*	'ælfə
Bb	Bravo	'brɑːvəʊ
Cc	Charlie	'tʃɑːli
Dd	Delta	'deltə
Ee	Echo	'ekəʊ
Ff	Foxtrot	'fɒkstrɒt
Gg	Golf	gɒlf
Hh	Hotel	həʊ'tel
Ii	India	'ɪndiə
Jj	Juliet	ˌdʒuːli'et
Kk	Kilo	'kiːləʊ
Ll	Lima	'liːmə
Mm	Mike	maɪk
Nn	November	nə'vembə
Oo	Oscar	'ɒskə
Pp	Papa	'pæpə
Qq	Quebec	kwɪ'bek
Rr	Romeo	'rəʊmiəʊ
Ss	Sierra	si'erə
Tt	Tango	'tæŋgəʊ
Uu	Uniform	'juːnɪfɔːm
Vv	Victor	'vɪktə
Ww	Whisky**	'wɪski
Xx	X-Ray	'eksreɪ
Yy	Yankee	'jæŋki
Zz	Zulu	'zuːluː

* Alfa in US English
** Whiskey in US English

Standard words and phrases

Word/Phrase	Meaning
Acknowledge	Let me know that you have received and understood this message.
Affirm	Yes
Approved	I give you permission for what you asked.
Cancel	Cancel the last clearance I gave to you.
Check	Examine a system or procedure.
Cleared	I give permission for you to continue, bearing in mind the conditions already given.
Confirm	Have I correctly received the following … ? *or* Did you correctly receive this message ?
Contact	Contact by radio …
Correct	That is correct.
Correction	An error was made in the last transmission. What follows is correct.
Disregard	Assume that the last transmission was not sent.
How do you read?	Tell me how good this transmission is on a 1 to 5 scale where 1 = unreadable (cannot understand) to 5 = excellent reception (no difficulty in understanding).
I say again	I am repeating in order to make my meaning very clear.
Over	My transmission is finished and I want a response from you.
Out	This exchange of transmissions is finished. I do not want a response from you.
Pass your message	Proceed with your message.
Read back	Repeat all, or the specified part of this message back to me exactly as received.
Request	I want to know *or* I want to have.
Roger	I have received all of your last transmission.
Say again	Repeat all, or the following part of your last transmission.
Speak slower	Speak more slowly.
Standby	Wait and I will call you.
Verify	Check and confirm with me.
Wilco	I understand your message and will comply with it.
Words Twice	*(as a request)* Communication is difficult. Please send every word or group of words twice. *(as information)* Because communication is difficult, every word or group of words in this message will be sent twice.

Aircraft registration codes

These codes are painted on all aircraft, showing their country of registration.

3A	Monaco	A3	Tonga
3B	Mauritius	A40	Oman
3C	Equatorial Guinea	A5	Bhutan
3D	Swaziland	A6	United Arab Emirates
3X	Guinea	A7	Qatar
4K	Azerbaijan	A9C	Bahrain
4R	Sri Lanka	AP	Pakistan
4U	United Nations Organisation	B	China & Taiwan
4X	Israel	B-H	Hong Kong
5A	Libya	B-M	Macau
5B	Cyprus	C	Canada
5H	Tanzania	C2	Nauru
5N	Nigeria	C3	Andorra
5R	Madagascar	C5	Gambia
5T	Mauritania	C6	Bahamas
5U	Niger	C9	Mozambique
5V	Togo	CC	Chile
5W	Samoa	CN	Morocco
5X	Uganda	CP	Bolivia
5Y	Kenya	CS	Portugal
6O	Somalia	CU	Cuba
6V	Senegal	CX	Uruguay
6Y	Jamaica	D	Germany
7O	Yemen	D2	Angola
7P	Lesotho	D4	Cape Verde
7Q	Malawi	D6	Comoros Islands
7T	Algeria	DQ	Fiji
8P	Barbados	EC	Spain
8Q	Maldives	EI	Ireland
8R	Guyana	EK	Armenia
9A	Croatia	EP	Iran
9G	Ghana	ER	Moldova
9H	Malta	ES	Estonia
9J	Zambia	ET	Ethiopia
9K	Kuwait	EW	Belarus
9L	Sierra Leone	EY	Tajikistan
9M	Malaysia	EZ	Turkmenistan
9N	Nepal	F	France
9Q	Democratic Republic of the Congo	F	New Caledonia (France)
9U	Burundi	F	Guadeloupe (France)
9V	Singapore	F	Martinique (France)
9XR	Rwanda	F	Tahiti (French Polynesia)
9Y	Trinidad and Tobago		
A2	Botswana	G	United Kingdom

Aircraft registration codes *continued*

H4	Solomon Islands	RA	Russian Federation
HA	Hungary	RP	Philippines
HB	Switzerland &	S2	Bangladesh
	Liechtenstein	S5	Slovenia
HC	Ecuador	S7	Seychelles
HH	Haiti	S9	Sao Tome and Principe
HI	Dominican Republic	SE	Sweden
HK	Colombia	SP	Poland
HL	South Korea	ST	Sudan
HP	Panama	SU	Egypt
HR	Honduras	SX	Greece
HS	Thailand	T2	Tuvalu
HV	The Vatican	T3	Kiribati
HZ	Saudi Arabia	T7	San Marino
I	Italy	T8A	Palau
J2	Djibouti	T9	Bosnia-Herzegovina
J3	Grenada	TC	Turkey
J5	Guinea Bissau	TF	Iceland
J6	St Lucia	TG	Guatemala
J7	Dominica	TI	Costa Rica
J8	St Vincent and the	TJ	Cameroon
	Grenadines	TL	Central African
JA	Japan		Republic
JU	Mongolia	TN	Congo-Brazzaville
JY	Jordan	TR	Gabon
LN	Norway	TS	Tunisia
LV	Argentina	TT	Chad
LX	Luxembourg	TU	Côte d'Ivoire
LY	Lithuania	TY	Benin
LZ	Bulgaria	TZ	Mali
N	USA	UK	Uzbekistan
OB	Peru	UR	Ukraine
OD	Lebanon	V2	Antigua and Barbuda
OE	Austria	V3	Belize
OH	Finland	V4	St Kitts and Nevis
OK	Czech Republic	V5	Namibia
OO	Belgium	V6	Micronesia
OY	Denmark	V7	Marshall Islands
P	North Korea	V8	Brunei
P2	Papua New Guinea	VH	Australia
P4	Aruba	VN	Vietnam
PH	Netherlands	VP, VQ	British Overseas
PJ	Netherland Antilles		Territories
PK	Indonesia	VP-A	Anguilla (UK)
PP	Brazil	VP-B	Bermuda (UK)
PZ	Suriname	VP-C	Cayman Islands (UK)

Aircraft registration codes *continued*

VP-F	Falkland Islands	YA	Afghanistan
VP-G	Gibraltar (UK)	YI	Iraq
VP-L	British Virgin Islands	YJ	Vanuatu
VP-M	Montserrat	YK	Syria
VQ-H	St Helena (UK)	YL	Latvia
VQ-T	Turks and Caicos	YN	Nicaragua
	Islands (UK)	YR	Romania
VR-B	Bermuda	YS	El Salvador
VR-C	Cayman Island	YU	Serbia and Montenegro
VR-G	Gibraltar	YV	Venezuela
VR-H	Hong Kong	Z	Zimbabwe
VT	India	ZA	Albania
XA	Mexico	ZK	New Zealand
XT	Burkina Faso	ZP	Paraguay
XU	Cambodia	ZS	South Africa
XY	Myanmar		

Airline codes

2J	Air Burkina	FG	Ariana Afghan Airlines
4U	GermanWings	FI	IcelandAir
9U	Air Moldova	FJ	Air Pacific
AA	American Airlines	FO	Airlines of Tasmania
AB	Air Berlin	FR	Ryanair
AC	Air Canada	GA	Garuda Indonesia
AF	Air France	GC	Gambia International Airlines
AH	Air Algerie		
AI	Air India	GF	Gulf Air
AM	Aeromexico	GH	Ghana Airways
AQ	Aloha Airlines	GL	Air Greenland
AR	Aerolineas Argentinas	GN	Air Gabon
AS	Alaska Airlines	GR	Aurigny Air Services
AT	Royal Air Maroc	GY	Guyana Airways
AY	Finnair	HA	Hawaiian Airlines
AZ	Alitalia	HM	Air Seychelles
BA	British Airways	HP	America West Airlines
BB	Seaborne Airlines	HV	Transavia Airlines
BD	bmi British Midland	HY	Uzbekistan Airways
BG	Biman Bangladesh Airlines	IB	Iberia
BH	Transtate Airlines	IC	Indian Airlines
BI	Royal Brunei Airlines	IE	Solomon Airlines
BL	Pacific Airlines	IR	Iran Air
BM	Air Sicilia	IV	Wind Jet
BO	Bouraq Indonesia Airlines	IY	Yemenia - Yemen Airways
BP	Air Botswana	JL	Japan Airlines
BR	EVA Air	JM	Air Jamaica
BU	Braathens ASA	JP	Adria Airways
BW	BWIA - West Indies Airways	JU	JAT Airways
		JY	Interisland Airways
CA	Air China International	KE	Korean Air Lines
CB	ScotAirways	KL	KLM Royal Dutch Airlines
CI	China Airlines	KM	Air Malta
CJ	China Northern Airlines	KP	Kiwi International Airlines
CM	COPA (Compania Panamena de Aviación)	KQ	Kenya Airways
		KU	Kuwait Airways
CO	Continental Airlines	KV	Kavminvodyavia
CU	Cubana	KX	Cayman Airways
CX	Cathay Pacific Airways	KY	Linhas Aereas de Air Sao Tome and Principe
CY	Cyprus Airways		
CZ	China Southern Airlines	LA	Lan-Chile
DL	Delta Air Lines	LG	Luxair
DS	Easyjet Switzerland	LH	Lufthansa
DT	TAAG Angola Airlines	LN	Jamahiriya Libyan Arab Airlines
DU	Hemus Air		
DY	Air Djibouti	LO	LOT Polish Airlines
EI	Aer Lingus	LY	El Al Israel Airlines
EK	Emirates	LX	Swiss
ET	Ethiopian Airlines	LZ	Balkan-Bulgarian Airlines
FC	Finncomm		

Airline codes *continued*

MA	MALEV Hungarian Airlines	RK	Royal Khymer Airlines
		RO	TAROM
MD	Air Madagascar	SA	South African Airways
MH	Malaysia Airlines	SD	Sudan Airways
MK	Air Mauritius	SK	SAS
MN	Commercial Airways	SN	SN Brussels Airlines
MR	Air Mauritanie	SQ	Singapore Airlines
MS	Egyptair	SU	Aeroflot Russian Airlines
NF	Air Vanuatu	SV	Saudi Arabian Airlines
NG	Lauda Air	SW	Air Namibia
NH	All Nippon Airways	TC	Air Tanzania
NO	Aus-Air	TE	Lithuanian Airlines
NQ	Air Japan	TG	Thai Airways International
NV	Nakanihon Airlines	TK	Turkish Airlines
NW	Northwest Airlines	TM	LAM - Lineas Aereas de Moçambique
NZ	Air New Zealand		
OA	Olympic Airlines	TN	Air Tahiti Nui
OB	Astrakhan Airlines	TP	TAP - Air Portugal
OK	Czech Airlines	TU	Tunisair
OM	MIAT - Mongolian Airlines	U2	Easyjet
		UA	United Airlines
ON	Air Nauru	UB	Myanmar Airways
OO	SkyWest Airlines	UI	Eurocypria Airlines
OS	Austrian Airlines	UL	SriLankan Airlines
OU	Croatia Airlines	UM	Air Zimbabwe
OV	Estonian Air	US	US Airways
PB	Provincial Airlines	UY	Cameroon Airlines
PC	Air Fiji	VE	AVENSA
PH	Polynesian	VH	Aeropostal
PK	Pakistan International Airlines	VJ	Jatayu Airlines
		VN	Vietnam Airlines
PR	Philippine Airlines	VO	Tyrolean Airlines
PS	Ukraine International Airlines	VR	TACV - Transportes Aereos de Cabo Verde
PU	Pluna Lineas Aereas Uruguayas	VS	Virgin Atlantic
		VU	Air Ivoire
PX	Air Niugini	VX	V Bird
PY	Surinam Airways	W6	Wizz Air
PZ	TAM - Transportes Aereos del Mercosur	WG	Wasaya Airlines
		WJ	Labrador Airways
QF	Qantas Airways	W6	Wizz Air
QM	Air Malawi	WG	Wasaya Airlines
QR	Qatar Airways	WJ	Labrador Airways
QU	East African Airlines	WN	Southwest Airlines
QV	Lao Airlines	WR	Royal Tongan Airlines
QX	Horizon Air	WY	Oman Aviation
RA	Royal Nepal Airlines	YK	Kibris Turk Hava Yollari
RB	Syrian Arab Airlines	YN	Air Creebec
RG	Varig	YU	Dominair
RJ	Royal Jordanian	ZB	Monarch Airlines

Airport codes

code	*airport*	*country*
ABJ	Abidjan	Côte d'Ivoire
ABZ	Aberdeen	UK
ACA	Acapulco	Mexico
ACC	Accra	Ghana
ADD	Addis Ababa	Ethiopia
ADL	Adelaide	Australia
AGP	Malaga	Spain
AKL	Auckland	New Zealand
ALC	Alicante	Spain
ALG	Algiers	Algeria
AMM	Amman	Jordan
AMS	Amsterdam	Netherlands
ANC	Anchorage	USA
ANK	Ankara	Turkey
ANR	Antwerp	Belgium
ANU	Antigua	Antigua
ARN	Stockholm Arlanda	Sweden
ASU	Asuncion	Paraguay
ATH	Athens	Greece
ATL	Atlanta	USA
AUH	Abu Dhabi	UAE
AXA	Wallblake	Anguilla
BAH	Bahrain	Bahrain
BCN	Barcelona	Spain
BDA	Bermuda	Bermuda
BER	Berlin	Germany
BEY	Beirut	Lebanon
BFS	Belfast	UK
BGI	Bridgetown	Barbados
BGO	Bergen	Norway
BHX	Birmingham	UK
BIO	Bilbao	Spain
BJL	Banjul	Gambia
BJM	Bujumbura	Burundi
BJS	Beijing	China
BKK	Bangkok	Thailand
BLQ	Bologna	Italy
BNE	Brisbane	Australia
BOD	Bordeaux	France
BOG	Bogota	Colombia
BOM	Mumbai	India
BOS	Boston	USA
BRE	Bremen	Germany
BRN	Berne	Switzerland
BRS	Bristol	UK

Airport codes *continued*

code	airport	country
BRU	Brussels	Belgium
BSL	Basle/Mulhouse	Switzerland
BTS	Bratislava	Slovakia
BUD	Budapest	Hungary
BUE	Buenos Aires	Argentina
BUH	Bucharest	Romania
BWI	Baltimore	USA
BZV	Brazzaville	Congo
CAI	Cairo	Egypt
CAS	Casablanca	Morocco
CBR	Canberra	Australia
CCS	Caracas	Venezuela
CCU	Calcutta	India
CDG	Paris Charles de Gaulle	France
CGK	Jakarta	Indonesia
CGN	Cologne	Germany
CHC	Christchurch	New Zealand
CHI	Chicago	USA
CLE	Cleveland	USA
CMB	Colombo	Sri Lanka
CMN	Casablanca Mohamed V	Morocco
CNS	Cairns	Australia
COO	Cotonou	Benin
CPH	Copenhagen	Denmark
CPT	Cape Town	South Africa
CUR	Curacao	Neth. Antilles
CVG	Cincinnati	USA
CWL	Cardiff	UK
DAC	Dhaka	Bangladesh
DAM	Damascus	Syria
DBV	Dubrovnik	Croatia
DCA	Washington National	USA
DCF	Dominica	Dominica
DEL	Delhi	India
DEN	Denver	USA
DFW	Dallas/Fort Worth	USA
DKR	Dakar	Senegal
DOM	Dominica	Oman
DRW	Darwin	Australia
DTT	Detroit	USA
DUB	Dublin	Ireland
DUR	Durban	South Africa
DUS	Dusseldorf	Germany
DXB	Dubai	UAE
EBB	Entebbe	Uganda

Airport codes *continued*

code	airport	country
EDI	Edinburgh	UK
EMA	East Midlands	UK
EWR	Newark	USA
FAO	Faro	Portugal
FCO	Rome Fiumicino	Italy
FIH	Kinshasa	Congo
FRA	Frankfurt	Germany
FUK	Fukuoka	Japan
GBE	Gabarone	Botswana
GCI	Guernsey	UK
GCM	Grand Cayman	Cayman Islands
GEO	Georgetown	Guyana
GIB	Gibraltar	Gibraltar
GIG	Rio de Janeiro	Brazil
GLA	Glasgow	UK
GND	Grenada	Grenada
GOA	Genoa	Italy
GOT	Gothenburg	Sweden
GRU	Sao Paulo	Brazil
GRZ	Graz	Austria
GUA	Guatemala City	Guatemala
GVA	Geneva	Switzerland
HAJ	Hanover	Germany
HAM	Hamburg	Germany
HAV	Havana	Cuba
HEL	Helsinki	Finland
HKG	Hong Kong	Hong Kong
HNL	Honolulu	USA
HOU	Houston	USA
HRE	Harare	Zimbabwe
IAD	Washington Dulles	USA
IAH	Houston Intl.	USA
INN	Innsbruck	Austria
ISB	Islamabad	Pakistan
IST	Istanbul	Turkey
JED	Jeddah	Saudi Arabia
JER	Jersey	UK
JFK	New York Kennedy Intl.	USA
JKT	Jakarta	Indonesia
JNB	Johannesburg	South Africa
KEF	Reykjavik	Iceland
KHI	Karachi	Pakistan
KIN	Kingston	Jamaica
KLU	Klagenfurt	Austria
KOJ	Kagoshima	Japan

code	*airport*	*country*
KRT	Khartoum	Sudan
KUL	Kuala Lumpur	Malaysia
KWI	Kuwait	Kuwait
LAD	Luanda	Angola
LAS	Las Vegas	USA
LAX	Los Angeles	USA
LBA	Leeds/Bradford	UK
LCA	Larnaca	Cyprus
LCY	London City	UK
LED	St Petersburg	Russia
LEJ	Leipzig	Germany
LGA	New York La Guardia	USA
LGW	London Gatwick	UK
LHR	London Heathrow	UK
LIL	Lille	France
LIM	Lima	Peru
LIN	Milan	Italy
LIS	Lisbon	Portugal
LJU	Ljubljana	Slovenia
LLW	Lilongwe	Malawi
LNZ	Linz	Austria
LOS	Lagos	Nigeria
LPA	Gran Canaria	Spain
LPB	La Paz	Bolivia
LPL	Liverpool	UK
LTN	London Luton	UK
LUN	Lusaka	Zambia
LUX	Luxembourg	Luxembourg
LYS	Lyons	France
MAA	Chennai	India
MAD	Madrid	Spain
MAN	Manchester	UK
MBA	Mombasa	Kenya
MCI	Kansas City Intl.	USA
MCO	Orlando	USA
MCT	Muscat	Oman
MEL	Melbourne	Australia
MEX	Mexico City	Mexico
MIA	Miami	USA
MIL	Milan	Italy
MKC	Kansas City	USA
MLA	Malta	Malta
MLW	Monrovia	Liberia
MME	Teeside	UK
MNL	Manila	Philippines

Airport codes *continued*

code	*airport*	*country*
MOW	Moscow	Russia
MPM	Maputo	Mozambique
MQS	Mustique	Grenadines
MRS	Marseilles	France
MRU	Mauritius	Mauritius
MSP	Minneapolis St Paul	USA
MSY	New Orleans	USA
MUC	Munich	Germany
MVD	Montevideo	Uruguay
MXP	Milan	Italy
NAP	Naples	Italy
NAS	Nassau	Bahamas
NBO	Nairobi	Kenya
NCE	Nice	France
NCL	Newcastle	UK
NGO	Nagoya	Japan
NOU	Nourrea	New Caledonia
NRT	Tokyo Narita	Japan
NUE	Nuremburg	Germany
NYC	New York	USA
ORD	Chicago O'Hare	USA
ORK	Cork	Ireland
ORL	Orlando	USA
ORY	Paris Orly	France
OSA	Osaka	Japan
OSL	Oslo	Norway
OTP	Bucharest Otopeni	Romania
PAR	Paris	France
PBM	Paramaribo	Surinam
PDX	Portland	USA
PEK	Beijing	China
PER	Perth	Australia
PHL	Philadelphia	USA
PHX	Phoenix	USA
PIT	Pittsburgh	USA
PLH	Plymouth	UK
PMI	Palma de Mallorca	Spain
POM	Port Moresby	Papua New Guinea
POS	Port of Spain	Trinidad and Tobago
PPT	Papeete	French Polynesia
PRG	Prague	Czech Republic
PSA	Florence Pisa	Italy
PTY	Panama City	Panama
RAR	Rarotonga	Cook Islands
REK	Reykjavik	Iceland

Airport codes *continued*

code	*airport*	*country*
RIO	Rio de Janeiro	Brazil
RIX	Riga	Latvia
ROM	Rome	Italy
RTM	Rotterdam	Netherlands
RUH	Riyadh	Saudi Arabia
SAH	Sana'a	Yemen
SAN	San Diego	USA
SAO	Sao Paulo	Brazil
SCL	Santiago	Chile
SEA	Seattle	USA
SEL	Seoul	South Korea
SFO	San Francisco	USA
SHA	Shanghai	China
SHJ	Sharjah	UAE
SIN	Singapore	Singapore
SKG	Thessaloniki	Greece
SLC	Salt Lake City	USA
SLU	Saint Lucia	Saint Lucia
SNN	Shannon	Ireland
SOF	Sofia	Bulgaria
SOU	Southampton	UK
STL	Saint Louis	USA
STN	London Stansted	UK
STO	Stockholm	Sweden
STR	Stuttgart	Germany
SVG	Stavanger	Norway
SVO	Moscow Sheremetyevo	Russia
SVQ	Seville	Spain
SXB	Strasbourg	France
SXF	Berlin Schoenefeld	Germany
SYD	Sydney	Australia
SZG	Salzburg	Austria
TCI	Tenerife	Spain
TGU	Tegucigalpa	Honduras
THF	Berlin Tempelhof	Germany
THR	Tehran	Iran
TLL	Tallinn	Estonia
TLS	Toulouse	France
TLV	Tel Aviv	Israel
TPA	Tampa	USA
TPE	Taipei	Taiwan
TRN	Turin	Italy
TUN	Tunis	Tunisia
TYO	Tokyo	Japan
UIO	Quito	Ecuador

Airport codes *continued*

code	airport	country
VCE	Venice	Italy
VIE	Vienna	Austria
VLC	Valencia	Spain
VNO	Vilnius	Lithuania
WAS	Washington DC	USA
WAW	Warsaw	Poland
WDH	Windhoek	Namibia
WLG	Wellington	New Zealand
YEA	Edmonton	Canada
YEG	Edmonton Intl.	Canada
YMQ	Montreal Mirabel	Canada
YOW	Ottawa	Canada
YTO	Toronto	Canada
YUL	Montreal Pierre Elliot Trudeau Intl.	Canada
YVR	Vancouver	Canada
YWG	Winnipeg	Canada
YYC	Calgary	Canada
YYZ	Toronto Lester Pearson	Canada
ZAG	Zagreb	Croatia
ZRH	Zurich	Switzerland

Local times around the world

London time	1200	London time	1200
Abu Dhabi	1600	Luanda	1300
Adelaide	2130	Luxembourg	1300
Algiers	1300	Madagascar	1500
Amsterdam	1300	Madrid	1300
Ankara	1400	Malé	1700
Astana	1800	Malta	1300
Athens	1400	Manila	2000
Baghdad	1500	Mexico	0600
Bangkok	1900	Minsk	1400
Beijing	2000	Montevideo	0900
Beirut	1400	Montreal	0700
Berlin	1300	Moscow	1500
Bern(e)	1300	Mumbai	1730
Bogota	0700	Nairobi	1500
Brasilia	0900	Nassau	0700
Brazzaville	1300	New York	0700
Brussels	1300	Oslo	1300
Bucharest	1400	Ottawa	0700
Budapest	1300	Panama	0700
Buenos Aires	0900	Paris	1300
Cairo	1400	Perth	2000
Calcutta (Kolkata)	1730	Phnom Penh	1900
Canberra	2200	Prague	1300
Cape Town	1400	Pretoria	1400
Caracas	0800	Pyongyang	2100
Chicago	0600	Quebec	0700
Colombo	1730	Rangoon	1830
Copenhagen	1300	Reykjavik	1200
Costa Rica	0600	Rio de Janeiro	0900
Damascus	1400	Riyadh	1500
Delhi	1730	Rome	1300
Dhaka	1800	San Francisco	0400
Dublin	1200	Santiago	0800
Gibraltar	1300	Seoul	2100
Hanoi	1900	Seychelles	1600
Harare	1400	Singapore	2000
Helsinki	1400	Stockholm	1300
Hong Kong	2000	Sydney	2200
Honolulu	0200	Taipei	2000
Istanbul	1400	Tallinn	1400
Jakarta	1900	Tbilisi	1600
Jerusalem	1400	Tehran	1530
Kabul	1630	Tirana	1300
Karachi	1700	Tokyo	2100
Khartoum	1400	Toronto	0700
Kiev	1400	Tripoli	1300
Kinshasa	1400	Tunis	1300
Kuala Lumpur	2000	Ulan Bator	2000
Kuwait	1500	Vienna	1300
Lagos	1300	Warsaw	1300
La Paz	0800	Washington DC	0700
Lima	0700	Wellington	0000 (+1 day)
Lisbon	1200	Yaoundé	1300

International dialling codes

Afghanistan	93	Egypt	20
Albania	355	El Salvador	503
Algeria	213	Equatorial Guinea	240
Andorra	376	Estonia	372
Angola	244	Ethiopia	251
Anguilla	264	Falkland Islands	500
Antigua and Barbuda	268	Fiji	679
Argentina	54	Finland	358
Armenia	374	France	33
Australia	61	French Guiana	594
Austria	43	Gabon	241
Bahamas	242	Gambia	220
Bahrain	973	Georgia	679
Bangladesh	880	Germany	49
Barbados	246	Ghana	233
Belarus	375	Gibraltar	350
Belgium	32	Great Britain	44
Belize	501	Greece	30
Benin	229	Grenada	473
Bermuda	441	Guatemala	502
Bhutan	975	Guinea	224
Bolivia	591	Guinea-Bissau	245
Bosnia	387	Guyana	592
Botswana	267	Haiti	509
Brazil	55	Honduras	504
Brunei	673	Hong Kong	852
Bulgaria	359	Hungary	36
Burkina Faso	226	Iceland	354
Burma (*see* Myanmar)		India	91
Burundi	257	Indonesia	62
Cambodia	855	Iran	98
Cameroon	237	Iraq	964
Canada	1	Irish Republic	353
Cape Verde Islands	238	Israel	972
Cayman Islands	345	Italy	39
Central African Republic	236	Ivory Coast	225
Chad	235	Jamaica	876
Chile	56	Japan	81
China	86	Jordan	962
Colombia	57	Kazakhstan	7
Comoros	269	Kenya	254
Congo (Republic of the)	242	Kuwait	965
Congo	243	Kyrgyzstan	996
(Democratic Republic of the)		Laos	856
Costa Rica	506	Latvia	371
Croatia	385	Lebanon	961
Cuba	53	Lesotho	266
Cyprus	357	Liberia	231
Czech Republic	420	Libya	218
Denmark	45	Liechtenstein	423
Djibouti	253	Lithuania	370
Dominica	767	Luxembourg	352
Dominican Republic	809	Macao	853
Ecuador	593		

International dialling codes *continued*

Macedonia	389	St Vincent	784
(Former Yugoslav Republic of)		Samoa	378
Madagascar	261	Saudi Arabia	966
Madeira	351	Senegal	221
Malawi	265	Serbia and Montenegro	381
Malaysia	60	Seychelles	248
Maldives	960	Sierra Leone	232
Mali	223	Singapore	65
Malta	356	Slovakia	42
Mauritania	222	Slovenia	386
Mauritius	230	Somalia	252
Mexico	52	South Africa	27
Moldova	373	South Korea	82
Monaco	377	Spain	34
Mongolia	976	Sri Lanka	94
Montserrat	664	Sudan	249
Morocco	212	Suriname	597
Mozambique	258	Swaziland	268
Myanmar	95	Sweden	46
Namibia	264	Switzerland	41
Nauru	674	Syria	963
Nepal	977	Taiwan	886
Netherlands	31	Tanzania	255
New Zealand	64	Thailand	66
Nicaragua	505	Togo	228
Niger	227	Tonga	676
Nigeria	234	Trinidad & Tobago	868
North Korea	850	Tunisia	216
Norway	47	Turkey	90
Oman	968	Turkmenistan	993
Pakistan	92	Tuvalu	688
Panama	507	Uganda	256
Papua New Guinea	675	Ukraine	380
Paraguay	595	United Arab Emirates	971
Peru	51	United Kingdom	44
Philippines	63	USA	1
Poland	48	Uruguay	598
Portugal	351	Uzbekistan	998
Puerto Rico	787	Vanuatu	678
Qatar	974	Venezuela	58
Réunion	262	Vietnam	84
Romania	40	Yemen	967
Russia	7	Zambia	260
Rwanda	250	Zimbabwe	263
St Lucia	758		

Standard symbols and abbreviations

Symbol	Meaning	Symbol	Meaning
+	positive	m	metre
-	negative	mb	millibar
Ω	ohm	mf, μf	microfarad
°	degree	mHz	millihertz
"	inch(es)	MHz	megahertz
'	foot (feet)	mi	mile(s)
amp	ampere	mm	millimetre
Btu	British thermal unit	MPH	miles per hour
C	Celsius	mv	millivolt
cal	calorie(s)	neg	negative
cal	large calorie(s)	oz	ounce(s)
cm	centimetre	pf, $\mu\mu$f	picofarad
cos	cosine	pos	positive
cu. cm, cc	cubic centimetre(s)	PPH	pounds per hour
cu. in	cubic inch(es)	PPM	parts per million
cu. ft	cubic foot (feet)	PSI	pounds per square inch
cu. m	cubic metre(s)	PSIA	pounds per square inch absolute pressure
dB	decibel		
deg	degree	PSID	pounds per square inch differential pressure
ESHP	equivalent shaft horsepower		
		PSIG	pounds per square inch gage
F	farad		
F	Fahrenheit	pt	pint
ft	foot (feet)	qt	quart
ft-lb(s)	foot-pound(s)	R	Rankine
g	gram	rev.	revolution(s)
gal	gallon	rpm, r.p.m.	revolutions per minute
HP	horsepower	sec.	second
hr	hour	SHP	shaft horsepower
Hz	hertz	sin	sine
in	inch(es)	sq. cm, cm^2	square centimetre(s)
in hg	inch(es) of mercury	sq. in	square inch(es)
IPS	inches per second	sq. ft	square foot (feet)
k	kilo	sq. m, m^2	square metre
K	kelvin	sq. mi	square mile(s)
kg	kilogram	sq. mil	square mil
kHz	kilohertz	tan	tangent
km	kilometre	TEHP	total equivalent horsepower
kW	kilowatt		
kW-hr	kilowatt hour	THP	total horsepower
l	litre	V	volt
lb	pound	yd(s)	yard(s)

Weights and Measures: Metric Measures

Length

1 millimetre (mm)		= 0.0394 in
1 centimetre (cm)	= 10 mm	= 0.3937 in
1 decimetre (dm)	= 10 cm	= 3.937 in
1 metre (m)	= 100 cm	= 1.0936 yds
1 kilometre (km)	= 1000 m	= 0.6214 mile

Area

1 square millimetre (mm^2)		= 0.0016 sq. in.
1 square centimetre (cm^2)	= 100 mm^2	= 0.155 sq. in
1 square metre (m^2)	= 10,000 cm^2	= 1.196 sq. yds
1 are (a)	= 100 m^2	= 119.6 sq. yds
1 hectare (ha)	= 100 ares	= 2.4711 acres
1 square kilometre (km^2)	= 100 hectares	= 0.3861 sq. mile

Weight

1 milligram (mg)		= 0.0154 grain
1 gram (g)	= 1000 mg	= 0.0353 oz
1 kilogram (kg)	= 1000 g	= 2.2046 lb
1 tonne (t)	= 1000 kg	= 0.9842 ton

Volume

1 cubic centimetre (cm^3)		= 0.061 cu. in.
1 cubic decimetre (dm^3)	= 1000 cm^3	= 0.0351 cu. ft
1 cubic metre (m^3)	= 1000 dm^3	= 1.308 cu. yds

Liquid Volume

1 litre (l)	= 1 dm^3	= 1.76 pt
1 hectolitre (hl)	= 100 l	= 22 gal

Weights and Measures: Imperial Measures

Length

1 inch (in)		= 2.54 cm
1 foot (ft)	= 12 in	= 0.3048 m
1 yard (yd)	= 3 ft	= 0.9144 m
1 rod (rd)	= 5.5 yds	= 4.0292 m
1 chain	= 4 rds	= 20.117 m
1 furlong	= 10 chains	= 201.17 m
1 mile	= 8 furlongs	= 1.6093 km
1 nautical mile	= 2025.4 yds	= 1.852 km

Area

1 square inch		= 6.4516 cm^2
1 square foot	= 144 sq. ins	= 0.0929 m^2
1 square yard	= 9 sq. ft	= 0.8361 m^2
1 acre	= 4840 sq. yds	= 4046.9 m^2
1 square mile	= 640 acres	= 259 hectares

Weight

1 ounce (oz)	= 437.6 grains	= 28.350 g
1 pound (lb)	= 16 oz	= 0.4536 kg
1 stone	= 14 lb	= 6.3503 kg
1 hundredweight (cwt)	= 112 lb	= 50.802 kg
1 long ton	= 20 cwt	= 1.0161 t

Volume

1 cubic inch		= 16.387 cm^3
1 cubic foot	= 1728 cu. ins	= 0.0283 m^3
1 cubic yard	= 27 cu. ft	= 0.7646 m^3

Liquid Volume

1 fluid ounce (fl. oz)	= 8 fl. drachms	= 28.413 cm^3
1 pint (pt)	= 20 fl. oz	= 568.26 cm^3
1 pint	= 4 gills	= 0.5683 l
1 quart (qt)	= 2 pt	= 1.1365 l
1 gallon (gal)	= 8 pt	= 4.5461 l
1 bushel (bu)	= 8 gal	= 36.369 l

Liquid Volume (US)

1 fluid ounce (US)		= 29.574 ml
1 pint (US)	= 16 fl. oz (US)	= 0.4723 l
1 gallon (US)	= 8 pt (US)	= 3.7854 l

Conversion factors: Imperial to Metric

Length

			Multiply by
inches	➤	millimetres	25.4
inches	➤	centimetres	2.54
feet	➤	metres	0.3048
yards	➤	metres	0.9144
statute miles	➤	kilometres	1.6093
nautical miles	➤	kilometres	1.852

Area

			Multiply by
square inches	➤	square centimetres	6.4516
square feet	➤	square metres	0.0929
square yards	➤	square metres	0.8361
acres	➤	hectares	0.4047
square miles	➤	square kilometres	2.5899

Volume

			Multiply by
cubic inches	➤	cubic centimetres	16.3871
cubic feet	➤	cubic metres	0.0283
cubic yards	➤	cubic metres	0.7646

Liquid Volume

			Multiply by
fluid ounces (UK)	➤	litres	0.0284
fluid ounces (US)	➤	litres	0.0296
pints (UK)	➤	litres	0.5682
pints (US)	➤	litres	0.4732
gallons (UK)	➤	litres	4.546
gallons (US)	➤	litres	3.7854

Weight

			Multiply by
ounces (avoirdupois)	➤	grams	28.3495
ounces (troy)	➤	grams	31.1035
pounds	➤	kilograms	0.4536
tons (long)	➤	tonnes	1.016

Conversion factors: Metric to Imperial

Length			*Multiply by*
millimetres	➤	inches	0.0394
centimetres	➤	inches	0.3937
metres	➤	feet	3.2806
metres	➤	yards	1.9036
kilometres	➤	statute miles	0.6214
kilometres	➤	nautical miles	0.54

Area			*Multiply by*
square centimetres	➤	square inches	0.155
square metres	➤	square feet	10.764
square metres	➤	square yards	1.196
hectares	➤	acres	2.471
square kilometres	➤	square miles	0.386

Volume			*Multiply by*
cubic centimetres	➤	cubic inches	0.061
cubic metres	➤	cubic feet	35.315
cubic metres	➤	cubic yards	1.308

Liquid Volume			*Multiply by*
litres	➤	fluid ounces (UK)	35.1961
litres	➤	fluid ounces (US)	33.8150
litres	➤	pints (UK)	1.7598
litres	➤	pints (US)	2.1134
litres	➤	gallons (UK)	0.2199
litres	➤	gallons (US)	0.2642

Weight			*Multiply by*
grams	➤	ounces (avoirdupois)	0.0353
grams	➤	ounces (troy)	0.0322
kilograms	➤	pounds	2.2046
tonnes	➤	tons (long)	0.9842

Temperature			*Operation (in sequence)*
Celsius	➤	Fahrenheit	x 9, ÷ 5, + 32
Fahrenheit	➤	Celsius	- 32, x 5, ÷ 9